The SAGE Handbook of

GIS and Society

SAGE has been part of the global academic community since 1965, supporting high quality research and learning that transforms society and our understanding of individuals, groups, and cultures. SAGE is the independent, innovative, natural home for authors, editors and societies who share our commitment and passion for the social sciences.

Find out more at: **www.sagepublications.com**

Contents

List of Contributors

Ryan M. Acton is an Assistant Professor in the Department of Sociology at the University of Massachusetts Amherst. His research interests include GIS, social network analysis, collection and sampling strategies for web-based data, information diffusion, technology, and disasters. In addition to his published work, Acton is the author of a special-purpose software package for web-based data collection. Ryan received his PhD in Sociology from the University of California, Irvine in 2010.

Marc P. Armstrong is Professor and CLAS Collegiate Fellow in the Department of Geography at the University of Iowa. His PhD is from the University of Illinois at Urbana-Champaign. Armstrong has served at the North American Editor of the *International Journal of Geographical Information Science* and is the author of more than 100 scholarly publications. His research interests include spatial analysis, spatial decision support systems, high performance computing and geographic visualization methods.

Dimitris Ballas is Senior Lecturer in GIS, in the Department of Geography at the University of Sheffield. His current research interests include economic geography, social and spatial inequalities, social justice, exploring geographies of happiness and socio-economic applications of geographical information systems (GIS). He is the lead author of the book *Geography Matters: Simulating the Impacts of National Social Policies* and co-author of the books *Post-Suburban Europe: Planning and Politics at the Margins of Europe's Capital Cities* and *Poverty, Wealth and Place in Britain, 1968 to 2005*. He has over a dozen papers in peer-reviewed international academic journals, eight peer-reviewed edited book chapters and over 50 conference papers.

Nathaniel Bell is Postdoctoral Research Fellow in the Department of Surgery at the University of British Columbia. He obtained his PhD from Simon Fraser University in 2009 under the mentorship of Dr Nadine Schuurman. He holds a joint appointment with the Centre for Clinical Epidemiology and Evaluation and the Section of Trauma Services at Vancouver General Hospital. His research focuses on the social and systems determinants of functional outcomes and health related quality of life following critical illness and injury. GIS/GIScience tools and principles, in conjunction with the use of linked health and administrative databases, form core components of his research.

Carter T. Butts is Associate Professor in the Department of Sociology and Institute for Mathematical Behavioral Sciences at the University of California, Irvine. He obtained his PhD from Carnegie Mellon University, and his BS from Duke University. His research involves the application of mathematical and computational techniques to theoretical and methodological problems within the areas of social network analysis, mathematical sociology, quantitative methodology and human judgement and decision making. Currently, his work focuses on the structure of spatially embedded large-scale interpersonal networks; models for informant accuracy, network inference, and graph comparison; representation and modeling of intertemporal relational data; and models for human behaviour in disrupted settings.

Gilberto Camara is General Manager of the Brazilian National Institute for Space Research – INPE, appointed by the Brazilian president for the period 2006–2010. He is responsible for the administration of INPE's research and development groups in space science, space engineering, earth observation and weather and climate studies. Previously, he was head of INPE's Image Processing Division from 1991 to 1996 and director for Earth Observation from 2001 to 2005. His research interests include geographical information science and engineering, spatial databases, spatial analysis and environmental modeling. He has published more than 120 full papers in refereed journals and scientific conferences.

Helen Couclelis is Professor of Geography at the University of California, Santa Barbara. She began her career as a planner in Greece and has held visiting appointments at the University of Waterloo and Princeton University. She is co-editor of the journal *Environment and Planning B: Planning and Design* and has served as associate director of the National Center for Geographic Information and Analysis (NCGIA) and on the executive committee of the Center for Spatially Integrated Social Science (CSISS). Her research interests are in the areas of geographic information science, urban and regional modeling and planning, and the geography of the information society.

Dr. Susan L. Cutter is a Carolina Distinguished Professor at the University of South Carolina. She directs the Hazards and Vulnerability Research Institute, has authored or edited twelve books and more than 100 peer-reviewed articles and book chapters. She serves numerous advisory boards and committees including the National Research Council, the AAAS, the National Science Foundation, the Natural Hazards Center, the H. John Heinz III Center, and the US Army Corps of Engineers IPET team. She also serves as co-editor of Environment and is associate editor of Weather, Climate, and Society. She is a past President of the Association of American Geographers, and of the Consortium of Social Science Associations.

Clodoveu Augusto Davis, Jr is Professor and Researcher at the Federal University of Minas Gerais. He received his BS degree in Civil Engineering from the Federal University of Minas Gerais (UFMG), Brazil. He obtained MSc and PhD degrees in Computer Science, also from UFMG. He led the team that conducted the implementation of GIS technology in the city of Belo Horizonte, Brazil, and coordinated several geographic application development efforts. His main research interests include geographic databases, urban GIS, spatial data infrastructures and multiple representations in GIS.

Danny Dorling is Professor of Human Geography at the University of Sheffield. His recent books include, Dorling et al. (2007) *Poverty, Wealth and Place in Britain, 1968 to 2005* and Thomas and Dorling (2007) *Identity in Britain: A Cradle-to-Grave Atlas*, Shaw et al. (2008), *The Grim Reaper's Road Map: An Atlas of Mortality in Britain,* Dorling et al. (2008), *The Atlas of the Real World: Mapping the Way We Live* and Dorling (2010) *Injustice: Why Social Inequalities Persist*?

Sarah Elwood is Professor in the Department of Geography at the University of Washington. Her research interests intersect critical GIS and urban and political geography. She studies the social and political impacts of spatial technologies such as GIS and the changing practices and politics of local activism, community organizing and other modes of civic engagement.

Dr. Christopher T. Emrich is a Research Assistant Professor at the Hazards and Vulnerability Research Institute within the University of South Carolina's Department of Geography. His research interests include the application of geospatial web-based technologies to emergency management planning and practice, long term recovery from disaster, and the intersection of social vulnerability and community resilience in the face of disaster. Dr. Emrich has been a strong advocate of the transition of knowledge from academia and research to real-world application and has been a key player in the development of theory, data, metrics, methods, applications, and spatial analytical models for understanding the newly emergent field of hazard vulnerability science.

Frederico T. Fonseca received his PhD in Spatial Information Science and Engineering from the University of Maine. He joined Penn State where he is an Associate Professor of the College of Information Sciences and Technology. His work on three areas of research, Geographic Information Science, Information Science and Information Systems, led to 18 journal papers, research grants from NSF and other agencies, and successful MA and PhD students. He received the 2006 Researcher Award from the University Consortium of Geographic Information Science (UCGIS) for his foundational work on ontologies in GIS.

Rina Ghose is Associate Professor in Geography at University of Wisconsin-Milwaukee. Her research interests intersect critical GIS, race and poverty studies, political economy and urban geography. She has conducted decade-long research on public participation GIS to examine the process of social activism and community organizing to combat inner-city poverty, and the use of GIS technologies as modes of resistance to inequities. Her current research projects include examining the impact of neoliberal policies in shaping PPGIS process and exploring the social construction of GIS in the non-western world.

Michael F. Goodchild is Professor of Geography and Director of the Center for Spatial Studies at the University of California, Santa Barbara. His research publications, including more than 400 scientific papers and a dozen authored and edited books, have laid a foundation for geographic information science and spatial analysis, extended the development of geo-libraries, contributed to understanding uncertainty in geographic data and advanced capabilities in location-allocation modeling. He is an elected member of the National Academy of Sciences and the American Academy of Arts and Sciences, and is a Foreign Fellow of the Royal Society of Canada.

Francis Harvey is Associate Professor at the University of Minnesota. His research interests include semantic interoperability, spatial data infrastructures, geographic information sharing, and GIS and societal issues. He serves on the editorial board of the *International Journal for Geographical Information System*, *Cartographica*, *GeoJournal*, *Europa Regional* and the *URISA Journal*. He published *A GIS Primer* with Guilford Press in 2008.

Donald G. Janelle is Research Professor at the University of California Santa Barbara. His primary research areas focus on temporal patterns of spatial behaviour in cities and on the social implications of transportation, telecommunication and information technologies in the development of urban-regional spatial systems. Recently edited books include *Information, Place, and Cyberspace: Issues in Accessibility* (Springer-Verlag, 2000, with David Hodge), *Spatially Integrated Social Science* (Oxford University Press, 2004, with Michael Goodchild) and *WorldMinds: Geographical Perspectives on 100 Problems* (Kluwer Academic Publishers, 2004, with Barney Warf and Kathy Hansen).

Piotr Jankowski is Professor in the Department of Geography and co-director of the Center for Earth System Analysis Research at San Diego State University. His previous faculty appointments were at the University of Idaho and Westfaelische Wilhelms Universitaet. His research focuses on spatial decision support systems, participatory geographic information systems, spatial optimization and visual analytics. He has published extensively in leading geography and GIScience journals and has been the PI and Co-PI on a number of research projects funded by NSF, NASA and various state agencies. He co-authored with Timothy L. Nyerges two books on participatory GIScience and spatial decision support.

Marinos Kavouras has served as Dean of the NTUA School of Rural and Surveying Engineering, Director of Cartography Laboratory, Director of the Geoinformatics Graduate Programme, Vice President of the Hellenic Cadastral Agency, chair of ISPRS Working Group II/6 – System Integration and Interoperability and Adjunct Researcher of the Institute for the Management of Information Systems (IMIS-ATHENA). He did his PEng, Dipl. Ing. from NTUA Athens, Greece, and MScE and PhD from UNB Canada. He has formed OntoGEO, a group conducting Ontological Research in GIScience, including knowledge engineering and theoretical cartography. He has co-authored one book and over 120 publications in scientific journals and conference proceedings.

Richard Kingston is Lecturer in spatial planning and GIS at the University of Manchester, United Kingdom. Over the past 15 years, he has been undertaking research investigating the use of ICT in spatial planning. This has focused more specifically on the development, testing and implementation of PPGIS methods to enhance the more traditional participatory processes within planning. His research has been funded by the ESRC, EPSRC the EU and the Joseph Rowntree Foundation. He is member of The Royal Town Planning Institute, The Town and Country Planning Association and the Urban and Regional Information Systems Association.

Margarita Kokla did her PEng, Dipl. Ing., MScE and PhD from the School of Rural and Surveying Engineering, National Technical University of Athens (NTUA). She has received the Dimitris Chorafas Foundation 2005 Prize in recognition of her work in knowledge representation and engineering in the geospatial domain. She is the secretary of ISPRS Working Group II/6 – System Integration and Interoperability. As a member of the OntoGEO research group, she specializes in GIScience. Her research interests include geospatial semantics, ontologies, semantic integration, interoperability and knowledge representation. She has co-authored one book and several publications in scientific journals and conference proceedings.

Peter A. Kwaku Kyem is Professor of Geography at Central Connecticut State University, New Britain, Connecticut. Dr Kyem holds a PhD in Geography from Clark University, Worcester, Massachusetts. He has presented papers on a number of topics at national and international conferences. His publications appear in books and reputable journals including the *Annals of the Association of American Geographers*, *Cartographica: the International Journal of Cartography*, *Transactions in GIS* and the *Journal of Planning Education Research*. His current research focuses on Participatory GIS Applications, GIS and Conflict Management and ICT deployment in Africa.

Melinda Laituri is Associate Professor at Colorado State University in the Forest, Rangeland, and Watershed Stewardship Department. She is the director of the Geospatial Centroid at CSU that provides information and communication about GIS across campus and community. Dr Laituri teaches graduate courses in GIS. Her research focuses on the intersection of science and culture using geospatial science. She has research projects in Mongolia, New Zealand, Ethiopia, Canada, Alaska and China. Other research work focuses on the role of the Internet and geospatial technologies of disaster management and cross-cultural environmental histories of river-basin management.

Roger Longhorn holds BSc and MSc degrees from MIT, Cambridge, MA, USA, and has been involved in the ICT industry since 1976. He developed marine information systems globally, then worked as an expert in information services for the European Commission and remains active in several EC R&D and information market programmes. He has been involved in developing the European Spatial Data Infrastructure strategy since 1995 and is currently helping to implement the INSPIRE Directive in three EU Member States. He co-authored a book on value, pricing and consumption of geographic information (2008) with Professor Mike Blakemore.

Ian Masser retired as Professor of Urban Planning at ITC in the Netherlands. Educated in geography and town planning at Liverpool University, Ian received his PhD and a LittD from the same University. He coordinated the UK Economic and Social Research Council's Regional Research Laboratory Initiative and co-directed the European Science Foundation's GISDATA scientific programme. His publications include 18 books and more than 300 contributions to conference proceedings, books and refereed journals. His most recent book, *Building European SDIs* was published by ESRI Press in 2007. Ian was founder chairman of the Association of Geographic Information Laboratories in Europe (AGILE), President of the European Umbrella Organisation for Geographic Information (EUROGI) and the Global Spatial Data Infrastructure Association (GSDI).

Robert B. McMaster is Professor of Geography and Vice Provost and Dean of Undergraduate Education at the University of Minnesota–Twin Cities. He received his PhD in Geography and Meteorology from the University of Kansas in 1983 and has held previous appointments at UCLA and Syracuse University. His research interests are in geographic scale and cartographic generalization, GIS and society, environmental risk assessment and the history of US academic cartography. He has published several books including *Map Generalization: Making Rules for Knowledge Representation* (with B. Buttenfield), *Generalization in Digital Cartography* (with K. Stuart Shea), *Thematic Cartography and Geographic Visualization* (with T. Slocum, F. Kessler and H. Howard), *A Research Agenda for Geographic Information Science* (with E.L. Usery) and *Scale and Geographic Inquiry* (with E. Sheppard).

Timothy L. Nyerges is Professor of Geography at the University of Washington. His current teaching and research involves participatory geographic information science and systems (GIS) enabled by cyberinfrastructure technology to support stakeholder-based problem solving for land use, transportation, water resources and coastal resources. He has authored or co-authored over 150 papers and chapters plus four books. A 2010 textbook about sustainability management is titled *Regional and Urban GIS: A Decision Support Approach,* co-author with Piotr Jankowski. Nyerges was chair of the GIS Specialty Group of AAG, research committee chair, president-elect and president of University Consortium for Geographic Information Science.

Laxmi Ramasubramanian is currently an Associate Professor of Urban Planning at Hunter College and the Graduate Center, both sister colleges of the City University of New York. She has a visiting professor appointment at Anna University, Chennai, India. She is a PhD, AICP and an architect and practicing planner. She is an expert in the design, implementation and evaluation of participatory planning projects that use affordable and accessible digital technologies. She has recently completed a book *Geographic Information Science and Public Participation*, published by Springer.

Martin Raubal is Associate Professor at the Department of Geography at the University of California, Santa Barbara. He received his PhD in Geoinformation from Vienna University of Technology in 2001. Martin's research interests lie in the area of cognitive engineering for geospatial services, more specifically he focuses on representing and modeling people's cognition and spatiotemporal behaviour, and the integration of such models into geospatial applications for the enhancement of people's decision-making support. Martin is currently a board member of UCGIS and serves on the editorial boards of *Transactions in GIS, Journal of Location Based Services, Journal of Spatial Information Science, Geography Compass* and the *Semantic Web Journal.* He has authored and co-authored more than 60 books and research papers published in refereed journals and conference proceedings.

Nadine Schuurman is Professor in the Department of Geography at Simon Fraser University. Her research is at the intersection of GIS and health informatics. She has worked on issues from ontology and metadata to spatial data integration. More recently, Dr Schuurman has focused on novel spatial approaches to global population health and location of health services.

Shih-Lung Shaw is Professor of Geography at the University of Tennessee, Knoxville. His research interests include GIS for transportation (GIS-T), temporal GIS, time geography, transportation, and spatial analysis and modeling. Dr Shaw is a fellow of the American Association for Advancement of Science (AAAS) and a recipient of the Edward L. Ullman Award for outstanding contributions to transportation geography from the Association of American Geographers (AAG). He served as chair of the Transportation Geography Specialty Group and secretary/treasurer of the GIS Specialty Group of the Association of American Geographers.

Daniel Z. Sui is Professor of Geography and Distinguished Professor of Social and Behavioral Sciences at Ohio State University. He also serves as the director for OSU's Center for Urban and Regional Analysis (CURA). Prior assuming his current position at OSU, Daniel Sui was a professor of geography and holder of the Reta A. Haynes endowed chair at Texas A&M University. His research interests include GIS-based spatial analysis and modeling for urban, environmental, and public health applications; theoretical issues in GIScience; and legal and ethical issues of using GIS in society. Sui is a current member of the National Mapping Science Committee.

Emily Talen is Professor at Arizona State University, where she has two affiliations: the School of Geographical Sciences and Urban Planning and the School of Sustainability. She holds a PhD in geography from the University of California, Santa Barbara. Her research focuses on topics dealing with new urbanism, urban design, sustainable communities and the social implications of community design. She has authored three books: *New Urbanism and American Planning: The Conflict of Cultures* (2005), *Design for Diversity* (2008) and *Urban Design Reclaimed* (2009).

Kenneth S.S. Tang is Senior Town Planner of the Planning Department (PlanD) of the Hong Kong SAR Government. He has substantial experience in both strategic and district planning. He has participated in the development of major IT systems for PlanD. He served as the Honorary Secretary of the Hong Kong Institute of Planners (HKIP) and currently a member of the editorial board of the HKIP journal *Planning and Development.* Over past 20 years, he has contributed to the teaching of quantitative methods, urban modelling and planning theories as part-time lecturer at a number of local universities.

Shaowen Wang is Associate Professor of Geography at the University of Illinois at Urbana-Champaign and Senior Research Scientist at the National Center for Supercomputing Applications. His research interests included computationally intensive spatial analysis and modeling, parallel and distributed computing, high-performance and collaborative geographic information systems, and cyberinfrastructure-based geospatial problem-solving environments and applications. Dr Wang has published over 40 peer-reviewed papers addressing these interests in various journals and conference proceedings in the domains of cyberinfrastructure, geographic information science and geography.

Stacy Warren is a Trained Cultural Geographer who also has been involved with GIS from numerous angles, including undergraduate instructor, freelance practitioner, programmer/developer and critical theorist. She has published several articles on the critical possibilities of GIS and social justice and its applications in undergraduate education. When not occupied with GIS pursuits, Dr Warren also publishes in the field of critical Disney studies with primary focus on the cultural and urban implications of Disney theme park-style development. She also serves as faculty advisor for the Walt Disney College Program.

Paul J. Weschler is a GIS Analyst for the Federal Emergency Management Agency in Washington D.C. He joined FEMA in 2004 and has participated in GIS response and recovery work for Hurricanes Charley, Frances, Ivan, Jeanne, Dennis, Katrina, Rita, Wilma, and Gustav. He served as GIS Unit Leader for FEMA's Mississippi Hurricane Katrina Recovery effort and has extensive knowledge of state and federal emergency management practices and procedures. He has a GIS Certificate from Penn State University and he is professionally interested in the integration of enterprise databases into GIS analysis and display as well as automating web-based geospatial analysis for public consumption.

Matthew Wilson is Assistant Professor in the Department of Geography at Ball State University. His research is situated across political, feminist and urban geography as well as science and technoculture studies, interfacing these with critical GIS. He studies the use of geographic information technologies in representations of the urban and the environment, with more specific interest in location-enabled mobile technologies and the proliferation of user-created, Internet-based locational data.

Dawn Wright is Professor of Geography and Oceanography at Oregon State University, with research interests in geographic information science, coastal web atlases, benthic terrain and habitat characterization and ocean informatics/ocean cyberinfrastructure. She serves on several editorial and advisory boards, as well as on the US National Academy of Sciences' Ocean Studies Board, Committee on Strategic Directions in the Geographical Sciences and Committee on an Ocean Infrastructure Strategy for US Ocean Research in 2030. Dawn holds a PhD in physical geography and marine geology from UCSB, and is a fellow of the American Association for the Advancement of Science.

Anthony G.O. Yeh is Chair Professor in Urban Planning and GIS at the University of Hong Kong and Academician of the Chinese Academy of Sciences. He has been doing research on the use of GIS in urban and regional planning since the early 1980s. He is the founding secretary-general of the Asian Planning Schools Association and Asia GIS Association. He has been the chairman of the Geographic Information Science Commission of the International Geographical Union (IGU) and founding president of the Hong Kong GIS Association. He is on the editorial boards of international journals and has published widely in international journals.

Hongbo Yu is Assistant Professor in the Department of Geography at Oklahoma State University. His research interests include transportation geography, time geography, spatial analysis, GIS for transportation and temporal GIS. He is a recipient of the 2006 Best PhD Dissertation Award in Transportation Geography from the Association of American Geographers (AAG) and a winner of the 2005 Honors Competition for Student Papers on Geographic Information Science of the AAG. He currently serves as a board member of the Transportation Geography Specialty Group of the AAG.

PART I

Introduction

Geographic Information Systems and Society: A Twenty Year Research Perspective

Timothy Nyerges, Robert McMaster, and Helen Couclelis

GIS AND SOCIETY RESEARCH WITHIN THE BROADER CONTEXT

'Society', in the general sense of the term, means 'a community, nation, or broad grouping of people having common traditions, institutions, and collective activities and interests, or more specifically an enduring and cooperating social group whose members have developed organized patterns of relationships through interaction with one another' (*Merriam-Webster Dictionary*, online edition); a heady concept indeed! So what does 'society' have to do with a technology such as geographic information systems (GIS), and what kinds of research linking these two notions does the title of this chapter imply? The 27 chapters in this book address many facets of those questions. Basically, the overarching theme in GIS and society research is how this technology influences, and is influenced by, the various structures, processes, mechanisms, and events that characterize today's post-industrial societies. A simpler way of expressing this may be to ask how geographic information technologies affect people and organizations and, conversely, how people and organizations use the technology and by using it, cause it to change. This question is of course part of the broader one concerning the relations between society and information technologies in general. However, geographic information technologies have unique characteristics that suggest a societal problematic of their own. The purpose of this book is to help unpack that problematic from a range of different perspectives that owe as much to the personal societal interests of the chapter authors as to their individual areas of technical expertise. The result is a broad panorama of GIS and society research that is neither complete nor the only one possible, but one that conveys a strong sense of the breadth and depth of the domain in question.

None of this was part of the picture some 40 or 50 years ago, when GIS was emerging out of the nascent fields of computer cartography, spatial statistics and analysis, and computer science. GIS research at that time was highly technical, much of it focused on algorithm development and map production. The early operational systems were primitive, with only those individuals in a select geospatial 'priesthood' able to contribute to, and actually work with them. The research community, focused on solving practical problems, had little idea of how these systems would evolve and mature, and little thought was given to the potential connections with society of the simple software packages of the day. Before too long however the impact of that novel kind of software was felt in a host of disciplines from demography to transportation planning to natural resource assessment, and it became increasingly clear that decisions made with the help of that software would have significant and long-lasting effects on many sectors of society. Indeed, by the 1980s and early 1990s GIS was beginning to be widely adopted by governments, businesses, and other kinds of organizations to address a wide variety of complex natural, social, and infrastructure issues. To the extent that society has a stake in these issues it soon became evident that the increasingly powerful software systems designed to help perform sophisticated analyses and to support significant decisions in these areas were having considerable and often unequal effects on different social groups. The field of GIS and society research was born out of this growing realization.

THE EARLY GIS AND SOCIETY DEBATES

What started as a gentle exchange between geographic information scientists and critical human geographers in the very early 1990s progressed to a full-scale controversy by the middle of that decade. A deciding moment came in the fall of 1993 when a group of researchers on both sides of the already heated debate came together in Friday Harbor, Washington, in an attempt to find some common intellectual ground for moving forward. From these discussions a robust research program in GIS and society eventually emerged that progressed in several different directions. Conferences and workshops, many sponsored by the National Center for Geographic Information and Analysis (NCGIA), which continued as the Varenius Project in the late 1990s, addressed a variety of GIS and society issues. Notable among these workshops was the NCGIA-sponsored Specialist Meeting held in Minnesota in 1996, where the concept of an alternative model for GIS was discussed, one that would not be constrained by the rigid geometrical paradigms of traditional GIS, and would thus be able to accommodate alternative ways of representing space and spatial processes. This was in response to a growing concern that stakeholder groups in society, especially those already marginalized, were being left out of a discourse that increasingly relied on GIS analyses too technical for non-experts to comprehend. There was already evidence that GIS was empowering certain segments of society and privileging certain groups and communities at the expense of others. Participants also espoused the view, by then well established in social theory, that different social groups outside the mainstream may have different conceptions of space and socio-spatial reality. GIS II, as this new model became known, was eventually operationalized as public participation GIS (PPGIS), although some argued that 'community-based GIS' was a better name. Some of the core concepts and debates from these early efforts were published in a special issue of *Cartography and GIS* (CaGIS) in 1995 (Sheppard and Poiker, 1995) and in the edited volume *Ground Truth* (Pickles, 1995). Other notable meetings and publications from that period and beyond are listed in Appendix A (at the end of this chapter). Each of the three editors of this Handbook took part in several of these meetings, sometimes as co-organizer, including the critical Friday Harbor and Minnesota workshops that are credited with initiating and broadening the exploration of GIS and society research.

Thus, initially, much of the motivation for research on the relations between GIS and society came from critics of GIS technology, resulting in a highly polarized view of these relations. On the one hand, GIS enthusiasts saw the technology as a force for good, stressing its role in enhancing scientific knowledge about the geographic world, human as well as natural, and in improving the quality of related decisions. On the other hand, there were those who were highly critical of GIS, seeing it as yet another technology leading to the 'colonization' of everyday lives, a technology with enormous potential to render people more locatable, traceable, objectified, and geo-coded, making them the 'geo-slaves' of a new 'governmentality'. These latter arguments fall within the broader critiques of Western philosophy, of masculinist perspectives in science, and of capitalist and neoliberal political economies, all of which purportedly conspire to demand a more 'visible' social (and sometimes also natural) world. There is no denying that GIS and related technologies provide extensive capabilities for surveillance and for tracking individual data-trails. The fear that 'big brother is watching us' is very real for many people. The thousands of video cameras monitoring automobile and pedestrian traffic in London and in other major cities around the world may be seen as the electronic eyes of sinister police departments, or as life-saving devices that help catch those who bomb trains.

The debate about the 'good' and 'evil' sides of geographic information technologies continues to this day, though in a much more qualified form. The naivety of sharply polarized thinking begins to unravel quite readily once one begins more fully to research,

deconstruct, and reconstruct the relationships at play. Simplistic perspectives on either side of the debate are being superseded by an understanding that the intents and actions of agents need to be situated within their social and institutional contexts in order for GIS technology development and use to be judged as good or evil. This more mature stance is part of a growing interest in creating an intellectual foundation for approaching the development and use of GIS as being itself a complex societal process.

GIS AND SOCIETY RESEARCH IN THE 2000s

As the discussions, debates, and engagements evolved and the research literature grew, a broad consensus eventually emerged regarding the relationship between GIS and society. In the meantime, geographic information *science* had emerged as the theoretical framework for geographic information *systems* (Goodchild, 1992), and conditions were ripe for a more systematic approach to GIS and society research. In 2004, a major report entitled *A Research Agenda for Geographic Information Science* (Elmes et al., 2004), written by delegates of the University Consortium for Geographic Information Science (UCGIS – http://www.ucgis.org), proposed that research on GIS and society should consider the following broad questions.

- In what ways have particular logics and visualization techniques, value systems, forms of reasoning, and ways of understanding the world been incorporated into existing GIS techniques, and in what ways do alternative forms of representation remain to be explored and incorporated?
- How has the proliferation and dissemination of databases associated with GIS, as well as differential access to these databases, influenced the ability of different social groups to utilize this information for their own empowerment?
- How can the knowledge, needs, desires, and hopes of non-involved social groups adequately

be represented in a decision-making process, and what are the possibilities and limitations of GIS technology as a way of encoding and using such representations?

The UCGIS report (Elmes et al., 2004) also proposed a formal classification of the research activity in GIS and society under five different approaches or perspectives, as follows.

Approach 1: The critical social theory perspective

This perspective continues and updates the original critical social theory interest in issues of marginalization and empowerment, access, surveillance, and other issues of social equity. It is concerned, among other things, with the limitations of current GIS representations of populations, locational conflicts, resource distributions, and other essential aspects of social geographies, and with the extent to which these limitations can be overcome by enhancing the capabilities of geographic information technologies. It is also concerned with how the evolution of geographic information technologies reflects both the societal structures and priorities as well as the practices of those who develop and utilize them, and with the more troubling question of whether the use of geographic information systems and other geospatial technologies actually benefits society (McMaster and Harvey, 2010). Another significant theme within the critical social theory perspective is that of data confidentiality. As pointed out in a recent National Research Council (NRC, 2007) study on the subject, 'The increased availability of spatial information, the increasing knowledge of how to perform sophisticated scientific analyses using it, and the growth of a body of science that makes use of these data and analyses to study important social, economic, environmental, spatial, and public health problems has led to an increase in the collection and preservation of these data and in the linkage of spatial and

non-spatial information about the same research subjects' (2007: vii). This issue is clearly of growing import as the spatial data in question become more accessible and ubiquitous, and the technologies that may be used to extract sensitive information from them becomes more powerful.

Approach 2: The institutional perspective

This perspective is concerned with the implementation of GIS within institutions, and more specifically with the costs and benefits associated with that implementation, the equity of the distribution of these costs and benefits among individuals and social groups, and the ongoing coordination and maintenance of geographic data by institutions. The institutional perspective also focuses on the development of theories, tools, and techniques for determining the impact of GIS on policy decisions, on how interactions between agencies and between citizens and government agencies are affected by the use of GIS, and on the technology's impacts on people's beliefs and actions in regard to the use and management of the land.

Approach 3: The legal and ethical perspective

This perspective is concerned with the institutional processes and pricing mechanisms governing access to spatial data, with the proliferation of proprietary spatial databases, with how these changes are rooted in governmental and legal regulation, with the ethical implications of these changes, and with possible legal remedies to related problems. Some argue that these two topics – legal issues and ethics – should not be coupled as each has a distinct history and relationship to GIS. For instance, a special branch of spatial law has developed in response to the proliferation of spatial databases, in particular those used for land and public records.

A critical question here deals with the ownership and accuracy of these data. Distinct from the legal concerns with spatial data are ethical debates surrounding their acquisition, use, and digital representation. For instance, as the spatial resolution of remote sensing imagery becomes finer, now commonly one meter or less, new ethical issues arise relating to privacy and surveillance. The use of geospatial technologies for tracking people also raises deep ethical questions. The Urban and Regional Systems Association (URISA) has now developed a Code of Ethics (http://www.urisa.org/about/ethics) to help GIS professionals make appropriate and ethical choices. The ethics code consists of four primary categories: obligations to society; obligations to employers and funders; obligations to colleagues and the profession; and obligations to individuals in society.

Approach 4: The intellectual history perspective

This is the fourth approach to understanding GIS and Society research, and it is concerned with tracing the evolution of geographic information technologies, the dynamics through which dominant technologies are selected out of a variety of potential alternatives at critical points in time, the societal, institutional, and personal influences governing these selection processes, and the question of whether and why other promising alternative technologies may have been overlooked. Some have argued that much of what makes up geographic information technology today resulted from research and development in the military-industrial complex (McMaster and Harvey, 2010). Others however can point to significant contributions by the private and governmental sectors, noting that the concept of topology as used in spatial databases comes out of the careful work of the United States Census in the 1970s within the context of building digital files of census units. This, and the work of the Harvard Laboratory for Computer Graphics and Spatial Analysis, institutionalized this particular data model (what eventually became the dominant georelational model) over other possibilities.

Approach 5: The public participation perspective

This final perspective identified in the UCGIS report (Elmes et al., 2004) is concerned with how a broader effective use of GIS by the general public and by community and grassroots groups can be attained, with implications for the empowerment of such groups as partners in discourses concerning their interests and rights. McMaster and Harvey (2010) identify a set of core questions that have emerged in public participation research.

- What technologies are most appropriate for community groups? How is the needed technological expertise maintained in communities? How do community groups gain access to the appropriate data?
- What models of access to the technologies are most appropriate?
- What are the methods of localized knowledge acquisition that are most appropriate?
- How may these technologies fundamentally change the political/social structures of community groups?
- What forms, including new forms, of representation are best suited for public participation work?
- How do neighborhood groups deal with issues of scale (e.g., relationships with municipal and state regulations)?

Some of the initial work in PPGIS identified a series of models by which the public could gain access to spatial data and digital maps (Leitner et al., 2000). Each of these models, which included

Community-based (in-house) GIS, University/Community Partnerships, GIS facilities in universities and public libraries, 'Map Rooms', Internet map servers, and Neighborhood GIS centers, has its own advantages and disadvantages. The one model that has dominated the PPGIS landscape is the Internet map server. Such servers have been developed at many scales, from the local (community-based mapping systems down to the neighborhood level) to the state level (e.g., sites displaying information on the distribution of natural resources), to global-scale sites built on universal resources such as Google Earth. (McMaster and Harvey, 2010)

ADDITIONAL PERSPECTIVES ON GIS AND SOCIETY

Following the perspectives directly addressing GIS and society connections, views about the nature of the technology itself have evolved over the years, making its socially relevant role part of its definition. In the late 1980s, a group of researchers, software industry experts, and US federal agency personnel developed a definition for GIS as a combination of hardware, software, data, people, procedures, and institutional arrangements for collecting, storing, manipulating, analyzing, and displaying information about spatially distributed phenomena for the purpose of inventory, decision making and/or problem solving within operations, management, and strategic contexts (Dueker and Kjerne, 1989). Three perspectives are represented within that definition, each providing a way to understand the societal dimensions of GIS (Nyerges, 1993). The first perspective views GIS as a system of components that include not just machines and data but also people and institutions. The second perspective addresses the processes involved in the use of the technology, making clear that the purpose of GIS is not mere data handling but the representation of spatially distributed phenomena, which are as often societal as they are natural or combined. The third perspective focuses on the practical applications of GIS in decision making, management, and so on, as used by governments, businesses, research, NGOs, and not-for-profit organizations, as well as by community groups. That complex definition thus clarifies 'from the inside out' how GIS connects with society in what it is, what it does, and for what purposes it does it.

As the breadth and depth of societally relevant applications grew over time, many researchers felt that the 'S' in GIS could legitimately be interpreted as 'services' as well as 'systems'. This view became more prevalent in the late 1990s when new developments of hardware and software associated with the expansion of the Internet gave a strong boost to the practical applications of GIS. The new technical possibilities for remote service delivery generated further interest in the potential of the technology to serve societal needs, and many more academic disciplines and segments of society were able to capitalize on the benefits of map use, which had by now become much more accessible to non-experts. As mentioned earlier, around the same time the field of GIS had sufficiently matured as an intellectual endeavor to fully justify another interpretation of the acronym as Geographic Information *Science* (Goodchild, 1992). Not coincidentally, a large part of geographic information science today focuses on the societal dimensions of the technology. These three perspectives on GIS – as systems, as services, and especially as science – are amply illustrated in the research presented in this volume.

Today most research in GIS and Society directly or indirectly touches on all three aspects of GIS as science, systems, and services. While distinct, these three perspectives build on each other: technical system developments affect practice, practice in turn identifies system shortcomings that need to be addressed, and basic research analyzes, anticipates, and provides new conceptual frameworks for approaching issues that emerge in both of these areas. This makes for a very broad umbrella under which computer scientists and mathematicians, social scientist, and geographers of every stripe, cognitive scientists, legal experts, philosophers, and academic activists can all find research themes to suit their interests and skills. It is no wonder that research relating to geographic information technologies is blossoming. By necessity the material in this handbook tends to emphasize the conceptual aspects of GIS research over the practical or technical ones, even though empirical research around case studies, or research fostering needed technological advances, may be just as valuable.

STRUCTURE OF THE HANDBOOK

Based on their first-hand experience of more than 20 years of research in geographic information and society, the handbook editors identified a tentative list of major themes and potential chapter titles and chose the prospective US and international chapter authors accordingly. Appendix A lists the major meetings and publications that influenced these choices. As the chapters came in, we were gratified to see that even though most authors had provided their own titles, the chapters still fell neatly into six broad categories that were very close to the ones we had anticipated. Even more importantly, these themes, and particularly the topics within the themes show considerable continuing research potential. It also appeared that a few topics were no longer considered as important as they had been a few years earlier, while other concerns or interpretations were emerging or becoming more prominent. The Handbook thus represents a snapshot in time, which is as it should be for a field as dynamic as that of GIS and Society research.

The themes that constitute the six sections of the Handbook are as follows:

1 Foundations of GIS and Society Research
2 GIS and Modern Life
3 Alternative Representations in GIS and Society
4 GIS in Organizations and Institutions
5 GIS in Public Participation and Community Development
6 Value, Fairness and Privacy in a GIS Context

Below we provide an overview of these sections and the respective chapters within each, starting with foundational issues in Section 1 and ending in Section 6 with considerations of value, fairness, and privacy as relating to geographic information. This sequence may be seen as a progression from topics that are basic to an understanding of the socio-spatial world to issues that deeply affect individuals and groups as members of society.

Section 1: Foundations of GIS and society research

Four chapters compose this section. We start with Chapter 2, 'Concepts, Principles, Tools, and Challenges in Spatially Integrated Social Science' by Donald Janelle and Michael Goodchild. Researchers in the social sciences beyond geography have been discovering the advantages of considering spatial location in the explanation of social relationships, leading to the notion that space acts as a strong integrative element for the social sciences. Spatially integrated social science deals with the growing understanding of how most of the social sciences connect with geospatial perspectives. Research is underway to explore the changing significance in the information age of key geographical concepts as applied to non-spatial social sciences and as reflected in the evolving character of GIS. Next, in Chapter 3, entitled 'Geographic Ontologies and Society', Marinos Kavouras and Margarita Kokla report on how the development of geographic ontologies has emerged as a fundamental research interest. Ontologies for fundamental spatial concepts can affect our interpretations of the world as seen through the prism of GIS. The linkage of spatial concepts with the technologies for processing, analyzing and displaying geo-referenced information is seen as an important objective to enhance social science insight for understanding and solving critical scientific and societal problems. The third chapter in the section, Chapter 4, entitled 'The Social Potential of GIS' is by Stacy Warren. Warren explores how GIS increasingly shapes society and in turn how society shapes what is important in GIS. The meaning of information in a socially constructed world deals with identity of place as relates to power relations of place, and of course the two issues are related. When seen as part of an assemblage grounded in a longer trajectory of participatory technologies constructed and transformed through mass-mediated, globalizing economies, GIS clearly embodies the social potentials and social perils of the contemporary social dialectic. Last in this section is Chapter 5, entitled 'Critical GIS' by Sarah Elwood, Nadine Schuurman, and Matthew Wilson. The chapter situates critical GIS amid the GIS and society tradition, and points to new modes of GIS practice that have emerged under the banner of critical GIS, including participatory, qualitative, and feminist GIS. Chapter 5 also traces the theoretical and epistemological bases of qualitative GIS, and shows how critical GIS scholarship demands an expanded understanding of the ways of knowing and producing knowledge that are possible with GIS. Finally, the chapter considers newly emerging spatial technologies, forms of geographic information, and modes of visualization that expand conventional forms of GIS and spatial data, and identify key questions that must be asked of all phenomena as critical GIS research enters its second decade.

Section 2: GIS and modern life

Four chapters also compose Section 2. The first, Chapter 6, entitled 'Connecting Geospatial Information to Society through Cyberinfrastructure' is by Marc Armstrong, Timothy L. Nyerges, Shaowen Wang, and Dawn Wright. The Internet and World Wide Web have had a tremendous impact on society over the past 15 years, providing unimagined access to information. More recently, new types of software are being developed that are combined with advanced hardware to create a new type of infrastructure called *cyberinfrastructure,* now one of the most important utilities that people have come to

rely upon in the developed world. A recounting of this recent phenomenon is presented along with some critical perspectives about the social dilemmas we could face as society continues to connect online. The next chapter, Chapter 7, entitled 'Environmental Sustainability: The Role of Geographic Information Science and Spatial Data Infrastructure in the Integration of People and Nature', is by Clodoveu A. Davis Jr, Frederico T. Fonseca, and Gilberto Camara, and provides an additional perspective on data within the cyberworld. However, this time, the focus is on how to bring the study of people and nature back together through spatial data infrastructures. Perspectives that connect people to nature are critical to understanding the relationships between humans and environmental sustainability. Several research questions are examined addressing the ways in which such integrative perspectives may be developed through access to spatial data infrastructures. Chapter 8, by Nadine Schuurman and Nathaniel Bell, is entitled 'GIScience and Population Health: An Overview'. Population health has always been an important research topic, but in the 21st century it could become one of the most important emerging research areas in GIS. The locational and environmental dimensions of health must be considered together with more traditional approaches dealing with how people can become and stay healthy as well as with the threats to health. The chapter presents a population health model and the primary techniques used to quantify and provide empirical evidence of geographic variations in health. It considers emergent GIS approaches for conceptualizing neighborhood influences on health, and for quantifying such relationships. The last chapter in this section, Chapter 9 entitled 'Cogito Ergo Mobilis Sum: The Impact of Location-based Services on Our Mobile Lives', is by Martin Raubal. Locational services and associated technologies are now rapidly expanding across the world. Next to providing valuable information on the users' surrounding areas, such technologies support the collection of information about the movements of individuals and vehicles and in turn seem to encourage further mobility. Location-based services show considerable potential for growth, but they also raise some difficult societal issues such as the threat to privacy.

Section 3: Alternative representations of GIS and society

Section 3 consists of four chapters exhibiting a high diversity of views as they explore previous research and point to directions forward. The first chapter is Chapter 10, 'Human-scaled Visualizations and Society', written by Dimitris Ballas and Danny Dorling. The authors identify the predominant trends in visualizing social phenomena using area-based cartograms and discuss how it is possible to tackle with this particular visualization method some of the problems associated with traditional cartographic approaches. They show how cartograms can be used to create maps of the world, with each country re-sized in proportion to some variable of interest (e.g., population, income, or unemployment rates). The chapter also discusses the societal implications of decisions to adopt a particular mapping and visualization method. The next chapter, Chapter 11 entitled 'Indigenous People's Issues and Indigenous Uses of GIS' is by Melinda Laituri. Laituri describes the state of the art in this domain, highlighting the politics of representation as a crucial aspect of the praxis for identifying and discussing how projects are conceptualized and implemented in indigenous communities. Geospatial technologies have been used by indigenous peoples for a variety of purposes including creating land tenure maps, managing natural resources, mapping cultural heritage, and for economic development. The chapter examines the role of online technology and its relationship to the presentation and dissemination of indigenous information. Various websites representing indigenous knowledge

explore how science and local culture may be intertwined for resource management and for local expression of empowerment. The third chapter in this section, Chapter 12, is entitled 'Spatial Modeling of Social Networks' and is co-authored by Carter Butts and Ryan Acton. Virtual social networks – on-line systems composed of social entities and the relationships among them – are 'spatialized', that is, given a spatial dimension, to help understand the role of space in the formation and strength of social relations supported on the internet. The authors review the core network terminology and concepts, the special data considerations for spatially embedded networks, and provide an overview of specification and estimation issues pertinent to the spatial modeling of network data. As a case study, Butts and Acton examine communication breakdowns that occurred following hurricane Katrina in 2005 on the US Gulf Coast. Lending a spatial dimension to communications networks fosters deeper understanding of social connections and reveals gaps in information flows. The last chapter in this section, Chapter 13, is 'GIS Designs for Studying Human Activities in a Space-time Context', by Hongbo Yu and Shih-Lung Shaw. Yu and Shaw describe how time geography offers an elegant framework for studying individual activities and their relationships in space-time contexts. Although early studies used time geography mainly as a conceptual framework, more recent developments in GIS demonstrate opportunities for implementing the framework, applying it to various social domains. Overviews of time geography, of major temporal GIS designs, and of GIS models for spatio-temporal activities are also included in the chapter. A space-time GIS design, which uses a 3D (i.e., 2D space + 1D time) GIS environment to simulate the integrated space-time system of time geography, is introduced. That design enables a 3D representation and visualization of space-time paths and prisms, and supports the spatiotemporal analysis of activities. Future research challenges are also discussed in the chapter.

Section 4: GIS in organizations and institutions

The fourth section focuses on the role of GIS within organizations and institutions. The first chapter of this section, Chapter 14: 'Emerging Frameworks in the Information Age: the Spatial Data Infrastructure Phenomenon', is by Ian Masser. The chapter reviews developments in spatial data infrastructures and examines some of the broader issues emerging from them. Three significant topics are: the concepts that underlie the spatial data infrastructure (SDI), the methods and organizational structures needed to facilitate SDI implementation, and issues concerning SDI applications at sub-national, national and supranational levels. The chapter also suggests future research directions that emerge from these issues. The second chapter in this section, Chapter 15, is 'Spatial Data Infrastructure for Cadastres: Foundations and Challenges', by Francis Harvey. Data about land ownership – the cadastre data – are among the basic elements of a SDI. Cadastral information is typically of major importance because it connects rights, restrictions, and responsibilities to land parcels and is used for taxation in most countries around the world. It also often provides crucial ancillary information for government and private activities such as for flood abatement districts, soil protection areas, and countless more. By its nature the cadastre serves conflicting interests, which an SDI needs to continue to support through the corresponding re-visioning of the notion of cadastre. This chapter reviews four examples to point out these challenges and the range of strategies for integration with SDI concepts. The third chapter, Chapter 16, is entitled 'GIS-based Computer-supported Collaborative Work Flow Systems in Urban Planning', and is written by Anthony Yeh and Kenneth S.S. Tang. Yeh and Tang describe how GIS-based planning support systems enable information flow within a planning office. They focus on how decisions on development control are made as well as

on the collection of public comments on planning applications and the dissemination of both textual and graphical information to the public at various stages of the planning process. The integration of a workflow system with planning support systems facilitate the tracking of progress at different stages in the decision-making process of development control. A case study on the application of a collaborative workflow system integrated with GIS developed by the Hong Kong Planning Department is used to show how an integrated system can be used to enhance development control and public consultation. The final chapter in this section, Chapter 17, is 'GIS and Emergency Management' and is written by Christopher T. Emrich, Susan L. Cutter, and Paul J. Wechsler. Current and future developments in geospatial technology promise to increase the use of geographic data and techniques in disaster response and recovery to save lives, protect property, and reduce the economic impacts of hazards. The chapter has four major sections that parallel the four tenets of the emergency management cycle, identifying and explaining GIS functions and capabilities within each of these four main steps. Future directions are outlined for both research and practice.

Section 5: GIS in public participation and community development

The fifth section begins with Piotr Jankowski's 'Designing Participatory Geographic Information Systems' (Chapter 18). Jankowski describes the conceptual bases for system design that derive from the notion of communicative rationality exemplified by a deliberative-analytic model of public participation. A framework called Enhanced Adaptive Structuration Theory helps with systematically considering the characteristics of anticipated participants, the process flow, and the interaction between technology and people. The chapter discusses fundamental Public Participation GIS (PPGIS) design considerations including participant information needs and the relationship between group size, participation setting, and information technologies. The chapter closes with pointing out opportunities and challenges for future PPGIS designs leveraging the widespread public familiarity with digital globes and the novel phenomenon of volunteered geographic information (VGI). The second chapter, Chapter 19, is 'Online Public Participation GIS for Spatial Planning', by Richard Kingston. Based on past research the chapter highlights where online PPGIS works best, drawing out the key strengths, weaknesses, opportunities, and challenges that the approach offers. The chapter proceeds to discuss issues in relation to e-government and the dilemma around the notions of the active citizen and the consumer citizen. It suggests that PPGIS is one possible approach that helps to unpack the theories and assumptions about e-government into a practical solution. This allows active citizens to contribute and participate in spatial decision making in their locality of interest while also fulfilling the transparency and efficiency requirements of good decision making. The third chapter is entitled 'Participatory Approaches in GIS and Society Research: Foundations, Practices, and Future Directions', Chapter 20, and is written by Sarah Elwood. Elwood frames participatory approaches in GIS and society research as encompassing substantive and methodological engagements with the related perspectives of participation in grassroots GIS research, participatory in action research that incorporates GIS, in group decision and collaborative GIS research. The chapter explores the range of ways in which GIS and society research has engaged theories and practices of participation, in these realms. It situates the epistemological and political roots of participation in GIS and society research within feminist critiques of science and pragmatist philosophies of knowledge. It reviews the range of ways in which GIS and society researchers have studied and practiced participation, reflecting on the key

contributions and limitations of these different approaches. Finally, it considers future questions for GIS and society research in this arena, with a particular focus on emerging spatial technologies that are transforming the possibilities and challenges of facilitating collaboration in the creation and sharing of spatial knowledge. The fourth chapter, Chapter 21, is 'PPGIS Implementation and the Transformation of US Planning Practice', by Laxmi Ramasubramanian. The chapter reflects on the changing nature of planning practice in the USA, arguing that the use of geospatial technologies can help make day-to-day planning practice more efficient, inclusive, transparent, and accountable only when coupled with credible participatory processes. Ramasubramanian describes the synergistic relationship between successful technology adoption and use by community groups, and changes in conventional planning practices in the USA. Ramasubramanian presents preliminary evidence that PPGIS developments have encouraged both citizen and official planners to use consensus-building approaches and pragmatic problem solving strategies. The last chapter in the section, Chapter 22 entitled 'Politics and Power in Participation and GIS Use for Community Decision Making', is by Rina Ghose. This chapter describes how spatial knowledge produced through bottom-up PPGIS can greatly assist community organizations to navigate the complexities of collaborative governance. The chapter draws upon the literature on urban geography, planning, and PPGIS, and the author's decade-long investigation of PPGIS activities in inner-city Milwaukee. Ghose explores how internal organizational factors shape the abilities of community organizations, leading to some being more successful than others in affirming their rights and obtaining resources in order to transform 'spaces of despair' into 'spaces of hope'. The chapter examines the critical role of actors and networks that shapes the PPGIS process and discusses the internal characteristics of community organizations that significantly affect their abilities to undertake PPGIS activities to negotiate better conditions for themselves.

Section 6: Value, fairness, and privacy in a GIS context

In the sixth and last themed section, several chapters focus on research concerning issues of value, fairness, and privacy relating to GIS use. The first chapter in this section is Chapter 23 'Geographic Information Value Assessment' and is written by Roger Longhorn. As SDI initiatives are emerging and being implemented around the world, funding agencies need to understand the value that related expenditures bring to their governments, societies, and economies. Geographic information is at the heart of all SDIs, yet quantifying the value of geographic information is problematic. The chapter explores several viewpoints, including what is meant by the term 'geographic information', how to determine its value, how to put a value on data tied to concrete locations, issues of value chains, and what further research may be needed in this area. The second chapter, Chapter 24 entitled 'Geovisualization of Spatial Equity', is written by Emily Talen. Traditionally, spatial equity has fundamentally been about access to people, services, and resources. The visualization of varying patterns of physical access currently helps characterize the degree of spatial equity, but an emerging information-age view sees spatial equity as being redefined in terms of the transactions that may take place in virtual as well as in physical space. When spatial equity is more widely defined as the equitably distributed ability to access either physically or virtually particular goods, services, or facilities, then, Talen argues, the visualization of spatial equity opens up a wider range of conceptual and methodological issues. The third chapter, Chapter 25, is 'Natural Resource Conflicts, their Management and GIS Applications', by Peter Kyem. The chapter explores how applications of a data-driven technology such

as GIS can influence decisions that stakeholders make to resolve or prolong a conflict. The chapter presents an overview of the role that GIS plays in the management of resource conflicts, starting with a discussion of their causes and consequences. That is followed by a review of theories on conflict and GIS applications. GIS-based decision support techniques for managing conflicts are then reviewed. The technology's contribution to the decision-making process is explained. The chapter concludes with an assessment of the role of GIS in conflict management. The fourth and last chapter of this section, Chapter 26, is entitled 'Legal and Ethical Issues of Using Geospatial Technologies in Society' and is written by Daniel Sui. Society has greatly benefited from the diverse applications of geospatial technology, but the latter has also raised a host of legal and ethical issues at individual, institutional, and international levels. The chapter provides an overview of the legal and ethical issues associated with GIS in connection with privacy, intellectual property, and national sovereignty. Legislative, ethical, and technical approaches to tackling these issues are also treated. To move beyond these challenges, a broader discussion must take palce among geographic information scientists, geographers, and legal scholars who are interested in the ethical and legal issues arising in the age of ubiquitous computing.

Finally, the last chapter of the Handbook is entitled 'GIS and Society Research: Reflections and Emerging Themes' and is written by the editors Helen Couclelis, Timothy L. Nyerges, and Robert McMaster. In the last chapter the editors reflect on the major issues, debates, and trends in geographic information and society research as presented in the Handbook. They also briefly touch on a few emerging information-age developments, in particular neogeography and volunteer geographies, both of which involve non-experts contributing and using online geographic information, motivated by their own interests and needs. The chapter closes with the identification of five cross-cutting themes which may well be part of tomorrow's major trends in research about GIS and society.

REFERENCES

Craig, W., Harris, T. and Weiner, D. (eds) (1998) *Empowerment, Marginalization and Public Participation GIS.* http://www.ncgia.ucsb.edu/varenius/ppgis/ncgia.html (accessed 15 July 2009).

Craig, W., Harris, T. and Weiner, D. (eds) (2002) *Community Participation and Geographic Information Systems.* London: Taylor & Francis.

Dueker, K. and D. Kjerne, (1989) *Multipurpose Cadastre: Terms and Definitions.* Falls Church, VA: American Society for Photogrammetry and Remote Sensing and American Congress on Surveying and Mapping (ASPRS-ACSM).

Elmes G., Epstein E., Shepard E. and Tulloch D. (2004) 'GIS and society: interrelation, integration, and trasnformation'. In R. McMaster and L. Usery (eds) *A Research Agenda for Geographic Information Science.* Boca Raton, Florida: CRC Press. pp. 287–312.

Goodchild, M. (1992) 'Geographical information science', *International Journal of Geographical Information Systems,* 6(1): 31–45.

Goodchild, M. and Janelle, D. (eds) (2004) *Spatially Integrated Social Science.* Oxford: Oxford University Press.

Harris, T. and Weiner, D. (eds) (1996) *GIS and Society: The Social Implications of How People, Space and Environment Are Represented in GIS,* Specialist Meeting 19. http://www.ncgia.ucsb.edu/Publications/Tech_Reports/96/96–7.PDF.

Janelle, D. and Hodge, D. (eds) (1998) *Varenius Workshop Geographies of the Information Society.* http://www.ncgia.ucsb.edu/conf/InfoSoc/.

Janelle, D. and Hodge, D. (eds) (2000) *Information, Place and Cyberspace.* Berlin: Springer.

Leitner, H., Elwood, S., Sheppard, E., McMaster, S., McMaster, R., (2000) 'Modes of GIS provision and their appropriateness for neighborhood organizations – examples from Minneapolis and St. Paul, MN', *Journal of the Urban and Regional Information Systems Association,* 12(4): 45–58.

McMaster, Robert B. and Harvey, F. (2010) 'Geographic information science and society'. In J.D. Bossler, J.B. Campbell and R.B. McMaster (eds), *A Manual of Geospatial Technology,* 2nd edn. London: Taylor & Francis.

McMaster, R.B. and Usery, E.L. (2005) *A Research Agenda for Geographic Information Science.* Florida: Taylor & Francis.

Nyerges, T. (1993) Understanding the Scope of GIS: Its Relationship to Environmental Modeling. In M. Goodchild, L. Steyaert and B. Parks (eds) *Environmental Modeling with Geographic Information Systems.* London: Oxford University Press, pp. 75–93.

National Research Council (2007) *Putting People on the Map: Protecting Confidentiality with Linked Social-Spatial Data,* Washington DC: National Academcy Press.

Nyerges, T. (2009) 'GIS and Society'. In R. Kitchin and N. Thrift (eds), *Encyclopedia of Human Geography.* Amsterdam: Elsevier Press, pp. 506–512.

Obermeyer, N.J. (1998) 'The Evolution of public participation GIS', *Cartography and Geographic Information Systems,* 25(2): 65–6.

Pickles, J. (eds) (1995) *Ground Truth: The Social Implications for Geographic Information Systems.* New York: Guilford Press.

Schroeder, P. (1996) *Report on Public Participation GIS Workshop.* http://www.geo.wvu.edu/i19/report/public.html.

Schuurman, N. and Kwan, M-P. (2004) 'Guest editorial: taking a walk on the social side of GIS', *Cartographica,* 39(1): 1.

Sheppard, E. and Poiker, T. (eds) (1995) 'Special issue: GIS and society', *Cartography and Geographic Information Systems,* 22(1): entire issue.

Sheppard, E., Couclelis, H., Graham, S., Harrington, J.W. and Onsrud, H. (1999) 'Geographies of the information society', *International Journal of Geographical Information Science,* 13(8): 797–823.

URISA (2003) 'Access and participatory approaches in using geographic information', *URISA Journal,* 15(1): entire issue.

URISA (2005) *PPGIS Conference topics 2005.* http://www.urisa.org/conferences/publicparticipation (accessed 15 July 2009).

APPENDIX A: LANDMARKS MEETINGS AND PUBLICATIONS

Varenius workshop: GIS and society (Harris and Weiner, 1996) http://www.ncgia.ucsb.edu/ Publications/Tech_Reports/96/ 96–7.pdf

- Limits of representation in GIS
- Societal impacts from GIS use
- Societal influences on GIS development/use
- Critical history of GIS
- Ethics in GIS
- Privacy and GIS
- Alternative GIS or GIS2
- Use of GIS in debates about global change
- Gender and GIS

Varenius workshop: public participation GIS (Schroeder, 1996) http://www.geo.wvu.edu/i19/report/ public.html

- Urban data sources and uses
- Dimensions of conflict and dispute resolution
- Current technological possibilities
- Future technological possibilities – GIS2
- Collaborative work
- Public process

Varenius workshop: empowerment, marginalization, and PPGIS (Craig et al., 1998) http://www.ncgia.ucsb. edu/varenius/ppgis/ncgia.html

- 'Successful' implementations of a public participatory GIS
- Changes in local politics and power relationships resulting from the use of GIS in spatial decision making
- What community groups need in the way of information and the role GIS plays or could play in meeting this need
- Current attempts to use GIS to 'empower' communities for spatial decision making
- The impacts on communities of differential access to hardware, software, data, and expertise in GIS production and use

- The educational, social, political, and economic reasons for lack of access and exemplary ways communities have overcome these barriers
- The implications of map-based representations of information for community groups
- The nature of GIS knowledge distortion from 'grassroots' perspectives
- The value of sophisticated analyses for understanding key issues as opposed to the negative impact of such analyses in confusing and marginalizing individuals and groups
- Implications of conflicting knowledge and multiple realities for spatial decision making
- The ways in which socially differentiated communities and their local knowledge are or might be represented within GIS
- GIS as local surveillance
- Identify which public data policies have positive influences on small neighborhood businesses and which are negative
- Develop prospective models (economic, organizational, legal, and technological) that might result in increased and more equitable opportunities among the diverse segments of society in accessing geographic information and tools
- Collaborative decision making involving the public

Varenius workshop Geographies of the Information Society (Janelle and Hodge, 1998) http://www.ncgia. ucsb.edu/conf/InfoSoc/

- Institutions and GIS: emerging frameworks in the information age
- Moving beyond the map as metaphor: representation and multiple realities
- Modeling and simulating geographies in a digital world
- Access to spatial data in networked environments
- Accessibility in a wired world
- Emergent social forms
- Social/geographic implications of information technologies
- Virtual geographies

Public participation GIS special issue of Cartography and GIS (Obermeyer, 1998)

- The evolution of public participation GIS

- Empowerment, marginalization, and community-integrated GIS
- GIS and community-based planning: exploring the diversity of neighborhood perspectives and needs
- Multimedia GIS for planning support and public discourse
- How and why community groups use maps and geographic information
- GPS public participation GIS – barriers to implementation
- Information technologies, advocay, and development: resistence and backlash to industrial shrimp farming

Varenius summary and prospective article (Sheppard et al., 1999)

- Theoretical (and methodological) perspectives on the societal implications of geographical information technologies
- The changing significance of key geographical concepts in the information age
- Societal aspects of the practical application of geographical information technologies
- Place and identity in an age of technologically regulated movement
- Measuring and representing accessibility in the information age (Information, Place, Cyberspace workshop)
- Empowerment, marginalization, and public participation GIS (PPGIS workshop)

Information, Place, and Cyberspace (Janelle and Hodge, 2000)

Contents:

Major themes in *Community Participation and GIS*

- GIS as tool of reason
- GIS as communicative tool
- GIS as tool for community resistance
- CPGIS as 'pioneering'
- CPGIS not a panacea
- GIS to support 'community participation'
- What is 'community' and 'public participation'?
- Consensus
- Local knowledge
- Empowerment and marginalization
- Political

Access to geographic information and participatory processes special issue of the *Urban-Regional Information Systems Association Journal* (URISA, 2003)

Part I – Workshop on access to geographic information and participatory approaches in using geographic information

- Toward a framework for research on geographic information-supported participatory decision making
- In search of rigorous models for policy-oriented research: a behavioral approach to spatial data sharing
- Cultural and institutional conditions for using geographic information; access and participation
- A new era of accessibility?
- World status of national spatial data clearinghouses
- Access to geographic information: a European perspective
- The future of participatory approaches using geographic information: developing a research agenda for the twenty-first century
- Transparency considerations for PPGIS research and development

Part II – Workshop on access to geographic information and participatory approaches in using geographic information

- Public participation GIS and local political context: propositions and research
- Directions
- The issue of access: an assessment guide for evaluating public participation
- Geographic information science case studies
- Reflections on PPGIS: A view from the trenches
- Geographic information and public participation: research proposal from a French perspective
- Digital participation and access to geographic information: a case study of local government in the United Kingdom
- The intersection of data access and public participation: impacting GIS users' success?
- Community-integrated GIS for land reform in South Africa
- A framework for the use of geographic information in participatory community planning and development

Special issue on GIS and Social Science in Cartographica (Schuurman and Kwan, 2004)

SPECIAL ISSUE: GIS AND SOCIAL SCIENCE: NEW RULES OF ENGAGEMENT

- Taking a walk on the social side of GIS
- The utopian potential of GIS
- The third domain: the spread and use of GIS within social science
- Rewiring for a GIS
- GIS and geographic governance: reconstruction the choropleth map
- Adapting to the machine: integrating GIS into qualitative research

UCGIS Research Agenda – chapter on GIS and society (McMaster and Usery, 2005)

GIS and society

- COLO-4 Study ethics of access, copyright, personal liability, and protection of intellectual property for spatial data and related products published, delivered or distributed electronically.
- MN-1 Institutional barriers to use of GIS in decision making
- OH-5 The social impacts of spatial information technologies
- WISC-5 The social impacts of spatial information technologies
- SDSU-4 Developing a critical social theory of GIS
- WVU-1 Representing multiple realities, new models of space

GIS in decision making

- CLRK-5 GIS and decision-making technique
- MN-1 Institutional barriers to use of GIS in decision making
- ORNL-5 Linkages between GIS research and business/government decision making
- WY-1 Decision support systems integrating spatial data with models, expert knowledge, and graphical user interfaces are needed for effective and efficient management of natural resources

Participatory GIS

- CLRK-3 Linking participatory approaches in institutional environments
- ME-4 Public forum GIS

Spatially Integrated Social Science (Goodchild and Janelle, 2004)

- Thinking spatially in the social sciences/Michael F. Goodchild and Donald G. Janelle
- Inferring the behavior of households from remotely sensed changes in land cover: current methods and future directions/Bruce Boucek and Emilio F. Moran
- Geovisualization of human activity patterns using 3D GIS: a time-geographic approach/Mei-Po Kwan and Jiyeong Lee
- Agent-based modeling: from individual residential choice to urban residential dynamics/Itzhak Benenson
- Too much of the wrong kind of data: implications for the practice of micro-scale spatial modeling/David O'Sullivan

Neighborhood-level analysis

- Identifying ethnic neighborhoods with census data: group concentration and spatial clustering/John R. Logan and Wenquan Zhang
- Spatial analyses of homicide with areal data/Steven F. Messner and Luc Anselin
- Spatial (dis)advantage and homicide in Chicago neighborhoods/Robert J. Sampson and Jeffrey D. Morenoff
- Measuring spatial diffusion of shots fired activity across city neighborhoods/Jacqueline Cohen and George Tita
- The spatial structure of urban political discussion networks/Munroe Eagles, Paul Bélanger, and Hugh W. Calkins

Region-level analysis

- Mapping social exclusion and inclusion in developing countries: spatial patterns of São Paulo in the 1990s/Gilberto Camara, Aldaiza Sposati, Dirce Koga, Antonio Miguel Monteiro, Frederico

Roman Ramos, Eduardo Camargo, and Suzana Druck Fuks
- Business location and spatial externalities: tying concepts to measures/Stuart H Sweeney and Edward J. Feser
- Updating spatial perspectives and analytical frameworks in urban research/Qing Shen
- Spatial analysis of regional income inequality/Sergio J. Rey
- Shaping policy decisions with spatial analysis/Ted K. Bradshaw and Brian Muller
- Geographical approaches for reconstructing past human behavior from prehistoric roadways/John Kantner

Multi-scale spatial perspectives

- Time, space, and archaeological landscapes: establishing connections in the first millennium BC/Patrick Daly and Gary Lock
- Spatial perspectives in public health/Anthony C. Gatrell and Janette E. Rigby
- The role of spatial analysis in demographic research/John R. Weeks
- Spatial interaction models of international telecommunication flows/Jean-Michel Guldmann
- Planning scenario visualization and assessment: a cellular automata based integrated spatial decision support system/Roger White, Bas Straatman, and Guy Engelen

URISA 2005 PPGIS Conference topics (URISA, 2005) http://www.urisa.org/PPGIS/ppgis.htm

Critical GIS

- Gender, race, class diversity of information use
- Types of power influencing information creation and use
- Access to information and implications for outcomes
- Subjectivity/positionality of information producers and users
- Correspondence of world, database, map database representation as validity
- Types of democracy and implications for public involvement

- Social/environmental justice
- Critical perspectives on cartography

Practice, monitoring and evaluation of GIS use

- Case studies illustrating a successful implementation of GIS
- Participatory use of GIS by stakeholder groups
- Use of GIS in specific sectors (e.g. social service provision and policy, health services, urban planning, environment, transit and disability)
- Development of applications to analyze and model data, collect and display information, inform and educate the public, and advocate for policy change
- Techniques (cartographic designs, visualization methods, computational and analytical methods) (probably belongs in GIScience below)
- Integration of GIS and other technologies (e.g., Internet, GPS and simulation software)
- Educational, social, political, and economic barriers to access and exemplary ways communities have overcome these barriers
- Techniques and measures for the evaluation of GIS

GIScience

- Ontology and scale in GIS for social science applications
- Implications of map-based representations of information for community groups
- The nature of GIS knowledge (e.g., local versus expert knowledge, transforming data into knowledge)
- Politics and power relationships resulting from the use of GIS for decision making
- Ethical issues in GIS
- GIS as used for surveillance and corporate control
- Models of economic, organizational, legal and/or technological issues that increase and

equalize access to GIS tools for diverse segments of society
- Data models that reflect the sanctity and values of local cultures
- Impacts on communities of differential access to hardware, software, data and expertise in GIS production and use
- Role of GIS in meeting the information needs of community groups
- Role of spatial analyses in understanding/marginalizing communities
- Virtual communities and physical communities in PPGIS
- Quality control for research
- Modeling participatory processes

Data issues

- Encryption, confidentiality, and privacy of spatial data
- Legal issues and information ownership
- Data sources, quality and accuracy
- Public information dissemination, sharing and access
- Data models that reflect values of the local culture
- Libraries as spatial data (including metadata) providers and educators

Organizations and institutions

- Role of public and private sectors in social use of GIS
- Education and learning structures for social use of GIS
- Funding structures and sources
- Sustaining PPGIS – securing funding after seed grants end, training and retaining staff, data maintenance and so on
- Emergence of technical assistance/data provision infrastructure
- Economics of GIScience/systems

GIS and Society Research

Foundations of GIS and Society Research

Concepts, Principles, Tools, and Challenges in Spatially Integrated Social Science

Donald G. Janelle and Michael F. Goodchild

INTRODUCTION

The historical legacies of using maps and spatial reasoning in the social sciences date back more than two centuries. However, early examples represent piecemeal applications by comparatively few scholars who saw that spatial context offered important clues to understanding human behavior and to resolving societal problems. A more widespread application of spatial perspectives in the social sciences has emerged in the past two decades, with the result that place, regional context, and spatial concepts are now increasingly seen as important contributors to social science theories and models and to empirical analyses about human processes and interactions. The expanded focus on spatial perspective has been made possible by improved computer capabilities for processing and storing large amounts of information, by advances in technologies for acquiring geographically referenced data and for making it accessible for researchers and policy decision makers, and by the development of new software tools and Internet capabilities to analyze, display, and disseminate spatial information.

This chapter describes how technologies for gathering, processing, analyzing, and displaying geo-referenced information have opened paths for spatial thinking and for the discovery of complex relationships that are revealed most clearly in geographical context. It outlines general principles of spatially integrated social science and some of the fundamental concepts of spatial thinking that are of most value to interdisciplinary perspectives on issues in the social sciences (Goodchild and Janelle, 2004). Through analytical cartography, spatial statistics, and geographic information systems (GIS), social scientists integrate theory and empirical analyses around five significant examples of spatial reasoning. These include: (1) identifying changes in the uses of, and regional differentiation of, space(s); (2) measuring the physical arrangement and clustering of phenomena to detect spatial patterns; (3) documenting spatial patterns over time to infer processes; (4) studying flows (e.g., migration, trade, and shopping patterns) between specific locations as indicators of spatio-temporal interactions; and (5) measuring spatial associations (and space–time associations) for testing hypotheses.

WHAT IS SPATIALLY INTEGRATED SOCIAL SCIENCE?

An underlying premise of spatially integrated social science (SISS) is that theories and problems intrinsic to the social sciences should govern the empirical issues for investigation and the applications of spatial concepts and tools (Goodchild et al., 2000). In the social sciences, primary research themes span problems at local through global scales. They range from the sense of place associated with daily life to the interdependences associated with regional and global interconnections. They also reflect needs for descriptive and predictive tools that enhance insights on the meanings of spatial patterns and how they relate to societal processes that impinge on all aspects of social well-being. Nonetheless, the case for embedding geospatial thinking into the foundations of interdisciplinary practice go beyond the application of techniques to a deeper understanding about the spatial patterning of social and environmental processes.

Researchers in anthropology, archaeology, economics, history, human geography, political science, and sociology, among other disciplines, are turning their attention to geo-referencing practices to capture locational information (e.g., matching a numeric street address with digital latitude–longitude coordinates), which contributes to a more complete understanding of social behavior, refinements in the prediction of human actions, and enhanced knowledge for

addressing societal issues. This was not the case a decade ago but, today, all of these disciplines have examples of pioneer academic departments that include geographic information systems and spatial statistics within their curricula.[1]

SISS owes its origins to the integration of spatial analytical methods with the theories and thematic problems of the social sciences and to the proposition that many social processes and problems are better understood through the mapping of phenomena and the analysis of spatiotemporal patterns. Maps and the application of cartographic visualization principles constitute important media for exploratory analysis and communication. Graphic design, cartographic symbolization, thematic mapping of statistical data over space and time, and geographic visualization for spatial data exploration and knowledge construction, are all of potential value to spatial approaches in the social sciences (Tufte, 1983). However, it is important to embed the use of such tools in a framework of basic principles.

PRINCIPLES OF SPATIALLY INTEGRATED SOCIAL SCIENCE

The primary principles of SISS include integration, spatiotemporal context, spatially explicit modeling, and place-based analysis. It is suggested that applications of these principles result in insights that would not be possible without the spatial perspective.

Integration

Spatially aware social science uses descriptive and analytic tools to integrate diverse information sources to help capture and understand the complexity of social and environmental processes and interactions across geographic scales. Space is the basis of integration. Location provides an essential link between the variously disparate forms of information, and between the distinct processes considered by different disciplines. Spatial analysis facilitates understanding such relationships by means of maps, spatial statistics, and other methods that exploit the representation of information according to the locations and spatial relationships of people, places, and their surroundings. Thus, a map depicting environmental quality can be overlaid with a map showing human health patterns to examine correlations that may suggest clues for additional data gathering and analysis and might extend future investigations into potential issues of environmental justice.

GIS technologies provide tools to explore complex relationships among interrelated social, economic, and environmental factors. Capitalizing on its representation of the multiple properties of places, GIS conceptualizes the world as a series of layers, each mapping a specific property, or class of properties, and allows for correlating and integrating information across layers. The explicit and tangible account of overlapping patterns permits insights on the integration of societal processes, a recognition of the importance of place in these processes, and the opportunity to integrate the perspectives of different disciplines.

The integration of social data by location is a core principle whereby space becomes an important mechanism for linking the analysis and understanding of social processes with data resources. An interesting variant of this is the increasingly widespread practice of posting pictures and information matched with locations on geo-browsers, such as Google Earth™, for global dissemination. This represents, potentially, a new domain of information for the social sciences that is discussed in this section under place-based analysis.

Spatiotemporal context

The understanding of social processes requires, in principle, an appreciation of all possible sources of variation and influence from within a spatial setting (place, neighborhood, region), from beyond its borders, and across time.

The co-location of economic and social processes may offer valuable perspectives on changes over time. However, the cross-sectional biases of most spatial data are assessed against the longitudinal data needs for investigating changes in social processes over time. General spatial concepts (e.g., distance, location, and adjacency) may serve as useful surrogates for interpreting patterns and processes but there are limits to the utility of GIS for capturing social process, and there is a need to structure new exploratory tools for space-time referencing of information (Anderton, 1996). Space–time representation and analytic approaches await further development in order to facilitate process-oriented analysis in the social sciences, though innovative efforts, such as STARS (Space Time Analysis of Regional Systems, Rey and Janikas [2006], http://regional-analysislab.org/), and the TerraSeer® Space-time Intelligence System™ (http://www.terraseer.com/products_stis.php) point to solutions in certain fields.

In drawing on important historical records (spanning decades or centuries), social scientists frequently confront information resources that are not accessible in digital form, that span multiple changes in the definitions of variables, and that include changes in the levels of temporal and spatial aggregation over time. Such inherent lack of comparability in the quality of data across changes in spatial and temporal scales illustrates the challenges of embracing a space–time perspective in research.

Conversely, through GPS tracking technologies, researchers can now exploit the technical capability to acquire geo-referenced data in real time at micro levels, including the individual level of trip traces and space–time diaries. In combination with the time-geographic perspective, introduced by Torsten Hägerstrand (1970) and expanded upon through GIS applications by Kwan and Lee (2004), Miller (2005), and others, the linking of GPS locations and diary entries allows researchers to focus specifically on the behavior represented by the space-time paths of individuals and subpopulations (e.g., the elderly).

Over the past few decades, there have been advances in modeling frameworks to focus directly on processes, especially through agent-based modeling and micro-simulation methods. The argument for micro-simulation spatial modeling and agent-based spatial modeling is certainly a reflection of their utility for thinking in process terms and for surmounting issues associated with data requirements for analy-sis-based research. However, computation requirements aside, cautionary notes about conflating plausible results with verification are at the heart of debate on the merits of simulation approaches (Couclelis, 2001; O'Sullivan, 2004).[2]

Spatially explicit modeling

Space and spatial perspective, often implicit in the theoretical frameworks adopted in the social sciences, can be made explicit through formalized models that link theory with process. Many such models are grounded in a scientific understanding that reflects the universality of space as a basic dimen-sion of reality. For instance, a feature asso-ciated with micro-simulation models is the assignment of parameter values about pro-pensities for human activities and land use patterns to reflect the influence of spatial attributes on human behavior. Thus, distance and direction, and the impact of spatial barriers, may be assigned central position in descriptive and predictive models of human interactions.

In economics, Krugman (1991) and others have pioneered a New Economic Geography that includes the addition of space to theories about the operation of markets and how they reflect impedance in the flows of infor-mation and the impact of transport costs.

The concept of distance decay in spatial behavior was the basis on which Dr. John Snow reasoned about the role of drinking water in the transmission of cholera in nineteenth-century London (Johnson, 2006; Snow, [1854] 1936). Similarly, the impact of distance is often reflected in models about the propensity to migrate, the out-comes of marketing strategies, the optimiza-tion of public facility locations, the allocation of land resources to enhance income or sustainability, and the space–time diffusion of innovations. All of these are examples where spatial patterns and processes are linked explicitly with the theoretical pers-pectives of the social sciences. Hence, it is argued that the incorporation of spatially explicit modeling adds new knowledge to our understanding of social processes. Recent advances in spatial econometrics have been especially valuable in measuring the independent contribution of space to explaining a broad range of social processes (see Anselin et al., 2004).

Place-based analysis

In spatially integrated social science, places (e.g., a neighborhood, city, county, or some other unit) are seen as natural repositories of the multiple social processes that occur simultaneously and that span the per-spectives of a broad range of disciplines. Scientific knowledge is most usefully applied when it is combined with specific knowledge of local and regional conditions. For example, instances of crime may be better understood when mapped to reflect the order and timing of occurrences exam-ined in relationship to the surrounding neighborhoods in which they occur (Tita and Cohen, 2004). Place-based analysis has been used to reveal hot spots in spatial distributions (e.g., of crimes or cases of dis-ease), and to reason about possible causes. GIS facilitates the understanding of such processes by combining local knowledge in the form of digital maps stored in databases with general principles in the form of algorithms, models, and analytical methods.

A comparatively new twist on place-based analysis is evolving through the insights of volunteered geographic information and Web 2.0 technologies (Goodchild, 2007). New web services, including geo-tagged entries in Wikipedia, place descriptions in Wikimapia, and sites such as OpenStreetMap support volunteer efforts to create public-domain geospatial data layers. Other examples include the geo-tagged photographs of Flickr™, and mashups with Google Earth™ and Google Maps™. Though researchers can learn a lot about places and geographic patterns through such sources, there is a need for rigorous assessments of how such information can be synthesized, verified, and integrated into scientific research.[3]

Aside from being a clue to scientific understanding, geographical location also has value for organizing information and for searching for information resources – often referred to as place-based search. New information resources, such as digital geolibraries (e.g., the Alexandria Digital Library, http://alexandria.sdc.ucsb.edu/) and even more general Internet search tools, increasingly use geographic location to find the data used in spatial analysis and GIS. Location holds one of the keys for integrating qualitative and quantitative information and for reconciling the fragmentation of data resources that are scattered among archives, censuses, and the holdings of individual scholars and public and private institutions.

FROM PRINCIPLES TO BASIC CONCEPTS

Long prior to the development of sophisticated software for mapping and analysis, innovative scholars and planners were incorporating the principles of integration, spatiotemporal context, spatially explicit modeling, and place-based analysis in research. Their theories, models, and descriptive analyses often reflected applications of basic spatial concepts to help understand the spatial imprint of human activities. Early applications of spatial concepts help document the historical legacies of using maps and spatial reasoning to understand social processes and to solve problems. Von Thünen (1826) modeled land use patterns of commodity production based on market locations, rent potentials, and transport costs, an approach replicated and expanded upon in urban economics by Alonso (1964) in the mid-twentieth century to explain land use structures of metropolitan areas.

In the heyday of the Industrial Revolution in Europe and North America, sociologists, such as Charles Booth (see Bales, 1999) and Florence Kelly (1895), were mapping social conditions in urban areas to help identify neighborhoods and regions of poverty and social need, and journalist/criminologist Henry Mayhew (1861) was exploring crime patterns in London and across England for evidence to social well-being. These pioneers used concepts of distance, location, and neighborhood. Charles Minard (see Robinson, 1967) used an innovative mapping of flows along invasion routes to depict the movement and attrition over time and space of Napoleon's troops in Eastern Europe and Russia.

By the mid- twentieth century, political scientist Vladimer Orlando Key (1949) was using maps to depict spatial associations between voting behavior and socioeconomic circumstances across the American South, sociologist Rupert Vance (1936) used maps to depict evidence of cultural and economic variations in regionalism in the South, and linguist Hans Kurath (1949) speculated about migration patterns and regional cultures in the eastern USA based on a mapping of the words that people used to describe features of everyday life (e.g., soda, tonic, or pop; see http://www.popvssoda.com). Zvi Grilihes ([1957] 1988), an economist, investigated the diffusion of hybrid corn seed to assess regional patterns of innovation adoption in the agricultural economy. Another economist, Robert Fogel (1971), employed distance buffers to isolate the impact of nineteenth-century canal development on American economic expansion.

Spatial graphics were also used to describe theoretical constructs about the regional division of social groups in cities, and maps were a basis for empirical documentation and validation (Park et al., 1925). This interest, extended in the mid-twentieth century with applications of social area analysis (Shevky and Bell, 1955) and factorial ecology (e.g., see Murdie, 1969), helped in the extraction of general patterns of social differentiation from census data at the tract level (and other small areas) for urban centers around the world.

As these early examples illustrate, the social sciences have a rich history of applying maps and spatial thinking to understanding social processes. Implicitly, if not explicitly, these pioneer researchers embraced the principles of integration, spatiotemporal context, spatially explicit modeling, and place-based analysis, making use of the fundamental concepts of location, distance, neighborhood, and region. Often, their work hinted at higher ordered spatial thought relating to scale effects, spatial associations, networks, spread effects, and spatial dependencies. These more advanced concepts, featured below, achieved significance among researchers in the last half of the twentieth century, coinciding with advancements in general quantitative reasoning and new computational capabilities in the social sciences.

CONCEPTUAL FOUNDATIONS FOR SPATIAL THINKING

Several scholars have attempted to identify the core geographical concepts of spatial thinking, notably Nystuen (1963) and Golledge (1995, 2002). Cutter et al. (2002) focus on the "big ideas" of geography and de Smith et al. (2009) expand on these and other earlier discussions, using the formalisms of contemporary geographic information science and their expression in GIS. They present a comprehensive set of concepts with explicit illustrations of their value for integrative modeling, analysis, and problem solving that are applicable to a cross-section of academic disciplines and societal issues.

Table 2.1 presents a synthesis of concepts of value to the geospatial analysis of phenomena in the social sciences. This includes the identity of problems associated with each concept, along with suggested tools and measures that may lead to solutions. The references listed in the table provide more complete discussions, including strategies for solving and mitigating problems associated with each concept.

The concepts listed in Table 2.1 are the foundation for practices of spatial reasoning in all branches of knowledge that focus on geo-space. They lie at the heart of the processes by which scientific knowledge emerges from spatial data. Although these concepts are now expressed in the tools of GIS and spatial statistics, a firm understanding of each concept is essential if these powerful tools are to be used effectively. Unlike the previous section, where emphasis was on historical precedents of applying spatial concepts, the remainder of this chapter focuses on contemporary applications of the concepts listed in Table 2.1.

CONCEPTS AND ANALYSIS TOOLS FOR SPATIOTEMPORAL REASONING IN THE SOCIAL SCIENCES

Applications of spatial thinking in the social sciences seldom make use of a single concept in isolation from others. Rather, applications generally integrate multiple spatial concepts simultaneously to engage general types of spatial reasoning to: (1) detect changes in the uses of, and regional differentiation of, space(s); (2) measure the physical

Table 2.1   Foundation concepts in spatial thinking[4]

Location	*Understanding formal and informal methods of specifying "where"*
	Primary concept: Point locations (e.g., street addresses and geographical coordinates) and divisions of the world (often recognized as place names, landmarks, or reporting units (e.g., postal zones, census tracts, counties, and other administrative units)) are the primary means of specifying where something is located.
	Subsidiary concepts: Locations may be abstracted within referencing systems as points (e.g., street addresses and coordinates), lines (e.g., polylines), and areas (e.g., polygons, rasters, grid cells, and tessellations). The attributes of places are assigned to such reference units.
	Problems: Important technical issues include uncertainty about positional accuracy, the need for planimetrically correct representations of spatial distributions, recognition of how the scale of measurement alters locational information, and assessing the consequences of using alternative mathematical approximations to the shape of the earth (geoid). In human discourse, placenames, prepositions, and movement verbs may reflect different cultures, different practices of land ownership, and different approaches to spatial thinking.
	Tools and measurements: Maps, map projections, and coordinate systems are primary tools for assigning location. Measurement and tracking of location through modern global positioning systems (GPS) have supplemented traditional surveying methods. Location is also important as a common key for searching information through Internet-based search tools.
	Key references: Hill, 2006
Distance	*The ability to reason from knowledge of relative position*
	Primary concept: Distances define relationships between places by measures of proximity.
	Subsidiary concepts: Examples include relative distances (e.g., relative location based on Euclidean and non-Euclidean metrics), distances in rasters, buffers, multidimensional scaling, weight matrices, and social distances.
	Problems: Accounting for the influence of distance on interaction and spatial behavior. Incorporating distance-decay effects in spatial interaction models and identifying optimum paths based on geodesics, potential fields, and cost surfaces. Specifying weights matrices for applications in spatial analysis and modeling.
	Tools and measurements: Metrics of distance on the plane and globe. Measures such as travel cost and travel time transform distances into measures of effort.
	Key references: Kimerling and Muehrcke, 2005
Neighborhood and Region	*Drawing inferences from spatial context*
	Primary concept: Understanding the situations and neighborhoods of places.
	Subsidiary concepts: Definitions of neighborhood based on the spatial behavior of humans and other organisms. Formal and functional regions and concepts of territory.
	Problems: Models of region design and political districting. The modifiable areal unit problem and the ecological fallacy.
	Tools and measurements: Metrics of fragmentation and shape. Techniques of areal interpolation. Clustering algorithms for aggregating spatial units.
	Key references: Montello, et al., 2003; Reibel, 2007
Networks	*Understanding the importance of connections and flows*
	Primary concept: Representation of linear networks for transportation, communication, and social interaction.
	Subsidiary concepts: Distinctions between planar and non-planar networks, circuits and trees, routes and paths, and networks as graphs and matrices.

Table 2.1   Cont'd

	Problems: Choosing among alternative ways of defining and weighting network nodes and links. Directional data (e.g., traffic flow) require specialized methods of analysis and may exhibit special characteristics (e.g., anisotropy). Specifying models of network development and design. Choosing alternative measures of connectivity and degrees of separation. Representing networks in spatial databases. Accounting for spatial dependencies in network structures.
	Tools and measurements: Many geographic phenomena are limited to the nodes and links of linear networks, such as roads or rivers, and require specialized measures of distance, connectivity, accessibility, and valence. Models of network flow assignment.
	Key references: Ahuja et al.,1993; Bialynicki-Birula and Bialynicki-Birula, 2004; Doreian 1990; Okabe et al., 2006
Overlays	*Inferring spatial associations by comparing mapped variables by locations*
	Primary concept: Superimposing maps to describe and analyze relationships between different features of the same location or geographic space.
	Subsidiary concepts: Intersections and unions of areas, lines, and points to identify patterns and relationships; mashups of different data registered to the same locations or areal units; merging, aggregating, and disaggregating areas based on joining areal units.
	Problems: Validating visualized associations among variables, adjusting for boundary mismatch for variables mapped by different spatial units, weighting different layers (attributes), or selecting class intervals to achieve different spatial configurations.
	Tools and measurements: Geographic information system (GIS); joins and unions.
	Key references: McHarg, 1969; O'Sullivan and Unwin, 2002; Reibel, 2007
Scale	*Understanding spatial scale and its significance*
	Primary concept: The level of detail of a geographic data set is one of its most important characteristics. Definitions of scale embrace spatial extent and level of resolution.
	Subsidiary concepts: Generalization, downscaling, and self-similarity (fractals).
	Problems: Scale is related to the uncertainty of how selection of spatial units can affect analytical results and interpretation of processes. The modifiable areal units problem (MAUP) demonstrates how analytic results depend on the sizes and shapes of geographic units chosen for analysis and can be influenced by ecological data.
	Tools and measurements: Procedures for downscaling, line and surface smoothing, recursive subdivision, variance decomposition, and multi-level analysis.
	Key references: Goodchild, 1997; Montello, 2001; Openshaw, 1983; Sheppard, 2004; Sinton, 1978
Spatial Heterogeneity	*The implications of spatial variability*
	Primary concept: The geographic world is fundamentally heterogeneous.
	Subsidiary concepts: First-order effects, non-stationarity, and uncontrolled variance.
	Problems: Implications of spatial heterogeneity for sampling and statistical inference.
	Tools and measurements: As opposed to complete description, spatial sampling is often used to characterize the attributes of geographic spatial units, with the results varying depending on the methods used (e.g., random, systematic, or stratified samples), measurable via landscape metrics (local indicators), place-based analysis, and geographically weighted analysis.
	Key references: Anselin, 2000; Forman, 1995; Fotheringham et al., 2002; MacArthur and Wilson, 1967
Spatial Dependence	*Understanding relationships across space*
	Primary concept: Attributes of places that are near to each other tend to be more similar than attributes of places that are far apart (Tobler's First Law).

Table 2.1   Cont'd

	Subsidiary concepts: The identification of spatial clusters, formal regions, distance-decay and spatial-lag effects, and autoregressive processes all display properties of spatial dependence. Understanding spatial dependence is important in the analysis of spatial interactions (such as migration, travel to work, or socializing), which tend to decline with increasing separation in predictable ways, influencing spatial choices and flows. Spatial dependence conditions the separation of activities in space, with notable impacts on the spatial organization of the economy (e.g., central services, location-allocation, functional regions, and service hinterlands).
	Problems: Statistical inference in the presence of spatial dependence; explicit models of spatial dependence; analysis of point patterns and cluster detection; the role of spatial dependence in uncertainty.
	Tools and measurements: Metrics of spatial dependence include the Moran, Geary, and Getis Indices. Geostatistics offers a theoretical framework for spatial data and spatial interpolation.
	Key references: Boots and Getis, 1988; Doreian, 1980; Isaaks and Srivastava, 1989; Journel and Huijbregts, 1978; Sweeney and Feser, 2004; Tobler, 1970
Objects and Fields	*Are phenomena continuous in space-time or discrete?*
	Primary concept: Discrete objects and continuous fields are fundamental conceptualizations of space and the basis for models of process.
	Subsidiary concepts: Spatial objects are the things that occupy the geographic world, described and measured in various ways as points, lines, areas, or volumes. The discrete-objects perspective is a traditional way of characterizing spatial patterns and is embedded in the uses of geospatial tools such as cartographic mapping and GIS. Yet, powerful insights into spatial processes often require a re-conceptualization of phenomena from objects to fields. Conceptualizing the geographic world as a series of continuous surfaces (fields), each mapping location to the value of some variable, permits representations of gradient, slope, and aspect, and allows for volumetric, visibility, and least-cost-path analyses.
	Problems: The spatial fields concept leads into issues of spatial interpolation (e.g., estimating the value of a field at places where it has not been measured). The object-field dichotomy poses alternative methods of spatial representation and analysis, with attendant issues of uncertainty in both conceptualizations.
	Tools and measurements: Tools for implementing the field concept include contour interpolation, inverse distance weighting, natural neighbor, radial basis functions, linear and non-linear triangulation, geostatistics, density estimation (e.g., density per unit area), and assessments of spatial probability (i.e., the likelihood of something happening at a place), presented as probability fields, species range maps, trade area estimations, or risk maps. Spatial correlation.
	Key references: Couclelis, 1992; Goodchild et al., 2007; Peuquet, 2002

arrangement and clustering of phenomena to identify spatial patterns; (3) document spatial patterns over time to infer processes; (4) study flows (e.g., migration, trade, and shopping patterns) between specific locations as indicators of spatiotemporal interactions; and (5) measure spatial associations (and space-time associations) to test hypotheses. The concepts in Table 2.1 can be combined in different ways to assist any of these applications in a broad range of investigations.

Consider, for example, a team of social scientists interested in the sociopolitical and population structures and dynamics of a metropolitan region in the USA. Drawing on theoretical constructs about such processes as population and economic growth, market forces and land use, housing and commuting choices, and social mobility and neighborhood transitions, there are a wide variety of potential academic and policy issues to investigate. By accommodating information and data at all scales of analysis – at the individual and household levels, as well as aggregations by standard census and political units – options for research topics and analytical methodologies are kept open. This framework permits use of any of the spatial analytic and information display tools, concepts, and spatial reasoning processes discussed in this chapter. Readers are invited to consider advanced discussions on specific research topics in leading textbooks and research reviews.[5] The examples suggested below are intended as illustrative rather than exhaustive and they are limited to questions about the structure and dynamics of a metropolitan region.

- Overlaying maps within a GIS may suggest relationships to explain variances across space in, for instance, ethnicity, political party allegiance, economic status, and social cohesion.
- GIS overlays and spatial analysis of neighborhood population characteristics with levels of toxic emissions or proximity to noxious facilities (e.g., a waste incinerator or a brownfield site) may be investigated for evidence of social or environmental injustice (Maantay, 2002).
- A search for correlates among variables aggregated by census tracts could shed understanding about patterns of disease transmission or exposures to environmental hazards.
- Analysis of spatial dependence in cross-sectional data can reveal insights into the spatial scale of causal mechanisms in domains as diverse as crime, housing markets, and job access. For example, how do car burglaries and acts of criminal violence relate to distances from clusters of liquor or drug outlets?
- Evidence of social pathology at community levels (Shaw and McKay, 1969) may show correlation with environmental factors and population densities, but considerations of spatial autocorrelations may suggest other forces at play (Loftin and Ward, 1981; Sampson et al., 2002).
- Researchers may reflect on correlations of individual activity behavior (from space–time diaries) with levels of obesity and the presence of park space or land use structures that encourage walking.
- A mapping of the concentration and clustering of ethnicity data by census units may help assess how assimilation processes alter the neighborhood foundations of ethnic groups in a metropolitan area (Logan and Zhang, 2004).
- Indices of segregation among ethnic and racial groups based on small-area data (e.g., census block groups) may change over time to reflect trends in social mobility, immigration, or other factors (Reardon and Firebaugh, 2002).
- Documenting residential moves within and across regions of the city may reveal if neighborhood demographic transitions respond to changing land markets and to public investments in social infrastructure.
- The graphic illustration of patterns as continuous variables over space (fields) makes sense for measures of average daily temperatures but might also be appropriate where theories and models permit the interpolation of values between sampled sites, as, for example, in estimating house values or the likelihood of noise exposure to traffic densities.
- Distance zones provide a basis of estimating a store's access to markets or to determine the potential client base for health clinics.
- Spatial dependencies in party voting tendencies at the precinct level may reflect the sense of shared community expectations and the spatial patterns of interpersonal networks (Eagles et al., 2004).
- Studying flows between specific locations within a neighborhood and beyond may reveal networks and spatiotemporal structures that foster interactions (e.g., social visits, commutes to work, or financial transactions). For instance, the origins of commodities sold in local markets may signal the level of the region's integration with national and global economies.

The examples above focus on topics at neighborhood and metropolitan scales, but they could be extended to integrate the micro geographies of households or global patterns of production and commerce, and environment–health interactions. Of course, the realm of social science research is forever unfolding with new hot topics, evolution in explanatory theories, and improved modeling and analysis tools. In addition, there are ongoing changes in infrastructures for communication, information retrieval and use, and analysis, all of which will impinge on the continued development of spatially integrated social science.

SPATIAL ANALYSIS SOFTWARE TOOLS

Beyond the many advances in GIS (reviewed by the editors in the introduction to this volume), analytic tools tailor-made for researchers in the social sciences have helped in the last decade to facilitate applications of the principles and practices of spatially integrated social science.[6] Some of the more easily accessed, affordable, and widely used of these software tools are listed below.

- GeoDa™ was released in 2003 as a free and easy-to-use software package. It provides an exploratory tool to describe, map, and analyze spatial data. More importantly, it has expanded the capabilities for social scientists to account for higher-order geographical effects on social patterns and processes, such as spatial autocorrelation and spatial heterogeneity. Rey and Anselin (2006) review the development and utility of *GeoDa*.
- Geographically weighted regression (GWR) (Fotheringham et al., 2002) recognizes that social processes usually vary depending on where they take place (i.e., spatial non-stationarity). GWR provides a method to account explicitly for localized multivariate spatial relationships in a regression framework, with local parameter estimates displayed usually as a continuous surface mapped within a GIS or with other software for data visualization.
- STARS (Space Time Analysis of Regional Systems, Rey and Janikas [2006]) is an open-source package for analyzing temporal trends in data aggregated by areal units for successive times or periods. It features dynamically linked graphical views to help researchers explore changing space–time relationships.
- R, a programming language for statistics and related graphics, features access to a number of specialized spatial analysis packages for point and areal data and cluster analysis (Baddeley and Turner, 2005). These programs provide significant flexibility for the analyst adept at writing customized scripts.
- CrimeStat® is tailored for use in crime analysis and crime mapping (Levine, 2007). It links GIS capabilities with descriptive tools for distance and hot-spot analysis of pattern distributions, spatial interpolation, and travel modeling, all of which are adaptable to a variety of social science applications.

CHALLENGES AND OPPORTUNITIES FOR THE FUTURE OF SPATIAL ANALYSIS IN THE SOCIAL SCIENCES

Applications of spatially integrated thinking in the social sciences reveal how the merger of spatial concepts with the processing power of GIS and other spatial technologies enhances opportunities to communicate results for research and teaching and to provide contextual real-world grounding for community discourse in solving societal problems. Nonetheless, there are impediments to embedding spatial concepts and spatial reasoning as standard practices within the social sciences and for problem solving. There are methodological challenges associated with the informed use of concepts and analytical tools, and with framing modeling approaches from a sound base of theoretical understanding. These are critically important but are treated elsewhere in this handbook and in the references noted in Table 2.1. In this section, the focus is on three interrelated challenges – information, communication, and infrastructure.

Information challenges

Social scientists explore and analyze a wide range of data resources, derived from diverse methodologies – from qualitative to quantitative, from field observation to laboratory experimentation, from standardized censuses to customized surveys, and from descriptive analysis to theory and modeling. This work yields thousands of heterogeneous data sources that relate to social and economic behavior around the world, but their unique data formats, customized subject categorizations, and diverse archival constraints preclude the ideal of a one-stop search capability for integrating such information. Even with sophisticated web tools, researchers must search separately and compile results from a multitude of different sources. Another common problem is that data gathered for political units (e.g., counties, states or provinces, or nations) are often not easily integrated with data collected from different underlying geographies (e.g., administratively defined regions, watersheds, buffers, or pixels). Furthermore, political and other administrative representations change over time as boundaries shift, units split or merge, or data-gathering organizations introduce new techniques that can affect the continuity and quality of time series data. Reibel (2007) describes strategies for coping with such issues in demography, but similar approaches would apply to other social sciences that rely on spatially aggregated data sources.

Although the task for integrating information for the social sciences is daunting, notable advances have helped to enhance resources in the spatial domain for social science research. The following projects focus on what may be termed re-spatialization (Goodchild et al., 1993) and new analysis tools tailored for broad social science applications, all of which are helpful to advancing the principles of spatially integrated social science.

- The National Historical Geographic Information System (NHGIS) addresses shifts in reporting zones of the US census since the eighteenth century, providing aggregate census data and GIS-compatible boundary files for the USA between 1790 and 2000. These cover a wide range of geographies, including blocks, census tracts, counties, metropolitan statistical areas, states, voting districts, zip codes, and many other tabulations. Hosted by the University of Minnesota's Minnesota Population Center, the NHGIS provides important facilitation for historical research on the changing demographic, economic, and social geographies of the United States (see http://www.nhgis.org/).
- The Gridded Population of the World (GPW) project, hosted by the Center for International Earth Science Information Network (CIESIN) at Columbia University transforms population data collected for national and subnational administrative units into population totals and densities on a grid defined by lines of latitude and longitude (Tobler et al., 1997). This permits researchers to integrate GPW with other gridded datasets (e.g., remote sensing data), to reaggregate population to alternative spatial units (e.g., watersheds, biomes, or metropolitan regions), and to weight other variables by population characteristics (see http://sedac.ciesin.columbia.edu/plue/gpw). Recent versions of GPW include urban and rural information that allow new insights on global patterns of human settlement.
- The Integrated Public Use Microdata Series (IPUMS) provides individual- and household-level census survey data over several decades in the USA and for several census years in many other countries. The Minnesota Population Center is creating an exceptional resource for cross-national and cross-temporal research (McCaa and Ruggles, 2002), collecting, preserving, harmonizing, disseminating, and documenting such data for the USA and, currently, for 26 other counties (see http://www.pop.umn.edu/data).

These data initiatives are exemplary in their attempts to resolve fundamental problems of linking data across different kinds of boundaries and across periods. Yet the task of embedding the perspectives of spatial analysis in the social sciences retains notable hurdles. A recent editorial in *Nature* (2008) makes the bold (but accurate) assertion that there is no excuse for not linking all survey and research observations with geo-referenced coordinates, whether or not they serve the immediate interests of the researchers. This editorial points to the information challenges that confront the adoption of spatially informed reasoning in all sciences but, also, to critical communication challenges that seem especially poignant for the social sciences.

Communication challenges

A second set of challenges relates to communication, manifested in the need to integrate social science knowledge with insight from the physical and environmental sciences. Increasingly, the social sciences, the natural sciences, and engineering need to exchange and integrate their respective expertise in solving problems. Thus, in research on environmental and global change, ecologists and earth scientists need socioeconomic knowledge to understand human influences on ecological and environmental processes (Chen, 1981; Miller, 1994; NRC, 1992, 1998, 1999). Similarly, engineers need background in socioeconomics to understand how public choices and behavioral patterns might interact with new engineering structures, and seismologists must consider social science perspectives to project natural hazard vulnerabilities and likely human responses (Cutter, 2001). The capacities to integrate data and to communicate across disciplinary boundaries are issues of considerable significance and will be key to the advancement of theory and the conduct of research across fields. The spatial framework and a common set of spatial concepts can provide a focus for defining and understanding problems and offer a basis for communication and integration.

Technologies for online collaboration and grid computing for computational support have seen successful, but limited, deployment through projects such as GEON (http://www.geongrid.org) in the geosciences and SEEK (http://seek.ecoinformatics.org) in ecology that distribute data and provide collaboration services and analytical tools in a seamless research environment. Other grid-computing initiatives support collaborative research in high-energy physics (GriPhyN), astronomy (NVO), biomedical applications (BIRN), and earthquake engineering (NEESGrid). Unfortunately, there are no parallel developments serving the social science community. Yet, a compelling task for such cyberinfrastructure in the social sciences would be the development of an interoperable platform to explore many disparate sources simultaneously in a single search to help uncover knowledge resources that run the gamut from bibliographies and publications to video and audio media, along with geo-spatial resources, data, model runs, tools for data visualization, simulations, and listings of experts.

Infrastructure challenges

The infrastructure challenges for resolving the data and communication needs are key to making social science more accessible, doable, transparent, and useful. This challenge embraces education and the need to embed the science tradition (including spatial awareness) for engaging students at all levels in practices of formulating testable propositions, gathering data, and modeling processes and interactions. Recent national initiatives to build infrastructure for spatial analysis in the social sciences have included the projects mentioned earlier from the Minnesota Population Center and CIESEN (focused on data issues) and from the Center for Spatially Integrated Social Science (CSISS), focused on developing new analytic tools and building expertise and awareness across disciplines.

Recent NSF reports (e.g., Atkins et al. 2003) highlight an infrastructure vision that works at the interfaces of computer science, communication technologies (using distributed computing resources and network-enabled tools for collaboration), and the social sciences, with outcomes directed to greater automation of routine procedures, easier access to data resources via web interfaces, and new tools for collaboration, both among social scientists and with researchers in other domains. The added potentials and issues related to web 2.0 technologies and practices highlight problems about validation and empirical verification of new information sources for use in scientific modeling and for social applications.

Individual institutions, recognizing the importance of building local collaborative efforts in this area, have acted to enhance support for spatial perspectives in research and teaching. Examples include Harvard University's Center for Geographic Analysis, Brown University's initiative on Spatial Structures in the Social Sciences, and spatial@ucsb – a spatial studies center to promote spatial thinking in all branches of knowledge – at the University of California, Santa Barbara. In addition, applications of GIS and spatial econometrics have figured prominently in some of the population research centers supported through the

National Institutes of Health, including the Geographic Information Analysis Core of the Population Research Institute at Pennsylvania State University, the Spatial Analysis Unit of the Carolina Population Center at the University of North Carolina, and the Applied Population Laboratory at the University of Wisconsin Center for Demography and Ecology.

DISCUSSION

Whatever the term, spatially integrated social science, or spatial social science, it is evident that the practice of spatial thinking through application of spatial concepts and the use of spatial data are expanding to help resolve gaps in our understanding of research questions in many disciplines. For instance, Knowles (2000) points to a spatial turn in history, Lobao (2003) makes a similar claim for sociology, and Voss (2007) argues that demography has been (historically), and is, a spatial social science. Academic leaders, including Norm Bradburn (2004) and Rita Colwell (2004), have flagged the importance of geographical perspective across the sciences, and Butz and Torrey (2006) suggest that spatial analysis is emerging as a fundamental growth area in pushing the frontiers of social science research. This momentum of growth, documented more fully by Janelle and Goodchild (2009), is buoyed, as well, by new kinds of geographical data resources and more easily acquired tools. However, many challenges remain, and it is not clear that the transition to spatial awareness in scholarship is keeping pace with societal needs.

The popularization of spatial technologies may be expanding faster than the acquisition of skills in fundamental spatial thinking (e.g., the understanding of geographical scale and the selection of map projections). The drivers of such change include the geovisualization of news in the popular press, new web 2.0 applications for embedding personal and other volunteered information on maps

(e.g., geotagging in Wikimapia and Flikr®), and commercial advertising (e.g., GPS navigation). They also include lay participation in the world of maps (e.g., Google Maps™, Google Earth™, and Microsoft's Bing Maps Interactive™), and reliance on map-based information search tools (e.g., location-based services). Opportunities to engage interactively with an integrated global network of producers and users of geographical information have expanded to the point of enabling new geographies of the information society. Foretold by Sheppard, et al. (1999), these new geographies and networking possibilities create demands for social scientists to build trans-disciplinary alliances based on improved spatial awareness to advance investigations of population dynamics, political issues, health problems, and other social concerns.

The National Research Council's (NRC) (2006) report on *Learning to Think Spatially* makes a compelling case for expanding the attention given to spatial reasoning and to the use of spatial tools in K–12 education. But, clearly, the rapidity of technological and social changes is so great that this education objective must be elevated and accelerated to reach all cohorts of citizens and scholars. The authors hope that the principles of spatially integrated social science, the concepts of spatial thinking, and the tools for spatial analysis and display, as discussed in this chapter and as summarized in the concluding chapter by the editors to this handbook, provide guidance in this direction. Nonetheless, the information, communication, and infrastructure challenges are likely to unfold in novel ways. They will pose ever-changing opportunities to employ spatial concepts for enriching our understandings and solutions to scientific and societal problems.

NOTES

1 The Center for Spatially Integrated Social Science (CSISS) maintains a collection of syllabi for

undergraduate and graduate courses about spatial analytic applications for social science disciplines. (See http://www.csiss.org/SPACE/directory/.)

2 A recent specialist meeting investigated issues surrounding the use and evaluation of space–time simulations in research. Access to diverse position statements by experts in the area are available at http://www.ncgia.ucsb.edu/projects/abmcss/.

3 Researchers from the academic, industrial, and governmental sectors met in Santa Barbara, CA in December 2007 to investigate these issues. The meeting was hosted by the National Center for Geographic Information and Analysis (NCGIA) with support from the Los Alamos National Laboratory, the Army Research Office, and the Vespucci Initiative. See http://ncgia.ucsb.edu/projects/vgi/ for copies of position papers and examples of applications of volunteered geographic information and associated issues.

4 Additional information on spatial concepts is available at http://spatial.ucsb.edu/resources/teach-learn/concepts.php. Since space does not permit a full discussion of the solutions to the problems noted in the table, readers are encouraged to examine the suggested key references.

5 Bailey and Gatrell (1996) provide a thoughtful reference, rich with examples of analytic methods and models for treating point patterns, spatially continuous data, area data, and spatial interaction data. Haining (2003) delves into the theoretical foundations of spatial analysis. O'Sullivan and Unwin (2002) integrate GIS capabilities with statistical procedures, and discuss applications of computationally intensive approaches to geo-spatial modeling (e.g., agent-based models, expert systems, and cellular automata). Steinberg and Steinberg (2006) introduce the basics of GIS for social science applications. Castro (2007), Voss, et al. (2006), Voss (2007), and Weeks (2004) review applications of spatial analysis specific to issues in demography; Cromley and McLafferty (2002) explore applications of GIS in public health research; Anselin et al. (2004) feature a selection of contemporary applications in spatial econometrics; and the journal *Political Analysis* released a special issue on spatial methods in political science (no. 10, 2002). For edited selections of important recent developments and applications in spatial data analysis, see Anselin and Rey (2010) and Fischer and Getis (2010).

6 The software systems described in this section are available at little or no cost and are downloadable from the web addresses that follow:

- GeoDa™ (http://geodacenter.asu.edu)
- Geographically Weighted Regression (http://ncg.nuim.ie/ncg/GWR)
- STARS (Space Time Analysis of Regional Systems, http://regionalanalysislab.org/)

- R, downloadable from http://www.r-project.org/, provides links to download a variety of spatial software to work with its open-source architecture
- CrimeStat® (http://www.icpsr.umich.edu/crimestat)
- Quantum GIS is a free open-source geographic information system. http://www.qgis.org/

Castro (2007) provides an alternative listing of freely distributed software tools that would be of special interest to demographers. In addition, commercial developers and venders of statistical software have augmented their products with capabilities for spatial analysis, and are recommended for consideration. For example, S+SpatialStats® (http://www.insightful.com/products/spatial) allows for data analysis and modeling of geostatistical data, point patterns, and lattice data with S-PLUS; SAS/GIS® (http://www.sas.com/products/gis/) provides integration of basic GIS functionality to its SAS statistical and exploratory tools; and TerraSeer® (http://www.terraseer.com) has a suite of tools for space-time analysis, cluster analysis, boundary analysis, and spatial econometric modeling.

Commercial GIS platforms may include sophisticated analytic capabilities for geospatial statistics, data modeling, 3D representations, trend analysis, and decision-support capabilities, either as add-ons to the main GIS platform (e.g., ESRI's ArcGIS® http://www.esri.com) or integrated into the platform (e.g., Clark Lab's IDRISI® http://www.clarklabs.org). Other GIS packages, offering different price points and capabilities, include MapInfo® http://www.mapinfo.com/, Maptitude® http://www.caliper.com/Maptitude, and Manifold® http://www.manifold.net.

REFERENCES

Ahuja, R.K., Magnanti, T.L. and Orlin, J.B. (1993) *Network Flows: Theory, Algorithms and Applications.* Englewood Cliffs, NJ: Prentice Hall.

Alonso, W. (1964) *Location and Land Use.* Cambridge, MA: Harvard University Press.

Anderton, D.L. (1996) 'Methodological issues in the spatiotemporal analysis of environmental equity', *Social Science Quarterly,* 77: 508–515.

Anselin, L. (2000) 'GIS, spatial econometrics and social science research', *Journal of Geographical Systems,* 2: 11–15.

Anselin, L., Florax, R.J. and Rey, S.J. (eds) (2004) *Advances in Spatial Econometrics: Methodology, Tools and Applications.* Berlin: Springer.

Anselin, L. and Rey, S.J. (eds) (2010) *Perspectives on Spatial Data Analysis*. Berlin: Springer.

Atkins, D.E., Droegemeier, K.K., Feldman, S.I., Garcia-Molina, H., Klein, M.L., Messerschmitt, D.J., Messina, P., Ostriker, J.P. and Wright, M.H. (2003) *Revolutionizing Science and Engineering Through Cyberinfrastructure: Report of the National Science FoundationBlue Ribbon Advisory Panel on Cyberinfrastructure*. Washington DC: National Science Foundation. http://www.nsf.gov/od/oci/reports/atkins.pdf (accessed 27 September 2010).

Baddeley, A. and Turner, R. (2005) 'Spatstat: An R package for analyzing spatial point patterns', *Journal of Statistical Software*, 12(6): 1–12. http://www.jstatsoft.org/ (accessed 27 September 2010).

Bailey, T.C. and Gatrell, A.C. (1996) *Interactive Spatial Data Analysis*. Harlow: Longman.

Bales, K. (1999) 'Popular reactions to sociological research: the case of Charles Booth', *Sociology*, 33(1): 153–168.

Bialynicki-Birula, I. and Bialynicki-Birula, I. (2004) *Modeling Reality: How Computers Mirror Life*. New York: Oxford University Press.

Boots, B.N. and Getis, A. (1988) *Point Pattern Analysis*. Newbury Park, CA: Sage Publications.

Bradburn, N.M. (2004) 'Foreword', In M.F. Goodchild and D.G. Janelle (eds), *Spatially Integrated Social Science*. New York: Oxford University Press. pp. v–vi.

Butz, W. and Torrey, B.B. (2006) 'Some frontiers in social science', *Science*, 312(5782): 1898–1900.

Castro, M.C. (2007) 'Spatial demography: An opportunity to improve policy making at diverse decision levels'. In P.R. Voss (ed.), *Special Issue on Spatial Demography: Population Research and Policy Review*, 26: 477–509.

Chen, R.S. (1981) 'Interdisciplinary research and integration: The case of CO_2 and climate', *Climatic Change*, 3: 429–447.

Colwell, R. (2004) 'The new landscape of science: A geographic portal', *Annals of the Association of American Geographers*, 94(4): 703–708.

Couclelis, H. (1992) 'People manipulate objects (but cultivate fields): beyond the raster vector debate in GIS'. In A.U. Frank and I. Campari (eds), *Theories and Methods of Spatio-temporal Reasoning in Geographic Space*. Berlin: Springer-Verlag, 639: 65–77.

Couclelis, H. (2001) 'Why I no longer work with agents: a challenge for ABMs of human-environment interaction'. In D. Parker, T. Berger and S. Manson (eds), *Agent-based Models of Land-use and Land-cover Change*. LUCC Report Series. 6: 3–5.

Cromley, E.K. and McLafferty, S.L. (2002) *GIS and Public Health*. New York: Guilford Press.

Cutter, S.L. (2001) 'Charting a course for the next two decades'. In S. L. Cutter (ed.), *American Hazardscapes: The Regionalization of Hazards and Disasters*. Washington DC: Joseph Henry Press. pp. 157–65.

Cutter, S.L., Golledge, R.G. and Graf, W.L. (2002) 'The big questions in geography', *The Professional Geographer*, 54(3): 305–17.

de Smith, M.J., Goodchild, M.F. and Longley, P.A. (2009) *Geospatial Analysis: A Comprehensive Guide to Principles, Techniques, and Software Tools*. Leicester: The Winchelsea Press, Troubador Publishing, Ltd. (a pdf e-book at http://www.spatialanalysisonline.com/).

Doreian, P. (1980) 'Linear models with spatially distributed data: spatial disturbances or spatial effects?', *Sociological Methods and Research*, 9: 29–60.

Doreian, P. (1990) 'Network autocorrelation models: problems and prospects'. In D. Griffith (ed.), *Spatial Statistics: Past, Present, and Future*. Ann Arbor, MI: Institute of Mathematical Geography. pp. 369–389.

Eagles, M., Bélanger, P. and Calkins, H.W. (2004) 'The spatial structure of urban political discussion networks'. In M.F. Goodchild and D.G. Janelle (eds), *Spatially Integrated Social Science*. New York: Oxford University Press. pp. 205–218.

Fischer, M.M. and Getis, A. (eds) (2010) *Handbook of Applied Spatial Analysis: Software Tools, Methods and Applications*. Berlin: Springer.

Fogel, R.W. (1971) *The Reinterpretation of American Economic History*. New York: Harper & Row.

Forman, R.T. (1995) *Land Mosaics: The Ecology of Landscapes and Regions*. Cambridge: Cambridge University Press.

Fotheringham, A.S., Brunsdon, C. and Charlton, M. (2002) *Geographically Weighted Regression: The Analysis of Spatially Varying Relationships*. New York: John Wiley.

Golledge, R.G. (1995) 'Primitives of spatial knowledge'. In T.L. Nyerges, D.M. Mark, R. Laurini and M.J. Egenhofer (eds), *Cognitive Aspects of Human–Computer Interaction for Geographic Information Systems*. Dordrecht: Kluwer Academic. pp. 29–44.

Golledge, R.G. (2002) 'The nature of geographic knowledge', *Annals of the Association of American Geographers*, 92(1): 1–14.

Goodchild, M.F. (1997) 'Scale in a digital geographic world', *Geographical and Environmental Modeling*, 1: 5–23.

Goodchild, M.F. (2007) 'Citizens as sensors: the world of volunteered geography', presentation to workshop on Volunteered Geographic Information. Santa Barbara CA, 13–14 December. http://ncgia. ucsb.edu/projects/vgi/ (accessed 27 September 2010).

Goodchild, M.F. and Janelle, D.G. (2004) *Spatially Integrated Social Science*. New York: Oxford University Press.

Goodchild, M.F., Anselin L. and Deichmann, U. (1993) 'A framework for the areal interpolation of socio-economic data', *Environment and Planning A, 25*: 383–397.

Goodchild, M.F., Anselin, L. Appelbaum, R.P. and Harthorn, B.H. (2000) 'Toward spatially integrated social science', *International Regional Science Review, 23*(2): 139–159.

Goodchild, M.F., Yuan, M. and Cova, T. (2007) 'Towards a general theory of geographic representation in GIS', *International Journal of Geographical Information Science, 21*(3): 239–260.

Griliches, Z. ([1957] 1988) 'Hybrid corn: An exploration of the economics of technological change', *Technology, Education and Productivity: Early Papers with Notes to Subsequent Literature*. New York: Basil Blackwell. pp. 27–52.

Hägerstrand, T. (1970) 'What about people in regional science?', *Papers of the Regional Science Association*, 24: 1–12.

Haining, R. (2003) *Spatial Data Analysis: Theory and Practice*. Cambridge: Cambridge University Press.

Hill, L.L. (2006) *Georeferencing: The Geographic Associations of Information*. Cambridge, MA: MIT Press.

Isaaks, E.H. and Srivastava, R.M. (1989) *Applied Geostatistics*. New York: Oxford University Press.

Janelle, D.G. and Goodchild, M.F. (2009) 'Location across disciplines: reflections on the CSISS experience'. In H.J. Scholten, R. van de Velde and N. van Manen (eds), *Geospatial Technology and the Role of Location in Science*. Dordrecht: Springer. pp. 15–29.

Johnson, S.B. (2006) *The Ghost Map: The Story of London's Most Terrifying Epidemic – And How It Changed Science, Cities, and the Modern World*. New York: Riverhead.

Journel, A.G. and Huijbregts, C.J. (1978) *Mining Geostatistics*. London: Academic Press.

Kelly, F. ([c1895] 1970) *Hull-House Maps and Papers: By the Residents of Hull-House*. New York: Arno Press.

Key, V.O. (1949) *Southern Politics in State and Nation*. New York: Knopf.

Kimerling, A.J. and Muehrcke, P. (2005) *Map Use: Reading, Analysis, and Interpretation*. Madison, WI: JP Publications.

Knowles, A.K. (ed.) (2000) 'Historical GIS: the spatial turn in social science history', *Social Science History*, 24(3): 451–470.

Krugman, P. (1991) *Geography and Trade*. Cambridge: MIT Press.

Kurath, H. (1949) *A Word Geography of the Eastern United States*. Ann Arbor, MI: University of Michigan Press.

Kwan, M.-P. and Lee, J. (2004) 'Geovisualization of human activity patterns using 3D GIS: a time-geographic approach'. In M.F. Goodchild and D.G. Janelle (eds), *Spatially Integrated Social Science*. New York: Oxford University Press. pp. 48–66.

Levine, N. (2007) *CrimeStat: A Spatial Statistics Program for the Analysis of Crime Incident Locations* (v 3.1). Houston, TX: Ned Levine & Associates.

Lobao, L. (2003) 'Rurals sociology and the "spatial turn" across the social sciences', *The Rural Sociologist*, 23(2): 1–2.

Loftin, C. and Ward, S.K. (1981) 'Spatial autocorrelation models for Galton's problem', *Behavior Science Research*, 16: 105–128.

Logan, J.R. and Zhang, W. (2004) 'Identifying ethnic neighborhoods with census data'. In M.F. Goodchild and D.G. Janelle (eds), *Spatially Integrated Social Science*. New York: Oxford University Press. pp. 113–126.

Maantay, J. (2002) 'Mapping environmental injustices: pitfalls and potential of geographic information systems (GIS) in assessing environmental health and equity', *Environmental Health Perspectives*, 110(2): 161–171.

McCaa, R, and Ruggles, S. (2002) 'The census in global perspective and the coming microdata revolution', *Scandinavian Population Studies*, 13: 7–30.

McHarg, I. (1969) *Design with Nature*. Garden City, NJ: Doubleday/Natural History Press.

MacArthur, R.H. and Wilson, E.O. (1967) *The Theory of Island Biogeography*. Princeton, NJ: Princeton University Press.

Mayhew, H. ([1861] 1967) *London Labour and the London Poor: a Cyclopaedia of the Condition and Earnings of Those That Will Work, Those that Cannot Work, and Those That Will Not Work*. New York: A.M. Kelley.

Miller, H.J. (2005) 'Necessary space–time conditions for human interaction', *Environment and Planning B: Planning and Design*, 32: 381–401.

Miller, R.B. (1994) 'Interactions and collaboration in global change across the social and natural sciences', *AMBIO: A Journal of the Human Environment*, 23(1): 19–24.

Montello, D.R. (2001) 'Scale, in geography'. In N.J. Smelser and P.B. Baltes (eds), *International Encyclopedia of the Social and Behavioral Sciences.* Oxford: Pergamon Press. pp. 13501–13504.

Montello, D.R., Goodchild, M.F., Gottsegen, J. and Fohl, P. (2003) 'Where's downtown? Behavioral methods for determining referents of vague spatial queries, special issue on spatial vagueness, uncertainty, granularity'. In B. Bennett and M. Cristani (eds), *Spatial Cognition and Computation,* 3: 185–204.

Murdie, R. (1969) 'Factorial ecology of metropolitan Toronto, 1951–1961', Research Paper No. 116, Department of Geography, University of Chicago.

National Research Council (NRC) (1992) *Global Environmental Change: Understanding the Human Dimensions.* Washington, DC: National Academy Press.

National Research Council (NRC) (1998) *People and Pixels: Linking Remote Sensing and Social Science.* Washington, DC: National Academy Press.

National Research Council (NRC) (1999) *Global Environmental Change: Research Pathways for the Next Decade.* Washington, DC: National Academy Press.

National Research Council (NRC) (2006) *Learning to Think Spatially: GIS as a Support System in the K-12 Curriculum.* Washington, DC: The National Academies Press.

Nature (2008) 'A place for everything (editorial)', *Nature,* 453: 2.

Nystuen, J.D. (1963) 'Identification of some fundamental spatial concepts', *Papers of the Michigan Academy of Science, Arts, Letters,* 18: 373–84.

Okabe, A., Okunuki, K. and Shiode, S. (2006) 'SANET: a toolbox for spatial analysis on a network', *Geographical Analysis,* 35: 57–66.

O'Sullivan, D. (2004) 'Too much of the wrong kind of data: implications for the practice of micro-scale spatial modeling'. In M.F. Goodchild and D.G. Janelle (eds), *Spatially Integrated Social Science.* New York: Oxford University Press. pp. 95–107.

O'Sullivan, D. and Unwin, D.J. (2002) *Geographic Information Analysis.* New York: John Wiley.

Openshaw, S. (1983) 'The modifiable areal unit problem', *Concepts and Techniques in Modern Geography: CATMOG Series.* 38. Norwich: GeoBooks.

Park, R., Burgess, E.W. and McKenzie, R.D. (1925) *The City.* Chicago, IL: University of Chicago Press.

Peuquet, D.J. (2002) *Representations of Space and Time.* New York: Guilford Press.

Reardon, S.F. and Firebaugh, G. (2002) 'Measures of multi-group segregation', *Sociological Methodology,* 32: 33–67.

Reibel, M. (2007) 'Geographic information systems and spatial data processing in demography: a review'. In P.R. Voss (ed.), *Special Issue on Spatial Demography: Population Research and Policy Review,* 26: 601–618.

Rey, S.J. and Anselin, L. (2006) 'Recent advances in software for spatial analysis in the social sciences', *Geographical Analysis,* 38: 1–4.

Rey, S.J. and Janikas, M.V. (2006) 'STARS: space-time analysis of regional systems', *Geographical Analysis,* 38: 67–86.

Robinson, A.H. (1967) 'The thematic maps of Charles Joseph Minard', *Imago Mundi,* 21: 95–108.

Sampson, R.J., Morenoff, J. and Gannon-Rowley, T. (2002) 'Assessing neighborhood effects: social processes and new directions in research', *Annual Review of Sociology,* 28: 443–78.

Shaw, C.R. and McKay, H.D. (1969) *Juvenile Delinquency and Urban Areas.* Chicago, IL: University of Chicago Press.

Sheppard, E.S. (2004) *Scale and Geographic Inquiry: Nature, Society, and Method.* Boston, MA: Wiley-Blackwell.

Sheppard, E., Couclelis, H., Graham, S., Harrington, J.W. and Onsrud, H. (1999) 'Geographies of the information society', *International Journal of Geographical Information Science,* 13(8): 797–823.

Shevky, E. and Bell, W. (1955) *Social Area Analysis: Theory, Illustrative Application and Computational Procedures.* Stanford, CA: Stanford University Press.

Sinton, D. (1978) 'The inherent structure of information as a constraint to analysis: mapped thematic data as a case study'. In G. Dutton (ed.), *Harvard Papers on Geographic Information Systems.* Reading, MA: Addison Wesley, 7: 1–17.

Snow, J. ([1854] 1936) *Snow on Cholera.* New York: The Commonwealth Fund, Oxford University Press.

Steinberg, S.J. and Steinberg, S.L. (2006) *Geographic Information Systems for the Social Sciences: Investigating Space and Place.* Thousand Oaks, CA: Sage Publications.

Sweeney, S.H. and Feser, E.J. (2004) 'Business location and spatial externalities'. In M.F. Goodchild and D.G. Janelle (eds), *Spatially Integrated Social Science.* New York: Oxford University Press. pp. 239–262.

Tita, G. and Cohen, J. (2004) 'Measuring spatial diffusion of shots fired activity across city neighborhoods'. In M.F. Goodchild and D.G. Janelle (eds),

Spatially Integrated Social Science. New York: Oxford University Press. pp. 171–204.

Tobler, W.R. (1970) 'A computer model simulation of urban growth in the Detroit region', *Economic Geography,* 46(2): 234–240.

Tobler, W.R., Deichmann, U., Gottsegen, J. and Maloy, K. (1997) 'World population in a grid of spherical quadrilaterals', *International Journal of Population Geography,* 3: 203–225.

Tufte, E.R. (1983) *The Visual Display of Quantitative Information.* Cheshire, CT: Graphics Press.

Vance, R.B. ([1936] 1982) 'The old cotton belt'. In J.S. Reed and D.J. Singal (eds), *Regionalism and the South: Selected Papers of Rupert Vance.* Chapel Hill, NC: University of North Carolina Press. pp. 86–127.

Von Thünen, J.-H. (1826) *Der Isolierte Staat* [The isolated state]. Hamburg, Germany: Perthes.

Voss, P.R. (2007) 'Demography as a spatial social science'. In P.R. Voss (ed.), *Special Issue on Spatial Demography: Population Research and Policy Review,* 26: 457–76.

Voss, P.R., White, K.J.C. and Hammer, R.B. (2006) 'Explorations in spatial demography'. In W. Kandel and D.L. Brown (eds), *The Population of Rural America: Demographic Research for a New Century.* Dordrecht: Springer.

Weeks, J.R. (2004) 'The role of spatial analysis in demographic research'. In M.F. Goodchild and D.G. Janelle (eds), *Spatially Integrated Social Science.* New York: Oxford University Press. pp. 381–399.

3

Geographic Ontologies and Society

Marinos Kavouras and Margarita Kokla

INTRODUCTION

Geographic information and its associated technologies no longer are privileged tools available only to geo-related scientists, such as geographers, surveyors, environmentalists, geologists, and so on. These tools are widely used by heterogeneous groups of scientists for analysis, planning, and decision making, since nearly all non-geographic data (social, economic, medical, and so on) may be associated to geographic data. Furthermore, aside from its role as a scientific tool for analysis, planning, and decision making, geographic information is also widely used by a steadily increasing group of non-experts varying in age, background knowledge, and interests. The increased availability of geographic information and the wide access to it especially through the World Wide Web and spatial data infrastructures (SDIs) have raised the need to explore new ways of semantic representation of geographic information in order for it to be properly understood and used even by non-experts.

Geographic information science, the science behind GIS, is thus confronted with the need to facilitate the understanding of geographic information and increase its use in society, as well as to facilitate efficient and meaningful information exchange, use, and analysis by heterogeneous groups of users and for their varying needs. The capability for meaningful integration, exchange, and reuse of geographic information requires that representations of geographic concepts be enriched with deeper knowledge of their meaning, shifting the focus on what is being represented and not on the representation per se. This necessitates the development of methods for the semantic representation of geographic information in order to preserve and clarify its meaning. The development of intelligent information and knowledge-based technologies and the need to formulate comprehensive methods for knowledge organization, representation, and elicitation have increasingly directed research towards the study of geographic concepts, semantics, and ontologies.

These studies focus on issues relating to geographic concepts and the conceptualization of geographic reality in general.

They deal with categories of geographic entities, phenomena, processes, their temporal dimensions, their defining properties, and their relations. The study of these issues relating to the meaning of geographic information may suggest new ways for its proper definition, representation, and communication among different groups of people or different information sources. Figure 3.1 shows some fundamental research topics (i.e., concepts, ontologies, meaning, properties, and relations) and some of their underlying issues as dealt with by five disciplines: philosophy, cognitive science, linguistics, computer science, and geographic information science. The list of items is indicative and by no means exhaustive; its aim is to highlight the interrelations among research subjects and disciplines.

Studies concerning the types of geographic concepts, their distinctive characteristics, and their differences compared to other types of concepts are also highly relevant to increasing the usability of geographic information. For example, geographically based socioeconomic concepts, such as administrative units (e.g., municipalities, counties, urban areas, metropolitan areas, and neighborhoods), exhibit great heterogeneity in their definitions among different countries or societies. Furthermore, they are often designated and analyzed according to different spatial, environmental, and socioeconomic criteria complicating the efforts for information exchange and reuse.

The expert–non-expert distinction also relates to the above considerations. The current wide access to geographic information by various groups of non-experts raises the question of proper information representation and organization in order to facilitate its understanding and support its proper use. Non-expert users may easily misinterpret the meaning of geographic information if it is not properly represented. Studies of commonsense conceptualizations of geographic concepts and their corresponding representations within geographic information systems are more crucial than ever.

In order to appreciate the importance of an ontological approach to geographic information, an example of the socioeconomic concept of urban area is presented. An urban area is a type of administrative concept used to fulfil multiple socioeconomic purposes and which differs among different countries. The definitions of administrative concepts also differ, ranging from general commonsense descriptions to detailed scientific definitions.

For example, Wikipedia presents a commonsense definition of an urban area and in addition provides major subclasses of the concept, such as cities and towns:

> An urban area is an area with an increased density of human-created structures in comparison to the areas surrounding it. Urban areas may be cities, towns or conurbations, but the term is not commonly extended to rural settlements such as villages and hamlets. (Wikipedia, 2009)

Canada's National Statistical Agency employs a detailed definition of an urban area using parameters such as population concentration and density:

> An urban area has a minimum population concentration of 1,000 persons and a population density of at least 400 persons per square kilometre, based on the current census population count. All territory outside urban areas is classified as rural. Taken together, urban and rural areas cover all of Canada. (Canada's National Statistical Agency, 2006)

The US Census Bureau classifies as "urban":

> densely settled territory, which consists of:
>
> - core census block groups or blocks that have a population density of at least 1000 people per square mile and
> - surrounding census blocks that have an overall density of at least 500 people per square mile. (US Census Bureau, 2008)

Two types of urban areas are distinguished: urbanized areas of 50,000 or more people and urban clusters of at least 2500 but fewer than 50,000 people.

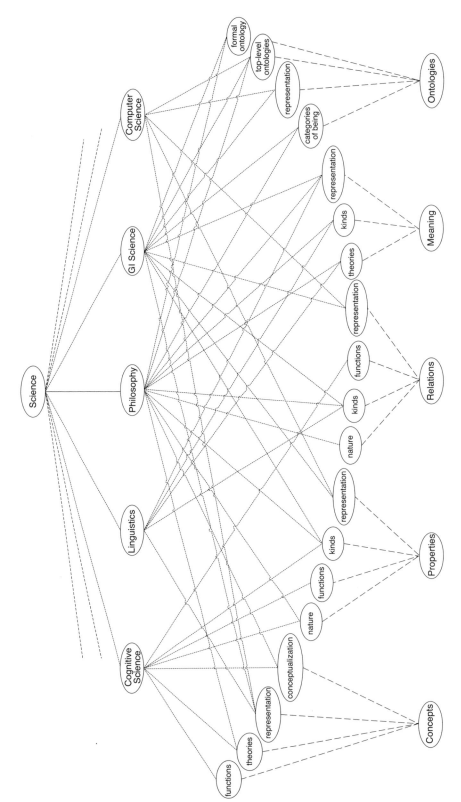

Figure 3.1 Association of research subjects and disciplines

The United Nations Statistics Division (2005) illustrates the problem of heterogeneity in the conceptualization of such a commonly used socioeconomic concept as an urban area by citing the differences in the definition of urban areas by different countries across the earth. The major criterion for the definition of an urban area is population concentration which ranges from 200 to 50,000 people.

Adherence to a single definition may avoid confusion, but this is not possible given the very different patterns and conditions of urbanization from country to country. Heterogeneities are revealed when different conceptualizations need to be combined, for example, for the development of a Global Spatial Data Infrastructure or for the comparison of statistical data across different countries. However, the aim is not to come up with a universal understanding and agreement on the meaning of terms but to develop methods and tools to properly formalize their meaning, in order for it to be readily understood and used even by non-expert users of geographic information.

The remainder of this chapter is organized as follows. The second section discusses the notion of ontologies in general, focusing on their realization in geographic information science. The third section studies the basic ontology components: concepts, properties, and relations. Special emphasis is placed on concepts and their semantic definition since they constitute the primary components. Finally, the last section presents the conclusions of this work, discussing future research directions.

ONTOLOGIES

Ontology in philosophy

Ontologies constitute one of the most salient recent research directions across various scientific fields. As used in science, ontologies encapsulate, illuminate, and designate the semantics of concepts in a particular domain (Kavouras and Kokla, 2008). They originate from considerations about the nature and kinds of relevant entities in that domain and the relations among these.

In its original sense, ontology is a branch of metaphysics and is defined as the science of being. It studies the categories of being (such as tangible or abstract, real or ideal, independent or dependent) as well as notions such as existence, life, essence, space, time, property, and relation. Different philosophical schools have formulated different ontological theories and have distinguished different categories of being according to their perspectives on reality. A basic distinction originates from a philosophical debate about our knowledge of reality: for those philosophers who believe that we can know reality to some extent, ontology is the science of being. For other philosophers who believe that it is not possible to know anything about an objective reality, ontology is the science of our thought about being (Lowe, 2001). Other distinctions relate to the basic constituents of ontology and the level of detail at which reality is observed and categories of being are formed (Smith, 2003). Substantialists consider substance as the key constituent of being in contrast to fluxists who focus on process or function or continuous variation. Adequatists are concerned with entities and their relations at all levels of focus and granularity, in contrast to reductionists, who restrict their observation of reality to an inclusive, minimum level of properties (Smith, 2003).

Another important ontological distinction in philosophy is that between universals, that is, mind-independent entities that encapsulate the properties of individual entities called individuals, or particulars, or instances (MacLeod and Rubenstein, 2006). This distinction, together with metaphysical views concerning the nature and knowledge of universals and their role in helping identify similarity among individuals, is called the problem of universals.

Ontologies in computer science

Increasingly over the past decade, computer science has focused on ontologies (in the plural) in order to provide a solid conceptual basis for knowledge-based tasks such as semantic integration, knowledge discovery and elicitation, intelligent reasoning, and the development of the semantic web. Computer science considers an ontology to be "an explicit specification of a conceptualization" (Gruber, 1995: 908), that is, a formal, language-dependent definition of the concepts and the relations between them that represent a domain or an application following specific functional constraints (Guarino, 1998; Smith, 2003). Ontologies in computer science are classified according to criteria such as formality and generality.

According to the degree of formality, ontologies may be classified into the following types (Uschold, 1996).

- *Highly informal ontologies* define concepts and relations using natural language.
- *Structurally informal ontologies* define concepts and relations using natural language but in structured manner.
- *Semiformal ontologies* define concepts and relations using a formal language such as Ontolingua.
- *Rigorously formal ontologies* define concepts and relations using a formal language accompanied by formal semantics, theorems, and proofs.

However, the classification of ontology types according to the level of formality raises some issues about their explicitness, since ontologies usually include both formal (e.g., axioms) and informal parts (e.g., definitions in natural language) in order to facilitate automated processing and human understanding tasks respectively (Gruber, 2003, 2004).

According to the degree of generality, ontologies may be classified into the following types (Guarino, 1998).

- *Top-level ontologies* define general concepts independent of any application domain such as entity, property, quality, identity, process, space, time, and so on.

- *Domain and task ontologies* define concepts pertinent to a domain or a task respectively; these concepts are specializations of the general concepts defined by the top-level ontology.
- *Application ontologies* define concepts relative to a particular application; these concepts are specializations of both domain and task ontology concepts.

Top-level ontologies are of primary importance, since they define the fundamental concepts and provide the framework for the development of new lower-level ontologies (domain, task, and application), as well as for the integration of existing heterogeneous ones; therefore they are the basis for knowledge-sharing across different domains (Sowa, 2000). Various initiatives to develop a top-level ontology exist focusing on different purposes, such as IEEE Standard Upper Ontology (SUO) (SUO WG, 2003), OpenCyc Upper Ontology (Cycorp, 2002), Descriptive Ontology for Linguistic and Cognitive Engineering (DOLCE) (Masolo et al., 2003), Basic Formal Ontology (BFO) (Grenon, 2003), WordNet (Fellbaum, 1998), Mikrokosmos Ontology (Mahesh, 1996; Mahesh and Nirenburg, 1996) and others. Figure 3.2 shows the diagram of the OpenCyc Upper Ontology (Cycorp, 2002). Despite their sophistication and usefulness, these initiatives underpin the speculation that the existence of various top-level ontologies does not solve interoperability and communication problems but just transfers them to a higher level. Opposite views about the advantages and disadvantages of top-level ontologies are reconciled by a third view, which holds that although it is not possible to develop a universally accepted ontology, there are significant communication advantages in the adoption of a top-level ontology for large communities of users.

Ontologies in geographic information science

During the last decade, geographic information science has also embraced ontologies as

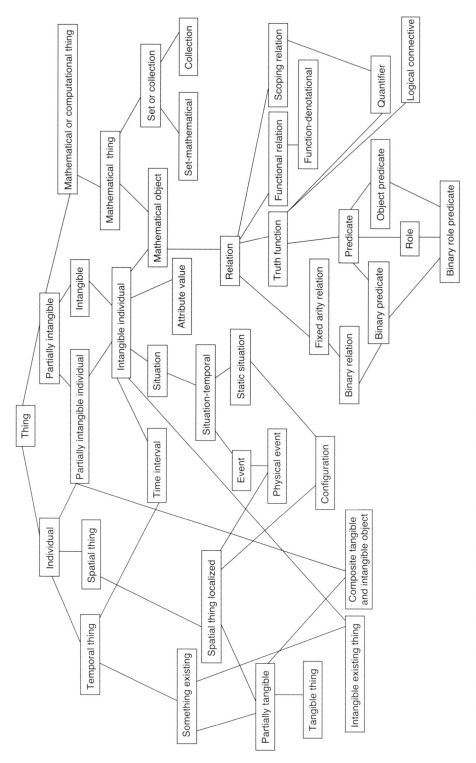

Figure 3.2   OpenCyc selected vocabulary and upper ontology (Cycorp, 2002)

a new and prominent research direction towards a better understanding, representation, and communication of geographic information (Smith and Mark, 1998; Fonseca et al., 2000). Despite the lack of consensus on ontological issues and the concerns about their status and usability (Winter, 2001; Hunter, 2002; Agarwal, 2005), ontologies "provide an indispensable conceptual vehicle" to facilitate tasks such as knowledge representation and discovery, semantic integration, data mining, intelligent reasoning, semantic-based query processing, semantic web development, and so on (Kavouras and Kokla, 2008).

Ontologies for geographic information science lie somewhere between the metaphysical perspectives of a single ontology related to the science of being and the information science perspective of multiple language-dependent and application-oriented ontologies. The solidity of geographic space and its existence independently of human cognition facilitates the convergence of the philosophical and the computer science perspectives (Mark et al., 2004). Ontological research in the geographic domain studies the ultimate components that constitute geographic reality, that is, geographic concepts, relations, processes, and so on, as well as the methods for their formalization, taking into account the pragmatic requirements of using this knowledge for various tasks in order to achieve information communication and exchange without loss of meaning.

Smith and Mark (2003) study Horton's (1982) distinction between *primary* and *secondary* theories for the convergence of the philosophical and computer science ontological views. *Primary theory* relates to the commonsense knowledge used by humans in order to function in their physical and social environment and results from the direct perception of entities, processes, and events. Therefore, primary theory is common to humans across different social and cultural contexts. On the other hand, *secondary theories* relate to knowledge of entities, processes, and events that are not directly perceived by humans and therefore vary among different social and cultural contexts.

The issues regarding the development of top-level ontologies are also rather pertinent to the geographic domain for two main reasons. The first reason is that a top-level ontology provides the basis for formulating domain concepts, in our case geographic ones, but also for integrating heterogeneous geographic ontologies. Since the development of an ultimate geographic ontology is considered to be an enormous (Mark et al., 2004) and even unachievable goal taking into account the interdisciplinarity of the geographic domain (Agarwal, 2005), a more realistic solution seems to be the association of heterogeneous geographic-domain ontologies within the solid basis of a top-level ontology (Kokla and Kavouras, 2001; Mark et al., 2004). Kokla and Kavouras (2001) propose a method for the integration of geographic domain ontologies under the solid framework provided by a top-level ontology. The method is based on the *principle of complementarity* (Bohr, 1934), which supports that different views represent different but interrelated aspects of reality, each of which may be suitable under specific contexts.

The second reason for the pertinence of top-level ontologies to the geographic domain is that a top-level ontology defines the most fundamental notions for geographic ontologies: space and time. The theories behind the definition of these fundamental concepts determine many aspects of the semantic definition and representation of geographic concepts. Some top-level ontological issues relative to geographic information science are (Casati et al., 1998; Muller, 1998).

- The distinction between spatial regions and spatial entities as primitives for geographic representation.
- The distinction between absolutist and relational theories of space; the first theory supports that space exists regardless of spatial entities and relations, whereas the second theory holds that only spatial entities and the spatial relations between them exist.

- The distinction between material entities which occupy a spatial area and immaterial entities which share a spatial area with other entities.
- The distinction between space and time considered to be different dimensions or viewed under a unified spatiotemporal perspective.
- The distinction between continuants, that is, objects whose existence persists through time and occurrents, that is, objects whose existence is temporally limited, such as processes and events.
- The notion of boundaries, their nature, their relation to geographic entities and the vagueness in their delineation.

In the context of the Basic Formal Ontology (BFO), Grenon and Smith (2004) developed a modular spatial ontology in order to represent the dynamic features of reality. The spatial ontology comprises two complementary ontologies: a SNAP ontology of endurants (continuants) in order to represent static views of the world (such as spatial regions and spatial locations), and a SPAN ontology of perdurants (occurrents) in order to account for processes (such as events, settings, and temporal regions) developing through time. Each ontology results in a partition of reality into categories or universals. Under this perspective, an excerpt of the formalization

of the concept "spatial region" in OWL (Web Ontology Language) is shown in Figure 3.3.

Geographic entities are not always static and unchanging. They often exhibit dynamic behaviors also in relation to human activities in space (Câmara et al., 2000; Kuhn, 2001; Raubal, 2001; Soon and Kuhn, 2004). Therefore, ontologies for the geographic domain should incorporate this distinctive characteristic and the ability to represent and reason about human activities. For that reason, Câmara et al. (2000) introduce the notion of action-driven ontologies, Kuhn (2001) proposes a methodology for developing geographic ontologies that would accommodate activities in geographic space, whereas Soon and Kuhn (2004) present a method for the formalization of user actions in geospace.

The information science perspective on geographic ontologies is mainly focused on ontology development, and integration. The first issue deals with the proper way to develop geographic ontologies, their principal components and how these may be properly defined and associated to each other, their structure, and so on. The second studies ways to compare, associate, and integrate

---

Class: a: Spatial Region

Complete Descriptions
Union Of (a: One Dimensional Region a: Two Dimensional Region a: Three Dimensional Region a: Zero Dimensional Region)

Super Classes
a: Continuant

Annotations
"Definition: A continuant that is neither bearer of quality entities nor inheres in any other entities"
"Comment: An instance of spatial region is a part of space. All parts of space are spatial region entities and only spatial region entities are parts of space. Space is the entire extent of the spatial universe, a designated individual, which is thus itself a spatial region"
"Examples: The sum total of all space in the universe, parts of the sum total of all space in the universe"
......

Figure 3.3   Excerpt of the formalization of the concept "spatial region" (IFOMIS, 2009)

geographic ontologies in order to facilitate information exchange and reuse without loss of meaning. Ontology integration is a prerequisite in order to allow heterogeneous information sources to communicate, analyze, and interpret the information exchanged. Ontology integration focuses on the semantic disambiguation of the underlying information sources, that is, on the intended meaning of the information.

Frank (2001) proposes an ontology meant to facilitate the association of different ontological approaches evolving at different abstraction levels consisting of five coordinated tiers: (1) physical reality; (2) observable reality; (3) object world; (4) social reality; and (5) cognitive agents.

In order to connect ontologies with the development of GIS, Fonseca, Egenhofer, and Agouris (2002) and Fonseca, Egenhofer, Davis, and Câmara (2002) define a model consisting of five "universes" that represent corresponding abstraction levels: (1) the physical universe, which represents the level of geographic reality; (2) the cognitive universe representing the level of human conceptualization of geographic concepts; (3) the logical universe representing the formalization of conceptualizations with logical mechanisms; (4) the representation universe depicting the adoption of representation paradigms, such as object-based and field-based; and (5) the implementation universe representing the final level of computer implementation. Two types of ontologies are defined within the abstraction model: (1) the phenomenological ontology which defines geographic concepts as part of the representation universe; and (2) the application domain ontology which defines specific subjects and tasks as part of the logical universe.

The development of a central reference ontology is used within the context of distributed geographic databases in order to resolve semantic heterogeneities among them (Leclercq et al., 1999; Hakimpour and Geppert, 2001, 2002; Cruz et al., 2002; Ram et al., 2002). The common reference ontology is used to define the semantics of the domain concepts. This knowledge facilitates the specification of mappings between the reference ontology and the local GISs. However, if the local GISs are not based on a single reference ontology, an ontology comparison and integration approach is necessary in order to facilitate the smooth communication of the underlying information sources. Rodríguez and Egenhofer (2003) develop a measure for computing semantic similarity among concepts from different ontologies taking into account sets of: (1) synonym terms; (2) distinguishing features (attributes, functions, and parts); and (3) is-a and part-whole relations. Fonseca et al. (2006) propose a framework for measuring the degree to which two ontologies are interoperable. The framework formalizes ontologies as models consisting of single hierarchies of concepts related to each other with specialization relations. The interoperability measure used is based on model management algebra (Bernstein, 2003). ONTOGEO (Kavouras and Kokla, 2002; Kokla and Kavouras, 2001, 2005) is a project which focuses on the semantic integration of heterogeneous ontologies. The project deals with three integration sub-processes: (1) semantic information extraction from the definitions of geographic concepts; (2) concept comparison and reconciliation; and (3) integration. Emphasis is placed on the extraction and formalization of semantic elements, such as properties and relations entailed in the definitions of geographic concepts. These semantic elements and their corresponding values are used in order to identify and resolve semantic heterogeneities among similar concepts and develop an integrated geographic ontology.

López-Pellicer et al. (2008) proposed a three-layered ontology for administrative units in order to describe the domain concepts and facilitate mappings among different types of administrative units in the context of SDIs. The higher level defines top-level, context-independent concepts using the DOLCE top-level ontology (Masolo et al., 2003). The second level defines the administrative domain concepts and relations which are common across different countries, such as "jurisdictional geographic object," "jurisdictional domain," "administrative division," "state," and so on. The third level represents the administrative application concepts, which are country-specific together with their corresponding instances. The application ontology is illustrated using an example of the administrative units of Spain.

ONTOLOGY COMPONENTS

Concepts

Since ontologies designate the knowledge about a domain, concepts are their most fundamental building blocks. Concepts are very prominent notions for various research fields such as philosophy, linguistics, cognitive science, conceptual analysis, and knowledge representation. These research fields study the ontological status and the nature, structure, and representation of concepts (Laurence and Margolis, 1999; Margolis and Laurence, 2006). Concepts are essential in performing human cognitive functions such as categorization and understanding and constitute the basic components of any ontological and linguistic system. Confusion around concepts relates to the use of the notion to denote either the things that exist in the world or their mental representations.

Sometimes in the literature the terms "concept" and "category" are used interchangeably. However, the two terms are not equivalent. A category is a set of entities that are connected to each other by a distinguishing property or a set of distinguishing properties. For example, the category "city" consists of all individual cities in the world, such as Paris, Rome, New York, or Athens. A concept, on the other hand embodies the knowledge that describes the meaning of a category. The concept "city" embodies all the relevant knowledge that connects these individuals, for example, that a city refers to a large urban area which is densely populated.

Concepts are rudimentarily specified using terms which may partially express their meaning. For example, the term "forest" assigned to a concept bears information about the concept, yet this is implicit and incomplete. Definitions are the primary means for clarifying the semantics of concepts used by most existing ontologies. Although they vary in type and formality, the purpose of definitions is to encapsulate the meaning of a concept ("A forest is a surface occupied by trees and shrubs"). Existing geographic ontologies employ natural language definitions to determine concept semantics. The role of natural language definitions is to specify the essential properties that define concept identity and thus to facilitate the unambiguous understanding, representation, and comparison of concepts.

The properties of geographic concepts as well as the relations between them are also very important components of geographic ontologies, since they provide a wealth of semantic information. Traditional spatial information sciences and standardization bodies, as well as other disciplines that study space such as psychology, cognitive science, and linguistics, conduct research on the types of spatial properties and relations; however, there is no universally agreed list of spatial property and relation types (Kavouras and Kokla, 2008). The types of semantic properties and relations are another issue of great importance for the generation of geographic ontologies. In contrast to spatial properties and relations that refer to instances, semantic properties and relations refer to geographic concepts; they contribute to the specification of their identity, that is, their semantic definition.

From a philosophical perspective, there are three main views on the notion of concepts: realism, conceptualism, and nominalism (Klein and Smith, 2005). Realism holds that concepts are mind-independent entities that represent the properties of individuals, in contrast to conceptualism which considers concepts to be mind-dependent entities. Nominalism on the other hand treats concepts as general terms in a controlled language (Klein and Smith, 2005). From a cognitive perspective, concepts are regarded as mental representations of categories; they bear all the relevant conceptual information about categories. Categories, on the other hand, are regarded as sets of entities bound by some properties that differentiate them from other entities outside the set.

The distinction between concepts that refer to entities and concepts that refer to cognitive representations of entities diminishes for geographic concepts, since space serves as a common basis for their grounding, formulation, and comparison (Kavouras and Kokla, 2008). By adopting a realist position, different views on geographic entities are likely to be more easily compared and reconciled as they are grounded on the same reference, that is, geographic reality (Kavouras and Kokla, 2008), which exists independently of human cognition. Furthermore, according to Smith (2004), the view of concepts as cognitive representations formed independently of reality is not suitable for developing ontologies in the natural sciences. A view of a concept as "the meaning of a term as agreed upon by a group of responsible persons" (Klein and Smith, 2005) is more pertinent to ontology and knowledge representation endeavors, since it accommodates the need for mutual understanding and information exchange among different people. Accordingly, geographic concepts are considered to represent the meaning of categories of entities existing in the geographic realm and not their cognitive representations. This realist position and the grounding in geographic reality provide a solid framework for mutual understanding of geographic concepts by different users and for different application needs.

Geographic concepts

Although there is still a lot of research needed in order to formulate a refined and profound theory of geographic semantics, there are some important studies of geographic concepts. These studies focus on issues relative to the special character of geographic concepts and the ways they may be properly defined and represented. However, space and spatial objects are not exclusively studied by geographic information science, they are also an important research subject in other disciplines such as linguistics and cognitive science. This is attributed to two main reasons (Zlatev, 2007). The first reason is the essential and universal status of spatial cognition for functioning in the physical and social environment. The second reason is that space is a solid, tangible domain, which may be used for facilitating the perception and understanding of other, more abstract domains.

Egenhofer (1993) and Fonseca and Egenhofer (1999) explore the nature and special characteristics of geographic concepts relative to other concepts. Varzi (2001a) examines whether the existence of geographic entities is dependent on their physical territory and boundaries. Mark et al. (1999) attribute the difficulty in the explication and formalization of geographic entities to two main reasons. The first is that, in contrast to objects of everyday experience such as tables, cars, people, and so on, geographic entities do not have determinate boundaries that clearly demarcate the area they occupy in relation to neighboring entities. The second reason is that it is not always possible to assign geographic entities to explicit categories. Mountains are an example of geographic entities with vague boundaries and not clearly defined categories (Smith and Mark, 2003; Mark and Smith, 2004).

Kavouras and Kokla (2008) examine the nature and degrees of "geospatiality" and identify three types of geographic concepts. First, there are those concepts that "possess a geospatial property essential to their existence" independently of the context under which they are observed, such as land property, landmark, geographic boundary (Kavouras and Kokla, 2008). These are usually directly connected to the physical world and are thus sometimes called bona fide concepts (Smith and Varzi, 2000). Another type of geographic concepts includes those that result from social agreement such as socioeconomic units and administrative regions; these are sometimes referred to as fiat concepts (Smith and Varzi, 2000). The third type of geographic concepts are those that do not possess a geospatial property essential to their existence resulting from their relation either to the physical world or to social reality, but that acquire such a property from the context in which they are observed. Vehicles in a traffic control system or ships in electronic charts are examples of this type of geographic concepts.

Couclelis (1996) formulates a typology of geographic entities with ill-defined boundaries. Casati et al. (1998) distinguish two types of boundaries for geospatial entities: bona fide boundaries which occur due to physical spatial discontinuities and fiat boundaries which occur due to social, political, and economic demarcations. Varzi (2001b) studies the notion of vagueness in the geographic domain from a philosophical point of view. Bennett (2001) examines the vagueness immanent in certain geographic concepts, such as the concept of forest. Kuhn (2003, 2005) proposes the notion of semantic reference systems in order to formalize the thematic data of geographic information parallel to the representation of spatial and temporal information by spatial and temporal reference systems.

Four groups of principal dimensions that describe geographic concepts may be defined (Kavouras and Kokla, 2008):

1   Reference – container
    • Spatial frame: a datum for the representation of the location of geospatial entities and their spatial properties and relations.
    • Temporal frame: a datum for the representation of the temporal location of geospatial entities and their temporal properties and relations.
    • Thematic frame: a datum for the representation of the thematic properties of geospatial entities.

2   Semantics
    • Context: a framework for the definition and understanding of geospatial entities.
    • Term: the name used to refer to a geospatial concept or entity.
    • Internal properties: properties of geospatial concepts formed independently of other concepts, either spatial such as: absolute location, shape, size, and so on or non-spatial such as: purpose, affordance, temporality, and so on.
    • External relations: relations of geospatial concepts relative to other concepts, either spatial such as: relative position, distance, orientation, adjacency, containment, and so on or non-spatial such: as is-a, part-whole, dependency, role, and so on.

3   Semiotics/pragmatics
    • Expression – symbolism: the signs (i.e., symbols, words, images, and so on) used to represent geospatial concepts.

4   Quality
    • Vagueness: the degree of inexactness, fuzziness, and indeterminacy of geospatial concepts, as well as of their properties and relations.
    • Approximation: the level of detail or granularity of the conceptualization, representation, and visualization of geospatial entities.

The meaning of concepts

Meaning is a central notion of many disciplines such as philosophy, linguistics, psychology, semiotics, communication theory and information science, especially as it concerns knowledge representation and engineering, and the development of the semantic web. Fundamental questions relative to the nature and ontological status of meaning and methods of semantic description and representation are the primary focus of the field of semantics. Geospatial semantics focuses on the meaning of geospatial entities, how it is conceptualized and whether the conceptualization of geospatial entities differs from conceptualizations of other types of entities, how it may be defined and represented, in order to be easily understood, used, and exchanged.

Ogden and Richards (1923) introduced the *meaning triangle* to illustrate the relation among an object, the concept (conceptualization) of the object, and the symbol used to represent the concept. Figure 3.4 shows an extension of the meaning triangle at a meta-level to illustrate that geographic information acquires meaning through the interrelation of three components: (1) geographic reality; (2) geographic conceptualization; and (3) geographic representation.

In general, there are two modes of meaning: (1) the *extension* or *reference* or *denotation*; and (2) the *intension* or *sense* or *connotation*. The *extension* of a concept refers to the set of entities, objects, things, and so on to which the concept properly applies. For example, the extension of the concept "river" includes all rivers that exist. On the other hand, the *intension* of a concept refers to the essential properties that describe the concept; these properties commonly apply to all things that fall under the extension of the concept. For example, the intension of the concept "river" includes such properties as "natural," "stream of water," and "flowing." A concept's intension and extension are interrelated. The intension designates the extension, since it provides the essential properties that serve as a criterion to determine which things belong to the extension. Moreover, they are inversely proportional (Swartz, 1997) since an intension increase results in an extension decrease. For example, if the intension of the concept "river" is augmented with the property "large," then the extension of the concept is diminished to only large rivers, excluding small ones.

The meaning of concepts is usually encapsulated by definitions. Definitions decompose the meaning of a concept into its components, that is, simpler concepts. The two modes of meaning consist in two methods of defining the meaning of concepts: (1) *extensional definitions* outline the objects that fall under the extension of a concept; whereas (2) *intensional definitions* specify the properties that constitute the intension of the concept.

The meaning of geographic concepts is usually described intensionally, that is, using intensional definitions that specify the properties of the entities that belong to the concept and provide a mechanism for the addition of new entities. For example, the definition: "forest: a large densely wooded area" determines the fundamental properties that constitute the concept's "forest" intension.

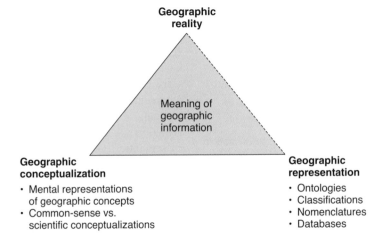

Figure 3.4   A meta-meaning triangle for geographic information

Exceptions are possible only for restricted concepts with closed-set domains such as "the Group of Eight (G8), which maybe defined extensionally as consisting of the following countries: Canada, France, Germany, Italy, Japan, Russia, the UK, and the USA.

Properties

Properties may be defined as the "attributes or qualities or features or characteristics of things" (Swoyer, 2000). Many scientific disciplines such as philosophy, cognitive science, and semantics study the nature, existence, types, and roles of properties. Properties are considered particularly salient due to their significance in fulfilling tasks such as qualitative similarity, recognition and classification of new instances, and explanation of the meaning of terms (Swoyer, 2000). Therefore, they may support the semantic definition of geographic concepts and facilitate their understanding by a wide range of users. Furthermore, they may be used in several semantic-based tasks, such as ontology development and integration, concept comparison, and information retrieval and extraction.

Several classifications of properties may be found in literature (Bigelow, 2000; Guarino and Welty, 2000a, 2000b; Swoyer, 2000), such as: (1) particularizing, characterizing and mass properties; (2) semantic and syntactic properties; (3) essential and non-essential properties; and (4) natural kind and artificial properties. Semantic properties are singled out as especially relevant to the semantic definition of geographic concepts; they describe the internal characteristics of a concept, which are independent of the existence or relations with other concepts (Kavouras and Kokla, 2008). Semantic properties may be both spatial (e.g., *size* and *shape*), and aspatial (e.g., *purpose*, *nature*, *cover*, *time*). For example, the following definition of a river expresses three semantic properties: *size*, *nature*, and *cover*.

River: *large, natural stream of water.*

Size is a spatial property and takes the value "large," whereas *nature* and *cover* are both aspatial properties; *nature* is assigned the value "natural" and *cover* the value "water." Different types of semantic properties are used to describe the meaning of different types of geographic concepts. Properties like *size*, *shape*, *nature*, and *cover* are used to describe concepts that relate to physical reality such as river, lake, and forest. Geographic concepts relative to water are further designated by the property of *water flow* which takes two values: "flowing" for concepts such as watercourse and 'stagnant' for concepts like lake. Artificial geographic concepts are described according to the *purpose* they are made to serve, as in the following definitions:

Canal: artificial waterway used for transportation.

Camp: a place usually in the country for recreation or instruction often during the summer. (Merriam–Webster online dictionary, 2009)

Administrative concepts, on the other hand, are defined according to administrative and socioeconomic parameters such as *population density* and *governmental jurisdiction*.

Town: a large densely populated urban area (Merriam–Webster online dictionary, 2009).

Municipality: an urban district having corporate status and powers of self-government (WordNet 3.0, Princeton University, 2006).

Semantic properties and relations have a twofold mission. On the one hand, they describe the essential characteristics that constitute the meaning of concepts. On the other, they contribute to the distinction between similar concepts. For example, a river is distinguished from a canal on the basis of the values of the property *nature*: a river is a natural watercourse, whereas a canal is an artificial or improved natural watercourse. Urban areas are distinguished from rural areas based on the value of *population density*. According to this, a town is defined as

an urban area with a fixed boundary that is smaller than a city (WordNet 3.0, Princeton University, 2006).

Relations

Like properties, relations have also attracted the attention of several disciplines. Depending on the context of study (e.g., philosophy, linguistics, cognition, information retrieval, and so on), several classifications of relations exist (Storey, 1993; Bean et al., 2002).

Is-a and *part-whole* relations are the most commonly used in geographic ontologies. The *is-a* relation (also called subtype/super-type, hyponymy, class, and kind of relation) refers to the subordination/superordination relation. It is based on the principle that each subordinate concept has all the properties of the superordinate concept plus at least one property that differentiates it both from its superordinate and its sibling concepts. This type of relation mainly refers to natural kinds, artifacts, states, and activities (Chaffin et al., 1988). For example, a broad-leaved forest *is-a* forest, a road network *is-a* transportation infrastructure, and retail trade *is-a* commercial activity.

Part-whole relations (also called mero-nymic and partonomy relations) are also an important relation type. They pertain to all entities, physical and abstract, spatial and temporal and are used for the semantic description of both concepts and instances (Pribbenow, 2002). Meronymic relations are further distinguished into subtypes (Winston et al., 1987; Gerstl and Pribbenow, 1995) such as *component – integral object*, *member – collection*, *portion – mass*, *stuff – object*, *feature – activity*, and so on *Part-whole* relations are dealt with by the theory called mereology; its combination with topology results in the theory of mereotopology which studies parts, wholes and boundaries (Smith, 1996; Varzi, 1996) and has made

important contributions in geographic information science.

Although several geographic ontologies are hierarchically structured using both *is-a* and *part-whole* relations, this should better be avoided. In case this is not possible, these two types of semantic relations should be thoroughly and cautiously managed under the same hierarchical structure in order to avoid confusion and misunderstanding on the ontological status of concepts, their superordinate concepts, their inherited properties, and so on. Figure 3.5 shows a hierarchical structure incorporating both *is-a* and *part-whole* relations.

Is-a relations usually result in single inheritance, that is, tree-structured hierarchies, allowing each concept to be associated to only one superconcept. However, some cases require the adoption of multiple inheritance in order to allow multiple views of the same information (Kavouras and Kokla, 2008). For example, the concept "private residence for the elderly" may be subconcept of both "commerce" and "social walefare" under different contexts. In order to retain both contexts in an integrated ontology, multiple inheritance would be established among these concepts as shown in Figure 3.6.

Analysis of definitions of geographic concepts has shown a number of essential semantic properties and relations of geographic concepts (Kokla and Kavouras, 2005; Kavouras and Kokla, 2008). The main semantic properties are: *purpose, cause, agent, cover, time, duration, frequency, size, shape*, and so on and the main semantic relations: *is-a, is-part-of, has-part, relative position, proximity, direction* and other topological semantic relations such as *separation, adjacency, connectivity, overlap, intersection, containment, exclusion, surroundness,* and *extension.* Figure 3.7 shows the analysis of the concept 'camp' into four semantic elements and their values according to the definition (Merriam–Webster online dictionary, 2009)

Camp: a place usually in the country for recreation or instruction often during the summer.

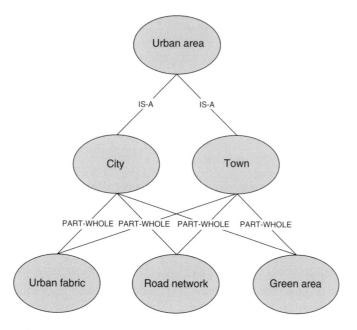

Figure 3.5   Mix of IS-A and PART-WHOLE relations

Darra (2009) defines some major properties of spatial socioeconomic entities, such as location, area, compactness, figure/shape, and distance/proximity, legal status, and positional stability.

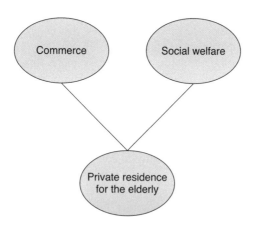

Figure 3.6   Example of multiple inheritance

CONCLUSION

In order to facilitate easy access, understanding, and use of geographic information through SDIs and the semantic web by society in general and not only by a small group of experts, it is important to develop advanced semantic information theories and corresponding technologies. Therefore, it is important to enrich geographic information sources with semantic information and to incorporate into geographic information systems semantic-enabled technologies, (e.g., the use of natural or controlled languages instead of formal languages) in order to facilitate the understanding of the meaning of geographic concepts. Advances in natural language processing present an important contribution towards this direction, since most semantic information on geographic concepts, properties, and relations is still conveyed through natural language. Natural language is an indispensable means of human expression, understanding, and communication.

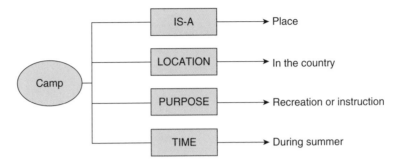

Figure 3.7   Analysis of the concept *camp* into its semantic elements and values

However, in order to be further utilized by information technologies, the meaning conveyed by natural language should be transformed into an appropriate formal language understood by computers. Controlled languages provide the necessary intermediate means for the association of natural and formal languages.

Another future research direction relates to the expert–non-expert issue: what are the differences between experts' and non-experts' conceptualizations of geographic reality? Do they decompose geographic reality into the same categories and at the same level of detail? Which is the proper way to represent the semantics of geographic information in order for it to be properly understood and used by non-experts? According to Smith and Mark (2001), an ultimate ontology of a domain should be developed based on good conceptualizations combining both scientific and commonsense knowledge. Although there are some experiments on people's understanding and representation of geographic concepts (Mark et al., 2001; Smith and Mark, 2001), there is still a lot of work needed in order to arrive at a complete and applicable theory of geographic concept perception and representation. Moreover, research has paid more attention to physical entities such as mountains, lakes, and rivers than to socioeconomic entities. Are there any differences between the conceptualization and representation of physical entities and socioeconomic entities? Are there any differences in the conceptualization and representation of socioeconomic entities between experts and non-experts? A theory able to answer the above questions would be of great importance for three main reasons: (1) to facilitate information exchange and reuse among different groups of users; (2) to reinforce the understanding and use of geographic information by a broader group of people, including non-experts; and (3) to explore the possibility of varying representations of geographic reality for different purposes and different users.

The distinction between "light" and scientific ontologies is also highly relevant (Kavouras and Kokla, 2008). "Light" ontologies are primarily based on common sense and may be used for enhancing the understanding of geographic information by non-experts. Scientific ontologies, by contrast, substantiate the knowledge of different scientific domains, providing a more robust and objective view of reality. The proliferation of the use of geographic information and intelligent services such as SDIs and the semantic web stress the need to investigate those cases that require a lighter, commonsense view of reality in contrast to the cases that demand a stronger scientific grounding. The association and parallel use of both ontology types is another stimulating research question that should be considered in the near future.

REFERENCES

Agarwal, P. (2005) 'Ontological considerations in Geographic information science', *International Journal of Geographical Information Science*, 19(5): 501–36.

Bean, C.A., Green, R. and Myaeng, S.H. (2002) 'Introduction'. In R. Green, C. A. Bean and S. H. Myaeng (eds), *The Semantics of Relationships: An Interdisciplinary Perspective*. Dortrecht: Kluwer Academic.

Bennett, B. (2001) 'What is a forest? On the vagueness of certain geographic concepts', *Topoi*, 20: 189–201.

Bernstein, P. (2003) 'Applying model management to classical meta data problems'. In C.A. Asilomar (ed.), *Proc. Conference on Innovative Database Research*, CIDR, pp. 209–20.

Bigelow, J. (2000) *Semantic Properties*. Monash University. http://www.wysiwyg://body.11 http: www.arts.mil/department/bigelow/semantic.html (accessed 10 June 2005).

Bohr, N. (1934) *Atomic Theory and the Description of Nature*. Cambridge: Cambridge University Press.

Câmara, G., Monteiro, A., Paiva, J. and Souza, R. (2000) 'Action-driven ontologies of the geographical space', in *Proc. 1st International Conference on Geographical Information Science (Geographic information science2000)*, Savannah, Georgia, USA, October 28–31, 2000.

Canada's National Statistical Agency (2006) Census metropolitan area (CMA) and census agglomeration (CA). *2006 Census Dictionary*. http://www12. statcan.ca/english/census06/reference/dictionary/ geo009.cfm (accessed 2 October 2009).

Casati, R., Smith, B. and Varzi, A.C. (1998) 'Ontological tools for geographic representation'. In N. Guarino (ed.), *Formal Ontology in Information Systems*. Amsterdam: IOS Press. pp. 77–85.

Chaffin, R., Herrmann, D.J. and Winston, M. (1988) 'An empirical taxonomy of part-whole relations: Effects of part-whole type on relation identification', *Language and Cognitive Processes*, 3(1): 17–48.

Couclelis, H. (1996) 'A typology of geographic entities with ill-defined boundaries'. In P.A. Burrough and A.U. Frank (eds), *Geographic Objects with Indeterminate Boundaries*. London: Taylor & Francis. pp. 45–56.

Cruz, I.F., Rajendran, A., Sunna, W. and Wiegand, N. (2002) 'Handling semantic heterogeneities using declarative agreements', *Proc. 10th ACM International Symposium on Advances in Geographic Information Systems*. New York: ACM Press. pp. 168–74.

Cycorp, Inc. (2002) 'OpenCyc selected vocabulary and upper ontology'. http://www.cyc.com/cycdoc/vocab/ vocab-toc.html (accessed 29 January 2009).

Darra, A. (2009) 'A framework for the development and comparison of spatial socioeconomic units', PhD thesis, National Technical University of Athens (in Greek).

Egenhofer, M. (1993) 'What's special about spatial? Database requirements for vehicle navigation in geographic space', *Proc. ACM SIGMOD International Conference on Management of Data*. Washington, DC: ACM Press. pp. 398–402.

Fellbaum, C. (ed.) (1998) *WordNet: An Electronic Lexical Database*. Cambridge, MA: MIT Press.

Fonseca, F. and Egenhofer, M. (1999) 'Ontology-driven geographic information systems'. In B. Medeiros, (ed.), *Proc. 7th ACM Symposium on Advances in Geographic Information Systems*. Kansas City, MO, pp. 14–9.

Fonseca, F., Câmara, G. and Monteiro, A.M. (2006) 'A framework for measuring the interoperability of geo-ontologies', *Spatial Cognition and Computation*, 6(4): 307–29.

Fonseca, F., Egenhofer, M. and Agouris, P. (2002) 'Using ontologies for integrated geographic information systems'. In F. Fonseca, M. Egenhofer, P. Agouris and G. Câmara (eds), *Transactions in GIS*, 6(3): 231–57.

Fonseca, F., Egenhofer, M., Davis, C. and Borges, K. (2000) 'Ontologies and knowledge sharing in urban GIS', *CEUS – Computer, Environment and Urban Systems*, 24(3): 232–51.

Fonseca, F., Egenhofer, M., Davis, C. and Câmara, G. (2002) 'Semantic granularity in ontology-driven geographic information systems', *AMAI Annals of Mathematics and Artificial Intelligence – Special Issue on Spatial and Temporal Granularity*, 36(1–2): 121–51.

Frank, A.U. (2001) 'Tiers of ontology and consistency constraints in geographic information systems', *International Journal of Geographical Information Science*, 15(7): 667–78.

Gerstl, P. and Pribbenow, S. (1995) 'Midwinters, end games and body parts: A classification of part-whole relations', *International Journal of Human-Computer Studies*, 43: 865–89.

Grenon, P. (2003) 'BFO in a nutshell: A bi-categorial axiomatization of BFO and comparison with DOLCE', *Technical Report, ISSN 1611–4019*, Institute for Formal Ontology and Medical Information Science (IFOMIS), University of Leipzig, Germany.

Grenon, P. and Smith, B. (2004) 'SNAP and SPAN: towards dynamic spatial ontology', *Spatial Cognition and Computation*, 4 (1): 69–104.

Gruber, T.R. (1995) 'Toward principles for the design of ontologies used for knowledge sharing', *International Journal of Human-Computer Studies*, 43(5–6): 907–28.

Gruber, T. (2003) 'It is what it does: The pragmatics of ontology', Invited talk at Sharing the Knowledge, International CIDOC CRM Symposium. Washington, DC, 26–27 March.

Gruber, T. (2004) 'Every ontology is a treaty', Interview for Semantic Web and Information Systems, SIG of the Association for Information Systems, *SIGSEMIS Bulletin*, 1(4).

Guarino, N. (1998) 'Formal ontology and information systems'. In N. Guarino (ed.), *Proc. 1st International Conference on Formal Ontologies in Information Systems (FOIS'98)*. Trento: IOS Press, pp. 3–15.

Guarino, N. and Welty, C. (2000a) 'A formal ontology of properties'. In R. Dieng and O. Corby (eds), *Proc. EKAW-2000: The 12th International Conference on Knowledge Engineering and Knowledge Management*. Lecture Notes on Computer Science, vol. 1937. New York: Springer Verlag. pp. 97–112.

Guarino, N. and Welty, C. (2000b) 'Ontological analysis of taxonomic relationships'., In A. Laender and V. Storey (eds), *Proc. ER-2000: The 19th International Conference on Conceptual Modeling*, Lecture Notes on Computer Science. New York: Springer-Verlag.1920: 210–24. http://www.cs.vassar.edu/faculty/welty/papers/er2000/LADSEB05–2000.pdf (accessed 29 January 2009).

Hakimpour, F. and Geppert, A. (2001) 'Resolving semantic heterogeneity in schema integration: An ontology based approach', *Proc. International Conference on Formal Ontology in Information Systems FOIS-2001*. pp. 297–308.

Hakimpour, F. and Geppert, A. (2002) 'Global schema generation using formal ontologies', *Proc. 21st International Conference on Conceptual Modeling ER2002*. New York: Springer-Verlag. 2503: 307–21.

Horton, R. (1982) 'Tradition and modernity revisited'. In M. Hollis and S. Luke (eds), *Rationality and Relativism*. Oxford: Blackwell. pp. 201–60.

Hunter, G. (2002) 'Understanding semantics and ontologies: They're quite simple really – if you know what I mean!', *Transactions in GIS*, 6(2): 83–7.

IFOMIS (Institute for Formal Ontology and Medical Information Science) (2009) *Basic Formal Ontology* (BFO). http://www.mygrid.org.uk/OWL/Presentation?url=http%3A%2F%2Fwww.ifomis.org%2Fbfo%2F1.1 (accessed 2 October 2009).

Kavouras, M. and Kokla, M. (2002) 'A method for the formalization and integration of geographical categorizations', *International Journal of Geographical Information Science*, 16(5): 439–53.

Kavouras, M. and Kokla, M. (2008) *Theories of Geographic Concepts: Ontological Approaches to Semantic Integration*. Boca Raton, FL: CRC Press.

Klein, G.O. and Smith, B. (2005) 'Concept systems and ontologies, recommendations based on discussions between realist philosophers and ISO/CEN experts concerning the standards addressing "concepts" and related terms', *CEN/TC 251/WGII Terminology and Knowledge Bases, WGII/N05–19*. http://ontology.buffalo.edu/concepts/ConceptsandOntologies.pdf (accessed 29 January 2009).

Kokla, M. and Kavouras, M. (2001) 'Fusion of top-level and geographical domain ontologies based on context formation and complementarity', *International Journal of Geographical Information Science*, 15(7): 679–87.

Kokla, M. and Kavouras, M. (2005) 'Semantic information in geo-ontologies: extraction, comparison, and reconciliation', *Journal on Data Semantics*, 35(34): 125–42.

Kuhn, W. (2001) 'Ontologies in support for activities in geographic space', *International Journal of Geographical Information Science*, 15(7): 613–31.

Kuhn, W. (2003) 'Semantic reference systems', *International Journal of Geographic Information Science*, 17(5): 405–409.

Kuhn, W. (2005), 'Geospatial semantics: why, of what, and how?', *Journal on Data Semantics*, 3: 1–24.

Laurence, S. and Margolis, E. (1999) 'Concepts and cognitive science'. In E. Margolis and S. Laurence (eds), *Concepts: Core Readings*. Cambridge, MA: MIT Press. pp. 3–81.

Leclercq, E., Benslimane, D. and Yétognon, K. (1999) 'ISIS: A semantic mediation model and an agent based architecture for GIS interoperability', *Proc. International Symposium Database Engineering and Applications (IDEAS)*, IEEE. pp. 87–91.

López-Pellicer F.J., Florczyk, A.J., Lacasta, J., Zarazaga-Soria, F.J. and R. Muro-Medrano, P. (2008) 'Administrative units, an ontological perspective'. In I.-Y. Song et al. (eds), *ER Workshops 2008, LNCS 5232, 2008*. Berlin: Heidelberg. pp. 354–63.

Lowe, E.J. (2001) 'Recent advances in metaphysics', *Proc. 2nd International Conference on Formal Ontology in Information Systems, FOIS 2001*, Ogunquit, Maine, 17–9, October ACM, http://www.cs.vassar.edu/~weltyc/fois/fois-2001/keynote/ (accessed 29 January 2009).

MacLeod, M.C. and Rubenstein, E.M. (2006) 'Universals', *Internet Encyclopedia of Philosophy*.

http://www.iep.utm.edu/u/universa.htm#H5 (accessed 29 January 2009).

Mahesh, K. (1996) 'Ontology development for machine translation: Ideology and methodology', *Technical Report MCCS 96–292, Computing Research Laboratory.* New Mexico State University, Las Cruces, NM.

Mahesh, K. and Nirenburg, S. (1996) 'Meaning representation for knowledge sharing in practical machine translation', *Proc. of the FLAIRS-96 track on Information Interchange.* AI Research Symposium, Florida.

Margolis, E. and Laurence, S. (2006) 'Concepts', *Stanford Encyclopedia of Philosophy, Metaphysics Research Lab.* CSLI, Stanford University. http://plato.stanford.edu/entries/concepts/ (accessed 29 January 2009).

Mark, D.M., Skupin, A. and Smith, B. (2001) 'Features, objects, and other things: Ontological distinctions in the geographic domain'. In D.R. Montello (ed.), *Spatial Information Theory: Foundations of Geographic Information Science.* Lecture Notes in Computer Science 2205. Berlin: Springer-Verlag. pp. 488–502.

Mark, D.M. and Smith, B. (2004) 'A science of topography: Bridging the qualitative-quantitative divide'. In M.P. Bishop and J. Shroder (eds), *Geographic Information Science and Mountain Geomorphology.* Chichester: Springer-Praxis. pp. 75–100.

Mark, D.M., Smith, B., Egenhofer, M. and Hirtle, S. (2004) 'Ontological foundations for geographic information science'. In R. McMaster and L. Usery (eds), *A Research Agenda for Geographic Information Science.* Boca Raton, FL: CRC Press. pp. 335–50.

Mark, D.M., Smith, B. and Tversky, B. (1999) 'Ontology and geographic objects: An empirical study of cognitive categorization'. In C. Freksa and D. Mark (eds), *Spatial Information Theory, Cognitive and Computational Foundations of Geographic Information Science.* Lecture Notes in Computer Science, Number 1661. New York: Springer. pp. 283–98.

Masolo, C., Borgo, S., Gangemi, A., Guarino, N., Oltramari A. and Schneider L. (2003) WonderWeb, Deliverable D17, The WonderWeb Library of Foundational Ontologies, Preliminary Report, version 2.1, ISTC-CNR.

Muller, P. (1998) 'Space-time as a primitive for space and motion'. In N. Guarino (ed.), *Proc. First International Conference in Formal Ontology in Information Systems (FOIS'98).* Trento, Italy: IOS Press, Netherlands. pp. 63–76.

Ogden, C.K. and Richards, I.A. (1923) *The Meaning of Meaning.* London: Routledge & Kegan Paul.

Pribbenow, S. (2002) 'Meronymic relationships: From classical mereology to complex part-whole relations'. In R. Green, C.A. Bean and S.H. Myaeng (eds), *The Semantics of Relationships: An Interdisciplinary Perspective*, Amsterdam: Kluwer Academic. pp. 35–50.

Princeton University (2006) 'WordNet 3.0'. http://wordnetweb.princeton.edu/perl/webwn

Ram, S., Khatri, V., Zhang, L. and Zeng, D.D. (2002) 'GeoCosm: A semantics-based approach for information integration of geospatial data'. In H. Arisawa and Y. Kambayashi (eds), *ER 2001 Workshops*, LNCS 2465. Berlin: Springer-Verlag. pp. 152–65.

Raubal M. (2001) 'Ontology and epistemology for agent-based wayfinding simulation', *International Journal of Geographical Information Science.* Taylor & Francis. 15(7): 653–65.

Rodríguez, A. and Egenhofer, M. (2003) 'Determining semantic similarity among entity classes from different ontologies', *IEEE Transactions on Knowledge and Data Engineering,* 15(2): 442–56.

Smith, B. (1996) 'Mereotopology: A theory of parts and boundaries', *Data and Knowledge Engineering*, 20: 287–304.

Smith, B. (2003) 'Ontology'. In L. Floridi (ed.), *Blackwell Guide to the Philosophy of Computing and Information.* Oxford: Blackwell. pp. 155–66.

Smith, B. (2004) 'Beyond concepts: Ontology as reality representation'. In A. Varzi and L. Vieu (eds), *Proc. International Conference on Formal Ontology and Information Systems (FOIS 2004)*, Turin.

Smith, B. and Mark, D. (1998) 'Ontology and geographic kinds'. In T.K. Poiker and N. Chrisman (eds), *Proc. 8th International Symposium on Spatial Data Handling (SDH'98).* Vancouver: International Geographical Union. pp. 308–20.

Smith, B. and Mark, D. (2001) 'Geographical categories: An ontological investigation', *Int. J. Geographical Information Science*, 15(7): 591–612.

Smith, B. and Mark, D.M. (2003) 'Do mountains exist? towards an ontology of landforms', *Environment and Planning*, 30(3): 411–27.

Smith, B. and Varzi, A.C. (2000) 'Fiat and bona fide boundaries', *Philosophy and Phenomenological Research*, 60: 401–20.

Soon, K. and Kuhn, W. (2004) 'Formalizing user actions for ontologies'. In M.J. Egenhofer, C. Freksa and H.J. Miller (eds), *Proc. Geographic information science 2004*, LNCS 3234, Berlin: Springer-Verlag. pp. 299–312.

Sowa, J.F. (2000) *Knowledge Representation: Logical, Philosophical and Computational Foundations.* Pacific Grove, CA: Brooks Cole.

SUO WG (2003) *IEEE P1600.1 Standard Upper Ontology Working Group Home Page.* http://suo.ieee.org/index.html (accessed 29 January 2009).

Storey, V.C. (1993) 'Understanding semantic relationships'. In F.J. Maryanski (ed.), *VLDB Journal*, 2: 455–88.

Swartz, N. (1997) 'Definitions, dictionaries, and meanings', Department of Philosophy, Simon Fraser University. http://www.sfu.ca/philosophy/swartz/definitn.htm (accessed 29 January 2009).

Swoyer, C. (2000) *Properties, Stanford Encyclopedia of Philosophy.* http://plato.stanford.edu/entries/properties/ (accessed 29 January 2009).

United Nations Statistics Division (2005) *Demographic Yearbook 2005.* http://unstats.un.org/unsd/demographic/sconcerns/densurb/Defintion_of%20Urban.pdf (accessed 2 October 2009).

United States Census Bureau (2008) *Census 2000 Urban and Rural Classification.* http://www.census.gov/geo/www/ua/ua_2k.html (accessed 2 October 2009).

Uschold, M. (1996) 'Building ontologies: Towards a unified methodology', paper presented at 16th Annual Conference of the British Computer Society Specialist Group on Expert Systems, Cambridge, 16–18 December.

Varzi, A.C. (1996) 'Parts, wholes, and part–whole relations: the prospects of mereotopology', *Data and Knowledge Engineering*, 20: 259–86.

Varzi, A.C. (2001a) 'Philosophical issues in geography – an introduction', *Topoi*, 20: 119–30.

Varzi, A.C. (2001b) 'Vagueness in geography', *Philosophy and Geography*, 4: 49–65.

Wikipedia (2009) *Urban Area.* http://en.wikipedia.org/wiki/Urban_area (accessed 2 October 2009).

Winston, M.E., Chaffin, R. and Herrmann, D. (1987) 'A taxonomy of part-whole relations', *Cognitive Science*, 11: 417–44.

Winter, S. (2001) 'Ontology – buzzword or paradigm shift in GI science?', *International Journal for Geographical Information Science*, Editorial for the special issue on Ontology in the Geographic Domain, 15(7): 587–90.

Zlatev, J. (2007) 'Spatial semantics'. In H. Cuyckens and D. Geeraerts (eds), *Handbook of Cognitive Linguistics.* Oxford: Oxford University Press.

4

The Social Potential of GIS

Stacy Warren

INTRODUCTION

The field of geographic information systems (GIS), once scorned by critical geographers as irretrievably positivist, is now being reconceptualized as a potentially liberating discourse that situates technology in social context. GIS is increasingly recognized as a technology, an activity, and a set of social relations that inserts itself into everyday life and thus embodies the social potential of other modern technologies to be both agent of control and agent of subversion. Significantly, the most sustained critical voices are just as likely to be GIS practitioners as outside observers, a transformation that points to a more constructive era of GIS activity in which GIS's social potential can be more fully realized.

Like the telephone, the radio, and the television long before it, GIS is one of many twentieth century communications technologies that promises – and threatens – to change our understanding and experience of time and space. Yet unlike other technologies, GIS requires the user(s) to construct the reality that will be conveyed to an unprecedentedly explicit degree. Whether utilizing high-end, production-quality software, like

ArcInfo, or accessible web-based programs like Google Earth™, the user must successfully choreograph an instance in which the software, hardware, data, and analytic capabilities at hand all cooperatively produce the desired spatial knowledge within the broader assemblage of social, political, and economic structures that shape the possibilities. Thus GIS stands apart as a superbly intriguing technology that invites critical review from numerous angles.

This chapter investigates the social potential of GIS applications by considering GIS as one of several communication technologies that have evolved throughout the twentieth century with potentially participatory capabilities. Against this backcloth, I first review the ways in which GIS has been theorized within the conventional GIS literature, and then consider alternative readings when viewed as an assemblage situated within broader communication theories. This allows for close examination of the ways in which GIS, or any communication technology, can have social potential. The chapter then presents two unique instances of GIS in action from very different geographic locations, in order to better explore the richly ambiguous nature of GIS's social potential as it plays out grounded in time and space. Each case brings a distinct (and essentially irreproducible) set of social and political conditions, from grasslands scientists in western China, to Israeli and Palestinian occupants of the West Bank. In each case, GIS plays a multi-faceted role that is neither wholly subversive nor wholly co-optive. Rather, GIS is at the center of contested spaces, utilized in quite different ways and to different ends by groups on either side (and sometimes on the same side). These examples serve as an important reminder that the technology of GIS, like other technologies of modernity, are adapted by and mutated through the social relations of the groups using it. Ultimately, the outcomes of GIS practices are strongly shaped by the power structures within which they exist, but not necessarily in predictable or consistent ways. In other words, GIS never quite looks the same twice.

HISTORICAL FRAMEWORK

Although humans have utilized some form of technology to answer geographic questions for millennia, the various computerized spatial technologies I group together under the name GIS date back to the early 1960s. Both raster and vector systems were pioneered during that decade, and the vast enterprise of spatial data capture begun. Cumbersome and expensive, the early tools of GIS attracted little if any critical discussion as to their social potential. In the ensuing years, however, a wide array of theoretical frameworks and their accompanying acronyms (GISystems, GIScience, GIStudies, PPGIS, GISoc, and so on) has emerged that locate GIS as both technology and science in broader social context. From thoughtful practitioners like Michael Goodchild (1992) who have argued for its role as science, to sharp denouncements of its insidious power from radical geographers like Neil Smith (1992), to gendered reconstructions of its

possibilities from feminist geographers like Mei Po-Kwan (2002), to eloquent veterans like Nicholas Chrisman (2005) who wisely argue it is time to move beyond the technological determinism implicit on all sides, GIS has attracted possibly more wide-ranging theoretical discussion than any other branch of geography in the past decade. To an outsider, the debate must appear rather disconnected at times; the various participants draw from quite distinct (and often virtually incommensurable) bodies of literature, and bring with them widely varying experience in the practice of GIS itself. In this section, I outline a historical evolution of GIS that focuses on the ways in which GIS has been used and critiqued as a potentially participatory communications technology.

The story of GIS's birth and development is no doubt quite familiar to most geographers, having been recounted so often it begins to take on fairy tale-like qualities. It is born of gentle innocence among Canadians seeking to protect threatened agricultural lands, and further explored by Harvard researchers who embraced Ian McHarg's vision of landscape overlays.[1] It falls into the hands of increasingly more sophisticated technologists who promote a pseudo-positivist objectivity, military personnel who embrace its destructive power, and clever marketing agents who grasp the civilian potential of both the technology and its supporting data.[2] At last, as the story goes, due to the watchful eyes of astute critical geographers, the proverbial finger is pointed. The emperor may be clothed, but in raiments that obfuscate and deceive.

At that point the story gets a bit murkier, with several possible readings. Does GIS, once exposed, forever gain the stigma of positivist enterprise used for nefarious purposes? Or, does the embarrassing revelation inspire a soulful rethinking of how a post-positivist GIS could be crafted? Or does the debate help shift focus to foundational ontologies of GIS that have been associated with the technology from the beginning? Though similar, each of these outcomes suggests fundamentally different assumptions about GIS's social potential. Indeed, several observers have come to the conclusion that analysis of the critiques can be just as informative as analysis of GIS itself (Schuurman, 2000; Sheppard, 2005; St. Martin and Wing, 2007). Schuurman's (2000) division of criticism into three chronological waves can be especially useful here, as it helps contextualize the various reactions in their discursive settings. I next review each briefly.

The earliest significant criticisms Schuurman identifies date back to the early 1990s. This first wave carried great rhetorical force even as it revealed little underlying understanding of the inner workings of GIS. Polemic attacks drew attention to, for example, GIS's ties to 'the very worst sort of positivism' that made it an 'intellectually sterile high-tech trivial pursuit' (Taylor, 1990: 212). Neil Smith famously blamed GIS for its tacit complicity in 'Iraq's killing fields' (Smith, 1992: 257). Underlying most of these early critiques was the assumption that GIS was completely incompatible with qualitative or subjective modes of knowledge (Lake, 1993). Not surprisingly, this first wave unleashed what Schuurman aptly calls a 'flurry' of responses, in part because the harshness of attack provoked immediate defensive posturing from many GIS practitioners, and in part because the tone of social critique effectively created a role for virtually everyone in subsequent debates surrounding the validity of GIS. No longer did one need to be a GIS expert, or even know how to turn on a computer, in order to participate. The parameters of discourse – vitriolic defense of positivist enterprise on the one hand (Openshaw, 1991), and what must have seemed like impenetrable philosophical arguments on the other (e.g., Lake, 1993) – virtually assured that the two sides would likely remain at antagonistic ends.

A key transition occurred by the mid-1990s with fledgling efforts on the part of human geographers and other social theorists to grapple with the critical implications of

the technology by engaging, not rejecting, GIS activity. During this second wave, a new generation of discussions surrounding GIS's social potential were entertained. NCGIA initiatives such as Friday Harbor and Initiative 19 date from this period and brought together GIS veterans on the one hand such as Michael Goodchild and Nicholas Chrisman, and critical geographers such as John Pickles, Eric Sheppard, and Michael Curry on the other. John Pickle's (1995) seminal edited volume *Ground Truth* crystallized the discussion in one location. However, as Schuurman reminds us, the boundaries of discussion were still tightly controlled by GIS critics – in essence, GIS supporters were welcome in the conversation as long as everyone agreed that GIS was by design a fundamentally non-democratic technology with extremely questionable ethical implications that privileged a quantitative, rational world view. The dominant message from the critical GIS community, thus, was that GIS's social potential would be forever limited to hegemonic support of the status quo until researchers and practitioners found ways to overcome GIS's many inherent problems.

To a small but growing number of GIS practitioners, the notion that GIS by definition automatically inherited a predefined set of problems was increasingly troublesome. A new set of questions emerged as these practitioners, many of whom were also trained in social and STS (Science, Technology, Society) theories, explored the problems and potentials that could be identified from critical understanding of actual daily GIS activity.[3] Thus the seeds were sown for the third wave of GIS criticism. This stage is defined broadly by Schuurman as a period when epistemological and ontological frameworks were being reconceptualized based on more nuanced understanding of GIS activity and especially its relation to structures of power. The rapid rise of PPGIS (Public Participation GIS), for example, is indicative of the spirit of the third wave. Within a few years of its inception, PPGIS grew into a widely accepted GIS subfield dedicated to achieving increased community participation in social and environmental justice issues through the use of GIS technology (Craig et al., 2002).

Since Schuurman initially wrote of the third wave in 2000, it has expanded to include a number of critical GIS practitioners informed by their research as feminist geographers, social theorists, post-colonialists, political economists, and the like. GIS is increasingly recognized as a valid research tool for mapping and counter-mapping[4] a host of urban, social, and environmental issues ranging from community-based land reform in South Africa (Weiner and Harris, 2003), the everyday life of households in economic transition in Moscow (Pavlovskaya, 2004), breast cancer activism in women's communities (McLafferty, 2005), neighborhood revitalization in American midwestern cities (Elwood and Leitner, 2003), unequal lending practices in American inner cities (Wylie et al., 2004), and the emotional landscape of a Muslim woman in Ohio (Kwan, 2007) to cite a few examples. These innovative and sometimes confrontational uses illustrate GIS's social potential to challenge conventional assumptions about the limits of GIS technology.

Many still lament, however, there is not greater continuity between critical GIS and its users. Six years after Schuurman's (2000: 582) Haraway-esque call to "engage in the construction of the [GIS] cyborg rather than critique it from afar," Pavlovskaya (2006) still found the climate hostile enough to craft a well-argued defense of GIS as qualitative methodology. Schuurman (2006) herself remarked on the still discouraging gap between (philosophical) conceptualization and (technological) formalization, specifically calling for critics to interrogate GIS's ontological structures on their own grounds. Both Schuurman (2006) and Georgiadou and Blakemore (2006), though working from somewhat different epistemological stances, found that the standard GIS journals rarely published articles that explicitly addressed critical GIS issues.[5] And perhaps most

notable of all, St. Martin and Wing (2007) discovered that surveyed undergraduates clung stubbornly to the belief that GIS alone is the sole branch of geography that can effectively be used to solve the problems of daily life (which apparently include getting a job).[6] Clearly the question of GIS's social potential is still being negotiated. Chrisman (2005) argues that as long as GIS research discourse tacitly perpetuates a version of social practice based upon technological determinism, fundamental qualities of GIS practice will remain undertheorized. "Technological determinism obscures the relationships between GIS technology and society ... [and] omits the people who practice the technology and the complex interactions required to maintain it" (Chrisman, 2005: 26). It is only by taking a longer historical view, Chrisman suggests, that these people and complex interactions can come to light. In the next section, I inquire what we can learn about GIS's social potential when it is repositioned as part of the broader historical trajectory of twentieth century communication technologies.

THE SOCIAL POTENTIAL OF TWENTIETH CENTURY COMMUNICATION TECHNOLOGIES

New technological space has been at one and the same time a new horizon and a closure, an intoxicating possibility and a dangerous suppression of something just beginning to happen.
(Jody Berland, cited in Dan Lander, 1999: np)

Our quick survey of GIS critiques illustrates that the notion that technology can have a "social potential" is itself an ambiguous, contextually grounded set of ideas. For many GIS critics, GIS's social potential is primarily dystopian, identified with negative social effects such as invasion of privacy or military aggression. GIS's association with positivism has also been characterized as an epistemological stance whose potential social impact is deeply negative. Others point to

GIS's more classically utopian potential to counteract social and environmental injustices. Yet others position GIS as the dialectical embodiment of both the positive and the negative. Consistent across all perspectives is the assertion that technology, far from being a neutral, objective tool, inexorably shapes the society within which it exists. While this relationship typically has been conceptualized as an inevitable one-way process, reflective of the technological determinism of which Chrisman refers, the actual "life stories"' of different technologies reveal a more complicated history.

Critics of GIS are stepping into a much longer tradition of complex and sometimes contradictory discourse about the social roles and social impacts of technology. The machines of modernity have been perceived across a vast spectrum that, to paraphrase Jody Berland's quote that opened this section, stretches from their intoxicating possibilities to their potential for dangerous suppression. Indeed, long before the diligent workers at Canada Land Inventory designed their first overlay map, the world has been nervous about technology. Communication technologies in particular, such as the telegraph, the radio, the telephone, and the television, both caused great excitement and evoked great fear. As Bagdikian (2004) comments, these particular machines can be especially tricky to study since they manufacture their own meaning as they disseminate knowledge and values. In other words, through them are communicated not only specific information but also the cultural value systems through which the public should interpret them. Seen in this context, GIS is but one of a longer string of modern technologies through which people have collected, transformed, and disseminated certain configurations of information and silenced others. In this section, I briefly outline the social trajectories that other related technologies have followed – highlighting in particular the radio – in order to then better theorize GIS's historic role as a communication technology with spatial capacities.

In spite of the dazzling number of inventions that appeared during the twentieth century that revolutionized the way humans conveyed information to each other, it has been argued that the end result did little to expand our communicative potential. Instead, due to the institutional structures within which the media were developed and disseminated, many media theorists believe that by the end of the century we paradoxically had far less control over information than we had at the beginning. Anecdotal histories capture the bewilderment of the age: through them we see glimpses of an astonished public flustered at hearing their first jazz record, or the vertigo early audiences reported upon seeing their first moving picture. Underlying critical social analyses suggest that the as the century progressed the public experienced these new technologies as passive subjects, with increasingly rare opportunities to capitalize on any participatory potential. Robert McChesney (1993, 2000) writes extensively on the systematic ways in which government and corporate powers worked together to ensure the public would have little or no voice in shaping content. He meticulously documents the gradual transformation in the USA from a print society committed to democratic access to a free press (noting even that the founding fathers agreed to heavily subsidize postal rates in order to ensure citizens received their newspapers in a timely manner), to a society in which a handful of corporations have seamlessly woven virtually every media outlet in the country into their merchandizing portfolios with almost complete collusion from the government.[7]

The struggle over communications media is perhaps most vividly illustrated through the history of radio. When "the wireless" was first popularized in the early twentieth century, it was a democratic device in the hands of thousands of amateur enthusiasts who essentially had free reign over the technology and the airwaves. However, the timing of its invention coincided with the rise of corporate monopolies, the privatization of leisure and consumption, increased militarization, and the growing sense that it was the role of the federal government to facilitate a rational utilitarian landscape in which US businesses could operate efficiently. Within 10 years the combined economic and legislative powers of the US government, the US military, and corporate America would ensure that radio instead became a highly controlled outlet for newly forming telecommunication giants like CBS and RCA (Douglas, 1987; Slotten, 2000). Nearly a century later, democratic access to the airwaves is still a ferociously contested issue, with narrow victories in the legalization of low-power FM radio decidedly overshadowed by increasing waves of media consolidation (Opel, 2004).

The history of communicative technologies, such as the radio, thus, on the surface appears to be the history of doors slamming shut for direct democratic involvement. Yet we also see that the most effective moments of resistance, from the stalwart radio pirates who spearheaded the LPFM movement to the WTO protesters who insert themselves into urban space as a form of disruption, utilize the same technologies that oppress them. That these resistant moments have not successfully dismantled the corporate structure should not detract from the underlying theoretical observation: the technology does not determine its social potential. Further, it is equally important to observe that the technology does not determine the discursive possibilities; that is, it does not limit one to either communication that perfectly reflects some inherent technological status quo, or, by contrast, its diametrical opposite. The technologies themselves can offer far more opportunity for inventive communication, even if their particular incarnation as a marketed product of a specific corporation appear to shut down those options. In some ways the popular history of communication technologies in the last century has made us collectively forget that a broader spectrum of practices is possible. It is instructive to recall Walter Benjamin's famous contemplation of the mechanically reproduced photographic image in 1935, before it became equated to a copyrighted, mass marketed product to which audiences are passively subjected: "With the close-up, space expands," he noted with some curiosity. He proposed that "by exploring commonplace milieus under the ingenious guidance of the camera," this new technology could "burst this prison-world asunder by the dynamite of the tenth of a second, so that now, in the midst of its far-flung ruins and debris, we calmly and adventurously go traveling" (Benjamin, 1968: 236). The question which Benjamin articulated decades ago still has relevance for GIS today: how can a new technology "extend our comprehension of the necessities which rule our lives?"

TOWARD A NEW THEORY OF GIS PRACTICE: LISTENING TO THE PRACTITIONERS

When placed in the broader context of other communicative technologies and infused with the enthusiasm of an earlier age, both GIS's shared history and its unique possibilities are highlighted. On the one hand, GIS is a product of many of the same economic, social, and political forces that shaped these other technologies. As with the other technologies, GIS's main task is the creation of information to communicate to others. It was born into an era during which powerful corporate/military enterprises had already developed substantial machinery, markets, and meanings that clearly privileged top-down communication. Through the media audiences learned of "science" – a logical progression conducted by white males in lab coats that either led to technological marvels like Sputnik, or a deep sense of national failure when it did not. The ways in which the machines were designed and marketed ensured that democratic participation would be minimal and highly controllable. The more scientific the enterprise, the less relevant multiple inputs or viewpoints would be.

It is therefore an entirely natural assumption, both on the part of early GIS users and later GIS critics, that the main role of GIS was necessarily the production of a scientifically objective model of reality whose underlying goal was the uncontested reproduction of the status quo.

On the other hand, GIS deviates from typical communication technologies in important ways. Its users are invited – if not actually forced – to bring their own information to the machine. And unlike technologies such as cell phones or GPS units whose uses are fairly transparent, or radio or television whose materials are highly scripted, GIS from the outside appears as a mysterious set of procedures that in the hands of trained experts somewhat inexplicably lead to a visible product. Where the data comes from, who was involved in its creation and to what capacity, and the degree to which a corporate infrastructure – ranging from the algorithms implemented in the software to the regulatory environment governing ownership – controlled the outcome are far harder to divine. To theorize GIS, one needs to spend considerable time on the inside, as it were, participating as a user. Sociologist Steve Woolgar (1991) introduced the phrase 'configuring the user' to capture the reciprocal nature of the relationship between user and machine. The concept is especially useful when the "machine" involves computer hardware and software. Woolgar's 18-month participant observation in the development and marketing of a new computer system exposed to him the ways in which the producers' "interpretations of what the machine is, what it's for, [and] what it can do," as well as the users input, mediated possibilities, and embedded constraints. 'The new machine becomes its relationship with its configured users' (Woolgar, 1991: 59).

When applied to GIS, "configuring the user" can help illuminate the shadowy corners of GIS activity by shifting focus to the ways in which users both participate in and are constrained by the (historically contingent) processes of software and data

development, as well as by the broader social environments that incubate knowledge in the first place. As outlined above, much has been written concerning GIS's legacy as a positivist technology. In doing so, these writers drape GIS in a modernist mantle, implicitly drawing associations with a version of scientific enterprise where the user is a passive tool of progress. Perhaps not surprisingly, one area of GIS research that remains provocatively undertheorized centers on the user. The GIS user typically has been constructed in much the same way that people have been theorized in other branches of critical theory – as passive subjects who unwittingly absorb the dominant world views that surround them. Like Fredric Jameson's classic "zombies in hyperspace" who could not mentally map the confusing spaces of post-modernity, GIS users often have been treated like zombies blinded by the shimmering illusion of rational modernity.[8] But the messy realities of GIS practice if anything make more explicit, not less, the underlying connections, representations, and configurations that critics claim go unnoticed. GIS inquiry that actively engages these everyday practices draws attention to those moments where humans collaborate with (or struggle against) specific tools of the software, specific constructions of data, other groups of people, organizations, and myriad different regulatory settings. In doing so, such research directly (re)configures the user.

What does a (re)configured GIS user look like? There are now numerous vantage points within GIS research to begin answering such a question. From interrogating the social history of spatial algorithms to reconceptualizing GIS practice as a form of performance media to tracing the ways GIS operates as a surveillant assemblage, recent GIS work increasingly explores the ways in which GIS users produce and transmit GIS's social potential. One of the most intriguing places to start is where one would least expect to find transformative potential: embedded deep inside the algorithms and programming code of GIS. Far from being neutral territory, careful examination suggests that each intersection, buffer, reclassification, and the like has its own social history. Chrisman (2001), for example, traces how the seemingly technical details of both registration and polygon overlay are in fact the contextual results of human decision making that privilege certain assumptions about acceptable levels of accuracy and divisions of labor. Schuurman (1999), similarly, follows the veritable fossilization of line generalization procedures based upon now nearly ancient cartographic concerns that bear little relevance to contemporary GIS data problems. The design of the human/machine software interface (the so-called GUI, or Graphical User Interface) also warrants investigation. An often-heard complaint among GIS users is that successive generations of GIS software, in manufacturer's quest to make GIS more user-friendly, have become more restrictive as more of the inner workings are obscured from the user. While on the surface this is true, at the same time developer-based advances such as ESRI's ArcObjects allow an unprecedentedly candid glimpse at GIS's innards – if one has the time and skills to learn how to participate in that particular dialogue. Rather than ubiquitously restricting access for all users, recent trends in GIS design intensify the division of labor that Chrisman (2001: 6) first identified and reveal them to be "social processes that divide labor and knowledge."

Our first observation, thus, is that the (re) configured GIS user chooses from a toolkit that may masquerade as objective but in fact is steeped in social processes. As Latour and Woolgar (1986: 105) remind us, when confronted with any seemingly objective scientific enterprise the next salient question is 'what processes operate to remove the social and historical circumstances on which the construction of a fact depends?' Here we can look to recent GIS research that highlights the ways in which the user experiences GIS as a socially and historically contingent communication technology. Sui and Goodchild's (2001, 2003) application of

media theorist Marshall McLuhan is one of the most literal attempts to theorize GIS as communication media. In applying McLuhan's four core questions to GIS media (i.e., what does GIS enhance? make obsolete? what does it retrieve? what does it reverse into?), they effectively present GIS as a constructed social activity that is in constant motion. From this perspective, the user neither objectively guides a neutral collection of "facts" nor is predestined to follow a technologically determined linear process whether it be "good" or "bad." GIS instead becomes the "paradoxical and ambivalent" medium through which the message is negotiated (Sui and Goodchild, 2001: 389; 2003: 5).

Recent contributions by other GIS practitioner/researchers deepen our understanding of GIS as media as they help focus more directly on what Kwan (2002) refers to as the "critical agency" of the GIS user. St. Martin and Wing (2007) encourage us to see GIS as discourse, to distinguish it from a monolithic unitary entity, or even a coherent set of practices. Further, it is a media discourse that, through its users, writes its own history – its consistent re-representation as positivist enterprise, St. Martin and Wing argue, have as much to do with the trajectories of dominant discourse as with the limits of the technology itself. Similarly, Elwood (2006: 324) considers GIS a "flexible spatial narrative" that is neither cooptation nor resistance. Rather, it embraces multiple practices that allow users to construct different world views through the ways in which they choose to arrange data, by the information they privilege and the information they marginalize, and through the many other implicit decisions that are made. She identifies this process as the manner in which "agency and authority are negotiated," thus positioning any particular individual GIS user squarely within the combined forces of state, business, and technology (Elwood 2006: 324). Kwan's explorations of the ways in which feminist theory can inform our understanding of GIS as performance, as "the articulation of emotional geographies," likewise reinforces the notion that in the cyborg activity of GIS practice both humans and machines actively engage in a process whose final product embodies the creativity of the participants who were involved (Kwan, 2007: 23).

It is important to recognize that by definition the (re)configured user is configured by the same forces that he or she is granted the agency to transform. In other words, the human being is not the only "user" with agency in the practice of GIS. Theorizing a social and technological context that is woven through yet materially separate from its users, an especial concern of STS studies, is highly relevant for GIS also. The challenge is to find a way to investigate this material context without simply declaring it a pure social construction (see, for example, the comparative overview by Palmas, 2007). Delueze and Guattari (2004) introduce the term *agencement*, translated in English to assemblage, to depict a heterogeneous configuration of what they refer to as "content" (bodies, both human and non-human) and "expression" (actions, statements, and other non-material aspects). Assemblages extend dendridically along thousands of tendrils that individually may not be directly related but taken together form an entity. Delueze and Guattari (2004: 7) liken its structure to the rhizome, a "subterranean stem … absolutely different from [unitary] roots" reminscent of tubers, crab grass, "rats swarm[ing] over each other." The competing forces of territorialization (stabilizing, homogenizing) and deterritorialization (destabilizing, rupturing) continually redefine the lines of connectivity. The assemblage effectively disintegrates many of the monolithic qualities both proponents and critics implicitly assigned to GIS. There can be no static totality, there can be no linear trajectory of progress, and there can not even be good or bad: "good and bad are only the products of an active and temporary selection, which must be renewed" (Delueze and Guattari, 2004: 10).

The notion of assemblage has recently entered the GIS literature in the form of Haggerty and Ericson's (2000) "surveillant assemblage." Developed to understand rapidly multiplying technologies of surveillance, many of them spatial, their concept helps bring attention to the ways that previously discrete systems operating at different scales converge, reformulate, and dissolve again by bringing together human, machine, institution, and territory. They bring out an explicitly spatial component of the assemblage in their identification of the "data double," a "decorporealized body" that has been abstracted from its geographic existence and "reassembled in different settings through a series of data flows" (Haggerty and Ericson, 2000: 611). Though referring to technologies that locate the (surveilled) human body in this case, the concept fits equally as well for reassembled places. These data doubles then become the material realities that other bodies – both human and non-human – interact with, make decisions based upon, and create new rhizomatic configurations because of. Philosopher of science Manuel De Landa (2006) interrogates more aggressively the material role that data play in the contemporary assemblage. Drawing upon Michel Foucault's classic study *Discipline and Punish*, de Landa (2006: 73) argues that the institutional structures through which contemporary assemblages are configured have inherited two centuries worth of ever-broadening data collection mandates for *ceaseless inspection* and *permanent registration*. Gradually it becomes more acceptable and more desirable to record the mundane and commonplace – the data double grows in complexity and scope. Yet though the material result may appear on the outside to be a sinisterly coherent whole, in reality the activities that result in the creation of GIS data, as all assemblage activities, are never "logically necessary but only contingently obligatory" (de Landa, 2006: 12). Just as it is impossible to point to a single author or a single causal force behind the data double, it is also impossible to know how any given user's contributions will be configured within the assemblage. Regarding the surveillant assemblage, Haggerty and Ericson conclude with a key observation:

> To the extent that the surveillant assemblage exists, it does so potentially, one that resides at the intersection of various media that can be connected for diverse purposes ... As it is multiple, unstable, and lacks discernible boundaries or responsible governmental departments, the surveillant assemblage cannot be dismantled by prohibiting a particularly unpalatable technology ... [or] attacked by focusing criticism on a single bureaucracy or institution. (2000: 609)

Much of the rhetoric of earlier critical GIS had focused on how to "overcome the limitations of conventional GIS" (Sheppard, 2005: 9), or indeed whether that would be possible without "bring[ing] contemporary GIS to a crashing halt" (Pickles, 1997: 366), and what, if left unchecked, the technologies "are going to do *to* us" (Sui and Goodchild, 2003: 14, italics in original). But by listening to the practitioners, we can move beyond this implicit technological determinism and instead see GIS as an assemblage where users, machines, state and private interests, datasets, and multiple realities configure and reconfigure current practice. From this perspective, we can conceptualize GIS as a participatory technology grounded in specific places and times that absorbs, filters, and sometimes mutates the social relations surrounding it. The next section examines how GIS's social potential is configured in specific places and times.

LISTENING TO THE PRACTITIONERS: TWO EXAMPLES

The examples presented here capture moments where GIS is used by multiple agents to achieve what are often diametrically opposed philosophical, scientific, and cultural purposes. Each instant represents a political struggle over territory defined and constructed in part through GIS technology, one situated in the grasslands of western

China, and the other in the occupied territories of Palestine. Though on the surface the various participants use GIS to characterize the same physical spaces, they employ different methodologies, focus on different data sources, engage different participants, have different levels of access to power, and consequently construct different realities. GIS technology is used to both stabilize and destabilize, to enforce and to resist. In the language of assemblages, the practice of GIS can be seen as the rhizome-like collection of numerous threads that manifest in distinct ways and through different players at different geographic scales. That neither example comes from North America (birthplace of GIS, home of the software developers), and that each places GIS in the hands of groups struggling against each other, accentuates the ways that within the assemblage, to quote de Landa, nothing is "logically necessary" but rather "contingently obligatory."

Grasslands in western China

In the first example, GIS technology has played a role in determining – or from another view suppressing – critical agency in the use and management of grasslands in Xinjiang Province in northwest China near the Kazak border (Figure 4.1). The region contains meadow, steppe, and desert grasslands that have been ancestral home to ethnic Kazak herders who engage in seasonal migrations from summer to winter pastures. Central authorities in the Chinese government have long maintained that such traditional herding practices are inefficient, irrational, and harmful to the environment, and in recent years have added GIS technology to their arsenal of scientific justification. Traditional herding communities, however, have attempted to incorporate GIS technology into efforts to maintain their locally developed approaches to livestock management through their participation in an international effort to reintroduce Przewalski's Horse in the region. In the final outcome,

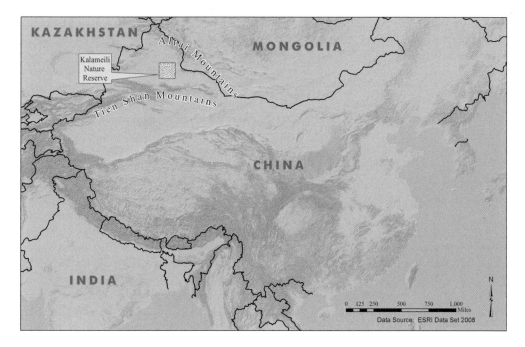

Figure 4.1   Grasslands of Western China

their efforts were overwhelmed by a rhizo-matic constellation of forces that when combined ensured that critical agency would shift into other hands.

Over centuries of tending animals in some-what inhospitable arid grasslands, distinct transhumance practices deeply embedded within kinship-based social relations emerged among the herders in Xinjiang Province. Anthropologist Michael Zukosky (2008) notes that many of their customary practices defy neat scientific categorization, let alone conventional GIS representation. Territorial grazing boundaries, for example, were deter-mined by a constantly shifting definition of "distance." "If an area is far from you, then it's not yours," one local informant explained to him, "but if it's close then it's yours"; the terms "far" and 'close' were actively con-structed according to the current environ-mental and social context (Zukosky, 2008: 50). While Maoist land collectivization initiatives introduced foreign cultural ele-ments into the region, the harshest conflicts

came later with decollectivization efforts in the 1980s when the government attempted to spur economic growth by transforming existing land allocation models. In spite of proceeding under the slogan "Implement in accordance with local conditions" and pur-porting to offer each village 15 different land tenure systems from which they could choose, in the end government mandates assigned a single system "independent small-family-operated holdings" to over ninety percent of the Chinese countryside (Unger, 1985: 587). Xinjiang was no exception, with married families allocated pasture use certificates that granted exclusive household rights to ration-ally bounded territories.

Local herders as well as local authorities found much of the new regime absurd, and Zukosky found little evidence that herders had made any attempts to comply. At the same time, central Chinese government offi-cials launched a widespread effort to estab-lish scientifically the inherent economical and environmental inferiority of traditional herding practices compared to the modern rational techniques they promoted. In the early 1990s, for example, government scientists announced that approximately twenty percent of the usable grasslands in Xinjiang Province had been seriously degraded due to overgrazing, a situation they equated to a "plundering" of grassland resources stemming directly from traditional nomadic herding practices (Committee on Scholarly Communication, 1992); Emily Yeh (2003) has found similar rhetoric applied to traditional herders in Tibet. By the end of the 1990s, Chinese government scientists began to make extensive use of GIS technology in order to map relationships between quality and yield (e.g., Chen and Fischer, 1998) and demonstrate that overgrazing had led to desertification and degradation (e.g., Zou et al., 2003). The causal links were clearly spelled out in government reports: "extensive nomadism with seasonal migration ... has led to high losses of energy [and] low efficiency of production" (Committee on Scholarly Communication, 1992: 117).

The Chinese government, thus, actively involved GIS technology in their efforts to propagate rational, scientific land use management in Xinjiang and other grasslands provinces. The local residents of Xinjiang, however, would encounter a "contingently obligatory" situation that somewhat serendipitously would present the opportunity for them to draw upon spatial technologies to gather information and stake claims on exactly the same land in ways that undercut dominant rhetoric. By almost complete spatial coincidence, a rare wild horse breed historically occupied the same territory, and international efforts were afoot to reintroduce them to the area. The reintroduction of Przewalski's Horse, identified as the last known surviving wild horse species and named after the Russian explorer who "discovered" them in the late 1800s, represented a great accomplishment for wildlife conservation but posed a distinct threat to these traditional Kazak herders who used the same grazing lands for their livestock. An international team comprised of Chinese, German, and American scientists calculated that approximately 200 families and their 300,000 animals would potentially be affected based on how families actually used the grazing territory, as opposed to how their allocations were arranged on paper. A small group of herders was invited by this international team to utilize GPS and GIS technologies in order to record their local knowledge of the land and their use of it as part of the reintroduction project ("Restoring Przewalski's Horses," 2007). Herders were trained to collect GPS data that would help identify their understanding and use of the land; additionally, their (qualitative) intimate knowledge of the landscape was valued as an advantage no remote sensing tool could match in the tracking of the wild horses. Thus, GPS/GIS technology was poised to be used to capture precisely the type of knowledge that government officials used GIS to discredit.

The herders' GIS project lasted "about a day" before the Chinese government put a stop to it (Zukosky, personal communication, 23 November 2009). While the end result was to silence an alternative voice, the circumstances behind the decision were multiple and varied, and not always motivated by censorship. An equine disease was ravaging the wild herd; Chinese officials were hesitant to allow local herders to expose their horses as well. The herders themselves were skeptical of the entire enterprise when they learned the exact locations they would need to visit; situated in particularly arid zones, herders argued they couldn't possibly survive those landscapes – for possibly weeks or months at a time – without traveling in much larger communities. Those who did ultimately participate in the project, with the blessing of the Chinese government, did so from motorized vehicles. This change introduced a new machine with its own unanticipated agency into the assemblage – the pickup truck. Przewalski's horses, while fairly tolerant of other equine visitors, turned out to be extremely wary of internal combustion engines. The startled horses would flee well in advance of the trucks' approach, losing themselves among hills and valleys unpenetrable by GPS (Zukosky, pers. comm). The entire project transformed unexpectedly into an inter-species surveillant assemblage, with the animals having a slight edge in this technological game of hide and seek.

The wall in Palestine

The second example moves from the remote hills of western China to the occupied territories of Palestine. Here, GIS is used as a part of everyday contestations over the immediate environment (Figure 4.2). Ever since Neil Smith first pointed the finger, the association of GIS with military agendas has been often cited as one of its unavoidable (i.e., logically necessary) social characteristics. However, by looking more closely at GIS's role in both Israeli and Palestinian hands, it becomes clear that GIS is not merely a single-minded instrument of war but rather simultaneously a technology of aggression and a technology of resistance. At once stabilizing and destabilizing, self-conscious and accidental, the boundaries can blur on both sides of the fence. Indeed, this example makes clear the degrees to

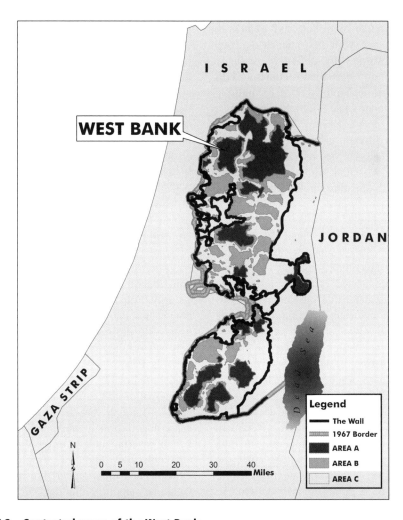

Figure 4.2   Contested areas of the West Bank

which the accepted parameters and philosophical implications of valid GIS practice are themselves actively configured and reconfigured at various flashpoints within the assemblage.

"Israeli occupation of Palestinian territory," comments communications theorist Gary Fields, "reveals two distinct but complementary faces" (Fields, 2004: n.p.). The first is evident through direct military presence, but the second is a more subtle occupation, where the "tools of the trade consist of aerial topographical photography, land use planning maps, Geographic Information Systems (GIS), and building regulations, backed by the bulldozer and construction crane" (Fields, 2004: n.p.). This GIS activity in Israel is state-controlled and treated in public discourse with the taciturn delicacy typically awarded to defensive security efforts. In return, Palestinians construct GIS as a pacifistic technology open to multiple inputs, and incorporate it into their resistance efforts in a more publicly staged manner. These quite different groups of human users are components of an assemblage where boundaries – spatial, linguistic, political, technological – are transgressed with alarming frequency.

Israeli architect Eyal Weizman (2007) traces in great empirical detail the ways in which Israel's GIS database is structured and populated – data doubles birthed – through a set of interconnected processes inseparable from broader defensive measures that ultimately defy easy categorization. On the one hand, the GIS initiative clearly enforces classic military aggression. An example is the recent completion of 3D models of the West Bank and Gaza where the Israeli Defense Forces (IDF) chose to map "intricate detail of individual houses, including the location of internal doors and windows" (Weizman, 2007: 195–6). These 3D models are data doubles of an urban space where, since the 2002 attack on Nablus, the next battlefield will likely be a domestic interior. On the other hand, though, other contradictory threads connect and transform the overall

GIS assemblage. The general dearth of public transparency makes it more challenging for either Israeli citizens or external critics to trace these threads. In a related example involving government data, the Israeli activist group Peace Now obtained an unofficial leaked copy of a database tracking Israeli settlers in Palestine ("A Third of Israeli Settlements," 2007). Using this contraband data, they calculated that 39 percent of Israeli settlements illegally occupied private Palestinian land. Peace Now then petitioned the Israeli High Court for official access to the same data. The government initially balked, requesting an extension because of 'a number of security and foreign relations considerations on the part of the State of Israel' that circulating such information to its citizens would raise (Etkes, 2007). When the official version of the data was finally distributed, Peace Now discovered that the percentage had dropped to thirty-two. The difference was attributed to "inaccuracies in the computerized system, or GIS," and consisted entirely of "corrections" where polygons identified as erroneously marked private were reclassified to State land ("A Third of Israeli Settlements," 2007). In one town alone, nearly 84 percent of land ownership officially transferred from private Palestinian hands to the Israeli government in one click of the GIS user's hand.

Israeli GIS data is shaped within an assemblage inextricably linked to a powerful state apparatus steeped in concerns about national security. Equally plentiful within the assemblage, however, are threads that connect users who desire to create and disseminate new ways of interpreting space. Peace groups such as Peace Now described above form more predictably traditional destabilizing forces within the assemblage, but Weizman (2007: 4) argues that the desire to re-image space materializes in unexpected ways as the Israeli government tries to inspect and register landscapes that are "fragmented and dynamic and thus unchartable by any conventional mapping technique." In fact, it is an assemblage that is self-consciously configured by people who know about assemblages.

In interviews with high-ranking IDF officers, Weizman reports that IDF command openly embrace poststructuralist and postcolonial theory as a starting point to develop contemporary military strategy. Delueze and Guattari's *A Thousand Plateaus*, in fact, is required reading. In the words of retired Brigadier General Shimon Naveh, *A Thousand Plateaus* "problematized our own paradigm ... to confront the 'striated' spaces of traditional, old-fashioned military practice with smoothness that allows for movement through space that crosses any borders and barriers" (Weizman, 2007: 201). Thus the assemblage self-consciously embeds its own threads of territorialization and deterritorialization.

While Israelis construct their efforts less as predatory occupation and more as preventative land management, the end result is material changes to the landscape – soldiers bursting through living room walls, buildings reduced to rubble, and most recently, an imposing barrier wall. Since 2002, the Israeli government has dedicated extensive GIS resources to determining the most appropriate route for a physical barrier that would completely enclose the West Bank. Official Israeli discourse refers to the wall as a "security fence," and explains its construction is a "preventative measure" taken "reluctantly" in their effort to stem acts of terrorism coming from the direction of the West Bank. In the absence of any natural barriers or obstacles, the fence provides an artificial one, its specific route a GIS smorgasbord of "topography, population density and threat assessments and ... humanitarian, archaeological and environmental concerns" (Ministry of Defense, 2007). The route was determined by the Ministry of Defense and approved by the Prime Minister. How exactly this was accomplished has not been well publicized. In an interview with Eyal Weizman, wall designer Danny Tirza stressed that planners refused to be swayed by political pressures but rather employed a "mathematical response to a variety of security issues and geographic conditions"

(Weizman, 2007: 166). Later the Israeli government could thus claim in an international court of law that the route of the Wall simply followed "the logic of security" (Weizman, 2007: 167). Two planning attributes conspicuous in their absence were political boundaries (though originally designed to follow it, the final fence line deviated significantly from the formal Green Line border), and input from local residents, a point that would later be contested at international scale (Beit Sourik Village Council vs. the Government of Israel, 2004).

Palestinians, by contrast, refer to the structure as a "separation wall," (and sometimes more polemically as an "apartheid wall,") and interpret its presence as an overt attempt by the Israeli government to expand into and ultimately annex Palestinian land ("Palestinian Minister," 2004). The Palestinian Ministry of Planning describes their use of GIS as a necessary defense weapon to "analyze the Israeli plans and ideas and develop Palestinian counter plans" (Ministry of Planning, 2007). A comprehensive body of GIS data and research has been developed and made publicly available by the Ministry of Planning and nonprofit agencies such as the Applied Research Institute of Jerusalem. Numerous maps document what are referred to as Israeli colonizing activities, tracking such changes as agricultural lands lost to Israeli bulldozers, house demolitions, changes in access to and depletion of water sources, the construction of settlers roads, changes in population settlement patterns, and sewage disposal dumping grounds. Since residents were typically given no advanced warning of impending wall construction and a legal period of seven days to contest announced plans, Palestinian authorities chose to be proactive with GIS as one of their preferred "tools of the trade." As a consequence, numerous legal claims have been brought forth into the Israeli courts, with the precise route of the fence being altered at the micro level on several occasions (Ministry of Defense, 2007). Weizman (2007: 174) estimates that "frequent reroutings" had cost the Israeli government over $200 million USD with construction not even halfway completed.[9]

The Wall once built – a circuitous combination of electric fences, ditches, control towers, and concrete slabs reaching 25 feet high that divide not only Israeli from Palestinian but Palestinian from Palestinian – is a flashpoint in an increasingly convoluted GIS assemblage. It is both material and symbolic, both local and global in scale: the physical manifestation of military strategies, counter-strategies, real estate agendas, international law, and global reactions. It becomes a GIS layer in itself and thus a (non-human) user in the assemblage, configuring its own new connections from land ownership battles to sewage dumps along its base to graffiti scrawled upon its surfaces. The Wall invites participation not only from its designers and engineers, but from those who live around it (both Israelis and Palestinians), as well as an international community expressing their opinion about it. Through the Wall's physical presence, the GIS used to create it communicates far more than a simple path of x, y coordinates; in Weizman's (2007) analysis, through its underlying foundation in post-structural theory it conveys to its own constituents a message of civilization and sophistication, while to its enemies the message is "You will never even understand that which kills you." But in an assemblage no communication is necessarily unilateral or uncontested. The Wall has sparked among Palestinians a "spatial turn in the discourse," where a group of people who a decade earlier literally had no mapped history of their own now embarked upon a mission to dynamically and openly map as much of the "physical facts of the territory, and its transformation by the occupying forces" as possible (Weizman, 2007: 263, see also Sauders [2008] on long-term institutionalized Palestinian separation from the materials of their own land use history). The Wall may be a prime example of a surveillant assemblage powered by GIS technology, but it is not entirely clear who, in the end, is surveilling whom.

CONCLUSION

In the broad-brush contradictions and everyday messiness illustrated in these two examples of GIS assemblages, we can now revisit observations made by critical GIS users hoping to invigorate the discipline with new sensitivity for the power of everyday practice. We have seen that GIS has social potential not because it has been rescued from its positivist prison-cell, but rather because it never was a clean-cut, positivist enterprise to begin with. Though extremely important GIS-enhanced research has been accomplished from the critical wing of the discipline, it is equally important to interrogate the so-called non-enlightened projects to understand how they, too, embody and transform social relations and hence construct the "flexible spatial narratives" to which Elwood referred.

Technological determinism remains a tempting and comforting analytic stance; it has been so embedded in theories of modernity from Marx onward that often it intuitively rings true. Certainly the degree to which technology shapes how GIS is used remains an important question, especially as GIS technology moves toward more user-friendly interfaces whose functions are more rigidly scripted, and as datasets become more widely available. The voices of GIS practitioners, however, whether from advanced university GIS labs, governmental agencies, local utilities companies, remote villages in China, or the West Bank help us move beyond technological determinism with their varied and unpredictable stories. Each voice points beyond itself to the heterogeneous and dynamic intersections that form the GIS assemblage. We are wise to recall Kwan's admonition that we need to engage in those daily struggles in the GIS Lab (or military briefing room, or West Bank apartment, or wildlife monitoring station) in order to expand the number of sites where the GIS orthodoxy can be disrupted (Kwan, 2002). Perhaps then geographers and other interested observers can look forward to a time when disputes concerning the validity of GIS will – as Walter Benjamin argued a technological generation ago with painting and photography – "seem devious and confused," and instead we will embrace a new crucial question: how the invention of the new technology might have entered into, and thus transformed, the act of spatial analysis itself. The transformative powers Benjamin (1968: 236) ascribed to photography fit remarkably well with GIS technology also: "it manages to assure us of an immense and unexpected field of action."

NOTES

1 The Canadian Geographic Information System (CGIS) is typically recognized as the first full-fledged GIS. Dating from the early 1960s, it was a joint federal-provincial effort to develop a vector-based method for storing and analyzing thematic map layers as part of the Canadian Land Inventory (Fisher and MacDonald, 1979). The Harvard Laboratory for Computer Graphics and Spatial Analysis also during the 1960s experimented with both raster and vector technologies, resulting in cult classics like SYMAP (raster) and ODYSSEY (vector) (Chrisman, 2006).

2 Environmental Systems Research Institute (ESRI) was founded in 1969 by Jack and Laura Dangermond. The GIS software company subsequently grew into the industry leader worldwide; their products are used in over 150 countries and most data providers format data to meet ESRI proprietary specifications.

3 While earlier GIS critiques tended to be grounded more in traditional social theory (which itself has been associated with blatant technological determinism – see for example Feenberg's [1999] excellent overview), the literature known as STS (Science, Technology, and Society, or alternately Science and Technology Studies) has been especially fruitful for more recent GIS critics. Drawing from foundational concepts such as Thomas Kuhn's scientific revolutions and paradigm shifts, STS explicitly questions the ways in which technology can be socially constructed and at the same time humans can be technologically constructed. Emergent configurations such as Donna Haraway's infamous "cyborg" have been instrumental in reconceptualizing GIS (and, it should be added, giving non GIS critics a whole new language to be baffled by). Chrisman (2001) and Schuurman (1999) provide accessible overviews of this trend.

4 Countermapping is a term that emerged from the environmental science literature in parallel to GIScience debates to distinguish mapping activity that attempts to destabilize existing power relations as a tactic to address questions of environmental and social justice. Its initial use is often attributed to Nancy Peluso's work on indigenous communities in Indonesia and their use of mapping technologies to document claims to local forest lands, and has since been adopted in support of a much more broadly defined notion of cultural resource mapping.

5 This is not to suggest that discussion of critical GIS has dwindled; rather, it continues at near frantic pace but is more likely to appear in core disciplinary journals such as the *Annals of the Association of American Geographers* or edgier specialized ones like such as, *Place, & Culture*.

6 Those undergraduates who believe GIS is the most reliable way geography majors will get a job are probably correct. Perhaps even more troubling for GIS critics is the fact that most GIS students do not appear to count existing theoretical critiques of GIS as an indispensable part of their GIS toolkit. When the author confessed at a recent panel discussion that she had finally abandoned attempts to assign Pickle's *Ground Truth* as required reading due to outright hostility from students, the audience responded with similar stories once the laughter died down.

7 This brief overview unfortunately can not do justice to important geographical variations in the ways in which different governments developed media policy; the discussion here focuses primarily on the trends in the USA. Important social critiques of American media also include Bagdikian (2004), Gitlin (2003), Herman and Chomsky (1988), and Starr (2004).

8 Fredric Jameson's (1984) superlative article "Postmodernism, or, The Cultural Logic of Late Capitalism" popularized the notion that postmodern culture left individual people bereft of the ability to mentally navigate their own environments. While his analysis of the relationship between cultural production and capitalism remains highly provocative, many culture theorists have since argued that his treatment of the human subject simply replicates earlier Marxian superstructural analyses of human agency B in which the inevitable conclusion nearly always was that agency did not exist.

9 Not a small fraction of petitions were generated by Israeli settlers themselves, in efforts to avoid their settlements falling on the Palestinian side of the wall, or to control the proposed paths of thoroughfares reserved for Israelis to travel unrestricted through the West Bank. Weizman does not indicate how much of the $200 million USD was spent to appease Israeli settlers. Total construction costs for the completed wall have been estimated at $2.5 billion USD based on an approximate final length of 500 miles (Gradstein and Schneider, 2009: A10).

REFERENCES

'A Third of Israeli Settlements are Built on Palestinian Land', (2007). AsiaNews.it. 15 March 2007. http://www.asianews.it/index.php?l=en&art=8742 (accessed 13 April 2009).

Bagdikian, B. (2004) *The New Media Monopoly.* Boston, MA: Beacon Press.

Beit Sourik Village Council vs. the Government of Israel (2004) *Petition to the Commander of the IDF Forces in the West Bank.* http://www.unhcr.org/refworld/docid/4374ac594.html (accessed 31 December complementarity 2007).

Benjamin, W. (1968) *Illuminations: Essays and Reflections.* New York: Schocken Books.

Chen, Y. and Fischer, G. (1998) *A New Digital Georeferenced Database of Grasslands in China.* Laxenburg: International Institute for Applied Systems Analysis.

Chrisman, N. (2001) 'Configuring the user: Social divisions of labor in GIS software'. http://chrisman.scg.ulaval.ca/Present/Configuring.pdf (accessed 9 April 2009).

Chrisman, N. (2005) 'Full circle: More than just social implications of GIS,' *Cartographica,* 40(4): 23–35.

Chrisman, N. (2006) *Charting the Unknown: How Computer Mapping at Harvard Became GIS.* Redlands, CA: ESRI Press.

Committee on Scholarly Communication with the People's Republic of China (1992) *Grasslands and Grassland Sciences in Northern China.* Washington, DC: National Academy Press.

Craig, W.J., Harris, T.M. and Weiner, D. (2002) *Community Participation and Geographical Information Systems.* London and New York: Taylor and Francis.

de Landa, M. (2006) *A New Philosophy of Society: Assemblage Theory and Social Complexity.* London and New York: Continuum.

Delueze, G. and Guattari, F. (2004) *A Thousand Plateaus: Capitalism and Schizophrenia.* Trans. Brian Massumi. London and New York: Continuum.

Douglas, S. (1987) *Inventing American Broadcasting, 1899–1922.* Baltimore, MD: Johns Hopkins University Press.

Elwood, S. (2006) 'Beyond cooptation or resistance: Urban spatial politics, community organizations, and GIS-based spatial narratives', *Annals of the Association of American Geographers,* 96(2): 323–41.

Elwood, S. and Leitner, H. (2003) 'GIS and spatial knowledge production for neighborhood revitalization: Negotiating state priorities and neighborhood visions', *Journal of Urban Affairs,* 25(2): 139–57.

Etkes, D. (2007) 'Legal News', Peace Now. http://www.peacenow.org.il/site/en/peace.asp?pi=370&docid=1662 (accessed 13 April 2009).

Feenberg, A. (1999) *Questioning Technology.* New York: Routledge.

Fields, G. (2004) 'Introduction: A presentation on Israeli unilateral action in Palestine,' *Logos,* 3(1). http://www.logosjournal.com/issue3.1.htm (accessed 30 November 2009).

Fisher, T. and MacDonald, C. (1979) 'An overview of the Canada geographic information system (CGIS)', *AutoCarto,* 4: 610–15.

Gradstein, L. and Schneider, H. (2009) 'Momentum slows for Israel's barrier; cost, legal concerns, and a drop in violence may leave controversial project unfinished,' *The Washington Post, Suburban Edition,* 20 August 2009, p. A10.

Georgiadou, Y. and Blakemore, M. (2006) 'A journey through GIS discourses', *Urisa.* http://www.urisa.org/publications/journal/articles/a_journey_through_gis (accessed 30 November 2009).

Gitlin, T. (2003) *Media Unlimited: How the Torrent of Images and Sounds Overwhelms Our Lives.* New York: Macmillan.

Goodchild, M. (1992) 'Geographical information science', *International Journal of Geographical Information Systems,* 6(1): 31–45.

Haggerty, K. and Ericson, R.V. (2000) 'The surveillant assemblage', *British Journal of Sociology,* 51(4): 605–22.

Herman, E.S. and Chomsky, N. (1988) *Manufacturing Consent.* New York: Pantheon Books.

Jameson, F. (1984) 'Postmodernism, or, the cultural logic of late capitalism', *New Left Review,* 146: 52–92.

Kwan, M.P. (2002) 'Is GIS for women? Reflections on the critical discourse in the 1990s', *Gender, Place, and Culture,* 9(3): 271–79.

Kwan, M.P. (2007) 'Affecting geospatial technologies: Toward a feminist politics of emotion', *Professional Geographer,* 59(1): 22–34.

Lake, R. (1993) 'Planning and applied geography: Positivism, ethics, and geographic information systems,' *Progress in Human Geography,* 17(3): 404–413.

Lander, D. (1999) 'Radiocasting: Musings on radio and art,' *eContact* 2.3. http://cec.concordia.ca/econtact/Radiophonic (accessed 30 November 2009).

Latour, B. and Woolgar, S. (1986) *Laboratory Life: The Construction of Scientific Facts*, 2nd edn. Princeton, NJ: Princeton University Press.

Ministry of Defense (Israeli) (2007) 'Israel Security Fence'. http://www.securityfence.mod.gov.il/Pages/Eng/default.htm (accessed 30 November 2009).

Ministry of Planning (Palestinian) (2007) *The General Directorate for Geographic Center and Technical Support.* http://www.mop.gov.ps/en/general_directorates/geographic_center2.asp (accessed 31 December 2007).

McChesney, R. (1993) *Telecommunications, Mass Media, and Democracy: The Battle for the Control of U.S. Broadcasting, 1928–1935.* Oxford: Oxford University Press.

McChesney, R. (2000) *Rich Media, Poor Democracy: Communication Politics in Dubious Times.* New York: The New Press.

McLafferty, S. (2005) 'Women and GIS: Geospatial technologies and feminist geographies', *Cartographica*, 40(4): 37–45.

Opel, A. (2004) *Microradio and the FCC: Media Activism and the Struggle Over Broadcast Policy.* Westport, CT: Praeger.

Openshaw, S. (1991) 'A view on the GIS crisis in geography, or, using GIS to put Humpty-Dumpty back together again,' *Environment and Planning A,* 23(5): 621–628.

Palestinian minister says Israeli separation wall is overt plan of expansion (2004) http://www.unis.unvienna.org/unis/pressrels/2004/gapal951.html (accessed 30 November 2009).

Palmas, K. (2007) 'Deleuze and DeLanda: A new ontology, a new political economy?'. http://www.isk-gbg.org/99our68/LSE_paper_jan_2007.pdf (accessed 9 April 2009).

Pavlovskaya, M. (2004) 'Other transitions: Multiple economies of Moscow households in the 1990s', *Annals of the Association of American Geographers*, 94(2): 329–51.

Pavlovskaya, M. (2006) 'Theorizing with GIS: A tool for critical geographies?', *Environment and Planning A*, 38(11): 2003–20.

Pickles, J. (ed.) (1995) *Ground Truth: The Social Implications of Geographic Information Systems.* New York: The Guilford Press.

Pickles, J. (1997) 'Tool or science? GIS, technoscience, and the theoretical turn,' *Annals of the Association of American Geographers*, 87(2): 363–372.

Restoring Przewalski's Horses to China's Steppes and Deserts (2007) *Conservation and Science*, 27 February 2007. http://nationalzoo.si.edu/ ConservationAndScience/SpotlightOnScience/phorsereintroduction.cfm (accessed 31 December 2007).

Sauders, R.R. (2008) 'Between paralysis and practice: Theorizing the political liminality of Palestinian cultural heritage', *Archaeologies*, 4(3): 471–94.

Schuurman, N. (1999) 'Critical GIS: Theorizing an emerging science', *Cartographica*, 36(4): 1–109 [Monograph #53].

Schuurman, N. (2000) 'Trouble in the heartland: GIS and its critics in the 1990s', *Progress in Human Geography*, 24(4): 569–90.

Schuurman, N. (2006) 'Formalization matters: Critical GIS science and ontology research', *Annals of the Association of American Geographers*, 96(4): 726–39.

Sheppard, E. (2005) 'Knowledge production through critical GIS: Review and assessment', *Cartographica*, 40: 5–22.

Smith, N. (1992) 'History and philosophy of geography: Real wars, theory wars', *Progress in Human Geography*, 16: 257–71.

Slotten, H.R. (2000) *Radio and Television Regulation: Broadcast Technology in the United States 1920–1960.* Baltimore, MD: Johns Hopkins University Press.

St. Martin, K. and Wing, J. (2007) 'The discourse and discipline of GIS', *Cartographica*, 42(3): 235–48.

Starr, P. (2004) *The Creation of the Media: Political Origins of Modern Communications.* New York: Basic Books.

Sui, D.Z. and Goodchild, M.F. (2001) 'GIS as media?', *International Journal of Geographic Information Science*, 15(5): 387–90.

Sui, D.Z. and Goodchild, M.F. (2003) 'A tetradic analysis of GIS and society using McLuhan's law of the media', *Canadian Geographer*, 47(1): 5–17.

Taylor, P. (1990) 'Editorial comment: GKS,' *Political Geography Quarterly*, 9(3): 211–212.

Unger, J. (1985) 'The decollectivization of the Chinese countryside: A survey of twenty-eight villages', *Pacific Affairs*, 58(4): 585–606.

Weiner, D. and Harris, T. (2003) 'Community-integrated GIS for land reform in South Africa', *URISA Journal*, 15(2): 61–73.

Weizman, E. (2007) *Hollow Land: Israel's Architecture of Occupation.* London: Verso.

Woolgar, S. (1991) 'Configuring the user: the case of usability trials' in J. Law (ed). *A Sociology of Monsters: Essays on Power, Technology, and Domination.* London: Routledge, pp. 57–99.

Wylie, E.K., Atia, M. and Hammel, D.J. (2004) 'Has mortgage capital found an inner-city spatial fix?', *Housing Policy Debate*, 15(3): 623–85.

Yeh, E.T. (2003) 'Tibetan range wars: Spatial politics and authority on the grasslands of Amdo', *Development and Change*, 34(3): 1–25.

Zou, Y., Zhang, Z., Zhou, Q. and Tan, W. (2003) 'Analysis of China grassland dynamic based on RS and GIS', *Proceedings IEEE International*, 5: 3389–91.

Zukosky, M. (2008) 'Reconsidering state effects of grassland science and policy in China', *Journal of Political Ecology*, 15(1): 44–60.

5

Critical GIS

Sarah Elwood, Nadine Schuurman
and Matthew W. Wilson

INTRODUCTION

Critical GIS is sometimes explained as the body of work that emerged in response to the GIS and Society critiques of the mid-1990s. While this framing of the field obscures a number of other lines of theory and practice that are also significant, there is a strong and contingent relationship between the GIS and society critiques and critical GIS. *Ground Truth*, a special issue of *Cartography and GIS*, and other critiques of GIS in the 1990s created a series of fractures in the practices surrounding and permeating GIS, as this handbook demonstrates. On the heels of these debates, GIS could no longer be (responsibly) viewed as a series of tools developed and implemented in a vacuum. Instead, this specific interplay of science and technology was recognized as 'socially implicated'. We see critical GIS as a diverse series of engagements that emerge from this moment of critique – spurred by the efforts of human geographers, geographic information science scholars, and hybrid scholars who identify themselves in both fields. As a result, these engagements have multiplied in diverse ways since Schuurman's monograph that named 'critical GIS' in 1999/2000, and

our chapter is meant to get at some of this diversity. The handbook editors invited us to frame critical GIS for this collection by bringing together parts of earlier single-authored contributions we have each made to the field. In doing so, we have sought not to create a comprehensive review of critical GIS scholarship, but rather, have sought to frame the core ideas around which the field coalesced, and illustrate the diversity of ways that these ideas have translated into new theory and practice with and about geographical technologies.

We begin in the first section below by offering a more extended discussion situating critical GIS, reviewing the ways in which this field appropriates and reworks the GIS and society tradition. One of the recent ways critical GIS is being taken up is under the banner of qualitative GIS, and this second section traces the theoretical and epistemological bases of this permutation. This section argues that qualitative GIS demands a critical stance that challenges the foundational arrangements of software/hardware and data/interpretation – a 'techno-positionality' that is framed in this section. These new developments in geospatial technologies and the new forms of geospatial data are discussed in the third section. Here, this emerging research agenda draws from the propositions of critical GIS. We have brought these texts together to describe the origins of critical GIS and position its contributions in relation to GIS and Society research.[1] In particular, we focused on selecting texts that would offer forward-looking perspectives upon ongoing contributions of the field, suggesting ways in which critical GIS theory and practice are further informing emerging research agendas in geographic information science.

Of course, this collaged approach cannot do all, and some readers will find the full individual papers to be richer.[2] In the spirit of this and other handbook projects, our goal has been to bring together texts that are both retrospective and prospective; and to frame some of the key debates and issues that have been part of critical GIS since its inception, and to give a sense of key issues that guide its future. Readers will have their own positions amid the technologies, theorizations, and points of debate and differentiation that we frame as part of the past and future of critical GIS. We invite and welcome the variety of ways that readers bring our text(s) to life in their own readings.

FRAMING CRITICAL GIS[3]

Critical GIS emerges from the intersection of social theory and geographic information science (Schuurman, 1999; Harvey et al., 2005; Sheppard, 2005). It is an approach to evaluating GIS technology that draws upon multiple intellectual tool kits (Schuurman, 2006). Critical GIS was until recently regarded as a vague and theoretical off-shoot of an otherwise perfectly acceptable sub-discipline in Geography (O'Sullivan, 2006). That position is changing as critical GIS begins to gain acceptance as a legitimate and perhaps even valuable component of the broad tent that is geographic information science.

Critical GIS did not materialize as a cohesive entity in the 2000s but rather descended from the struggles between human geographers and GIS scientists in the 1990s (Schuurman, 2000). The previous decade witnessed an intellectual struggle between human geographers who were wary of the increasing dominance of GIS and GIS scientists who were generally surprised at the amount and virulence of resistance to their work (Wright et al., 1997a). That antagonism – known colloquially as the 'Science Wars' in Geography – was based upon a suspicion that GIS was not attentive to the theoretical advances in human geography that increasingly acknowledged the roles of social theory and feminism (Curry, 1995; Pickles, 1995; Taylor and Johnston, 1995). At the same time, critics were concerned that GIS served large corporations, public agencies and governments while eschewing the disenfranchised. The legacy of the quantitative revolution contributed to this general discomfort with GIS (Taylor and Johnston, 1995).

Two seminal collections characterized the unease with which human geographers viewed the emerging sub-discipline of critical GIS – both published in 1995. The first was a book anthology edited by John Pickles (1995), entitled *Ground Truth*. The second was a collection of papers in *Cartography and GIS* edited by Eric Sheppard. Complaints about the technology included: the 'masculinist' overtones of the technology (e.g., emphasis on engineering rather than people); its part in a cybernetic grid of control; its role in geodemographics and marketing, a lack of attention to explicit epistemology; reliance on 'Cartesian perspectivalism' (e.g., rational map-based analysis); and general inaccessibility to those without a high level of technical skill (Schuurman, 2006). Though an initial antagonism characterized these academic conversations (Taylor and Johnston, 1995; Pickles, 1997; Wright et al., 1997b), they were ultimately productive in that they stimulated debate within geography about the role of technology and its social responsibilities.

By the late 1990s, the emphasis of critiques had shifted from the ethical shortcomings of

GIS to epistemology and ontology (Curry, 1997a; Curry, 1997b). While the occasional critique still focused on surveillance and Cartesian perspectivalism (Katz, 2001), there was a general acknowledgement that technology was embedded in a larger social fabric (Sheppard et al., 1999; Sheppard, 2001). A détente gradually formed, allowing critical GIS to emerge from the early struggles in geography over GIS. Perhaps the most defining characteristic of critical GIS today is that its ranks are primarily composed of practicing GIScientists who were influenced by early debates about GIS and its social and philosophical responsibilities.

It is difficult to characterize a group as diverse as critical GIS scholars. A typical critical GIS session at a major conference might include papers on topics as diverse as feminism, participatory GIS, Marxism and epistemology (Kwan, 2002b; Crampton, 2005; Harvey et al., 2005; Sheppard, 2005; Elwood, 2006b; O'Sullivan, 2006; Ghose, 2007). Yet somehow there is an implicit understanding that these disparate issues fall under the same category. The invisible thread that links these issues constitutes critical GIS. In what follows, we will characterize some aspects of critical GIS.

First and foremost critical GIS pays attention to the philosophical genealogy of the technology – the controversial issues of epistemology and ontology. Epistemology refers broadly to the tools that we use to study the world (Schuurman, 2004); it certainly influences the perspective through which researchers interpret entities on the earth's surface. Ontology – in a traditional interpretation – refers to what something really is, its foundational essence (Gregory, 2000; Agarwal, 2005). Every epistemological perspective imbues an observation with different meanings, and different ontologies come into view depending on the epistemology of the GIS user. However, in GIS, we do not rely upon the philosophical interpretation of ontology. Rather the computing science interpretation – developed in the 1970s – is used (Gruber, 1995). In this interpretation,

an ontology is a fixed universe of discourse in which each data field or attribute is precisely defined – as are its possible relationships to other data elements. In other words, in the information sciences, there are no foundational ontologies. Instead, each classification system, map legend, or cultural context will produce a different ontology (Schuurman and Leszczynski, 2008a; Schuurman and Leszczynski, 2008b). In this interpretation, each unique epistemological interpretation of a set of events (e.g., refugee movement or ancient glaciation) will also result in a different ontology. Ironically, this recognition of diverse ontologies links GIS more closely to postmodernism than many other sub-disciplines of geography.[4]

We have argued elsewhere that it is this attention to the role of ontologies that has drawn mainstream technically oriented GIScientists into the realm of critical GIS (Schuurman, 2006). There is a deep concern in Geographic information science about the role of ontologies in differentiating context (e.g., the same entity in a different ontology or nomenclature has a very different meaning and implications). As a result much recent geographic information science research has focused on how to incorporate multiple ontologies or contexts into GIS – thus permitting more diverse and context-based representation of the human and physical world (Frank, 2001; Brodeur et al., 2003; Winter and Nittle, 2003). These efforts are primarily directed towards developing computational strategies to permit multiple ontologies to be included in one GIS. These efforts address many of the concerns of early critics of GIS (Aitken and Michel, 1995; Pickles, 1995; Sheppard, 1995).

These debates and conceptual underpinnings have been taken up by critical GIS scholars to re-imagine and rework GIS theory and practice in a variety of ways. In particular, critical GIS has given rise to some productive collisions of geographic information science and feminist geography, as qualitative research with GIS. Critical GIS-inspired research of course includes a host of other approaches and contributions, including public participation GIS, and several of the chapters in this handbook offer rich examples.

Understanding the effectiveness of GIS and the production of truth within and through GIS, requires a specialist's knowledge. Critical GIS scholars have argued that it is possible to influence the products of the technology as well as interpretation of results; they see tactical ways of using existing GIS technologies to further goals for social justice and feminism in particular. Kwan (2002a) argued, for instance, that critical GIS in a feminist context needs to be more reflexive in order to produce truths otherwise concealed. Likewise, Kwan (2002b) has demonstrated that it is possible to develop feminist discourses in GIS using visualization. The technology can, in fact, be used to enrich feminist geography and practices. More recently, Kwan (2007) has gone farther and argued that emotions and feelings can and should be incorporated into GIS and that this addition would decrease the potentially oppressive effects of geographic technologies. McLafferty conducted ground-breaking epidemiological research on the spatial distribution of breast cancer and links to potential environmental co-factors (Timander and McLafferty, 1998; McLafferty, 2002). This research has been extended by her demonstration that GIS queries can be developed to include context and a sense of place by including links to oral histories and narratives – that personalize the analysis. McLafferty has traced means by which GIS has been 'feminized' as there is greater introspection among GIScientists (McLafferty, 2005).

Perhaps one of the most valuable contributions of critical GIS has been to draw attention to the potential of incorporating qualitative data and research into GIS analysis. Bell and Reed (2004) initiated this discussion by illustrating how feminist participatory research could be incorporated into GIS analysis. Pavlovskaya (2006) has theorized how GIS might be re-shaped by

incorporation of qualitative data. She posits that GIS is a product of dynamic social processes rather than a static entity. In this respect, quantitative methods are linked to conservative social ideologies just as social theory and more qualitative methods are linked to more progressive social agenda. The qualitative/quantitative divide is thus exacerbated by political differences. This view is actually not factional but unifying as it posits that factor analysis and other methods of systematically looking for pattern are not so different from deconstruction. Certainly both support theory development; thus the line between methods is blurred (Pavlovskaya, 2006).

This theoretical work was incorporated earlier into an analysis of household economies in Moscow as it emerged from communism (Pavlovskaya, 2004). In this study, Pavlovskaya combined qualitative survey data with GIS to model parallel economies. Likewise, Knigge and Cope (2006) developed an analytical method for using both qualitative and quantitative data in GIS that enables them to 'ground theory'. Their paper highlights the axiom that there is no single way of representing map data. Moreover, it demonstrates that GIS can incorporate many data types from geo-referenced address data to photos and interviews.

Ethnography is another important avenue through which qualitative methods are integrated into geographic information science. Matthews et al. (2005) introduce a means for incorporating qualitative data gathered from ethnographic interviews into GIS. Their team incorporated 'life-at-a-glance' calendars, photos, as well as time travel data into GIS representations. This strategy resulted in a fuller, more dimensional representation than might otherwise have been possible. Kwan and Ding (2008) focus specifically on extending current GIS to accommodate ethnographic materials including oral histories, biographies, and other qualitative narratives. They employ a sophisticated approach that includes visualization capabilities and the dimension of time. This fusion of qualitative and the quantitative data and the technical means to implement them both are a hallmark of the *new* critical GIS – with its emphasis on qualitative data.

POSITIONING CRITICAL GIS, QUALITATIVELY[5]

A source of great debate in the GIS and society research that gave rise to critical GIS was the question of insiders and outsiders to the technology (Taylor, 1990; Openshaw, 1991, 1992; Taylor and Overton, 1991; Clark, 1992). Insider–outsider questions still matter in critical GIS work (Schuurman, 1999, 2000; Kwan, 2002a; Schuurman and Pratt, 2002; Pavlovskaya, 2009), but not in exactly the same way as they did in the earlier and mid-1990s. In this section, we argue that this tension can be productively engaged in critical GIS praxis – an argument we demonstrate using the emerging field of qualitative GIS. That is, here we urge us toward a situated qualitative GIS, which is responsive to the critiques and contributions of critical GIS. Critical GIS is of course one of the conceptual hearths from which qualitative GIS has emerged, but it is imperative that qualitative GIS continually and actively engage in critical perspectives. In this section, we offer some ways in which it might do so. We offer two points of departure in this situation, arguing that a qualitative GIS situated as a qualitative-ness of GIS theory and practice has implications for both critique and for critical praxis.

First, qualitative GIS can be considered a political intervention. In addition to being a host of technical and methodological considerations for 'out-of-the-box' thinking in GIS development and use, qualitative GIS is constructed by a series of academic debates around the fit of GIS within disciplinary geography. Those advocating a more qualitative GIS are potentially responding to an assumption that GIS is quantitative, or lacks a qualitative capacity – a dichotomy

problematized by Pavlovskaya (2009). Pavlovskaya does not insist that GIS is either quantitative or qualitative; rather, she argues that GIS was always non-quantitative. Her claims to an originally non-quantitative GIS enable, for her, a powerful rethinking of the practice and theorization of GIS. This kind of discussion of the quantitative/qualitative-ness of the GIS are indicative of the kinds of tensions which are important in Schuurman's (2000) critical GIS – to be concerned with the technology on its own terms, in its terminologies. Qualitative GIS, like critical GIS, also serves to remind critical geographers of the importance of *doing* GIS in critical contexts, extending calls for a critical cartographic literacy (Harris and Harrower, 2005; Johnson et al., 2005). Qualitative GIS inherits this tradition, via critical GIS, and enables this critical praxis. By reading qualitative GIS through the lens of critical GIS as it emerges in debate and from contestation, we introduce the second point of departure in situating qualitative GIS – the construction of an *insider gaze* that is privy to and constitutive of the terms and terminologies of the technology.

Second, an insider gaze is central to critical GIS, and enables, we argue, the more recent move to qualitative GIS. We need to preface this claim, however, with the recognition that the critical GIS first articulated by Schuurman in 1999 has now mutated into various forms taking up different dimensions of the 'critical' (qualitative GIS among them). This earlier critical GIS, as bounded by Schuurman's research monograph, is where this insider gaze is manifested. It emerges as a counter-argument to a certain form of critique, whereby the critic is challenged for their positionality in relation to the technology. Schuurman, in her history of GIS critique, provokes a rejoinder to earlier critics of GIS. In her remarks concluding a review of the GIS debates, she worries that critique which employs language outside the terminology of GIS will not 'gain the ear of GIS researchers' (Schuurman, 2000: 587). Critiques of technology must remain

Table 5.1 Insider–outsider discourse in early critical GIS

Insider	Outsider
Vocabularies of the technology	Vocabularies of social theory
Care for the subject	Care for the critic
Bolstering	Trashing
Relevant	Irrelevant
Legitimate	Illegitimate
Constructive	Destructive
Positive	Negative
Proximate	Distant

'relevant to the technology', she writes, and to do so, critics of technology must acquire the 'vocabulary of the technology' (2000: 587). Schuurman and Leszczynski (2006) take this call up in later research about metadata standards; highlighting the importance of ontology-based metadata. Here, they investigate the inner-workings of these systems to remain responsible to the issues of the technology. The early critical GIS project is furthered by this kind of insider–outsider discourse, where proponents of the project are positioned as insiders (see Table 5.1).

Feminist geographers are attentive to these kinds of discussions of internal critique. Kim England (1994, 2002) discusses how our own understandings of self mitigates our abilities (or inabilities) to conduct research. Lynn Staeheli and Patricia Martin (2000) point to the blurring of boundaries between the field and the researcher, and power relations that underlie this relationship. Staeheli and Martin write, 'positioning oneself in relation to the field…become[s] immanently political processes' (2000: 145). This positioning has been described as 'in-betweenness' (Katz, 1994, as cited by Staeheli and Martin, 2000: 146) and as 'borderlands' (Marshall, 2002). Marshall considers insider–outsider tensions a borderland in her ethnographic research; her positionality as the researcher was multiply defined with various human relationships in the study. The status of being *inside to* or *outside of* defined the moments of research, further nuancing Marshall's narrations. In this way, Marshall places insider–outsider

relations in dialog in her ethnography. Likewise, Gillian Rose (1997) proposes a reflexivity that problematizes the distance constituted by various borderlands, including insider–outsider positions.

These two points of departure highlight two ways we might situate qualitative GIS, as a troubling of the kind of political intervention undertaken and of the positionality of critique. We have discussed these departures as emerging from the work by Schuurman to define a critical GIS. More recent work in critical GIS/cartography contributes to new understandings of these departures, particularly new understandings of the 'critical'. The practicing of qualitative GIS might be understood as engaging a kind of double critique, echoing Crampton and Krygier (2005) in their discussion of implicit and explicit cartographic critique. Critique, they suggest, can be understood as both an interrogation of knowledge-making practices and an alteration of these practices in ways that affect change. Qualitative GIS is emblematic of these new understandings, and yet, as we shall discuss, the way in which the 'insider gaze' constitutes its field of operation is cause for further genealogical investigation. We must ask, therefore, what kinds of positionalities are afforded this gaze, and what are the implications for this kind of critical, qualitative GIS?

By maintaining that certain critical positions wage more relevant GIS critique, Schuurman (1999) constitutes a site to place her research – what she termed critical GIS – and further invokes a way of thinking about technologies and critique (see also Schuurman, 2006). As a sub-disciplinary label, critical GIS marks research which seeks to critique technology through re-construction – by engaging the technology on its own terms. Schuurman and Pratt (2002) point to examples of research by Sarah Elwood, Mei-Po Kwan, and Sarah McLafferty, where GIS is framed as a non-neutral tool in state-community dynamics and where GIS is mobilized as a tool to interrogate these more material dynamics.

These research projects, they argue, are emblematic of a kind of constructive critique that recognizes the transformative potential of the technology itself – a potential recognized through the insider-ness of this form of GIS critique. This, as we discussed previously, is a kind of positionality, and one to which we shall return. There are other positionalities in GIS and Society research, which take up different relations with the technology. In order to situate qualitative GIS, we discuss how related branches of GIS and Society research enact certain research positionalities in relation to the technology. These positionalities crystallize around specific technology–researcher relationships, or the degree to which the researcher actively re-works the technology as the means or the end point of the research. Here, we propose four clusters of GIS and Society research and discuss their specific positionalities: science, technology, and society (STS) studies of GIS; ethno(carto)graphic studies; socio-behavioral studies; and qualitative GIS.

STS studies within GIS research uses discourse analysis and actor-network theory to problematize the power–knowledge relationships between science, technology, and society. This research draws upon Latour (2005) and Haraway (1991) to articulate the interconnectivities of technology and society, to historicize their co-embeddedness (Pickles, 1997, 2004; Curry, 1998; Harvey and Chrisman, 1998; Chrisman, 2005; Poore and Chrisman, 2006; Ghose, 2007). This approach, emerging out of the GIS critiques of the mid-1990s, draws upon the perspective of science and technology to historicize GIS. Their positionality as researchers is to intervene through renewed storytellings of geographic information systems, of its origins and implications. This form of critique is not an admonishment of GIS; rather, this work seeks to place GIS in broader narratives of global capital, institutional networks, and information sciences. When employing discursive and actor-network analysis, the researcher negotiates a position that actively re-reads the histories and implications of

technology. This positionality is about reading the technology through various (social) theoretical perspectives, be they poststructuralist or historical-materialist. STS studies of GIS, from the perspective of the insider advocate, may be criticized as being too distant from the code-based realities of the technology (Schuurman 2000, Leszczynski, 2007). Their positionality, in other words, remains too divested from the mechanisms of the technology.

It is helpful to read STS studies in juxtaposition with ethnographic studies. Ethnography, or within GIS and society what we term ethno(carto)graphy, is a method popularized due to the belief that ethnographies appropriately place the researcher *within* the process of doing research. Here, researchers attempt to correct or ground their inquiry *in* the phenomena of their study (Herbert, 2000; Marshall, 2002; Matthews et al., 2005; Knigge and Cope, 2009). It is also a methodology of collaboration, or of participatory research (Williams and Dunn, 2003; Pain, 2004; Benson and Nagar, 2006; Elwood, 2006a; Brown and Knopp, 2008). Ethno(carto) graphic methodologies are both ethnographic and cartographic – a production of critique through the discursive work that collaborative cartographies enable. The positionality of the researcher in ethno(carto) graphy is explicitly invoked in the process of doing research. Elwood's positionality as a 'technical expert' in relation to the organization bolsters her analysis and findings. Her ability to perform research, therefore, is mediated through this positionality – of being marked both as an insider *and* outsider to the process of spatial knowledge production. The ethnographer's implicated position of being a participating observer is one requiring cautious introspect and reflection (Marshall, 2002). Ethnography in GIS and Society, as Elwood (2006a) demonstrates and Elwood and Martin (2000) discuss, requires an exposed consideration of place and incorporates critical map and critical GIS reading. Ethno(carto)graphy necessitates this positionality of preoccupation with interiority and exteriority as productive of critical research practices.

By some accounts, socio-behavioral studies of GIS maintain a close relationship to the technology. This relationship is one that constructs and configures the codes and practices of the technology itself (Jankowski and Nyerges, 2001a; Peng, 2001; Dragicevic and Balram, 2004; Nyerges et al., 2006). In contrast to STS studies of GIS and ethno(carto) graphies, these studies base much of their legitimacy and relevancy on this relationship. From the perspective of the insider gaze, the socio-behavioral researcher positionality is intensely insider. The command and control of the technology in research situations allows these researchers to build technological agendas for replication and extension. The socio-behavioral researcher makes use of scientific distance in this way, underlining the separation between researcher and subject – all while requiring the insider positionality of technical proficiency. This research is often not framed as critique, due to its own ambivalences about relevancy to the terminologies of the technology. And yet, socio-behavioral research engages the technology in a way that enacts the kind of technological engagement that the insider positionality advocates.

Qualitative GIS, we argue, engages a different researcher positionality from the three categories of GIS and Society research that we previously discussed. We propose two departures for situating qualitative GIS. We enter qualitative GIS as distinct from other GIS and Society research. And yet, it explicitly and implicitly inherits from these three traditions. From an STS perspective, qualitative GIS is a technology *being* situated within its institutional, capitalistic, and disciplinary histories. This perspective enables its recognition as a political intervention. From an ethno(carto)graphic perspective, qualitative GIS is a technology which recognizes the qualitative-ness of collaborative knowledge production. It is a participatory action technology. From a socio-behavioral GIS perspective, qualitative GIS implicitly inherits

the motivation to alter the technology and the techniques, to change the configurations and propose new specifications. It is a re-constructed technology. These congeries of partial histories co-shape qualitative GIS.

Qualitative GIS enables a kind of positionality that is attentive to the ins and outs of geographic information systems, and is motivated to complicate the rules and responsibilities of the software and its practice. Therefore, it is energized by the insider–outsider tension, and yet moves beyond this framing. It necessitates a *techno-positionality* of a conflicted insider, confronting colliding epistemologies and embracing incongruities. Qualitative GIS exceeds the insider–outsider tensions that constituted 'critical GIS', and additionally, enacts the researcher–technology relationship differently from other GIS and Society research. In this section, we consider what is entailed by foregrounding the qualitative-ness of GIS theory and practice, in the work of Jung, Kwan, and Knigge and Cope. Here, we draw on a notion of qualitative-ness that is about the embeddedness of practice and the context of counting (Moss, 1995). It is a qualitative-ness of fixity. As a system of representation, qualitative GIS necessitates a moment of fixity captured by the image and the database. One might assume that this fixity gives GIS its strength as a tool of generalization and exploration, and yet, the question of what becomes fixed, when, and by whom, is a site of contestation. In this tone, qualitative GIS has the potential to work more as a system of re-presentation, by opening up these questions of what, when, and whom, (as well as how and, of course, where) to multiple authorings and re-creation. Fixity is nuanced here as temporary fixes. While qualitative GIS requires these moments of fixity, it enables a qualitative-ness in doing so.[6] It offers an active re-characterization of the underlying logics in GIS. This is a techno-positionality, a research positionality not of the historical-materialist, nor of the technical expert or embedded ethno(carto) grapher.

Techno-positionality is a positionality in conducting research that is simultaneously about and with the technology. It is 'techno' in the sense that its relationship with technology is hybrid – a taking up of the discourses and the technicalities of the machine. It is a way of *doing* research through 'machinic vision' (Johnston, 1999).[7] Furthermore, it is a way of *doing* technology as a craft – of practicing technocritique. Qualitative GIS invokes this techno-positionality to recognize how these technologies enable shifts in discourse, while actively re-working the technology to enable an openness to incongruity and irreverence, that is productive of new forms of knowledge. As such, this techno-positionality is a conflicted insider – privy to the terminologies of the technology, and yet uninterested in the continuities of the technology. It is a way of relating to technology that is neither entirely inside nor outside, relevant nor irrelevant, constructive nor destructive, in the sense of an earlier, strategic critical GIS, as depicted in Table 5.1.

This 'conflicted insider' techno-positionality is steeped in the technicalities of GIS, and yet seeks resistive practices, new collusions, and irreconcilables to challenge GIS at the level of code. From this perspective, the technology (of hardware and software) is conceptualized as a site of opening, of the possibility for new encodings, interactions, and interpretations. Jin-Kyu Jung (2009) and LaDona Knigge and Cope (2006, 2009) each move 'inside' the technology to re-work what is meant by surface (in Jung's fantastic mosaic of embodied landscapes) and by meta-data (in Knigge's reversal of coordinate-laden ground and ground-laden coordinates). Each challenges what we imagine to be map-like, and yet also bring analytical tools and procedure to bear on these new visualizations. In effect, they have constituted new visualizings. Their qualitative GIS is about multiplicities and contingencies – about joining together previously separated objects and practices.

Qualitative GIS researchers artfully connote a kind of *mashup*. Mashups popularly refer to the co-joining of two or more instances of a particular medium, or of media. For instance, the use of Internet map applications for other purposes beyond the original intent of the map application, constitutes a mashup (Miller, 2006). Mashups become a political intervention in qualitative GIS, as they refigure data, source, meta-data, image, and anecdote. Knigge and Cope allude to this conceptualization by describing how, in combining quantitative data with ethnographic data and 'iterative, reflexive rounds of analysis', this re-figuration happens and is thereby 'attuned to multiple subjectivities, truths, and meanings' (2006: 2035). While 'mashup' has not been used to describe qualitative GIS research, it is appropriate because the term draws in other efforts in geographic information science (both academic and non-academic), including research in volunteered geographic information (Goodchild, 2007), affective GIS (Kwan, 2007; Aitken and Craine, 2009), and web development using Google Maps™ and Google Earth™.[8] We cite/site these efforts together as mashups to consider their potential relatedness. Volunteered geographic information (VGI) demarcates a new area of study, emerging from a specialist meeting held in December of 2007 at Santa Barbara, California (see 2008 special issue of *GeoJournal*). Michael Goodchild refers to VGI as depicting the 'flood of new web services and other digital sources [that] have emerged [and] can potentially provide rich, abundant, and timely flows of geographic and geo-referenced information' (2007). The concern here is with shifting data-scapes or new ways of creating, storing, manipulating, and analyzing geographic information. Mashups, a kin of VGI, elude our traditional ways of knowing and seeing. Similarly, Aitken and Craine (2009) and Kwan (2007) have explored alternative (non)representative practices with GIS, to de-tether GIS from its fixed usages, and further, as Kwan writes, to demonstrate her restlessness with these technologies' involvement in war, conflicts, and surveillance.

These new visualizings mash together different ways of knowing. Much has been written about the epistemology of GIS (c.f. Smith, 1992; Lake, 1993; Pickles, 1997; Schuurman, 2000; Brown and Knopp, 2008), and while we can be certain that this is contested terrain, one reason for the appeal and excitement of qualitative GIS is that what qualitative GIS seeks to know challenges earlier epistemological critiques of GIS. Jung's (2009) collage of georeferenced images with systematized relations to a qualitative analysis engine and Kwan's (2007) artful renderings of triangulated irregular networks surprise us. This surprise, a grotesque discourse, enables an active rethinking of *how we know* with GIS. Traditional GIS is often assumed to be positivistic, enabling a separation of subject from object. This separation becomes untenable in these instances of qualitative GIS. The surprises that this sort of technology engenders are due to the shifts in knowing necessitated by such new creations, a kind of playful mimesis. This element of surprise emerges in part due to the breakdown of insider–outsider relations with GIS technologies; qualitative GIS reworks knowledge by using the tools in ways that exceed their original purposes. These multiple claims to knowing, while seemingly incongruous, are foregrounded in qualitative GIS. These incongruities surprise and reveal. Qualitative GIS is an exploration of these incongruities.

Qualitative GIS also challenges our understanding of distance, location, and anecdote. While traditional GIS is assumed to use geometrically-determined systems of distance and location, and 'anecdotal' knowledge is stored within meta-data, qualitative GIS codes images, anecdotes, and coordinates in ways which exceed systematization. Again, qualitative GIS reconfigures these staples of GIS, to produce knowledges differently. There is no whole story provided by the qualitative GIS, but only a partial and situated storytelling. Knigge and Cope's (2009) research is emblematic of this kind of re-conceptualization (see also Knigge and Cope, 2006). Her recursive analysis with grounded visualization is about situating knowledges and configuring the GIS to bring these multiple knowledges into collusion. The dissonance created by these juxtapositions, and of these reversals of coordinates, images, and anecdotes, provides for her the necessary elements of 'strong conclusions' (Knigge and Cope, 2006: 2021). Her qualitative GIS resists the hegemony of flat cartography, by demonstrating how these cartographies are always-already interpolated by databases, images, imaginations, and narrative. Qualitative GIS is not only about placing numbers in context, as Moss (1995) has proposed, but also about allowing these numeracies to mingle with the non-numeric.

The techno-positionality of qualitative GIS engages in knowledge-making practices through the mixing of methods and analysis, both to create different knowledges and to permanently alter the technology, materially and discursively. The qualitative-ness of such an endeavor underlines its resistance to prevalent discourses that associate GIS with quantification, logical positivism, and technophilia. However, this agenda is not solely being advanced in the academy, as practitioners are already looking to the next mashup and the next widget to capture the qualities of lives lived in Google Earth™. Qualitative GIS, and its techno-positionality, is implicated in global capital; see for instance, the acquisitions made in online mapping technologies (Francica, 2007). It becomes primarily our responsibility, as academics, to continue to open these movements to interrogation and to consider the shifts in discourse that such technologies and techno-positionalities are enabling. There will be new combinations, and new ways of juxtaposing. As a form of critical GIS research, qualitative GIS should continue to inquire about these emerging ways of creating knowledge, to ask: What is symptomatically not seen in this mode of visuality? Who cannot protest? How is this sort of techno-positionality productive of new sightings and silences?

GUIDING CRITICAL GIS IN NEW TECHNOLOGICAL FRONTIERS[9]

In his 2005 discussion of the genealogy and futures of critical GIS, Eric Sheppard notes that a plethora of new technologies necessitate re-working of conventional definitions of a geographic information system, with concomitant shifts in our understandings of the boundaries and core concerns of geographic information science. He pointed in particular to then very new web-based technologies for gathering, sharing, and mapping spatial data, many of which are rooted in so-called 'Web 2.0' practices that enable user-generated online content and new forms of interactivity and connectivity among users. A growing number of geographers have turned their attention to different aspects of these new technologies, cartographies, and forms of geographic information, in emerging research on the 'geospatial web' (Scharl and Tochtermann, 2007), 'new spatial media' (Crampton, 2009b), and 'volunteered geographic information' or VGI (Goodchild, 2007). VGI refers specifically to user-generated geographic content online, such as the thousands of images on photo sharing services like Flickr that are geo-referenced, or a host of 'citizen science' initiatives that assemble geospatial data sets from the contributed observations reported by citizens. In this section, we consider how ideas from critical GIS inform emerging research on the social and political significance of volunteered geographic information (VGI) and its related technologies and practices.

Critical, feminist, and participatory GIS research share in common a notion that the societal impacts of GIS are in part wrought by the ways that geographic information is created, represented, communicated, and accessed in a digital environment. But they also hold that the ways in which these procedures are handled in a digital environment are themselves the product of social, political, and economic relationships, histories, and practices. This integrated conceptual framework is precisely the sort of foundation from which we might build a better understanding of the social and political impacts of VGI. But more specifically, these three research areas in GIS also offer a number of conceptualizations that can inform VGI research – specifically efforts to understand how and with what implications VGI may alter spatial data production, its content and characteristics, and the knowledge practices it advances.

Emerging debates about the societal impacts of VGI include a concern about the potential of this phenomenon to disempower and to worsen existing inequalities and exclusions. Critical, participatory, and feminist GIS offer a number of conceptualizations that might inform our efforts to understand precisely what forms of disempowerment are occurring and how they are produced. Especially important is the notion that in their representation of people and places, spatial data are a central loci or mechanism of inclusion and exclusion, empowerment and disempowerment. Specifically, the exclusion and under-representation of information from and about marginalized people and places in existing data records is linked to the ensuing exclusion of their needs and priorities from policy and decision making processes (Elwood and Leitner, 2003; Weiner and Harris, 2003; Elwood, 2008). For example, national census data records reflect undercounts in places that have a large number of homeless people, a high level of household mobility, or many informal settlements. Local government data on property conditions and housing abandonment are frequently incomplete in those areas in greatest need – those places where residents are less likely to contribute information and where field-based staff members may be reticent to go. Individuals' isolation, language barriers, frequent moves, fear, or other barriers may inhibit their involvement even in explicitly participatory efforts to create data. But these gaps are simultaneously constructed through mismatches between existing data structures and lived experiences. Consider for example the difficulty posed by single racial categorizations in the US Census prior to 2000, for those individuals who identify as multi-racial.

In short, when the epistemologies, vocabularies, and categories of data structures do not or cannot encompass the experiences, knowledge claims, and identities of some social groups or places, this produces their under-representation in digital data. These under-representations have all sorts of social and political implications and so must be part of our investigation of the empowerment and disempowerment potential of VGI. But further, this notion that spatial data are representative *and* constitutive of unequal access and power needs to inform efforts to use VGI for the 'patchwork' practices discussed in the previous section. While the vision that VGI might be used to flesh out incomplete public data sets is important and promising, these ideas from critical, participatory, and feminist GIS suggest that the very mechanisms that produced these gaps in the first place may well perpetuate them. The social and technological barriers that inhibited representation of some people and places from existing data records will likely challenge their participation in efforts to generate volunteered geographic information to fill the gaps. This is not to suggest that such efforts are futile or should not be undertaken. Rather, it is imperative to shape 'patchwork' VGI initiatives in ways that respond to what we already know from critical, participatory, and feminist GIS research about how exclusion and representation are constituted in digital spatial data.

A second important proposition from critical, feminist, and participatory GIS research (drawing from feminist theory and critiques of science) is that identity, power, and spatial knowledge are inseparably linked (Hanson, 2002; Kwan, 2002b; Pavlovskaya, 2002). Put more succinctly, who we are shapes what we know, and vice versa. For example, in research with community-based organizations in a Chicago neighborhood, we have found that Latino residents and community activists tend to characterize an

enclave of Puerto Rican businesses and community agencies in their community as a vibrant center of economic activity, community services and capacity building, and neighborhood revitalization (Elwood, 2006a). In contrast, Wilson and Grammenos' (2005) research in the same neighborhood documents how real estate agents, mostly white and from outside the neighborhood, typically frame the neighborhood as gang-ridden, dangerous, and dilapidated. These cases show how identity shapes knowledge, as seen in different articulations of neighborhood characteristics. But the authors of each also emphasize how characterizations of place (whether in maps, spatial data, and public media) also influence the identities and power of individuals and social groups in those places.

These theorizations of the situated nature of spatial knowledge and the co-productive relationship between knowledge and identity may be woven into VGI research in many ways. Even early studies of VGI services show that contributors will seek to use these services to generate and share diverse forms of knowledge (Miller, 2006; Turner, 2006). This suggests that VGI research must consider the extent to which the data structures and visualization services that foster VGI can support the inclusion of multiple knowledges. As well, we may wish to consider whether the data structures and visualization services commonly used with VGI are able to store or communicate anything about the situated context in which volunteered information was generated. Schuurman and Leszczynski (2006) and others have illustrated that such details about the context of spatial knowledge production (and its representation as digital data) are centrally important to understanding the data themselves and their societal applications and impacts. The situated nature of spatial knowledge is also important to questions of accuracy and reliability in volunteered information. Given the diverse range of contributors who may contribute information through VGI services, we suspect we will see especially high levels of contradictory or contrasting information. Most existing discussions of VGI frame these differences in information contributed as problems of accuracy and reliability. A critical GIS-informed reading of these differences would suggest that these contradictions in volunteered information may well be indications of social and political difference. An important dimension of VGI research could be examining how these contradictions might inform new understandings of the places and people represented in this information.

A third way in which critical and participatory GIS might inform VGI research is through its rich evidence of how spatial data access, management, and sharing are socially and politically constructed. Research from PPGIS/PGIS and critical GIS has developed detailed accounts of the social and political structures, practices and relationships mediate geospatial data access, sharing, and administration. For example, research in this arena illustrates that locally and nationally situated laws, institutional policies, and political or organizational cultures affect what data are integrated into spatial data infrastructures, as well as public access to these data (Craglia and Masser, 2003; Harvey and Tulloch, 2006; Rajabifard et al., 2006). Other research in this arena shows how spatial data integration and sharing is affected not just by the technology-rooted procedures used to do so, but also by the sorts of practices that are used to ensure consistency and interoperability, such as data standards or metadata standards (Nedovic-Budic et al., 2004; Schuurman, 2006). PPGIS/PGIS research emphasizes the capacity of unequal social and political relationships to influence spatial data access and sharing (Onsrud and Craglia, 2003; Tulloch and Shapiro, 2003; Weiner and Harris, 2003). Our own work suggests that in local political cultures that restrict access to information or in the face of relationships of mistrust, inequality and exploitation, spatial data comes to function as a commodity, a resource to be traded upon for influence or political power.

This political commodification of information produces strong disincentives for spatial data access and sharing (Elwood, 2008).

Many of these same socio-political structures and mechanisms may well affect the production, sharing, and administration of VGI. Further, investigating how they operate in this new context is an important first step in understanding the nature and genesis of limits or barriers in producing and using VGI. As well, many of the potential new knowledge practices or 'patchwork' uses of VGI that are envisioned in these discussions are presented with the caution that their possibility rests upon the ability to consistently share or integrate these data. Critical and participatory GIS offer a framework to guide our interrogation of the socio-political side of this equation. Some research is already drawing on these ideas, as in Zook and Graham's (2007) demonstration of how search and retrieval algorithms may be altered in response to government pressure, such that they retrieve only certain spatial information about a place.

However, this research on the socio-political construction and administration of spatial data in a distributed environment is also useful in highlighting the limits of existing practices to deal with new challenges posed by VGI. For instance, consider the expressed concerns about ensuring consistency and reliability in volunteered information. Research on SDIs, data standards, and metadata standards has well documented that these existing structures are quite limited in their capacity to foster consistence in traditionally-conceived and managed spatial data (Nedovic-Budic et al., 2004; Onsrud et al., 2005; Schuurman and Leszczynski, 2006). The potential heterogeneity of volunteered geographic information and the openness of many platforms for collecting and visualizing it may mean that existing structures and practices for ensuring spatial data consistency and completeness are even less appropriate in this context.

In this section, we have charted some ways in which conceptualizations and findings from critical, participatory, and feminist GIS might fruitfully inform VGI research. It also bears noting that ideas from these research trajectories do not map onto VGI research needs exactly. Grappling with the phenomenon of VGI requires us to rethink and rework ideas from these research areas, and branch out to fill critical gaps. For example, GIS and Society research has developed detailed accounts of how hardware, software, data, and expertise needed to use GIS can function as barriers to spatial data access. But the hardware, software, data, and expertise needed to contribute or use VGI are quite different. Uneven access to high-speed Internet connectivity, for example, is likely to be tremendously important in shaping the impacts of VGI, but has been given less attention in the context of GIS. In another example, PPGIS/PGIS research clearly points to the difficulty of integrating spatial data that originate from different epistemologies, as 'local knowledge' and 'official knowledge' often do (Weiner and Harris, 2003; Dunn, 2007). But this research area has focused very little on the challenges of integrating local and official knowledge, which will surely be a central concern in VGI research. Much of critical GIS research on the production, administration, and sharing of spatial data has focused on government and academic data producers and users, such that this existing work may be limited in conceptualizing the engagement of ordinary citizens and their local knowledge in VGI development and use. As Budhathoki et al. (2008) assert, the phenomenon of VGI pushes us to re-think our conceptualization of 'the user'.

Nonetheless, ideas from critical, participatory, and feminist GIS are centrally important as we formulate a VGI research agenda. Many of the same questions posed in the GIS and Society research agenda are equally important to ask of VGI as we develop a research agenda that includes considering the social and political impacts of this phenomenon. The central issues raised in *Ground Truth* (Pickles, 1995) and other early

agenda-framing publications from GIS and Society (Smith, 1992; Lake, 1993; Poiker, 1995) suggest a multitude of questions for VGI research. What are the mechanisms through which VGI will tend to alter participation, power, and knowledge? What kinds of representations of world can these mapping interfaces be used to produce, and how is the authority of these representations produced and challenged? What institutions originated the hardware, software, and interfaces that are used to create and share VGI, and how do these origins shape the sociopolitical construction and impacts of VGI? How are the challenges of cartographic representation, data storage and retrieval, and data integration handled in various VGI environments and initiatives, and with what consequences? What new forms of interaction, communication, or political practice may be advanced through VGI and VGI services? What is the potential of these new forms of information and technological practice to advance emancipatory projects, and how might they worsen existing digital divides, unequal 'information politics', and other exclusions? Finally, the converse is true as well: VGI research will have much to contribute to other research areas in GIS. As Sui (2008) describes, GIS and spatial data handling are themselves being fundamentally altered by the emergence of new geo-enabled technologies. As such, the data and practices fostered through VGI services are an increasingly central consideration in GIS practice, suggesting the necessity of situating VGI research in close conversation with a diversity of geographic information science research.

THE FUTURES OF CRITICAL GIS

As practices surrounding geographic technologies proliferate and diversify, conceptualizations of a 'GIS' continue to shift. Qualitative enquiry and 'volunteered' geospatial data represent two contemporary trajectories that re-work the GIS and Society project (Cope and Elwood, 2009; Goodchild, 2007). Here, we have discussed how these modalities intersect the broader project of critical GIS – an approach that frames its own contingencies to changing spatial technologies as a necessary, productive relationship. Critical GIS provides a framework to continue interrogating the challenges of massive databases and the hope of interoperability (Schuurman, 2005, 2006, 2009; Schuurman and Leszczynski, 2006). In the age of 'data about everything' (Anderson, 2008), critical GIS draws upon the GIS and Society tradition to contribute to studies of ubiquitous computing, technocultures, urban natures, and other cyborg geographies (Dodge and Kitchin, 2005, 2007; Zook and Graham, 2007; Wilson, 2008, 2009). And critical GIS also informs emerging research that theorizes emerging geotechnologies as 'new spatial media', as part of efforts to understand the shifting cultural politics of visual representation that are emerging in connection with the technologies (Zook and Graham 2007; Crampton, 2009b; Dodge and Perkins, 2009; Elwood, 2010). Within these varied trajectories of work, critical GIS scholars ask, what forms of geographic knowledge and spatial politics are being practiced with the newest forms of geographic information technologies, as these expand well beyond conventional GIS? How are the ever-expanding institutions, corporations, and individual actors taking part in these proliferations? What practices of mapping are emerging? How do we evaluate their ethics?

Certainly, critical GIS has flourished over the past decade. There are two emerging scenarios for the future of critical GIS – both optimistic. The first possible picture of critical GIS's future is that it increasingly attracts graduate students and scholars who are trained in both geographic information science as well as qualitative techniques and social theory. In this view, critical GIS might seamlessly integrate emerging qualitative and theoretical research into the technology,

algorithms and underlying epistemology. A good example of this possibility is seen in the pervasive emphasis on incorporating multiple ontologies into geographic technologies. The second scenario is that critical GIS – as a discernable entity – fades from view as researchers just consider it an implicit necessity of working in geographic information science. In either case, the important work that has been achieved in ontologies, feminism and GIS, incorporating qualitative methods and PPGIS has positively affected geographic information science and geography over the past decade – and may in decades to come.

ACNKOWLEDGMENTS

We extend our thanks to Tim Nyerges for the invitation to create this chapter from our past writing, and also to four anonymous reviewers whose thoughtful feedback we have tried to accommodate in this piece.

NOTES

1 Although the selections emerge from single-authored works, we have replaced the original language of 'I' with 'we' throughout the three main sections.

2 For another recent collage of commentaries on the topic of theory and practice in critical GIS, see Wilson et al. (2009).

3 The material in this section and the conclusion appeared originally in Schuurman, N. 2009. Critical GIScience in Canada in the new millennium. *The Canadian Geographer* 53(2): 139–45. It is reprinted here with kind permission of Wiley-Blackwell.

4 For further discussion of ontologies in this context, see Leszczynski (2009a and 2009b) and Crampton (2009a).

5 The material in this section appeared originally in Wilson, M. 2009. Towards a genealogy of qualitative GIS, in M. Cope and S. Elwood (eds), *Qualitative GIS: A Mixed Methods Approach*. London: Sage Publications. pp. 156–70. It is reprinted with kind permission of Sage Publications.

6 Thanks to Meghan Cope and Sarah Elwood for suggesting 'qualitativeness' here, as it appropriately

characterizes the multiple interventions that qualitative GIS enables.

7 Thanks to an anonymous reviewer for this point.

8 See, for example, the handful of paper sessions at the 2007 AAG Meeting on this topic, including 'Google Earth as the "view from nowhere"', organized by Martin Dodge and Chris Perkins; 'Virtual Globes', organized by Josh Bader and J. Alan Glennon; 'Visualization and Map Communications', chaired by Molly Holmberg; and 'Mapping and the Internet', chaired by Ron McChesney.

9 The material in this section appeared originally in Elwood, S. 2008. Volunteered geographic information: future research directions motivated by critical, participatory, and feminist GIS. *GeoJournal*, 72(3&4): 173–83. It is reprinted here with kind permission of Springer Science and Business Media.

REFERENCES

Aitken, S. and Craine, J. (2006) 'Guest editorial: Affective geovisualizations', *Directions Magazine*. 7 February.

Aitken, S. and Craine, J. (2009) 'Into the image and beyond: Affective visual geographies and geographic information science'. In M. Cope and S. Elwood (eds), *Qualitative GIS: A Mixed Methods Approach*. London: SAGE. pp. 139–55.

Aitken, S. and Michel, M. (1995) 'Who contrives the "real" in GIS? Geographic information, planning, and critical theory', *Cartography and Geographic Information Systems*, 22(1): 17–29.

Agarwal, P. (2005) 'Ontological considerations in geographic information science', *International Journal of Geographical Information Science*, 19(5): 501–36.

Anderson, C. (2008) 'The end of theory: The data deluge makes the scientific method obsolete', *Wired Magazine*. Available at: http://www.wired.com/science/discoveries/magazine/16–07/pb_theory.

Bell, S. and Reed, M. (2004) 'Adapting to the machine: Integrating GIS into qualitative research', *Cartographica*, 39(1): 55–66.

Benson, K. and Nagar, R. (2006) 'Collaboration as resistance? Reconsidering the processes, products, and possibilities of feminist oral history and ethnography', *Gender, Place and Culture*, 13(5): 581–92.

Brodeur, J., Bedard, Y., Edwards, G. and Moulin, B. (2003) 'Revisiting the concept of geospatial data interoperability within the scope of human communication processes', *Transactions in GIS*, 7(2): 243–65.

Brown, M. and Knopp, L. (2008) 'Queering the map: The productive tensions of colliding epistemologies', *Annals of the Association of American Geographers*, 98(3): 1–19.

Budhathoki, N., Bruce, B. and Nedovic-Budic, N. (2008) 'Reconceptualizing the role of the user of spatial data infrastructures', *GeoJournal*, 72(3/4): 149–60.

Chrisman, N. (2005) 'Full circle: More than just social implications of GIS', *Cartographica*, 40(4): 23–35.

Clark, G. (1992) 'GIS – what crisis?', *Environment and Planning A*, 24(3): 321–2.

Cope, M. and Elwood (eds) (2009) *Qualitative GIS: A Mixed Methods Approach*. London: SAGE.

Craglia, M. and Masser, I. (2003) 'Access to geographic information: A European perspective', *The URISA Journal*, 15(APAI): 51–60.

Crampton, J. (2005) 'Critical GIS', *GeoWorld*, 18(1): 22.

Crampton, J. (2009a) 'Being ontological: Response to "Postructuralism" and GIS: Is there a "disconnect"?', *Environment and Planning D: Society and Space*, 27(4): 603–8.

Crampton, J. (2009b) 'Cartography: Maps 2.0?', *Progress in Human Geography*, 33(1): 91–100.

Crampton, J. and Krygier, J. (2005) 'An introduction to critical cartography', *ACME*, 4(1): 11–33.

Curry, M. (1995) 'GIS and the inevitability of ethical inconsistency'. In J. Pickles. (ed.), *Ground Truth: The Social Implications of Geographical Information Systems*. New York: Guilford Press. pp. 68–87.

Curry, M. (1997a) 'Digital people, digital places: Rethinking privacy in a world of geographic information', *Ethics and Behaviour*, 7(3): 253–63.

Curry, M. (1997b) 'The digital individual and the private realm', *Annals of the Association of American Geographers*, 87(4): 681–99.

Curry, M. (1998) *Digital Places: Living With Geographic Information Technologies*. London, New York: Routledge.

Dragicevic, S. and Balram, S. (2004) 'A Web GIS collaborative framework to structure and manage distributed planning processes', *Journal of Geographical Systems*, 6(2): 133–53.

Dunn, C. (2007) 'Participatory GIS: A people's GIS?', *Progress in Human Geography*, 31(5): 617–38.

Dodge, M. and Kitchin, R. (2005) 'Codes of life: Identification codes and the machine-readable world', *Environment and Planning D: Society and Space*, 23(6): 851–81.

Dodge, M. and Kitchin, R. (2007) '"Outlines of a world coming into existence": Pervasive computing and the ethics of forgetting', *Environment and Planning B: Planning and Design,* 34(3): 431–45.

Dodge, M. and Perkins, C. (2009) 'The "view from nowhere"? Spatial politics and cultural significance of high-resolution satellite imagery', *Geoforum,* 40(4): 497–501.

Elmes, G., Dougherty, M., Callig, H., Karigomba, W., McCusker, B. and Weiner, D. (2004) 'Local knowledge doesn't grow on trees: Community-integrated geographic information systems and rural community self definition', in P. Fisher (ed.), *Developments in Spatial Data Handling.* Berlin: Springer-Verlag. pp. 29–39.

Elwood, S. (2008) 'Grassroots groups as stakeholders in spatial data infrastructures: Challenges and opportunities for local data development and sharing', *International Journal of Geographic Information Science,* 22(1): 71–90.

Elwood, S. (2002) 'GIS and collaborative urban governance: Understanding their implications for community action and power', *Urban Geography,* pp. 737–59.

Elwood, S. (2006a) 'Beyond cooptation or resistance: Urban spatial politics, community organizations, and GIS-based spatial narratives', *Annals of the Association of American Geographers,* 96(2): 323–41.

Elwood, S. (2006b) 'Critical issues in participatory GIS: Deconstructions, reconstructions, and new research directions', *Transactions in GIS,* 10(5): 693–708.

Elwood, S. (2006c) 'Negotiating knowledge production: The everyday inclusions, exclusions, and contradictions of participatory GIS research', *The Professional Geographer,* 58(2): 197–208.

Elwood, S. (2010) 'Geographic information science: Emerging research on the societal implications of the geoweb', *Progress in Human Geography,* 34: 256–263.

Elwood, S. and Martin, D. (2000) '"Placing" interviews: Location and scales of power in qualitative research', *The Professional Geographer,* 52(4): 649–57.

Elwood, S. and Leitner, H. (2003) 'GIS and spatial knowledge production for neighborhood revitalization: Negotiating state priorities and neighborhood visions', *Journal of Urban Affairs,* 25(2): 139–57.

England, K. (1994) 'Getting personal: Reflexivity, positionality and feminist research', *The Professional Geographer,* 46(1): 80–9.

England, K. (2002) 'Interviewing elites: Cautionary tales about researching women managers in Canada's banking industry'. In P. Moss (ed.),

Feminist Geography in Practice: Research and Methods. Oxford: Blackwell. pp. 200–13.

Francica, J. (2007) 'How much is location technology worth?', *Directions Magazine,* 7 October.

Frank, A. (2001) 'Tiers of ontology and consistency constraints in geographical information systems' *International Journal of Geographical Information Science,* 15(7): 667–78.

Ghose, R. (2007) 'Politics of scale and networks of association in PPGIS', *Environment and Planning A,* 39(8): 1961–80.

Goodchild, M. (2007) 'Citizens as sensors: The world of volunteered geography', *GeoJournal,* 69(4): 211–21.

Gregory, D. (2000) 'Ontology'. In R. J. Johnston, D. Gregory, G. Pratt and M. Watts (eds), *The Dictionary of Human Geography,* 4th edn. Oxford: Blackwell. pp. 561–4.

Gruber, T. (1995) 'Toward principles for the design of ontologies used for knowledge sharing', *International Journal of Human-Computer Studies,* 43(5–6): 907–28.

Hanson, S. (2002) 'Connections', *Gender, Place and Culture,* 9: 301–3.

Haraway, D. (1991) *Simians, Cyborgs and Women: The Reinvention of Nature.* New York: Routledge.

Harvey, F., Kwan, M. and Pavlovskaya, M. (2005) 'Introduction: critical GIS', *Cartographica,* 40(4): 1–4.

Harvey, F. and Tulloch, D. (2006) 'Local-government data sharing: Evaluating the foundations of spatial data infrastructures', *International Journal of Geographic Information Science,* 20(7): 743–68.

Harvey, F. and Chrisman, N. (1998) 'Boundary objects and the social construction of GIS technology', *Environment and Planning A,* 30(9): 1683–94.

Harris, L.M. and Harrower, M. (2005) 'Critical interventions and lingering concerns: Critical cartography/GIS, social theory, and alternative possible futures', *ACME: An International E-Journal for Critical Geographies,* 4(1): 1–10.

Herbert, S. (2000) 'For ethnography', *Progress in Human Geography,* 24(4): 550–68.

Jankowski, P. and Nyerges, T. (2001a) *Geographic Information Systems for Group Decision Making: Towards a Participatory, Geographic Information Science.* London: Taylor and Francis.

Jankowski, P. and Nyerges, T. (2001b) 'GIS-supported collaborative decision-making: Results of an experiment', *Annals of the Association of American Geographers,* 1: 48–70.

Jankowski, P., Robischon, S., Tuthill, D., Nyerges, T. and Ramsey, K. (2006) 'Design considerations and evaluation of a collaborative, spatio-temporal decision support system', *Transactions in GIS,* 10(3): 335–54.

Johnson, J., Louis, R. and Pramono, A.H. (2005) 'Facing the future: Encouraging critical cartographic literacies in indigenous communities', *ACME: An International E-Journal for Critical Geographies,* 4(1): 80–98.

Johnston, J. (1999) 'Machinic vision', *Critical Inquiry,* 26(1): 27–48.

Jung, J. (2009) 'Computer-aided qualitative GIS: A software-level integration of qualitative research and GIS'. In M. Cope and S. Elwood (eds), *Qualitative GIS: Mixed Methods in Theory and Practice.* London: Sage Publications. pp. 115–35.

Katz, C. (1994) 'Playing the field: Questions of fieldwork in geography', *The Professional Geographer,* 46(1): 67–72.

Katz, C. (2001) 'Vagabond capitalism and the necessity of social reproduction', *Antipode,* 33(3): 709–28.

Knigge, L. and Cope, M. (2006) 'Grounded visualization: Integrating the analysis of qualitative and quantitative data through grounded theory and visualization', *Environment and Planning A,* 38(11): 2021–37.

Knigge, L. and Cope, M. (2009) 'Recursive analysis of community spaces using ethnography and GIS', in S. A. Elwood and M. Cope (eds), *Qualitative GIS: A Mixed-Methods Approach.* London: Sage. pp. 95–114.

Knigge, L. and Cope, M. (2009) 'Grounded visualization and scale: A recursive analysis of community spaces'. In M. Cope and S. Elwood (eds), *Qualitative GIS: Mixed Methods in Theory and Practice.* London: Sage Publications. pp. 95–114.

Kwan, M. (2002a) 'Is GIS for women? Reflections on the critical discourse in the 1990s', *Gender, Place and Culture,* 9(3): 271–79.

Kwan, M. (2002b) 'Feminist visualization: Re-envisioning GIS as a method in feminist geographic research', *Annals of the Association of American Geographers,* 92(4): 645–61.

Kwan, M. (2007) 'Affecting geospatial technologies: Toward a feminist politics of emotion', *The Professional Geographer,* 59(1): 27–34.

Kwan, M. and Ding, G. (2008) 'Geo-narrative: Extending geographic information systems for narrative analysis in qualitative and mixed-method research', *The Professional Geographer,* 60(4): 443–65.

Lake, R. (1993) 'Planning and applied geography: Positivism, ethics, and geographic information systems', *Progress in Human Geography,* 17(3): 404–13.

Latour, B. (2005) *Reassembling the Social: An Introduction to Actor-Network-Theory.* Oxford, New York: Oxford University Press.

Leszczynski, A. (2007) 'Critique and its discontents: GIS and its critics in postmillennial geographies', Unpublished MA Thesis, Simon Fraser University, Burnaby, British Columbia.

Leszczynski, A. (2009a) 'Poststructuralism and GIS: Is there a "disconnect"?', *Environment and Planning D: Society and Space,* 27(4): 581–602.

Leszczynski, A. (2009b) 'Rematerializing Geographic information science', *Environment and Planning D: Society and Space,* 27(4): 609–15.

Marshall, J. (2002) 'Borderlands and feminist ethnography'. In P. Moss (ed.), *Feminist Geography in Practice: Research and Methods.* Oxford, UK; Malden, MA: Blackwell Publishers. pp. 174–86.

Matthews, S., Detwiler, J. and Burton, L. (2005) 'Geo-ethnography: Coupling geographic information analysis techniques with ethnographic methods in urban research', *Cartographica,* 40(4): 75–90.

McLafferty, S. (2002) 'Mapping women's worlds: Knowledge, power, and the bounds of GIS', *Gender, Place and Culture,* 9(3): 263–9.

McLafferty, S. (2005) 'Women and GIS: Geospatial technologies and feminist geographies', *Cartographica,* 40(4): 37–45.

Miller, C. (2006) 'A beast in the field: The Google Maps mashup as GIS/2', *Cartographica,* 41(3): 187–99.

Moss, P. (1995) 'Embeddedness in practice, numbers in context: The politics of knowing and doing', *The Professional Geographer,* 47(4): 442–9.

Nedovic-Budic, Z., Feeney, M., Rajabifard, A. and Williamson, I. (2004) 'Are SDIs serving the needs of local planning? Case study of Victoria, Australia, and Illinois, USA', *Computers, Environment and Urban Systems,* 28(4): 329–51.

Nyerges, T. (2005) 'Scaling-up as a grand challenge for public participation GIS', *Directions Magainze.* http://www.directionsmag.com/article.php?article_id=1965&trv=1 (accessed 20 September 2005).

Nyerges, T. and Jankowski, P. (1997) 'Enhanced adaptive structuration theory: A theory of GIS-supported collaborative decision making', *Geographical Systems,* 4(3): 225–59.

Nyerges, T., Ramsey, K. and Wilson, M. (2007) 'Design considerations for an Internet portal to support public participation in transportation improvement decision making'. In S. Balram and S. Dragicevic (eds), *Collaborative Geographic Information Systems.* Hershey, PA: Idea Group. pp. 208–36.

Nyerges, T., Jankowski, P., Tuthill, D. and Ramsey, K. (2006) 'Collaborative water resource decision support: Results of a field experiment', *Annals of the Association of American Geographers,* 96(4): 699–725.

Onsrud, H. and Craglia, M. (2003) 'Introduction to special issues on access and participatory approaches in using geographic information', *The URISA Journal,* 15(APAI): 5–7.

Onsrud, H., Poore, B., Rugg, R., Taupier, R. and Wiggins, L. (2005) 'Future of the spatial information infrastructure'. In R. McMaster and L. Usery (eds), *A Research Agenda For Geographic Information Science.* Boca Raton: CRC Press. pp. 225–55.

Openshaw, S. (1991) 'A view on the GIS crisis in geography, or, using GIS to put Humpty-Dumpty back together again', *Environment and Planning A,* 23(5): 621–8.

Openshaw, S. (1992) 'Further thoughts on geography and GIS: A reply', *Environment and Planning A,* 24(4): 463–6.

O'Sullivan, D. (2006) 'Geographical information science: Critical GIS,' *Progress in Human Geography,* 30(6): 783–91.

Pain, R. (2004) 'Social geography: Participatory research', *Progress in Human Geography,* 28(5): 652–63.

Pain, R., MacFarlane, R., Turner, K. and Gill, S. (2006) '"When, where, if, and but": Qualifying GIS and the effect of streetlighting on crime and fear', *Environment and Planning, A,* 38(11): 2055–74.

Pavlovskaya, M. (2002) 'Mapping urban change and changing GIS: Other views of economic restructuring', *Gender, Place and Culture,* 9: 281–9.

Pavlovskaya, M. (2004) 'Other transitions: Multiple economies of Moscow households in the 1990s', *Annals of the Association of American Geographers,* 94(2): 329–51.

Pavlovskaya, M. (2006) 'Theorizing with GIS: A tool for critical geographies?', *Environment and Planning A,* 38(11): 2003–20.

Pavlovskaya, M. (2009) 'Critical GIS and its positionality', *Cartographica,* 44(1): 8–10.

Peng, Z. (2001) 'Internet GIS for public participation', *Environment and Planning B: Planning and Design,* 28(6): 889–905.

Pickles, J. (1991) 'Geography, GIS and the surveillant society', *Papers and Proceedings of Applied Geography Conferences,* 14: 80–91.

Pickles, J. (ed.) (1995) *Ground Truth: The Social Implications of Geographic Information Systems.* London: Guilford.

Pickles, J. (1997) 'Tool or Science? GIS, technoscience, and the theoretical turn', *Annals of the Association of American Geographers,* 87(2): 363–72.

Pickles, J. (2004) *A History of Spaces: Cartographic Reason, Mapping, and The Geo-Coded World.* New York: Routledge.

Poiker, T. (1995) 'Preface', *Cartography and Geographic Information Systems,* 22(1): 3–4.

Poore, B. and Chrisman, N.R. (2006) 'Order from noise: Towards a social theory of geographic information', *Annals of the Association of American Geographers,* 96(3): 508–23.

Pratt, G. (1996) 'Trashing and its alternatives', *Environment and Planning D: Society and Space,* 14, Binns, A., Masser, I. and Williamson, I. (2006) 'The role of sub-national government and the private sector in future spatial data infrastructures', *International Journal of Geographical Information Science,* 20(7): 727–41.

Rose, G. (1997) 'Situating knowledges: Positionality, reflexivities and other tactics', *Progress in Human Geography,* 21(3): 305–20.

Scharl, A. and Tochtermann, K. (2007) *The Geospatial Web: How Geo-Browsers, Social Software and the Web 2.0 are Shaping the Network Society.* Dorchrect: Springer.

Schuurman, N. (1999) 'Critical GIS: Theorizing an emerging science', *Cartographica,* 36(4): 1–108.

Schuurman, N. (2000) 'Trouble in the heartland: GIS and its critics in the 1990s', *Progress in Human Geography,* 24(4): 564–90.

Schuurman, N. (2004) *GIS: A Short Introduction.* Oxford: Blackwell.

Schuurman, N. (2005) 'Social perspectives on semantic interoperability: Constraints on geographical knowledge from a data perspective', *Cartographica,* 40: 47–61.

Schuurman, N. (2006) 'Formalization matters: Critical GIS and ontology research', *Annals of the Association of American Geographers,* 96(4): 726–39.

Schuurman, N. (2009) 'Metadata as a site for imbuing GIS with qualitative information'. In M. Cope and S. Elwood (eds), *Qualitative GIS: A Mixed Methods Approach.* London: Sage Publications. pp. 41–56.

Schuurman, N. and Leszczynski, A. (2006) 'Ontology-based metadata', *Transactions in GIS,* 10(5): 709–26.

Schuurman, N. and Leszczynski, A. (2008a) 'A method to map heterogeneity between near but non-e quivalent semantic attributes in multiple health data registries', *Health Informatics Journal,* 14(1): 39–57.

Schuurman, N. and Leszczynski, A. (2008b) 'Ontologies and the reorganization of biological databases in the age of bioinformatics', *Bioinformatics and Biology Insights,* 2(1): 187–200.

Schuurman, N. and Pratt, G. (2002) 'Care of the subject: Feminism and critiques of GIS', *Gender, Place and Culture,* 9, Couclelis, H., Graham, S., Harrington, J.W. and Onsrud, H. (1999) 'Geographies of the information society', *International Journal of Geographical Information Science,* 13(8): 797–823.

Sheppard, E. (1993) 'Automated geography: What kind of geography for what kind of society?', *The Professional Geographer,* 45(4): 457–60.

Sheppard, E. (1995) 'GIS and society: Towards a research agenda', *Cartography and Geographic Information Systems,* 22(2): 5–16.

Sheppard, E. (2001) 'Quantitative geography: Representations, practices, and possibilities', *Environment and Planning D: Society and Space,* 19(5): 535–54.

Sheppard, E. (2005) 'Knowledge production through critical GIS: genealogy and prospects', *Cartographica,* 40(4): 5–21.

Smith, N. (1992) 'History and philosophy of geography: Real wars, theory wars', *Progress in Human Geography,* 16(2): 257–71.

Staeheli, L. and Martin, P. (2000) 'Spaces for feminism in geography', *Annals of the American Academy of Political and Social Science,* 571(1): 135–50.

Sui, D. (2008) 'The wikification of GIS and its consequences: Or Angelina Jolie's new tattoo and the future of GIS', *Computers, Environment and Urban Systems,* 32(1): 1–5.

Taylor, P. (1990) 'GKS', *Political Geography Quarterly,* 9(2): 211–2.

Taylor, P. and Overton, M. (1991) 'Further thoughts on geography and GIS', *Environment and Planning A,* 23(8): 1087–90.

Taylor, P. and Johnston, R.J. (1995) 'GIS and geography'. In J. Pickles (ed.), *Ground Truth: The Social Implications of Geographic Information Systems.* New York: Guildford Press. pp. 68–87.

Timander, L. and McLafferty, S. (1998) 'Breast cancer in West Islip, NY: A spatial clustering analysis with covariates', *Social Science and Medicine,* 46(12): 1623–35.

Tulloch, D. and Shapiro, T. (2003) 'The intersection of data access and public participation: Impacting GIS users' success?', *The URISA Journal,* 15(APAII): 55–60.

Turner, A. (2006) 'An introduction to neogeography', *Sebastapol,* CA: O'Reilly Media.

Weiner, D. and Harris, T. (2003) 'Community-integrated GIS for land reform in South Africa', *The URISA Journal,* 15(APAII): 61–73.

Williams, C. and Dunn, C. (2003) 'GIS in participatory research: Assessing the impacts of landmines on communities in North-west Cambodia', *Transactions in GIS,* 7(3): 393–410.

Wilson, D. and Grammenos, D. (2005) 'Gentrification, discourse and the body: Chicago's Humboldt Park', *Environment and Planning D: Society and Space,* 23(2): 295–312.

Wilson, M. (2005) *Implications for a Public Participation Geographic Information Science: Analyzing Trends in Research and Practice,* MA Thesis, Department of Geography, University of Washington, Seattle.

Wilson, M. (2008) 'On focus groups and interactive mappings: Reviewing the rhythms of the neighborhood advocate,' Presented at *Tracking the rhythms of daily life,* an Economic and Social Research Council seminar of the Time-Space and Life Course seminar series, organized by R. Pain and S. Smith. London, UK. http://time-space-life-course.ncl.ac.uk/seminar3.html.

Wilson, M. (2009) 'Cyborg geographies: Towards hybrid epistemologies', *Gender, Place and Culture,* 16(5): 499–516.

Wilson, M., Poore, B., Harvey, F., Kwan, M.-P., O'Sullivan, D., Pavlovskaya, M., Schuurman, N. and Sheppard, E. (2009) 'Theory, practice, and history in critical GIS: Reports on an AAG panel session', *Cartographica,* 44(1): 5–16.

Winter, S. and Nittle, S. (2003) 'Formal information modelling for standardization in the spatial domain', *International Journal of Geographical Information Science,* 17(8): 721–41.

Wright, D., Goodchild, M. and Proctor, J. (1997a) 'Demystifying the persistent ambiguity of GIS as "tool" versus "science"', *Annals of the Association of American Geographers,* 87(2): 346–62.

Wright, D., Goodchild, M. and Proctor, J. (1997b) 'Reply: Still hoping to turn that theoretical corner', *Annals of the Association of American Geographers,* 87(2): 373.

Wolf, M. (1992) *A Thrice-Told Tale: Feminism, Postmodernism, and Ethnographic Responsibility.* Palo Alto, CA: Stanford University Press.

Zook, M. and Graham, M. (2007) 'The creative reconstruction of the Internet: Google and the privatization of cyberspace and DigiPlace', *GeoForum,* 38(6): 1322–43.

GIS and Modern Life

6

Connecting Geospatial Information to Society Through Cyberinfrastructure

Marc P. Armstrong, Timothy L. Nyerges,
Shaowen Wang and Dawn Wright

INTRODUCTION

Infrastructure refers to the provision of fundamental services that members of society use to sustain modern civilization. The composition of infrastructure has evolved from basic services, such as the roads and water supplies built by the Roman Empire, to other services such as electricity and telephony that were introduced into many societies during the twentieth century. As computer technologies have advanced, it has become widely accepted that broadband networking and other information technologies have evolved to comprise an important element of infrastructure. Access to this cyberinfrastructure, defined more completely in the following section, has fundamentally changed how computer systems and services are conceived and how the latter are delivered.

The purpose of this chapter is to describe the nature of these changes and the ways

that they are manifested in the collection, processing and dissemination of geospatial information. It is important to recognize that these changes in access to technologies, and the technologies themselves, are also altering perspectives of the user community; people are able to conceptualize problems and interact with others in ways that they were unable to only a few years ago. The remainder of the chapter is organized as follows. First, we provide an elaborated definition of cyberinfrastructure and the architectures used to implement it. Then we narrow our focus to a collection of application domains that are germane to geographic information science; these include volunteered geospatial information, wireless and ubiquitous GIS, geospatial web portals and support for virtual organizations. The chapter concludes with an assessment of past effects of cyberinfrastructure developments and future prospects for transforming human-computer-human interaction within society.

CYBERINFRASTRUCTURE

During the late 1980s and 1990s, researchers and computer manufacturers began to rethink their conceptualizations of computer systems. Sun Computer, for example, proffered the tagline 'The network is the computer' during the 1980s. In the following decade, Larry Smarr and Charlie Catlett (1992) began to develop the concept of a metacomputer, a system of computers that to the user appears to be a single machine. At the turn of the century, these concepts were developed even further. In an introduction to the seminal work on grid computing (Foster and Kesselman, 1999), Smarr (1999) described a vision in which computing would be transformed into another effectively ubiquitous utility that requires an infrastructure to provide service delivery. Similar concepts that are variants on this theme are: utility computing and cloud computing. These and related ideas are now having additional effects, as new services are beginning to expand outside of research labs, into the commercial sector and transforming the way society organizes itself (e.g. social networking services).

The term used to describe the evolving computational and information infrastructure is called cyberinfrastructure (CI). Though this term is unwieldy, it is now widely adopted, largely as a consequence of its promotion by the US National Science Foundation (NSF) (2007) in a series of whitepapers, proposal solicitations and names bestowed on new units in the Foundation. CI refers to a coordinated and flexibly configured collection of heterogeneous networked devices (e.g. high-performance computers, sensors, instruments and data repositories), software and human resources that are needed to address computational and data-intensive problems in science, engineering and commerce. One additional term is gaining widespread acceptance in the commercial computing sector; cloud computing (Hayes, 2008; Leavitt, 2009) refers to a group of concepts related to the provision of computing services that bears many similarities to CI.

Cyberinfrastructure architectures

Cyberinfrastructure is implemented through the use of multiple, interconnected layers of software and hardware with communication protocols that mediate among them. In addition, as conventionally construed, CI refers not only to abstract machine terms, but also to the human resources that support and use the technology. CI architectures are often described in terms of the following abstract layers: hardware, software, middleware and human resources.

The key computational elements of CI are increasingly being transformed into networked assemblages of computers that contain multiple cores. This is taking place because chip manufacturers have reached an economic limit on their ability to improve clock speeds and achieve significant steps in manufacturing processes that lead to shrinking chip form-factors. Instead, manufacturers are turning to architectures that enable them to execute multiple instructions during each time period. This shift towards massive parallelism has recently been recognized by software designers and can best be illustrated by examining what is taking place at Microsoft® and two leading research institutions.

- Microsoft® has begun a Parallel Computing Initiative and has released a whitepaper that describes a basic change in programming models from single to multiple cores (The Manycore Shift whitepaper). It has also developed and released parallel extensions to .Net, one of their major application development environments.
- University of California, Berkeley and University Illinois, Urbana-Champaign have established Universal Parallel Computing Research Centers (with funding provided by Microsoft® and Intel®). Research at these centers is focused on the development of a complete and widely accessible pipeline of parallel computing technologies from hardware and software to applications.

In addition to Microsoft® and university research centers, other corporate efforts are particularly notable. In many ways, Google™ defines the current state-of-the-practice: it has developed massive parallel server farms to analyze and monetize the billions of user queries they receive each day. They have also entered into cooperative agreements with IBM® on cloud computing education. Amazon has followed a similar path and now sells computer cycles on demand to customers. These trends in hardware are driving computing costs down to negligible levels, so low that they are, effectively, free (Anderson, 2009).

Middleware

Middleware is specialized software that links disparate systems and data formats to support interoperability. Middleware is also used to coordinate resource allocation and schedule distributed computational tasks. In some instances, middleware is generic and handles routine tasks and widely available data types. In other cases, domain-specific inputs are encountered, thus calling for an additional layer of middleware tailored to that particular domain. Geographic problems have just such a requirement since they must confront the anisotropy that is present in the environment. This lack of geographic uniformity can induce extreme load imbalances among computational resources and services, thus significantly reducing parallel efficiency. Geographic information, therefore, requires the use of a specific type of middleware called geo-middleware (Wang et al., 2002; Wang and Armstrong, 2009).

Other middleware is needed to support different types of geospatial analyses. For example, research on middleware to support large-scale participation in structured processes has been part of the Participatory GIS for Transportation (PGIST) project (Nyerges et al., 2006). Results of the PGIST project demonstrated that a structured discussion tool developed as a combination of structured participation techniques can support larger groups of participants within an analytic-deliberative workflow (Lowry et al., 2008). However, emergent workflow engines are more difficult to design for web services than for integrated server applications.

CYBERINFRASTRUCTURE IN APPLICATION

CI is being used in numerous applications that link members of society. These social linkages are typically fluid, having flexible rules for joining and leaving and may be driven by political, social or scientific agendas.

Social networks

Computer-mediated social networking services have developed rapidly during the past several years. Starting with SixDegrees in 1977, other social networking services, such as MySpace™ (released in 2003) and Facebook (in 2004) and micro-blogging services such as Twitter™ (in 2006) have continued to fuel explosive growth in interpersonal communication (Howard, 2008). CI plays a key role in supporting social interaction in such environments. The mobile web (3G, 4G and WiFi), for example, makes Twitter™ possible. While individual 'tweets' are miniscule consumers of bandwidth, cumulatively they form a cacophony. Even more important, however, are trends in which users introduce prodigious amounts of content as they move inexorably towards increased levels of resolution of images and other media. Clearly, shifts to increased megapixel images and to high-definition video clips will require CI to handle the burden of interactivity.

The rise of social networks is having important effects on personal interactions, information search and the diffusion of ideas (memes), all concepts that are not foreign to geographic researchers. While geographic researchers have written about 'friends and neighbors effects', they were hardly anticipating the rise of Facebook friends.

As CI penetrates more deeply into social arrangements and the routine use of geospatial information, it is useful to distinguish several levels of coordination that are supported by the technology. Shirky (2008) describes several on a ladder of such activities; each rung characterized by a higher degree of interaction and agreement:

1   Sharing – this most basic activity is now well-supported by CI. In the geospatial realm, for example, photos that have been georeferenced are widely shared using technologies such as Flickr®, which is a photo-sharing and content tagging service.
2   The second rung, cooperation, is more difficult since it requires individuals to synchronize with others and often modify their behaviour, to accomplish a goal. In a sense, moving beyond Flickr® with additional meta-data enables the creation of Photosynth™-like applications (Photosynth™ is a web service that allows users to contribute and link photos to produce mosaics and three-dimensional scenes). In this case agreement must be shared about how to identify and represent geospatial information so that others can use and interact with it more readily.
3   Collaboration is yet more difficult since it requires, as a basic premise, that no single individual gets 'credit' for the production of some good or service. Wikimapia is one such example where a digital base image is annotated by a large number of individuals who achieve some type of consensus about feature labels.
4   Collective action is the final rung. In this case, individuals are required to commit themselves to a unified effort in which the decision of the group binds the behaviour of individuals. Shirky (2008) cites Hardin's 'tragedy of the commons' as an instance of collective action overcoming individual benefit.

CI is able to support each of these levels of activity. It is important to note that as we move up levels, increasing amounts of coordinated social interaction and agreement are required. In effect, we must crawl before we walk, walk before we run.

Cyberinfrastructure in geospatial information collection

Goodchild (2007) describes how enabling technologies have empowered individuals to act as volunteer geospatial data collection agents. The collection of geospatial information by members of society is supported by the ubiquity of mobile computing devices ranging in computing capacity from cell phones, PDAs and tablets, to laptops; such devices enable untethered *in situ* computing (Bennett et al., 2007). When these devices are configured with WiFi (or a different radio technology such as WiMax), they are able to communicate with other devices and serve as metaphorical 'leaves on a CI tree'. In fact when appropriately configured, a PDA can be used to access powerful computer resources available through the NSF TeraGrid, which is arguably the most capable CI in the world (see Figure 6.1). Geo-middleware supports the linkage of applications to CI resources. Together they are connected through cloud and Grid computing to achieve high performance and distributed computations for ubiquitous access.

The proliferation of advanced mobile technologies also enables individuals to make contributions to the development of the spatial data infrastructure, often using Web 2.0 software models. Goodchild (2007) describes several key issues in this transformative process:

• Motivation – people must have a desire to contribute to efforts such as Wikimapia.
• Authority – control over what is added in both the spatial and attribute domains can be contested.
• Access – the digital divide is real and limits what can be added to volunteered geospatial data products.

Haklay and Weber (2008) describe the process through which individuals contribute spatial information to the OpenStreet Map (OSM) database (see http://www.openstreetmap.org). Unlike other contributed sites (e.g. Wikipedia), OSM brings people together, before they begin data collection, in what are called 'mapping parties' that are intended to not only inform contributors about mapping protocols, but also to foster a sense of community and user group support, thus contributing to both the authority and motivation issues described by Goodchild.

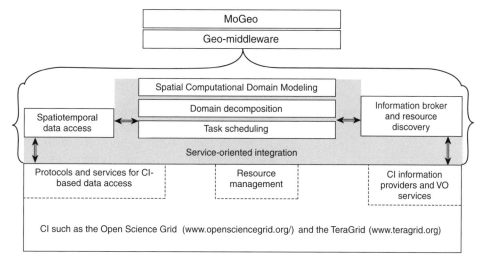

Figure 6.1   Linking spatially aware mobile utilities with CI via geo-middleware

Elwood (2008) explores how new Web 2.0 (web service) technologies associated with volunteered geographic information (VGI) are part of broad shifts in the social and technological processes that support the generation of digital spatial data. She reviews the debates about whether the content and characteristics of geospatial data and the social and political practices that promote their use are different from previous CI-related GIS developments. She suggests that VGI research could be improved by drawing upon conceptualizations from participatory, feminist and critical GIS research that have emerged from similar foundations.

Cyberinfrastructure-enabled information delivery services

When mobile devices are equipped with GPS, they are able to support the provision of information services that are context-dependent. Such awareness represents a significant departure in the ability of systems to provide information that is tailored to the user in a particular location and context.

Cyberinfrastructure in data analysis and visualization

Data-intensive, large-scale and multi-scale geospatial problems are becoming increasingly important in scientific discovery and decision making in many fields (e.g. ecology, environmental engineering and sciences, geosciences, public health and social sciences). As the size of spatial data and complexity of relevant analysis approaches have increased, spatial data analysis and visualization have become much more dependent on the emerging CI.

Geo-middleware services tailored to the handling of massive spatiotemporal data need to be developed to adapt the generic CI data and visualization services such as the Storage Resource Broker (SRB) (Rajasekar et al., 2002) and the Replica Location Service (Chervenak et al., 2004). Visualization is an essential element of GIS functions but has been mainly used as a post-processing step in part due to limited visualization resources available in conventional GIS environments. As CI-based visualization hardware resources have become available (e.g. the NSF TeraGrid visualization resources at several supercomputing centers), remote visualization services are able to accommodate on-demand visualization computations. Furthermore, CI-based data and visualization services facilitate interactive visualization for better understanding of intermediate or final data analysis results and, thus, effectively steer data-intensive exploratory analysis.

Geoportals

A geoportal is a type of web portal used to find and access geographic information (geospatial information) and associated geographic services (e.g. display, editing and analysis) via the Internet (Maguire and Longley, 2005; Goodchild et al., 2007; Wang and Liu, 2009). This approach greatly simplifies access to such services, thus substantially broadening the community of potential users. Geoportals are important for effective use of GIS and are a key element of the emerging spatial data infrastructure.

Virtual Organizations

CI supports the formation and activities of virtual organizations that address complex problems using geospatial information. A virtual organization (VO) is a '... collection of geographically distributed, functionally and/or culturally diverse entities that are linked by electronic forms of communication and rely on lateral, dynamic relationships for coordination' (DeSanctis and Monge, 1999: 693). Research into VOs has been called out as important within the Cyberinfrastructure Vision for the twenty-first century strategic plan as a '... group of individuals whose members and resources may be dispersed geographically while the group functions as a coherent unit through the use of CI (NSF, 2007: 31).

VOs can be particularly useful when public policy problems arise. Such problems contain multiple, often conflicting criteria that must be considered as part of a process of searching for solutions to them. To provide a general perspective, Nyerges and Jankowski (2010: 67) provide a framework for policy decision problems based on four terms

simple, difficult, complicated and *complex.* The four types of decision problems are differentiated in terms of the changes in four components – content, structure, process and context of a problem. When the *content* changes, but structure (relationships), process and context remain the same, then a problem is considered simple. When the *content and structure* (that is relationships) between those elements change, the problem is called difficult. When the content, structure and process components change, the problems can be called difficult. Finally, when all four components are susceptible to change, then we can call the problem complex. VOs are particularly suitable to address complex problems, often requiring inputs from many people.

Complex decision problems often involve criteria that span broad areas of expertise and require experts in multiple domains of knowledge. Moreover, complex decision problems may contain aspects that cannot be quantified and easily incorporated into computer-based solution processes. Consequently, decision-making processes are often conducted by panels, committees, boards, councils and other types of deliberative groups. GIS software can be used by such groups (Rinner, 2001; Balram and Dragićević, 2006; Nyerges et al., 2006; Jankowski and Nyerges, 2007) and one branch of the research literature refers to the process as collaborative spatial decision making.

A key element of collaborative spatial decision processes is a focus on the use of maps. In fact, a map forms a central metaphor: the campfire around which people gather to explore and gain an understanding about the geographical characteristics of complex policy problems. But a map in isolation is an insufficient tool. Maps must be linked to other spaces, be transparently interactive and give feedback about consequences of alternative plans in the public realm (Armstrong and Densham, 2008). As shown in Figure 6.2, individual members of a distributed VO can develop their own set

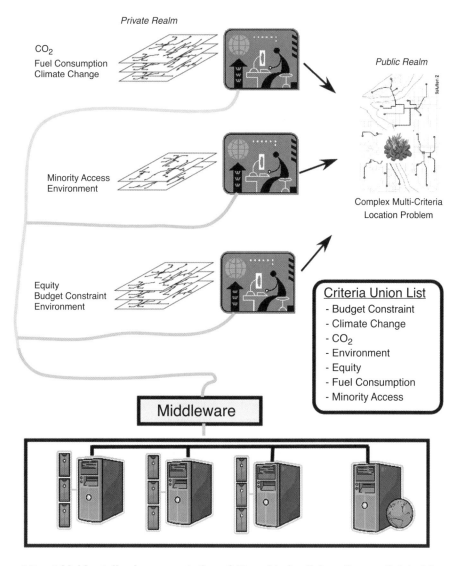

Figure 6.2   A highly stylized representation of CI-enabled collaborative spatial decision making

of criteria that figure prominently in the course of searching for solutions to a complex problem (e.g. one VO member in this example places a high value on maintaining access by minority groups, as well as minimizing environmental effects). These criteria are realized through their application in models (processed with CI resources); results are then evaluated and placed in a public realm for discussion and debate. CI enables users to analyze complex problems

expediently, during the course of a meeting, rather than as multi-hour batch processes that could play no role in deliberation during, say, a one-hour meeting.

Maps as analytic devices can be linked to structured online discussions and inform the geographic perspective of analytic-deliberative decision support processes about regional-scale projects (National Research Council, 1996, 2005). Maps at different scales are also advantageous in grounding structured discussions (Aguirre and Nyerges, in press). Rinner and his colleagues have been working on structured discussion capabilities linked to maps, called argumentation maps, for several years (Rinner, 2001; Kirschner et al., 2003). Argumentation maps provide discussion contributions embedded at the feature locations where those contributions are relevant 'on the ground'. Using such maps, one should be able to follow a discussion via maps or follow map-to-map sequences through a conversation.

Looking deeper into the process of collaborative decision making, Jankowski and Nyerges (2001) recognize that at least four cumulative levels of 'social interaction' can be elucidated under the umbrella term of 'participation' – *communication, cooperation, coordination and collaboration*. At a basic level of participation, people communicate with each other to exchange ideas as a fundamental process of social interaction. In public decision contexts, the traditional forum of a public meeting provides for *communicative* interaction – but only at a most basic level, a drawback to such meetings when 'truly constructive' comments are desired. At the next level of social interaction, building on a set of ideas developed through basic communication can be considered to be *cooperative* interaction. Participants in a cooperative activity each agree to make a contribution that can be exchanged, but each can take the results of the interaction away with them and act on the results as they see fit, with no further interaction required. A *coordinated* interaction is one whereby participants agree to cooperate, but in addition they agree to sequence their cooperative activity for mutual, synergistic gain. A *collaborative* interaction is one whereby the participants in a group agree to work on the same task (or subtask) simultaneously or at least with a shared understanding of a situation in a near-simultaneous manner.

One of the recent directions for CI-enabled participatory GIS research is scaling analytic-deliberative processes to very large groups (Nyerges et al., 2006). CI middleware

capabilities are needed for language processing in order to establish shared meaning among deliberative contributions at multiple levels of granularity. A formal ontology consisting of shared meaning terms is needed to scale deliberative discussions. Connections between natural language processing and the mapping of ontologies to computational lexicons like OpenCyc look promising for exploitation. The spatial characteristics of such connections, and those represented using maps, are crucial to the effective design of geo-middleware for user-centric collaborative spatial problem solving based on cyber-infrastructure capabilities (Figure 6.3).

Science communities

Cyberinfrastructure in service to both science and society has developed in many scientific domains, such as the iPlant collaborative for the plant science community (http://iplantcollaborative.org), the Geosciences Network (GEON) for the geology and geophysics community (http://www.geongrid.org), the National Ecology Observatory Network (NEON) for terrestrial ecology (http://www.neoninc.org) or the Thematic Real-Time Environmental Distributed Data Services (THREDDS) for the atmospheric science community and related earth system science research (http://www.unidata.ucar.edu/projects/THREDDS). While it is beyond the scope of this chapter to cover all science communities, one exemplar is that of oceanography and marine resource management, where researchers have been concerned for many decades with the acquisition, management, analysis and publication of geographic data from the world's deep oceans and near-shore/coastal environments. The societal motivation for this is from the standpoint of economics, public safety, public education and regional governance, as well as science. For example, the oceans are home to many fish, birds and mammals, as well as a zone that is critical to coastal economies via sport and commercial fishing and tourism. Data

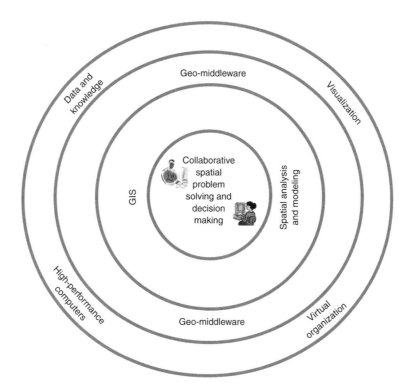

Figure 6.3   Geo-middleware as the bridging layer between major CI capabilities and GIS, spatial analysis and modeling for user-centric collaborative spatial problem solving

collection and monitoring of fishing grounds is necessary to keep the abundance of commercial species at sustainable levels. Mapping of the seafloor within the territorial seas and Exclusive Economic Zones of the US west coast will greatly improve tsunami inundation modeling, which is critical to protecting life and property in coastal towns. And knowledge of sea surface temperature and wind stress, as well as the chemical and physical structure of shallow depths is needed to track severe storms, to monitor the heat budget of the planet (global warming), as well as to gain an improved understanding of climate systems at a range of scales.

Massive data volumes from the ocean are now available through innovations in remote sensing (both satellite based and *in situ* acoustic), ocean sensor arrays, telemetry tracking of marine animals, submersibles, remotely operated vehicles, hydrodynamic

models and other emerging data collection techniques. These observations have been added to the information data streams now available to answer research questions in basic science and exploration and applications in ocean protection, preservation and management. The three-dimensional nature of the marine domain, the temporal dynamics of marine processes and the hierarchical interconnectedness of marine systems grossly increase the complexity of effective spatial solutions to these questions (e.g. Wright and Halpin, 2005; Baker and Chandler, 2008). Approaches to studying and managing the oceans are evolving as ocean-observing systems with an emphasis on real-time collection, discovery and dissemination of data for hurricane tracking and storm surge prediction, global climate change monitoring and general environmental protection. All of these approaches have geographic space as a crucial component (e.g. Graybeal et al., 2005; Wright, 2005; Arrot et al., 2006; Gomes et al., 2007) and the choice of where to locate the arrays is of crucial importance. These observing systems are based on a conceptual infrastructure design for information management and system control that allows access to the real-time data and assimilation of that data into predictive models, while integrating with deep archives of legacy data. A central architectural element is a federated data management system, implemented on a continuum from local clusters to a national grid and providing data catalog and repository services to the oceanographic communities (Arrot et al., 2006).

CI for the ocean/coastal realms is emphasizing interoperability as a key requirement for success, where access to data and information become truly universal and translations exist between the terms and understandings as expressed by ocean/coastal biologists, physicists, chemists, geologists, engineers and resource managers (e.g. Helly et al., 2003; Chandler, 2008). As such, semantic interoperability is being designed, developed and evaluated via controlled vocabularies and ontologies, semantic web technologies, system support of machine access in addition to human clients and metadata systems to support automated, accurate, machine-to-machine exchange of information (e.g. Chandler, 2008; Marine Metadata Interoperability, 2009). A growing number of research projects and initiatives in global ocean science are finally seeking to implement CI to serve diverse approaches to science (Baker and Chandler, 2008). For the coast and oceans, it is clear that CI is now crucial, but its use in this challenging environment can also advance the body of knowledge in CI design and architecture in many other application domains.

SOCIETAL ISSUES

The provision of geospatial information using CI can cause a wide variety of social

and economic problems and create opportunities for malicious behaviour. In this section we describe several issues that either have emerged or are likely to emerge in the not-too-distant future.

Access

Differential use of geospatial information through CI creates imbalances among social and economic groups. This can take place not only as a consequence of the 'digital divide', which is often construed as an access to hardware issue, but may also have its genesis in the ability of some groups to use geospatial information to marshal persuasive arguments. With respect to physical access, a large proportion of individuals on this planet have no Internet connectivity. While there are efforts to change this (the so-called US$100 laptop, for example, Kraemer et al. 2009), differentials in information access will remain in place. The issue of conceptual access is also largely, but not exclusively, rooted in class and income differentials, which also often have a racial component.

Privacy

Access to high-resolution geospatial information can also enable individuals to compromise certain aspects of privacy. For example, it is relatively easy to link disparate databases using geographic identifiers. Such linked data can yield insights into behaviours that are not otherwise available. Geospatial information can also be used to transform information in ways that might make individuals uncomfortable. For example, an inverse geocoding transformation can turn relatively anonymous pin maps into address lists that can then be linked with other databases (Armstrong and Ruggles, 2005).

Dobson (2009) expresses similar concerns about a study conducted by computer scientists at a US university whose observations about the daily movements of humans are potentially important for improving public safety and homeland security, as well as the forecasting of infectious disease spread, traffic flows, and other diffusion processes related to human mobility (González et al., 2008). However, their observations were based on the cell phone records of individuals who had not given their consent and whose identities had not been masked. This and other examples (Lane, 2003; National Research Council, 2007a, 2007b, 2008; VanWey et al., 2005; Bertino et al., 2008;) underscore the difficulties faced by researchers today.

Quality

In the past, the creation and dissemination of geospatial information was dominated by government agencies and large corporations. These organizations imposed controls on the type, quantity, and quality of information that was contained in their products. As the amount of content contained in online repositories is increasingly contributed by individuals with unknown skill levels, quality can become suspect. As a consequence, any use of the information in analyses may contain large errors.

Aggression

The quality issues described in the previous section are assumed to be the result of errors of omission and accidental errors of commission. However, it is well within the realm of possibilities that intentional errors could be introduced into geospatial information in much the way that revisionist and even malicious Wikipedia entries occur.

Piracy

Contributed or volunteered geospatial information is given freely for the idealized common good. Considerable effort may be expended on such contributions. And the results can be a rich and useful compendium. It may become so rich and useful, however, that individuals would be motivated to appropriate and repackage it for commercial or other uses. Such 'piracy' is hardly new. It was widely rumored, for example, that commercial map companies would introduce intentional small 'signature' errors into their products to enable them to detect whether a competitor or user had copied their intellectual property without permission.

Educational shallowness

Just as the exclusive use of Wikipedia is sometimes viewed as the gold standard of shoddy research, online access to geospatial information may limit the pursuit of richer, more difficult to obtain or use, resources. And what of the quality of VGI? Studies such as Flanagin and Metzger (2008) assess the level of trust users have now in, for example, Wikipedia, Google Earth™, and Citizendium and develop new analyses and rubrics for geographic training and education of novices by experts.

CONCLUSION

CI can be characterized as a disruptive technology, in the sense that it is providing a new mode of access to geospatial information and processing services. Moving away from the single desktop model of computing, CI uses distributed processing models supported by high-speed networks and specialized middleware to expand the range of capabilities that are available to users. CI moves beyond the capabilities that were provided by web geospatial applications which mainly altered information at the presentation level. With the development of CI and associated software environments, information now flows bi-directionally. Applications for public decision support are of this nature. They offer opportunity for more meaningful participation than traditional forms of public participation. The big challenge is how to scale out that participation to thousands of people, while at the same time scale high to increase technical competence for those involved (Aguirre and Nyerges, in press).

Beyond these applications are those that provide users with increased control over content and presentation. We might think of this as the next step beyond Web 2.0 applications. This inversion of Web Services has enabled the rise of contributed geospatial information and has diminished the centralized control of geospatial information and services by command bureaucracies. The rise of two-way completely distributed web apps, however, raises both epistemic and ontological problems.

Despite such problems, large investments, in both the public and private sectors are being made to support the development of CI: NSF, Department of Energy and National Institutes of Health among other federal funding agencies are providing millions of dollars of research funding each year. In the private sector, major IT and e-commerce companies are also vigorously pursuing the design, development and adoption of CI-based access to information and services. Given these substantial investments, there are abundant opportunities for research and development in the general area of geospatial CI and its role in society. Geographical researchers have unique perspectives that can be used to contribute in many ways, ranging from critical theory to GIScience approaches to distributed geographic information analysis. A particularly promising avenue of research lies in the use of CI to address complex geospatial problems by members of virtual organizations.

REFERENCES

Aguirre, R. and Nyerges, T. (in press) 'Geovisual evaluation of public participation in decision making: The 4D grapevine technique', *Journal of Visual Languages and Computing*.

Anderson, C. (2009) *Free: The Future of a Radical Price*. New York: Hyperion.

Armstrong, M.P. and Densham, P.J. (2008) 'Cartographic support for locational problem-solving by groups', *International Journal of Geographical Information Science*, 22(7): 721–749.

Armstrong, M.P and Ruggles, A. (2005) 'Geographic information technologies and personal privacy', *Cartographica*, 40(4): 63–73.

Arrot, M., Chave, A., Graybeal, J., Kruieger, I., Guillemot, E. and Pirotte, B. (2006) *Ocean Research Interactive Observatory Networks (ORION) Cyberinfrastructure Concept Architecture*. Available online at http://orionprogram.org/advisory/committees/ciarch/ (accessed 16 June 2009).

Baker, K.S. and Chandler, C.L. (2008) 'Enabling long-term oceanographic research: Changing data practices, information management strategies and informatics', *Deep-Sea Res. II*, 55, doi:10.1016/j.dsr2.2008.05.009.

Balram, S. and Dragićević, S. (eds) (2006) *Collaborative Geographic Information Systems*. Hershey, PA: Idea Publishing.

Bertino, E., Thuraisingham, B., Gertz, M. and Damiani, M.L. (2008) 'Security and privacy for geospatial data: Concepts and research directions', *SPRINGL '08: Proceedings of the SIGSPATIAL ACM GIS 2008 International Workshop on Security and Privacy in GIS and LBS*. New York: Association for Computing Machinery. pp. 6–19.

Bennett, D.A., Armstrong, M.P. and Mount, J.D. (2007) 'MoGeo: A location-based educational service'. In G. Gartner, W. Cartwright and M.P. Peterson (eds), *Lecture Notes in Geoinformation and Cartography: Location Based Services and Telecartography*. New York: Springer. pp. 493–508.

Catlett, C. and Smarr, L. (1992) 'Metacomputing', *Communications of the Association for Computing Machinery*, 35(6): 45–52.

Chandler, C. (2008) 'Introduction to interoperability', *Proceedings of the 2008 Ocean Observing Systems Interoperability Planning Workshop*. Huntsville: Alabama. Available online at http://marinemetadata.org/workshops/oosinterop2008/oosip/oosipoverview/ (accessed 16 June 2009).

Chervenak, A.L., Palavalli, N., Bharathi, S., Kesselman, C. and Schwartzkopf, R. (2004) 'Performance and scalability of a replica location service', *Proceedings of the 13th IEEE International Symposium on High Performance Distributed Computing*. IEEE Computer Society.

Desanctis, G. and Monge, P. (1999) 'Communication processes for virtual organizations', *Organization Science,* 10(6): 693–703.

Dobson, J.E. (2009) 'Big Brother has evolved', *Nature,* 458(7241): 963.

Elwood, S. (2008) 'Volunteered geographic information: future research directions motivated by critical, participatory, and feminist GIS', *GeoJournal,* 72(3/4): 173–183.

Flanagin, A.J. and Metzger, M.J. (2008) 'The credibility of volunteered geographic information', *GeoJournal,* 72: 137–148.

Foster, I. and Kesselman, C. (eds) (1999) *The Grid: Blueprint for a New Computing Infrastructure.* San Francisco, CA: Morgan Kaufman.

Gomes, K.J., Graybeal, J. and O'Reilly, T.C. (2007) 'Data management issues in operational ocean observatories', *Sea Technology,* 48(5): 17–20.

González, M.C., Hidalgo, C.A. and Barabási, A.L. (2008) 'Understanding individual human mobility patterns', *Nature,* 453: 779–782. http://www.nature.com/nature/journal/v453/n7196/full/nature06958.html, (accessed 14 October 2010).

Goodchild, M.F., Fu, P. and Rich, P.M. (2007) 'Geographic information sharing: The case of the Geospatial One-Stop portal', *Annals of the Association of American Geographers,* 97(2): 250–266.

Goodchild, M.F. (2007) 'Citizens as sensors: The world of volunteered geography', *GeoJournal,* 69: 211–221.

Graybeal, J., Bellingham J.G. and Chavez, F.P. (2005) 'Data systems for ocean observation programs', *Sea Technology,* 46(9): 23–24, 26.

Haklay, M. and Weber, P. (2008) 'OpenStreetMap: User-generated street maps', *IEEE Pervasive Computing,* 7(4): 12–18.

Hayes, B. (2008) 'Cloud computing', *Communications of the Association for Computing Machinery,* 51(7): 9–10.

Helly, J., Staudigel, H. and Koppers, A. (2003) 'Scalable models of data sharing in earth sciences', *Geochemistry Geophysics Geosystems,* 4(1): 1010, doi: 10.1029/2002GC000318.

Howard, B. (2008) 'Analyzing online social networks', *Communications of the ACM,* 11(8): 14–16.

Jankowski, P. and Nyerges, T. (2001) *Geographic Information Systems for Group Decision Making.* New York: Taylor & Francis.

Jankowski, P. and Nyerges, T. (2007) 'GIS and participatory decision making'. In J. Wilson and S. Fotheringham (eds), *Handbook of Geographic Information Science.* Blackwell. Chapter 27.

Kirschner, P.A., Shum, J.B. and Carr, C.S. (ed.) (2003) *Visualizing Argumentation: Software Tools for Collaborative and Educational Sense-Making.* New York: Springer.

Kraemer, K.L., Dedrick, J. and Sharma, P. (2009) 'One laptop per child: Vision vs. reality', *Communications of the Association for Computing Machinery,* 52(6): 66–73.

Lane, J. (2003) *Key Issues in Confidentiality Research: Results of an NSF Workshop.* Washington, D.C: National Science Foundation. http://www.nsf.gov/sbe/ses/mms/nsfworkshop_summary1.pdf (accessed 16 June 2009).

Leavitt, N. (2009) 'Is cloud computing really ready for prime time?', *IEEE Computer,* 42(1): 15–20.

Lowry, M., Nyerges, T. and Rutherford, G.S. (2008) 'An internet portal for large group participation in transportation programming decisions', *Transportation Research Record,* Publication 2077, National Academy of Sciences, Washington, D.C.

Maguire, D.J. and Longley, P.A. (2005) 'The emergence of geoportals and their role in spatial data infrastructures', *Computers, Environment and Urban Systems,* 29: 3–14.

Marine Metadata Interoperability project, hosted by Monterey Bay Aquarium Research Institute and Woods Hole Oceanographic Institution. http://marinemetadata.org (accessed 16 June 2009).

National Research Council (1996) *Understanding Risk: Informing Decisions in a Democratic Society.* Washington, DC: The National Academies Press.

National Research Council (2005) *Decision Making for the Environment: Social and Behavioral Science Research Priorities.* Washington, DC: The National Academies Press.

National Research Council (2007a) 'Engaging privacy and information technology in a digital age'. In J. Waldo, H.S. Lin and L.I. Millett (eds), *Committee on Privacy in the Information Age, Computer Science and Telecommunications Board, Division of Engineering and Physical Sciences.* Washington, DC: The National Academies Press.

National Research Council (2007b) 'Putting people on the map: Protecting confidentiality with linked social-spatial data'. In M.P. Gutmann and P.C. Stern (eds), *Panel on Confidentiality Issues Arising from the Integration of Remotely Sensed and Self-Identifying Data, Committee on the Human Dimensions of Global Change.* Division of Behavioral and Social Sciences and Education. Washington, DC: The National Academies Press.

National Research Council (2008) 'Protecting individual privacy in the struggle against terrorists: A framework for assessment'. In W.J. Perry and C.M. Vest (eds), *Committee on Technical and Privacy Dimensions of Information for Terrorism Prevention and Other National Goals.* Computer Science and Telecommunications Board, Division of Engineering and Physical Sciences. Washington, DC: The National Academies Press.

National Science Foundation (2007) *Cyberinfrastructure Vision for 21st Century Discovery.* http://www.nsf.gov/pubs/2007/nsf0728/nsf0728.pdf (accessed January 2009).

Nyerges, T. and Jankowski, P. (2010) *Regional and Urban GIS: A Decision Support Approach.* New York: Guilford Press.

Nyerges, T., Ramsey, K. and Wilson, M. (2006) 'Design considerations for an internet portal to support public participation in transportation improvement decision making'. In S. Balram and S. Dragićević (eds), *Collaborative Geographic Information Systems.* Hershey, PA: Idea Publishing. pp. 208–230.

Rajasekar, A., Wan, M. and Moore, R. (2002) 'MySRB and SRB: Components of a data grid', *Proceedings of the 11th IEEE International Symposium on High Performance Distributed Computing.* IEEE Computer Society.

Rinner, C. (2001) 'Argumentation maps: GIS based discussion support for on-line planning', *Environment and Planning B: Planning and Design,* 28: 847–863.

Shirky, C. (2008) *Here Comes Everybody: The Power of Organizing without Organizations.* New York: Penguin.

Smarr, L. (1999) 'Grids in context'. In I. Foster and C. Kesselman (eds), *The Grid: Blueprint for a New Computing Infrastructure.* San Francisco, CA: Morgan Kaufman. pp. 1–14.

VanWey, L.K., Rindfuss, R.R., Gutmann, M.P., Entwisle, B. and Balk, D.L. (2005) 'Confidentiality and spatially explicit data: Concerns and challenges', *Proceedings of the National Academy of Sciences,* 102(43): 15337–15342.

Wang, S. and Armstrong, M.P. (2009) 'A theoretical approach to the use of cyberinfrastructure in geographical analysis', *International Journal of Geographical Information Science,* 23(2): 169–193.

Wang, S., Armstrong, M.P. and Bennett, D.A. (2002) 'Conceptual basics of middleware design to support grid computing of geographic information', *Proceedings of 2nd International Conference on Geographic Information Science.* 25–28 September. Boulder: CO, USA. pp. 197–200.

Wang, S. and Liu, Y. (2009) 'TeraGrid GIScience gateway: Bridging cyberinfrastructure and GIScience', *International Journal of Geographical Information Science,* 23(5): 631–656.

Wright, D.J. (2005) 'Data management a top priority?', *Sea Technology,* 46(2): 93.

Wright, D.J. and Halpin, P.N. (2005) 'Spatial reasoning for terra incognita: Progress and grand challenges of marine GIS'. In D.J. Wright and A.J. Scholz (eds), *Place Matters: Geospatial Tools for Marine Science, Conservation and Management in the Pacific Northwest.* Corvallis, OR: Oregon State University Press. pp. 273–287.

7

Environmental Sustainability: The Role of Geographic Information Science and Spatial Data Infrastructures in the Integration of People and Nature

Clodoveu A. Davis, Jr, Frederico T. Fonseca
and Gilberto Camara

INTRODUCTION

The process of global change is altering the Earth's environment and climate. The implications of these changes for sustainability call for an approach that integrates the natural sciences and the human sciences. Scientists need to develop an understanding of the complexity of physical-ecological-anthropogenic systems. In this new paradigm, the Earth's environment is seen as being influenced by the dynamic interaction of natural and social systems.

One of the most important research questions today is then "How is the Earth's environment changing and what are the consequences for human civilization?" The science disciplines necessary to address this question are so many that only a solid interdisciplinary approach can succeed. One of the attempts to understand global change in an interdisciplinary way is what is called Sustainability Science. This new undertaking has recently gained recognition in the National Academy of Sciences, which approved, in 2006, a new section dedicated to Sustainability Science (Clark and Dickson, 2003; Clark, 2007).

Sustainability science purports to understand, integrate, and model nature and society. Since most of the interventions affecting the environment are the result of human choices, we need modeling tools that represent the world as seen and modified by human beings. Geographic Information Science (GIScience) is crucial for this purpose (Goodchild, 2003). In order to create environmental models that include humans, we need GIScience. The key question for GIScience is whether it has the methods and techniques to support sustainability research. We argue that GIScience is able to contribute to sustainability research, since it reviews some fundamental themes in traditional spatially oriented fields, such as geography, cartography, and geodesy, while incorporating more recent developments in cognitive and information science (Mark, 2000).

This chapter identifies the necessary key research questions for GIScience to support environmental sustainability. We discuss the main topics necessary for extending the capability of GIScience to understand, represent, and model sustainability related activities, and to support public policies of adaptation and mitigation. GIS for sustainable development has been subject of research for many years (Wheeler, 1993). The constant development in information technology is always providing new opportunities (Wilhelmi and Brunskill, 2003). We argue that the combination of technologies, people, and policies that defines a spatial data infrastructure (SDI) is probably the best approximation we have to solve these problems.

GISCIENCE RESEARCH AND SUSTAINABILITY SCIENCE

The challenges facing GIScience in its support of sustainability actions can be understood as being part of a cycle (for a full annotated bibliography of the early years, see [Shortridge, 1995] and for more recent work see [Campagna, 2006]). We need to improve our modeling skills, in order to address more complex systems and the interaction between human actions and natural systems. We also need to refine our data collection and data

management tools, so that we can work in a globally distributed way, and manage increasingly large amounts of online data. Furthermore, our knowledge discovery assets need to be revised to work with such large amounts of distributed data, in order to generate relevant and timely information. This information can then be used as a basis for policymaking, and for simulations and other kinds of advanced studies. Whatever knowledge is gained in the process will probably indicate the need to improve our models and collect data again, thus forming a cycle of continuous improvement.

The four main proposed topics for the new GIScience research agenda that will help the understanding of the process of global change involve *modeling*, *data collection*, *knowledge discovery*, and *support for policymaking*. A similar framework, although with a focus on Spatial Decision Support Systems, was introduced earlier by Densham (1991). These topics are briefly discussed next.

Modeling

A model is a construct that is developed to help us focus on what is important and relevant in our goal to understand a system. Modeling tries to reduce the complexity of a real-world element or phenomenon to combinations of elements, such as a set of mathematical equations (*mathematical modeling*), a number of descriptive characteristics (*database modeling*), or a set of rules and behaviors (*dynamic* or *predictive modeling*).

Scientists must use simplifications and approximations to model aspects of reality. The inaccuracies that result from such simplifications need to be assessed, in order to check the validity of the model. One way to do so is to create *simulations*, in which the scientist uses the modeled elements and past data to verify how accurately the present conditions can be predicted. The insight on reality that can be obtained from such a process enables the formulation of *forecasting models*, by means of which trends and the effects of new policies can be anticipated.

Modeling usually reflects a particular view on reality. Modelers must select and use elements from reality, as required to solve a specific range of problems, within that particular world view. For a geographic information scientist, however, there is the additional challenge of creating representations of geographically located real-world elements that can be used by researchers in other fields of expertise (Frank, 2003). Therefore, incorporating semantics in the models is an important requisite. Furthermore, an additional challenge is posed by semantic differences that result from modeling some real-world elements in different representation scales (Bruegger, 1995; Myers et al., 2003), along with the creation of realistic and practical spatiotemporal modeling tools.

In order to adequately support the needs of sustainability science, we must be able to do all of the above, and also to evolve our modeling tools and skills to the point where modeling the connections between society and nature becomes feasible. There must be ways for scientists to develop a better understanding of human actions and motivations, especially in situations that affect the environment. This can only be done by making the various world views explicit, and making sure these conceptions can be adequately represented in computational tools such as GIS. The path to achieving that involves using ontologies (Fonseca et al., 2002) as a modeling step that precedes conceptual modeling (Fonseca et al., 2003).

Data collection

Data collection has certainly improved over the last decade, to the point where concerns have shifted from availability to accessibility and discovery of data sources. The Internet has certainly helped, but a relative lack of universally accepted data transfer standards makes it hard to integrate data from several sources in a meaningful and practical way.

Much work on interoperability originates in such data transfer and translation difficulties (Rajabifard and Williamson, 2001). A partial solution has been found by establishing neutral standards (such as the Geography Markup Language [GML]) as a common ground between different data sources, but practical ways to automatically deal with semantics for integration purposes are still the subject of much research (Fonseca, 2008).

Many research initiatives currently need to: (1) collect and organize large amounts of data using various methods; (2) integrate data from several different and distributed sources; and (3) adapt data collected within different semantic frameworks to fulfill their needs. It is usually possible, although time-consuming and error-prone, to perform such tasks manually. Research and development in fields such as data warehousing and records linkage have managed to produce a few tools and techniques, but there is still much to do.

Furthermore, when someone assembles a dataset from several different sources, the chances are the data will soon become outdated. Therefore, some applications would rather rely on methods of accessing data sources directly, instead of being caught in the extraction–transformation–load cycle. Current service-based architectures and content management technology can be combined and adapted to fulfill dynamic requests for data, thus enabling the creation of *loosely coupled information systems*. Such systems require, fundamentally, that adequate sources of metadata are created and maintained (Kashyap and Sheth, 1996). This is not a simple task, considering semantic concerns and the need to synchronize metadata and actual data, although some international metadata creation standards are available (International Standards Organization [ISO], 2003).

Collecting data for models that integrate nature and society (implying distributed global data management) requires understanding the collaborative monitoring of the Earth. There is a definite need for technologies and services that allow combining data from various (dynamic, distributed) sources to improve our capacity of measuring the state of the planet and acting upon the results.

Knowledge discovery

Dealing with large amounts of distributed data, as explained in the previous section, is already very difficult. Trying to make sense of all that data to generate useful and meaningful information is an even more complex task. There are currently data warehousing (DW), data mining (DM), and knowledge discovery from databases (KDD) techniques that are able to do so from centralized repositories (Shekhar and Chawla, 2003; Han and Kamber, 2005), and even some initiatives that allow for decentralized data sources, thus creating distributed data warehousing (Lau and Madden, 2006). A range of DM techniques, geared towards mining data streams, can also be useful (Gaber et al., 2005).

GIScience takes on the challenge of putting together all kinds of knowledge discovery tools and techniques, adapting them wherever necessary to use the full potential of spatial and temporal information, in order to generate knowledge from observations, measurements, and other types of data available on the Internet. In the process, it is necessary to consider semantic frameworks to achieve integration (Fonseca et al., 2006), and to allow for ways of integrating without having to create centralized repositories or transferring large volumes of data. Ideally, DM and KDD should be performed in a decentralized fashion, combining results at some location.

In the case of environmental sustainability, the challenges for knowledge discovery are even larger. It is necessary to combine and extract knowledge from spatial and temporal data (Fonseca and Martin, 2004). It is also important to understand that data representing human actions and data representing nature may behave differently and generate incompatible trends. In summary, the problem of knowledge discovery, which is already complicated enough, becomes more complex when it is applied to environmental issues, understood as the result of society–nature interactions (Miranda and Saunders, 2003).

There is also the technological challenge of mining data from streams of environmental measurements, then applying these data to models to be used to monitor environmental changes, and also to support mitigation work. Therefore, we need to improve our capacity to discover new facts and trends in order to meet the demands of sustainable development. It is also necessary to find ways to share the new knowledge broadly and quickly (Goodchild et al., 2007).

Support for policymaking

In order to support policymaking, we need to use the knowledge that we acquired through the previous processes to develop policies to act upon the dynamic interactions of nature and society (Blackman and Köhlin, 2008; Burtraw et al., 2008). It is necessary to communicate the results of knowledge discovery to policymakers. They also need access to the data and to well-explained versions of the models. In the case of global policies, we need also to make explicit any cultural assumptions behind the data and the models.

GIScience can be used to support the creation of new environmental policies (Walsh and Crews-Meyer, 2002). How can we take action to preserve the environment now and still keep growing economically? We need to create different ways of modeling, to implement and study these models (for instance, using simulation techniques), and to use them to create and support policies that address sustainable development. Currently with people becoming more aware of sustainability issues and starting to take immediate and long-term action, we need to check if our models, data, and policies are correct.

GIScience can help in many ways, including the creation of sustainability indices to support our decision making and to measure its effectiveness (Kates et al., 2001), and by facilitating the dissemination of information.

CONNECTIONS BETWEEN GISCIENCE RESEARCH AND SUSTAINABILITY SCIENCE

In this section we list the core questions that sustainability science needs to address as outlined in *Science* by Kates et al. (2001), and discuss their repercussions. From this discussion, we propose new questions, this time specific to GIScience. Each new question is then related to one or more of the topics presented above, namely modeling, data collection, knowledge discovery, and support for policymaking.

Question 1. *How can the dynamic interaction between nature and society – including lags and inertia – be better incorporated in emerging models and conceptualizations that integrate the Earth system, human development, and sustainability?*

This question poses, for GIScience and for other areas with an interest in modeling human behavior and its interactions with nature, a very big challenge. In short, it is about understanding how human societies shape and are shaped by nature, including cultural, political, social, and economic aspects. The broad scope of the question requires the capacity to generalize on a global scale, while considering local aspects and peculiarities. It also implies the need to cope with development policies and their impact on societies and on nature (see Table 7.1).

Question 2. *How are long-term trends in environment and development, including consumption and population, reshaping nature-society interactions in ways relevant to sustainability?*

This question is intrinsically related to the previous one, since knowing more about long-term trends requires more advanced modeling and conceptualization skills. However, it presents GIScience with the need to improve monitoring methods and tools, in order to assess the correctness of models and the effectiveness of sustainability policies (see Table 7.2). Kates et al. (2001) suggest

Table 7.1   Questions related to modeling and conceptualizing interactions between nature and society

Questions	Modeling	Data collection	Knowledge discovery	Support for policymaking
How do conceptualizations of sustainability vary across different cultures?	X			
How do we represent human actions in computer systems?	X			X
What is the impact of human actions in different geographical scales?	X		X	
How to deal with the variations in the perception of natural phenomena at various levels of detail?	X			
How can we merge geographic and georeferenced data from heterogeneous sources?	X	X		
How to establish the trustworthiness of data sources?		X		
How can we generate knowledge without experimenting with nature? Can we integrate and use alternative sources of knowledge, such as data from the past?		X	X	
How to assess and demonstrate the effects of development policies over natural systems?			X	X

Table 7.2   Questions on trends in environment and development

Questions	Modeling	Data collection	Knowledge discovery	Support for policymaking
How can we agree on a set of societal and environmental variables from which indicator components can be chosen?	X	X		
How can we establish firm goals and quantifiable objectives for the sustainability effort?	X			X
How can we collect relevant data for sustainability indicators at different spatial and temporal granularities?		X		
How can we generate time series of indicators that reflect the situation in the past, so we can detect tendencies for the immediate future?		X	X	
How can we present indicators in a way that the general public can understand the evolution towards sustainability?			X	X
What kind of policies will accelerate and what kind will slow down the processes we want to control?				X

the creation of sustainability indicators. We observe that such indicators should be built upon adequate spatial and temporal reference granularities, and should probably be assembled from local data, in a bottom-up fashion.

Question 3. *What determines the vulnerability or resilience of the nature-society system in particular locations and for particular types of ecosystems and human livelihoods?*

Different societies and cultures may interpret and value differently vulnerability and environmental threats. Nevertheless, the actions of each society on the environment are shared by all. This is another example on how local activities affect the global environment, and on how a society (or all societies) should be held accountable for the consequences of its actions on the environment.

There are examples of fragile ecosystems that are affected by human actions both directly and indirectly, as in the case of the Great Barrier Reef, in Australia. Recently, the Reef has been affected both by farming, which causes pesticide- and fertilizer-based pollution in nearby river basins (Devlin and Brodie, 2004), and by rising sea water temperatures, that result from global warming (Great Barrier Reef Marine Park Authority, 2008). Such an observation

shows how, in several environmental issues, national borders become meaningless and the need to face problems becomes a global undertaking.

Therefore, within a GIScience understanding, the challenge presented by this question concerns reaching comprehensive agreements, first on data and models, then on policies and monitoring (see Table 7.3).

Question 4. *Can scientifically meaningful "limits" or "boundaries" be defined that would provide effective warning of conditions beyond which the nature-society systems incur a significantly increased risk of serious degradation?*

In a way, this question touches again on the issue of indicators, and asks whether is there a "point of no return" in relation to human actions causing degradation. If this is the case, the question implies the need for a monitoring system, from which early warnings could be issued and action could be taken before a threshold is reached. For GIScience, this constitutes the main challenge related to this question, even though we can imagine geographic information scientists being involved in the determination of the thresholds themselves.

As a result, many demands to GIScience arise from the need to collect and analyze large amounts of data on nature–society

Table 7.3   Questions on vulnerability and resilience

Questions	Modeling	Data collection	Knowledge discovery	Support for policymaking
How do conceptualizations of vulnerability and resilience vary across different cultures?	X			
How to express vulnerability and resilience spatially?	X			
How can we overcome national boundaries when dealing with data collection?		X		
How can we propose and implement global standards for data collection, documentation, and distributed access?		X	X	
How can we develop policies that are effective and, at the same time, fair to different cultures and lifestyles?			X	X

systems, and to present results in a meaningful way (see Table 7.4).

Question 5. *What systems of incentive structures – including markets, rules, norms, and scientific information – can most effectively improve social capacity to guide interactions between nature and society toward more sustainable trajectories?*

Incentive systems are among the most interesting and cost-effective ways for public authorities to deal with environmental issues. In short, authorities must develop policies that make damaging the environment more costly than their prevention or compensation. There can be rewards for reducing impact, and/or penalties for causing degradation. In a best-case scenario, such rewards and penalties should be applied so that it becomes economically beneficial for the source of degradation to invest in strategies and technologies to reduce the impact it has on the environment and on populations (National Center for Environmental Economics [NCEE], 2001).

However, incentive systems alone cannot ensure that society learns about threats to itself or to the environment. There are numerous cases of litigation, either involving governments and corporations, or groups of citizens and corporations, in which reparation is sought in the courts for health or environmental damage. Awareness of such situations should be foremost in the agenda for sustainability. For that purpose, regulations

Table 7.4   Questions on limits or boundaries for permanent degradation risk

Questions	Modeling	Data collection	Knowledge discovery	Support for policymaking
How can we identify natural systems at risk, communities at risk, and cases of dependency between communities and natural systems? Which are the populations at immediate and long-term risk?	X	X	X	X
What are the human inputs to global climate models (land use change, carbon cycle, water cycle, and atmospheric chemistry, for instance), and where are their sources?	X	X		
How can we demonstrate and present tendencies and predict degradation risk?			X	X
How to tap into and learn from the globally distributed efforts to monitor the environmental systems?			X	
How can we isolate facts that can be used as examples and arguments to demonstrate degradation risk?			X	X
How can we isolate causes of degradation so that more efficient action can be taken against them?			X	X
How can we support the creation of a global schedule or timetable for acting against sources of degradation?			X	X

Table 7.5   Questions on incentive structures

Questions	Modeling	Data collection	Knowledge discovery	Support for policymaking
What are the relations between markets and sustainability at various spatial scales?	X	X	X	
How can economic factors for sustainability be expressed and viewed spatially?	X		X	
How can we integrate structured and unstructured data for information transparency purposes?	X	X		
How does the spatial expression of markets contribute to public policies that promote sustainability?				X

and norms that require information transparency are becoming commonplace, but communicating complex data to the general public is still a big challenge (Table 7.5).

Question 6. *How can the current operational systems for monitoring and reporting on environmental and social conditions be integrated or extended to provide more useful guidance for efforts to navigate a transition toward sustainability?*

In our data-intensive era, numerous data collection efforts take place simultaneously, generating large volumes of measurement data. Considering the historical accumulation of such data, these volumes are ever increasing, to the point where the problem of data availability has become a problem of finding and getting access to *relevant* data.

Naturally, if every environmental and social data source found a way to publish their data on the Internet, much of the access problem would be solved, but the data discovery problem would still remain. Furthermore, there are semantic aspects related to the paradigms that guided the data collection effort, that have to be considered when scientists decide whether the existing data fit their needs or not.

Metadata, in this case, become fundamentally important. Standards for geographic metadata are in place, in the form of ISO 19115 (2003) (International Standards Organization [ISO], 2003), and projects such as INSPIRE (Smits, 2002) have already assembled searchable sources of geographic metadata. The current efforts can be extended to include alternatives to keyword-based

searching, so that language becomes less of a hindrance and semantic aspects can be included.

There is also the matter of the integration of data sources. Metadata should be sufficient to allow a scientist to decide whether two datasets could be reasonably combined, but adequate (and possibly automatic) treatment of uncertainty, level of detail, and – once again – semantics is still an issue (Table 7.6).

Question 7. *How can today's relatively independent activities of research planning, monitoring, assessment, and decision support be better integrated into systems for adaptive management and societal learning?*

The integration of scientific disciplines to promote research on interdisciplinary themes is often hard to achieve. Different world views, along with divergent research agendas and pigeonholed funding opportunities, constitute hurdles to groups of scientists that work on similar subjects and wish to develop integrated work.

GIScience is recognized as being essentially interdisciplinary, and geography can often provide a good basis for the integration of scientific work and data from several disciplines. Therefore, the answer to this question, from a GIScience point of view, implies continuing the search for more and better ways to integrate models, people, and data, and for more and better ways to communicate results and act upon them (Table 7.7).

When applied to sustainability, implying various social and environmental conditions and a multiplicity of actors, with points of

Table 7.6   Questions related to information technology support for monitoring and reporting on environmental and social conditions

Questions	Modeling	Data collection	Knowledge discovery	Support for policymaking
How can we achieve interoperability between models that are created under different scientific paradigms?	X			
How can we achieve interoperability between environmental monitoring systems?	X	X		
Can we build intelligent systems that work on the border between the environmental and the social worlds, joining data sources from both?	X		X	
Can we quickly put together new systems based on multiple and distributed data sources?	X		X	X
How can we create systems that help the design of policies and the evaluation of policies' results?				X

view ranging from the political to the scientific to the common citizen, Clark's questions pose enormous challenges for information science and technology, and for GIScience in particular. SDIs have the potential to address many of these problems (Keßler et al., 2005; Czerwinski et al., 2007; de Man, 2007), although they have to evolve in many ways to face the enormous challenges posed by sustainability.

SPATIAL DATA INFRASTRUCTURES AND SUSTAINABILITY

Scientists involved in sustainability must be able to combine spatial data from different sources to produce new information for a region of interest. This activity can be very complex for many reasons. First, phenomena occur and are modeled in various geographic scales, ranging from microbiology in specific locations to planetary climate impacts. Even though there is a general understanding about the semantic variation of phenomena across multiple geographic scales, our current tools and techniques are still primitive when compared to the breadth of this challenge. Second, there are multiple views on the reality of the environment, including many scientific disciplines and the view of local populations. These views are sometimes complementary, and sometimes conflicting, each one based on a particular set of concepts. Third, the complexity and level of

Table 7.7 Questions on interfaces and integration for planning

Questions	Modeling	Data collection	Knowledge discovery	Support for policymaking
How can we build interdisciplinary models that reach across different and sometimes incompatible fields of knowledge?	X			
How can we integrate data coming from different sciences?		X		
How can we incorporate unstructured data coming from informal sources?	X	X		
How can we build geographical visualization systems that help public policy makers and societal stakeholders?			X	X
How do good GIS user interfaces help planners and decision makers?				X
How can a planner build scenarios using spatial decision support systems?	X	X	X	X

detail of activities, such as data collection and analysis, range from large volumes of scientific data down to news and descriptions suited to the cultural level of local populations. From a GIScience standpoint, such requirements involve, at least: (1) efficient access to data; (2) widely accepted interoperability mechanisms (Wilhelmi and Betancourt, 2005); and (3) semantic integration of data sources (Claramunt and Theriault, 1996; Laurini, 1998; Hakimpour and Timpf, 2001).

SDI is a new approach to the creation, distribution, and use of geographic information that tries to address the shortcomings listed above. SDI tries to avoid the old view of GIS as an automated map distribution system, which focuses on map production and distribution of existing sources on an "as-is" basis. SDI is an enabler for understanding space. SDI does not simply deliver maps. It disseminates spatial data with associated quality control, metadata information, and semantic descriptions. In this view SDI can play an important role in the management of the environment and in the sustainable growth of our society.

The expression "spatial data infrastructure" was initially used to describe a standardized way to access to geographic information (Maguire and Longley, 2005). An SDI implies the existence of some sort of coordination for policy formulation and implementation, along with more complete and standardized metadata, possibly including the means to provide online access to data sources.

The first generation of SDI focused on granting a broad thematic scope, which is consistent with the current analogy between SDI and other types of infrastructure: fostering economic development by granting access to publicly available and multiple-use goods or services. Evolution from the first generation of SDI was made possible by the recent expansion of Web-based information systems. In the USA, the Geospatial One-Stop (GOS) Web portal was created to provide widespread access to geographic information, inaugurating the concept of *geoportals* (Maguire and Longley, 2005; Tait, 2005), currently viewed as SDI components. While an SDI is the overarching environment formed by the confluence of several geographic data providers, each of which granting data access through specific Web services, a geoportal provides the means to give humans some level of interactive access to these data resources, including Web-based viewers and metadata-based discovery tools (Figure 7.1).

The use of Web services to grant direct access to data is the most important distinction between first- and second-generation SDIs. In fact, the numerous possibilities that arise from using such services to encapsulate data from multiple sources, and thereby achieve interoperability, have led Bernard and Craglia (2005) to propose a new meaning to the SDI acronym: *Service-driven Infrastructures*. In fact, current SDIs include Web services as one of the possible data access channels, while maintaining links to downloadable data and existing Web applications.

The most current view on spatial information infrastructures considers their evolution into the perspective of *service-based distributed system architectures*, which have been proposed as part of a strategy for developing complex information systems based on reusable components. One of the most interesting approaches in this field is the one of *service-oriented architectures* (SOA) (Papazoglou and Georgakopoulos 2003). Services, their descriptions, and fundamental operations, such as discovery, selection, and binding, form the basis of SOA. SOA supports large applications through the sharing of data and processing capacity, network-based distributed allocation of applications, and use of computational resources. In this architecture, services are self-contained, which means that information on the service's description, including its capabilities, interface, behavior, and quality, can be obtained from the service itself, through a standardized set of functions. The Open Geospatial Consortium

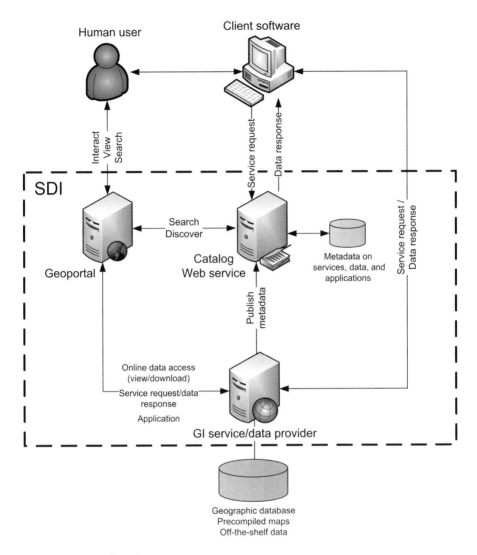

Figure 7.1   Geoportals and SDI

(OGC) has proposed many standards for Web service-based data access, such as the Web Feature Service (WFS), the Web Map Service (WMS), and several more, including some which are under evaluation at the time of writing (Klopfer, 2005). Of these, one of the most important is the Web Processing Service (WPS), which allows services to encapsulate analysis operations and algorithms, and provides the means for service chaining, that is, establishing sequences of steps using services, in a sort of workflow.

RESEARCH CHALLENGES

We consider SDIs to be a valuable asset in the development of practical solutions to the huge challenges posed by sustainability science. By organizing existing data in an unobtrusive setting of multiple and distributed sources, scientists can discover and gain direct access to relevant data, avoiding the need for time-consuming data transfer and translation. By "unobtrusive" we mean that data providers can keep their data collection and maintenance routines intact, based on the information technology tools of their choice, while being able to provide direct access to data in a timely and technologically neutral way.

The resulting framework points towards the idea of *loosely coupled GIS* (Alves and Davis, 2007), especially if the possibilities for developing and deploying more sophisticated processing and analysis services are taken into account. For instance, consider the existence of various separate sources of data on rainfall, temperature, soil types, and vegetation. From these data, a climate scientist needs to perform an analysis to determine evaporation averages. Algorithms to perform such an analysis can be documented with metadata and implemented as services, such as the WPS. As a result, by chaining selected data-provision services for the four sources to a selected analysis or processing service, information can be generated without the need to transfer and install sophisticated tools at the scientist's site, and can even dismiss the need for locally available computing power. The scientist could, in principle, execute such an analysis in the field, equipped only with some sort of mobile computing device connected to the Internet. This is a form of *cloud computing*, a concept related to Web 2.0 in the direction of providing "software as a service" (SaaS) (Buyya et al., 2008; Pierce, 2008). Note that selection from various data and processing sources is an integral part of the task, and the scientist needs to have means to discern between such alternatives. This indicates the need for *semantic discovery of services*, meaning that simple metadata schemes with keyword-based searches may not suffice.

Even though there is a potentially large number of data sources, there is a definite challenge in finding and combining them adequately. One view of SDI (Craglia et al., 2008) associates it with official mapping agencies. We think it is unreasonable to expect that systematic cartography can keep up with spatial data needs, especially in environmental frontiers, such as the Amazon.

However, this point has been the subject of much debate recently. While cartography advocates stand for a more traditional approach, with an SDI based on a broad agreement on its data contents, others envision a multitude of apparently disconnected datasets, each of which with its own intended uses, but with possible applications in other areas as well. The first approach implies a stronger presence of official data providers in the definition of what should be available, while the second expects users to proactively discover the data they need, in a broader definition of the SDI concept. This redefinition of SDIs is based on the strong need for data availability, requiring simple and practical Web-based resources. We understand that, in such an SDI, a user should be able to assess data provenance (Myers et al., 2003), and to make an informed choice between official and other data sources.

Modeling in such a complex setting is also a challenge. We need to create different ways to implement and study these models (possibly using simulation techniques), and use them to create and support policies that address sustainable development. Currently, with people becoming aware of sustainability issues and starting to take immediate and long-term action, we need to check if our models, data, and policies are correct. One of the solutions points toward the creation of sustainability indices to support our decision making and to measure its effectiveness, as suggested by Kates et al. (2001). This is a definite requirement if we intend our models to succeed in situations that are much more complex than the usual geographic application, such as in the broad modeling of the interaction between society and nature.

FUTURE TRENDS AND PROSPECTS

The potential volume of data sources and the complexity of geospatial analysis algorithms pose interesting and important challenges for loosely coupled GIS and cloud computing.

Application requirements for large volumes of data transfer can be costly and time consuming, indicating that users might prefer to keep copies at more convenient (although also Web-based) locations, and therefore some kind of synchronization should take place. There is also the need for more research and development on services integration, chaining, and orchestration, with better and easier to use tools, along with the need for specialized services, designed to assist the use of geospatial cloud computing resources with temporary data storage and synchronization methods (Alves and Davis, 2007). Furthermore, more and better tools for mobile SDI-based geospatial computing need to be developed, including geospatial viewers specifically designed for small screens, and location-aware services, which can rely on the growing availability of GPS receivers in cellular phones and other devices. There are also several concerns about computational performance, protection of sensitive data, and the security of partial results, although these concerns are shared by the general SOA and cloud computing development efforts.

The kind of sharing that motivates the creation of SDIs can be extended towards the establishment of communities of practice (Lesser et al., 2000; de Man, 2007), in which the central theme or subject is approached in various levels of detail and complexity. In order to support sustainability efforts, there is clearly the need to improve information dissemination not only among members of the same group (scientists, policymakers, citizens), but among groups. The recent phenomenon of online communities of social interaction on the Web demonstrates that this kind of integration is possible, and highly desirable as a means to motivate people to participate and contribute to solve real problems.

In our point of view, the center of a community of practice for a subject as wide as environmental sustainability should be built along the lines of the Digital Earth paradigm (Craglia et al., 2008), which consists on a very wide array of data and information sources, ranging from the governmental mapping agency cartographic data (SDI), to data collected in research projects, associated to academic publications. It should also include structured data sources, such as remote sensing products, and simplified and less structured sources, such as volunteered geographic information about themes of interest for the community. Geobrowsers can play the role of integrators for popular contributions, and should be enhanced by scientific data and elements from official policies. Furthermore, we expect that a new generation of semantic integration tools and techniques will be able to enrich community building, by providing actors with some level of semantic support, such as translation of concepts, automatic links to educational resources, and discovery of services or applications.

ACKNOWLEDGMENTS

Clodoveu A. Davis' work was partially supported by the Brazilian National Institute of Science and Technology for the Web (CNPq grant 573871/2008–6), CNPq (grants 302090/2009-6, 551037/2007-5, and 560027/2010-9), and Fapemig (CEX PPM-00168-09), Brazilian agencies in charge of fostering research and development.

Frederico Fonseca's work was partially supported by Fapemig (CEX 00038/07), and by the generous support of Penn State's College of Information Sciences and Technology.

Gilberto Camara's work is partially funded by CNPq (grant PQ 304752/2010-0 and grant 560130/2010-4) and FAPESP (grant 2008/58112-0).

REFERENCES

Alves, L.L. and Davis Jr, C.A. (2007) 'Evaluation of ogc web services for local spatial data infrastructures and for the development of clients for geographic information systems'. In C.A. Davis Jr and A.M.V. Monteiro (eds), *Advances in Geoinformatics.* Berlin: Springer. pp. 217–34.

Bernard, L. and Craglia, M. (2005) 'SDI: From spatial data infrastructure to service driven infrastructure', *Research Workshop on Cross-Learning between Spatial Data Infrastructures (SDI) and Information Infrastructures (II).* Enschede: Holanda.

Blackman, A. and Köhlin, G. (2008) 'Environment for development: RFF joins initiative to strengthen green policies in developing countries', *Resources.* Fall 2008: pp. 4–5.

Bruegger, B. (1995) 'Theory for the integration of scale and representation formats: Major concepts and practical implications'. In A. Frank and W. Kuhn (eds), *Spatial Information Theory – A Theoretical Basis for GIS, International Conference COSIT '95, Semmering, Austria.* Berlin: Springer-Verlag. 988: 297–310.

Burtraw, D., Sweeney, R. and Walls, M. (2008) 'Crafting a fair and equitable climate policy: A closer look at the options', *Resources.* (Fall 2008, Number 170). Fall: 20–3.

Buyya, R., Yeo, C.S. and Venugopa, S. (2008) 'Market-oriented cloud computing: Vision, hype, and reality for delivering IT services as computing utilities', *10th IEEE International Conference on High Performance Computing and Communications (HPCC-08),* Dalian: China.

Campagna, M. (2006) *GIS For Sustainable Development.* Boca Raton: CRC Press.

Claramunt, C. and Theriault, M. (1996) 'Toward semantics for modelling spatio-temporal processes within GIS', *International Symposium on Spatial Data Handling,* Delft, NL. pp. 47–63.

Clark, W.C. (2007) 'Sustainability science: A room of its own', *Proceedings of the National Academy of Sciences,* 104(6): 1737.

Clark, W.C. and Dickson, N.M. (2003) 'Sustainability science: The emerging research program', *Proceedings of the National Academy of Sciences, National Acad Sciences.* 100: 8059–61.

Craglia, M., Goodchild, M.F., Annoni, A., Câmara, G., Gould, M., Kuhn, W., Mark, D., Masser, I., Maguire, D., Liang, S. and Parsons, E. (2008) 'Next-Generation digital earth', *International Journal of Spatial Data Infrastructures Research,* 3: 146–67.

Czerwinski, A., Sandmann, S., Stšcker-Meier, E. and Pluemer, L. (2007) 'Sustainable SDI for EU noise mapping in NRW – best practice for INSPIRE', *International Journal of Spatial Data Infrastructures Research,* 2: 90–111.

de Man, E. (2007) 'Beyond spatial data infrastructures there are no SDIs – so what?', *International Journal of Spatial Data Infrastructures Research,* 2: 1–23.

Densham, P.J. (1991) 'Spatial decision support systems'. In D.J. Maguire, M.F. Goodchild and D. Rhind (eds), *Geographical Information Systems: Principles and Applications.* London: Longman Scientific and Technical. pp. 403–12.

Devlin, M.J. and Brodie, J. (2004) 'Terrestrial discharge into the Great Barrier Reef Lagoon: Nutrient behavior in coastal waters', *Marine Pollution Bulletin,* 51(1–4): 9–22.

Fonseca, F., Camara, G. and Monteiro, A. (2006) 'A framework for measuring the interoperability of Geo-ontologies', *Spatial Cognition and Computation,* 6(4): 307–29.

Fonseca, F., Egenhofer, M., Agouris, P. and Câmara, G. (2002) 'Using ontologies for integrated geographic information systems', *Transactions in GIS,* 6(3): 231–57.

Fonseca, F. and Martin, J. (2004) 'Space and time in eco-ontologies', *AI Communications – the European journal on Artificial Intelligence,* 17(4): 259–69.

Fonseca, F.T. (2008) 'Ontology-based geospatial data integration'. In S. X. Shekhar and H. Xiong (eds), *Encyclopedia of GIS.* London/New York: Springer.

Fonseca, F.T., Davis Jr., C.A. and Câmara, G. (2003) 'Bridging ontologies and conceptual schemas in geographic applications development', *Geoinformatica,* 7(4): 355–78.

Frank, A. (2003) 'Ontology for spatio-temporal databases'. In M. Koubarakis and T. Sellis (eds), *Spatio-Temporal Databases: The Chorochronos Approach.* Berlin Heidelberg New York: Springer-Verlag. pp. 9–78.

Gaber, M.M., Zaslavsky, A. and Khrishnaswami, S. (2005) 'Mining data streams: A review', *ACM SIGMOD Record,* 34(2): 18–26.

Goodchild, M.F. (2003) 'Geographic information science and systems for environmental management', *Annual Review of Environment and Resources,* 28: 493–519.

Goodchild, M.F., Fu, P. and Rich, P. (2007) 'Sharing geographic information: An assessment of geospatial one-stop', *Annals of the Association of American Geographers,* 97(2): 250–66.

Great Barrier Reef Marine Park Authority (2008) 'Coral bleaching on the great barrier reef'. http://www. gbrmpa.gov.au/corp_site/key_issues/climate_ change/climate_change_and_the_great_barrier_ reef/coral_bleaching_on_the_great_barrier_reef (accessed 25 August 2008).

Hakimpour, F. and Timpf, S. (2001) 'Using ontologies for resolution of semantic Heterogeneity in GIS 4th', *AGILE Conference on Geographic Information Science, Brno, Czech Republic.* pp. 385–95.

Han, J. and Kamber, M. (2005) *Data Mining: Concepts and Techniques*, 2nd edn., Morgan-Kaufmann.

International Standards Organization (ISO) (2003) 'Geographic information – Metadata'. http://www.iso.org/iso/iso_catalogue/catalogue_tc/catalogue_detail.htm?csnumber=26020 (accessed 25 August 2008).

Kashyap, V. and Sheth, A. (1996) 'Semantic heterogeneity in global information system: The role of metadata, context and ontologies'. In M. Papazoglou and G. Schlageter (eds), *Cooperative Information Systems: Current Trends and Directions.* London: Academic Press. pp. 139–78.

Kates, R.W., Clark, W.C., Corell, R., Hall, J.M., Jaeger, C.C., Lowe, I., McCarthy, J.J., Schellnhuber, H.J., Bolin, B. and Dickson, N.M. (2001) *Environment and Development: Sustainability Science*, 292: 641–2.

Keßler, C., Wilde, M. and Raubal, M. (2005) 'Using SDI-based public participation for conflict resolution', *11th EC-GI and GIS Workshop*, Alghero: Sardinia.

Klopfer, M. (2005) 'Interoperability and open architectures: An analysis of existing standardisation processes and procedures'. In O.G. Consortium (ed.), *OGC White Paper. Open Geospatial Consortium.* p. 26.

Lau, E. and Madden, S. (2006) 'An integrated approach to recovery and high availability in an updatable, distributed data warehouse', *Proceedings of the 32nd International Conference on Very Large Databases.* Seoul, Korea. pp. 703–14.

Laurini, R. (1998) 'Spatial multi-database topological continuity and indexing: A step towards seamless GIS data interoperability', *International Journal of Geographical information Science*, 12(4): 373–402.

Lesser, E.L., Fontaine, M.A. and Slusher, J.A. (2000) *Knowledge and Communities.* Boston: Butterworth-Heinemann.

Maguire, D.J. and Longley, P.A. (2005) 'The emergence of geoportals and their role in spatial data infrastructures', *Computers, Environment and Urban Systems*, 29(1): 3–14.

Mark, D. (2000) 'Geographic information science: Defining the field'. In M. Duckham, M.F. Goodchild and M.F. Worboys (eds), *Foundations of Geographic Information Science.* New York: Taylor & Francis. pp. 3–18.

Miranda, S.M. and Saunders, C.S. (2003) 'The social construction of meaning: An alternative perspective on information sharing', *Information Systems Research*, 14(1): 87–106.

Myers, J.D., Pancerella, C., Lansing, C., Schuchardt, K.L. and Didier, B. (2003) 'Multi-scale science: Supporting emerging practice with semantically derived provenance', *Semantic Web Technologies for Searching and Retrieving Scientific Data Workshop at the 2nd International Semantic Web Conference*, Sanibel Island, FL.

National Center for Environmental Economics (NCEE) (2001) 'Chapter 3: The cost effectiveness and environmental effects of incentive systems', *The U.S. Experience with Economic Incentives for Protecting the Environment.* Washington, DC: Environmental Protection Agency (EPA).

Papazoglou, M.P. and Georgakopoulos, D. (2003) 'Service-oriented computing', *Communications of the ACM*, 46(10): 25–8.

Pierce, M.E. (2008) 'Grids and geospatial information systems', *Concurrency Computation: Practice and Experience*, 20: 1611–5.

Rajabifard, A. and Williamson, I.P. (2001) 'Spatial data infrastructures: concept, hierarchy, and future directions', *GEOMATICS'80*, Tehran: Iran.

Shekhar, S. and Chawla, S. (2003) *Spatial Databases: A Tour.* Prentice Hall.

Shortridge, A. (1995) 'Multiple roles for GIS in US global change research: Annotated bibliography'. Santa Barbara, CA: University of California, Santa Barbara.

Smits, P. (2002) *INSPIRE Architecture and Standards Position Paper.* http://inspire.jrc.it/reports/position_papers/inspire_ast_pp_v4_3_en.pdf (accessed April 2005).

Tait, M.G. (2005) 'Implementing geoportals: Applications of distributed GIS', *Computers, Environment and Urban Systems*, 29(1): 33–47.

Walsh, S.J. and Crews-Meyer, K.A. (eds) (2002) *Linking People, Place, and Policy: A GIScience Approach.* Berlin: Springer.

Wheeler, D.J. (1993) 'Commentary: Linking environmental models with geographic information systems for global change research', *Photogrammetric Engineering and Remote Sensing*, 59(10): 1497–501.

Wilhelmi, O.V. and Betancourt, T.L. (2005) 'Evolution of NCAR GIS initiative: Demonstration of GIS interoperability', *Bulletin of American Meteorological Society*, 86(2): 176–8.

Wilhelmi, O.V. and Brunskill, J.C. (2003) 'Geographic information systems in weather, climate, and impacts', *Bulletin of American Meteorological Society*, 84(10): 1409–14.

8

GIS and Population Health: An Overview

Nadine Schuurman and Nathaniel Bell

INTRODUCTION

In this chapter, we illustrate a number of methodological contributions by geographers in the field of geographic information science (GIS) that have strengthened or offer the potential to contribute to the known empirical relationship between socioeconomic conditions and gradients in health. The intersections between GIS and population health, while few, are differentiated from traditional spatial epidemiology as the two approaches to health outcomes research arise from different theoretical models. GIS is potentially a powerful tool for elucidating and communicating trends in population health and understanding patterns in health outcomes because it can offer both confirmatory and exploratory data solutions to a variety of questions on health and wellness. The research intersection between GIS and population health is still being developed, and there is much potential in the future for GIS to serve as a means of analysis and communication of health trends and their graded nature.

This chapter begins with a descriptive overview of the population health model and the primary techniques used to quantify and provide empirical evidence of variations in health status. This is followed with an evaluation of emergent GIS approaches to population health that will potentially influence how we (1) conceptualize neighbourhood influences on health, (2) optimize the scale in which these processes are observed, and (3) construct benchmarks to quantify such relationships. We conclude with a case study illustrating how to integrate participatory surveys into GIS for building composite measures of socioeconomic status.

DEFINING AND MEASURING POPULATION HEALTH STATUS

The population health model

Health and the myriad factors that affect it including 'lifestyle', biological and psychological characteristics have long been under scrutiny within developed countries. Yet, their combined influence has never explained why certain populations are healthier than others, encouraging many to conclude that the structure of the social environment is likely the most profound means by which the health status of the general population is shaped (Mustard and Frank, 1994; Syme, 1994; Tarlov, 1996; Hayes, 2004). Collectively, these findings are part of a wider discussion of health inequality rooted in the pathways and mechanisms by which an individual's health outcomes parallel his or her social class or socioeconomic position. The impetus for this paradigm resulted from questions raised in *The Black Report* (Black et al., 1982), and which continues to be strengthened by research about intersections between the individuals and society and the effects of power relationships, however measured (social position, income, employment stability, social cohesion, family structure), on health status (Evans et al., 1994; Hertzman, 1999; Marmot and Wilkinson, 2006; Wilkinson and Pickett, 2006).

The *population health* model – which focuses on determinants and health inequalities – uses empirical evidence demonstrating the socioeconomically graded nature of health outcomes among population groups; much of this research is then filtered back into policy in Canada, the UK, and the USA (Collins and Hayes, 2007). Central to the thesis of the population health model is a recognition of how and why social gradients in health – the stepwise rise in health where health outcomes improve as one moves upward from the lowest social stratum to the next higher social stratum – are manifest throughout society and how individual health outcomes are affected in the process (Marmot, 1986). While geographers have long been engaged with this discussion and advocated for stronger recognition of the social environment in shaping health status and its ensuing spatial expression, others have noted that, albeit with few exceptions (Taylor, 1993; Hayes, 1994; Dunn and Hayes, 2000), there has been insufficient advocacy directed at the pathways by which health inequalities are embedded in the context of our routine encounters with others and the graded nature that these encounters produce over the entire life-course (Hayes, 2004).

Antecedents to population health research

Since the early 1990s, the term *population health* has come to define an integrative approach toward health and well-being under the premise that responding to the causes of diseases from a *population* perspective will influence the lives of more people and for longer periods of time than individual or clinically-based interventions alone (Yen and Syme, 1999). Its roots, however, can be traced back to the pioneering work on suicide compiled by French sociologist Émile Durkheim (1858–1917), who found that suicide rates among population groups exhibited relatively stable patterns over time even though new individuals continued to move in and out of the groups and take their place (Durkheim, 1952). Ensuing research from the ongoing *Whiltehall* studies (1967–2007), a longitudinal study of cardiovascular disease among graded levels of British civil servants, offered additional early and critical evidence that health outcomes are not isolated, individual events, but share an overwhelmingly strong linkage to an individual's position as he or she moves along the social ladder (Marmot et al., 1991). Subsequent national research platforms, notably the 1998 publishing of the *Acheson Report* in England, and the 1994 *Strategies for Population Health* initiatives in Canada, further evoked similar appraisal for population-level policies toward health and wellness and the ongoing findings that groups that exhibit similar social characteristics also share similar health outcomes.

While population health encompasses a broader understanding of mechanisms that influence health beyond disparities in the social environment alone, it is the scale and relative distribution of social and economic differences between individuals within society that leads to a focus on understanding the step-wise variations in health outcomes across the population stratum (Keating and Hertzman, 1999). This is a startling contrast from more exclusive risk-factor or resource-oriented models of traditional clinical or disease epidemiology – often focused on individual behaviour – toward one that is more inclusive of broader social influences. Adding up the benefits of medical care or the affects of genetics, coupled with 'lifestyle' factors or reductions in point-source pollution exposures fails to fully explain why certain populations are healthier than others (Hayes, 2004) – while a population health model can accommodate these healthy populations. This framework has been strengthened from the paradoxical finding that increased spending on health care no longer corresponds with a positive increase in the overall health status, and the ensuing realization that beyond a very low threshold in income disparity, relative income distributions remain stronger markers of overall health status both *within* and *between* countries (Wilkinson, 1996). Similarly, and in the face of collectively funded health care systems such as in Canada and the UK, medical or resource-based models have failed to address why privileged populations continually live longer, healthier lives than those who experience greater disadvantage (Black et al., 1982; Ross et al., 2001; Dunn, 2002). Epidemiologists have thus become increasingly aware that general health status is most closely linked to characteristics and distribution of wealth *within* countries, using the population health model as a framework for understanding these patterns. The question, of course, is how best to transform this evidence into health care policy and health promotion.

Quantifying population health status

Evidence that health corresponds to social and structural variations in class or socioeconomic position has been linked to individual social and economic circumstance (Townsend et al., 1987; Carstairs, 1989), but also to the social and physical environment, so much so that it is liable to change according to the neighbourhood where one lives. This latter finding is the primary emphasis of attempts to quantify the various effects of features such as feelings of safety, resource sharing, or the amalgamation of other features that are thought to be a part of more equitable societies, such as social cohesion, levels of trust, and group membership that, in their absence or unequal distribution, may converge on or buffer the influence of one's individual circumstances (e.g., income, employment status) (Kawachi et al., 1999; Ross et al., 2004). This emphasis has also coincided with a resurging interest in quantifying the role of 'place' and the significance of intra-individual relationships in characterizing one's health (Macintyre et al., 1993; Diez-Roux et al., 1997; Kennedy et al., 1998). However, both strategies recognize that individual and neighbourhood geographies are nested within larger systems and that interventions must ultimately emerge from wider social and political processes.

Evidence of this effect, however derived, is primarily taken from national censuses – a practice that has been in use since at least the early 1970s in the UK and continues to be the primary approach for small-scale approaches toward measuring health inequalities within Canada, the USA, and elsewhere (Townsend et al., 1987; Carstairs, 1989; Frohlich and Mustard, 1996; Krieger et al., 1997; Salmond et al., 2006). Reliance on the national census as the primary source of population-level data stems from its availability and its broad representativeness of all political jurisdictions, but also due to its inclusion of extensive number of direct or indirect indicators of an individual's or area's class or socioeconomic position relative to the surrounding population. These datasets are also regularly used to assess small-area class or socioeconomic variations due in part to their embedded spatial and attribute linkages, making it by far the most robust spatialised dataset to evaluate socioeconomic patterns across local or nationwide scales. The indices take on numerous forms, but the majority are based on the aggregation or single instances of variables by either a z or log-transformation or through more computationally robust techniques such as a principle component analysis (Pampalon and Raymond, 2000). Likewise, multilevel modelling techniques are quickly becoming the standard for capturing and isolating the unique combination of neighbourhood influences on health over and above the personal characteristics of the resident individuals (Stafford et al., 2001; Wiggins et al., 2002; Ross et al., 2004; Oliver et al., 2007).

In conjunction with specially designed health surveys, national censuses have served as the data cornerstone for population health research as they are the most viable means of obtaining a broad range of information about the population in the absence of having to conduct intense, focused, and spatially discrete investigations. Census geographies are also some of the most practical boundaries for highlighting local gradients in health outcomes as municipal and state-wide officials often rely on these boundaries for allocating health and social services. Thus, reporting health and socioeconomic gradients using similar bounds helps ensure a more fluid transformation between research and policy implementation.

Limitations and pitfalls

Census-based analyses are rich in detail, but have a number of profound shortcomings. Widespread critique has been placed on their retrospective nature as they often negate important information regarding yearly changes in mobility or migration as well as their lack of representativeness (Crampton, 2004). In Canada, for instance, the census is particularly poor in capturing meaningful information among First Nations peoples living on reserves (Statistics Canada, 2003).

An ensuing conceptual problem has been entangled in the often interchangeable use of the terms poverty, deprivation, class, and socioeconomic position. Townsend (1987) noted that a person is said to be deprived if they lack the type of income, employment skills, or housing that are customary to society at-large, but only impoverished if they lack the means to escape deprivation (Townsend, 1978).

There has also been substantial cross-discipline engagement over the potentially negating effects of aggregating inversely valued variables (e.g., house rich, income poor) and the possible misconceptions introduced from this effect (Noble et al., 2006). In a similar vein, rise in popularity of multilevel modelling is a response to aggregation bias and hidden clustering stemming from areal effects. The shift to multilevel modelling, however, has amassed substantial critical scrutiny as one's position in the social hierarchy is clearly influenced not only by 'space' (neighbourhood of residence), but also by 'place' (the social meanings attached to residence). The latter are, however, often immeasurable given the nature of the census questionnaires and the partitioning of its geography (Macintyre et al., 2002). Thus, current quantitative models of population health invariably rely and come to be limited by the boundaries and attributes circumscribed by the census. This is a critical concern if one is to ascribe meaningful dimensions of social space to evidence raised from their use (Longley, 2003).

Combined, these shortcomings within the current framework for quantifying the graded nature of health outcomes are potentially damaging to establishing long-term community health needs and maximizing the fulfilment of social, political, and health care policy initiatives intended to reduce their effect. Emerging developments in GIS have the potential to refine our current understanding of linkages between 'place' and 'space' that can be drawn from population-level databases as well as generate new tools for deriving powerful evidence that is possibly more revealing of its nature than is currently known. In the ensuing sections, we review key examples taken from current literature where integration between GIS and population health is in the process of transforming how we (1) conceptualize neighbourhood influences on health, (2) optimize the scale for deriving empirical evidence of this relationship, and (3) develop measures to quantify this effect.

GIS AND MAPPING HEALTH OUTCOMES

Antecedents to mapping health outcomes

Maps have long played an important role in the geographical study of disease and there are numerous case studies and textbooks that illustrate how its inclusion has provided important clues as to how to approach disease aetiology, model its diffusion across the landscape, or assess small-scale trends in various health outcomes. However, one of the earliest and most well-known attempts to map health events is generally credited to British physician, Dr John Snow (1813–1858).

In early and mid-nineteenth century, cholera epidemics devastated major cities throughout Europe, resulting in the deaths of tens of thousands of Europeans. Cholera is an acute infection characterized by severe vomiting and diarrhoea, which in extreme cases may result in death due to dehydration. Between the 1830s and 1840s, cholera caused the deaths of over 20,000 Londoners. The onset was brought on, at least in part, by the economic distress from the Industrial Revolution, which resulted in massive urban overcrowding, poor sanitation, and impoverished living conditions among the urban poor. Snow, a London sanitation physician, theorized that the cholera epidemic was water-borne rather than transmitted through inhalation. Combining insight from both

statistics, cartography and epidemiology, Snow mapped confirmed cholera cases using a series of 'dots' to represent count and proximal location between patients who had died from cholera in relation to various public water pumps. From these data, he derived incident rates for each of the public water pumps currently in service to the population. Ultimately, his study helped convince leading medical authorities that the transmission of a localized outbreak of cholera could be traced back to a single point source.

Snow's cholera map is showcased in nearly all medical geography textbooks as the quintessential model of the use of maps and statistical analysis for studying disease aetiology. However, his study is not the only, nor the earliest, example of how maps have been used for understanding disease patterns. Works from German physicians Heinrich Berghaus (1848) and Leonhard Finke (1792), and American physician Valentine Seaman (1798) are some of the earliest disease maps of the world, predating Snow's work by over half a century. Edwin Chadwick's (1800–1890) *Report on the Sanitary Condition of the Labouring Population in Great Britain* (1842) relied heavily on mapping and statistical analysis to draw linkages between the poor sanitary conditions of English squalors and the early deaths and health of the English working poor. Modern disease atlases, including *The New Social Atlas of Britain* (Dorling, 1995) and *The World Atlas of Diseases* (Cliff et al., 2004) continue to serve as powerful accounts of population health status.

GIS and population health

In recent years, integration of GIS into mainstream health research has helped redefine how we understand and conceptualize the spatial patterning of diseases (Lawson and Denison, 2002). GIS is a powerful medium for conveying trends in population health and offers an expansive set tools for exploring a variety of questions pertaining to the spatial patterning of health and wellness. Its integration into the population health research domain has grown considerably. A recent application from Mitchell et al. (2002) traced the changing geography of mortality in the UK to determine whether composition of the population's age and class structure alone accounted for changing pattern of mortality (Mitchell et al., 2002). The various table operation features of the GIS enabled scalable joining of numerous disparate databases, borrowing from the more granular tables to infer sub-aggregate class/age/gender breakdowns within existing census boundaries (Mitchell et al., 2002). In other cases, GIS has been used to remove temporal mismatches between decennial census wards, allowing researchers to build numerous connections across historical population movements that could find additional application investigating large-scale longitudinal variations between social and economic characteristics and patterns of mortality (Martin et al., 2002). Similarly, Szwarcwald et al. (2000) drew heavily on GIS for merging disparate demographic, economic, and mortality databases with infrastructure data (e.g., health care facilities) to draw linkages to features in the communities that might lead to explanations for individual health experiences and build from these findings future strategies for health promotion (Szwarcwald et al., 2000).

Yet much of the integration between GIS and population health, however well-intended, largely underscores internal practices of broadly segregating social inequalities into dichotomous classifications ('deprived/privileged', 'unemployed/employed', 'low income/high income') and has thus far been largely absent from drawing further evidence to the graded relationship between status and health. A recent account linking both geographical and social space by Gatrell et al. (2004) found a broad division between affluent and deprived neighbourhoods, but fails to fully reference the extent that these differences translate across social space

(Gatrell et al., 2004). While assessing the graded socio-spatial nature of health outcomes can largely be seen as a conceptual rather than a methodological challenge, there remains a need to explain causal mechanisms. Geographers undoubtedly play a key role in furthering our understanding of the linkages between 'space', 'place', and 'health', and, as the next section will attempt to demonstrate, there is great potential to not only further embrace the strengths of this technology, but also to use its tools to help explain the complex social processes that parallel population health outcomes and provide evidence of this relationship.

Conceptualizing neighbourhood influences on health

Data availability, coupled with the ensuing demand for population-wide evidence of power relationships and the underlying emphasis on how social gradients manifest themselves across local spaces from one group to the next have, somewhat paradoxically, meant that researchers draw evidence from health surveys or other data sources and then tie these findings back to the census boundaries. However, recent applications from the literature raise the possibility of integrating GIS to construct digital representations of more meaningful spaces and are illustrative of new research areas where this technology might be used to reduce the conceptual challenges of differentiating between 'place' and 'space' while still retaining the contextual data found in the census to conduct population-level analyses.

In their analysis of disability and variations in average income, Lebel et al. (2007) devised a methodology for linking historical (e.g., parish boundaries), census-based socioeconomic units, and concept mapping boundaries derived from local stakeholder perspectives into a composite spatial model of relative deprivation. This linking enabled them to develop a complex analysis from what would normally be isolated geographic characteristics. The historical boundaries were selected based on their present day relevance and, where applicable, digitally rectified to correspond with the other datasets. Municipal stakeholders were asked to draw neighbourhood boundaries according to what they believed to be the most relevant in terms of various local characteristics and the local actors returned and assisted in qualifying the data variations produced from the various scales (Lebel et al., 2007). The flexibility of this approach allowed the authors to construct quantitative measurements using a range of socioeconomic indicators while also facilitating a mechanism for apportioning these values onto spatial extents viewed by local participants to be meaningful representations of social space.

Variations of concept mapping approaches for building neighbourhood boundaries within a digital environment are emergent elsewhere in the literature. Aronson et al. (2007) found that amalgamating mapping, statistical and primary data sources – including walkthroughs and participatory interviews and focus groups, provides a more complex understanding of how social and political features operate at the neighbourhood level and influence risk of poor health (Aronson et al., 2007). A similar study by Wheeler (2008) incorporated historic texts, aerial photographs, and GIS to analyse the evolution and understand the consequences of the built environment on urban form, thus illustrating that the boundaries one has at their disposal for such a task are seemingly endless (Wheeler, 2008).

Both Lebel et al. (2007) and Aronson et al. (2007) point out that determining which characteristics of the environment are conducive to influencing health outcomes needs to be carefully considered when operationalising 'mixed methods' GIS-based models. Yet, the overall conclusion is that there is increasing potential to integrate GIS into what has traditionally been a very 'non-GIS' research area and derive from this exchange more meaningful representations of social space that is transferable at the municipal or district

scale. The utility of GIS makes it well-suited for deriving scalable solutions pertaining to boundary construction and there are numerous 'out-of-the-box' tools imbedded within GIS to create spatial connections between neighbouring units. This protocol provides researchers with a dynamic geographic modelling environment to conceptualize community variations in health outcomes and quantify the spatial arrangement of any ensuing gradient, which, like many phenomena, are known to have varying effects across regional, neighbourhood and personal space (Openshaw, 1984).

This integration suggests that if we are to continue drawing from the census to infer meaningful descriptions of neighbourhood influences on health, there is a need for greater inclusion of GIS-based methods for amalgamating scalable datasets. Consequently, the aforementioned methodologies, while capable of fulfilling this objective, may or may not be as capable of disentangling the hierarchical nature of social processes on individual health outcomes as multilevel modelling (Diez-Roux, 2000). So long as the GIScientist has access to data from multiple scales, however, these methods should be considered as viable and valuable approaches toward building more meaningful boundaries of social space.

It should be noted, however, that there are currently no standards, such as those used to legislate 'safe housing', defining what exactly a 'meaningful neighbourhood' entails. While GIS techniques help to conceptualize interactions between hierarchical data elements, the problem of how we differentiate a desirable from an undesirable neighbourhood will undoubtedly remain. Emergent research from 'mixed communities' studies is one area actively investigating how changes might be made in future housing developments to help minimize the polarities between neighbourhoods (Homes, 2006). There is ample potential for GIS to engage with ongoing developments in the use of geographically defined neighbourhoods to better understand health outcomes.

Optimizing scale for population health research and analysis

The challenges of rational neighbourhood definition are a larger part of a long-standing cross-discipline focus on the demonstrable affect of boundaries on empirical models of health inequalities. Statistical conclusions are susceptible to the magnitude of data aggregation and the way in which the units are subdivided whenever researchers work with data that was partitioned by administrative fiat. This problem, more formally referred to as the *modifiable areal unit problem* (MAUP), has long been the focus of attempts to disentangle the statistical effects that arise out of various partitioning of areal datasets – especially those derived from the census (Soobader and LeClere, 1999; Soobader et al., 2001; Martin et al., 2002; Schuurman et al., 2007). A complex description of its origins beyond a very basic summary are beyond the scope of this text and for further discussion the reader is encouraged to review (Openshaw, 1984; Fotheringham and Wong, 1991; Martin, 1998; Krieger et al., 2002).

Briefly, attempts to address the MAUP are primarily condensed into two distinct, but closely related problems. The first is the well-known scale effect. As the name implies, different statistical results are obtained from the same set of geographic units when they are organized into an increasingly higher (or lower) spatial extent (Openshaw, 1984). Not unrelated, the zoning effect refers to the effect of basing a hypothesis from areal geographic units, which, if subdivided differently *at the same spatial extent*, may or may not lead the investigator to conclude differently (Haynes et al., 2007).

Concern for patient or respondent confidentiality often necessitates that individual-level data is organized into areal geographic units. This reduces the spatial resolution of data and restricts the kinds of research questions that can be addressed – limiting the overall effectiveness of (geographical) health research. Until recently, however, many policy safeguards were somewhat irrelevant

as GIS-led investigations primarily employed choropleth techniques for mapping regional or intra-urban variations in health events (Rushton, 1998). Rushton (1998) further notes that this was largely due to the encoding of individual-level data into aggregate form, but also due in-part because researchers tended to request information that was in commensurate geographic units with other datasets. Today, however, public health organizations predominantly use electronic information systems capable of measuring the interaction between multiple exogenous variables and possible or probable individual health outcomes that may arise as a result of knowledge gained from their embedding. Increasingly, GIS is integrated into these platforms and used to amalgamate data from multiple scales into real or potential health outcome scenarios in real-time (Shershakov et al., 1996; Buckeridge et al., 2002; Sugimoto et al., 2007). Thus, at least on some levels, data availability and need would suggest that population health investigators break from reliance on aggregate data and return to working with data in point form.

Patient and respondent confidentiality prohibits many investigations from using the individual-level analyses techniques proposed by Rushton (1998) and Armstrong et al. (1999). However these concerns can be met by conducting fine-scale spatial analysis on individual-level data and then using statistical or geographic masking of the published output. Armstrong et al. (1999) proposed that geographic masks be used as an alternative approach to areal aggregation to insure privacy while also removing the artificial effects that boundaries impart on cluster detection analyses. Geographical masks add stochastic or deterministic noise to the original data by modifying the geographic coordinates of the data points, while avoiding areal aggregation. In addition to aggregation (a form of statistical masking), there are two main techniques for geographical masking: (1) affine transformations; and (2) random perturbation. Affine transformations translate, contract or expand a point pattern, while random perturbation randomly displaces a point along a line feature, or within a circle or other polygon defined relative to original point.

Kwan et al. (2004) examined the effectiveness of the three random perturbation masks using the following approach. Original point data were mapped and analyzed using several point pattern analysis methods; three radii (r) were tested (98 ft, 915 ft, and 4273 ft) to approximate the size in square feet of particular census areal units (census-block, census-block group, and census tract); and a weighting factor (w) was assigned using population density to introduce less error where population density is higher and the risk of disclosure is lower. The authors found '... a rather consistent trade-off between protection of geoprivacy and accuracy of analytical results. Increasing accuracy of results means introducing error and necessarily increases the risk of disclosure' (Kwan et al. 2004: 26). The authors conclude that the middle r (915 ft or approximately the size of census-block group) represents the optimum trade-off between accuracy and privacy protection for the specific area and data tested.

Both, Armstrong et al. (1999) and Kwan et al. (2004) point out that a geographic masking approach should be implemented with purpose-specific masks (i.e. each project will have a different spatial distribution of data points and local context that needs to be carefully considered to ensure confidentiality is maintained). Nonetheless, the overall conclusion drawn is that geographic masking offers a workable approach for protecting geoprivacy that still allows the use of geo-referenced individual-level data for social science research. These conclusions appear to be further substantiated within ongoing investigations that find the *scale* problem of the MAUP remains a more substantial problem than the *zoning* problem, thus possibly pointing further to the need to devise alternative models to conceptualize social and economic variation across population groups (Boulos et al., 2006).

Recent interest in moving toward a finer resolution analysis of population health outcomes

parallels an emerging cross-discipline critical engagement on the optimization of scale for health surveillance (Nakaya, 2000; Krieger et al., 2002; Haynes et al., 2007). Thus far, the evidence suggests that as scale increases so too does homogeneity, but that this relationship only becomes artefact as one moves away from the smaller administrative units into larger, municipal, postal or zip code catchments. Likewise, recent findings raised by Lebel et al. (2007) offer a somewhat dissenting opinion over concern for the zoning effect so long as geographical units are based on the consensus made by local actors, which could reasonably be seen to '... qualify their idiosyncrasy and be less vulnerable to the MAUP' (Lebel et al., 2007: 13).

Cross-disciplinary methodologies have rarely have moved beyond the manipulation of geographic units defined by the census to model neighbourhood influences on health – thus retaining the areal artifice now under scrutiny. The task ahead is to demonstrate if social gradients in health might be made more visible if modelled at both the level of the individual and the aggregate. In some respects this has been one of the central principles of multilevel modelling approaches, which would suggest that cluster detection models are an equally valuable or at least complementary technique to pursue further given the additional level of detail that mapping or more advanced spatial analyses would provide. However, such practices also run the risk of becoming too microscopic and could fail to construct clear 'big picture' accounts of the structural and social processes that manifest themselves across population groups. Somewhat paradoxically, the greatest strengths of boundaries is that they enable investigators to illustrate how social gradients play out across the landscape.

The role of expert knowledge in quantitative analysis

Earlier sections of this chapter have shown that local actors more frequently play a pivotal role in the design of digital and empirical representations of social boundaries than those provided by the census. Decision makers in health care are in a unique position to assess the conditions that influence population health given their educational and professional expertise. Additionally, many have the responsibility of overseeing the health outcomes of communities, to trace diseases outbreaks and provide direction and oversight in assisting community residents. In short medical health officers are an invaluable – and relatively untapped – information source for deriving indicators for characterizing relative health outcomes.

A recent study of core housing need in Vancouver, British Columbia, found that juxtaposing survey data with the census produced a more nuanced understanding of core housing need—which has historically been undercounted due to the nature of the coarsely aggregated census aggregation units (Fiedler et al., 2006). The authors' methodology provides strong evidence that surveys offer a similar complementary role for small-scale population studies of health inequalities. Extending this approach for constructing deprivation indices also provides researchers a new vantage point from which to assess the conditions that influence health outcomes as medical health officials may be in a better (or at least in as good as) position to comment on the specific importance of each factor (e.g. income, housing) as one moves from one community to the next. Moreover, depending on their level or expertise or political power, their inclusion may further link policy with evidence given a knowledgeable level of working knowledge of the day-to-day conditions that impact local health outcomes.

Following a similar protocol, both Rinner and Taranu (2006) and Bell et al. (2007) have suggested that more meaningful indicators of local context could be constructed from a multi-user approach if derived from a multi-criteria analysis (MCA) framework (Rinner and Taranu, 2006; Bell et al., 2007).

Rinner and Taranu (2006) suggested the use of the Analytical Hierarchy Process (AHP) to help offset problems associated with weighting a large number of sentinel indicators, weighting the criteria fairly and lessening the effects that different methods will generate different results (Rinner and Taranu, 2006). Similarly, Bell et al. (2007) proposed the use of the Order Weighted Average (OWA) as a validation technique of the variable weighting schemes chosen by local stakeholders, using the continuous scaling framework of the OWA to lessen the historic tension that arises from incorporating user-defined indicator weights (Bell et al., 2007).

Until recently, GIS-based MCA has primarily been utilized in solving site suitability conflicts (Eastman et al., 1995; Malczewski, 1999). MCA condenses complex problems involving multiple criteria (e.g. variables) into an optimal ranking of the best variable scenarios from which an alternative is chosen, typically by deriving alternatives based on the spatial arrangement of areas that meet the minimum or maximum of each of the evaluation criteria. In a GIS, this might involve a set of geographically defined criteria, such as soil grade, commercial or residential zoning, or hypsography and deriving alternatives for land use development based on the spatial arrangement of areas that exceed a minimum, maximum or critical value of each of the evaluation criteria. Weights can be assigned to the criteria according to the importance of each variable in deriving the alternative and each combination of the variables and their weights may have a more or less favourable influence on the final decision than another.

Both the AHP and OWA weighting procedures are conceptually distinct. AHP techniques are particularly well-suited at offsetting the challenges of assigning relative weights across a large number of indicators when each indicator is conceptualized as having a pair-wise relationship with all other factors (Saaty, 1980). Such an approach previously lent itself to establishing priorities in community health services need within the growing hierarchy of health data (Rinner and Taranu, 2006). Each pair-wise relationship has an ensuing reciprocal relationship (e.g. if income is twice as important as employment ratios for characterizing local health outcomes then the reciprocal must be true of the reversal). The AHP incorporates a confidence index to test whether the continuity between all comparisons corresponds with the patterns exhibited in the data.

Similarly, user-defined weights are inherently subjective and biased by personal opinion, thus challenging the validation of an unbiased effect or the extent that their value represents meaningful depictions of the data. OWA can balance the influence of user-defined weights against the values exhibited in the data using a variety of scaling factors that either restrict, release, or average out the weights originally assigned by the respondent (Jiang and Eastman, 2000). This framework allows the index to be simultaneously represented by the weighting parameters assigned by the experts but also introduces a mechanism to allow the data to enforce local variations where other socioeconomic characteristics may dominate.

The AHP and OWA models are two strategies for integrating local knowledge from key actors in constructing population-level indices of relative health outcomes while also including mechanisms to gauge or modify the ensuing challenges of incorporating user-defined weights.

An ongoing shortcoming of singularly relying on raw data for building 'big picture' views of population health status has been the lack of mechanisms to validate *why* the indicator was assigned its relative importance or how variable interactions after aggregation will either intensify or attenuate the final deprivation score (Noble et al., 2006). MCA provides a number of solutions for these limitations while also introducing additional mechanisms to contextualize what has previously been a very insular construction process.

Rarely, however, have census-based measures of socioeconomic inequality based on data obtained from small- or large-scale surveys of local actors, owing in large part to critique stemming from earlier attempts (Carr-Hill and Sheldon, 1991; Davey-Smith, 1991). Current strategies, rather, tend to be derived from variations of principal component analysis. The growing affinity toward data reduction models is due in part to the inclusion of expansive datasets such as the census. There is a rather parallel association between the number of variables included in the index and the potential for data collinearity, thus yielding a greater likelihood of unnecessary complexity and possibly confounding the results. Additionally, these methods alleviate the need for individuals to ascribe importance to one indicator over the next, thereby decreasing bias.

In certain respects, however, the AHP method may not completely curtail pressures to eliminate or reduce bias from the construction process as there is no mechanism that prevents the expert from going ahead with a decision even though the pair-wise groupings selected by the expert are incongruent with the internal structure of the data. While the OWA model eliminates this problem as both the experts *and the data* weight the individual criteria, ascribing meaning to the various weighting combinations may equally be seen as a somewhat dubious task. Combined, these mutually reinforcing caveats may detract others from moving toward this type of decision model, though it is presumable that further integrating health and policy experts into the research process would considerably outweigh these limitations. Nonetheless, matching expansive datasets with local expert knowledge sources has the potential to amalgamate the rich level of detail of the 'mixed methods' approach popularized in other health research models with the traditionally broad deprivation models, but these approaches are only recently beginning to receive wider attention as a viable and valuable means for quantifying gradients in health outcomes.

CASE STUDY

Building local deprivation indices using Order Weighted Average (OWA) MCA framework

In this section we illustrate a case study using an OWA multi-criteria model for constructing area-based deprivation indicators (ABDI) of population socioeconomic status (SES). The case study illustrates the use of available protocols for visualizing and validating subjective and objective variable strategies associated with quantifying socioeconomic gradients in health outcomes when they are derived from expert group surveys. Our study draws on a survey distributed to provincial health officials in Canada on the social and economic factors that best characterize relative health outcomes. A Canadian city is used to illustrate the different weighting scenarios that can be assigned to the same variables selected by the panel.

Methods background

OWA is a unique type of MCA weighting strategies in that it incorporates a dual weighting strategy; one local (order weights) and one global. The global weights are based on pre-existing scores assigned by consensus from the expert group (e.g. tallying up the frequency of their responses for each variable and scaling these scores across 100 per cent). The local, or order weights, rather, are assigned after the global weights and are also allowed to change as one moves from one census area to the next. For example, the highest weighted variable assigned by the expert groups (e.g. education) is only assigned the highest local weight if the value of the education variable is larger than all other n variables within a particular census unit. Otherwise, the highest local weight is assigned to the weighted variable with the largest value. This is an important distinction as it implies that weights assigned by the experts are only maintained when a census unit reflects the same hierarchical proportions of all n variables. Otherwise, each census unit is assigned an additional weight based on the proportional arrangement of the individual variables.

For example, in Census Tract (CT) 002 in Figure 8.1 the three criteria to be evaluated are unemployment rates, the proportion of lone parent families, and average income. Assuming that each of the variables was ranked by an expert according to its importance in characterizing relative health outcomes, the product of their weights with the standardized values results in 0.6, 0.2, 0.5, respectively. If the associated local weights are 0.5, 0.3, 0.2, then the value for CT 002 if the expert wished to *maximize* the level of socioeconomic deprivation would be $(0.6 \times 0.5) + (0.2 \times 0.2) + (0.5 \times 0.3) = 0.49$. Similarly, in certain instances it may be desirable to keep only the highest or lowest ranked variable from a series on n variables selected by a group of health experts such that the deprivation score is either maximized (MAX) or minimized (MIN) according to a single variable. Using the same four criteria as the example above, the results from a MAX OWA decision model would carry the local weights [1, 0, 0] and in this particular case the CT deprivation score would be represented by the areas employment rate. Conversely, the MIN OWA model would carry the local weights [0, 0, 1] and would be represented by the proportion of lone parent families. Although the objective in many health studies is to identify populations who experience multiple deprivation the MIN and MAX decision models provide a window to observe if certain areas tend to exhibit similar socioeconomic conditions that stand out more than others. These scenarios change depending on: (1) how confident one is that the weights assigned by the experts also reflect the structure of the data; and (2) how much flexibility the decision maker wishes to assign to local nuance. In this sense, the OWA model enables both the experts *and the data* to weight the individual criteria.

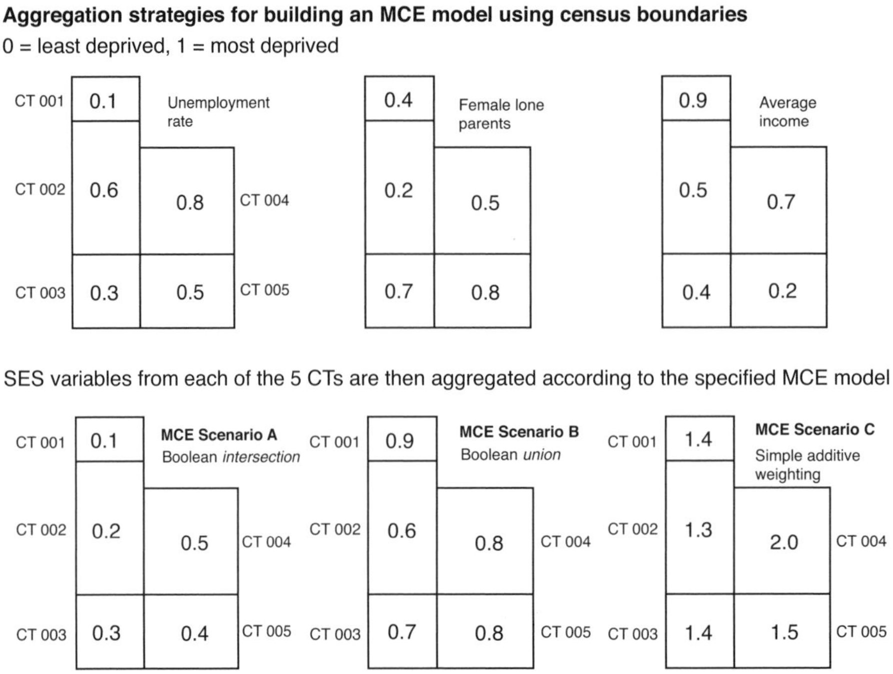

Aggregation strategies for building an MCE model using census boundaries

0 = least deprived, 1 = most deprived

SES variables from each of the 5 CTs are then aggregated according to the specified MCE model

Figure 8.1   Three MCE variable aggregation strategies – note unemployment rate, lone parent and average income values are shown as tied to separate geographies for purposes of clarity

Similar examples are provided in greater detail in Table 8.1.

Note that the MIN OWA model is synonymous to the risk-adverse Boolean *intersection* model whereby the deprivation score is based on the lowest of the n criteria. The MAX OWA model, conversely, is synonymous to the risk-seeking Boolean *union* model whereby the deprivation score is selected using the largest of the n criteria. The continuous scaling mechanism of the OWA model is bounded by both Boolean crisp sets with a full trade-off (averaging) of the decision criteria weights located in between. The averaging mechanism will have a neutral effect on the global weights as each local weight is identical. Thus, the full trade-off OWA model provides a window to observe the original deprivation index scores as chosen by the experts.

Each OWA weighting phase is classified using measures of ANDness, ORness and

TRADE-OFF associated with the set of criteria (Jiang and Eastman, 2000). The three measures are calculated as follows:

$$ANDness(w) = \frac{1}{n-1}\sum_r (n-r)w_r$$

$$ORness = 1 - ANDness$$

$$TradeOff(w) = 1 - \left[\frac{n\sum_r (w_r - 1/n)^2}{n-1}\right]^{0.5}$$

where n is the number of criteria, r is the position of each criterion, and w_r is the importance assigned to the particular criterion, r (Malczewski, 1999). As Table 8.2 illustrates there is no limit to the number of variables that can be included in the OWA, nor is there any predefined theory as to how far each of the scaling increments between variable weights should be placed although logic should dictate that as more variables

Table 8.1   Order weights are assigned on an area-by-area basis and their rank order varies according the individual criteria values in each census boundary.

Census tract 0011				Census tract 0012			
	Scenario 1 w^a = [1,0,0]				Scenario 1 w^a = [1,0,0]		
Census indicator	x_i	w^a	Value	Census indicator	x_i	w^a	Value
Income	0.37	0	0	Income	0.15	1	0.15
Employment	0.22	1	0.33	Employment	0.81	0	0
Tenancy	0.61	0	0	Tenancy	0.35	0	0
	Scenario 1 w^b = 0.5,0.3,0.2				Scenario 1 w^b = 0.5,0.3,0.2		
Census indicator	x_i	w^b	Value	Census indicator	x_i	w^b	Value
Income	0.37	0.3	0.11	Income	0.15	0.5	0.07
Employment	0.22	0.5	0.11	Employment	0.81	0.2	0.16
Tenancy	0.61	0.2	0.12	Tenancy	0.35	0.3	0.10
	Scenario 1 w^c = [0,0,1]				Scenario 1 w^c = [0,0,1]		
Census indicator	x_i	w^c	Value	Census indicator	x_i	w^c	Value
Income	0.37	0	0	Income	0.15	0	0
Employment	0.22	0	0	Employment	0.81	1	0.81
Tenancy	0.61	1	0.61	Tenancy	0.35	0	0

Source: Adapted from Malczewski (1999).

are added to the equation the significance of the weights will lessen.

Data

A web-survey was administered to a group of medical health officers asking them to comment on the social and economic variables selected from the census that best characterize relative health outcomes in urban areas throughout a Canadian province. Each variable was obtained from a master list of 21 census variables and were selected based

on the frequency of the expert responses. The corresponding global weights (listed in parentheses) were similarly assigned to the seven variables based on the frequency of expert responses and standardized to sum to 100 per cent. The OWA model was constructed from the seven census indicators that received the greatest number of responses from the expert panel, including: population without a high school diploma (0.250), unemployment rate (0.214), population with a university degree (0.179), lone parent families (0.143), average income (0.089), home ownership (0.089) and the employment ratio (0.036).

Table 8.2   Various weighting scenarios using the OWA decision model

Operator	Order weights	ANDness	Orness	Trade-off
MIN (Boolean AND)	1, 0, 0, 0	1	0	0
	0.6, 0.25, 0.1, 0.05	0.79	0.21	0.5
	0.4, 0.3, 0.2, 0.1	0.66	0.34	0.74
Trade off (Avg)	0.25, 0.25, 0.25, 0.25	0.5	0.5	1
	0.1, 0.2, 0.3, 0.4	0.33	0.67	0.74
	0.05, 0.1, 0.25, 0.6	0.20	0.80	0.5
MAX (Boolean OR)	0, 0, 0, 1	0	1	0

Analysis

The seven indicators are represented as the criteria for the OWA model and constrained by the Boolean union and intersection weighting parameters. The intersection, or *AND* ($\cap$) OWA model assigns an order weight of 1 to the indicator within each census unit that has the lowest of the seven scores and a 0 to the remaining variables. In other words, the full *intersection* is synonymous to viewing the decision outcome as 'a chain is only as strong as its weakest link', and SES is evaluated according to variable that produces the 'least deprived' area score out of the seven factors within its own geography. The union, or OR ($\cup$) OWA model assigns an order weight of 1 to the indicator within each census unit that produces the highest area score of the seven factors and a 0 to all subsequent variables. Five additional criteria scenarios were constructed using different local weighting schemas, four of which were variations of the Boolean approach, but also included additional criteria. The final model was a full trade-off and the local weights were averaged across each of the seven variables. The order weights are illustrated in Table 8.3.

Results from the analysis are shown in Figure 8.2. The core OWA model most reflective of the original variable weights assigned by the expert group frequency responses is the full trade-off model (0.142, 0.142, 0.142, 0.142, 0.142, 0.142, 0.142). Each variation towards either the full

intersection [1, 0, 0, 0, 0, 0, 0] or full union [0, 0, 0, 0, 0, 0, 1] model assigns greater significance to the individual census areas values and less significance to the order assigned by the expert panel. The decision analyst controls the number and value associated with the local weights. Although there is no underlying framework that governs the number of variables or the proportional value assigned to each criteria, it is generally followed that the weights sum to 100 per cent and increase/decrease in rank order as they approach either the full ANDness or ORness.

Results and discussion

In our case study the census areas classified as the 'most deprived' remain consistent regardless of the weight attributed to the criteria and the number of criteria used to model areal SES. This trend is reversed when viewing areas coded as the 'least deprived'. We can see that trends toward a more definitive gap between the least and most deprived areas grows along the east–west axis when more emphasis is placed on either the full averaging and full union weighting scenarios and becomes less definitive as greater decision uncertainty is placed on the expert group variable selections. Thus, visualizing the various modelling scenarios offers some indication that the weighting parameters selected by the expert panel are not incongruous with way that their relevance appears to be

Table 8.3 OWA local (order) weighting scenarios assigned to the expert scores

Operator	Order weights	ANDness	Orness	Trade-off
MIN (Boolean AND)	1, 0, 0, 0, 0, 0, 0	1	0	0
	.7, .15, .1, .05	0.92	0.08	0.35
	.4, .25, .15, .1, .05, .025, .025	0.78	0.22	0.63
Trade off (Avg)	.142, .142, .142, .142, .142, .142, .142	0.5	0.5	1
	.025, .025, .05, .1, .15, .25, .4	0.22	0.78	0.63
	.05, .1, .15, .7	0.08	0.92	0.35
MAX (Boolean OR)	0, 0, 0, 0, 0, 0, 1	0	1	0

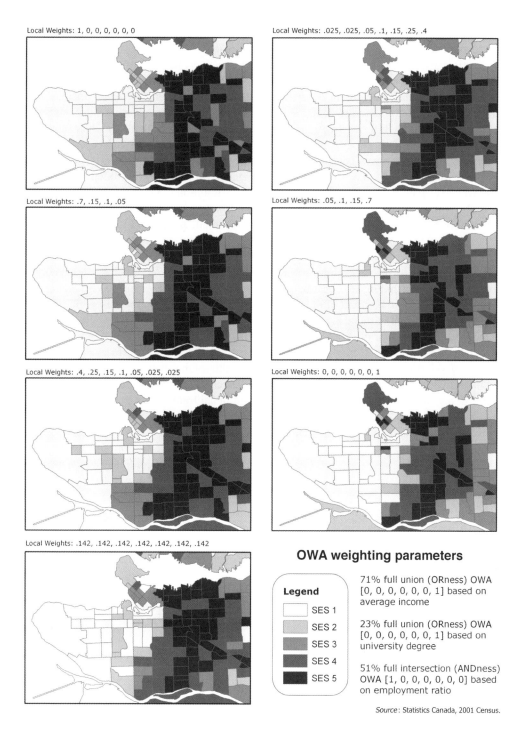

Figure 8.2   **Map of various OWA comparisons based on different combination of local and global weights (SES 1 = least deprived quintile, SES 5 = most deprived quintile).**

apportioned in the population. Simple pair-wise tests can be used to determine if there are statistically significant differences between different weighting scenarios, as well contrasting each weighting scenario against different health outcomes data.

Similar to classic ABDI construction, the MCA framework allows experts to assign weights to the indicator variables weights and each combination of the variables and their weights may have a more or less favourable influence on the final decision than another. However, the MCA framework offers a greater level of transparency in the construction process. This framework lends itself to a number of research areas within population health, including (1) constructing sensitivity analyses of the impact of indicator strength across neighbourhoods, (2) deter-mining what combination of different varia-ble weighting scenarios will produce higher or lower deprivation scores, (3) measuring how sensitive various indicator weighting scenarios are to the index variables, and (4) testing the validity of a deprivation index constructed from health policy administrators.

CONCLUSION

We have provided a broad background to population health and GIS including a his-tory and description of many practices and their justification. A case study was presented as a means of illustrating – in concrete terms – the challenges and potential of this disciplinary intersection. Techniques associ-ated with spatial analysis are far more sophis-ticated than their inclusion in current population health studies and there is much future potential for GIS to serve as a means of analysis and communication of health patterns and their graded nature.

At present, evidence illustrating social gradients in health has been largely con-structed from a diverse mesh of frameworks derived from either multivariate or multilevel regression models. Hierarchical approaches

are increasingly used to explore many aspects of 'place' linked to health inequalities; their advantage is that they avoid problems arising from aggregation bias and hidden clustering stemming from areal effects. Increasingly, however, these frameworks, as they currently stand, are still limited by their common reliance on administrative data and continue to be criticized in their ability to represent meaningful depictions of social space. While these traditional mapping and hierarchical models are often only capable of providing very broad, population-level hypotheses of why some people are healthier than others, they nevertheless contribute to understanding health inequalities and their graded nature.

One of the chief virtues of visualizing data in graphic form is that it makes the informa-tion more accessible; indeed the ability of GIS to represent social and physical proc-esses of the Earth's surface is one of the strengths of the technology. Population health researchers are currently expanding their traditional frameworks and methodologies to include GIS and quickly finding an array of methodological and conceptual benefits that tailoring this merger affords. However there remains ample work at this research intersec-tion as there has been little 'spatial' analysis in any of the GIS methods commonly used thus far to identify social gradients in health outcomes. One approach is to incorporate spatial autocorrelation statistics to better account for the contiguity or spatial connec-tion between areas with similar or dissimi-lar qualities. More complicated techniques involving geographically weighted regres-sion to control for the confounding effects of location and better account for the changing spatial pattern of health outcomes can also be constructed (Fotheringham et al., 2002). Both approaches can be brought together within the current multilevel modelling framework or used in conjunction with any one of the techniques highlighted in this chapter. This adaptation is one of many strengths of GIS as it can often build on top of traditional ana-lytic methods while recognizing that these events might also be spatially linked. Such approaches will play a key part in future development of spatial analysis techniques for linking broader social influences to individual health outcomes.

Geoprivacy is another pending issue that must continue to be addressed as GIS and health research intersect more closely. As individual-level health data become increasingly available, the underlying privacy issues that animated GIS research to date will be exacerbated. Moreover, this shift will likely continue to parallel the recent surge in constructing spatial point process models from individual-level health data and growing trends to reduce our reliance on areal units to quantify variations in health status. While event mapping is often more revealing of the distribution of disease patterns which would otherwise be veiled if modelled using aggregate census data, neither individual nor aggregate data alone – as is often illustrated from multilevel modelling – account for the graded nature of health outcomes. Future research applying more complex individual-level interactions while also drawing linkages of this effect to wider social processes merits particular attention and is a field which will undoubtedly come to rely on geomasking techniques that can ensure patient or respondent anonymity.

Ultimately GIS and population health research is designed to contribute to evidence-based policies. At present there is limited transfer of GIS findings to health administrators. Geographers have a mandate to pursue development of broad, policy-relevant analysis from individual level data and analysis – and its *effective dissemination*. In addition, there is a need for GIS specialists to work with domain experts in health in order to effect a more thorough technology transfer. Benefits of this cross-fertilization potentially include better geoprivacy methods, more sophisticated methods of maintaining health surveillance systems, and more nuanced methods of understanding the spatial pattern of health outcomes. GIS is poised to make a significant contribution to this research domain and has considerable potential to increase our understanding of the spatial and graded nature of population health.

REFERENCES

Armstrong, M.P., Rushton, G. and Zimmerman, D.L. (1999) 'Geographically masking health data to preserve confidentiality', *Statistics in Medicine*, 18(5): 497–525.

Aronson, R.E., Wallis, A.B., O'Campo, P.J. and Schafer, P. (2007) 'Neighborhood mapping and evaluation: A methodology for participatory community health initiatives', *Maternal and Child Health Journal*, 11(4): 373–83.

Bailey, T.C. and Gatrell, A.C. (1995) *Interactive Spatial Data Analysis.* Harlow: Longman Group.

Bell, N., Schuurman, N. and Hayes M.V. (2007) 'Using GIS-based methods of multicriteria analysis to construct socio-economic deprivation indices', *International Journal of Health Geographics*, 6(17): np.

Beral, V., Roman, E. and Martin, B. (eds) (1993) *Childhood Cancer and Nuclear Installations.* London: BMJ Publishing Group.

Black, D., Townsend, P. and Davidson, N. (1982) *Inequalities in Health: The Black Report.* Harmondsworth, Middlesex: Penguin Books.

Boulos, M.N.K., Cai, Q., Padget, J.A. and Rushton, G. (2006) 'Using software agents to preserve individual health data confidentiality in micro-scale geographical analyses', *Journal of Biomedical Informatics*, 39(2): 160–70.

Buckeridge, D.L., Mason, R., Robertson, A., Frank, J., Glazier, R., Purdon, L., Amrhein, C.G., Chaudhuri, N., Fuller-Thomson, E., Gozdyra, P., Hulchanski, D., Moldofsky, B., Thompson, M. and Wright, R. (2002) 'Making health data maps: A case study of a community/university research collaboration', *Social Science and Medicine*, 55(7): 1189–206.

Carr-Hill, R. and Sheldon, R. (1991) 'Designing a deprivation payment for general practitioners: The UPA (8) wonderland', *British Medical Journal*, 302: 393–6.

Carstairs, V. (1989) 'Deprivation: Explaining differences in mortality between Scotland and England and wales', *British Medical Journal*, 299: 886–9.

Cliff, A.D., Haggett, P. and Smallman-Raynor M. (2004) *World Atlas of Epidemic Diseases.* London: Oxford University Press.

Collins, P. and Hayes, M.V. (2007) 'Twenty years since Ottawa and Epp: Researchers' reflections on challenges, gains and future prospects for reducing health inequities in Canada', *Health Promotion International*, 22: 337–45.

Crampton, J.W. (2004) 'GIS and geographic governance: Reconstructing the choropleth map', *Cartographica*, 39(1): 41–53.

Croner, C.M., Sperling, J. and Broome F.R. (1996) 'Geographic information systems (GIS): New perspectives in understanding human health and environmental relationships', *Statistics in Medicine*, 15(17/18): 1961–77.

Davey-Smith, G. (1991) 'Second thoughts on the Jarman index – claims being made for the under-privileged area score are unproved', *British Medical Journal*, 302: 359–60.

Diez-Roux, A., Nieto, F., Muntaner, C., Tyroler, H.A. and Comstock, G.W. (1997) 'Neighborhood environments and coronary heart disease: A multilevel analaysis', *American Journal of Epidemiology*, 146: 48–63.

Diez-Roux, A.V. (2000) 'Multilevel analysis in public health research', *Annual Review of Public Health*, 21: 171–92.

Dorling, D. (1995) *A New Social Atlas of Britain.* Chichester: John Wiley & Sons.

Dunn, J.R. (2002) 'Housing and inequalities in health: A study of socioeconomic dimensions of housing and self reported health from a survey of Vancouver residents', *Journal of Epidemiology and Community Health*, 56(9): 671–81.

Dunn, J.R. and Hayes, M.V. (2000) 'Social inequality, population health, and housing: A study of two Vancouver neighbourhoods', *Social Science and Medicine*, 51(4): 563–87.

Durkheim, E. (1952) *Suicide: A Study in Sociology* [tr. by Spalding J, Simpson G]. London: Routledge and Kegan Paul.

Eastman, R., Jin, W., Kyem, P. and Toledano, J. (1995) 'Raster procedures for multi-criteria/multi-objective decisions', *Photogrammetric Engineering and Remote Sensing*, 61: 539–47.

Elliott, P. and Wartenberg, D. (2004) 'Spatial epidemiology: Current approaches and future challenges', *Environmental Health Perspectives*, 112(9): 998–1006.

Evans, R.G., Barer, M.L. and Marmor, T.R. (eds) (1994) *Why are Some People Healthy and Others Not?* New York: Aldine de Gruyter.

Fiedler, R., Schuurman, N. and Hyndman, J. (2006) 'Improving census-based socioeconomic GIS for public policy: Recent immigrants, spatially concentrated poverty and housing need in vancouver', *Acme*, 4(1): 145–71.

Fotheringham, A.S., Charlton, M. and Brunsdon, C. (2002) *Geographically Weighted Regression: The Analysis of Spatially Varying Relationships.* Chichester: Wiley.

Fotheringham, A.S. and Wong, D.W.S. (1991) 'The modifiable areal unit problem in multivariate statistical-analysis', *Environment and Planning A*, 23(7): 1025–44.

Frohlich, N. and Mustard, C. (1996) 'A regional comparison of socioeconomic and health indices in a Canadian province', *Social Science and Medicine*, 42(9): 1273–81.

Gatrell, A.C., Popay, J. and Thomas, C. (2004) 'Mapping the determinants of health inequalities in social space: Can Bourdieu help us?', *Health and Place*, 10(3): 245–57.

Hayes, M.V. (1994) 'Evidence, determinants of health and population epidemiology: Humming the tune, learning the lyrics'. In M.V. Hayes, L.T. Foster and H.D. Foster (eds), *The Determinants of Population Health – A Critical Assessment.* Victoria: University of Victoria. pp. 121–34.

Hayes, M.V. (2004) 'Gradients, inequality and the social geography of health'. In P. Boyle, S. Curtis, E. Graham and E. Moore (eds), *The Geography of Health Inequalities in the Developed World.* Aldershot: Ashgate. pp. 371–88.

Haynes, R., Daras, K., Reading, R. and Jones, A. (2007) 'Modifiable neighbourhood units, zone design and residents perceptions', *Health and Place*, 13(4): 812–25.

Hertzman, C. (1999) 'Population health and human development'. In D.P. Keating and C. Hertzman (eds), *Developmental Health and the Wealth of Nations.* New York: Guilford.

Homes, C. (2006) *Mixed Communities: Success and Sustainability.* York: Joseph Rowntree Foundation.

Jiang, H. and Eastman, R. (2000) 'Application of fuzzy measures in multi-criteria evaluation in GIS', *Int J of Geographic Information Systems*, 14: 173–84.

Kawachi, I., Kennedy, B.P. and Glass, R. (1999) 'Social capital and self-rated health: A contextual analysis', *American Journal of Public Health*, 89(8): 1187–93.

Keating, D.P. and Hertzman, C. (eds) (1999) 'Population health and human development', *Developmental Health and the Wealth of Nations.* New York: Guilford.

Kennedy, B.P., Kawachi, I., Glass, R. and Prothrow-Stith, D. (1998) 'Income distribution, socioeconomic status, and self rated health in the United States: Multilevel analysis', *British Medical Journal*, 317(7163): 917–21.

Krieger, N., Chen, J.T., Waterman, P.D., Soobader, M.J., Subramanian, S.V. and Carson, R. (2002) 'Geocoding and monitoring of US socioeconomic inequalities in mortality and cancer incidence: Does the choice of area-based measure and geographic level matter? The public health disparities geocoding project', *American Journal of Epidemiology*, 156(5): 471–82.

Krieger, N., Williams, D.R. and Moss, N.E. (1997) 'Measuring social class in US public health research: Concepts, methodologies, and guidelines', *Annual Review of Public Health*, 18: 341–78.

Kwan, M.-P., Casas, I. and Schmitz, B.C. (2004) 'Protection of Geoprivacy and accuracy of spatial information: How effective are geographical masks?', *Cartographica*, 39(2): 15–28.

Lawson, A. and Denison, D.G.T. (eds) (2002) *Spatial Cluster Modelling*. Boca Raton, FL: Chapman and Hall/CRC.

Lebel, A., Pampalon, R. and Villeneuve, P.Y. (2007) 'A multi-perspective approach for defining neighbourhood units in the context of a study on health inequalities in the Quebec City region', *International Journal of Health Geographics*, 6: 27.

Longley, P. (2003) 'Geographical information systems: Developments in socio-economic data infrastructures', *Progress in Human Geography*, 27(1): 114–21.

Macintyre, S., Ellaway, A. and Cummins, S. (2002) 'Place effects on health: How can we conceptualise, operationalise and measure them?', *Social Science and Medicine*, 55(1): 125–39.

Macintyre, S., Maciver, S. and Sooman, A. (1993) 'Area, class and health – should we be focusing on places or people', *Journal of Social Policy*, 22: 213–34.

Malczewski, J. (1999) *GIS and Multicriteria Decision Analysis*. New York: John Wiley & Sons.

Marmot, M. and Wilkinson, R. (2006) *Social Determinants of Health*. Oxford: Oxford University Press.

Marmot, M.G. (1986) 'Social inequalities in mortality: The social environment'. In R.G. Wilkinson (ed.), *Class and Health: Research and Longitudinal Data*. London: Tavistock. pp. 21–33.

Marmot, M.G., Davey Smith, G., Stansfeld, S., Patel, C., North, F., Head, J., White, L., Brunner, E. and Feeney, A. (1991) 'Health inequalities among British civil servants: The whitehall II study', *Lancet*, 337: 1387–93.

Marshall, R.J. (1991) 'A review of methods for the statistical-analysis of spatial patterns of disease', *Journal of the Royal Statistical Society Series a-Statistics in Society*, 154: 421–41.

Martin, D. (1998) 'Optimizing census geography: The separation of collection and output geographies', *International Journal of Geographical Information Science*, 12(7): 673–85.

Martin, D., Dorling, D. and Mitchell, R., (2002) 'Linking censuses through time: Problems and solutions', *Area*, 34(1): 82–91.

Matthew, G.K. (1992) 'Health and environment: The significance of chemicals and radiation'. In P. Elliott, J. Cuzick, D. English and R. Stern (eds), *Geographical and Environmental Epidemiology: Methods for Small-Area Studies*. New York, Oxford University Press. pp. 22–34.

Mitchell, R., Dorling, D. and Shaw, M. (2002) 'Population production and modelling mortality – an application of geographic information systems in health inequalities research', *Health and Place*, 8(1): 15–24.

Mustard, J.R. and Frank, J. (1994) 'The determinants of health'. In M.V. Hayes, L.T. Foster and H.D. Foster (eds), *The Determinants of Population Health: A Critical Assessment*. Victoria: University of Victoria.

Nakaya, T. (2000) 'An information statistical approach to the modifiable areal unit problem in incidence rate maps', *Environment and Planning A*, 32(1): 91–109.

Noble, M., Wright, G., Smith, G. and Dibben, C. (2006) 'Measuring multiple deprivation at the small-area level', *Environment and Planning A*, 38(1): 169–85.

Nuckols, J.R., Ward, M.H. and Jarup, L. (2004) 'Using geographic information systems for exposure assessment in environmental epidemiology studies', *Environmental Health Perspectives*, 112(9): 1007–15.

Oliver, L.N., Dunn, J.R., Kohen, D.E. and Hertzman, C. (2007) 'Do neighbourhoods influence the readiness to learn of kindergarten children in Vancouver? A multilevel analysis of neighbourhood effects', *Environment and Planning A*, 39(4): 848–68.

Openshaw, S. (1984) 'Ecological fallacies and the analysis of areal census-data', *Environment and Planning A*, 16(1): 17–31.

Openshaw, S. (1984) 'The modifiable areal unit problem', *Concepts and Techniques in Modern Geography*, p. 38.

Pampalon, R. and Raymond, G. (2000) 'A deprivation index for health and welfare planning in Quebec', *Chronic Diseases in Canada*, 21(3): 104–13.

Ricketts, T.C. (2003) 'Geographic information systems and public health', *Annual Review of Public Health*, 24: 1–6.

Rinner, C. and Taranu, J.P. (2006) 'Map-based exploratory evaluation of non-medical determinants of population health', *Transactions in GIS*, 10(4): 633–49.

Ross, N.A., Tremblay, S. and Graham, K. (2004) 'Neighbourhood influences on health in montréal, Canada', *Social Science and Medicine*, 59: 1485–94.

Ross, N.A., Wolfson, M.C., Berthelot, J.M. and Dunn, J.R. (2004) 'Why is mortality higher in unequal societies? Interpreting income inequality and mortality in Canada and the United States'. In P. Boyle, S. Curtis, E. Graham and E. Moore (eds), *The Geography of Health Inequalities in the Developed World*. Aldershot: Ashgate. pp. 103–28.

Ross, N.A., Wolfson, M.C. and Dunn, J.R. (2001) 'Why is mortality higher in unequal societies? Interpreting income inequality and mortality in Canada and the United States', *The Geography of Health Inequalities in the Developed World*. Boyle: Curtis, Gatrell, Graham and Moore.

Rushton, G. (1998) 'Improving the geographic basis of health surveillance using GIS'. In A.C. Gatrell and M. Löytönen (eds), *GIS and Health*. London: Taylor & Francis. pp. 63–80.

Saaty, T. (1980) *The Analytical Hierarchy Process*. New York: McGraw Hill International.

Salmond, C., Crampton, P., King, P. and Waldegrave, C. (2006) 'NZiDep: A New Zealand index of socioeconomic deprivation for individuals', *Social Science and Medicine*, 62(6): 1474–85.

Schuurman, N., Bell, N., Dunn, J.R. and Oliver, L. (2007) 'Deprivation indices, population health and geography: An evaluation of the spatial effectiveness of indices at multiple scales', *Journal of Urban Health*, 84: 591–603.

Shershakov, V.M., Baranov, A.Y., Borodin, R.V., Golubenkov, A.V., Godko, A.M., Kosykh, V.S., Korenev, A.I. and Meleshkin, M.A. (1996) 'Informatics support for analysing the radiological impact of areas affected by the Chernobyl accident', *Radiation Protection Dosimetry*, 64(1–2): 149–55.

Soobader, M.J. and LeClere, F.B. (1999) 'Aggregation and the measurement of income inequality: Effects on morbidity', *Social Science and Medicine*, 48(6): 733–44.

Soobader, M.J., LeClere, F.B., Hadden, W. and Maury, B. (2001) 'Using aggregate geographic data to proxy individual socioeconomic status: Does size matter?', *American Journal of Public Health*, 91(4): 632–6.

Stafford, M., Bartley, M., Mitchell, R. and Marmot, M. (2001) 'Characteristics of individuals and characteristics of areas: Investigating their influence on health in the Whitehall II study', *Health and Place*, 7(2): 117–29.

Statistics Canada (2003) *2001 Census: Aboriginal Peoples of Canada: A Demographic Profile*. Statistics Canada.

Sugimoto, J.D., Labrique, A.B., Ahmad, S., Rashid, M., Klemm, R.D.W., Christian, P. and West, K.P. (2007) 'Development and management of a geographic information system for health research in a developing-country setting: A case study from Bangladesh', *Journal of Health Population and Nutrition*, 25(4): 436–47.

Syme, J.L. (1994) 'The social environment and health', *Daedalus,* 94(123): 79–86.

Szwarcwald, C.L., Bastos, F.I., Barcellos, C., Pina, M.D. and Esteves, M.A.P. (2000) 'Health conditions and residential concentration of poverty: A study in Rio de Janeiro, Brazil', *Journal of Epidemiology and Community Health*, 54(7): 530–6.

Tarlov, A. (1996) 'Social determinants of health: The sociobiological translation'. In D. Blane, E. Brunner and R. Wilkinson (eds), *Health and Social Organization: Towards a Health Policy for the Twenty-First Century*. London: Routledge. pp. 71–93.

Taylor, S.M. (1993) 'Geography of urban health'. In L.S. Bourne and D.F. Ley (eds), *The Changing Social Geography of Canadian Cities*. Montreal, McGill-Queen's University Press.

Townsend, P. (1978) 'Deprivation', *Journal of Social Policy,* 16: 125–46.

Townsend, P., Phillimore, P. and Beattie, A. (1987) *Health and Deprivation: Inequality and the North*. London: Croom Helm.

Wheeler, S.M. (2008) 'The evolution of built landscapes in metropolitan regions', *Journal of Planning Education and Research*, 27(4): 400–16.

Wiggins, R.D., Joshi, H., Bartley, M., Gleave, S., Lynch, K. and Cullis, A. (2002) 'Place and personal circumstances in a multilevel account of women's long-term illness', *Social Science and Medicine*, 54(5): 827–38.

Wilkinson, R.G. (1996) *Unhealthy Societies: The Afflictions of Inequality*. London: Routledge.

Wilkinson, R.G. and Pickett, K.E. (2006) 'Income inequality and population health: A review and explanation of the evidence', *Social Science and Medicine*, 62(7): 1768–84.

Yen, I.H. and Syme S.L. (1999) 'The social environment and health: A discussion of the epidemiologic literature', *Annual Review of Public Health*, 20: 287–308.

9

Cogito Ergo Mobilis Sum: The Impact of Location-Based Services on Our Mobile Lives

Martin Raubal

INTRODUCTION

Over the most recent decades most of the world's civilization has turned into a *mobile information society*. Increased mobility has impacted various areas, such as travel and tourism, communication, social behavior, and the environment. Mobile persons have to face and solve novel spatiotemporal problems, such as during navigation or multimodal trip planning. Finding one's way from the airport to a hotel in an unfamiliar city is not trivial and requires a number of decisions to be made on the spot (Rüetschi and Timpf, 2005; Winter et al., 2001): Do I take the bus, train, or taxi into the city? Where do I buy my tickets? Where and when do I change to the subway? Which train and direction do I take? Where do I exit the subway station?

Location-based services (LBS) support users during their mobile decision making. They are information services that are sensitive to the location of a mobile user and relate their location to the surrounding environment, which in turn provides location-based information to facilitate the successful completion of spatiotemporal tasks. For example, LBS inform clients about the locations of nearby hotels, restaurants, and cultural sites; they support users of public transport systems; and they help people to locate nearby friends. They also affect society as a whole through their capabilities for tracking people's behavior in space and time, location-based social networking, or potential privacy invasion.

LBS emerged in part due to a general shift in geographic information science (GIScience) from *Big GIS* to *Small GI* (Frank, 1999). In the past, geographic information systems (GIS) were mainly used by large organizations, such as public utility companies, regional planning offices, and highway departments, to support them in their decision-making processes. These organizations collected the necessary data, managed them in their own databases, and produced reports and maps for various internal uses. Nowadays, different providers offer services for geospatial problem solving and by that means sell geographic information (GI) to many users in small quantities. Although the search for a "killer application" is ongoing, the use of LBS in various application areas has risen dramatically over the years and in the longer term, many expect the technology to impact our lives in unpredictable ways, similar to the initial development of the Internet (Jensen et al., 2002; Turner and Forrest, 2008). Based on the multidisciplinary nature of location-based services – involving GIScience, the cognitive sciences, computer science, and the social sciences – research in these fields will contribute to achieving the highest objective for location-based services, namely improving their utility to help people in making good decisions in their mobile everyday lives (Raper et al., 2007b). Personalization of services is thereby a critical factor.

This chapter continues with an overview of location-based services and mobile decision making. I discuss aspects of personalization, briefly describe some technical issues such as positioning, and identify LBS applications. The third section identifies core domains of LBS that strongly relate to GIS and society research. I focus on traditional application areas, where LBS can have positive impacts, for example, navigation and emergency services, and discuss innovative ideas on mobile social networking and social positioning. In addition, critical issues regarding privacy and security, and their potential dangers and consequences are highlighted. In order to demonstrate how LBS can impact our daily lives, the fourth section introduces a specific location-based decision service (LBDS), the *HotelFinder*. This novel application shows how users can be supported in their mobile decision making. The chapter ends with conclusions and directions for further research.

LOCATION-BASED SERVICES

Progress in the areas of geospatial technologies and wireless communication in recent years has led to the development of information services that are sensitive to the location of a mobile user. These services, LBS or more specifically *mobile location-based services* (mLBS), have been defined as "the delivery of data and information services where the content of those services is customized to the current or some projected location and context of the user" (Brimicombe and Li, 2006: 7). It is important to emphasize that such content may include information on how, when, and with whom an activity can be performed, in addition to where. LBS therefore deliver applications to a mobile terminal, such as a mobile phone or personal digital assistant (PDA), by exploiting geospatial information about a user's surrounding environment, their proximity, and distance to other entities in space (Urquhart et al., 2004). This facilitates the successful completion of spatiotemporal tasks such as navigation (Winter et al., 2001).

Tremendous benefits may be achieved from the widespread adoption of these services, providing large segments of the population real-time decision support for purposes ranging from trivial (wayfinding and friend-finder services) to critical (emergency response). LBS also have great potential to serve as tools for collecting disaggregate activity-travel data from users, providing researchers and planners detailed information with regard to spatiotemporal patterns of interaction in urban environments (Ahas and Mark, 2005; Miller, 2005). However, while current services often provide multiple thematic layers to choose from, such as points-of-interests (POIs), restaurants, or bus stations, they still assist the user's decision making based on a small number of constraints – typically only distance and one additional thematic attribute.

Mobile decision making and personalization

There is still little knowledge about how *mobile* location-based decision making is different from generic decision making (Raper et al., 2007b). General decision theory covers a wide range of models with different foci on describing how decisions could or should be made and on specifying decisions that are made (Golledge and Stimson, 1997). It has been found that human decision making is not strictly optimizing in an economical and mathematical sense (Simon, 1955), such as proposed by the algorithms of classical decision-making theories, therefore behavioral decision theory has been emphasized in the cognitive literature. In order to investigate whether principles of generic decision making can be transferred to mobile decision making and find potential differences, researchers have developed tools to study the interaction between environments, individuals, and mobile devices. Most case studies focus on pedestrian navigation in various settings, such as urban environments (Li and Longley, 2006) – see also Raper et al. (2007b) for an overview. Raubal et al. (2004) proposed a user-centered theory of LBS, which specifically focuses on individuals' mobile decision making. It integrates spatial, temporal, social (using affordances), and cognitive (using decision-making theory) aspects of a LBS.

Recent research activities have focused on aspects of *personalization* – the customization and adaptation of LBS to their users. This trend to highly specialized geospatial services has been intensified by people's increased need to acquire and use spatial information. In today's world of vast mobility and change we frequently face new situations in unfamiliar environments, such as finding one's way in an unfamiliar city or airport. Personalized LBS can only be achieved by considering various dimensions of context, which includes more than location (Schmidt et al., 1999). People's information needs depend highly on temporal, situational, and personal context, such as time of day, the physical and social environment they are situated in, and their preferences, abilities, activities, and knowledge (Reichenbacher, 2007). For example, when looking for a place to stay overnight a business traveler has fewer constraints due to price, and at the same time higher demands

with respect to the quality of accommodation, than a low-budget traveler. Disabled people require different route instructions from a navigation service than other wayfinders. Several researchers in the area of cartography and geovisualization have stressed the need for mobile map adaptation (Reichenbacher, 2005; Sarjakoski and Sarjakoski, 2008) and the utilization of multimedia presentations for mobile mapping (Dransch, 2007). Recently, Raubal and Panov (2009) proposed a formal model for mobile map adaptation that can be employed for different LBS applications.

Architectures and positioning

LBS are imbedded within complex technical infrastructures, including positioning infrastructures, application servers, and handheld location-aware devices (Küpper, 2005). Their technological place lies at the intersection of GIS, the Internet, and new information and communication technologies (NICTs) (Brimicombe and Li, 2009). The recently evolving *geospatial web*, "an interconnected, online digital network of discoverable geospatial documents, databases, and services" (Turner and Forrest, 2008: 2), provides a rich foundation for LBS. A user situated in the real world may access information through a variety of NICTs such as 3G phones. Queries and responses are communicated to and from a server with GIS software through a wireless network. The server in turn has access to additional services and databases, including the World Wide Web, which facilitates answering a particular query.

Position determination is crucial and the requirement by the US Federal Communications Commission that all cellular carriers must identify the position of a 911 caller (Wireless Communications and Public Safety Act 1999)[1] was in fact one of the main drivers of LBS (the European version was established in 2003 through the EU Directive E112).[2] Positioning of mobile devices works either *actively*, that is, the device can recognize its current position such as through a GPS (global positioning system) receiver (Leick, 2003), or *passively*, that is, the position is accessed over a network connection such as the mobile phone network. A disadvantage of GPS is that it does not work well or not at all in dense urban and indoor environments. Other technologies, such as infrared sensors, RFID (Radio Frequency Identification), or Wi-Fi technology can be utilized for indoor positioning. The most important methods for network-dependent outdoor positioning include Cell-ID, Time of Arrival (TOA), and Observed Time Difference (OTD). Detailed information about local positioning systems can be found in (Kolodziej and Hjelm, 2006).

Applications

LBS applications can be classified into business-to-consumer (B2C) and business-to-business (B2B). The various types of services are utilized by individuals, businesses, and governments to facilitate their spatial and temporal decision making. Two core questions of individual users are "where am I?" and "where is a certain object?," for example, when trying to find the nearest Italian restaurant or gas station. Once such an object is found, an LBS supports the user in getting there through guided route instructions. Businesses can make use of LBS through targeted advertising or finding optimal delivery routes for shipping goods based on customers' locations and traffic conditions. Typical application areas for administrations and government are local commerce, emergency dispatch, and asset management (Francica, 2008). A comprehensive overview of LBS applications is given by (Raper et al., 2007a).

LOCATION-BASED SERVICES AND SOCIETY

This section identifies areas where location-based services impact individuals,

organizations, and our society as a whole. The domains in which these areas fall are widespread and affect different aspects of our daily lives, some of them trivial, others critical. The spaces in which LBS are used are based on complex interactions between physical, social, and cultural aspects, and it is therefore important to account for these when looking at the encounters between people and location-based technology (Dourish and Bell, 2007). Although there are potential dangers that must not be ignored, LBS have a vast potential to improve our decision making in significant ways.

Navigation services and mobile guides

Car navigation systems have been one of the early accomplishments of LBS and their commercial success is still on the rise. Decreasing costs of this technology and the availability of up-to-date street network data have made car navigation systems almost a commodity. The advantages are obvious: support in finding optimal routes for the driver, easy communication through verbal turn-by-turn instructions and maps, and low maintenance. On the downside, it has been argued that the use of such systems results in higher visual and cognitive demands for the driver (Burnett et al., 2004), and that the operation of automatic navigation systems may lead to an overall degradation in spatial knowledge acquisition (Parush et al., 2007).

Navigation services are also available to pedestrians, although the wayfinding behavior of pedestrians is much more complex because they are not bound to a given street network. These services are especially helpful for disabled people because their route instructions can be adapted to the type of disability. For example, route instructions for people in wheelchairs must not include segments with stairways. There is also a large body of literature on navigation systems for the visually impaired (Golledge et al., 1998) and indoor routing algorithms for the blind that can be utilized in wayfinding services have been developed (Swobodzinski and Raubal, 2009).

Over the last decade it has been realized that route instructions from existing navigation services lack cognitive adequacy (Strube, 1991), because they mainly rely on quantitative values, such as "go straight for 1.35 km, then turn left, go 0.76 km, and so on," instead of providing landmark-based instructions, such as "go straight until you reach the large yellow building, turn right after the building, and so on." Researchers have therefore investigated methods for the automatic detection of landmarks to be used in wayfinding instructions (Sadeghian and Kantardzic, 2008). Raubal and Winter (2002) addressed the question of how to enrich instructions from a wayfinding service with local landmarks in order to make them compatible with human thinking.

Navigation services are often an integral part of *mobile guides*, currently the largest group of LBS applications. Mobile guides are portable and location-sensitive digital guides that provide a wealth of information about the user's surroundings (Raper et al., 2007a), therefore replacing traditional guidebooks and paper maps. One of the main advantages is that the data behind digital mobile guides can be easily revised, providing both spatially and temporally up-to-date

information to their users. Furthermore, these LBS can be adapted to user preferences and with regard to the visualization of geographic information (Krüger et al., 2007). These features allow for personalized information and interaction, a tremendous improvement over conventional tourist guides or maps. Recent research has focused on the integration of small mobile displays and large static paper maps to get the best of both worlds (Rohs et al., 2007). For example, *Wikeye* (Hecht et al., 2007) is an approach to improve the understanding of places that combines digital Wikipedia content with a paper-based map. When the user views a small portion of a map through the mobile device, Wikipedia-derived content relating to chosen objects is offered. Through its extension *WikEar* (Schöning et al., 2008), this content is automatically organized according to principles derived from narrative theory and creates an educational audio tour starting and ending at stationary city maps (Figure 9.1).

Location-based transportation and emergency services

The use of location-based transportation services can have a positive impact on both the environment and the safety of people. They provide more efficient transportation, which

Figure 9.1   WikEar is a novel mobile guide that generates location-based audio tours (by Johannes Schöning, Institute for Geoinformatics, University of Münster, Germany)

in turn leads to less pollution, and location-based information and driver assistance enhance the protection of drivers. Location-based transportation services impact different application levels and people, such as individual car drivers but also businesses that depend on vehicle management (Raper et al., 2007a).

Emergency services are one key application of LBS. As described above, all cellular carriers are required to be able to identify the position of a 911 caller. This automatic position determination and communication technology can save critical time during rescue operations in car accidents, where injured people are unable to report their location. The OnStar[3] system combines a GPS device and wireless communication to provide both emergency response and other services, such as roadside assistance and stolen vehicle tracking. LBS can also contribute to the efficiency of geo-collaborative crisis management through the improvement of effective response operations (Rinner, 2007). An emergency operations center (EOC) can thereby locate and coordinate their emergency crews in the field through GPS. First responder teams use mobile client software to receive updated information and decision-making parameters from the EOC.

Social networking

The deployment of location-aware technologies and wireless networks not only affects people's experience and interaction with computation (Dourish and Bell, 2007) but also their social interaction with others. Location-based social networking is a novel social possibility offered by LBS technology. These services can be used to determine the locations of friends and family members. After subscribing to a service provider, the subscriber receives notification when one of their network members comes within a specified geographic proximity. These are essentially friend-finder services, which visualize the locations of contacts on a mobile map. Such services enable groups of users to spontaneously meet in order to perform common activities such as having dinner together. The selection of a meeting point, as well as a place for the activity, such as a restaurant, requires a group decision process. Current research investigates the integration of multiple criteria decision-making methods (Jankowski, 1995) into LBS with the goal of creating personalized location-based services that support user groups in their everyday decision-making (Espeter and Raubal, 2009).

Parents can utilize such services for the surveillance of their children's mobility. Fotel and Thomsen (2004) relate various parental monitoring strategies to the welfare and socioeconomic structures in the families. They discuss both the positive and negative implications of children's mobility surveillance by cellular phones. One of their conclusions is that the remote control of children's movements has implications on the levels of independence regarding the children's mobility while their actual reach in terms of geographical space may not be affected.

An extension to the functionality of mobile guides was suggested by Baus et al. (2005). Mobile guides could be integrated within a collaborative network, thereby utilizing the possibility of location-based social networking. Users will not only be able to locate their friends but also view their friends' spatiotemporal tracks and recommendations of places. This essentially constitutes an application of the social navigation approach to mobile devices (Höök, 2003; Persson et al., 2003). A currently popular service for social networking is Twitter™,[4] which allows its users to send and receive short text-based updates in real time. It was also used in combination with Google Maps™[5] for some of the 2008 US presidential campaigns to present real-time updates of their ballot access teams across the country.

Social positioning

The availability of people's location data has offered the possibility of automatically tracking people's behavior in space and time. Such deployment of LBS technology creates social, legal, and ethical questions, including privacy and security of the individual as discussed below. The social positioning method (SPM) (Ahas and Mark, 2005; Ahas et al., 2007) integrates the location coordinates of people with their social characteristics in order to study the space–time behavior of society (Mountain and Raper, 2001). It is envisioned that SPM will have a major positive impact on our future society in areas such as planning, marketing, and public participation. The resulting data and their analyses could be used to improve upon existing transportation infrastructures between cities and their suburbs, or to estimate the impact of projects on various social groups and their dynamic spatiotemporal patterns. Figure 9.2 shows a three-dimensional representation of

personal activity tracks of a commuter in greater Tallinn, Estonia. SPM has been applied to the study of tourism, resulting in a higher spatial and temporal preciseness than for regular tourism statistics. One of the outcomes of this study was the mapping of typical routes for tourists categorized by their nationalities (Ahas et al., 2008) (see Figure 9.3). In essence, SPM data helps to project people's behavior into the future through simulation and therefore foresee and prevent potential problems arising from such behavior and movement.

Privacy and security

The rapid spread and use of geospatial technologies and LBS has brought up concerns in our society about information privacy and the

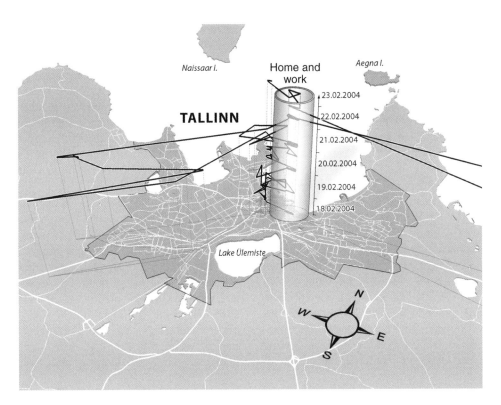

Figure 9.2   3D representation of personal activity tracks of a commuter in greater Tallinn, Estonia (by Raivo Aunap and Rein Ahas, Department of Geography, University of Tartu, Estonia)

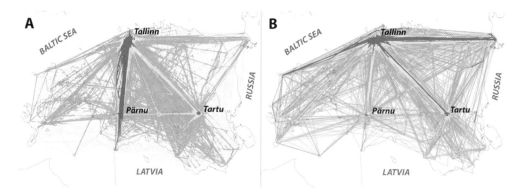

Figure 9.3   Linear movement corridors of Latvians (A) and Russians (B) during holidays in Estonia (by Rein Ahas, Department of Geography, University of Tartu, Estonia)

security of individuals. Virtual globes such as Google Earth™[6] have contributed to these concerns through their high-resolution imagery, which makes it possible to virtually identify individual houses and cars. The main threat is seen to be the capacity for real-time integration of location information and personal data, which in extreme cases may lead to geoslavery. *Geoslavery* has been defined as "a practice in which one entity, the master, coercively or surreptitiously monitors and exerts control over the physical location of another individual, the slave" (Dobson and Fisher, 2003: 47–8). This potential for real-time control is made possible by commercially available human tracking systems and therefore several initiatives have called for laws to regulate and restrict their use. Different forms of surveillance have raised concerns during the recent Beijing Olympics. For example, taxi drivers had devices in their cars, which were linked to the vehicles' navigation systems and allowed a central monitoring station to listen to anything inside the taxi (Magnier, 2008). Blakemore (2005) provides an overview of various issues regarding the use of location-based technologies for surveillance in workplaces.

As is the case with most technology in general, there can be positive and negative uses. For location-based services it is necessary to find the right balance between customer service and privacy invasion. Several studies have investigated these issues and produced valuable results. Barkhuus (2004) has discovered that if LBS are sufficiently attractive to their users and provide adequate protection, then the users are less concerned about privacy issues. In a comprehensive field study in Finland it was found that users show high acceptance and trust towards service providers. There seem to exist strong cultural differences though to what counts as privacy invasion of the individual and therefore extended studies in different countries involving different cultural groups are required to arrive at a more comprehensive picture.

There has been research on technical measures to help provide the user's privacy and safety. Regarding GPS signals, encryption and licensed access are one way to go and have been actively discussed by the European Union in the context of *Galileo*, its global navigation satellite system that is currently under construction. On a larger scale, monitoring of the whole LBS industry may be required to keep LBS from serving unethical purposes (Dobson and Fisher, 2003). Duckham et al. (2006) developed a formal model of spatiotemporal aspects to be employed for safeguarding location privacy. Their "obfuscation" approach tries to minimize the information about a user's location.

The model also includes strategies for third parties to invade the user's location privacy through global and local refinement operators. A survey of other location privacy protection methods can be found in (Duckham and Kulik, 2006).

LOCATION-BASED DECISION SERVICES

Improving user acceptance of LBS in our society depends critically on enhancing their utility in helping people to make good decisions in their mobile everyday lives. One key to achieving this is *personalization*, that is, the personal managing of space and place through user preferences and characteristics. Recent research has focused on the conception and development of mobile *location-based decision services* (LBDS) that provide personalized spatial decision support to their users. These services are based on the integration of multicriteria decision analysis (MCDA) and can therefore provide analytic evaluations of the attractiveness of alternative destinations and choices being offered (Rinner, 2008). This section presents a mobile hotel-finder service to demonstrate how this novel form of LBS can support users in their mobile decision making.

The *HotelFinder* was developed as a mobile LBDS and integrates MCDA methods, which had been introduced to GIS in the 1990s for applications such as site suitability analysis (Malczewski, 1999). The software features multicriteria decision support for the task of finding suitable hotels in an unfamiliar environment depending on the user's location and preferences. The original application (Raubal and Rinner, 2004) was extended in (Rinner and Raubal, 2004) by integrating the ordered weighted averaging (OWA) decision rule (Yager, 1988). The OWA method allows users to choose a decision strategy as part of their decision-making preferences. This leads to different answers by the LBS depending on people's level of

risk-taking. Decision strategies range from "optimistic" (i.e., risk-taking) to "pessimistic" (i.e., cautious), and allow from a full trade-off to no trade-off between the different decision criteria. OWA uses a second set of weights (besides criterion importance weights), namely order weights, to emphasize either high or low standardized criterion outcomes. For example, with a pessimistic strategy, decision makers focus on the lower outcomes of each decision alternative to avoid the risk of selecting an alternative with poor performance in any criterion. In contrast, with the optimistic strategy, decision makers focus on the higher outcomes, thus incurring the risk of accepting an alternative with excellent performances in some criteria but possibly poor performances in other criteria.

The service was tested using profiles for a business traveler, a tourist, and a low-budget tourist. Simulated users run through the steps of an MCDA process that includes determining decision alternatives (hotel destinations), selecting decision criteria (e.g., room rate, checkout time), standardizing the criterion values for all alternatives, determining importance weights for criteria, and using a multi-criteria decision rule to aggregate the weighted standardized criterion values to an evaluation score and rank for each alternative (Rinner and Raubal, 2004). The user interface of the mobile device provides both the functionality for displaying the geographic data as well as a dialog component to elicit the user's input of MCDA parameters. A discussion of user interface design for LBDS can be found in Rinner et al. (2005). The test cases demonstrated that different users can and should be offered specific choices through their LBS. Figure 9.4 shows the user interface of the original *HotelFinder* application for the city of Münster, Germany (Raubal and Rinner, 2004). Figure 9.5 demonstrates another version for the city of Toronto, Canada, where the map window is provided by map servers such as Google Maps™ or Microsoft® Virtual Earth®.[7] It presents the user standardization and

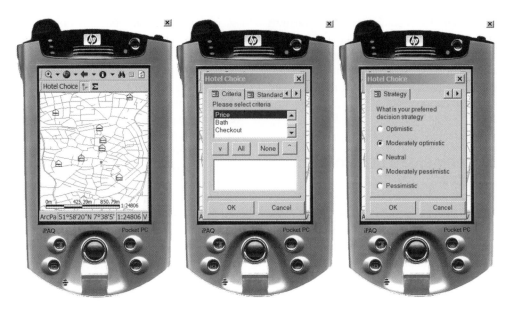

Figure 9.4   User interface for the Münster HotelFinder
Source: Raubal and Rinner, 2004

weighting of criteria, the selection of a decision strategy, and the presentation of the
results with the additional option of calculating the route to the optimal hotel.

The usefulness of the *HotelFinder* was
demonstrated through a comprehensive user
test showing that MCDA can be employed

for optimizing location-based decision processes (Bäumer et al., 2007). The goal of this
test was to focus on the benefits and draw-
backs of a personalized mobile LBDS. The
results confirmed that applying the multicriteria decision strategy enhances people's
decision support in unfamiliar environments.

Figure 9.5   User interface for the Toronto HotelFinder

CONCLUSION AND FUTURE TRENDS

LBS have become an integral part in various domains of our lives and therefore impact the decision making of individuals, organizations, and our society as a whole. It is important to realize that although LBS can offer major benefits, there are also large risks to be considered. On the one hand, LBS help people in making good and efficient decisions. Navigation and transportation services, or emergency services provide fine examples. On the other hand, privacy and security issues must not be ignored when engaging in activities such as mobile social networking and social positioning. Technological development has been moving at an incredibly high speed and nowadays geospatial technologies allow for real-time tracking and monitoring of people. Analyzing this wealth of data helps in modeling the space-time behavior of our society and can in a positive way be utilized to forecast and solve potential future problems. In the worst case though, it may lead to geoslavery.

Further research is needed to arrive at a comprehensive picture of LBS and their effects on our society. Although companies put different LBS on the market day by day, many of these services work inefficiently, are difficult to use, and have the potential to serve unethical purposes. Changes in technology happen so fast that research on critical issues is often lagging behind. In the following, we identify some of the important future research directions.

In order to enhance both the usability and usefulness of LBS, they must be designed by considering principles of human spatial cognition regarding the representation and processing of spatiotemporal aspects of phenomena. One of the goals of applying *spatial cognitive engineering* (Raubal, 2009) methods to LBS is the personalization of geospatial services due to the differences of geographic information users in their cognitive styles, abilities, preferences, and information needs. Research in this area should focus on formal conceptual representations

that minimize the gap between system and user, theories of mobile real-time decision making and how it differs from classical decision making, and necessary context parameters to be accounted for by the services depending on the user's background, perspectives, and situation. In addition, continuing research on augmented reality visualization will eventually result in interfaces, where information and objects can be visually referred to in a direct way (Höllerer et al., 2007). A better understanding of these issues will provide the basis for LBS that facilitate mobile human-computer interaction and provide high-quality spatiotemporal decision-making support.

It is a widely accepted estimate that 80 percent of human decisions affect space or are affected by spatial situations (Albaredes, 1992). This number also indicates the future potential of LBS for governments, businesses, and individuals. For Europe it has been forecasted that LBS revenues will grow by 50 percent annually (Berg-Insight, 2006). More research is necessary to develop business models that account for the exact value of location for mobile decision making. Such research has to investigate cost and pricing of geospatial information and how these should be distributed among content providers, information brokers, service providers, and users. The main questions from a user perspective are thereby: What is the value of a particular piece of geoinformation, what improvement in the decision is achieved when this piece of information is available, and how much am I willing to pay for it (Frank, 2008)?

LBS technology nowadays allows for the tracking and monitoring of our spatiotemporal behavior and it is not clear yet what the exact consequences will be in the future in terms of privacy and security issues. Some research has been done but in order to get a more comprehensive picture of the potential dangers and how to counter these, studies have to be conducted over a wider range of domains and geographic space, including diverse social groups and cultures.

Geopositioning in the wired world has become more precise and accurate, therefore paving the way for optimal targeting of people through triggered location services, where users receive advertising messages when they come within a certain distance of a store or business. What are the impacts of such services? Does our society really want or need them? What are the effects of excluding people on the lower socio-economic end who might be left out from these geographies of Wi-Fi infrastructures and use (Torrens, 2008)?

In this chapter I have selectively identified areas where LBS affect individuals, organizations, and our society as a whole. Many more applications are possible and have been in use, such as location-based gaming or the use of tracking and monitoring functionality for health applications. There will no doubt be novel application areas in the future including mobile group-decision making and mobile public participation among others. The recently finished Android Developer Challenge I,[8] where LBS developer teams have been competing in the creation of novel LBS applications, provides convincing evidence that the search for the "killer application" still continues.

ACKNOWLEDGEMENTS

I would like to thank the three reviewers for their support and constructive comments. Their feedback helped me to enhance the quality and content of the chapter. Gwen Raubal helped improving the grammar and style of this work.

NOTES

1 http://www.fcc.gov/pshs/services/911-services/
2 http://ec.europa.eu/environment/civil/prote/112/112_en.htm
3 http://www.onstar.com/
4 http://twitter.com/
5 http://maps.google.com/
6 http://earth.google.com/
7 http://maps.live.com/

REFERENCES

Ahas, R., Aasa, A., Roose, A., Mark, Ü. and Silm, S. (2008) 'Evaluating passive mobile positioning data for tourism surveys: An Estonian case study', *Tourism Management*, 29: 469–86.

Ahas, R., Aasa, A., Silm, S., Aunap, R., Kalle, H. and Mark, Ü. (2007) 'Mobile positioning in space–time behaviour studies: Social positioning method experiments in Estonia', *Cartography and Geographic Information Science*, 34(4): 259–73.

Ahas, R. and Mark, Ü. (2005) 'Location based services – new challenges for planning and public administration?', *Futures*, 37: 547–61.

Albaredes, G. (1992) 'A new approach: User oriented GIS', *Paper Presented at the EGIS '92*, Munich.

Barkhuus, L. (2004) 'Privacy in location-based services, concerns vs. coolness', *Paper Presented at the Workshop on Location Systems Privacy and Control (Mobile HCI 2004)*. Glasgow: UK.

Bäumer, B., Panov, I. and Raubal, M. (2007) 'Decision improvement through multi-criteria strategies in mobile location-based services'. In A. Car, G. Griesebner and J. Strobl (eds), *Geospatial Crossroads @ GI_Forum: Proceedings of the First Geoinformatics Forum Salzburg*. Heidelberg: Wichmann. pp. 17–25.

Baus, J., Cheverst, K. and Kray, C. (2005) 'A survey of map-based mobile guides'. In L. Meng, A. Zipf and T. Reichenbacher (eds), *Map-Based Mobile Services*. Berlin: Springer. pp. 197–216.

Berg-Insight (2006) *Strategic Analysis of the European Mobile LBS Market*.

Blakemore, M. (2005) *Surveillance in the Workplace – an Overview of Issues of Privacy, Monitoring, and Ethics: Britain's General Union*. http://www.gmb.org.uk/shared_asp_files/uploadedfiles/0577B12A-09E2–4B67-B1B2–28DDA5B44426_Surveillance.pdf (accessed 1 December 2009).

Brimicombe, A. and Li, B. (2009) *Location-Based Services and Geo-Information Engineering*. Chichester: Wiley-Blackwell.

Brimicombe, A. and Li, Y. (2006) 'Mobile space-time envelopes for location-based services', *Transactions in GIS*, 10(1): 5–23.

Burnett, G., Summerskill, S. and Porter, J. (2004) 'On-the-move destination entry for vehicle navigation systems: Unsafe by any means?', *Behaviour and Information Technology*, 23: 265–72.

Dobson, J. and Fisher, P. (2003) 'Geoslavery', *IEEE Technology and Society Magazine*, (Spring 2003).

Dourish, P. and Bell, G. (2007) 'The infrastructure of experience and the experience of infrastructure: Meaning and structure in everyday encounters with space', *Environment and Planning B: Planning and Design*, 34(3): 414–30.

Dransch, D. (2007) 'Designing suitable cartographic multimedia presentations', in B. Cartwright, M. Peterson and G. Gartner (eds), *Multimedia Cartography*. Heidelberg: Springer. pp. 75–85.

Duckham, M. and Kulik, L. (2006) 'Location privacy and location-aware computing', in J. Drummond, R. Billen, D. Forrest and E. Joao (eds), *Dynamic and Mobile GIS: Investigating Change in Space and Time*. Boca Raton, FL: CRC Press.

Duckham, M., Kulik, L. and Birtley, A. (2006) 'A spatio-temporal model of strategies and counter strategies for location privacy protection'. In M. Raubal, H. Miller, A. Frank and M. Goodchild (eds), *Geographic Information Science – Fourth International Conference, GIScience 2006*. Berlin: Springer. 41(97): 47–64.

Espeter, M. and Raubal, M. (2009) 'Location-based decision support for user groups', *Journal of Location Based Services*, 3(3): 165–87.

Fotel, T. and Thomsen, T. (2004) 'The surveillance of children's mobility', *Surveillance and Society*, 1(4): 535–54.

Francica, J. (2008) 'Location-based services: Practices and products'. In S. Shekhar and H. Xiong (eds), *Encyclopedia of GIS*. New York: Springer. pp. 623–7.

Frank, A. (1999) 'The change from big GIS to small GIS', *Paper presented at the ICTPA'99, Fourth International Conference on Information and Communications Technology in Public Administration*, 25–27 October, Bucharest, RO.

Frank, A. (2008) 'Economics of geographic information'. In K. Kemp (ed.), *Encyclopedia of Geographic Information Science*. Los Angeles: Sage Publications. pp. 120–2.

Golledge, R., Klatzky, R., Loomis, J., Speigle, J. and Tietz, J. (1998) 'A geographical information system for a GPS based personal guidance system', *International Journal of Geographical Information Systems*, 12(7): 727–49.

Golledge, R. and Stimson, R. (1997) *Spatial Behavior: A Geographic Perspective*. New York: Guilford Press.

Hecht, B., Rohs, M., Schöning, J. and Krüger, A. (2007) 'Wikeye – using magic lenses to explore georeferenced wikipedia content', *Paper Presented at the 3rd International Workshop on Pervasive Mobile Interaction Devices (PERMID)*. Toronto: Canada.

Höllerer, T., Wither, J. and DiVerdi, S. (2007) '"Anywhere augmentation": Towards mobile augmented reality in unprepared environments'. In G. Gartner, M. Peterson and W. Cartwright (eds), *Location Based Services and TeleCartography*. Springer. pp. 393–416.

Höök, K. (2003) 'Social navigation: From the web to the mobile', *Paper Presented at the Mensch and Computer 2003*. Interaktion in Bewegung, Stuttgart.

Jankowski, P. (1995) 'Integrating geographical information systems and multiple criteria decision-making methods', *International Journal of Geographical Information Systems*, 9(3): 251–73.

Jensen, C., Kligys, A., Pedersen, T. and Timko, I. (2002) 'Multidimensional data modeling for location-based services', *Proceedings of the Tenth ACM International Symposium on Advances in Geographic Information Systems*. McLean, VA. pp. 55–61.

Kolodziej, K. and Hjelm, J. (2006) *Local Positioning Systems: LBS Applications and Services*. Boca Raton, FL: CRC Press.

Krüger, A., Baus, J., Heckmann, D., Kruppa, M. and Wasinger, R. (2007) 'Adaptive mobile guides'. In P. Brusilovsky, A. Kobsa and W. Nejdl (eds), *The Adaptive Web*. Berlin: Springer. pp. 521–49.

Küpper, A. (2005) *Location-Based Services – Fundamentals and Operation*. Chichester, England: Wiley.

Leick, A. (2003) *GPS Satellite Surveying*, 3rd edn. New York: Wiley.

Li, C. and Longley, P. (2006) 'A test environment for location-based services applications', *Transactions in GIS*, 10(1): 43–61.

Magnier, M. (2008) 'Beijing Olympics visitors to come under widespread surveillance', *Los Angeles Times*, 7 August 2008.

Malczewski, J. (1999) *GIS and Multicriteria Decision Analysis*. New York: John Wiley.

Miller, H. (2005) 'What about people in geographic information science?' In P. Fisher and D. Unwin (eds), *Re-Presenting Geographical Information Systems*. New York: John Wiley. pp. 215–42.

Mountain, D. and Raper, J. (2001) 'Modelling human spatio-temporal behaviour: A challenge for location-based services', *Paper Presented at the 6th International Conference on GeoComputation*, 24–26 September, University of Queensland, Brisbane, Australia.

Parush, A., Ahuvia, S. and Erev, I. (2007) 'Degradation in spatial knowledge acquisition when using navigation systems'. In S. Winter, M. Duckham, L. Kulik and B. Kuipers (eds), *Spatial Information Theory – 8th International Conference, COSIT 2007, Melbourne*, Australia, September 2007, Berlin: Springer. 47(36): 238–54.

Persson, P., Espinoza, F., Fagerberg, P., Sandin, A. and Cöster, R. (2003) 'GeoNotes: A location-based information system for public spaces'. In K. Höök, D. Benyon and A. Munro (eds), *Designing Information Spaces: The Social Navigation Approach*. Berlin: Springer. pp. 151–73.

Raper, J., Gartner, G., Karimi, H. and Rizos, C. (2007a) 'Applications of location-based services: A selected review', *Journal of Location Based Services*, 1(2): 89–111.

Raper, J., Gartner, G., Karimi, H. and Rizos, C. (2007b) 'A critical evaluation of location based services and their potential', *Journal of Location Based Services*, 1(1): 5–45.

Raubal, M. (2009) 'Cognitive engineering for geographic information science', *Geography Compass*, 3(3): 1087–104.

Raubal, M., Miller, H. and Bridwell, S. (2004) 'User-centred time geography for location-based services', *Geografiska Annaler B*, 86(4): 245–65.

Raubal, M. and Panov, I. (2009) 'A formal model for mobile map adaptation'. In G. Gartner and K. Rehrl (eds), *Location Based Services and TeleCartography II – From Sensor Fusion to Context Models: Selected Papers from the 5th International Symposium on LBS and TeleCartography 2008, Salzburg, Austria*. Berlin: Springer. pp. 11–34.

Raubal, M. and Rinner, C. (2004) 'Multi-criteria decision analysis for location based services', *Paper Presented at the Geoinformatics 2004, 12th International Conference on Geoinformatics*, 7–9 June 2004, Gävle, Sweden.

Raubal, M. and Winter, S. (2002) 'Enriching wayfinding instructions with local landmarks'. In M. Egenhofer and D. Mark (eds), *Geographic Information Science – Second International Conference, GIScience 2002, Boulder, CO, USA, September 2002*. Berlin: Springer. 24(78): 243–59.

Reichenbacher, T. (2005) 'Adaptive egocentric maps for mobile users'. In L. Meng, A. Zipf and T. Reichenbacher (eds), *Map-based Mobile Services: Theories, Methods and Implementations*. Heidelberg: Springer. pp. 141–58.

Reichenbacher, T. (2007) 'Adaption in mobile and ubiquitous cartography'. In W. Cartwright, M. Peterson and G. Gartner (eds), *Multimedia Cartography*. Heidelberg: Springer. pp. 383–97.

Rinner, C. (2007) Multi-criteria evaluation in support of emergency response decision-making', *Paper Presented at the Joint CIG/ISPRS Conference on Geomatics for Disaster and Risk Management*, 23–25 May 2007, Toronto, Canada.

Rinner, C. (2008) 'Mobile maps and more – extending location-based services with multi-criteria decision analysis'. In L. Meng, A. Zipf and S. Winter (eds), *Map-Based Mobile Services*. Berlin: Springer. pp. 335–52.

Rinner, C. and Raubal, M. (2004) 'Personalized multi-criteria decision strategies in location-based decision support', *Journal of Geographic Information Sciences*, 10(2): 149–56.

Rinner, C., Raubal, M. and Spigel, B. (2005) User interface design for location-based decision services. *Paper Presented at the 13th International Conference on GeoInformatics, 17–19 August 2005, Proceedings (CD-ROM)*, Toronto, Canada.

Rohs, M., Schöning, J., Raubal, M., Essl, G. and Krüger, A. (2007) 'Map navigation with mobile devices: Virtual versus physical movement with and without visual context', *Proceedings of the Ninth International Conference on Multimodal Interfaces (ICMI 2007), 12–15 November 2007, Nagoya, Japan*: ACM Press. pp. 146–53.

Rüetschi, U. and Timpf, S. (2005) 'Modelling wayfinding in public transport: Network space and scene space'. In C. Freksa, M. Knauff, B. Krieg-Brückner, B. Nebel and T. Barkowsky (eds), *Spatial Cognition IV*. Berlin: Springer. 33(43): 24–41.

Sadeghian, P. and Kantardzic, M. (2008) 'The new generation of automatic landmark detection systems: Challenges and guidelines', *Spatial Cognition and Computation*, 8(3): 252–87.

Sarjakoski, L.T. and Sarjakoski, T. (2008) 'User interfaces and adaptive maps'. In S. Shekhar and H. Xiong (eds), *Encyclopedia of GIS*. Berlin: Springer. pp. 1205–12.

Schmidt, A., Beigl, M. and Gellersen, H. (1999) 'There is more to context than location', *Computers and Graphics*, 23(6): 893–901.

Schöning, J., Hecht, B. and Starosielski, N. (2008) 'Evaluating automatically generated location-based stories for tourists', *Paper Presented at the Conference on Human Factors in Computing Systems (CHI '08), Extended Abstracts*, Florence, Italy.

Simon, H. (1955) 'A behavioral model of rational choice', *Quarterly Journal of Economics*, 69: 99–118.

Strube, G. (1991) 'The role of cognitive science in knowledge engineering'. In F. Schmalhofer, G. Strube and T. Wetter (eds), *Proceedings of the*

First Joint Workshop on Contemporary Knowledge Engineering and Cognition, 21–22 February 1991. London: Springer. 6(22): 161–74.

Swobodzinski, M. and Raubal, M. (2009) 'An indoor routing algorithm for the blind: Development and comparison to a routing algorithm for the sighted', *International Journal of Geographical Information Science*, 23(10): 1315–43.

Torrens, P. (2008) 'Wi-Fi geographies', *Annals of the Association of American Geographers*, 98(1): 59–84.

Turner, A. and Forrest, B. (2008) *Where 2.0: The State of the Geospatial Web*. O'Reilly Media, Inc.

Urquhart, K., Miller, S. and Cartwright, W. (2004) 'A user-centered research approach to designing useful geospatial representations for LBS', *Paper Presented at the 2nd Symposium on Location Based Services and TeleCartography*. Vienna, Austria.

Winter, S., Pontikakis, E. and Raubal, M. (2001) 'LBS for real-time navigation – a scenario', *GeoInformatics*, 4: 6–9.

Yager, R. (1988) 'On ordered weighted averaging aggregation operators in multi-criteria decision making', *IEEE Transactions on Systems, Man and Cybernetics*, 18(1): 183–90.

Alternative Representations in GIS and Society Research

10

Human-Scaled Visualizations and Society

Dimitris Ballas and Danny Dorling

INTRODUCTION

We must create a new language, consider a transitory state of new illusions and layers of validity and accept the possibility that there may be no language to describe ultimate reality, beyond the language of visions.

(Denes, 1979: 3)

When you look out of the window you can see a great deal in an instant. The mind has an extremely powerful system for processing imagery, which can instantly analyze a pattern of colours, of light and shade and know (or at least think) that these are trees, houses or people out there. How long would it take to describe all that you can see in words? Yet we still have to argue that in the study of societies there are many things that cannot be eloquently described in words or succinctly captured by equations. We depend on vision, we think visually, we talk in visual idioms and we dream in pictures, but we cannot easily turn a picture in our mind into something other people can see. An artist will take days to paint a single portrait. Suddenly, just as the last generation now dead was given the camera, we have received

the computer, which can turn a huge amount of data into pictures – snapshots of our society. Increasingly people are being able to speak visually.

Spatial information about the world and its people has always been at the forefront of visualization. As map-making developed into the art of cartography, rules were formalized and conventions defined (for early work see Peucker, 1972; Friis, 1974; Bertin, 1978; Howe, 1986). Most people are used to conventional maps of their regions, countries and the world. Such conventional maps appear on television every evening in the weather reports, showing geographical regions and countries as they appear from space (e.g. see Figure 10.1, which is an equal area land map of the world that is also revisited and redrawn in the third section of this chapter).

Conventional maps are very good in showing where oceans lie and rivers run. Their projections are calculated to aid navigation by compass or depict the quantity of land under crops. These maps are typically based on area projections such as that of Gerardus Mercator, developed in 1569, which was and

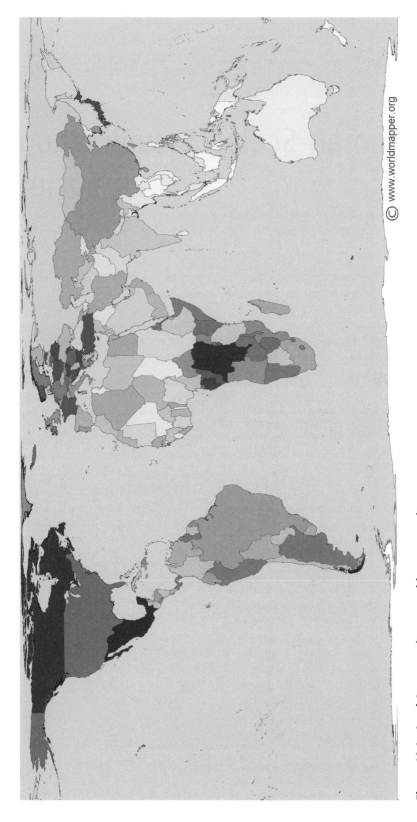

Figure 10.1   Land Area map (www.worldmapper.org)

is suitable as an aid for ships to sail across the oceans because it maintains all compass directions as straight lines. All projections inevitably result to a degree of distortion as they transfer the area of the earth being mapped (or the whole globe) into a flat surface such as a piece of paper or a display unit such as a computer screen. For instance, the Mercator projection stretches the earth's surface to the most extreme of extents and hence introduces considerable visual bias. Areas are drawn in ever expanding proportions to how near territory is to the poles and this results in areas such as India appearing much smaller than Greenland (when in reality India has an area more than seven times the size of Greenland). The degree to which such a distortion may be acceptable depends on the intended use of the map. There are a number of alternative projections that correspond to the actual land area size and these are much more suitable for the visualization and mapping of environmental variables and for pinpointing the location of physical geographical features of interest than Mercator's map ever was.

However, looking at a city, region or country from space is not the best way to see their human geography. For instance, mapping the distribution of human population on a conventional map means that urban areas with large populations, but small area size, are virtually invisible to the viewer. Conversely, the large rural areas with small populations dominate the map. When mapping data about people, it is therefore sensible to use a different spatial metaphor, one that reflects population size. Most conventional maps, regardless of the projection method that was adopted to create them, are not designed to show the spatial distributions of humans, although the single spatial distribution of people upon the surface of the globe, at one instance in time, can be shown on them. They cannot illustrate the simplest human geography of population. People are points on the map, clustered into collections of points called homes, into groups of points known as villages or cities. Communities of people are not like fields of crops. The paths through

space which they follow are not long wide rivers of water, and yet, to see anything on maps of people they must be shown as such.

As noted above, conventional maps cannot show how many people live in small areas, instead they show how little land supports so many people. They cannot show who the people are, what they do, where they go. They show no temporal distribution, they do not need to – how quickly do rivers move or mountains shrink on a human timescale? They will not show the distributions of people changing – international migration, moving house or just going to work. They cannot portray the distribution of the wealthy or the poor; on the map, at almost any scale, both groups can be found to live in much the same square inch of paper. Nor will they show where and when people had certain jobs, certain power, voted, were out of work, lived and died.

This chapter presents alternative ways of mapping human societies and demonstrates that they are more suitable for human-scaled visualization than conventional maps. In particular, the chapter argues that it is 'human cartograms' that should be used conventionally to visualize societies instead of conventional thematic mapping. Such cartograms can be defined as maps in which at least one scalar aspect, such as distance or area, is deliberately distorted to be drawn in proportion to a socioeconomic or demographic or any other 'human' variable of interest. Human cartograms are similar to conventional maps in that they also involve a degree of visual bias and distortion. However, this distortion is aimed to aid the examination and deeper understanding of issues, problems and research questions pertaining to human societies rather than environmental, geological or meteorological issues. It is also argued that visualization methods that have been developed in cartography and related disciplines provide enhanced capabilities when adapted for use in human-scaled visualizations. These methods can be used to make the huge volumes of data and figures that have been collected and recorded about human populations and their actions understandable without misrepresenting their meaning, and without reducing them to tables, graphs, crude maps or models.

The remainder of the chapter is organized as follows: first, the next section reviews the historical development of human cartograms in relation to conventional cartography. It also discusses the societal impacts of traditional maps and how these may differ from the impacts of non-conventional maps such as human cartograms. The following section then identifies the predominant current trends in visualizing human populations and discusses how they may tackle the problems associated with traditional approaches. In particular, this section introduces and discusses equal area cartogram methods (also known as density-equalizing maps), which typically re-size each area according to the variable being mapped. The next section shows how such methods can be used to create maps of the world, with each country re-sized and re-shaped according to a particular variable. Furthermore, it discusses the societal implications of decisions to adopt a particular mapping and visualizing method. The following two sections give similar examples with regards to visualizing the 'nation' and the 'city' respectively. The chapter concludes by illuminating issues and problems that are inherent in visualizing human populations and outlines possible new areas of research that could improve existing approaches and ways of thinking.

REVIEW OF THE STATE OF THE ART IN HUMAN GEOGRAPHY

The world is complex, dynamic, multidimensional; the paper is static, flat. How are we to represent the rich visual world of experience and measurement on mere flatland? (Tufte, 1990: 9)

The term 'human cartography' is credited to Swedish cartographer Janos Szegö (1984, 1987, 1994) who criticized the use of conventional mapping to depict people. Human cartography pertains to mapping where the focus is on people, where they live, where they go and what they do. Human cartograms were based on the development of ideas that underpin traditional cartograms, focusing on human variables. In this section we provide a brief history of conventional cartograms and show how human cartograms have been developed on that basis.

Conventional cartography tends to focus on land, even if there are human aspects in the mapping of landownership or the navigability of the terrain for armies of men. Conventional cartograms can be thought of as maps in which at least one scalar aspect, such as distance or area, is deliberately distorted to be drawn in proportion to a variable of interest. Many conventional maps are cartograms, but few cartograms appear like conventional maps. An equal area conventional map is a type of area cartogram, as is the Mercator projection briefly described in the introduction. The Mercator projection is just one of many that draws land areas in proportion (albeit non-linear) to their distance from the poles. This definition of cartograms sees them as a particular group of map projections.

The map projection definition is just one of a plethora of definitions that have been offered for cartograms. The cartography of cartograms during the twentieth century and its continuing rapid development in the twenty-first century has been so multifaceted that no solid definition could emerge – and the multiple meanings of the word continue to mutate. During the first three-quarters of the twentieth century it is likely that most people who drew cartograms also believed that they were inventing them or at least inventing a new variant of them. This was because what we know now as cartograms did not arise from cartographic orthodoxy but were instead mainly produced by mavericks and consequently only tolerated in cartographic textbooks – often referred to as being on the margins of the subject: map-like rather than map.

The heterogeneous development of cartograms in the twentieth century is partly reflected in the many names that exist for cartograms. For instance, the area distorting kind alone have been termed: *anamorphosis* (Dorling, 2006); diagrammatic maps; map-like diagrams; *varivalent* projections; density-equivalized maps; isodensity maps; value-by-area maps; and even mass distributing (*pycnomirastic*) map projections. The sub-category of those where area is drawn in proportion to population have gone under many names also, including: political map; demographic map; population scale map; and many very specific titles such as 'a map for health officers' (Dorling, 1996). There are non-continuous (Olson, 1976) as well as contiguous (Tobler, 1973) varieties, and – as an infinite number of correct continuous area cartograms can be produced (Sen, 1975) for any given variable – very many different cartograms have been drawn scaled to the same quantity, usually population. However, by the end of the century it became clear that only one area cartogram will approximate the best, least distorting solution (Tobler, 2004) and a practical means to achieving that solution became available shortly after the end of the century (given in Gastner and Newman (2004) and discussed in the following section). These are, of course, just part of the start of the history of cartograms. Tobler's (2004) review is an excellent place to begin to go further – for work since then see Henriques et al. (2009), Keim et al. (2002, 2004, 2005), Dorling (2006) and Dorling et al. (2006, 2007a,b).

The motivations for drawing cartograms have in most cases been related to the rapidly changing political geography of the twentieth century and the period shortly before that century began, which followed the upheavals of industrialisation and the concretisation of nation-states and the consequence visualization of 'state-istics'. The earliest known area cartogram was Levasseur's 1870 cartogram of Europe, which depicted countries in their 'correct' (in this case correct physical area) size. That cartogram is reproduced on page 29 of Tobler (2004) and is shown in Figure 10.2.

The very first cartogram is a good example to begin with to understand that these have never been neutral maps (of course no maps can be neutral). In studying Figure 10.2 it is hard to imagine that part of Levasseur's aim was not to imply that Russia was somehow balanced by, or a threat to, the combined land weight of Europe. Levasseur's cartogram, seen in the context of political mapping and visualization of its time added to the images of the apparent invulnerability of Russia and the threat of its land area in a way uncannily similar to its depiction using the Mercator projection on Cold War US television screens a century later.

By many, in the years leading up to the start of the twentieth century Russia was seen as the largest potential threat to new emerging political systems in Europe; and some images such as Figure 10.2 were drawn suggesting that it should have been taken more seriously than its traditional depiction on maps suggested. It is very important to stress the possible societal and political implications of choosing a particular cartographic method to draw a map. It has also often been argued that all forms of mapping are forms of social control in the sense that they are created to serve the purposes and designs of their creators rather than to inform the 'public' and that the organizations controlling most cartographic production choose what information they collect and how they show it in quite partisan ways (e.g. see Harley, 1988; Pickles, 1995). Undoubtedly, the choice of a method has a potentially huge influence on the message that comes across. It should always be borne in mind that all mapping and cartographic approaches represent alternative views and at the same time propagate a particular doctrine by choosing to present (or hide!) information in a suitable way (Monmonier, 1991; Dorling, 1996).

Although both area and linear cartograms were drawn before the advent of the twentieth century, only a handful of examples of explicitly created cartograms have ever been referred to from those times. All these, to the best of our knowledge, dated from the last half of the nineteenth century. Many ancient maps do, of course, look like modern day

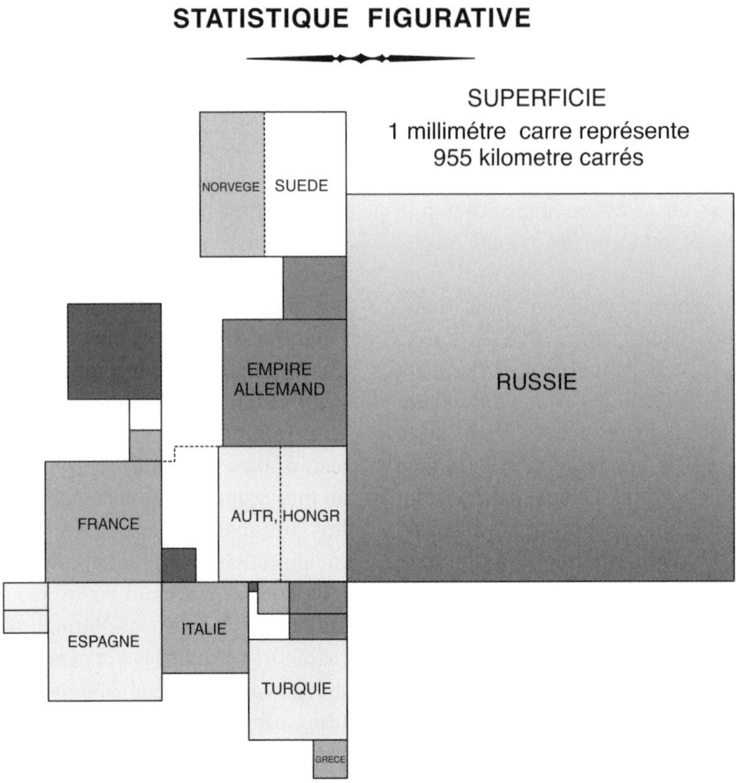

STATISTIQUE FIGURATIVE

SUPERFICIE
1 millimétre carre représente
955 kilometre carrés

NORVEGE   SUEDE

EMPIRE
ALLEMAND

RUSSIE

FRANCE

AUTR, HONGR

ESPAGNE

ITALIE

TURQUIE

GRECE

Figure 10.2   Levasseur's 1870 cartogram of Europe (Reproduced from Tobler (2004: 29))

cartograms and land was often drawn in rough proportion to perceived social importance in *mappa mundi* for instance – but the modern day cartogram really is a product of very recent generations. The increasing availability of a wide range of new data sources in digital format, coupled with computer hardware and software advances including high-quality computer graphics and presentation facilities were key. Orthodox cartographic methodology has been translated onto the computer screen (Bickmore, 1975; Hagen, 1982; Taylor, 1985; Jupe, 1987; Goodchild, 1988; Visvalingham, 1989; Muller, 1989). Swirling images were produced from the simplest formulae (Davis, 1974; Mandelbrot, 1983; Andrews et al., 1988). So, during the twentieth century methods of cartogram projection developed from manual drawing and the manipulation of hundreds of cardboard

tiles (Hunter and Young, 1968); through to the use of thousands of ball bearings and hinged metal joints (Skoda and Robertson, 1972); to early computer modelling (Dougenik et al., 1985), to a plethora of algorithms becoming available towards and shortly after the end of the century that were developed to cope with the shifting of millions of vertices (House and Kocmound, 1998; Kocmound, 1997; Gusein-Zade and Tikunov, 1993). At the same time, map makers were still using paper and pen to draw several social atlases worth of cartograms, albeit with a little aid from computers, to achieve effects that computer algorithms alone could not (Dorling, 1995).

The twentieth century also saw the description of cartograms in theory that have yet to exist in practice (Angel and Hymen 1972). These included cartograms where travel time is shown as distance not just from a single point but between all points on the map (approximated by Ahmed and Miller, 2007; Ewing, 1974; Muller, 1978; Spiekermann and Wegener, 1994). Such a linear cartogram would be possible (it has been proved mathematically if not visually) were the map to be drawn as a two-dimensional surface (manifold) undulating within, wrapped up in and occasionally torn within three-dimensional space – no longer the flat map of tradition. Linear and area cartograms could be combined in this way and together merged into quantity as volume cartograms where, for instance, each life that had existed were given an equal amount of volume in a deliberately distorted block of space-time. Such possibilities have been described and a few developed (Dorling, 1996), but it often takes several decades between the proof of what is possible and its realization. Thus part of the history of cartograms in the twentieth century has been in imagining new possibilities that have yet to be realized. Many may never be realized.

The actual construction of what are now seen as traditional cartograms remains problematic for most of those who wish to draw cartograms and was near impossible for most people living in most places in the twentieth century. Many months, even years could be spent creating a cartogram by hand, of – for instance – the parliamentary constituencies of Britain in 1964, only for their boundaries to be redrawn by 1970 and the cartogram then abandoned.

Instrumental in all this work and in the development of automated methods of cartogram production and the theories behind them was Dr Waldo Tobler (1930) whose work inspired all those who worked in this area in the last third of the century. His seminal publication (Tobler, 1973) was related to the need for cartograms that arises periodically in America with the political redistricting following each decadal population census. Thirty-seven years later, as we say above, his review of the development of computer cartograms remains one of the most useful summaries of the field (Tobler, 2004).

Due to the recent availability of new algorithms, more cartograms were drawn in the first few years of twenty-first century than were produced throughout the whole of the twentieth (see Dorling et al., 2008). Software to produce linear cartograms (and sophisticated flow maps) has lagged that used in creating area cartograms and so there are fewer examples to discuss of linear cartograms in which distance (or the width of lines) is rescaled to be proportional to a variable of interest (see Figure 10.3 below for an example). Figure 10.3 is a traditional travel time map of Switzerland. Such time-scaled maps are created by transforming the physical locations into new ones that satisfy travel-time linear constraints (see Axhausen et al., 2006, 2008, for more details).

The significant developments in cartographic methodologies aided by increasing computational power and sophisticated graphical capabilities has led to many alternative maps and visualizations of societies that were not based on physical geography. These cartogram-based visualizations differ considerably from traditional thematic maps. The latter drastically distort the reality they purport to contain, at worse reversing the patterns that exist. People who study people, who are interested in societies, politics, history, economics and increasingly even human geography, usually do not use these maps. They usually use no maps at all. A topographic map base allows, at most, the depiction of human land use. People have created maps based on human geography in the past, but only with the advent of sophisticated image and graphics software has it become possible to do this on an easily replicable basis.

Human cartography concentrates on the human experience of space and portrays the human encounters with 'reality', rejecting the view that behaviour (and, therefore, features such as population distribution and the location of industrial activity) is governed totally by the framework of the earth and the 'tyranny of distance'. Figure 10.4 gives a

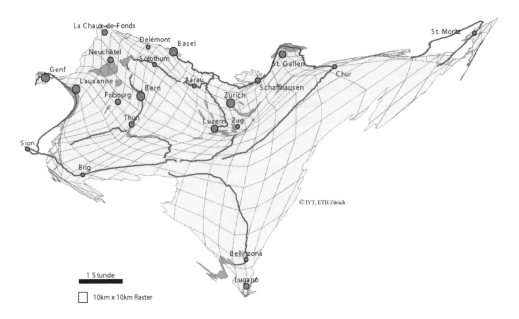

Figure 10.3   1950 time-scaled map (Axhausen et al. (2008: 402))

Figure 10.4   Using Chernoff faces in a human cartogram of voting, housing, employment and industrial composition (Dorling, 1991; note that the original is in colour)

good example of how human cartograms should be used to depict the spatial distribution of a variable that has been systematically mapped using conventional maps: voting. In particular, it shows the spatial distribution of voting in Britain and how Chernoff (1973) faces combined with the appropriate use of colour can be used in a human cartogram of the distribution of voting, housing, employment and industrial compositions in the 1983 general election in Britain. The 633 parliamentary constituencies are each represented by a face whose features express the various variables, and which is coloured by the mix of voting – drawn on the equal population cartogram (for more details and the original colour version of this cartogram see Dorling, 1991).

During the 19th century, as interest in population statistics grew and as people who had been peasants became consumers, the relative value of land to human life fell and human geography began to matter more. The emergence of detailed census cartography after the Second World War grew out of these shifting priorities. However, most of the thematic maps of census variables were still governed by the logic of physical geography. For instance, choropleth maps of population data typically shade regions with boundaries defined on the basis of their area size in proportion to the measurement of a variable of interest. It can be argued however, that such maps, apart from often being bad examples of physical geography's cartography, are bad social science. They make concentrations appear where they are not, and dissolve existing patterns.

Human cartography can address these issues by redrawing the location of boundaries (dasymetric mapping) and size of territories on the basis of a population variable of interest. In this way the relative values of objects on a map are reflected by the size of the area and this is much easier for the human eye-brain system to assess when compared to trying to translate shades of colour into rates and then to imagine what they imply. Rescaling area to the variation in particular variables is very effective in terms of visual communication and a good example of this is the traditional homunculus used in medical science to portray the human body in terms of the degree of sensitivity: the skin is rescaled in proportion to even out number of nerve endings[1] (also see Dorling, 2007a,b).

In addition, using human population cartograms instead of traditional maps has very important societal implications. An early example of using human cartograms to promote a particular viewpoint or support an argument is the publication of a map in *The Washington Post* on Sunday 3 November 1929 with state areas equal to population and taxation, accompanied by a proposal to the Congress to modify the allocation of tariffs (Tobler, 2004). A more recent example is the work of Kidron and Segal (initially in 1981 and 1984; and in recent years updated by various authors and published by Earthscan) who drew an alternative State of the World Atlases, in which they used area cartograms to show how inequitably the world's health, weapons and food were distributed. These cartograms were designed by hand to keep the shape of the world familiar while still showing clearly how unfair the distribution of resources and power was at the time (it is now more unfair). The cartograms and maps used in these atlases were perhaps some of the best remembered by the school children that were taught in the 1980s with such books and therefore may have had very important social effects upon this generation.

Other examples of using human cartography in advocacy include the work of Seager and Olson (1986) who described the geography of women's rights in the world, Gilbert's (1982) *Atlas of the Holocaust* and Bunge's (1988) *Nuclear War Atlas* illustrating what would be the devastating impact of a possible nuclear war. A more recent example is shown in Figure 10.5. This is a map produced by Social Watch.[2] This map treats population sizes in the same way that a conventional method such as Peter's projection treats land area. In this map countries are represented by rectangles of varying size, which is determined by how many people live there and not by how many hectares the country occupies. The rectangles are then coloured according to their rank in the Basic Capabilities Index, which a way of identifying poverty situations not based on income. By not using income this index is consistent with the definitions of poverty based on capabilities (promoted by Sen, 1982; Nussbaum and Sen, 1993) and lack of human rights (Social Watch, 2007). Countries in blue on the map (see source Web site for the original colour version of this map) are those that provide their inhabitants with a minimum level of social services, whereas countries in red face critical situations of deprivations. In addition, the colour scale of the circles shows degrees of progress towards gender equity.

The map shown in Figure 10.5 depicts very different societal impacts on the views of its readers compared with traditional mapping approaches. This becomes clear by comparing the size of countries, for instance the Russian Federation, Australia and Canada and their respective sizes in a land area map (see Figure 10.1). Figure 10.5 has a very

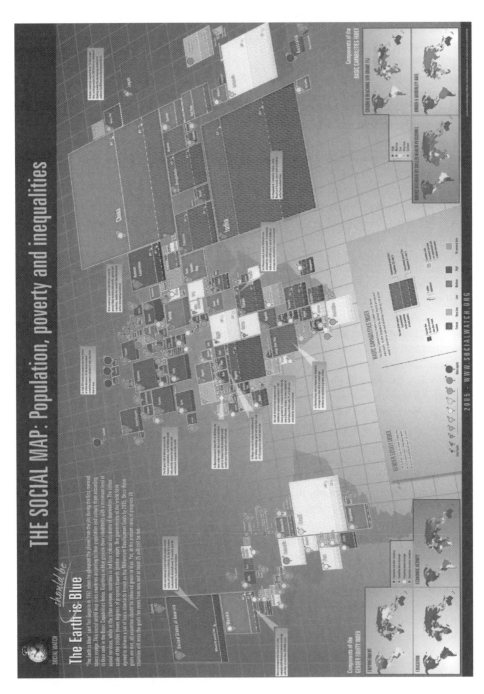

Figure 10.5   The social map (http://www.socialwatch.org)

different impact upon the public's perception regarding the progress in achieving a set of basic standards known as the Millennium Development Goals for the majority of the planet's population (if all these standards are met then all countries in the map will be coloured blue or green).

It is increasingly and convincingly argued that conventional maps should not be used to map human data and that cartograms such as that shown in Figure 10.5 should be used instead. However, it is also argued that it would be useful if population cartograms approximate the shapes of the regions and countries as much as possible, while at the same time preserving orientation and contiguity, so that areas on them can be easily recognizable and familiar to the map reader (Dent, 1996). The following section discusses new approaches that have been adopted and implemented in order to produce cartograms that distort the least on the surface of the sphere while still scaling areas correctly.

MAPS AND SOCIETY: THE SOCIETAL IMPACTS OF TRADITIONAL/ CONVENTIONAL MAPS VS. HUMAN CARTOGRAMS

What use are Mercator's North Poles and Equators, Tropics, Zones and Meridian Lines?
So the Bellman would cry: and the crew would reply,
They are merely conventional signs!
(*Hunting of the Snark* by Lewis Carroll, quoted in Truss, 2003: 200–1)

Cartograms such as that shown in Figure 10.5 represent good examples of how social scientists should be using maps for human-scaled visualization. However, a disadvantage of this cartogram is that it distorts the original regions' real shapes and this affects the degree to which it is familiar and recognizable by a map-reader. As suggested by the brief review in the previous section, there have been numerous methodological developments aimed at creating cartograms on the

basis of automated computer algorithms. These methods attempted to address a number of key challenges:

- Develop a method which is as simple and easy to understand and implement as possible.
- Generate 'readable' maps by minimizing the distortion of the shape of the geographical areas being mapped, while at the same time preserving accuracy and maintaining topological features.
- Determine the cartogram projection uniquely.
- Minimize computational speed.
- Make the end result independent of the initial projection being used.
- Make the end result look aesthetically acceptable.
- Have no overlapping regions.

As noted in the previous section the work of Tobler (1963, 1973) was instrumental in facing these challenges. In particular, Tobler constructed the first computer algorithm that created an equal density approximation by compressing or expanding lines of latitude and longitude until a least root mean square error solution is obtained. The method generates pseudo-continuous cartograms according to partial differential equations in order to fix a planimetrically correct base map to an underlying continuous surface. This was then projected onto a distorted plane, which represented the variable transformation (Tobler, 1963; Dougenik et al., 1983). The original Tobler algorithm is regarded as imaginative but highly inaccurate as the resulting cartograms may contain extensive area errors, slow due to the number of iterations required by the algorithm and guilty of producing an overgeneralized end product. There have been several attempts to build upon Tobler's original work, including the work of Nicholas Chrisman, which uses a different distorted plane approach. In this scheme, each region or polygon has an amount of 'force' applied to it based on the variable's value being mapped (Dougenik et al., 1983). More recently, a Cellular Automaton approach has been developed (Dorling, 1996; Henriques et al., 2009) to create cartograms. This approach involves superimposing a grid on a map. The individual cells are then swapped on this grid until every geographic region has a number of cells corresponding to its desired area. This method is very effective at achieving the correct area, but regions tend to lose their unique contours and acquire a shape reflecting the grid. An example is given in Figure 10.6 reproduced from the more recent work of Henriques and collaborators (see Henriques et al., 2009).

The problems of distortion and projection-dependence have been successfully addressed by Gastner and Newman (2004) who developed computer software that creates unique cartograms that can be adapted to minimize distortion on the surface of the sphere while still scaling areas correctly. The process is essentially one of allowing population to flow-out from high-density to lower-density areas, which used the linear diffusion method from elementary physics to model this process. The computer algorithm has been altered

so that it re-projects the boundaries of territories on the surface of the sphere – rather than on the plane. It can also be described as using a diffusion equation from the physics of heat transfer and molecular mixing (for a detailed formal discussion see Gastner and Newman [2004]). The resulting maps remain recognizable and incorporate the striking re-sizing used previously in 'rectangular maps'. Furthermore, unlike its predecessor projections, Gastner and Newman's method does not reflect the arbitrary choice of initial projection (for instance, it joins East–West unlike any other equal population projection) and produces an image that approximates a unique least distorting solution. This means that the cartogram reader has only one new projection to learn should they wish to map upon population rather than land. The remainder of this chapter shows how this projection

Figure 10.6   USA county population cartogram (Henriques et al., 2009: 508)

method can be used to visualize countries around the world, regions within countries and areas within cities.

VISUALIZING THE WORLD

The pioneering diffusion method of Gastner and Newman described above was first applied by them in order to depict the results of the 2000 US presidential election, as well as to investigate the distribution of lung cancer cases among the male population in the state of New York and to also study the geographical distribution of news stories in the USA. Following on from this work, there have been a number of extensive applications of the technique to generate world cartograms. The first such cartogram was presented by Richard Webb (2006) in *Nature* showing how Mark Newman had overlaid a grid of 4096 by 2048 squares on a rectangular world map based on a cylindrical equal-distance projection and then computed a starting population-density function by dividing the population of each country equally between the squares covering its territory. In this way population was allowed to diffuse away from higher to lower density areas with national boundaries moving such that the net population flow through them was zero at all times. The 'Gastner and Newman' diffusion technique has also been used extensive to generate a series of world cartograms in the context of Worldmapper,[3] which is a collaborative project between researchers at the Social and Spatial Inequalities Research Group of the University of Sheffield, UK and Mark Newman, from the Center for the Study of Complex Systems at the University of Michigan in the USA. The project has so far produced nearly 700 world maps where territories are re-sized on each map on the basis of a number of subjects, ranging from health, life and death to income, poverty and wealth (Dorling, 2006; Barford and Dorling, 2007a,b; Dorling et al., 2008). Figure 10.7 shows a Worldmapper cartogram of the world population distribution

across territories, similar to the first such cartogram by Richard Webb (2006) briefly discussed above.

It is noteworthy that, unlike conventional choropleth maps of population data (as well as the Mercator-projection maps briefly reviewed above), the Worldmapper cartogram shown in Figure 10.7 reveals more of the real pattern of population distribution by showing where the highest population concentrations are and therefore how human population can be more revealingly mapped by social scientists. China and India which account for about a third of the world population are the largest territories on the map. In contrast, the size of territories of countries with large land sizes but low population densities such as Russia, Canada and Australia are diminished when compared with conventional land-based choropleth maps.

It is also interesting to see how the sizes of the territories change in relation to the population cartogram when mapping other socioeconomic variables and to also think about the societal effects of such a cartogram on collective imaginations. As we have also shown above, using a cartogram instead of a conventional map has a very different impact upon the public's perception regarding the World's progress in achieving the United Nations Millennium Development goals. One of these goals is the eradication of extreme poverty and hunger and a more specific target in relation to this goal is to halve between 1990 and 2015 the number of people who suffer from hunger (United Nations, 2008). A useful indicator pertaining to this target is the prevalence of underweight children under five years of age, which is also discussed in this context in latest recent report by the United Nations Children's Fund (UNICEF) on the state of the World's children (UNICEF, 2007). According to data collected and calculations made by the Worldmapper project, between 1995 and 2002 almost a quarter of all children aged under 15 years old were estimated to be underweight.[5] Figure 10.8 shows a world map of all underweight children in the world.

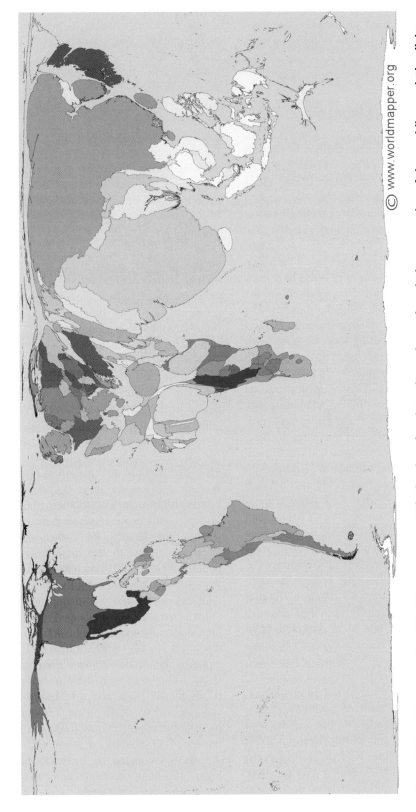

Figure 10.7   Total population (Worldmapper map 002). The size of each territory shows the relative proportion of the world's population living there (United Nations Development Programme, 2004, Human Development Report)

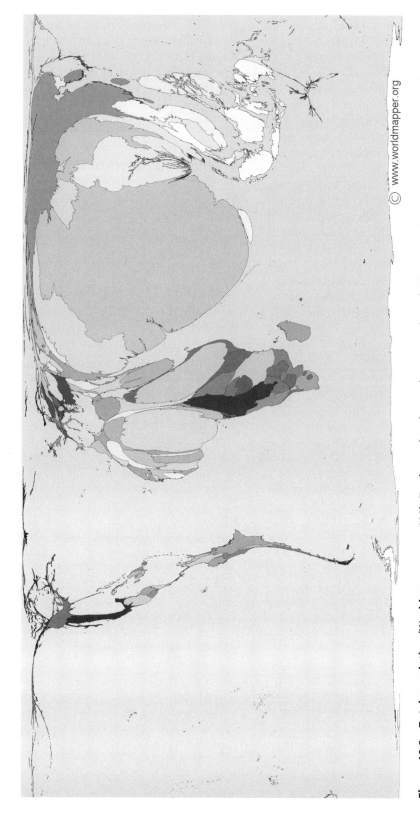

Figure 10.8 Total population (Worldmapper map 182). Territory size shows the proportion of all underweight children in the world that live there. (United Nations Development Programme, 2004, Human Development Report)

It is interesting to consider at this stage the impact that Figure 10.8 may have on the public's perception of progress regarding the achievement of Millennium Goals, when compared to conventional maps. Figure 10.8 is a much better representation of the spatial inequality and in particular it highlights that half of all underweight children under the age of five years live in Southern Asia, whereas Southeastern Africa, Asia Pacific, Northern Africa and Eastern Asia also have very large numbers of underweight children, especially Ethiopia, Indonesia, Nigeria and China. In contrast, it is very difficult to distinguish the shapes of most countries in Europe and the Americas because they are hardly visible. When compared with conventional maps a human-scaled visualization such as that presented in Figure 10.8 is possibly presenting a much more accurate, appropriate and powerful depiction of the magnitude of issues such as child poverty as well as the associated social and spatial inequalities. Apart from the statistical human population data that this map communicates, it can be argued that it also has a very effective and emotionally powerful visual impact. Or, as one of us has argued elsewhere with regards to the social and spatial inequalities that underpin inequalities in health: 'You can say it, you can prove it, you can tabulate it, but it is only when you show it that it hits home' (Dorling, 2007a: 13). Cartograms have been around for many years and thus it is perhaps surprising that human cartograms have not been used more by organizations such as UNICEF as well as a number of non-governmental organizations to increase awareness and improve the quality of information that the public have about global issues.

Figure 10.8 is just one example of how new innovative cartogram creation methodologies can be used to draw alternative human-scaled visualizations by keeping the shape of the world familiar, while at the same time showing clearly striking patterns of inequalities. There are, of course, numerous other examples of variables that can be and have been mapped in a similar way: there are over 600 such maps created so far by the Worldmapper project alone. In principle, any variable pertaining to human population could be mapped in this way at the world scale in order to address research questions and policy issues pertaining to human societies.

VISUALIZING THE NATION STATE

The cartogram methods discussed above in a world mapping context, can also be very powerful tools in depicting socioeconomic information for smaller geographical levels, within nation states. Among the first applications of the Gastner and Newman method was to provide an alternative visualization of the results of the 2000 US presidential election and subsequently it was also used to depict the 2004 presidential and the 2006 congressional election results.[6] One of the key arguments against using conventional maps to depict election results is that they may give the superficial impression that electoral regions that have a large topographic area but relatively small populations dominate the political landscape. For instance, in the case of the US 2000 and 2004 presidential elections conventional maps were dominated by the red colour (the republican candidate) whereas the blue colour (democratic candidate) was much less visible, despite the fact that the 'blue' states had very large numbers of voters. Gastner et al. (2004) show how such biases can be corrected by resizing each state according to its population and they also conduct the same analysis at the county level. In 2008, Barack Obama did not appear to win on the conventional map.

In this section we further demonstrate the power of cartogram technologies for human-scaled visualizations by mapping regions within a country, resizing the areas of the regions on the basis of a variable that is increasingly used in the social sciences: subjective happiness. In particular, we use data from the British Household Panel Survey (BHPS) which is one of the most comprehensive social surveys in Britain drawn from a representative sample of over 5,000 households and which includes a number of questions pertaining to subjective happiness and well-being, such as: *Have you recently been feeling reasonably happy, all things considered?*

It has often been argued that responses to such questions may not be readily comparable between countries due to various kinds of cultural bias (Diener, 1995; Diener and Diener, 1995). For instance, it has often been suggested that Americans have a tendency to claim that they are very happy because the term 'happiness' is positively valued in their

society, whereas in other countries such as Japan and France, there is the exact opposite tendency (Frey and Stutzer, 2002). It can be argued therefore that the subjective happiness variable is more suitable for analysis and visualization at the national and sub-national level, when such data is available. Figure 10.9 is based on data from the BHPS and represents the 'mirror image' of happiness and unhappiness in Britain. In particular, the cartogram on the left-hand side was created using the Gastner and Newman's diffusion method to rescale the sizes of all areas according to the number of the 'unhappy'

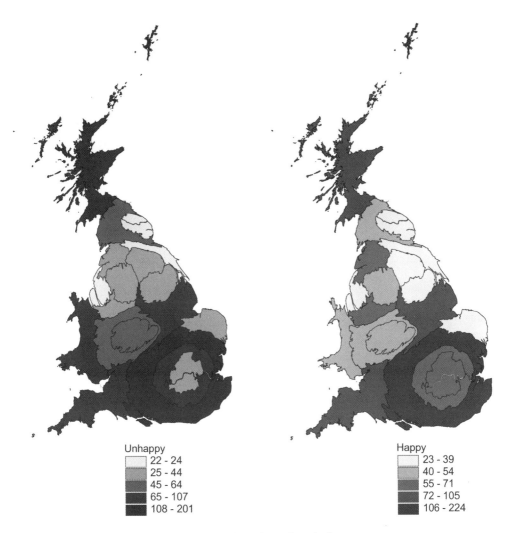

Figure 10.9 Mirror image of happiness/unhappiness in Britain

respondents in the survey. Likewise, the same method was used to create the cartogram on the right-hand side of Figure 10.9, in which the sizes of all areas are rescaled on the basis of the number of 'happy' respondents. As can be seen, these human cartograms are very different from conventional maps of Britain, as they give more prominence to regions with large concentrations of a human variable of interest, which in this case is the number of 'happy' and 'unhappy' people. Taking a closer look at these cartograms, we observe similarities in terms of the shape and size of most regions. For instance, the region 'Rest of South East', coloured in red in both cartograms, has very similar numbers of both 'happy' and 'unhappy' people. Nevertheless, there are also some notable differences. In particular, the sizes of Scotland and Wales is slightly larger in the cartogram of 'unhappy' people. The shades of the region vary because the different shades show populations happy and unhappy, whereas the areas show the absolute numbers. The regions of Inner and Outer London have considerably larger sizes in the cartogram of 'happy people' (for a more detailed discussion of the happiness data used to create Figure 10.9 see Ballas et al., 2007).

A key societal implication of using cartograms such as those shown in Figure 10.9 in order to depict areas within nation states is that, if widely reproduced, it may influence considerably the public's mental map of the nation, which is typically constructed by mainstream media representations.

VISUALIZING THE CITY

In this section we show how the Gastner and Newman diffusion cartogram method can be employed to visualize human variables at sub-regional and sub-city level, drawing on recent research on poverty, wealth and place in Britain (Dorling et al., 2007) and focusing on the city of London.

As noted above, one of the key advantages of the diffusion cartogram method is that it minimizes the distortion of the shape of the geographical areas being mapped, while at the same time it maintains the topological features. This advantage is perhaps more important when mapping countries or regions within countries that have shapes with which most people likely to read the cartograms are familiar. However, it can be argued that people are perhaps much less familiar with administrative, census or postal geographical units that are typically used when mapping socio-economic and demographic variables at the sub-regional or intra-city level. In this section we have chosen the parliamentary constituency as the unit of analysis for intra-city, human-scaled visualization. UK parliamentary constituencies are a very useful unit of analysis of socio-economic and demographic data as they each contain roughly the same number of people. In addition, it can be argued that they are an intra-region and intra-city unit of analysis with which the public is familiar, given that election results are mapped at this level and such maps are extensively used by the media, especially at the time of parliamentary elections.

The Greater London metropolitan area, which is used as an example here, comprise 74 in 2009 parliamentary constituencies which are shown in Figure 10.10.

As can be seen, the shapes and the size of each area vary considerably and this variation introduces undesirable visual bias, given that all areas have roughly the same population. As it was the case with regions and countries, such bias can be corrected by using cartogram methods. In the UK case of parliamentary constituencies, a population cartogram would result in all areas having roughly the same size (see Dorling, 2005; Dorling and Thomas, 2006). However, cartogram methods can also be used to distort the size of each constituency on the basis of a socioeconomic variable that pertains to the political agenda of national and local government authorities. A policy-relevant theme in this context is the spatial distribution of poverty and wealth, which according to recent research has been characterised by high

Figure 10.10   Map of Greater London parliamentary constituencies

degrees of spatial polarization increasing within Britain at regional and local levels (Dorling et al., 2007; Dorling and Ballas, 2008). In particular, the highest wealth and lowest poverty rates in Britain tend to be clustered in the South East of England, with the exception of some areas in inner London (Dorling et al., 2007). The geographical patterns of social and spatial inequalities can be explored further with the use of human cartograms. For instance, Figures 10.11 and 10.12 show an alternative human-scaled visualization of the geography of poverty and wealth in London. In particular, they show how the London parliamentary constituencies can be distorted on the basis of the number of households living in them classified as 'core poor' and 'exclusive wealthy', respectively.

As can be seen in Figure 10.11, the 'core poor' map of the locations of the poorest of the poor in London is dominated by inner city areas and areas in the South East. 'Core poor' are defined as people who are simultaneously income poor materially deprived and subjectively poor, and who have very little money coming in, very few possessions and resources and they also consistently perceive themselves as poor (Dorling et al., 2007). The parliamentary constituencies with the largest numbers of this group of households, those which dominate the map (and also dark shaded) are Poplar and Canning Town, Vauxall, Hackney South and Shoreditch, North Southward and Bermondsey and Bethnal Green, all located in the east end of London.

In contrast, Figure 10.12 shows a very different picture of London, as it distorts the size of all parliamentary constituencies on the basis of the number of households classified

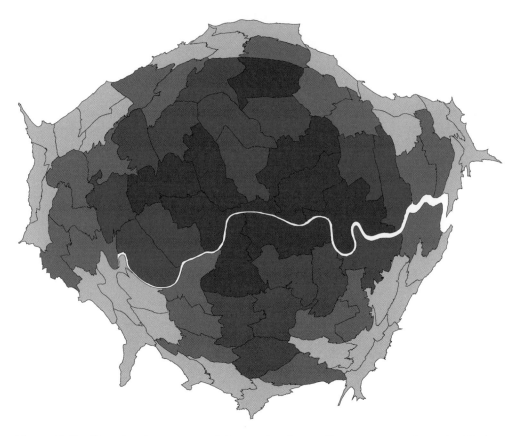

Figure 10.11 'Core Poor' cartogram of Greater London parliamentary constituencies (darker areas show higher concentrations of 'core poor')

as 'exclusive wealthy'. These are households that have sufficient wealth to exclude themselves from the norms of society, if they so wish (Dorling et al., 2007). As can be seen, the west end of London dominates the map, but also some of the wealthy suburbs in the outskirts of the city, whereas the size of most of the areas in the east end of London has shrunk. Kensington and Chelsea (the largest dark shaded area in the middle of the cartogram) is the parliamentary constituency with the highest number of exclusive wealthy households, which is nearly double that of Richmond Park which comes second, followed by Finchley and Golders Green and Twickenham (all areas in the west end of London). On the other hand, most of the areas in the shrinking (in Figure 10.12) east end of London have very few households that could exclude themselves by dint of wealth

from the norms of society if they wished to do so. Many households there are excluded by their poverty.

Maps such as those shown in Figure 10.11 and 10.12 may have a very different impact on the public perception about the state of societal inequality when compared to conventional maps. They can also be used to raise awareness about social disparities and their geographical manifestations within cities and regions and to monitor progress (or lack of progress!) with regards to stated government, social, regional and urban policy goals.

CONCLUSION

In this chapter we provided an overview of the state of the art in human area population

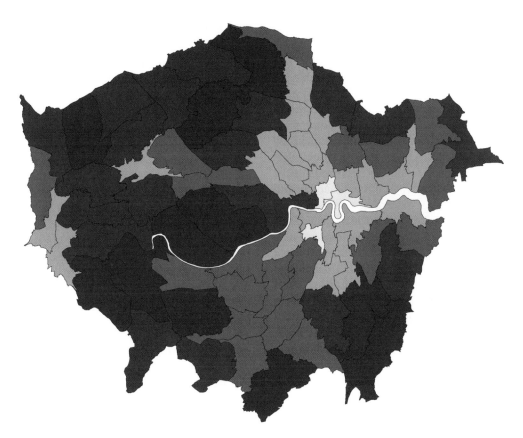

Figure 10.12 *Exclusive Wealthy* **cartogram of Greater London parliamentary constituencies (darker areas show higher concentrations of 'exclusive wealthy')**

cartograms and also gave a number of examples at different geographical scales in order to illuminate issues and problems that are inherent in visualizing human populations. We have argued strongly that conventional maps that show how cities, regions and countries appear from space are not depicted in an appropriate way to show the spatial distributions of humans and their characteristics. Human cartography provides the appropriate methods and tools for the depiction of the spatial distribution of variables pertaining to human societies rather than environmental, geological or meteorological problems.

As we argued throughout this chapter, the visual impact of human cartograms may have a considerable influence upon the public's perception about very important issues at different geographical scales: from achieving World Millennium Goals planet wide to ameliorating income and wealth inequalities within cities or regions.

Undoubtedly there has been progress in human cartography over the past 20 years. It can be argued that the new developments in human cartogram technologies, some of which were reviewed here, provide the tools and the enabling environment for social scientists across disciplines to map their data using methods that are appropriate for human-scaled visualizations. The new methods are relatively easy to understand and use and the resulting cartograms can be extremely powerful images to support the arguments of social science researchers. They are also much more successful than previous attempts in retaining recognizable aspects of the physical geographical zones that they seek to represent. It should be noted however, that the ability to deliver this 'recognizability' is always subject to the nature of the geography concerned and therefore automatic cartograms are not a panacea. The products of cartogram algorithms such as those discussed in this chapter should always be subject to scrutiny by the cartogram creator as well as the viewer (ideally through computer–user interaction through appropriate interfaces) and it should be acknowledged that non-automatic manual cartograms may be sometimes more appropriate. Also, it could be argued that the effectiveness of human cartograms of smaller sub-regional or intra-urban areas the physical shapes of which are less recognizable by viewers could be enhanced with the use of interactive tools ('mouseover', links to bar charts and alternative visualization and conventional maps) so that the cognitive effort in order to make comparisons between areas is minimized. More simply, some place name labels could just be added!

Finally, it can be argued that one of the ways in which human cartography can be improved is the enhancement of visual impact of human cartograms through the use of computer animation (Herzog, 2003) showing the changing shape and size of neighbourhoods, cities, regions and countries on the basis of different variables. It would also be useful to link human cartography to other new mapping technologies such as Google Earth™ in order to allow the viewers to spin around the sphere and allow viewers to zoom in and out of the globe and query where they were looking–to find out more about each place, to learn more, more quickly and even to see one image morph into another. This is one of the immediate priorities of projects such as the Worldmapper, which was discussed in above and it is possible that by the time you read this chapter, the Worldmapper Web site may well have enhanced 3D human cartograms (it already has some basic animations of map transformations).

ACKNOWLEDGEMENTS

The authors would like to thank John Pritchard for his help with the illustrations presented in Figure 10.9. They would also like to thank the editors and three anonymous reviewers for their very useful comments and suggestions on an earlier draft. The British Household Panel Survey data which were used to create this figure were made available through the UK Data Archive. The data were originally collected by the ESRC Research Centre on Micro-social Change at the University of Essex, now incorporated within the Institute for Social and Economic Research. Dimitris Ballas and Danny Dorling were funded by the UK Economic and Social Research Council (research fellowship grant number RES-163–27–1013) and the British Academy and Leverhulme Trust (British Academy Research Leave Fellowship and Leverhulme Trust grant) respectively, while writing this chapter.

NOTES

1 Also see: http://en.wikipedia.org/wiki/Homunculus.

2 http://www.socialwatch.org/.

2 http://www.socialwatch.org/.

3 http://www.worldmapper.org/.

4 The Worldmapper maps and data files cover 200 territories, mainly United Nation Member States plus a few others to include at least 99.95% of the world's population.

5 http://www.worldmapper.org/display.php?selected=182#.

6 http://www-personal.umich.edu/~mejn/election/.

REFERENCES

Ahmed, N. and Miller, H.J. (2007) 'Time-space transformations of geographic space for exploring, analyzing and visualizing transportation systems', *Journal of Transport Geography*, 15: 2–17.

Andrews, D.F., Fowlkes, E.B. and Tukey, P.A. (1988) '*Some approaches to interactive statistical graphics*'.

In W.S. Cleveland and M.E. McGill (eds) *Dynamic Graphics For Statistics.* Wandsworth: California.

Angel, S. and Hyman, G.M. (1972) 'Transformations and geographic theory', *Geographical Analysis*, 4: 350–67.

Axhausen, K.W., Dolci, V., Fröhlich, Ph., Scherer, M. and Carosio, A. (2006) Constructing time-scaled maps: Switzerland 1950–2000. Arbeitsberichte Verkehrs und Raumplanung 342, IVT, ETH Zürich, Zürich, Available at: http://www.ivt.ethz.ch/vpl/publications/reports/ab342.pdf (accessed 20 May 2008).

Axhausen, K.W., Dolci Frhlich, P., Scherer, M. and Carosio, A. (2008) 'Constructing time-scaled maps: Switzerland from 1950 to 2000', *Transport Reviews*, 28(3/5): 391–413.

Ballas, D., Dorling, D. and Shaw, M. (2007) 'Social inequality, health and well-being'. In J. Hawrorth and G. Hart (eds), *Well-Being: Individual, Community & Social Perspectives*. Palgrave: Basingstoke. pp. 163–86.

Barford, A. and Dorling, D. (2006a) 'Worldmapper: the world as you've never seen it before', *Teaching Geography*, 31(2): 68–75.

Barford, A. and Dorling, D. (2006b) 'A new approach to mapping the world: Visualizing facets of international health', *National Medical Journal of India*, 19(4).

Barford, A. and Dorling, D. (2007a) 'Re-ordering the world', *Geography Review*, 20(5): 8–11.

Barford, A. and Dorling, D. (2007b) 'A map a day, for every day of the year: A new view of the world', *GeoInformatics,* April/May 2007.

Bertin, J. (1978) 'Theory of communication and theory of "the graphic"', *The International Yearbook of Cartography*, 18: 118–26.

Bickmore, D.P. (1975) 'The relevance of cartography'. In J.C. Davies and M.J. McCullagh (eds), *Display and Analysis of Spatial Data*. London: John Wiley & Son. pp. 328–51.

Bunge, W. (1988) *The Nuclear War Atlas*. Oxford: Basil Blackwell.

Chernoff, H. (1973) 'The use of faces to represent points in k-dimensional space graphically', *Journal of the American Statistical Association*, 68: 361–68.

Davis, P.J. (1974) 'Visual geometry, computer graphics and theorems of perceived type, *Proceedings of Symposia in Applied Mathematics*, vol. 20, The Influence of Computing on Mathematical Research and Education, American Mathematical Society, Providence, Rhode Island.

Dent, B.D. (1996) *Cartography Thematic Map Design*, 4th edn. Dubuque, IA: C. Brown Publishers.

Denes, A. (1979) *Isometric Systems in Isotropic Space: Map Projections: From the Study of Distortions Series 1973–1979*. New York: Visual Studies Workshop Press.

Diener, E. (1995). 'A value based index for measuring national quality of life', *Social Indicators Research*, 36: 107–127.

Diener, E., & Diener, C. (1995). 'The wealth of nations revisited: Income and quality of life', *Social Indicators Research*, 36: 275–286.

Dorling, D. (1991) 'The visualization of spatial structure', PhD Thesis, Department of Geography, University of Newcastle upon Tyne.

Dorling, D. (1995) *A New Social Atlas of Britain.* Chichester: John Wiley.

Dorling, D. (1996) *Area Cartograms: Their Use and Creation Concepts and Techniques in Modern Geography*, series 59. (Norwich: Environmental Publications, University of East Anglia).

Dorling, D. (2006) 'New maps of the world, its people and their lives', *Society of Cartographers Bulletin*, 39(1/2): 35–40.

Dorling, D. (2007a) 'Worldmapper: The human anatomy of a small planet', *PLoS Medicine*, 4(1): 13–18.

Dorling, D. (2007b) Anamorphosis: 'The geography of physicians and mortality', *International Journal of Epidemiology*, 36(4): 745–50.

Dorling, D. and Ballas, D. (2008) 'Spatial divisions of poverty and wealth'. In T. Ridge and S. Wright (eds), *Understanding Poverty, Wealth and Inequality: Policies and Prospects*. Bristol: Policy Press.

Dorling, D., Barford, A. and Newman, M. (2006) 'Worldmapper: The world as you've never seen it before', *IEEE Transactions on Visualization and Computer Graphics*, 12(5): 757–64.

Dorling, D. and Fairbairn, D. (1997) *Mapping: Ways of Representing the World*. Harlow: Longman.

Dorling, D., Newman, M. and Barford, A. (2008) *The Real World Atlas*. London: Thames and Hudson.

Dorling, D., Rigby, J., Wheeler, B., Ballas, D., Thomas, B., Fahmy, E., Gordon, D. and Lupton, R. (2007) *Poverty, Wealth and Place in Britain, 1968 to 2005*. Bristol: Policy Press.

Dorling, D. and Thomas, B. (2004) *People and Places: A Census Atlas of the UK*. Bristol: Policy Press.

Dougenik, J.A., Chrisman, N.R. and Niemeyer, D.R. (1985) 'An algorithm to construct continuous area cartograms', *Professional Geographer*, 37(1): 75–81.

Dougenik, J.A., Niemeyer, D.R. and Chrisman, N.R., (1983) A Computer Algorithm to Build Continuous Area Cartograms, Harvard Computer Graphics Week, Harvard University Graduate School.

Ewing, G.O. (1974) 'Multidimensional scaling and time-space maps', *The Canadian Geographer*, 18(2): 161–7.

Frey, B. and Stutzer, A. (2002) *Happiness and Economics*. Princeton, NJ: Princeton University Press.

Friis, H.R. (1974) 'Statistical cartography in the United States prior to 1870 and the role of Joseph C.G. Kennedy and the U.S. census office', *The American Cartographer*, 1(2): 131–57.

Gastner, M.T. and Newman, M.E.J. (2004) 'Diffusion-based method for producing density equalizing maps' *Proc Natl Acad Sci USA*, 101: 7499–7504.

Gastner, M., Shalizi, C. and Newman, M. (2008) Maps and cartograms of the 2004 US presidential election results. Available from: http://www-personal.umich.edu/~mejn/election (accessed 15 April 2008).

Gilbert, M. (1982), *Atlas of the Holocaust*. London: Michael Joseph.

Goodchild, M.F. (1988) 'Stepping over the line: Technological constraints and the new cartography', *The American Cartographer*, 15 (3): 311–19.

Gusein-Zade, S. and Tikunov, V. (1993) 'A new technique for constructing continuous cartograms', *Cartography and Geographic Information Systems*, 20(3): 167–73.

Hagen, C.B. (1982) *Maps: An overview of the producer-user interaction*, ACSM-ASP 42nd Annual Convention, March, Denver Colorado, pp. 325–38.

Harley, J.B. (1988) 'Maps, knowledge and power'. In D. Cosgrove and S. Daniels (eds), *The Iconography of Landscape*. New York: Cambridge University Press.

Herzog, A. (2003) 'Developing cartographic applets for the internet', in M.P. Peterson (ed.), *Maps and the Internet, 1*: 115–28.

Henriques, R.A.P. (2005) *CARTO_SOM: Cartogram creation using self-organising maps*, Masters in GIS dissertation, Instituto Superior de Estatistica e Gestao de Informacao, Universidade Nova de Lisboa, http://www.isegi.unl.pt/servicos/documentos/TSIG010.pdf (accessed 5 February 2008).

Henriques, R., Bação, F. and Lobo, V. (2009), Carto-SOM: Cartogram creation using self-organizing maps, *International Journal of Geographical Information Science*, 23(4), 483–511

House, D. and Kocmoud, C. (1998) 'Continuous cartogram construction', *Proceedings of IEEE Visualization*. IEEE: Research Triangle Park, NC.

Howe, G.M. (1986) 'Disease mapping'. In M. Pacione (ed.), *Medical Geography: Progress and Prospect*. London: Croom Helm.

Hunter, J.M. and Young, J.C. (1968) 'A technique for the construction of quantitative cartograms by physical accretion models', *The Professional Geographer*, 20(6): 402–7.

Jupe, D. (1987) 'The new technology: will cartography need the cartographer?', *The Canadian Surveyor*, 14(3): 341–6.

Keim, D.A., North, S.C. and Panse, C. (2004) 'CartoDraw: A fast algorithm for generating contiguous cartograms', *IEEE Transactions on Visualization and Computer Graphics,* 10(1): 95–110.

Keim, D.A., North, S.C. and Panse, C. (2005) 'Medial-axes based cartograms', *IEEE Computer Graphics and Applications*, 25(3): 60–8.

Keim, D.A., North, S.C. Panse, C. and Schneidewind, J.O. (2002) 'Efficient cartogram generation: A comparison', *Proceedings of the IEEE Symposium on Information Visualization*, 2002: 33.

Kidron, M. and Seegal, R. (1981) *The State of the World Atlas*. London: Heinemann.

Kidron, M. and Seegal, R. (1984) *The New State of the World Atlas*. London: Pluto Press.

Kidron, M. and Seegal, R. (1991) *New State of War and Peace: An International Atlas*. London: Grafton Books.

Kocmound, C. (1997) 'Constructing continuous cartograms: A constraint-based approach', Office of Graduate Studies. Master of Science: Texas, Texas A&M University.

Mandelbrot, B.B. (1983) *The Fractal Geometry of Nature*. San Francisco: W.H. Freeman & Co.

Monmonier, M. (1991) *How to Lie with Maps*. Chicago, IL: University of Chicago Press.

Muller, J. (1978) 'The mapping of travel time in Edmonton, Alberta', *The Canadian Geographer*, 22(3): 195–210.

Muller, J.C. (1989) *Changes Ahead for the Mapping Profession*, Auto Carto 9 (International Symposium on Computer-Assisted Cartography), pp. 675–83.

Nussbaum, M. and Sen, A. (eds) (1993), *The Quality of Life*, Oxford: Clarendon Press, 1993.

Olson, J.M. (1976) 'Noncontiguous area cartograms', *The Professional Geographer*, 28: 371–80.

Peucker, T.K. (1972) *Computer Cartography: A Working Bibliography*, Discussion Paper No. 12, Department of Geography, University of Toronto.

Pickles, J. (ed.) (1995) *Ground Truth: The Social Implications of Geographic Information Systems*. New York: Guilford Press.

Seager, J. and Olson, A. (1986) *Women in the World: An International Atlas*. New York: New York, Simon and Schuster.

Sen, A.K. (1975) 'A theorem related to cartograms', *American Mathematics Monthly*, 82: 382–85.

Sen, A.K. (1982) *Choice, Welfare and Measurement*. Oxford: Blackwell.

Skoda, L. and Robertson, J.C. (1972) *Isodemographic Map of Canada,* Geographical Paper No. 50, Department of the Environment, Ottawa, Canada.

Social Watch (2007) *The Social Map,* available from: http://www.socialwatch.org/.

Spiekermann, K. and Wegener, M. (1994) 'The shrinking continent: New time-space maps of Europe', *Environment and Planning B,* 21: 653–73.

Szegö, J. (1984) *A Census Atlas of Sweden,* Statistics Sweden, Central Board of Real Estate Data, Swedish Council for Building Research and The University of Lund, Stockholm.

Szegö, J. (1987) *Human Cartography: Mapping the World of Man.* Stockholm: Swedish Council for Building Research.

Taylor, D.R.F. (1985) 'The educational challenges of a new cartography', *Cartographica,* 22(4): 19–37.

Tobler, W.R. (1963) 'Geographic area and map projections', *The Geographical Review,* 53: 59–78.

Tobler, W.R. (1973) 'A continuous transformation useful for districting', *Annals of the New York Academy of Sciences,* 219: 215–20.

Tobler, W. (2004) 'Thirty Five Years of Computer Cartograms', *Annals of the Association of American Geographers,* 94: 1, 58–73.

Truss, L. (2003) *Eats, Shoots and Leaves.* London: Profile Books.

Tufte, E.R. (1990) *Envisioning Information.* Chesire, CT: Graphics Press.

UNICEF (2007) *The State of the World's Children 2008: Child Survival,* UNICEF, ISBN: 978–92–806–4191–2; also available online: http://www.unicef.org/publications/files/The_State_of_the_Worlds_Children_2008.pdf

United Nations (2008), The Millennium Goals Development Report, New York, United Nations; available on-line: http://www.un.org/millenniumgoals/pdf/The%20Millennium%20Development%20Goals%20Report%202008.pdf

Visvalingham, M. (1989) 'Cartography, GIS and maps in perspective', *The Cartographic Journal,* 26: 26–87.

Webb, R. (2006) 'Cartography: A popular perspective', *Nature,* 439: 800.

11

Indigenous Peoples' Issues and Indigenous Uses of GIS

Melinda Laituri

INTRODUCTION

A discussion about Indigenous Peoples and their relationship to map-making technologies is necessarily situated within the meta-narratives of the Columbian Exchange, the Scientific Revolution, the Industrial Revolution, and twentieth-century development and globalization strategies (Hodgson, 2002). Representations of place are inextricably linked to power, politics, and culture; demonstrating knowledge transformation and cultural change often in concert with the silencing of alternative voices. Maps are the product of a complex mix of history, geography, science, myth, art, and power relationships reflecting a selective outcome in representation: maps are as much about what is represented as about what is *not* represented (Wood, 1992; Monmonier, 1996). They are the result of the interface between different cultures filtered through a set of common themes: inequality, exploitation, poverty, adaptation, resistance, and resilience. As such, they are situated in a contentious and controversial context.

The Columbian Exchange refers to the "discovery" of the Americas and the subsequent exchange of plants, animals, humans, ideas, and disease (Crosby, 2003). The global legacy of this exchange and consequent colonial enterprises was profoundly felt by Indigenous Peoples through the loss of their lives, lands, religions, languages, and ways of life (Blaut, 1993, Diamond, 1997; Mann, 2005). Paralleling the events of the Columbian Exchange was the occurrence of the Scientific Revolution in Europe. The development of scientific method and inquiry was predicated upon not only exploration by Europeans of the Americas, but realignments between church and state and changing economic structures in trade and finance via capitalism (Berman, 1984; Merchant, 1995). The intersection of capitalism, technology, and science informed a powerful world view based upon control, utility, and the commodification of nature for economic gain. This separation of humans from nature led to the systemized classification of the world by European explorers, colonialists, and travelers replacing and displacing

Indigenous Peoples and perspectives (Johnson and Murton, 2007). The Western[1] world view and imperialist expansion emphasized divisions between "Europeans and their 'others'" (Said, 1993: xxviii) laying the groundwork for diffusionist myths of European superiority (Blaut, 1993). The Industrial Revolution, built upon the slave trade and the slave plantation system, resulted in technological innovations that increased material production. This Revolution was predicated upon global capitalist expansion and notions of progress, relying on the continued exploitation of indigenous communities and natural resources by dominant world powers (Zinn, 1995). Building upon the colonial legacies of the past, twentieth-century development and globalization strategies coupled with technological advances further impacted Indigenous ways of life and marginalized Indigenous populations.

Central to the Indigenous response to colonization, imperialism, and globalization has been the capacity for adaptation, resistance, and resilience. This response has been articulated through work to recover their rights, reestablish collective identity, and reclaim land (Cant et al., 2005). The interplay between traditional identities and contemporary perspectives reflect the dynamic nature of Indigenous cultures situated in local struggles over resources and rights. These struggles are linked to global initiatives and international agendas creating a significant cultural and political force, the global diffusion of Indigenous rights, and trans-national legal practices (Brantenberg and Minde, 1995; Minde and Hilsen, 2003; Nyseth and Pederson, 2005). Central to this activity is the recognition of Western world views as juxtaposed with Indigenous ways of knowing. Oliveira (2005) states: "Western ways of knowing differ from that of Indigenous peoples" (p. 122). Further, Indigenous ways of knowing are multiple and do not represent a monolithic counter to Western epistemologies. This is evidenced by the myriad ways Indigenous people

interact, respond, and manage their environments (e.g., Maori Iwi (Tribes) of New Zealand: Barton, 1980; Inuit hunters: Aporta and Higgs, 2005; Andaman Island tribes: Bhattacharyya, 2006; Sammi of Scandinavia: Lawrence, 2007; South Australian Aborigines: Aguis et al., 2007).

One arena to examine these differences is in maps and map making. Several researchers discuss the comparisons between Indigenous and Western cartography (Lewis, 1993; Peat, 1996; Cajete, 2000; Kelley and Francis, 2005; Pearce and Louis, 2008). Peat (1996) describes Indigenous groups such as Australian Aboriginal's dream tracks and the Naskapi, Blackfoot, and Cree's "maps in their heads." These maps reflect the values and knowledge passed from elders through stories and linked to landmarks and seasons (Peat, 1996), reflecting the intergenerational transmission of indigenous landscape knowledge. Cajete describes the direct relationship Indigenous Peoples have with the land, where place is a living presence and culture and nature are integrated through ritual, experience, and responsibility (2000: 183). Pearce and Louis (2008) describe the Hawaiian perspective that exhibits a "depth of place knowledge" linked to the spiritual realm and where all natural and cultural resources are interrelated. Similarly, Western maps are equally embedded in cultural claims of objectivity and the Western world view through the decoupling of culture and nature where places are physical features devoid of a living force (Cajete, 2000).

Maps can be defined as cultural representations of time and place situated within a historical context through a variety of media. Kelley and Francis (2005) describe maps as "tangible (visual, 'artifactual') and intangible (verbal, 'mental', performed)" (p. 85). They describe an example of Navajo traditional wayfinding based upon verbal narrative sharing the verbal map of a portion of their creation stories. Monmonier (1996) points out that multiple maps can be constructed of the same place using the same data about the same situation. Additionally, maps can be constructed of the same place using different culturally explicit data such as stories and collective memory creating constructions of place as defined by the local community. Cultural mapping is the integration of cartography with other cultural resources and information recorded by alternative techniques (UNESCO.org, 2005, http://www. unescobkk.org/culture/our-projects/protection-of-endangered-and-minority-cultures/cultural-mapping/).

Cultural mapping is of particular relevance to Indigenous Peoples driven in part by the outcomes of the United Nations Decade for Indigenous Peoples (1994–2004) and the Declaration on the Rights of Indigenous Peoples (2007). The UN Decade for Indigenous Peoples saw increasing indigenous mobilization with respect to demanding recognition of property rights and protection of traditional practices and knowledge (Hodgson, 2002). The Declaration on the Rights of Indigenous Peoples further emphasizes indigenous rights to self-determination and the protection of cultural knowledge (Pearce and Louis, 2008; Charters and Stavenhagen, 2009). Cultural mapping of Indigenous struggles over land tenure and resources has become a crucial tool for Indigenous communities increasingly adopting the use of geospatial information technologies. Indigenous Peoples have used the "power of maps" to create counter maps that integrate global databases with local data to reclaim traditional territories and develop maps and databases for their own purposes (Poole, 1995; Harris and Hazen, 2006).

STATE OF INDIGENOUS USES OF GEOSPATIAL TECHNOLOGIES

Overview of Indigenous mapping

Indigenous mapping has taken on new forms due to advances in geospatial technologies (geographic information systems, global positioning systems, remote sensing,

and internet mapping services). Indigenous peoples[2] have adopted these technologies for land tenure issues (Duerden and Keller, 1992), natural resource management (Harmsworth, 2002), preservation of cultural heritage (Aporta and Higgs, 2005), and intergenerational educational projects (Johnson et al., 2006). The cornerstone of Indigenous uses of GST resides in utilizing, understanding, and expressing Indigenous knowledge (IK).[3] IK is embedded within a particular culture and place. It is inherently geographic and dynamic; expressed as a set of skill and adaptations to the environmental and socio-economic conditions of a particular place (Thrupp, 1989; Warren, 1991; Flavier et al., 1995). IK is the result of the collaborative construction of the Indigenous historical experience spread out across a heterogeneous landscape. This knowledge is often held in a distributed database among members of a community based upon experience and social status and shared through cultural norms and practices specific to different cultural groups. IK systems represent a scientific system with its own taxonomic structure, particular methodologies, and a set of experts (Rundstrom, 1995; Brodnig and Mayer-Schonberger, 2000). Cajete refers to this a Native Science that "operates according to cognitive and linguistic 'maps' that chart both collective and individual wisdom" (2000: p. 65).

Environmental managers, scientific researchers, politicians, and local decision makers recognize the significant contributions that indigenous people have made to the global knowledge base, particularly in the identification of important medicinal plants (Berkes, 1999) and veterinary medicine (Kohler-Rollefson, 2004). Increasingly, IK is recognized as having critical importance for complex environmental issues such as natural resource management (Laituri and Harvey, 1996) and climate change (Minang and McCall, 2006). Disaster management and mitigation is an emerging area where IK systems have demonstrated an adaptability to and integration with GST due to long-term observation and practice (Tran, et al., 2009). Additionally, various indigenous groups are adopting geo-spatial technologies for their specific needs and gaining the requisite skills to maintain and develop their own GIS databases and systems (see for tribal activities in GIS: http://www.nativemaps. org/?q=top_menu/1/88/90/23).

The use of Indigenous mapping for land claims and natural resources began in the 1960s in Canada and Alaska (Chapin et al., 2005). Coupled with the emerging environmental justice movement of the 1990s, the United Nation's International Decade on the World's Indigenous Peoples (1994–2004), the World Bank 1998 strategy for Indigneous issues and development, the Declaration on the Rights of Indigenous Peoples (2007), and the development of desktop GIS, the integration of geospatial technologies with indigenous mapping has resulted in an impressive array of applications, methods, and case studies throughout the world. There are several reviews that provide an overview of this complex literature focusing on Indigenous mapping, the adoption of GIS, and the use of participatory approaches (Poole, 1995; Brodnig and Mayer-Schonberger, 2000; Tripathi and Bhhattarya, 2004; Chapin et al., 2005; McCall, 2005; Dunn, 2007). Several guidebooks and handbooks have been written that document mapping procedures, explain participatory methods, and explain community mapping practices (Fox, 1998; Harrington, 1999; Flavelle, 2002; Rambaldi and Collosa-Tarr, 2002; Fox et al., 2005). There are numerous documents developed by international agencies and non-governmental organizations that address issues related to IK and mapping. Some examples include African Indigenous People's Workshop on effective use of Information Communication Technology (ICTs) in environmental advocacy (Indigenous Peoples of Africa Coordinating Committee, 2008), Good practices in participatory mapping (International Fund for Agricultural Development, 2009), Indigenous Peoples Mapping and Biodiversity

Conservation (The Biodiversity Support Program, USAID, 1995), IK in Disaster Management in Africa (United Nations Environmental Program, 2008), and Mapping Communities: Ethics, Values, Practice (East-West Center, 2005).

There exist several important compendiums of indigenous mapping projects that include an overview of the geographic distribution of these activities. The "Indigenous Peoples, Mapping and Biodiversity Conservation: An Analysis of Current Activities and Opportunities for Applying Geomatics Technologies" (Poole, 1995) describes the ways indigenous communities are using maps and advanced mapping technologies for local purposes such as land claims and natural resource management. The "Nexus of GeoData Analysis and Local Spatial Knowledge: Applications of P-Mapping and PGIS to issues in NRM and Community Development: A Partial Review" (McCall, 2005) builds upon Poole's analysis reviewing indigenous mapping efforts using geospatial technologies and participatory approaches. These reviews are global in scope and include land-based communities utilizing local and Indigenous spatial knowledge.

Several websites provide links to numerous resources for Indigenous mapping. For example, the Integrated Approaches to Participatory Development (IAPAD) website (http://www.iapad.org/) hosts the Community Mapping Virtual Library (http://www.iapad. org/bibliography.html) that has become a clearinghouse for articles on integrated approaches to participatory development and management of natural resources using geospatial technologies focusing on indigenous mapping and development issues throughout the globe. A review of these publications from 1991 to 2007 demonstrate the upsurge in interest, activities, and applications in this arena. The site also supports links to other web pages that address "GIS and Development" and "Community-based Mapping" providing access to resources and practitioners. Further, the Open Forum on Participatory Information Systems and

Technologies (http://ppgis.iapad.org/) is an electronic forum for discussion of the participatory uses of geo-spatial information systems and technologies focusing specifically on the developing world and Indigenous groups. Another example is the The Aboriginal Mapping Network (http://www.nativemaps.org) established in 1998. It supports the efforts of Indigenous peoples to address land claims, treaty negotiations, and resource development using common tools, such as community GIS capacity building and GIS mapping. The goals of AMN are to create connections between Indigenous mapping professionals and mitigate the geographic and professional isolation many experience; and to increase the effective use of local knowledge in the decision-making process. The Indigenous Mapping Network (http://indigenousmapping.net/), established in 2005, aims to bridge the gap between traditional mapping practices and modern mapping technologies.

There are several recurrent themes in the voluminous literature on IK and mapping. Indigenous knowledge is important as it has made significant contributions to global knowledge and can be transferred, adopted, and adapted to other places (McCall, 2005). It should be preserved particularly for the rural poor who depend upon such place-based knowledge for specific skills and survival strategies (Poole, 1995). However, IK is under assault and in danger of becoming extinct due to the forces of globalization that encourage homogenization of culture replacing local knowledge systems with consumerism, capitalism, and westernization (Harmsworth, 2002). For example, pressures for economic assimilation have been identified as one of the reasons for loss of language diversity accelerating the loss of cultural identity (Razak, 2003).

Tensions exist between Indigenous and Western epistemologies embedded in the legacy of colonialism and the social construction of separation between culture and nature (Cajete, 2000; Coombes, 2007; Johnson and Murton, 2007). Indigenous mapping is composed of a complex mix of songs, myths, ritual, dance, stories, and place names often linked to knowledge of the elders in a community (Grenier, 1998). The empirical nature of modern science necessarily separates the indigenous "data" into different layers, extracting the geographical information and severing the link to the underlying cultural knowledge system (Rundstrom, 1995; Brodnig and Mayer-Schonberger, 2000). Therefore, the Indigenous view is often incompletely represented in GST (Chapin et al., 2005).

Despite these tensions, the integration of IK into GIS projects has the potential to expand the breadth of science and improve the effectiveness of resource management strategies. In 2002, UNESCO launched the Local and Indigenous Knowledge Systems (LINKS) project to cultivate interdisciplinarity and contribute to the Millennum Development Goals to alleviate world poverty (http://www.uniesco.org/links). IK provides "added value" to data systems to better map and communicate products and decisions for sustainable development (Poole, 1995; Harmsworth et al., 2005). IK will "bridge a gap" (Anderson et al., 1993; Laituri and Harvey, 1996; Brodnig and Mayer-Schonberger, 2000) or "close a chasm" (Brodnig and Mayer-Shconberger, 2005) to develop synergies between different epistemologies: traditional knowledge systems and modern science.

GIS is a tool of power that has spread rapidly throughout the world (Dunn et al., 1997; Chapin et al., 2005), providing avenues for empowerment to marginalized populations (Harris and Weiner, 1998). However, issues of access and equity can result in differential use of GIS data and equipment within communities and between nations (Laituri, 2003). There is a need for explicit indigenous applications and approaches to the use of GIS (Pearce and Louis, 2008) that is informed by spatial literacy (Laituri, 2002), a critical cartography (Johnson et al., 2006), and appropriate technologies (Poole, 2006). GST adoption within communities has repercussions that can affect power relationships and cultural practice. Palmer (2009) warns of the need to recognize both the "marginalizing and transformative impacts of technoscience that can potentially disenfranchise tribal elders: (p. 38).

These themes are found throughout the literature on Indigenous mapping that is largely based upon case studies. Case studies can be divided into geographical areas (Poole, 1995; Chapin et al., 2005; McCall, 2005), tool-based applications (e.g., land tenure systems), and issue-based applications (e.g., monitoring slum conditions) (IIED, 2006). Emerging topics include issues related to theory (Wilson and Memon, 2005), ethics (Rambaldi et al., 2005), and best practices (http://www.unesco.org/most/bpikreg.htm). This literature is scattered throughout scholarly journals or concentrated in special edition journals dealing exclusively with Indigenous People and mapping technologies such as *Geographical Research* (2007: 45(2)), *Geografiska Annaler, Series B: Human Geography* (2006: 88(2)), *Progress in Human Geography* (2007: 31(5)), *Futures* (2003: 35), and the *International Institute for Environment and Development: Mapping for Change* (2006: 54) and *An International E-Journal for Critical Geographies Critical Geographies (ACME)* (2006:4(1)).

Evolution of adoption

The theoretical basis, the fundamental concepts, and methodological approaches for Indigenous uses of GIS reveal important issues in how projects are implemented. Rundstrom (1995) defines GIS as a technoscience, meaning that the technology modifies and transforms the world while delivering a particular "reality" where GIS activities and products can have far-reaching implications, modifying and transforming the world (Johnson et al., 2006). The digital database from which GIS maps are produced

represent the intersection of world views and the conceptual foundation of the Indigenous map (Poole, 1995). Geographic information that make up the digital database presents specific problems in the representation of data and information and this is of particular interest and concern to Indigenous groups in terms of how IK, especially special or sacred knowledge, is depicted and communicated (Rundstrom, 1995; Pearce and Louis, 2008). Ethical dilemmas present themselves for researchers, experts, and local representatives in terms of the appropriate use of this information that can result in unintended consequences in the adoption of Western technology (Louis, 2007).

Map as theory

Lewis (1993) describes the close relationship between the origins of language and the development of spatial consciousness in humans and suggests that cognitive maps may have been a major influence in human intellectual development. Recognizing the role of space in ordering our knowledge and experience reveals the ubiquity of the map as metaphor for theory, culture, and language (Turnbull, 1989). Further, spatiality may be critical to all cultures, but how cultures locate themselves in space is one of the variables that express how the world is experienced differently. All maps are selective and represent some parts of the landscape (Wood, 1992; Monmonier, 1996; Harris and Hazen, 2006). These graphic representations spatially order information and provide a powerful mode of inference based upon observation. Maps represent the cognitive schema in which knowledge, space, and practical action intersect – the theoretical construct of "one's" world (Turnbull, 1989). Observations and theories are linked in the manifestation of a map and are fundamental to science as a set of practices (Harley 1989; Turnbull, 1989; Blaut et al., 2003). Maps represent the outcome of a shared set of practices based upon cultural context and linked to human purpose and action (Barton, 1980;

Turnbull, 1989). Examples include stick charts of the Marshall Islands that represent currents and islands, carved wooden coastal charts of the Greenland Inuit, and dream maps of the Australian Aborigines that depict the homeland where a crocodile' body parts are synonymous with landforms (Turnbull, 1989).

Geospatial technologies impose a particular method of representation, the adoption of binary code to define space, the use of layers of data that are overlaid to identify pattern, and derivation of new information through analytical procedures of spatial data (Longley et al., 1999). Several articles provide a systematic overview of the role of culture in the use and adoption of GIS (Rundstrom, 1995; Aporta and Higgs 2005; Chambers, 2006). There have been important developments such as the Nunavut Atlas (1992), the Maya Atlas, (1977) (http://geography.berkeley.edu/ProjectsResources/MayanAtlas/MayaAtlas/MayanAtlas2.htm), the Gaia Atlas of First Peoples, (1990), and the Aboriginal Mapping Network (http://www.nativemaps.org/). These activities have created connections between Indigenous communities and their land/resources with the cultural mapping efforts of other Indigenous communities. If it is agreed that GIS is a technoscience, then it is critically important to understand the recursive relationship between GIS and culture. How do GIS products affect the cognitive schema of different cultural groups (Aporta and Higgs, 2005)? Johnson et al. (2006) argue that Indigenous communities should become literate in cartographic methods and develop a "critical consciousness" of GIS technology.

Representation in GIS: Politics of Representation/Politics of Position

The issue of representation is significant in devising strategies that use and share IK as it is necessary to acknowledge and consider the implications of representing another group in techno-ethnographic activities. Efforts to understand and utilize knowledge have

increasingly recognized problems with cultural differences (Malone, 2007), issues related to trust (Riseth, 2007), and controversies over who should collect such information (Kelley and Francis, 2005). Representation of the "other" is a serious play of power (Katz, 1992); and the position of observation reveals the political nature of knowledge production. Turnbull (1998) suggests that comparisons between Western and Indigenous mapping reveal that distinct knowledge systems are locally produced. Therefore, the partiality of the observer needs to be explicitly acknowledged to cross-cultural boundaries and validate alternative perspectives.

Strategies blending Indigenous and scientific approaches need to be developed and explored without privileging one culture over the other (Rundstrom, 1995; Laituri and Harvey, 1996; Turnbull 2003, Chambers, 2006; Pearce and Louis, 2008). Resource management laws requiring planning documents and assessment procedures as in New Zealand (1993), South Africa (1998), and Canada (2000) resulted in coordinated efforts to integrate Indigenous information into GIS databases. The range of information is extended, including cultural/social information that has a spatial component that can assist in the local resource decision making process (Meszaros, 1991; Tripathi and Bhattarya, 2004). However, an important caveat is to recognize the inherent bias in the base layers that are often employed in a GIS. These base layers are derived from governmental agencies that reflect the dominant Western paradigm, are the inheritors of the post-colonial geography, and have previously excluded IK (Blaut, 1993; Brondnig and Mayer-Shonberger, 2000; Tripathi and Bhattarya, 2004; Johnson et al. 2006). The challenge is to combine IK with Western technology in order to devise alternative natural resource management and conservation strategies that may be more efficient, and environmentally and culturally sensitive (Laituri and Harvey, 1996).

Self-determination and Empowerment

A trend in the use of Indigenous uses of GIS is the adoption of the technology by Indigenous users. There are numerous issues associated with this activity (access to hardware and software, expertise with GIS tools, mapping "special" information), however, Indigenous researchers and GIS practitioners acknowledge the importance of using geospatial technologies for self determination, cultural respect, and empowerment (Weiner et al., 2002; McCall, 2003; McCall and Minang, 2005). Key to promoting this activity has been the UNESCO Universal Declaration on Cultural Diversity that has created opportunities for Indigenous peoples to defend their cultural self-determination and participate on an equal basis with dominant peoples (Crawhall, 2003). Projects include place name mapping, mapping hunting territories, ethno-ecological knowledge, language mapping, and medicinal plant mapping (Poole, 1995; Crawhall, 2003). Other governmental projects have also facilitated the involvement of Indigenous peoples into media and mapping activities. For example, "Digital Dreaming: A National Review of Indigenous Media and Communication", undertaken by Indigenous Management Australia (1999) identifies factors that affect the Aboriginal and Torres Strait Islander people in media and communication services. A crucial finding was the need to involve Indigenous people in the development of projects, at all levels of production and decision making.

An essential element of Indigenous uses of GST is that the GIS is utilized by Indigenous peoples for *their* needs (McKinnon, 2001; Louis, 2007). The need to assert self-determination in the GIS process for resource management (Meszaros, 1991), research (Louis, 2007), or planning activity (Waldron and Sui, 1999) is essential to the success of such efforts. For example, the passage of the Resource Management Act 1993 in New Zealand included a requirement that *iwi* or tribes draft management plans for development and conservation purposes

resulting in the widespread adoption and use of GIS by Maori (Harmsworth, 2002). Maori have identified GIS as an enabling technology that allows them to "speak the same language" through culturally relevant data layers and cartographic products (Laituri, 2002).

Access and Negotiated Research

Access and equity are critical in terms of the ability to adopt GIS technologies and how such adoption affects Indigenous communities. Access is composed of several aspects: context, connectivity, capabilities, and content (Laituri, 2003). Context refers to the nature of the spatial questions under consideration, the community social structure, and the role of elders in Indigenous mapping. Connectivity refers to the existing infrastructure and access to funding to improve technology access and infrastructure needs. An important caveat is the recognition of appropriate technology. Poole (2006) and Rambaldi and Callosa-Tarr (2005) have demonstrated that GIS can be conducted simply without high-end computers or sophisticated software using alternative techniques such as 3D mapping and hand-held global positioning system (GPS) units.

Access to the skills to conduct GIS is crucial for Indigenous mapping that reflects self-determination and empowerment. Aspects of Indigenous mapping has been found to be highly compatible with the fundamental concepts of GIS (McKinnon, 2001), competency in these areas will assist in the further development of bottom up approaches (Harris and Weiner, 1998). With Indigenous peoples gaining skills in GIS, their perspectives and approaches to GIS development and use expands the range of GIS conceptions and research through explorations of multiple cartographies and Indigenous Geography (Johnson et al., 2006; Louis, 2007). However, GIS applications tend to be based on Western perspectives of land-use; they do not include Indigenous legal conditions, traditional tribal perceptions of land-use, or unique resource management goals such as the protection of sacred sites. Appropriate education and training for the specific needs, applications, and analyses of Indigenous entities is needed (Palmer, 2009). Pearce and Louis (2008) demonstrate the flexibility of GST to demonstrate Indigenous concepts through mapping "depth of place" in Kauai, Hawaii.

An important aspect of Indigenous mapping is the unique and special knowledge that reflect their world view resulting in meaningful community-based mapping and requiring close consultation with community elders. A key challenge of Indigenous mapping is the ability to identify, map, and protect sensitive information. There are two levels in the protection of sensitive information: (1) to ensure that such information is not generally accessible to a wider audience (Harmsworth, 2002); and (2) that sensitive information remains intact – meaning that it is not disconnected from the cultural context that makes it meaningful (Rundstrom, 1995; Johnson et al., 2006). A contradiction in the recording of IK is that it can be both exploited for development purposes and used to protect culturally-sensitive sites (Dunn et al., 1997; Agusto, 2008). There is the risk that such databases may have broader accessibility and be mined or exploited in ways that may have harmful effects upon local communities. Inappropriate use of sensitive information (e.g., about sacred sites, cultural areas, hunting and gathering sites) may also pose problems. Restricted access to information may be critical not only to protect specific sites, but also to reinforce the integrity of knowledge systems dependent on ritualized processes of knowledge acquisition (Turnbull, 1989).

In situations where "outside" researchers or experts are participants in the project, delineations of data exchange and development must be clearly articulated and negotiated (Rambaldi et al., 2005; Louis, 2007). In part, "outsiders" or facilitators of GIS practice control how knowledge is represented as well as the transfer process (Corbett

et al., 2006). The relationship between the outside expert and local informants or knowledge brokers is a critical aspect of Indigenous mapping projects where local expertise is limited. Investments in time and trust by outside experts in the local community result in the exchange of reliable information reflecting the current views of the people (Waldron and Sui, 1999; Corbett et al., 2006). Negotiated research and project development result in shared benefits built upon trust and the establishment of long-term relationships between facilitators, local knowledge brokers, and the end users (Chambers, 2006). These shared benefits include data collection techniques, participatory mapping protocols, and cross-cultural awareness, understanding, and respect. However, there are numerous examples of participatory projects that were largely driven by the "outside" experts who extract community information, publish papers, and the end result has limited or no impact on community empowerment (Waldron and Sui, 1999; Weiner et al., 2002; Kyem, 2004; Rambaldi, et al., 2005).

Participatory GIS and Indigenous Mapping

GIS is increasingly used in research and development projects that include community participation. Participatory GIS (PGIS) is a spatial decision-making tool used to represent local people's spatial knowledge for development activities, resource management, local planning, communication, and community advocacy (Rambaldi et al., 2005). The North (Canada, the USA, and Europe) and South (Africa, Asia, and South America) exhibit different paths of development with regard to participatory practices and the use of geospatial technologies. Rambaldi et al. (2005) suggest that differences exist between the North and South in a number of ways. The South has necessarily focused on appropriate technology that has included innovative mapping strategies using a mixture of high and low technologies. Participation is process driven, in that there is a proactive collaboration between local knowledge brokers and GIS facilitators. There are numerous projects that are non-documented, carried out by partnerships between non-governmental organizations, community organizations, and Indigenous groups. The North exhibits a different organizational approach that include community–university partnerships, grass-roots organizations, and tribal-governmental ventures with an emphasis on participatory planning and the adoption of sophisticated technology and approaches.

Data problems and adoption of information technologies exist throughout the South where information and knowledge sharing and availability remains limited (Gregson, 2000). For example, Puginier (2001) identifies issues related to data ownership that has increasingly shifted to governmental and outside agencies in the creation of land use maps often resulting in land confiscation by the government in rural Thailand. Dunn et al. (1997) describes issues related to disparities in data between North and South where census data remains particularly problematic in developing countries. Nevertheless, numerous techniques have been used for data collection that include Rapid Rural Assessment, Participatory Rural Appraisal, and Participatory Learning and Action (Chambers, 2006) as well as sketch mapping resulting in ephemeral maps (Poole, 1995).

One of the key criteria for identifying participatory projects is mapping applications of local/IK that are locally initiated and managed (Poole, 1995). Products of these projects range from informal maps (ephemeral or hand-drawn maps) used primarily for local needs to technical maps (derived from GIS) for use with external agencies. Results from activities using these techniques reveal that local people are quite adept at making their own maps for their own needs (McKinnon, 2001). Increasingly traditional cartography is supplemented with contemporary geospatial technologies and approaches (Poole, 1995). For example, the use of Global Positioning Systems (Aporta and

Higgs, 2005) and remotely sensed imagery (Tabor and Hutchinson, 1994; Cumbi, 2002) have both been used in the development of Indigenous databases. McCall (2010) maintains an up-dated bibliography of PGIS utilizing Indigenous spatial knowledge identifying over 1000 PGIS projects as well as a bibiliography of urban PPGIS activity (http://ppgis.iapad.org/pdf/pgis_psp_itk_cbnrm_biblio_mccall.pdfaw).

Following Poole (1995) and McCall (2005), the general categories of this body of research includes: (1) land claims and land tenure; (2) resource management; (3) conflict and conflict resolution; (4) equity issues; and (5) community awareness. Embedded in this body of literature is the contentious nature of participatory mapping activities and the questions that surround access, control, and ownership of the process and the output (Dunn, 2007). Fundamentally, these research categories speak to power relationships within and between Indigenous communities, between Indigenous groups and government agencies and external groups, and between Indigenous Peoples and researchers or outside experts. The concept of counter-mapping (Peluso, 1995) addresses the underlying power relations that inform cartographic/GIS production and identify methods that local groups can adopt (Rambaldi, 2005) while using appropriate technology for their needs (Poole, 1995). Harris and Hazen (2006) define counter mapping as "efforts to contest or undermine power relations and asymmetries in relation to cartographic products and processes" (p 155). Indigenous peoples use GST for identifying areas of historic and current use and land claims (Aboriginal Mapping Network, http://www.nativemaps.org/), recognizing resources to maintain legitimacy and ownership (Nietschmann, 1995); addressing conflict and competition with multi-national corporations (Hearn, 2007), developing resource management and facilitating conservation plans demanded by national legislation (Harmsworth, 2002), and economic development opportunities (Kyem, 2002).

However this is not a neutral process and these GST activities and applications result in compromises by Indigenous communities with respect to their knowledge systems. Johnson et al. (2006) identify three problems with GIS use of IK: (1) IK becomes tangible and accessible to others; (2) IK may be used beyond its original intent and context; and (3) the separation from context (in space and time) makes it difficult to ensure moral restraint in its further use (p. 89). Augusto (2008) describes the importance of "visuality, orality, and setting" in the practice of African traditional medicine. He describes the "inherent multiplicity of [indigenous] systems of knowledge" which includes "multiple modes of cognition from empirical observation to dreams and messages from the ancestors" (p. 216). With respect to Hawaiian spatial knowledge, Pearce and Louis (2008) similarly note that cartographies are linked to "interactive performances of oration" (p. 123); further emphasizing the intangible elements of IK that are beyond GST capabilities and the possibilities for misuse and misrepresentation in using decontextualized knowledge.

Challenges to integrating IK and GST and the attendant power issues are explicitly discussed in several of articles from the Mapping for Change Conference (see IIED, Issue 54, April, 2005). The underlying theme of this conference was the belief the PGIS practice could have a profound impact for marginalized groups in society to enhance capacity, stimulate innovation and encourage social change (Corbett et al., 2006). However, the issues identified at the 1998 University of Durham workshop are still being addressed at conferences such as the Mapping for Change event several years later: can a top-down technology such as GIS have a place in participatory research; can a technology developed by commercial companies in North America and western Europe be used appropriately in the South; and can local knowledge be integrated and represented in an information system that has rejected such knowledge in favor of

spatially defined "expert" information? (Abbot et al., 1998: 30).

The track record in identifying answers to these questions remains mixed. Conceptual and methodological problems plague boundary demarcation that often defy digital representation such as "flexible" or "fuzzy" boundaries based upon social-cultural identities (McCall, 2005, from Cousins, 2000). Fox et al. (2003) describe impacts on local social dynamics and increased conflicts between local stakeholder groups due to the oversimplification of overlapping land title claims within GIS. Harris and Hazen (2006) describe how advanced technologies may both exacerbate inequities and improve power relations. A key purpose of many Indigenous mapping efforts is the protection of local and sacred knowledge and cultural heritage for the community (McCall and Minang, 2005; Bhattacharyya, 2006). The intersection of the Internet and GST has played a key role in building community awareness locally, but also in building a global indigenous community (http://www. nativemaps.org/).

Indigenous Cyberspace: Implications

The role of the Internet cannot be overlooked in the development of Indigenous mapping. The ability to disseminate information and create a global community of Indigenous users have reinforced the recognition of Indigenous rights and sparked a renaissance for the Indigenous land rights and human rights movements (Aust et al., 1996; Crawhall, 2003; Dyson, 2004). Discussion lists and ring webs have provided important arenas for discussion of cutting edge topics between researchers, community and Indigenous activists, and students (http://t.webring.com/hub?ring=ppgis). Virtual space is not limited to only the Internet; alternative mobile technologies have developed new networks and innovative spaces in remote and rural areas (McKinnon, 2001). The intersection of culture and cyberspace creates an arena for cultural hybrids and reveals the dynamic, adaptive nature of IK systems (Nathan, 2000), (i.e., Four Directions Teaching, http://www.four-directionsteachings.com). Digital Drum builds upon Internet technology to provide a forum for indigenous cultural expression and to "stake a claim in cyberspace to adapt, advance, use and share" such resources and to encourage intercultural exchange (http://www.digitaldrum.ca/en/node/755).

In an increasingly homogenized, globalized world, cyberspace provides a supplementary means of belonging or creating a sense of place. For example, multi-media technologies integrate oral histories and native languages creating cultural atlases with access for tribal members only (e.g., Alaska Native Knowledge Network (http://ankn.uaf.edu/index.html). The Living Cybercartographic Atlas of Indigenous Perspectives and Knowledge (https://gcrc.carleton.ca/confluence/display/GCRCWEB/Living+Cybercartographic+Atlas+of+Indigenous+Perspectives+and+Knowledge) uses multimedia stories and local knowledge to "capture the richness and uniqueness of IK" using via electronic media.

Indigenous cyberspace provides networks for knowledge sharing (e.g., The Indigenous People's Literature: http://www.indigenous-people.net/ipl_final.html) and connectivity (Indigenous Mapping Network, http://indigenousmapping.net/; The Aboriginal Mapping Network, http://www.nativemaps.org/). Explicit tribal plans include linking Navajo information technology islands to ensure the sharing of resources, infrastructure and strategies within and between Indigenous users that specifically target cyberspace to bridge the cultural digital divide (Skow, 2004). Resources (e.g., best practices of IK protection), databases (e.g., historical maps; password-protected digital data), and social networks are provided via tribal webpages. The Native American Nations identifies and maintains links to Canadian and US tribes (http://www.nativeculturelinks.com/nations.html). Additionally, the Indigenous Node of the World Wide Web Virtual Library provides links to global resources and activities around the world (http://www.cwis.org/wwwvl/indig-vl.html#other).

Mobile Interactive Geographic Information Systems (MIGIS) demonstrate the technological advances of GIS and GPS for use by local communities for local level planning (McKinnon, 2001; Verplanke, 2004). The combination of a portable GIS unit for field data collection combined with a GPS register and an easily understood graphical user interface (GUI) has served to integrate IK and scientific information. Cybertracker was designed to enhance tracker capabilities using a hand-held field computer, a unique user interface with easy to recognize icons and the ability for quick downloads and data accessibility (Liebenberg et al., 1998). Cybertracker has since expanded to tracking pests in farming, disaster relief, and biodiversity monitoring. These projects highlight several important issues: MIGIS can be successful when a representative group is involved (Verplanke, 2004), that technology can be successfully and respectfully integrated with IK (Liebenberg, 1998), and the recognition by local communities that this activity has real meaning for their communities in terms of building capacity and managing their own resources (McKinnon, 2001).

However, the Internet, new mobile technologies, and geospatial technologies illuminate the multi-faceted digital divide of access, equity, and differences that exist between the North and South. Access, adoption, and diffusion of the Internet in general and geospatial techniques specifically have accelerated unevenly across the globe revealing striking differences between the North (Canada, the USA, and Europe) and the South. There are equally striking differences within countries between remote and rural areas and urban centers as well as within urban centers in developing countries and their peri-urban regions. Dodge and Kitchin (2001) present a series of maps that track Internet connectivity globally and reveal large concentrations of Internet hosts in North America, Europe, and an growing hub in East Asia. The North–South divide is obvious with countries in Africa, South America, and central Asia having fewer hosts.

Even as Internet access and connectivity improves in developing countries, efforts to develop digital repositories of Indigenous and local knowledge are underway. Sen (2005) describes efforts to document IK in electronic databases for the purposes of preservation and utilization. Indian efforts protect Indian knowledge about medicinal plants from misappropriation through the Traditional Knowledge Digital Library (http://www.tkdl.res.in/tkdl/langdefault/ common/Abouttkdl.asp?GL=Eng). Lessons learned from India provide valuable insights for South–South collaboration in the development of digital databases (Dunn et al., 1997). A major challenge of these digital databases (including geospatial databases) is in the abstraction and reduction of knowledge through the practice of cataloging and archiving where IK is generalized and decontextualized (Augusto, 2008). Such databases need "datadiversity" that include historical processes, indigenous meaning and beliefs, and descriptions of the social interaction associated with knowledge (Bowker, 2000; Augusto, 2008). While there are numerous non-governmental agencies involved in creating registers and repositories for documentation, validation, protection, and dissemination, there are few legal safeguards. Sen (2005) notes that western intellectual property rights laws favor individuals and corporations rather than local communities.

PROSPECTS AND DIRECTIONS

There exists an extensive case study history in participatory and Indigenous uses of GIS activities. The Mapping for Change International Conference on Participatory Spatial Information Management and Communication (2005) created a pivotal moment in terms of direction and prospects for PGIS Indigenous activity. The conference continued to build upon the case study approach as a forum for sharing PGIS practices. Two other important areas identified to facilitate effective Indigenous mapping activities include (1) enhancing communication networks communities and practitioners and (2) developing guidelines for PGIS projects that include best practices and ethical considerations (Corbett et al., 2006). Creating multiple venues for meetings and the exchange of ideas are critical in continuing the dialogue about Indigenous uses of GST as Internet communication cannot replace face to face exchange and interaction (e.g., Indigenous Mapping Network Conference; Indigenous Peoples Specialty Group of the Association of American Geographers' Subcommittee on Research and Indigenous Peoples; ESRI International User Conference Tribal/ Indigenous GIS sessions).

Exploring new technologies is an important avenue for Indigenous mapping activities. Interactive web applications (Rantanen, 2005) and the potential of Open Source software applications are both possible avenues for Indigenous user-specific needs and developing countries (Camara and Onsrud, 2008). However, Open Source development efforts in developing countries need to establish public supported projects adapted to local needs (Camara and Onsrud, 2008). While PGIS has been touted as a democratizing influence in terms of the flow and dissemination of information (Obermeyer, 1998), a key aspect of Indigenous uses of GIS is the protection of special, sensitive, or sacred information. Understanding the limitations that should be placed on knowledge sharing and how that will impact partnerships among resource managers, governmental agents, and Indigenous communities need to be further understood. Louis (2007) offers insights into how indigenous methodologies can be used in geographic research highlighting the need to build ethical research relationships.

The assessment of on-going and past projects needs to be undertaken. Part of the process of identifying best practices includes determining metrics of success and evaluating the rich case studies available to determine what has worked in which types of environments. Participation, technology, and the notion of empowerment need to be carefully examined within the context of praxis and outcomes (Kyem, 2002). Fully developing an understanding of participatory activities along with the introduction of levels and types of technology would help in identifying impacts on the socio-cultural landscapes of different communities. Further the need for appropriate technologies and culturally appropriate techniques and methods cannot be overstated. The large number of case studies suggest the ability for practitioners to develop, design, implement, and manage projects that are sensitive to Indigenous demands, adopt participatory approaches, and include community elders (Dyson, 2004). Louis (2007) describes methods to address the rift between knowledge systems and ways to narrow that divide – such efforts need to be identified and examined with the aim to learn and improve the collective research effort.

Many practitioners may consider theoretical underpinnings as the purview of academicians. However, the importance of recognizing the theoretical basis of Indigenous mapping generally, and Indigenous uses of GIS specifically, will yield important insights to epistemologies and ontologies. Turnbull (1998) argues that there is a critical link among human development, spatial cognition, and language. Research on landscape semantics between different cultural groups can inform not only a group's complex relationship to the land, but also how GIS can be adapted (or not) to spatio-cultural landscapes (Mark, 2006). The development of culturally appropriate GIS that allows for intergenerational transmission of Indigenous landscape knowledge is needed.

Limitations of Indigenous uses of GIS are linked to issues related to access. Access issues include the costs of technology, inadequate telecommunications links in remote areas, and poor computer literacy. Access to culturally appropriate education and training in computer literacy and GIS are essential to the future development and sustainability of Indigenous uses of GIS that is truly developed by these communities for their explicit needs. Palmer (2009) suggests the term "indigital" to describe the relationship between IK and digital technologies. He recommends three critical approaches in furthering GST adoption: (1) the need to develop adequate tribal data protection methods that include data storage, public access, secure proprietary information, and policies and procedures for sharing tribal data with other governmental agencies; (2) the development of peer-to-peer training of applications that are important to tribal communities; and (3) creating activities that include both tribal elders and youth in the development and use of map and GIS.

CONCLUSION

Indigenous mapping using GIS provides a unique opportunity for exploring the recursive relationship between technology and culture. Rambaldi (2005) poses the question, "who owns the map legend?" and describes the cartographic power of maps embedded in their construction and exercised in their use. Pearce and Louis (2008) note that IK is "distorted, suppressed, and assimilated into the conventional Western map" (p. 109). However, they further state: "the need for indigenous communities to adapt to Western mapping techniques for the representation of local knowledge remains essential to both the preservation of indigenous cultural diversity and the realization of indigenous self-determination in the face of global change" (p. 109).

Rundstrom (1995, 1998) reminds us that intellectual inquiry is political, space is culturally constructed, and that power relationships are explicit in the use of GST. He calls for comparative cross-cultural studies of knowledge transformation that examine cultural change built upon a sound conceptual framework. Such efforts must include ethical standards that address the controversial nature of a "culturally appropriate" GIS. Use of GST will continue to be brokered through those with geospatial skills (Chambers, 2006) and the knowledge representation and transfer process have to be carefully negotiated.

Johnson and Murton (2007) suggest that "place" offers a common ground between Western and Indigenous thought. They state, "perhaps this reunification of culture and nature is possible within an ethic which heightens our awareness of the 'subtle qualities of place' and one which recognizes 'many new voices', including Indigenous voices, in its production" (p. 127). Examining Indigenous uses of GST reveals a rich literature on complex problems on survival, cultural change, resistance, and resilience. The challenge is to develop ways of using GST that are inclusive of multiple ways of knowing building on institutional and interpersonal trust while exploring new and different cartographic landscapes.

ACKNOWLEDGEMENT

The author wishes to acknowledge the editors of this book for their guidance and the anonymous referees who commented most helpfully on an earlier draft of this chapter.

NOTES

1   In this chapter, Western world views refers to Western European Rationality based on Cartesian-Newtonion scientific and technological perspectives.

2   Indigenous peoples are diverse in their culture, religion, and socioeconomic organization. They have shared a common experience in that they were the original inhabitants of their lands, share a legacy of colonialism, have a set of values that are in contrast to Western priorities, and seek to maintain a spiritual and sustainable connection to their homelands (Burger, 1990). The term, indigenous peoples, refers to heterogenous groups throughout the world that have a strong sense of identity as unique peoples and claim the right to define what is meant by indigenous and to be recognized as such.

3   There is a significant terminology associated with indigenous mapping. Terms include: indigenous knowledge, folk wisdom, traditional knowledge, traditional ecological knowledge, local knowledge. For the purposes of this paper, I will use the term indigenous knowledge (IK).

REFERENCES

Abbot, J.R., Chambers, C., Dunn, Harris, T., de Merode, E., Porter, G., Townsend, J. and Weiner, D. (1998) 'Participatory GIS: Opportunity or oxymoron?', *PLA Notes*, 33: 27–33.

Agosto, G. (2008) 'Digitzing IKS: Epistemic complexity, datadiversity and cognitive justice', *The International Information and Library Review*, 40: 211–18.

Aguis, P., Jenkin, T., Jarvis, S., Howitt, R. and Williams, R. (2007) '(Re)asserting indigenous rights and jurisdictions within a politics of place: Transformative nature of native title negotiations in South Australia', *Geographical Research*, 45(2): 194–202.

Anderson, M., Hill, S. and Wavey, R. (1993) 'GIS as a bridge between cultures', *GIS World*, 10 (18).

Aporta, C. and Higgs, E. (2005) 'Satellite culture: Global positioning systems, inuit wayfinding and the need for a new account of technology', *Current Anthropology*, 46 (5/12): 729–53.

Aust, R., Newberry, B. and Resta, P. (1996) *Internet Strategies for Empowering Indigenous Communities in Teaching and Learning*. INET '96 Montreal, Canada. http://www.isoc.org/inet96/proceedings/h4/h4_4.htm (accessed 30 September 2010).

Barton, P.L. (1980) 'Maori geographical knowledge and mapping: A synopsis', *The Turnbull Library Record*, 13(1): 5–15.

Berkes, F. (1999) *Sacred Ecology: Traditional Ecological Knowledge and Resource Management*. Philadelphia, PA: Taylor & Francis.

Bhattacharyya, A. (2006) 'Using participatory GIS to bridge knowledge divides among the onge of little Andaman Island, India', *Knowledge Management for Development Journal*, 2(3): 97–110.

Blaut, J. (1993) *The Colonizer's Model of the World: Geographical Diffusionism and Eurocentric History*. New York: Guilford Press.

Blaut, J., Stea, D., Spencer, C., Blades, M. (2003) 'Mapping as a cultural and cognitive universal',

Annals of the Association of American Geographers, 93(1): 165–185.

Berman, M. (1984) *The Reenchantment of the World*. New York: Bantom Books.

Bowker, G. (2000) 'Biodiveristy, datadiversity', *Social Studies of Science*, 30(5): 643–83.

Brantenberg, T. and Minde, H. (1995) 'Introduction: The indigenous perspective. In: Becoming visible: Indigenous politics and self government'. In T. Brantenberg, J. Hansen and H. Minde (eds), *Proceedings of the Conference on Indigenous Politics and Government 8–10 No 1993, Tromso*. Tromso: Center for Saami Studies.

Brodnig, G. and Mayer-Schonberger. V. (2000) 'Bridging the gap: The role of spatial information technologies in the integration of traditional environmental knowledge and western science', *The Electronic Journal on Information Systems in Developing Countries*, 1(1): 1–15. http://www.ejisdc.org/.

Brodnig, G. and Mayer-Schonberger, V. (2005) 'Closing the chasm'. In R. M. Davison, et al. (eds), *Information Systems in Developing Countries – Theory and Practice*, 9 City University of Hong Kong Press.

Burger, J. (1990) *The Gaia Atlas of First Peoples: A Future for the Indigenous World*. Ringwood: Penguin Books.

Cajete, G. (2000) *Native Science: Natural Laws of Interdependence*. Sante Fe, NM: Clearlight Publishers.

Cant, G., Goodall, A. and Inns, J. (eds) (2005) *Discourses and Silences: Indigenous Peoples, Risks and Resistance*. Christchurch, New Zealand: Department of Geography, University of Canterbury.

Camara, G. and Onsrud, H. (2008) 'Open-source geographic information systems software: Myths and realities', *Open Access and the Public Domain in Digital Data and Information for Science*, 30: 127–33.

Chambers, R. (2006) 'Participatory mapping and geographic information systems: Whose map? Who is empowered and who disempowered? Who gains and who loses?', *The Electronic Journal on Information Systems in Developing Countries*, 25(2): 1–11.

Charters, C. and Stavenhagen, R. (2009) Making the Declaration Work: The United Nations Declaration on the Rights of Indigenous Peoples. International Work Group for Indigenous Affairs.

Chapin, M., Lamb, Z. and Threlkeld, B. (2005) 'Mapping indigenous lands', *The Annual Review of Anthropology*, 34: 619–38.

Coombes, B. (2007) 'Postcolonial conservation and Kiekie harvests at Morere New Zealand – abstracting indigenous knowledge from indigenous polities', *Geographical Research*, 45(2): 186–93.

Corbett, J., Rambaldi, G., Kyem, P., Weiner, D., Olson, R., Muchemi, J., McCall, M. and Chambers, R. (2006) 'Overview: Mapping for change: The emergence of a new practice', *Participatory Learning and Action*, 54(4): 13–20.

Cousins, B. (2000) 'Tenure and common property resources in Africa'. In C. Toulmin and J. Quan (eds), *Evolving Land Rights, Policy and Tenure in Africa*. London: DFID/IIED/NRI.

Crawhall, N. (2003) *Giving New Voice to Endangered Cultures. International Forum on Local Cultural Expressions and Communication*, UNESCO, November 3. http://www.iapad.org/publications/ppgis/crawhall_nigel.pdf

Crosby, A. (2003) *The Columbian Exchange: Biological and Cultural Consequences of 1492*. Westport, CT: Praeger.

Cumbi, J. (2002) *Combining local traditional knowledge with modern remote sensing techniques: A pilot study from Buzi and Save Basin in Central Mozambique.* http://www.unoosa.org/pdf/sap/2002/ethiopia/presentations/2speaker03.pdf (accessed 8 December 2008).

Diamond, J. (1997) *Guns, Germs and Steel: The Fate of Human Societies*. New York: W.W. Norton and Co.

Dodge, M. and Kitchin, R. (2001) *Atlas of Cyberspace*. Harlow: Addison Wesley.

Duerden, F. and Keller, C.P. (1992) 'GIS and land selection for native claims', *La Geographie Applique*, 10: 11–4.

Dunn, C. (2007) 'Participatory GIS – a people's GIS?', *Progress in Human Geography*, 31(5): 616–37.

Dunn, C., Atkins, P. and Townsend, J. (1997) 'GIS for development: A contradiction in terms?', *Area*, 29(2): 151–9.

Dyson, L. (2004) 'Cultural issues in the adoption of information and communication technologies by indigenous Australians'. In F. Sudweeks and C. Ess (eds), *Proceedings Cultural Attitudes towards Communication and Technology*. Australia: Murdoch University. pp. 58–71.

Flavelle, A. (2002) *Mapping Our Land: A Guide to Making Your own Maps of Communities and Traditional Lands*. Connecticut: Lone Pine Foundation.

Flavier, J.M. (1995) 'The regional program for the promotion of indigenous knowledge in Asia'. In D.M., Warren, L.J. Slikkerveer and D. Bronkensha (eds), *The Cultural Dimension of Development: Indigenous Knowledge Systems*. London: Intermediate Technology Publications. pp. 479–87.

Fox, J. (1998) 'Mapping the commons: The social context of spatial information technologies', *The Common Property Resource Digest*, 45: 1–4.

Fox, J., Surayanta, K., Hershock, P. and Pramono, A. (2003) *Mapping Power: Ironic Effects of Spatial*

Information Technology. Working Paper No. 63. Environmental Change, Vulnerability, Honolulu: East-West Center.

Fox, J., Suryanata, K. and Hershoc, P. (eds) (2005) *Mapping Communities: Ethics, Values, Practice.* Honolulu: East-West Center.

Gregson, J. (2000) '"Breathing the thin air of cyberspace": Global knowledge and the Nepal context', *Information Technology for Development*, 9(3/4): 141–52.

Grenier, (1998) *Working with Indigenous Knowledge.* Otawa: International Development Center.

Harley, J. (1989) 'Deconstructing the map', *Cartographica*, 26: 1–20.

Harmsworth, G. (2002) *Indigenous Concepts, Values and Knowledge for Sustainable Development: New Zealand Cast Studies.* 7th Joint Conference: Preservation of Ancient Cultures and the Globalization Scenario. School of Maori and Pacific Development & International Center for Cultural Studies (ICCS), India, 22–24 November.

Harmsworth, Garth, Mick Park, and Dean Walker (2005) Report on the development and use of GIS for iwi and hap: Motueka case study, Aotearoa-New Zealand. Auckland: Landcare Research NZ Ltd. (p. 33) MaoriGISreport.doc, (accessed 8 December 2008). Available from http://www.landcareresearch.co.nz/sal/documents/ICM.

Harrington, S. (1999) *Giving Land a Voice: Mapping our Home Places.* Saltspring Island: Land Trust Alliance of BC.

Harris, L. and Hazen, H. (2006) 'Power of maps: (counter) mapping for conservation', *An International E-Journal for Critical Geographies (ACME)*, 4(1): 99–130.

Harris, T. and Weiner, D. (1998) 'Empowerment, Marginalization and "Community-integrated" GIS', *Cartography and Geographic Information Systems*, 25(2): 67–76.

Hearn, K. (2007) 'Tribes effectively barred from making high-tech maps', *National Geographic News.* http://news.nationalgeographic.com/news/2007/04/070426-asia-maps.html (accessed 8 December 2008).

Hodgson, D. (2002) 'Introduction: Comparative perspectives on the indigenous rights movement in Africa and the Americas', *American Anthropologist*, 104(4): 1037–49.

Indigenous Management Australia (1999) 'Digital dreaming: A national review of indigenous media and communications'. Executive Summary. Available from http://pandora.nla.gov.au/pan/41033/20060106 –0000/ATSIC/programs/Broadcasting/Digital_ Dreaming/preface.html. (accessed 8 December 2008).

International Institute for Environment and Development (IIED) (2006) *Mapping for change: Practice, technologies and communication*, 4: 54.

Johnson, J. and Murton, B. (2007) 'Re/placing native science: Indigenous voices in contemporary constructions of nature', *Geographical Research*, 45(2): 121–9.

Johnson, J., Louis, R.P. and Pramono, A.H. (2006) 'Facing the future: Encouraging critical cartographic literacies in indigenous communities', *An International E-Journal for Critical Geographies IACME*, 4(1): 80–98.

Katz, C. (1992) 'All the world is staged: Intellectuals and the projects of ethnography'. *Environmental Planning D: Soc. Space*, 19: 495–510.

Kelley, K. and Francis, H. (2005) 'Traditional Navajo maps and wayfinding', *American Indian Culture and Research Journal*, 2(2): 85–111.

Kohler-Rollefson, I. (2004) *Indigenous Knowledge of Animal Breeding and Breeds*, http://www2.gtz.de/dokumente/bib/04–5104a2.pdf (accessed 17 December 2007).

Kyem, P. (2002) 'Promoting local community participation in forest management through a PPGIS application in Southern Ghana'. In W. Craig, T. Howard and D. Weiner (ed.), *Community Empowerment, Public Participation and Geographic Information Science.* New York: Taylor & Francis. pp. 218–31.

Kyem, P. (2004) 'Power, participation and inflexible institutions: An examination of the challenges to community empowerment in participatory GIS applications', *Cartographica*, 38(3/4): 5–17.

Laituri, M. and Harvey, L.E. (1996) 'Bridging the space between indigenous ecological knowledge and New Zealand conservation management using geographic information systems'. In D. A. Saunders, J. L. Craig and E. M. Mattiske (eds), *Nature Conservation 4: The Role of Networks.* Chipping North, NSW, Australia: Surrey Beatty and Sons. pp. 122–31.

Laituri, M. (2002) 'Equity and Access to GIS for Marginal Communities'. In W. Craig, T. Howard and D. Weiner (eds), *Community Empowerment, Public Participation and Geographic Information Science.* London: Taylor & Francis. pp. 270–82.

Laituri, M. (2003) 'The issue of access: An assessment guide for evaluating public participation geographic information science case studies', *Journal of the Urban and Regional Information Systems Association* 15, APA II, 25–31. http://www.urisa.org/files/Laiturivol15apa2–3.pdf (accessed 8 December, 2008).

Lawrence, R. (2007) 'Corporate social responsibility, supply chains and Saami claims: tracing the political in the Finnish forestry industry', *Geographical Research*, 45(2): 167–76.

Liebenberg, L., Blake, E., Steventon, L., Benadie, K. and Minye, J. (1998) 'Integrating traditional knowledge with computer science for the conservation of biodiversity'. *Paper presented at the 8th International Conference on Hunting and Gathering Societies, Osaka, Japan, October 1998*, http://www.cybertracker.org/index.html (accessed 8 June 2009).

Lewis, G. (1993) 'Metrics, geometries, signs and language: Sources of cartographic miscommunication between Native and Euro-American cultures in North American', *Cartographica,* 30(1): 98–106.

Longley, P., Goodchild, M., Maguire, D. and Rhind D. (eds) (1999) *Geographical Information Systems: Principles, Techniques, Management and Applications.* New York: John Wiley.

Louis, R. (2007). 'Can you hear us now? Voices form the margin: Using indigenous methodologies in geographic research', *Geographical Review,* 45(2): 130–9.

Malone, G. (2007). 'Ways of belonging: Reconciliation and Adelaide's public space indigenous cultural markers', *Geographical Research,* 45(2): 158–66.

Mann, C. (2005) *1491: New Revelations of the Americas before Columbus.* New York: Vintage Books.

Mark, D. (2006) 'Cultural difference, technological imperialism and indigenous GIS', *Directions Magazine*, 18 May, http://www.directionsmag.com/printer.php?article_id=2173 (accessed 8 December 2008).

Meszaros B. (1991) 'The role of geographic information systems in American Indian land and water rights litigation', *American Indian Culture and Research Journal*, 15(3): 77–93.

McCall, M. (2003) 'Seeking good governance in participatory GIS: A review of processes and governance dimensions in applying GIS to participatory spatial planning', *Habitat International, 27:* 549–73.

McCall, M. and Minang, P. (2005) 'Assessing participatory GIS for community-based natural resource management: claiming community forests in Cameroon', *Geographical Journal, 171:* 340–56.

McCall, M. (2005) *DRAFT: Nexus of GeoDatat Analysis and Local Spatial Knowledge: Applications of P-Mapping and PGIS to Issues in NRM and Community Development: A Partial Review* (Draft), April, http://www.iapad.org/publications/ppgis/ITKNRMmapsLitReview_IAPAD.pdf (accessed 8 December 2008).

McCall, M. (2010) *Pgis-Psp-lsk: Applying Participatory-Gis and Participatory Mapping to Participatory Spatial Planning (in Particular to Local-Level Land and Resource Management) Utilizing Local and Indigenous Spatial Knowledge: A Bibliography*, May 2008, http://ppgis.iapad.org/pdf/pgis_psp_itk_cbnrm_biblio_mcall.pdf (accessed 30 September 2010).

McKinnon, J. (2001) 'Mobile interactive GIS: Bringing indigenous knowledge and scientific information together: A narrative account'. Paper given at: International Workshop on Participatory Technology Development and Local Knowledge for Sustainable Land Use in Southeast Asia, Chiang Mai, June.

Merchant, C. (1995) 'Reinventing Eden: Western culture as a recovery narrative'. In W. Cronon (ed.), *Uncommon Ground: Toward Reinventing Nature.* New York: W.W. Norton and Co. pp. 132–67.

Minang, P. and McCall, M.K. (2006) 'Participatory GIS and local knowledge enhancement for community carbon forestry planning: An example from Cameroon', *Participatory Learning and Action Number*, 54(4): 85–91.

Minde, H. and Hilsen, R. (2003) 'Conclusion', In S. Jentoft, H. Minde and R. Nilsen (eds), *Indigenous Peoples: Resource Management and Global Rights.* Delft: Eburon.

Monmonier, M. (1996) *How to Lie with Maps*, 2nd edn. Chicago, IL: The University of Chicago Press.

Nathan, D. (2000) 'Plugging in indigenous knowledge: Connections and innovations', *Australian Aboriginal Studies*, 2000(2): 39–47.

Nietschmann, B. (1995) 'Defending the Miskito Reefs with maps and GPS', *Cultural Survival Quarterly*, Winter: 34–37.

Nyseth, T. and Pedersen, P. (2005) 'Globalization form below: The revitalization of a Coastal Sami community in northern Norway as part of the global discourse in Indigenous identity', In G. Cant, A. Goodall and J. Inns (eds), *Discourse and Silences: Indigenous Peoples, Risks and Resistance.* Christchurch: University of Canterbury. pp. 71–85.

Obermeyer, N. (1998) 'PPGIS: The evolution of public participation GIS', *Cartography and Geographic Information Systems*, 25(2): 65–6.

Oliveira, K.R.K. (2005) 'Two Worldviews War: The struggles of a Hawaiian connection to the land'. In G. Cant, A. Goodall and J. Inns (eds), *Discourses and Silences: Indigenous Peoples, Risks and Resistance.* Christchurch: University of Canterbury. pp. 115–25.

Palmer, M. (2009) 'Engaging the indigital geographic information networks', *Futures*, 41: 33–40.

Pearce, M. and Louis, R. (2008) 'Mapping indigenous depth of place', *American Indian Culture and Research Journal*, 23(3): 107–26.

Peat, F. (1996) 'I have a map in my head', *Revision*, 18 (3): 11–17.

Peluso, N.L. (1995) 'Whose woods are these? Counter-mapping forest territories in Kalimantan, Indonesia', *Antipode*, 27(4): 383–406.

Poole, P. (1995) *Indigenous Peoples, Mapping and Biodiversity Conservation,* Biodiversity Support Program and World Wildlife Fund, Washington DC, http://rmportal.net/tools/biodiversity-support-program/indigenous_people.pdf/view (accessed 8 December 2008).

Poole, P. (2006) 'Is there life after tenure mapping?', *Participatory Learning and Action*, 54: 41–9.

Puginier, O. (2001) 'Can participatory land use planning at community level in the highlands of northern Thailand use geographic information systems (GIS) as a communication tool?'. Paper presented at the International Workshop 'Participatory Technology Development and Local Knowledge for Sustainable Land Use in Southeast Asia' Chaing Mai: Thailand. 6–7: 6.

Rambaldi, G. (2005) 'Who owns the map legend?', *URISA Journal*, 17(1): 5–13.

Rambaldi, G. and Callosa-Tarr, J. (2002) *Participatory 3-Dimensional Modeling: Guiding Principles and Applications.* ASEAN Regional Center for Biodiversity Conservation (ARCBC), Los Banos, Laguna, Phillipines, July.

Rambaldi, G., Kyem, P., Mbile, P., McCall, M. and Weiner, D. (2005) 'Participatory spatial information management and communication in developing countries', Mapping for Change International Conference, Nairobi, Kenya, 7–10 September.

Rantanen, H. (2005) 'Mapping local knowledge: Possibilities of Web GIS in a planning process', TED Workshop: e-Participation in Environmental Decision Making, 19–22 May, Helsinki and Conference Ship, Finland, http://www.ted.tkk.fi/Abstract_Rantanen.rtf

Razak, V. (2003) 'Can indigenous cultures survive the future?', *Future*, 35: 907–15.

Riseth, J. (2007) 'An indigenous perspective on national parks and Sami reindeer management in Norway', *Geographical Review*, 45(2): 177–85.

Rundstrom, R. (1995) 'GIS, Indigenous peoples and epistemological diversity', *Cartography and Geographic Information Systems*, 22(1): 45–57.

Rundstrom, R. (1998) 'Mapping, the white man's burden', *Common Property Resource Digest*, 45: 7–9.

Said, E. (1993) *Culture and Imperialism.* London: Vintage Press.

Sen, B. (2005) 'Indigenous knowledge for development: Bringing research and practice together', *The International Information and Library Review*, 37: 375–82.

Skow, H. (2004) Navajo Nation Digital Technology Plan. Department of Information Technology, Window Rock, AZ, 30 June, http://www.dit.navajo.org/images/Docs/NAVAJO%20NATION%20Strategic%20Information%20Technology%20Plan%201.3.pdf (accessed 8 December 2008).

Tabor, J. and Hutchinson, C. (1994) 'Using indigenous knowledge, remote sensing and GIS for sustainable development', *Indigenous Knowledge and Development Monitor*, 2(1): 2–6.

Thrupp, L. (1989) 'Legitimizing local knowledge: From displacement to empowerment for Third World people', *Agriculture and Human Values*, Summer: 13–24.

Tran, P., Shaw, R., Chantry, G. and Norton, J. (2009) 'GIS and local knowledge in disaster management: a case study flood risk mapping in Vietnam'. *Disasters.* March 33(1):152–69.

Tripathi, N. and Bhattarya, S. (2004) 'Integrating indigenous knowledge and GIS for participatory natural resource management: State-of-the-Practice', *The Electronic Journal on Information Systems in Developing Countries*, 17(3): 1–13.

Turnbull, D. (1989) *Maps are Territories: Science is an Atlas.* Chicago, IL: University of Chicago Press.

Turnbull, D. (2003) *Masons, Tricksters and Cartographers: Comparative Studies in the Sociology of Scientific an Indigenous Knowledge*, 2nd edn. London: Routledge.

UNESCO (2005) 'Local and Indigenous knowledge of the natural world: An overview of programmers and projects', *International Workshop on Traditional Knowledge*, Panama City, Panama, 21–23 September. http://www.un.org/esa/socdev/unpfii/documents/workshoop_TK_castro.pdf

Verplanke, J. (2004) Combining mobile GIS and indigenous knowledge in community managed forests. Proceedings of the 3rd annual URISA Public Participation GIS (PPGIS) Conference, University of Wisconsin, Madison, 18–20 July.

Waldron, J. and Sui, D. (1999) 'Integrating indigenous knowledge and GIS in land use suitability analysis', Paper presented at GISOC'99, Conference on Geographic Information and Society, Minneapolis, June. http://www.socsci.umn.edu/~bongman/gisoc99/new/waldron.htm. Accessed 30 September 2010.

Warren, D.M. (1991) *Using Indigenous Knowledge in Agricultural Development*, World Bank Discussion Paper No. 127. Washington, DC: The World Bank.

World Bank (1998) *Indigenous Knowledge for Development – a Framework for Action, Knowledge and Learning Center Africa Region.* Washington, DC: World Bank. http://www.worldbank.org/afr/ik/ikrept.pdf

Weiner, D., Harris, T. and Craig, W. (2002) 'Community participation and geographic information systems' In W. Craig, T. Harris and D. Weiner (eds), *Community Participation and Geographic Information Systems.* London: Taylor & Francis. pp. 3–16.

Wilson, G.A. and Memon, P.A. (2005) 'Indigenous forest management in 21st-century New Zealand: towards a "postproductivist" indigenous forest-farmland interface?', *Environment and Planning A,* 37: 1493–518.

Wood, D. (1992) *The Power of Maps.* New York: Guilford Press.

Zinn, H. (1995) *A People's History of the United States: 1492 – Present.* New York: Harper Perennial.

12

Spatial Modeling of Social Networks

Carter T. Butts and Ryan M. Acton

INTRODUCTION

From the broad perspective of relational analysis, it is natural to view both spatial analysis and network analysis as important special cases of a more general structural approach. Although often seen as separate areas of endeavor, both spatial analysis and network analysis are alike in treating the relationships among entities – rather than their intrinsic properties – as being the focus of primary interest. Within spatial analysis, these relationships are construed as arising from the embedding of entities within a spatial structure, as represented by the action of a distance function on a set of possible positions. The constraints placed upon the distance function (e.g., identity, symmetry, and frequently the triangle inequality) define the nature of the space of positions and serve as the primary "levers" of analysis and theory construction. Alternately, network analysis typically assumes relations to be comprised of pair-wise interactions, whose states depend upon one another primarily through configural mechanisms (e.g., reciprocity [Holland and Leinhardt, 1981], transitive closure bias

[Holland and Leinhardt, 1971], or Markov dependence [Frank and Strauss, 1986]) or covariate effects (e.g., homophily [McPherson et al., 2001]). While consequential, these differences are not insuperable. As analysts in both fields have long recognized, spatial interactions can be viewed as comprising a network structure of distances, and seemingly non-spatial network structures can be represented (at least approximately) by locations in a latent space (McPherson, 1983; McPherson and Ranger-Moore, 1991; Hoff et al., 2002).

A natural consequence of this view is the notion that spatial and other types of relationships – for instance, social ties among persons, groups, or organizations – are themselves related. While substantiated by a long tradition of empirical research (e.g., Bossard, 1932; Stewart, 1941; Zipf, 1949; Morrill and Pitts, 1963; Irwin and Hughes, 1992), the fact that social ties are often structured by spatial relationships has not been fully recognized within the social sciences. Likewise, models for the spatial distribution of groups and individuals typically omit the consequences of these arrangements for social structure per se. A unified treatment of social and spatial structure requires the joint analysis of both relationships, using methods which bridge both analytical traditions.

Like geography, the social network field has an extensive methodological literature. As detailed by Freeman (2004), the network analytic field arose as the result of an interplay and eventual integration among several initially independent streams of research within a number of disciplines, including anthropology, sociology, psychology, mathematics, and computer science. Undoubtedly the most comprehensive treatment of this union to date has been the canonical text of Wasserman and Faust (1994), whose synthesis of concepts and methods has become the standard reference for what may now be considered "classical" social network analysis. The classical approach stresses exploratory and descriptive methods, as well as graph visualization, with a strong focus on the identification of key positions within networks (e.g., Freeman, 1979), classification of subgroups and social roles (Everett, 1985; Freeman, 1992), description of connectivity and path structure (Travers and Milgram, 1969), and analysis of local structure (particularly properties such as reciprocity, transitivity, and clustering (e.g., Holland and Leinhardt, 1971; Granovetter, 1973; Hammer, 1985]). A number of accessible introductions to this tradition exist (in addition to Wasserman and Faust, above), including well-known texts by Scott (1991) and Degenne and Forsé (1999). Moreover, classical network analytic concepts and techniques continue to experience rapid development, as summarized by more recent reviews such as those of Brandes and Erlebach (2005), Carrington et al. (2005), and Doreian et al. (2005). At the same time, much recent work has centered on the development of statistical modeling approaches for network data, many of which follow from the seminal papers of Holland and Leinhardt (1981) and Frank and Strauss (1986) on what have come to be called *exponential random graph models*. (See Butts [2008] for a recent review of these

and related approaches.) As an outgrowth of the classical tradition, the network modeling literature has also been concerned with problems such as the measurement of local structure (Snijders et al., 2006), differences in activity across individuals (Jones and Handcock, 2003), and the effect of group membership on tie formation (Morris, 1991). Placing these problems within a statistical framework has also facilitated treatment of more complex problems such as data quality and measurement error (Butts, 2003a), structural dynamics (Snijders, 1996), network sampling (Thompson and Frank, 2000), non-local dependence (Pattison and Robins, 2002), and network comparison (Butts, 2007). While some work on this area has focused on the development of null hypothesis testing procedures (e.g., Holland and Leinhardt, 1970; Krackhardt, 1987; Anderson et al., 1999; Pattison et al., 2000), emphasis in recent years has turned towards parametric modeling, which allows for direct measurement of multiple, competing effects, and for the evaluation of quantitative theoretical predictions (Wasserman and Robins, 2005; Robins and Morris, 2007).

While the general network modeling literature is rich and growing, specific guidance for the use of GIS or other spatial information in parametric modeling of social ties has been difficult to obtain. The use of latent (non-observed) spatial structure as a tool for modeling networks has been explored in a number of recent contributions (e.g., Hoff et al., 2002; Handcock et al., 2007; Krivitsky and Handcock, 2008), but this is obviously different from the use of geographical information to predict ties. Butts (2002) developed a simple scheme for modeling network data from spatial information, demonstrating in Butts (2003b) that this approach is sufficient to account for certain aspects of large-scale structure under fairly weak conditions. (An alternative approach for smaller networks, with some similarities to the combinatorial methods of Gale et al. [1983] can be found in Butts [2007].) Recent work by Hipp and Perrin (2009) also uses a model of this kind to analyze ties within neighborhoods, showing the impact of both social factors and physical distance in predicting interaction across households. Drawing on this recent line of work, we here provide an introduction to the use of spatial relationships in the parametric modeling of social networks. The methods we employ are themselves "hybrids" of techniques developed in spatial and network contexts, combining the use of spatial interaction functions (taken from the gravity modeling tradition of geographical analysis) and inhomogeneous Bernoulli graph models (taken from the statistical literature in social network analysis). Using these methods, we demonstrate how one can obtain maximum likelihood estimates (and associated standard errors) for interaction function parameters, and how one can choose among competing models on a principled basis. This presentation is prefaced by a brief introduction to the basic concepts of social network analysis, and considerations regarding the collection and representation of network data in spatial contexts.

To illustrate these methods, we apply them to the analysis of inter-organizational collaboration during the first several days of the response to the Hurricane Katrina disaster of 2005 (Butts et al., 2011). As we show, field interactions among the organizations were strongly associated with proximity among their respective headquarters. Emergent, local interactions within the disaster are thus shown to be constrained by long-standing spatial relationships, contrary to what would be expected from a myopic view of the event as independent of prior context. This simple example highlights the value of a combined treatment of geographical and social structure, and the use of model-based methods for elucidating the relationship between the two.

Core concepts and notation

As with spatial analysis, researchers in the social network field employ specialized terminology and notation. Much of this is borrowed from *graph theory*, the branch of mathematics that is concerned with discrete relational structures (for an overview, see West [1996] or Bollobás [1998]; for historic applications in geography, see Nystuen and Dacey [1961] or Kansky [1963]). While the graph theoretic formalisms used within the social network field can seem daunting to the newcomer, the core concepts and notation are easily mastered. We begin, therefore, by reviewing some of these elements before advancing to a discussion of network data and methods.

A social network, as we shall here use the term, consists of a set of *entities*, together with a *relation* on those entities. For the moment, we are unconcerned with the specific nature of the entities in question; persons, groups, or organizations may be objects of study, as may more exotic entities such as texts, artifacts, or even concepts. We do assume, however, that the entities which form our network are distinct from one another, can be uniquely identified, and are finite in number. Likewise, we constrain the set of potential relations to be studied not by content, but by their formal properties. Specifically, we require that relations be defined on pairs of actors (called *dyads*), and that there exists a qualitative distinction between relationships which are present and those which are absent. A wide range of relations can be cast in this form, including collaboration, attributions of trust or friendship, and interpersonal communication.

Within the above constraints, we may represent social relations as *graphs*. A graph is a relational structure consisting of two elements: a set of entities (called *vertices* or *nodes*), and a set of entity pairs indicating connections among them (called *edges* or *ties*). Formally, we represent such an object as $G = (V, E)$, where V is the vertex set and E is the edge set. Where multiple graphs are involved, it can sometimes be useful to treat V and E as operators: thus, $V(G)$ is the vertex set of G, and $E(G)$ is the edge set of G. When used alone (as V and E) these elements are tacitly assumed to pertain to the graph under study. We represent the number of elements in a given set by the cardinality operator, $|\bullet|$, and hence $|V|$ and $|E|$ are the numbers of vertices and edges in G, respectively. The number of vertices in a given graph is known as its *order* or *size*, and will be denoted here by $n = |V|$ where there is no danger of confusion. (Some graph theory texts use "order" to refer to $|V|$ and "size" to refer to $|E|$, but this convention is not followed among social network analysts.) It is also standard in the network literature to employ simple set theoretic notation to describe various collections of objects. In particular, $\{a,b,c,...\}$ refers to the unordered set containing the elements a, b, c, and so on, and $(a,b,c,...)$ refers to an ordered set (or *tuple*) on the same objects. Note that the order of elements matters only in the latter case; thus $\{a,b\} = \{b,a\}$, but $(a,b) \neq (b,a)$. Set membership is similarly denoted by $\in$, with $a \in A$ indicating that object a belongs to set A. While this notation may be unfamiliar to some readers, it provides a precise and compact language for describing structure which cannot be obtained using natural language. This notation is frequently encountered within the network literature, particularly in more technical papers.

Returning to the matter of graphs, we note that they appear in several varieties. These varieties are defined by the type of relationships they represent, as reflected in the content of their edge sets. Graphs that represent dyadic relations which are intrinsically symmetric (i.e., no distinction can be drawn between the "sender" and the "receiver" of the relation) are said to be *undirected*, and have edge sets which consist of unordered pairs of vertices. By contrast, other graphs represent relations which are not inherently symmetric, in the sense that each relationship involves distinct "sender" and "receiver" roles. These graphs (which are called *directed graphs* or *digraphs*) have edge sets that are composed of ordered pairs of vertices. An edge from a vertex to itself is a special type of edge known as a *loop*, and may or may not be meaningful for a particular relation.

Relations which are *irreflexive* (i.e., have no loops) and which are not *multiplex* (i.e., do not allow duplicate edges) are said to be *simple*. For purposes of this chapter, we will focus primarily on simple graphs – network structures discussed here should be assumed to be of this kind unless otherwise indicated.

Finally, we note that the networks of primary interest for purposes of this chapter have the special property that their vertices can be associated with some position in a geographical space. (More general notions of space – such as the *Blau spaces* of McPherson and Ranger-Moore [1991]; McPherson [1983] – provide no particular difficulty, but we will focus on the geographical case.) Let S be such a space, and let there exist some *location* operator, l, which takes V into S; we then say that the associated graph, G is *spatially embedded*. In practice, we generally work not with vertex locations per se, but rather with some *distance* between those locations. Let d be a distance on the elements of S; we will then denote the distance $d(l(v_i), l(v_j))$ between the locations of any two vertices v_i and v_j by the shortened form D_{ij}.[1]

DATA CONSIDERATIONS

This section provides a brief overview of data considerations for spatial network analysis. This includes a short summary of basic network data collection and representation strategies. Specific issues related to geocoding of vertex locations is also discussed, with some additional comments on practical challenges, which can arise when geocoding network elements from archival sources.

Network data

Before considering the analysis of network data within a spatial context, we first begin with a brief discussion of network data per se. Since network data is represented in a different form from the matrix/vector format familiar to most social scientists, we start with a short discussion of how such data may be numerically represented. This is useful both notationally (for the discussion which follows) and also pragmatically, since most available network analysis tools (e.g., Pajek [Batagelj and Mrvar, 2007], statnet [Handcock et al., 2008], StOCNET [Huisman and van Duijn, 2003], and UCINET [Borgatti et al., 1999]) assume some basic familiarity with the representation of network data. We also say a few words about the collection of network data (designs and instruments), briefly reviewing some methods which are in common use.

Data representation

Network data can be represented in a number of ways, depending upon the type of network and the intended application. We have already seen that networks can be represented using graph theoretic notation, a representation which is frequently employed in conceptual discussions. For practical purposes, however, network data is more often represented in other ways. The most common data representation in empirical contexts is the *adjacency matrix*, an $n \times n$ matrix whose ijth cell is equal to 1 if vertex i sends an edge to vertex j, and 0 otherwise. For an undirected graph G with adjacency matrix $\mathbf{A}$, it is clear that $A_{ij} = A_{ji}$ (i.e., the adjacency matrix must be symmetric). This is not generally true if G is a digraph. If G is simple (i.e., G has no loops), then all elements of the diagonal of $\mathbf{A}$ will be identically 0. Otherwise, $A_{ii} = 1$ if vertex i has a loop (this being identical for directed and undirected graphs). In spatial contexts, the same representation is often employed to represent *contiguity* (i.e., sharing of pointwise or linear borders between regions); indeed, contiguity structures may be viewed as graphs containing loops, and the *contiguity matrix* of such a structure is simply the corresponding graph adjacency matrix.

While the above describes the pure adjacency structure of a graph, it is not always

the case that connections between entities are dichotomous. In the special case of networks with valued edges, we employ the above representation with the minor modification that A_{ij} is the value of the (i,j) edge (conventionally 0 if no edge is present). Here again, we have the direct spatial analogs of the distance matrix (where A_{ij} is the spatial distance between locations i and j) and the flow matrix (where A_{ij} represents a flow of people, goods, or other objects from location i to location j).

Although adjacency matrices are simple to work with, they can be unwieldy where n is very large (especially if G is very sparse). In such cases, it is common to store networks via *edge lists*, or pairs of vertices which are tied to one another. Another representation which is sometimes useful is the *incidence matrix*, a $n \times |E|$ matrix $\mathbf{I}$ such that $I_{ij} = 1$ if vertex i is an endpoint of edge j and 0 otherwise. Direction within incidence matrices is denoted via signs, such that $I_{ij} = -1$ if i is the source of the jth edge of G, and $I_{ij} = 1$ if i is instead the destination of the jth edge. Incidence matrices are relatively unwieldy, and are not often used in conventional network research. However, incidence matrices are very useful for representing *hypergraphs* (i.e., networks whose edges involve more than two endpoints) and for two-mode data (i.e., networks consisting of connections between two disjoint types of entities). We do not treat these applications here, although the interested reader may turn to Wasserman and Faust (1994: Chapters 3 and 4) for an introductory account.

Data collection

Relational data is collected in many forms, and data on social networks is no exception to this rule. The most common data type encountered in traditional social network studies (and treated at great length in standard volumes such as Wasserman and Faust [1994]) consists of dichotomous edge observations from a *complete* or *network census* design, measuring the interactions among all pairs of entities from some fixed set. For instance, one might consider all advice ties among members of a given firm, or all migration relationships among US counties. In a network census design, a single observation is present for each edge – these observations are traditionally taken to be error-free, although challenges to this assumption (see, for example, Killworth and Bernard, 1976, 1979; Bernard and Killworth, 1977; Bernard et al., 1979, 1984) have led to the development of more systematic measurement models (Romney et al., 1986; Batchelder and Romney, 1988; Butts, 2003a). Some extensions of the network census design include the *cognitive social structure* design (Krackhardt, 1988), in which multiple sources report their perceptions of all dyad states, and subsets of this such as the balanced arc-sampling designs suggested by Butts (2003a). Though most work in this tradition has focused on elicitation of edge reports from human informants, archival or other sources are also possible; for instance, Baker and Faulkner (1993) use court records to reconstruct networks of illegal behavior, Comfort and Kapucu (2006) and Tierney (2003) employ institutional documents and media reports to reconstruct organizational interaction during disasters, Wimmer and Min (2006) draw on historical records to study war between nations, and Choudhury and Pentland (2003) use sensors to measure human interaction. Although variable in other respects, all designs in this family are intended to provide at least one measurement on each dyad, and hence permit (in principle) direct calculation of global structural properties.

While census designs in their various forms remain the gold standard of network analysis, the impossibility of census sampling on large populations has forced the development of alternative approaches. Many of these are reviewed at greater length in Marsden (1990, 2005) and Frank (2005); only a brief description of the more common variants will be given here. In *personal network* or *egocentric* studies, selected individuals (referred to as "egos") are sampled in some fashion (typically at random), and information on their local structural properties are obtained. Usually, measurements are obtained for all dyads of which ego is a member; ego and those to whom he or she is tied (known as "alters") collectively define ego's personal network. In a *complete egocentric* design, measurements are also made of all dyads having only the alters as endpoints (i.e., all potential ties among ego's alters). Egocentric designs (complete or otherwise) based on probability samples of egos from a large population are popular in survey studies such as the General Social Survey (Davis and Smith, 1988), due to their compatibility with traditional survey instruments. Although such data only provides information on local structure, the approach can still be employed in studies of personal network size and composition. One major family of variants on the egocentric design employs a form of adaptive sampling (Thompson, 1997) in which alters nominated in the initial sampling process are then selected as egos in a later wave of the study (a process which may be further iterated in successive waves). Such designs are often called *link-trace* designs, and incorporate traditional snowball sampling (Goodman, 1961), respondent-driven sampling (Heckathorn, 1997, 2002), random-walk sampling (Klovdahl, 1989), among many others. Although complicated to execute, link-trace designs are a favored means of sampling hard-to-reach populations (e.g., IV drug injectors) who are nevertheless socially connected. Like other egocentric designs, link-trace designs do not provide measurements on all edges, and hence are limited in their ability to show global structure (although estimation for some such properties is possible using exponential family models; see Thompson and Frank [2000]). As with complete network designs, it should be noted that ego-net and link-trace studies can be employed with organizational or other non-human networks (e.g., using informant- or observer-based measurement).

Geospatial data

In order to analyze spatially embedded networks, it is frequently necessary to collect and/or code geospatial information regarding vertex locations. This subsection comments on some of the issues surrounding this problem, with a discussion of pitfalls which have affected past research. Given that available data are rarely perfect, our emphasis here is on practical considerations; some additional comments are included in a later section, which discusses Butts et al.'s (2011) study of organizational collaboration networks during the Hurricane Katrina response as an illustrative case.

Geocoding for spatially embedded networks

It is rarely the case in social network studies that the researcher is provided with rich geographic location information regarding each element in the target network – given this, some ingenuity is often necessary. When studying sets of people, organizations, or animals, for instance, it may be possible to obtain the location attributes of those entities in different ways. Location might be obtained through technological mechanisms such as GPS tracking of the individuals at various points in time, though less sophisticated means such as asking a person or a representative of an organization in a survey to provide a current street address can also prove effective. While exact locations may not be available, it may in some cases be possible to georeference an entity to a Census tract or some other known, bounded region after the network data have already been collected. Unfortunately, most existing social network data contains little to no information about vertex locations, making them artificially "aspatial." Collection of geospatial data should thus be a priority when initiating new studies, taking care to ensure that the data which is collected will be sufficiently precise to use. Some early residential network studies, for instance, did collect spatial data, but did so in a fashion that rendered it insufficient for future use: common problems included using idiosyncratic units to measure distance (e.g., "four doors away" in an apartment setting), using purely ordinal distance measures, excessive binning of distances into a small number of highly variable categories, and presenting distances/ locations via maps without an associated scale. Such errors can render an otherwise excellent study largely useless for spatial network analysis, and can be avoided by systematic use of appropriate geocoding and georeferencing methods.

Considerations for the specificity of spatial information

Prior to collecting spatial information, one must first choose the level of precision desired. At one extreme, one may be interested in knowing the location of a vertex at a given point in time within a range on the order of meters. This kind of precision is warranted when dealing with relationships which attenuate over very short distances, and/or where the total range covered by entities included within the study is reasonably small. When studying long-range ties, however, location to the county, state, or even national level may be sufficient in order to analyze broader spatial patterns. In such cases, vertex positions may be georeferenced to Census tract or ZIP-code centroids, city center coordinates, or perhaps a state or national capitol. The level of detail required is governed both by the study objectives, and by the above-mentioned attenuation property. In general, greater precision is required for accurate simulation of networks from geospatial data than for inference regarding spatial interaction functions (described below). Likewise, interaction functions with long tails require data over greater spatial scales in order to accurately estimate tail weight; it can be difficult to discriminate between interaction functions with similar properties (e.g., arctangent and power law models) unless precise spatial information is available.

SPATIAL ANALYSIS OF NETWORK DATA

Having discussed network data in general – and issues affecting spatially embedded network data, in particular – we now proceed to a discussion of methods for the spatial analysis of network data. Our approach here is model-based, drawing upon a general and extensible family of models which combine geographical and network analytic elements. We begin by discussing this model family, next moving to a discussion of the core formalism expressing the relationship between distance and social structure (the spatial interaction function). Finally, we conclude this section with a treatment of likelihood-based inference (parameter estimation and model selection) for spatial Bernoulli graphs.

Spatial Bernoulli graphs

To model the effect of space on network structure, it is helpful to begin with a model family which is simple enough to be easily employed, yet powerful enough to be interesting. The basic family employed here is the *spatial Bernoulli graphs* (Butts, 2002), a simple discrete exponential family model which takes edges as independent conditional on an observed distance structure (see Wasserman and Robins [2005] for an accessible discussion of exponential families and dependence structures for network data). While conditional independence given distance – that is, the assumption that the dependence of one edge upon another is completely contained within the underlying distance structure – should be regarded as an approximation to a more complex reality, Butts (2003b) has shown that spatial models based on this assumption can be very powerful under fairly general conditions. In particular, the spatial Bernoulli graphs will account for many aspects of network structure, so long as the spatial scale is reasonably large compared to distance at which edges become improbable on average. (See the above

reference for a formal discussion.) Perhaps more importantly, spatial Bernoulli graphs can be used to study the empirical relationship between geographical distance and tie probability, a matter which is of considerable interest for the geographical study of social systems.

The spatial Bernoulli graphs are defined as follows. Let us consider a set of vertices, V, which are embedded in some space, S, with distance matrix $\mathbf{D}$. Further, let G be random graph on V, with stochastic adjacency matrix $\mathbf{Y}$. We then write the probability mass function (pmf) of G (via its adjacency matrix) given $\mathbf{D}$ as

$$\Pr(\mathbf{Y} = y \mid \mathbf{D}, \mathcal{F}_d) = \prod_{\{i,j\}} B(y_{ij} \mid \mathcal{F}_d(D_{ij})), \quad (12.1)$$

where $B(x|\theta)=x\theta+(1-x)(1-\theta)$ is the Bernoulli pmf, and $\mathcal{F}_d$ is a *spatial interaction function*. The spatial interaction function (SIF) is defined as a function from $(0, \infty)$ into $[0, 1]$, thereby mapping *distance* into *tie probability*. Given $\mathcal{F}_d$ and $\mathbf{D}$, the spatial Bernoulli graph arises with a series of independent Bernoulli trials, with the probability of each edge determined by the distance between vertices and the SIF. This distribution is thus a general linear model with link function $\mathcal{F}_d^{-1}$, and is also a special case of the *gravity models* long used by geographers to model spatial interaction (Haynes and Fotheringham, 1984). This last is discussed in more detail below. Although Equation 1 is written for the case of simple graphs, it should be noted that directed graphs can be treated as well. In the latter case, one simply defines the joint probability of $\mathbf{Y}$ as a product over all ordered pairs (i, j) instead of all unordered pairs; the model is otherwise identical.

While the spatial Bernoulli graphs do incorporate an assumption of conditional independence, this should not be equated with unconditional independence (e.g., as in the homogeneous Bernoulli graphs often credited to Erdös and Rényi [1960]). Indeed, phenomena such as transitivity, formation of locally dense clusters, and (in the directed case) reciprocity can emerge as a byproduct of the underlying distance structure. Indeed, this insight has been used by Hoff et al. (2002) and Handcock et al. (2007) to argue for the utility of *latent distance models* as tools for capturing social structure. In this framework, **D** is taken to result from a set of latent vertex positions within a Euclidean space, with $\mathcal{F}_d$ taken as fixed (e.g., a logistic link). Given an observed graph, latent positions are then inferred based on the structure of ties among vertices; the framework is thus a model-based analog of metric multidimensional scaling (Torgerson, 1952) for network data. In our case, conversely, it is **D** and *G* which are observed, and $\mathcal{F}_d$ which is the target of primary interest. We thus proceed to a discussion of the spatial interaction function.

The spatial interaction function

Geographers have long been concerned with the modeling of interaction between spatially distant elements (particularly areal or other aggregate units, for example, cities, countries, regions, and so on). A general and powerful approach to this problem is the use of the aforementioned *gravity models* (Wilson, 1970; Tobler, 1976; Haynes and Fotheringham, 1984), which model the strength of interaction between elements in terms of marginal rates, together with a function which attenuates these rates in some fashion which depends upon the distance between them. Specifically, the expected volume of interaction between two distinct elements *A* and *B* in a gravity model is taken to be proportional to $P(A)P(B)\mathcal{F}_d(d(A,B))$, where *P* is the *interaction potential* of a given element, and $\mathcal{F}_d$ is the *impedance* or SIF governing the spatial interaction. Despite the name, "gravity" models need not take $\mathcal{F}_d(d) = d^{-2}$ – indeed, many functional forms may be chosen for both $\mathcal{F}_d$ and *P*. Gravity models have proven highly successful in characterizing such diverse phenomena as telecommunications volume (Guldmann,

2004), international trade (Linnemann, 1966), and daily commuting behavior (Oppenheim, 1995). More importantly, the family provides a simple and intuitive way of parameterizing the relationship between distance and interaction strength: by choosing the functional form of the spatial interaction function, one can succinctly express a great deal of information regarding the manner in which distance affects social interaction.

While the gravity model is sometimes seen as a distinctly geographical tool, we have already alluded to the fact that it can also be viewed as a network model. Given a possibly valued graph *G* with adjacency matrix **A**, the gravity model posits that $\mathbf{E}A_{ij} \propto P(v_i)P(v_j)\mathcal{F}_d(d(l(v_i),l(v_j)))$; this is a family of edge-independent network formation models with marginal and/or dyadic covariate effects, and includes a number of existing models as special cases. For instance, if we take $P(v_i) = \exp(\theta^T \mathbf{x}_i)$ and $\mathcal{F}_d = \exp(-\phi d)$, then the gravity model becomes a standard *network regression* model (Krackhardt, 1988) on ln*A*. The gravity model is also closely related to the p_1 model family of Holland and Leinhardt (1981), which represents edge probabilities as functions of marginal fixed effects, an overall activity level, and a symmetry bias. The spatial Bernoulli graphs described above are likewise a gravity model family for which $P \propto 1$, with model behavior therefore governed by $\mathcal{F}_d$. The approach taken here to the analysis of spatially embedded networks is thus as closely tied to geographical as to network analytic modeling traditions.

As the above suggests, the explicitly spatial aspects of network interaction – neglecting *locational* effects which may enter into marginal interaction tendencies – are driven by the spatial interaction function. Although the choice of spatial interaction function can be (and often has been) conducted as a purely exploratory curve-fitting exercise, this need not be the case. Indeed, the functional form governing the distance/tie probability relationship is of central *theoretical* importance, as it forms the essential "bridge" between micro-level phenomena such as boundaries and interaction costs and the structural properties of large-scale networks. Knowledge of the substantive properties of the relation being modeled places a priori bounds on the set of plausible spatial interaction functions; by turns, knowledge of a spatial interaction function reveals much about the process with which it is associated. Similarly, the form of the spatial interaction function determines many macroscopic properties of the networks generated by them. Information regarding the incidence of those properties in a relation of interest thus aids in identifying the associated spatial interaction function, even as knowledge of the interaction function obviously provides a basis for structural prediction. The position taken here, then, is that the spatial interaction function should be viewed as an important theoretical object, and its properties are worth considering in some depth.

While many aspects of $\mathcal{F}_d$ could be considered, we here focus our discussion on a few qualitative features which serve to separate families of interaction functions. While many others could be chosen, the following properties – monotonicity, tie probability at the origin, local curvature, and tail weight – are of particular import for features of interest when analyzing spatially embedded social networks. We here discuss each in turn, concluding with some comments on the heuristic use of these features for selecting candidate interaction functions in practical settings.

Monotonic versus non-monotonic interaction functions

Perhaps the most basic property of any spatial interaction function is that of whether it is monotonic in distance. The classical assumption is that marginal interaction probabilities are at least weakly monotone decreasing in distance; ceteris paribus, two individuals who are further apart are no more likely to interact than individuals who are closer to one another. Although this assumption is reasonable in many circumstances (for reasons discussed at length by Zipf [1949]),

cases may arise in which it does not hold. Although monotone increasing interaction functions are rarely plausible (see below), non-monotonic interaction functions may be encountered in certain settings. In practice, such functions will generally arise either from intrinsic properties of the relation of primary interest, or as an artifact of inadequate relational sampling. Here, we briefly consider each of these possibilities.

Substantively non-monotonic interaction functions are most likely to arise in contexts where there are significant negative incentives for local tie formation. A classic example of this is marital exogamy, in which residents of a particular social unit (e.g., village or household compound) are expected to seek partners from more distant units. Although it is reasonable to expect a preference for partners from nearby (and hence accessible) units over ones which are extremely far away, the prohibition on local ties will similarly reduce edge probabilities for closely placed vertices. Another possible generator of nonmonotonic interaction functions may be relations which are based on the exchange of spatially autocorrelated goods; gains from trade would be expected to increase (on average) with the distance between actors, but would eventually be overcome by transaction costs at more extreme distances. Exactly how prevalent such conditions are is not currently known, but few if any well-verified examples are present in the current literature. For most purposes, then, relations which are fundamentally non-monotonic in distance may be suspected to be rare, though the possibility should be investigated where factors such as the above are present.

While non-monotonic interaction functions may be generated by intrinsic properties of the social relation in question, they may also be produced as a byproduct of inadequate measurement. Many fundamental relationships – such as communication – can be enacted in various ways, and/or through various media. For instance, modern persons in the developed world can communicate with one another through physical contact, face-to-face conversation, telephony, email, and epistolary mechanisms (to mention only a few). Each such mechanism has a profile of both cost and effectiveness which varies with distance, but all can be used to convey information. Thus, we may reasonably expect to find *substitution effects* within interpersonal communication, in which different mechanisms are used to effect communication at various distances. Importantly, such effects may result in interaction frequencies which are non-monotonic when disaggregated by mechanism, despite an overall communication pattern that is itself monotonic in distance. Such a scenario is illustrated in Figure 12.1, where various non-monotonic interaction functions are depicted together with the resulting probability of interaction by any mechanism (heavy line). Although the cumulative probability of interaction here is plainly monotonic, a study which sampled from only one of the potential mechanisms would draw very different conclusions. In such circumstances, the presence of unexpectedly non-monotonic interaction functions may be a clue that the relations in question have not been properly sampled (and, in particular, that one or more mechanisms of interaction have been omitted).

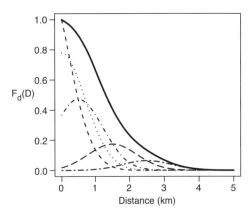

Figure 12.1   Decomposition of a monotonic interaction function into multiple non-monotonic inter-action functions, due to substitution effects

Alternately, it is also important to bear in mind that the monotonicity of an aggregate relationship may not imply that its components are similarly monotonic. Where an interaction can occur via multiple mechanisms with disparate spatial properties, and where there is a potential incentive to substitute one mechanism of interaction for another at varying distances, interaction frequencies for particular mechanisms may be expected to be non-monotonic in distance.

As a final observation, it should be noted that if space (and population) is effectively unbounded, then bounded degree[2] implies that $\mathcal{F}_d$ must be either decreasing or identically equal to 0 at sufficiently large distances. (Since, otherwise, degree would grow without bound.) In most practical settings, the range of degree scores is sufficiently small relative to the number of possible long-range alters to ensure monotone decreasing (or 0) interaction probabilities in the large-d limit.

Structural effects of monotonicity

Monotonically decreasing interaction functions will tend to produce (spatially) "short" edges; that is, the distance between endpoints will be shorter, on average, than the distance between non-adjacent individuals. Such correlations between proximity and interaction are almost ubiquitous for social networks embedded in both physical and non-physical spaces. While (as noted above) nearly all plausible interaction functions will be monotonically decreasing at large distances, locally non-monotone functions are possible. Non-monotone functions that are unimodal will be less locally cohesive than equivalent monotone functions, but may exhibit more distal connectivity (to the extent that tie probabilities are higher at longer distances). These effects are illustrated in Figure 12.2, which compares typical networks produced by monotone decreasing (top panels) and non-monotonic (bottom panels) interaction functions. As can be seen, a side effect of the tendency for edges in the bottom panel to be of a characteristic length (between 1 and 2 units) is the generation of connections

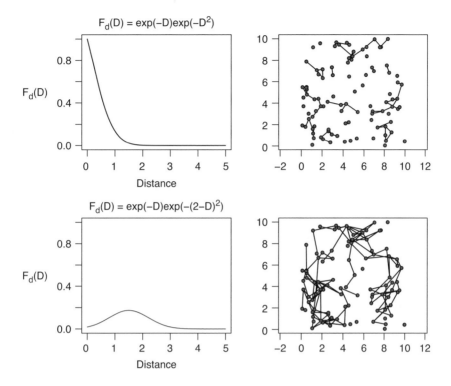

Figure 12.2   Comparison of monotonic and non-monotonic interaction functions, with typical network realizations

between groups of vertices which would not otherwise be connected by proximate ties (e.g., top panel). On the other hand, these same groups of vertices tend not to be internally cohesive, due to their proximity; thus while the monotonic interaction function tends to produce local clustering, the non-monotonic interaction function tends to produce locally *k-partite* behavior. Such properties have a number of implications for the spectra of the resulting graph adjacency matrices (see, for example, Seary and Richards, 2003).

Tie probability at the origin

Another fundamental property of $\mathcal{F}_d$ is its behavior at the origin (i.e., as $d \to 0$). This reflects, intuitively enough, the probability of a tie between two persons who are arbitrarily close to one another in physical space. The behavior $\mathcal{F}_d$ of at the origin will depend on

whether the relation in question is *proximity-sufficient*; that is, whether immediate proximity is in and of itself sufficient to guarantee interaction. For relations such as simple communication, parties who are sufficiently close to one another have little alternative but to interact. These relations can be expected to have $\mathcal{F}_d \to 1$ as $d \to 0$. By contrast, relations such as friendship or kinship have additional requirements which are not satisfied by proximity alone. Even where they are monotone decreasing in distance, then, we must admit the possibility that $\mathcal{F}_d$ will be less than 1 at the origin for such relations.

Structural effects of origin behavior

Higher values $\mathcal{F}_d(0)$ of tend to result in networks which are more locally cohesive; for monotonic interaction functions, this value also places an upper bound on edge probability generally. The former effect can be seen in the right-hand panels of Figure 12.2, where immediate neighbors are nearly always tied in the upper panel ($\mathcal{F}_d(0) = 1$) and rarely tied in the lower panel ($\mathcal{F}_d(0) \ll 1$).

Local curvature

In addition to tie probability at the origin itself, interaction functions vary consequentially in their curvature near the origin. This is typically well-summarized by the second derivative of $\mathcal{F}_d$ near 0, where this derivative exists. Specifically, we identify the *local curvature* of $\mathcal{F}_d$ with the sign of $\lim_{d \to 0} \partial^2 \mathcal{F}_d(d) / \partial d^2$; interaction functions with positive limiting derivatives are said to have locally positive curvature, while those with negative derivatives are said to have locally negative curvature. For monotone decreasing interaction functions, positive local curvature implies that the impact of distance is strongest near the origin, diminishing as one moves farther way. By contrast, interaction functions that have locally negative curvature will have distance effects which start slowly and grow as more distance is accumulated. (This relationship is reversed for interaction functions which are increasing near the origin.)

Relationships that are monotone decreasing and negatively curved can arise from compositions of multiple interaction modes with differing cost structures, as was discussed above. For instance, the costs of employing a given transportation mode (e.g., pedestrian travel) may scale linearly with distance over a certain range, only to increase supra-linearly at longer distances. Such differential costs may result from intrinsic properties of the transportation technology, or may represent the marginalized effects of discrete barriers that occur at varying spatial location. Grannis (1998), for instance, has found that small, "trivial" streets enhance pedestrian travel, while major roads inhibit it. This implies (in urban areas) an interaction function that falls slowly at short distances, decaying more rapidly as one approaches the average distance between major roads. By contrast, relationships with decreasing

marginal costs in distance can be expected to exhibit positive local curvature.

For locally increasing interaction functions, negative curvature may arise as a result of a reaction enhancement that grows slowly with distance from the origin, or from a local reaction inhibition which falls similarly slowly. Relationships with positive payoffs for spatial mixing (but some penalty for long-range interactions) may be expected to behave in this manner. In contrast, positive curvature is to be expected where local inhibition is sharply bounded, or where local interaction enhancement is active within a narrowly specified band. Relations with a prohibition on interaction with those inside a specified local neighborhood (e.g., normatively exogamous marriage in small villages) may demonstrate such behavior; intuitively, this is the inverse of the local interaction process described by Grannis (1998).

Note that local curvature may be of limited use with interaction functions defined on non-physical attribute spaces. Although $\mathcal{F}_d$ may itself be differentiable, highly discrete attribute bases may yield distance increments which are too widely spaced to give the local derivatives of $\mathcal{F}_d$ much meaning. On the other hand, Blau spaces which incorporate continuous attributes such as age, and/or which are high-dimensional, may show enough variation near the origin for curvature measures to be useful. These details notwithstanding, the fundamental interpretation of local curvature in terms of the change in the marginal impact of small distances can be applied in at least an approximate fashion to most settings.

Structural effects of local curvature

Under negative curvature, tie probabilities either fall more slowly (monotone decreasing) or rise more rapidly (monotone increasing) at short distances than at slightly longer distances; thus, negatively curved interaction functions tend to produce more locally cohesive networks than their positively curved counterparts. This is illustrated graphically in Figure 12.3, in which the realization for the

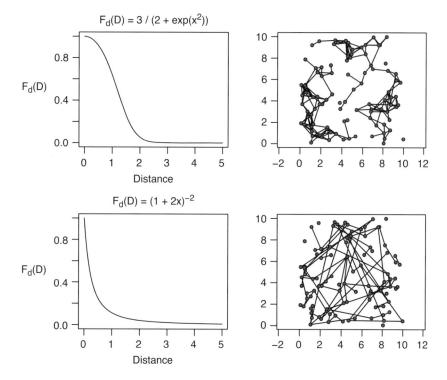

Figure 12.3 Comparison of light and heavy-tailed interaction functions with differing local curvature, with typical network realizations

negatively curved interaction function (top right) clearly shows a much higher rate of attachment to nearby alters than the realization for a negatively curved interaction function with identical tie probability at the origin (bottom right). The presence of local negative curvature in monotone decreasing interaction functions tends to produce a "local region" in which the behavior of the function is more representative of the origin than of the tails; this provides a useful means of discriminating among potential interaction functions, and is discussed in greater detail below. By contrast, positive curvature in monotone decreasing interaction functions leads to networks which exhibit no local region. The reverse is true for locally increasing functions, however, which exhibit local regions (here, regions of exclusion) under positive local curvature.

In understanding the structural effects of local curvature, it is useful to consider the extreme limit in which tie probabilities change radically at a given threshold. For instance, monotone decreasing models with strong negative curvature will include ties in the graph containing all dyads of length less than a particular threshold at a higher rate than other dyads. (The reverse is true of monotone increasing models with strong positive curvature.) This is the basis for the local cohesion/local exclusion effect described above, and can be useful for deriving approximations to the behavior of models based on certain interaction functions.

Tail weight
The last of the features to be discussed here is tail weight. Although it can be defined in different ways, we here consider tail weight in terms of the behavior of $\mathcal{F}_d(d)$ as $d \to \infty$ (where defined). While this value must approach 0 in most settings of interest (since

degree would otherwise diverge), we are here interested primarily in the *rate* of convergence. One obvious distinction in this regard is between functions that decay exponentially (i.e., $o(\exp(-cd))$) and those that decay as power laws (i.e. $o(d^{-c})$). For simplicity, spatial interaction functions decaying at least exponentially fast will generally said to be light tailed, while those decaying as a power law (or more slowly) are said to be heavy tailed. Of course, gradations of tail weight beyond these simple categories can be consequential (see Kleinberg [2000] for an example regarding searchability), but we will focus our present discussion on this basic distinction.

Relationships with effectively insuperable barriers to long-range edges are likely to give rise to light-tailed interaction functions. Face-to-face communication in cultures without vehicular technology, for instance, is essentially limited to persons within a relatively narrow radius of one's home range. Indeed, it is conceivable that a transition from light to heavy-tailed interaction functions for such relations may be a signature of the acquisition of domesticable riding animals and/or boatmaking technology, both of which have had well-verified impacts on the capacity for spatial expansion of the cultures that acquire them (Diamond, 1999). Light-tailed interaction functions have also been observed for intra-urban migration patterns (Morrill and Pitts, 1963; Freeman and Sunshine, 1976), presumably due to the substantially increasing costs of longer-range geographical moves. Long-tailed interaction functions, by contrast, may be particularly likely to arise where marginal interaction costs are diminishing in distance. In such settings, long-range interaction may be expensive, but relatively small variations in capacity to interact will lead to substantial differences in edge length. Such conditions can come about through technology mixing, where actors are able to choose among communication and/or transportation technologies that have low fixed but high variable costs (on the one hand) and high fixed but low variable costs (on the other). Modern transportation systems have precisely this structure which may account for the long-tailed interaction structures reported by Zipf (1949) and Latané et al. (1995).

Structural effects of tail weight

Tail weight governs the incidence of long edges within a spatially embedded network, and thus has dramatic implications for network structure. As Figure 12.3 illustrates, even differences in long-distance tie probability that appear small to the unaided eye can have an easily discernible effect on the number of realized long-range ties. Sociograms such as that in the bottom right of Figure 12.3 make this effect especially salient, since long edges are much more easily seen than short edges. (Such displays can also make long-tailed networks appear much more dense than they really are in some cases, and may give the false impression that no propinquity effect is present.) The shortage of long-range ties in light-tailed models can lead to locally "grid-like" behavior, particularly in the presence of high origin tie probability and substantial negative curvature. Long-tailed models, on the other hand, generate networks with relatively large numbers of non-local ties. These ties create short paths between spatially distant regions of the network, a phenomenon which is well-known from the work of Pool and Kochen (1979) Travers and Milgram (1969).

As with local curvature, the effects of tail weight can also be thought of in terms of stylized threshold models. The family of threshold models in which all edges beyond a given radius are excluded provides the limiting case of light-tailed models, with the associated restriction of realized networks to subgraphs of the threshold-induced graph. The heavy-tailed limit for monotone decreasing interaction functions, by contrast, is the uniform graph. As this suggests, increasing tail weight tends to lead to graphs with properties like those of (uniform) random graphs, an observation reminiscent of the findings of Watts and Strogatz (1998) regarding rewired lattice models. The rewired lattice studies would likewise seem to suggest that relatively modest non-local tie probabilities are required to obtain "uniform-like" behavior, provided that the interaction function is sufficiently flat in the upper tail.

Parametric forms

As the above suggests, a wide range of forms may be posited for $\mathcal{F}_d$. In practice, however, it is often useful to restrict attention to a smaller set of parametric forms having known properties. To that end, we briefly present several families of spatial interaction functions, which are likely to prove helpful in modeling spatially embedded social networks. Insofar as each form incorporates particular assumptions regarding tail weight, local curvature, and the like, it behooves researchers to view the selection of interaction functions (whether empirically or due to a priori considerations) as a matter of substantive theoretical importance. Although various SIFs may look similar to the naked eye, each may give rise to networks with very different properties.

Power laws

One of the most commonly proposed types of SIF is that which decays as a power law in distance. While a law of the general form $p = \alpha d^\beta$ with $\beta < 0$ is unacceptable due to its divergence in small distances, "protected" forms are viable. An obvious choice in this regard is $\mathcal{F}_d(x) = p_b(1 + \alpha x)^{-\gamma}$, where $0 \le p_b \le 1$ is a baseline tie probability, $\alpha \ge 0$ is a scaling parameter, $\gamma > 0$ and is the exponent that controls the distance effect. In terms of the qualitative features described in the previous section, this function is monotone decreasing in distance, with positive local curvature and relatively heavy tails. Tail weight is parametrized primarily through γ, although the scale parameter (α) determines the actual range over which distance effects are realized. Tie probability at the origin is parametrized directly by p_b and (like scale) may be varied independently of other features. Networks generated by the power law

model, then, will tend to have relatively frequent long-range ties (compared to frequencies in the vicinity of $d \le \alpha$), with local tie frequency declining most rapidly immediately about the origin. This last means that power law-generated networks may not be locally cohesive, even where γ implies a strong impact of distance overall.

A minor variant on the above can be obtained by allowing the effect of distance to attenuate close to the origin. Such an "attenuated power law" can be achieved by a function such as $\mathcal{F}_d(x) = p_b(1 + (\alpha x)^{-\gamma})$, with each parameter having the same interpretation as in the simple power law model above. Like the previous model, the attenuated power law interaction function is monotone decreasing and heavy tailed. Unlike the simple power law model, however, the attenuated variant exhibits negative local curvature. This model thus tends to produce both a high proportion of long-range edges and a high degree of local cohesion (the scale of these effects being dependent upon α). Where $(\alpha d)^\gamma \gg 1$, both variants exhibit similar behavior.

Exponential and logistic laws

The power law models are characterized by the presence of heavy tails: while tie probability initially falls rapidly with distance, small but non-negligible tie probabilities remain at large distances. In contrast with such models, an exponential decay law corresponds to \a process in which edge probabilities are virtually zero beyond some given range. The SIF for such a law can be written simply as an inverse exponential effect, that is, $\mathcal{F}_d(x) = p_b \exp(-\alpha x)$ where p_b is the usual baseline tie probability and $\alpha \ge 0$ is a scaling parameter. Like the simple power law, the exponential decay model is monotone decreasing with positive local curvature, and its scale and base tie probabilities are independently parametrized. Unlike the power law models, however, the exponential tails of the latter family damp out long-range ties, reducing the incidence of such "spatial shortcuts" in its associated networks.

Just as the simple power law admitted an attenuated form, so too is there an attenuated analogue to the exponential decay law. Such a law is the logistic probability law, which is recognizable as being a one-sided logit transform of the (additively inverted) distance. The spatial interaction function in this case is given by $\mathcal{F}_d(x) = (1+\beta)p_b / (1+\beta\exp(\alpha x))$, where α and p_b are the usual scaling parameters for distance and tie probability at the origin (respectively). Although this model is constrained to have light, exponential tails, its local curvature can be controlled via the β parameter. For $\beta < 1$, the logistic law has negative local curvature, creating a local region of attenuated distance effects extending to $\ln(1/\beta)/\alpha$ units from the origin. As such, it may useful in modeling settings for which interaction is only weakly impeded at short distances, while becoming essentially impossible as one moves beyond a threshold region.

Piecewise linear laws

Although the above examples all constitute smooth curves that descend from an initial high edge probability to a low probability at great distances, it is also possible to define interaction functions that treat the effect of distance in a more discontinuous fashion. From the perspective of these models, distance acts via a series of *thresholds*, which serve to structure the world into "near/far" regions (with corresponding effects on tie probability). A trivial case of this is the "degenerate" constant probability model $\mathcal{F}_d = p_b$, which occurs as the limiting case of a completely flat interaction function. A more interesting variant is a truncated linear model, in which edge probabilities descend linearly from an initial value until they reach a given threshold distance; from this point outward, tie probabilities are constant. Such a SIF can be written as $\mathcal{F}_d(x) = \max(\min(\beta - \alpha x, p_b), \gamma p_b)$, with "intercept" parameter $\beta > 0$, long-range attenuation parameter $0 \le \gamma \le 1$, and other parameters as treated elsewhere. For this

function, edge probabilities begin at a base value of p_b, holding constant until
$$x = \frac{\beta - p_b}{\alpha}.$$
At this point, the tie probability falls linearly (with slope α) until
$$x = \frac{\beta - \gamma p_b}{\alpha},$$
at which point it remains constant at γp_b. Note that this implies the existence of two thresholds – a high-probability "inner circle" and a low-probability "outer circle" – such that the marginal effect of distance is negligible within or beyond these limits. In this way, the truncated linear model somewhat resembles the sigmoid functions of the attenuated models, although (by setting the inner circle width to zero) it can model a linearized version of the strictly concave functions as well.

Maximum likelihood estimation for spatial Bernoulli graph models

Given a parametric form for $\mathcal{F}_d$, we may still seek to estimate its unknown parameters from observed network data; similarly, where competing theories suggest alternative interaction functions, we may wish to discriminate among the contenders on a principled empirical basis. The simplest means of approaching such inferential problems when using spatial Bernoulli models is generally via maximum likelihood methods. The complete-data likelihood for an observed graph under a spatial Bernoulli model was shown previously in Equation 1; for convenience, we shall here reframe it in terms of a more compact data structure. Given an observed graph, we may group together all vertex pairs observed at the same distances to create m *dyad collections*. We represent these by a vector of dyad counts ($\mathcal{P}$, the number of possible edges at each distance), a vector of edge counts (**Z**, the number of edges at each distance, with corresponding observation vector **z**), and a vector of distances (**d**). Conditional on d_i and $\mathcal{F}_d$, it follows from Equation 1 that Z_i is the sum $\mathcal{P}_i$ of iid

Bernoulli variables, and hence is binomially distributed. By the assumption of conditional independence, it further follows that the joint likelihood of observed count vector $\mathbf{z}$ given $\mathcal{P}$, $\mathbf{d}$ and $\mathcal{F}_d$ will simply be the product of the likelihoods for the elements of $\mathbf{z}$. Explicitly stated, we thus have:

$$\Pr(\mathbf{Z} = \mathbf{z} \mid \mathcal{F}_d, \mathcal{P}, \mathbf{d}) = \prod_{i=1}^{m} \mathrm{Bin}(z_i \mid \mathcal{P}_i, \mathcal{F}_d(d_i)),$$

treating any unknown parameters in $\mathcal{F}_d$ as implicit. Note that, in many cases, it is more practical to work with the log of Equation 2 than its untransformed value. Writing this log with the parametric dependence of $\mathcal{F}_d$ made explicit, we then have

$$
L(\mathbf{z} \mid \theta, \mathcal{P}, \mathbf{d}) = \sum_{i=1}^{m} \left[\ln \binom{\mathcal{P}_i}{z_i} \right.
$$
$$
+ z_i \ln \mathcal{F}_d(d_i, \theta) + (\mathcal{P}_i - z_i)
$$
$$
\left. \ln(1 - \mathcal{F}_d(d_i, \theta)) \right]
$$
(12.2)

where θ is a vector of parameters of $\mathcal{F}_d$. Inference for this model family is a straightforward nonlinear regression problem, of which familiar binomial GLMs such as logistic and probit regression are special cases (McCullagh and Nelder, 1989).

Parameter estimation

Given a tuple of observations $(\mathbf{Z}, \mathcal{P}, \mathbf{d})$ arising from a spatial Bernoulli graph model with log-likelihood function L, we may estimate any unknown parameters by finding the solution to $\hat{\theta} = \arg\max_\theta L(z \mid \theta, \mathcal{P}, \mathbf{d})$, where θ is the vector of unknown parameters. Any $\hat{\theta}$ that are a solution to this equation are said to be a *maximum likelihood estimator* of θ, with maximized likelihood $\hat{L} = L(\mathbf{z} \mid \hat{\theta}, \mathcal{P}, \mathbf{d})$. The elements of $\mathbf{z}$ are assumed to form conditionally independent draws from a curved exponential family, and under fairly mild regularity conditions $\hat{\theta}$ thus has an asymptotic normal distribution with mean vector θ and variance–covariance matrix $\left(\mathbf{E}_{\hat{\theta}} \left[\frac{\partial^2}{\partial \hat{\theta}} L(\mathbf{z} \mid \hat{\theta}, \mathcal{P}, \mathbf{d}) \right] \right)^{-1}$ where the MLE

exists (Brown, 1986). Using this property, one can obtain asymptotic frequentist confidence regions (and associated *p*-values) in the usual fashion.

Model selection

As with estimation, model selection for the spatial Bernoulli graphs can be performed via a straightforward application of existing methods. Typically, such selection will involve a choice among competing parametric forms for the spatial interaction function, and as such may not be framed in terms of nested hypotheses. Formal model selection criteria such as Akaike's Information Criterion (AIC) and the Bayesian Information Criterion (BIC) are reasonable alternatives, particularly on large data sets. In the above notation, the AIC for a spatial Bernoulli model is $-2\hat{L} + 2k$, where k is the number of parameters of $\mathcal{F}_d$ (i.e., the length of θ). The corresponding BIC value is

$$-2\hat{L} + k \ln\left(\sum_{i=1}^{m} \mathcal{P}_i \right).$$ The BIC differs from the AIC both in justification and in the weight given to parsimony, although lower scores are preferred for both indices. Two useful comparative reviews of these selection criteria are Bozdogan (2000) and Wasserman (2000).

ILLUSTRATIVE APPLICATION: ORGANIZATIONAL COLLABORATION IN THE HURRICANE KATRINA RESPONSE

To illustrate the above methods, we here apply our spatial network modeling approach to data on interorganizational collaboration in the 2005 Hurricane Katrina response (Butts et al., 2011). This data was collected via the use of archival sources to identify responding organizations during the 13-day period from initial storm formation through the first week following landfall in Louisiana. From these resources, the researchers identified organizations that were involved in collaboration during the period; using additional information sources, the nominal (pre-disaster) headquarters of each organization was also located. Georeferencing of these locations provides a spatial embedding of the interaction network, allowing us to relate the actions taken during the disaster with the spatial proximity of responding organizations during normal operations. As we shall show, these spatial relationships are indeed associated with collaboration within the disaster itself, with a long-tailed interaction function governing the probability of collaboration given distance between headquarters.

Network data

Butts et al. (2011) employed publicly available documents to obtain information on the changing status of Hurricane Katrina and the response to it by various persons and organizations. The primary materials for the study came from a collection of situation reports (or "SITREPs") obtained from 21 source organizations located throughout the USA. SITREPs constitute a genre of documents, typically released online by emergency management agencies and various other local, state, and federal agencies that find themselves involved in some managerial role in response to an emergency or disaster situation. The documents, which are usually released in some periodic manner (e.g., hourly, daily, or weekly), generally contain information such as a weather report at the time of the document's release for a given area, a description of any existing and new emergencies for a given area (e.g., downed power lines, destruction to structures, or an account of fatalities), and some account of those persons and/or organizations known to be currently responding to the situation. These accounts of organizational activity were employed by the researchers to construct a collaboration network for the Hurricane Katrina response.

After identifying 187 SITREPs from the collected materials, the research team coded all mentions of organizations that were involved in the Katrina response, as well as all indicators of collaboration among those organizations. This effort ultimately produced a list of 1577 organizations, with 857 instances of collaboration among them. For purposes of this chapter, we consider the network formed by collaborative ties occurring at any time during the 13-day study period; that is, the simple graph on the set of organizations in which organization i is adjacent to organization j if i and j are described by any source as collaborating at any point in time.

Exploratory analysis

The combined network obtained by taking the union of all mentions of organizations and collaborations across the study period is depicted in the network diagram (or *sociogram*) of Figure 12.4. In comparing this figure with cartographic depictions frequently used in geographical contexts, several points bear mention. First, each grey circle represents one vertex in the network, and each black line represents one instance of collaboration between two vertices. Second, only the edge structure of the figure is interpretable – in particular, the spatial layout of the vertices within the figure does not correspond to geographical structure. Rather, the layout algorithm employed to generate the display (Fruchterman and Reingold, 1991) attempts to maximize readability of the underlying structure. It is thus the crude "space" formed by the adjacency relation which is displayed here, rather than associated geography.

One will immediately notice in Figure 12.4 that the network contains a large cluster of connected vertices and their respective edges on the left side of the image, around which are scattered a few smaller clusters of vertices and many more isolate vertices. The large component indicates that, at least in theory, a "collaboration path" connects all members

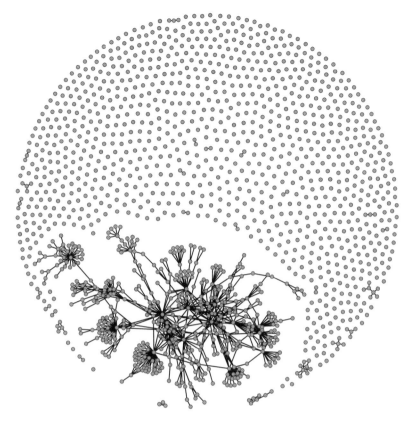

Figure 12.4   Sociogram of the combined network of organizational collaboration in the Hurricane Katrina response

of the component. For example, a path exists between a given vertex in the lower portion of the component and a vertex in the upper portion of the component, indicating that – assuming compatible edge timing – a message or some unit of resources could traverse its way through the network from one vertex to the other. (More definitely, elements *not* connected by such a path could not have exchanged information or resources in this manner.) This primary component in the graph consists of the organizations among which collaboration activity is the greatest. The vertices that form smaller clusters, but which are not connected to the central component, indicate smaller "islands" of collaboration. Finally, the isolate vertices in the network represent instances of organizations

that were present and active in the early days of the Katrina response, but that did not collaborate with other organizations during the study period.

The average number of alters with which a given organization collaborated (the mean degree) in the Katrina network is 1.09. This value is relatively low, despite the large component of collaboration activity seen in Figure 12.4, because the degree of every vertex in the graph is accounted for. As there are many isolate vertices (997 of them, or 63 percent of the vertices in the graph), the mean degree is thus pulled down. There are considerably more isolate vertices in the graph than there are vertices that are members of the largest component. The largest component accounts for 467 vertices

(31.5 percent of the vertices in the graph). Those vertices not accounted for as either isolates or as members of the main component are the ones that make up the smaller components, of which there are relatively few.

Spatially locating the organizations in the data

Although spatial information is of clear interest within emergency management settings, the Katrina SITREPs do not supply sufficient geographical information to clearly identify the locations of most organizations within the field. Given this, the research team made the decision to georeference all organizations to the locations of their primary headquarters. Given that the responding organizations originated from across the North American continent, it was determined that resolution within several kilometers would provide adequate proportional accuracy for most analyses. Based on a pilot sample of approximately 30 of the organizations in our data set, it was determined that city, state, and country information was reliably available for most organizational headquarters of organizations within the data set. Since street addresses could not be reliably obtained, it was decided to resolve organizational locations to the city level.

Headquarter location information was collected from multiple sources. Online sources enabled, for the vast majority of the organizations in the data set, relatively straightforward collection of the desired information. In many cases, organizations' own websites indicated their headquarters locations (typically on a "Contact Us" or "Customer Service" page on the site). In some cases further investigation was required, as an organization's website may not directly provide the city/state/country location of the desired division or branch. In other instances, searches through Google or other similar search engines for general references to the organization proved helpful – for instance, documents or directories listing

an organization would often contain its contact and/or location information. In such situations, however, it was important to triangulate the information obtained from these searches across multiple sources, as websites and directories that provide information of this kind can easily become outdated (or generally contain incorrect information). The online collaborative encyclopedia Wikipedia[3] also contained in many cases entries for the desired organizations, often providing location information for their headquarters. The same caveats about incorrect information, of course, apply to sites like Wikipedia, and triangulation was thus employed here as well.

A map depicting the geocoded organizations, as well as the path of Hurricane Katrina itself, is given in Figure 12.5. In this representation of the data, the vertices are located by their headquarter coordinates (contrary to the layout of vertices in Figure 12.4. Network edges are omitted from Figure 12.5, as their inclusion would obstruct much of figure and prevent the reader from gleaning much about the spatial dispersion of the vertices.

It is important to note that geocoding accuracy can only be as high as the quality of the inputs fed to the computer software. Krieger et al. (2001) report on an empirical study of accuracy in geocoding using inputs with errors, suggesting that geocoding accuracy rates could be very low should the geocoder fail to correct those errors. They caution researchers to verify the accuracy of their geocoded results, and to be critical of geocoding practices when they are presented in research. Within our dataset, we obtained 98 percent match rate of our headquarter location coordinates against existing points in a shapefile of populated point locations in the USA. For most of the 2 percent of organizations which were not geocoded, many were headquartered in small towns. For a small fraction of the organizations we were unable to obtain complete location information, thus accounting for their absence in the geocoded set of data points. For a review of the

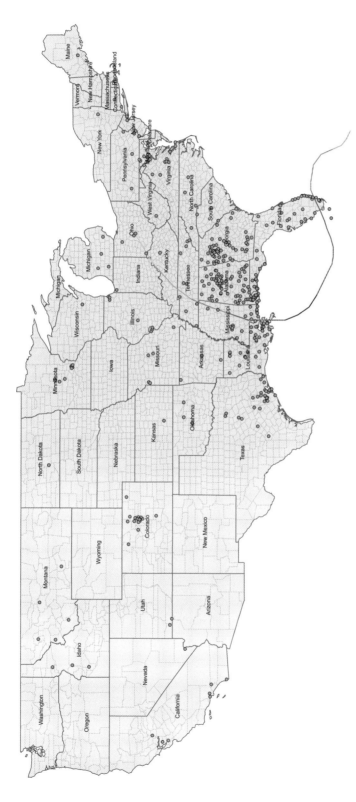

Figure 12.5 City/state locations of geocoded organizations in the Katrina data (showing only the 48 contiguous USA)

accuracy of several popular geocoding tools, see Yang et al. (2004).

Modeling

Given the geocoded data, we now proceed to estimate the relationship between distance and tie probability for organizational collaboration in the Hurricane Katrina response. We begin by fitting the spatial Bernoulli model of Equation 1 to the Katrina data for various choices of $\mathcal{F}_d$. In addition to the functional forms described above, we also include a "uniform disk" model (in which tie probability is constant out to a threshold distance, then falls to a lower constant) and an arctangent law (which is much like the simple power law, but with heavier tails). Goodness of fit information for the resulting models is shown in Table 12.1, with models listed in descending order of fit (as assessed by the BIC). As the table indicates, the best model in terms of AIC, BIC, and model deviance is clearly the simple power law, followed closely by the attenuated power law. Falling somewhat behind is the arctangent, with the uniform disk and truncated linear laws next in line. Finally, we have the exponential, logistic, and constant probability models, which perform substantially worse than the other models on all counts.

Several things can be immediately discerned from this ordering. First, all distance models outperform the null model of constant probability by a large margin: thus, there is clearly an effect of headquarter distance on collaboration within the event. Second, we see that models with light tails (the exponential and logistic families) do very poorly – this tells us that the nature of the dependence in question is long range. Third, the large gap between the smooth heavy-tailed SIFs and the discontinuous models (uniform disk and truncated linear laws) suggests that the effect of distance is not simply a threshold property, but is rather a smooth decline. This also rules out negative curvature at distances several kilometers from the origin, although we would note that the data is not precise enough for us to be extremely confident in ruling out a very small radius of negative curvature.

To take a closer look at the spatial relationship in question, we examine the MLEs (and associated standard errors) for the power law model. Table 12.2 shows the baseline tie probability (p_b), scaling factor (α), and exponent (γ) for the power law model. As might be expected, base tie probability for such a sparse model is low – approximately 0.9 percent. Nevertheless, this is over 12 times the baseline density of approximately 0.07 percent, indicating that organizations headquartered in the same city are far more likely than average to collaborate with one another. While this rate declines rapidly at first, the long tail of the power law function ensures that long-range ties remain

Table 12.1 Goodness of fit for spatial Bernoulli model, various interaction functions

SIF	Model df	Model Deviance	AIC	BIC
Power Law	3	1478.77	3758.22	3794.2
Attenuated Power Law	3	1471.85	3765.14	3801.11
Arctangent Law	2	1427.23	3807.77	3831.75
Uniform Disk	3	1360.94	3876.05	3912.02
Truncated Linear Law	4	1304.09	3934.9	3982.86
Exponential Law	2	746.69	4488.3	4512.28
Logistic Law	3	746.6	4490.4	4526.37
Constant Probability (Null Model)	1	0	5232.99	5244.98

Table 12.2 Parameters and asymptotic standard errors for the power law model

Parameter	MLE	Standard error
pb	0.0092	0.0004
α	0.1154	0.0209
γ	0.7048	0.0288

possible even at great distances. Indeed, the power law exponent in this case is approximately 0.7, meaning that the probability of collaboration is estimated to fall with the 0.7 power of distance between headquarters. Put another way, a five-fold increase in distance between two organizations would be expected to cut the collaboration probability by a factor of approximately one-third. (Compare this to an inverse square law, for which the same increase would reduce the collaboration probability to one twenty-fifth of its initial value.)

Another view of the interaction function can be obtained by plotting the MLE of $\mathcal{F}_d$ against distance. This is depicted by the heavy line in Figure 12.6, which clearly shows both the steep descent of tie probability over the first few hundred kilometers, and

the long tail with non-negligible interaction probability out to 1400 km or more. Also shown in Figure 12.6 are binned means for interaction rates at various distances, with upper/lower approximate 95 percent confidence bounds. The estimated rate function can be seen to provide a good qualitative fit to the data, particularly in the upper and lower tails. Some deviation is present, for example, between 250 and 450 km where observed tie probabilities are somewhat below predictions, but even here the power law model provides a reasonably good approximation to the actual rates. The figure does not, in any event, suggest that an alternate functional form would provide superior performance, and we may provisionally conclude that the marginal distance dependence in this case is at least approximately captured by the power law model.

If this result is typical of disasters like Hurricane Katrina, what conclusions can we draw regarding collaboration in emergency settings? First, we can see that pre-disaster geography does indeed predict in-situ collaboration, and that this effect scales smoothly with distance between headquarters – it is neither the case that distance has no effect, nor that its effect acts as a simple threshold. Second, we can see that the scale on which this effect operates is quite large; in the Katrina case, organizations from more than 1500 km away were seen to work together on-site, although they were less likely to do so than more proximate organizations. This elongated scale is a telling artifact of a modern technological society: distance continues to matter, but its influence is spread over much larger areas. In pre-modern times, it simply would not have been possible to bring responders (much less whole teams) from across a continent to alleviate a regional crisis, much less to do so within a few days time. As transportation and telecommunication costs continue to fall, we may conjecture that the scale of such interactions will continue to expand – whether this will manifest through a simple adjustment of the phenomenological distance unit (i.e, α an effect) or a

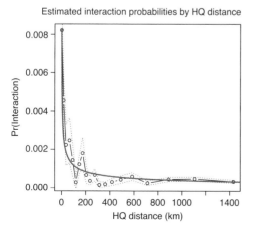

Figure 12.6 Estimated spatial interaction function for the Katrina data, with binned mean rates

change in the form of the interaction (e.g., a γ effect) is an important question for theoretical inquiry. Being able to formulate such questions directly, and to evaluate them against empirical data, is an important advantage of this approach.

CONCLUSION

In this chapter, we have provided a brief introduction to the parametric modeling of social network data using spatial information. We began by introducing network concepts and representation schemes, then proceeding to a discussion of data collection issues. We articulated a simple approach to the analysis of spatially embedded networks based on the use of the spatial Bernoulli graphs, a family of distributions that draws on both standard network approaches and the gravity models long used within the geographical tradition. Like the gravity models, spatial Bernoulli graphs take the spatial interaction function as a core formalism; we thus described a number of key qualitative features by which such functions can be classified, and related those features to the networks produced by the resulting Bernoulli graph models. After discussing parameter estimation and model selection for the spatial Bernoulli graphs, we then turned to the illustrative example of organizational collaboration in the 2005 Hurricane Katrina response. While both "pure" network and geospatial analyses can prove insightful, much is gleaned by a joint analysis. In this case, we showed that there was a strong association of headquarter location with collaboration during the response, with the probability of collaboration falling as a power law of distance between the organizations in question. Even during a turbulent event such as the Katrina response, therefore, pre-disaster geography exerted a lingering effect; at the same time, the heavy-tailed nature of the interaction function indicates a relatively large fraction of long-range ties. While this example is illustrative in nature, we believe it underscores a more general point: social structure and geographical structure can and should be studied together. It is hoped that this chapter will help facilitate more work in this area by researchers in a range of disciplines.

ACKNOWLEDGMENTS

This work was supported in part by US National Science Foundation awards BCS-0827027 and CHE-0555125, and by US DoD Office of Naval Research award N00014–08-1-1015. The input of the members of the UCI Social Network Research Group is gratefully acknowledged.

NOTES

1 We do not assume here any additional properties of d (e.g., that d is a metric or ultrametric on S), although such constraints may provide analytical leverage in some settings.

2 In graph theory, the degree of a given vertex is the count of its direct ties.

3 http://www.wikipedia.org.

REFERENCES

Anderson, B.S., Butts, C.T. and Carley, K.M. (1999) 'The interaction of size and density with graph-level indices', *Social Networks*, 21(3): 239–67.

Baker, W.E. and Faulkner, R.R. (1993) 'The social organization of conspiracy: illegal networks in the heavy equipment industry', *American Sociological Review*, 58: 837–60.

Batagelj, V. and Mrvar, A. (2007) 'Pajek – program for large network analysis'. Electronic data file.

Batchelder, W.H. and Romney, A.K. (1988) 'Test theory without an answer key', *Psychometrika*, 53(1): 71–92.

Bernard, H.R. and Killworth, P. (1977) 'Informant accuracy in social network data II', *Human Communication Research*, 4(1): 3–18.

Bernard, H.R., Killworth, P. and Sailer, L. (1979) 'Informant accuracy in social networks IV: a comparison of clique-level structure in behavioral and cognitive network data', *Social Networks*, 2: 191–218.

Bernard, H.R., Killworth, P., Kronenfeld, D. and Sailer, L. (1984) 'The problem of informant accuracy: the validity of retrospective data', *Annual Review of Anthropology*, 13: 495–517.

Bollobás, B. (1998) *Modern Graph Theory*. New York: Springer.

Borgatti, S.P., Everett, M.G. and Freeman, L.C. (1999) *UCINET 5.0* Version 1.00. Natick, MA: Analytic Technologies.

Bossard, J.H.S. (1932) 'Residential propinquity as a factor in marriage selection', *American Journal of Sociology*, 38: 219–44.

Bozdogan, H. (2000) 'Akaike's information criterion and recent developments in information complexity', *Journal of Mathematical Psychology*, 44: 61–91.

Brandes, U. and Erlebach, T. (eds) (2005) *Network Analysis: Methodological Foundations*. Berlin: Springer-Verlag.

Brown, L.D. (1986) *Fundamentals of Statistical Exponential Families, with Applications in Statistical Decision Theory*. Hayward, CA: Institute of Mathematical Statistics.

Butts, C.T. (2002) 'Spatial models of large-scale interpersonal networks'. PhD dissertation, Carnegie Mellon University.

Butts, C.T. (2003a) 'Network inference, error, and informant (in)accuracy: a Bayesian approach', *Social Networks*, 25(2): 103–40.

Butts, C.T. (2003b) 'Predictability of large-scale spatially embedded networks'. In R. Breiger, K.M. Carley and P. Pattison (eds), *Dynamic Social Network Modeling and Analysis: Workshop Summary and Papers*. Washington, DC: National Academies Press.

Butts, C.T. (2007) 'Permutation models for relational data', *Sociological Methodology*, 37(1): 257–81.

Butts, C.T. (2008) 'Social networks: a methodological introduction', *Asian Journal of Social Psychology*, 11(1): 13–41.

Butts, C.T., Acton, R.M. and Marcum, C. (2011) 'Interorganizational collaboration in the Hurricane Katrina response', *Journal of Social Structure*, Forthcoming.

Carrington, P.J., Scott, J. and Wasserman, S. (eds) (2005) *Models and Methods in Social Network Analysis*. Cambridge: Cambridge University Press.

Choudhury, T. and Pentland, A. (2003) 'Sensing and modeling human networks using the sociometer', *Proceedings of the International Conference on Wearable Computing*. White Plains, NY.

Comfort, L.K. and Kapucu, N. (2006) 'Interorganizational coordination in extreme events: the world trade center attack, 11 September 2001', *Natural Hazards: Journal of the International Society for the Prevention and Mitigation of Natural Hazards*, 39(2): 309–27.

Davis, J.A. and Smith, T.W. (1988) *General Social Survey, 1988*. Chicago, IL: National Opinion Research Center.

Degenne, A. and Forsé, M. (1999) *Introducing Social Networks*. London: Sage.

Diamond, J.M. (1999) *Guns, Germs and Steel: The Fates of Human Societies*. New York: W. W. Norton and Company.

Doreian, P., Batagelj, V. and Ferlioj, A. (2005) *Generalized Blockmodeling*. Cambridge: Cambridge University Press.

Erdös, P. and Rényi, A. (1960) 'On the evolution of random graphs', *Public Mathematical Institute of Hungary Academy of Sciences*, 5: 17–61.

Everett, M.G. (1985) 'Role similarity and complexity in social networks', *Social Networks*, 7: 353–59.

Frank, O. (2005) 'Network sampling and model fitting'. In P.J. Carrington, J. Scott and S. Wasserman (eds), *Models and Methods in Social Network Analysis*. Cambridge: Cambridge University Press. pp. 31–56.

Frank, O. and Strauss, D. (1986) 'Markov graphs', *Journal of the American Statistical Association*, 81: 832–42.

Freeman, L.C. (1979) 'Centrality in social networks: conceptual clarification', *Social Networks*, 1(3): 223–58.

Freeman, L.C. (1992) 'The sociological concept of group: an empirical test of two models', *American Journal of Sociology*, 98: 152–66.

Freeman, L.C. (2004) *The Development of Social Network Analysis: A Study in the Sociology of Science*. Vancouver: Empirical Press.

Freeman, L.C. and Sunshine, M.H. (1976) 'Race and intra-urban migration', *Demography*, 13(4): 571–5.

Fruchterman, T. and Reingold, E. (1991) 'Graph drawing by force-directed placement', *Software – Practice and Experience*, 21(11): 1129–64.

Gale, N., Hubert, L.J., Tobler, W.R. and Golledge, R.G. (1983) 'Combinatorial procedures for the analysis of alternative models: an example from interregional migration', *Papers of the Regional Science Association*, 53: 105–15.

Goodman, L.A. (1961) 'Snowball sampling', *Annals of Mathematical Statistics*, 32: 148–70.

Grannis, R. (1998) 'The importance of trivial streets: residential streets and residential segregation', *American Journal of Sociology*, 103: 1530–64.

Granovetter, M. (1973) 'The strength of weak ties', *American Journal of Sociology*, 78(6): 1369–80.

Guldmann, J.-M. (2004) 'Spatial interaction models of international telecommunication flows'. In M. F. Goodchild and D. G. Janelle (eds), *Spatially Integrated Social Science*. New York: Oxford University Press. pp. 400–19.

Hammer, M. (1985) 'Implications of behavioral and cognitive reciprocity in social network data', *Social Networks*, 7: 189–201.

Handcock, M.S., Hunter, D.R., Butts, C.T., Goodreau, S.M. and Morris, M. (2008) 'Statnet: software tools for the representation, visualization, analysis and simulation of network data', *Journal of Statistical Software*, 24(1).

Handcock, M.S., Raftery, A.E. and Tantrum, J.M. (2007) 'Model based clustering for social networks', *Journal of the Royal Statistical Society, Series A*, 170: 301–54.

Haynes, K.E. and Fotheringham, A.S. (1984) *Gravity and Spatial Interaction Models*. Beverly Hills, CA: SAGE.

Heckathorn, D.D. (1997) 'Respondent-driven sampling: a new approach to the study of hidden populations', *Social Problems*, 44(2): 174–99.

Heckathorn, D.D. (2002) 'Respondent-driven sampling II: deriving valid population estimates from chain-referral samples of hidden populations', *Social Problems*, 49(1): 11–34.

Hipp, J.R. and Perrin, A.J. (2009) 'The simultaneous effect of social distance and physical distance on the formation of neighborhood ties', *City and Community*, 8(1): 5–25.

Hoff, P.D., Raftery, A.E. and Handcock, M.S. (2002) 'Latent space approaches to social network analysis', *Journal of the American Statistical Association*, 97(460): 1090–98.

Holland, P.W. and Leinhardt, S. (1970) 'A method for detecting structure in sociometric data', *American Journal of Sociology*, 70: 492–513.

Holland, P.W. and Leinhardt, S. (1971) 'Transitivity in structural models of small groups', *Comparative Group Studies*, 2: 107–24.

Holland, P.W. and Leinhardt, S. (1981) 'An exponential family of probability distributions for directed graphs (with discussion)', *Journal of the American Statistical Association*, 76(373): 33–50.

Huisman, M. and van Duijn, M.A. J. (2003) 'Stocnet: software for the statistical analysis of social networks', *Connections*, 25(1): 7–26.

Irwin, M.D. and Hughes, H.L. (1992) 'Centrality and the structure of urban interaction: measures, concepts and applications', *Social Forces*, 71(1): 17–51.

Jones, J.H. and Handcock, M.S. (2003) 'An assessment of preferential attachment as a mechanism for human sexual network formation', *Proceedings of the Royal Society, Series B*, 270: 1123–28.

Kansky, K.J. (1963) *Structure of Transportation Networks: Relationships Between Network Geometry and Regional Characteristics*. Chicago: University of Chicago Press.

Killworth, P.D. and Bernard, H.R. (1976) 'Informant accuracy in social network data', *Human Organization*, 35(8): 269–86.

Killworth, P.D. and Bernard, H.R. (1979) 'Informant accuracy in social network data III: a comparison of triadic structure in behavioral and cognitive data', *Social Networks*, 2: 10–46.

Kleinberg, J.M. (2000) 'Navigation in a small world', *Nature*, 406: 845.

Klovdahl, A.S. (1989) 'Urban social networks: some methodological problems and possibilities', In M. Kochen (ed.), *The Small World*. Norwood: Ablex. pp. 176–210.

Krackhardt, D. (1987) 'QAP partialling as a test of spuriousness', *Social Networks*, 9(2): 171–86.

Krackhardt, D. (1988) 'Predicting with networks: nonparametric multiple regression analyses of dyadic data', *Social Networks*, 10: 359–82.

Krieger, N., Waterman, P., Lemieux, K., Zierler, S. and Hogan, J.W. (2001) 'On the wrong side of the tracts? Evaluating the accuracy of geocoding in public health research', *American Journal of Public Health*, 91: 1114–16.

Krivitsky, P.N. and Handcock, M.S. (2008) 'Fitting latent cluster models for networks with latentnet', *Journal of Statistical Software*, 24(5).

Latané, B., Liu, J.H., Nowak, A., Bonevento, M. and Zheng, L. (1995) 'Distance matters: physical space and social impact', *Personality and Social Psychology Bulletin*, 21(8): 795–805.

Linnemann, H. (1966) *An Econometric Study of International Trade Flows*. Amsterdam: North-Holland.

Marsden, P.V. (1990) 'Network data and measurement', *Annual Review of Sociology*, 16: 435–63.

Marsden, P.V. (2005) 'Recent developments in network measurement'. In P. J. Carrington, J. Scott and S. Wasserman (eds), *Models and Methods in Social Network Analysis*. Cambridge: Cambridge University Press. pp. 8–30.

McCullagh, P. and Nelder, J.A. (1989) *Generalized Linear Models*, 2nd edn. London: Chapman and Hall.

McPherson, J.M. (1983) 'An ecology of affiliation', *American Sociological Review*, 48: 519–32.

McPherson, J.M. and Ranger-Moore, J.R. (1991) 'Evolution on a dancing landscape: organizations and networks in dynamic Blau space', *Social Forces*, 70: 19–42.

McPherson, J.M., Smith-Lovin, L. and Cook, J.M. (2001) 'Birds of a feather: homophily in social networks', *Annual Review of Sociology*, 27: 415–44.

Morrill, R.L. and Pitts, F.R. (1963) 'Marriage, migration and the mean information field: a study in uniqueness and generality', *Annals of the Association of American Geographers*, 57: 401–22.

Morris, M. (1991) 'A log-linear modeling framework for selective mixing', *Mathematical Biosciences*, 107: 349–77.

Nystuen, J.D. and Dacey, M.F. (1961) 'A graph theory interpretation of nodal regions', *Papers in Regional Science*, 7(1): 29–42.

Oppenheim, N. (1995) *Urban Travel Demand Modeling: From Individual Choices to General Equilibrium*. New York: John Wiley and Sons.

Pattison, P. and Robins, G. (2002) 'Neighborhood-based models for social networks', *Sociological Methodology*, 32: 301–37.

Pattison, P., Wasserman, S., Robins, G. and Kanfer, A.M. (2000) 'Statistical evaluation of algebraic constraints for social networks', *Journal of Mathematical Psychology*, 44: 536–68.

Pool, I.D.S. and Kochen, M. (1979) 'Contacts and influence', *Social Networks*, 1(1): 5–51.

Robins, G. and Morris, M. (2007) 'Advances in exponential random graph ($p\,*$) models', *Social Networks*, 29: 169–12.

Romney, A.K., Weller, S.C. and Batchelder, W.H. (1986) 'Culture as consensus: a theory of culture and informant accuracy', *American Anthropologist*, 88(2): 313–38.

Scott, J. (1991) *Social Network Analysis: A Handbook*. London: Sage.

Seary, A.J. and Richards, W.D. (2003) 'Spectral methods for analyzing and visualizing networks: an introduction'. In R. Breiger, K.M. Carley and P. Pattison (eds), *Dynamic Social Network Modeling and Analysis*. Washington, DC: National Academies Press. pp. 209–28.

Snijders, T.A.B. (1996) 'Stochastic actor-oriented models for network change', *Journal of Mathematical Sociology*, 23: 149–72.

Snijders, T.A.B., Pattison, P.E., Robins, G.L. and Handcock, M.S. (2006) 'New specifications for exponential random graph models', *Sociological Methodology*, 36: 99–153.

Stewart, J.Q. (1941) 'An inverse distance variation for certain social influences', *Science*, 93: 89–90.

Thompson, S.K. (1997) 'Adaptive sampling in behavioral surveys'. In L. Harrison and A. Hughes (eds), *The Validity of Self-Reported Drug Use: Improving the Accuracy of Survey Estimates*. Rockville, MD: National Institute of Drug Abuse. pp. 296–319.

Thompson, S.K. and Frank, O. (2000) 'Model-based estimation with link-tracing sampling designs', *Survey Methodology*, 26(1): 87–98.

Tierney, K.J. (2003) 'Conceptualizing and measuring organizational and community resilience: lessons learned from the emergency response following the 11 September 2001 attack on the World Trade Center', paper presented at the Third Comparative Workshop on Urban Earthquake Disaster Management, Kobe, Japan.

Tobler, W.R. (1976) 'Spatial interaction patterns', *Journal of Environmental Systems*, 6(4): 271–301.

Torgerson, W.S. (1952) 'Multidimensional scaling: I, theory and method', *Psychometrika*, 17: 401–19.

Travers, J. and Milgram, S. (1969) 'An experimental study of the small world problem', *Sociometry*, 32: 425–43.

Wasserman, L. (2000) 'Bayesian model selection and model averaging', *Journal of Mathematical Psychology*, 44(1): 92–107.

Wasserman, S. and Faust, K. (1994) *Social Network Analysis: Methods and Applications*. Cambridge: Cambridge University Press.

Wasserman, S. and Robins, G. (2005) 'An introduction to random graphs, dependence graphs and $p\,*$'. In P. J. Carrington, J. Scott and S. Wasserman (eds), *Models and Methods in Social Network Analysis*. Cambridge: Cambridge University Press. pp. 192–214.

Watts, D.J. and Strogatz, S.H. (1998) 'Collective dynamics of "small-world" networks', *Nature*, 393: 440–42.

West, D.B. (1996) *Introduction to Graph Theory*. Upper Saddle River, NJ: Prentice Hall.

Wilson, A.G. (1970) *Entropy in Urban and Regional Modeling*. London: Pion.

Wimmer, A. and Min, B. (2006) 'From empire to nation-state: explaining wars in the modern world, 1816–2001', *American Sociological Review*, 71(6): 867–97.

Yang, D.-H., Bilaver, L.M., Hayes, O. and Goerge, R. (2004) 'Improving geocoding practices: evaluation of geocoding tools', *Journal of Medical Systems*, 28(4): 361–70.

Zipf, G.K. (1949) *Human Behavior and the Principle of Least Effort*. New York: Hafner.

13

GIS Designs for Studying Human Activities in a Space–Time Context

Hongbo Yu and Shih-Lung Shaw

INTRODUCTION

Individuals are the fundamental elements of a society. Their daily activities and interactions support the normal operations of a society. Each activity or interaction has its own specific spatial and temporal characteristics because the occurrence of an activity or interaction is associated with a specific geographic location and a specific time period. The spatiotemporal characteristics of people's activities and interactions reflect a society's footprint in space and time. Therefore, they are important factors in the investigation of various research problems related to a society. For example, knowing where and when people participate in various activities can help transportation researchers and city planners understand how individuals arrange their trips and why a particular traffic pattern emerges in a region; examining the activity opportunities in space and time that are available to different socioeconomic or ethnic groups has received increasing

attention in studies of social exclusion (Miller, 2006); and tracking the movements and physical contacts of individuals who have been diagnosed with a contagious disease (e.g., avian flu) can help epidemiologists examine the spread of the disease. Geographic information systems (GIS), which specialize at spatial data handling, have been employed in various studies to support the management and spatial analysis of individual activities and interactions.

During the past decades, we have witnessed the significant improvements of GIS in terms of their capability of representing and analyzing various spatial problems. However, due to their strong connections to cartography at the formative stage, the mainstream GIS designs have adopted a static view to model and represent geographic phenomena (Spaccapietra, 2001; Peuquet, 2002; Yuan et al., 2004). A time dimension is missing in most traditional GIS designs. Without a time dimension, it is difficult to represent and examine the dynamic aspect of geographic phenomena. Many researchers have suggested the importance of including a time dimension in activity studies. While spatial dimensions offer a means to describe where activities take place, a time dimension can help coordinate the temporal organization of activities and record the dynamic process of activities. In the late 1960s, Torsten Hägerstrand and his colleagues developed a conceptual framework for studying the relationships between human activities and their constraints in a space–time context. This framework now is well known as time geography. Treating time and space as equally important factors, time geography adopts an orthogonal three-dimensional (3D) system (i.e., two dimensions for space and a third dimension for time) to examine human activities (Hägerstrand, 1970). This 3D system is known as the space–time system of time geography. Since the space–time system allows researchers to examine activities in their space–time contexts, many researchers have argued that time geography offers an effective and efficient conceptual framework to investigate the spatiotemporal characteristics of human activities (Kwan, 2000a; Miller, 2005a).

Recent developments of information and communication technologies (ICT), such as the Internet and cell phones, have extended human activities to a hybrid physical-virtual space (Batty and Miller, 2000; Janelle and Hodge, 2000). People now can enjoy additional flexibility in space and time to perform activities and to interact with others. For example, a person can purchase a movie online, download it, and then watch it on a computer at home instead of going to a local movie theater; a scholar can have 24/7 access to numerous research articles through online journal subscriptions without being limited to the open hours of a local library; a person can participate in a social network that consists of members from all around the world through online services such as myspace™ and Facebook™. Under these circumstances, the traditional concepts of distinct places, such as home and work place, become

tangled with one another, and the concept of physical proximity is unable to capture the expanding spatial extent of human interactions via various telecommunication connections. The freedom gained by the use of ICT introduces a re-distribution of activities in space and time (Shaw, 2006). How can we capture and represent these emerging characteristics of activities and their interactions in a hybrid physical-virtual environment? How will the spatiotemporal re-distribution of activities affect various aspects of our society, such as travel patterns, spatial organization of urban environment, social dynamics, and interactions? These research questions have drawn increasing attention among social scientists who aim to gain a better understanding of the spatiotemporal characteristics of various activities in our society. Meanwhile, the GIS community is facing new challenges of representing and analyzing activity patterns and interactions at the individual level. Without an appropriate data model to handle a time dimension, traditional GIS designs fall short of providing an effective environment to support the representation and analysis of spatial and temporal characteristics of human activities under the time geography context. Thus, efforts are needed to develop a GIS design that can better support the study of human activities and interactions in a space–time context.

The rest of this chapter is organized into four sections. In the next section, we briefly review several key concepts in time geography and how the time geography framework can effectively manage the spatial and temporal characteristics of human activities. The third section discusses recent developments in GIS, especially temporal GIS, which contribute to the representation of spatial and temporal information. The fourth section presents selected space–time GIS designs that can accommodate the concepts and framework of time geography and support activity studies within a space–time context. Conclusions and future research directions of GIS for activity studies are provided at the end of this chapter.

TIME GEOGRAPHY AND HUMAN ACTIVITIES IN SPACE AND TIME

Human activities are conditioned by various spatial and temporal constraints. First of all, in today's society, people can rarely find a single location that meets all their needs. Multiple locations are usually involved in an individual's daily activity routine. The spatial distribution of these daily activities influences how a person arranges these activities and schedules corresponding trips. Second, an individual usually organizes his/her activities in a particular temporal order so that the activities can be coordinated to fulfill this person's needs. The sequential order of these activities sometimes indicates a cause-and-effect relationship among the activities. For example, a face-to-face meeting of two individuals in a local café usually is the result of a previous arrangement such as a phone conversation between the individuals to set up a meeting. Finally, how efficient an individual can carry out various activities is closely related to this person's capability of trading off time for space. As activity sites are often dispersed across space, travel is required for individuals to overcome the spatial separations of these activity sites. Since time is a limited resource and travel takes time, more travel time implies less time for other activities. Consequently, an individual must balance the time allocated to various activities at different locations and trips for moving between activity locations. As activities occur in a space–time context, a framework that supports an explicit representation of space and time can facilitate the research needs of examining how people organize and carry out their activities.

The time geography approach proposed by Hägerstrand (1970) offers an elegant conceptual framework to study the relationships of human activities and their constraints in a space–time context. The classical time geography framework identifies three types of constraints that limit an individual's freedom of performing activities (Golledge and Stimson, 1997). First of all, every individual must spend time to meet his/her physiological needs (e.g., sleeping and eating), which limit the time a person has for other activities. Also, based on the available resources (e.g., automobile ownership), people posses different levels of capability to trade time for space. For example, driving allows an individual to overcome a longer distance than walking under a fixed time budget. This implies that more activity opportunities may become available to this person due to the expanded activity space. In time geography, these conditions that limit an individual's movements due to physical or biological factors are called *capability constraints*. The second type of constraints, *authority constraints*, addresses general rules or laws that limit an individual's access to certain activity opportunities at particular locations (e.g., a military base) or during specific time periods (e.g., a store's business hours). Finally, *coupling constraints* are spatial and temporal requirements that allow an individual to bundle with other individuals and/or entities in order to perform certain activities (e.g., face-to-face meeting with other people, or presence at the workplace during work hours). These constraints work together to shape the spatiotemporal patterns of people's movements and activities. An integrated space–time environment therefore is desired to support the investigation of human activities and their constraints in a space–time context.

Based on an integrated space–time system, time geography proposes several key concepts to represent and examine human activities under various constraints. A *space–time path* concept represents the observed trajectory of an individual's movements across space and over time. A 3D line is used to represent a path in the space–time system (see Figure 13.1). Composed of a sequence of vertical and sloped line segments, a path effectively stores an individual's activity history, including activities conducted at specific locations, movements between those locations, and the sequential order of the activities and movements. Therefore, the

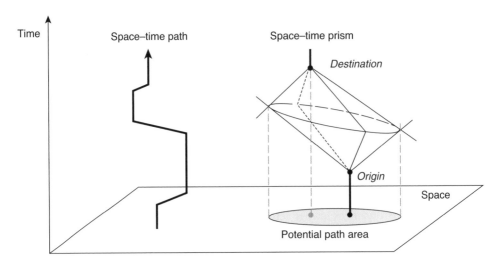

Figure 13.1   The space–time system, space–time path, and prism of time geography

space–time path concept provides an integrated space–time representation of an individual's movements and activity history (Miller, 2005a).

While a space–time path describes the observed movements of an individual, a *space–time prism* is used in time geography to depict the potential action space accessible to an individual under a specific set of constraints (Lenntorp, 1976). Since activities are often dispersed at different locations, how efficiently an individual can travel has a significant effect on the number of opportunities available to the individual. The more efficiently a person can travel, the larger space the person can cover within a given time budget and the higher the number of activity opportunities can be reached. A space–time prism therefore defines the extent within which an individual can reach under certain constraints, and the extent defines the maximum activity opportunities available to the individual. Figure 13.1 includes a space–time prism defined by two cones. The forward cone demarcates the spatial limit that an individual can reach within a given time budget by starting from the marked origin location, and the backward cone delineates the boundary where and when the individual must leave a location and will still be able to arrive

at the destination within the designated time window. Therefore the space between these two cones represents the space–time prism, which defines the feasible activity opportunities to an individual when a person leaves the origin at a specific time and must reach the destination at a pre-determined time. The slope of the prism's boundary lines indicates the space–time tradeoff efficiency. A flatter line suggests a higher travel speed, which translates to a larger potential activity area under a fixed time budget. The projection of a space–time prism onto a 2D plane becomes a region, which is known as a *potential path area*.

Using the space–time system and related concepts, time geography offers an elegant framework to represent observed human activities with their spatiotemporal characteristics and to examine the potential activity opportunities in a space–time context. This framework also provides a good foundation to support investigations of various spatiotemporal relationships among people. As social beings, people frequently interact with one another to fulfill their social and other needs. With the influences of the recent ICT developments, human activities have been extended to a hybrid physical-virtual space and the constraints for people to interact with others over space and time have been relaxed. In addition to participating in activities via physical presence, people can choose tele-presence, which allows people to carry out activities from remote locations via electronic connections (e.g., e-banking and e-shopping). ICT also permit many interactions to take place in an asynchronous manner that removes coupling constraints. For example, we can perform transactions of our bank account from home at midnight without having to worry about physically visiting the bank when it is open and bank tellers are available. Based on the different combinations of spatial (physical presence vs. tele-presence) and temporal (synchronous vs. asynchronous) characteristics of interactions, researchers have identified four modes of communications and interactions (Janelle, 1995, 2004; Harvey and Macnab, 2000; Miller, 2005b). A face-to-face meeting is an example of *synchronous physical presence* (SP). Dropping a package at a location for someone to pick it up later represents an interaction through the *asynchronous physical presence* (AP) mode. A phone conversation is done by a *synchronous tele-presence* (ST) interaction between individuals and emails are exchanged among individuals

through an *asynchronous tele-presence* (AT) interaction. Space–time paths can effectively support the representation of these four interaction modes. Three spatiotemporal relationships of paths, which are co-existence, co-location in space, and co-location in time, have been discussed in the literature (Parkes and Thrift, 1980; Golledge and Stimson, 1997). A *co-existence* relationship describes a scenario when several people stay at the same location during the same time. When people visit the same location during different time periods, they have a *co-location in space* relationship. Finally, a situation in which people at different locations are available to interact with one another during the same time period is defined as a *co-location in time* relationship. These relationships among individual space–time paths can represent the SP, AP, and ST types of interactions respectively. Recent efforts have extended the space–time paths relationships to include a fourth spatiotemporal relationship, *no co-location requirement in either space or time* (e.g., email communication), to represent the AT interactions (Yu, 2006; Yu and Shaw, 2007). Figure 13.2 shows the four interaction modes and their respective spatiotemporal relationships between individual

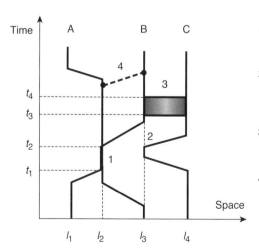

1. A and B had a meeting (*synchronous physical presence*): **co-existence**

2. C left a note which was picked up by B later (*asynchronous physical presence*): **co-location in space**

3. B phoned C (*synchronous tele-presence*): **co-location in time**

4. A sent an e-mail to B (*asynchronous tele-presence*): **no co-location in either space or time**

Figure 13.2   Spatiotemporal relationships of human interactions (adapted from Yu and Shaw, 2007)

space–time paths. It is also feasible to apply the concept of space–time prisms to exploring potential interaction opportunities among individuals under different interaction modes (Yu and Shaw, 2007, 2008).

Time geography provides a spatially and temporally explicit framework to study the relationships of constraints and human activities in a space–time context. Recently, we have seen renewed interests in time geography. The time geography framework has been applied to various activity studies related to different aspects of our society, including transportation studies (Miller, 1991, 1999), daily activity patterns of individuals (Ellegård, 1999; Adams, 2000), location-based services (Raubal et al., 2005), gender studies (Kwan, 1999; Ren and Kwan, 2007, 2009), social exclusions (Miller, 2006), diffusion of health risks (Mark et al., 1999; Sinha and Mark, 2005), geography of the homeless (Rollinson, 1998), among others. Although the structure of time geography is simple and straightforward, most studies used the framework as a conceptual model and limited efforts were made to operationalize the framework in a computer system in the past (Yuan et al., 2004). Some researchers have suggested GIS as a useful platform to accommodate the time geography framework and support the study of spatiotemporal characteristics of human activities (Miller, 1991; Pipkin, 1995). An operational GIS that supports the time geography framework can open up many opportunities for researchers to study human activity in our society and gain a better understanding of their spatiotemporal characteristics.

TEMPORAL GIS AND MODELING HUMAN ACTIVITIES IN GIS

Developing an efficient and effective GIS framework to model human activities presents a great challenge to the GIS community due to the complex nature of human activities in space and time. Many efforts have been devoted to modeling human activities in GIS, from simply storing and managing activity data to developing a spatiotemporal analysis environment to help researchers investigate human activities and their interactions. Traditional GIS designs have been strong in spatial information representation. A wide range of spatial data handling functions makes GIS capable of managing the spatial aspect of human activity data. Lacking an adequate design consideration of the time dimension, conventional GISs fall short of supporting the research needs of representing and analyzing the temporal characteristics of human activities. Many researchers have addressed the importance of including time in the GIS design so that GIS can support the representation of changes and help explore the dynamic nature of geographic phenomena (Frank, 2001; Frank et al., 2001; Yuan et al., 2004; Goodchild et al., 2007). A number of studies have been dedicated to integrating time into GIS and the initial efforts can be traced back to late 1980s (Renolen, 2000).

A straightforward approach to including temporal information in GIS is to add timestamps to geographic objects. Timestamp methods are originally used in temporal databases to represent the evolution of non-spatial data. However, similar methods can be employed in spatial databases. Depending on where a timestamp is attached in a relational database, three major timestamp methods have been developed to add temporal information (Yuan, 1999), including attaching a timestamp to an entire table (Gadia and Vaishnav, 1985), to a record in a table (Snodgrass and Ahn, 1985), or to a cell in a table (Gadia and Yeung, 1988). Applied to a spatial database, a timestamp attached to a table indicates that all geographic entities in a table share the same temporal information, which is equivalent of creating a snapshot of a geographic phenomenon. Attaching a timestamp to each record in a table allows each geographic entity in a spatial database to have its own temporal information. Finally, attaching a timestamp to a cell in a spatial database permits a single geographic entity to have different temporal attributes associated with different fields (i.e., cells). Due to the ease of implementation, attaching timestamp has been frequently adopted in various temporal GIS applications to add temporal information in a database, including managing travel and activity records. For example, attaching a timestamp to a record has been widely used to store the GPS tracking information of a moving vehicle and record individual trips with their starting and ending times in a travel diary database (Shaw and Wang, 2000).

The timestamp methods provide a basic approach to modeling spatiotemporal entities. However, by treating temporal information as additional attributes stored in a relational database, the timestamp approach does not offer an effective spatiotemporal modeling environment and it falls short of representing entities with complex spatiotemporal characteristics. Moving beyond the timestamp approach, several spatiotemporal data models have been proposed to represent spatiotemporal entities and their changes in various application domains, including the snapshot model (Armstrong, 1988), space–time composite model (Langran and Chrisman, 1988), object-oriented spatiotemporal model (Worboys, 1992), three-domain model (Yuan, 1999), among others. The object-oriented spatiotemporal model adopts a multidimensional approach, which includes two dimensions for space and one dimension for time (Worboys, 1992). The basic element in the data model is a spatiotemporal atom (ST-atom) which possesses homogeneous properties in both space and time. ST-atoms are used to form spatiotemporal objects that represent changes of real world entities. Since this model uses a 3D system, it offers some insights for the development of a GIS that implements the concepts in time geography, which also is based on a 3D space–time system.

Different spatiotemporal applications require different methods to represent spatiotemporal objects. Tryfona and Jensen (1999) categorize spatiotemporal applications into three types: (1) applications for objects with discrete changes of shapes; (2) applications for objects with continuous motion but without changes of shapes; and (3) applications for objects with continuous motion and changes of shapes. GIS applications of modeling the movements of human beings belong to the second application type. These objects, which change locations while maintaining shape and identity, are known as moving objects in the literature (Erwig et al., 1999). Since no shape changes are involved during the movements, moving objects are usually represented as point features in a GIS database.

Wolfson et al. (1998) and Porkaew et al. (2001) represent moving objects in a 2D space and propose methods to predict moving objects' future locations based on their previous locations and recent movement parameters (i.e., direction and velocity). Bian (2000) takes an object-oriented design and a simulation approach to studying the movements of fish in a 3D space. Vazirgiannis and Wolfson (2001) and Brinkhoff (2002) develop models to record real-time object movements along road networks. Both their models use universal time as the temporal reference system (for simulation purposes) and apply a timestamp method to attach temporal information to an object's location. Each new location is added into the database as a separate record containing spatial coordinates, time, and object ID. Erwig et al. (1999) and Güting et al. (2000) also propose their conceptual framework to model moving objects in a 3D system (2D space + 1D time). They use abstract data types to represent spatiotemporal objects and discuss potential operations applied to them. More recently, several studies have focused on analyzing the trajectories of a group of moving objects to recognize specific spatiotemporal patterns (e.g., converging, diverging, leading, expanding, and so on) presented by the objects (Laube et al., 2005; Andersson et al., 2008; Huang et al., 2008). Using the methods proposed in these studies, researchers can explore spatiotemporal patterns among moving objects hidden in a large dataset of trajectories. In general, studies of moving objects focus solely on physical location changes of observed objects, including storing tracked locations, predicting future locations, and analyzing spatial patterns presented by the objects. They offer a useful approach to supporting the construction of trajectories associated with individual activities and examination of their spatiotemporal relationships in physical space.

Managing activity data is more than recording the spatial and temporal information of the activities. Researchers have been aware of the needs to represent complex information and relationships related to human activities (e.g., scheduling multiple activities in space and time to complete a task) in GIS to support the exploration and understanding of activity patterns and organizations. Several attempts have been made to organize activity/travel data at the individual level in GIS to facilitate queries of trips/ activities and exploration of their spatiotemporal characteristics. In a relational GIS environment, Shaw and Wang (2000) develop a model to maintain the complex relationships among the spatial, temporal, and attribute components of travel activities in a travel diary dataset. The system allows users to retrieve and visualize disaggregate travel data according to various perspectives related to individual's trips. Adopting an activity-based approach to travel behavior, Wang and Cheng (2001) conceptualize human activity patterns as a sequence of stays and movements between different locations and organized the activity/travel data in a GIS environment to support spatiotemporal queries on both trips and activities. Allowing activities to be associated with their corresponding trips, this model emphasizes on an important concept of activity-based approach, in which travel is considered as derived demand. Taking an object-oriented approach, Frihida et al. (2002) present a spatiotemporal data model and implemented it with an object-oriented GIS shell to support the navigation and representation of individual

travel behavior over space and time. In their model, individual activities and trips are organized according to their temporal order. Therefore, the sequential order of an individual's activities can be conveniently maintained and such information can be used to investigate how individuals organize their daily activities.

The above studies contribute to the efforts of representing complex relationships among activities besides maintaining their spatial, temporal, and attribute information. Treating temporal information as an additional attribute, these approaches can support basic temporal queries of trips and activities in GIS. However, without an integrated representation of space and time, the spatial and temporal nature (e.g., trip chaining and activity sequencing) of human activities cannot be properly modeled, and exploration of interactions among individuals is cumbersome.

SPACE–TIME GIS TO SUPPORT HUMAN ACTIVITY STUDIES

Many researchers have suggested time geography as an elegant framework to facilitate activity studies due to its focus of examining activities in a space–time context. The lack of computational support in the past however has limited practical uses of this framework. During the past two decades, the GIS community made good progress in temporal GIS and enhanced the capability of GIS to handle spatiotemporal information and represent the dynamics of geographic phenomena. Such progress facilitates research of implementing the concepts of time geography and its framework in a GIS environment.

As the space–time prism concept can be used to identify potential activity opportunities in space and time that are available to an individual, it has been frequently used in activity studies to compute space–time constrained accessibility measures. Miller (1991) first implements the space–time prism concept in a GIS environment and calculates the network-based potential path area for studying individual accessibility. Recently, several more attempts have been made to use GIS to measure space–time constrained individual accessibility under various spatial and temporal circumstances and to identify available activity opportunities (Kwan and Hong, 1998; Miller, 1999; Miller and Wu, 2000; Weber and Kwan, 2002; Kim and Kwan, 2003). GIS procedures are provided in these studies to delimit the extent in a road network that is physically accessible to an individual under certain constraints in space and time. These studies represent space–time prisms in a 2D space as potential path areas. It remains a challenging task to model space–time prisms in a 3D GIS environment (2D space + 1D time). A 3D GIS model, which offers a better representation of the original concept of space–time prism, can enhance the visualization of prisms and provide additional spatiotemporal analysis capabilities for examining prisms (e.g., finding the overlapping space and time between two prisms in order to identify the opportunities for two individuals to interact with each other).

Several studies have attempted to realize the prism concept in a 3D GIS environment. Forer (1998) develops a raster approach to representing prisms in a 3D GIS. In his approach, a prism is calculated and represented as a collection of space–time cubes. The size of space–time cubes is determined by the granularity of the spatial and temporal resolution of the 3D raster GIS. Although this approach provides a valuable practice to identify accessible activities in space and time with a 3D model of prisms, it is less suitable to portray available activity opportunities in an urban environment, where most human travels are confined to a channelized network. Neutens et al. (2008) propose a 3D model of network-based prisms. They provide a mathematical description of network-based prisms and eventually employ a computer-aided design (CAD), rather than GIS, environment to visualize the prisms.

Yu and Shaw (2008) develop a space–time GIS design and implement the computation and visualization of network-based prisms in a 3D form. Their approach provides a spatially and temporally explicit 3D GIS implementation of prisms. This 3D GIS environment consists of two dimensions for space (x,y) and another dimension for time (t). Figure 13.3 shows the conceptual 3D design of the network-based prism and its implementation in a space–time GIS. In this approach, a network-based 3D prism is constructed by computing a forward cone and a backward cone to identify the enclosed prism between a pair of origin and destination locations. A shortest path tree algorithm is used to construct the forward cone from the origin location and the backward cone from the destination location. The derived space–time prism is composed of a set of vertical spatiotemporal lines, each of which indicates the earliest possible time that an individual can arrive at the location, the latest time that this individual must depart from the location, and how long this individual can stay at that location to participate in activities without violating the spatial and temporal constraints. Since space and time are explicitly represented in this model, this approach can support spatiotemporal analysis functions applied to the prisms (Yu and Shaw, 2008). As an initiative study with an operational prototype of the 3D GIS model for prisms, this approach demonstrates the potential of GIS to implement the prism concept in a 3D form and support activity analysis under various spatial and temporal constraints.

There are also many efforts dedicated to representing the space–time path concept in a spatiotemporal GIS environment. Kwan (2000b) develops a method to construct the trajectories of individuals from their travel dairy data records and model them as space–time paths. A 3D GIS environment called space–time aquarium is used to visualize the paths. Using similar techniques, Kwan and Lee (2004) report a 3D GIS visualization result of space–time paths representing trajectories constructed from GPS data. As ICT

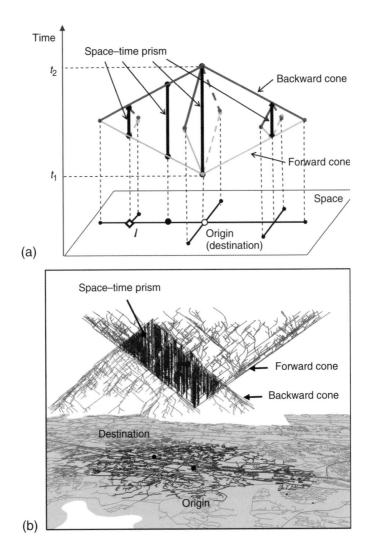

Figure 13.3   Implementing the space–time prism concept in a space–time GIS: (a) a conceptual design of a network-based prism; and (b) a network-based prism realized in a space–time GIS (adapted from Yu and Shaw, 2008)

become widely adopted in our society and an increasing number of activities are carried out in virtual space, researchers have attempted to use the space–time path concept to accommodate the representation of activities in both physical and virtual spaces.

Using the space–time path concept, Adams (2000) develops a conceptual model to represent an individual's daily communications and social connections. Six levels of spatial scopes, rather than accurate locations, are used to capture the different impact ranges of various activities conducted by individuals. While a face-to-face contact takes place at the physical proximity level of people, a telepresence communication (e.g., a phone call) may have impacts at the regional level or international level. Using 3D CAD diagrams, Adams represents the spatial and temporal scopes of individual activities as horizontal bars reaching out a 3D pillar, which represents the path. Kwan (2000a) proposes a similar idea based on a multi-scale GIS representation to illustrate the concept of human beings as agents with extensibility. Communications through virtual space are modeled as links stretching out from a space–time path. While a space–time path records an individual's trajectory in physical space, the links are used to model connections among people in virtual space. Using either bars or links for connections among people, these studies present useful approaches to the representation and visualization of virtual activities in a space–time format.

The space–time path concept also provides an elegant way to organize individual activities in a space–time context. A space–time path, which records an individual's movements in physical space over time, can function as a thread to connect all activities conducted by an individual in space and time according to their temporal sequence. This offers a useful framework for researchers to explore the spatiotemporal characteristics of activities and their interactions. Buliung and Kanaroglou (2006) apply the space–time path concept to study household level activity/travel behavior. They visualize space–time paths in a 3D GIS environment and develop a toolkit to analyze the patterns of individual space–time paths. A similar approach is adopted by Kang and Scott (2007) to investigate intra-household interactions in GIS.

Yu (2006) offers a detailed discussion of developing a spatiotemporal GIS model to support the representation, visualization, and analysis of activities that are organized in the form of space–time paths. A 3D GIS environment is established to simulate the space–time system of time geography. In this system, every location is referenced by a triplet of coordinates (x,y,t), which describes an object's spatial location (x,y) at a specific time instance (t). A line feature, which is constructed and represented by a sequence of (x,y,t) triplets, is used to represent the trajectory of a moving object. Since every activity takes place at particular locations during a specific time period and the activity's spatiotemporal information is recorded

with its corresponding space–time path, an activity can be modeled as an *episode* associated with a space–time path. Once an individual's space–time path is constructed (e.g., from GPS tracking data), each activity of this individual can be located on the path with the starting and ending times of the activity. Therefore, the spatial and temporal characteristics of an activity can be retrieved from the corresponding segment on a space–time path. Since this approach is similar to the linear referencing and dynamic segmentation method used in a transport system to measure locations along a route (e.g., highway mileposts), it is named a *temporal linear referencing and dynamic segmentation* method (Yu, 2006). Because this method permits multiple activities to overlap on a space–time path, it is capable of handling multi-tasking situations (such as calling someone on a cell phone while riding a bus), which have become common practices in today's society with the increasing use of ICT. Thus, this model provides a powerful approach to the representation of individual activities.

Besides representing each individual activity, a GIS design should be able to model the complex relationships among individuals and their activities to effectively support activity analysis. Two general types of relationships among individual activities can be identified. The first type includes relationships of activities among multiple individuals, which are usually recognized as interactions among people. For example, an interaction can be two groups of people having a conference call or a person sending an email to another person. The other type of relationship focuses on the sequential organization of activities of one or multiple individuals because the sequential order of activities presents a key to the understanding of the process of activities. For instance, a person can use the Internet to compare prices of a digital camera at different stores and then visit a local store to purchase the camera. Time geography uses the concept of *project* to define a series of activities conducted by a person or a group of people to achieve a specific goal

(Golledge and Stimson, 1997). It presents a major challenge to model the above relationships of activities in GIS because the relationships may possess complex spatiotemporal patterns. When people interact with others, they can choose any of the four interaction modes (i.e., SP, AP, ST, and AT – also known as co-existence, co-location in space, co-location in time, or no co-location in either space or time). In addition, activities associated with an individual's project may not be contiguous in either space or time. A project can last for hours, days, or years and different locations may be involved in various activities associated with the project. When a project involves multiple individuals, interactions among the participating individuals can be carried out with different spatiotemporal modes that result in complex spatiotemporal patterns.

Figure 13.4 shows a space–time GIS model that presents an attempt to manage various relationships of activities. Each individual has one space–time path, which stores the person's observed movements in space and time. An individual can have multiple activities. Each activity can be associated with its corresponding space–time path through the aforementioned temporal linear referencing and dynamic segmentation method. An *event* object is included to help us track the interactions among individuals. Each event is composed of one or more activities. When an event involves multiple activities, it represents an interaction of

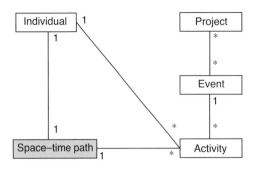

Figure 13.4   A space–time GIS to model relationships of human activities

multiple individuals. A *project* object is composed of multiple events that are organized in a particular sequence to achieve a goal set by an individual or a group of individuals. An event is allowed to be associated with more than one project because an event may function as a part of multiple projects. Interactions among individuals, events, and projects are modeled as relationships. Using these objects and relationships, it is feasible to organize complex relationships among activities and interactions in a space–time GIS. Since activities are associated with their corresponding space–time paths, it is very easy to explore and visualize the spatiotemporal patterns hidden among the interactions and projects. Shaw and Yu (2009) offer detailed discussion of the above concepts and present a GIS approach to implementing these concepts. Figure 13.5 shows two examples of implementing a space–time GIS to organize and visualize interactions and projects.

In addition to the capability of organizing complex relationships among activities and visualizing their spatiotemporal patterns, a good space–time GIS design should also provide useful analysis functions to help uncover the hidden spatiotemporal relationships among individuals and their activities. Analysis functions to examine the four possible human interaction relationships (i.e., co-existence, co-location in space, co-location in time, and no co-location in either space or time) have been reported in the literature (Yu, 2007). These operations allow users to examine potential interactions among individuals. For example, a co-existence analysis can be used to find people who visited the same location during the same time as a person with a contagious disease. These people therefore have a chance of being infected with the disease. Similar analysis functions also can be developed for space–time prisms (Yu and Shaw, 2008). For instance, an intersect operation between two space–time prisms can help identify the locations and time windows that two or multiple individuals can meet (i.e., a

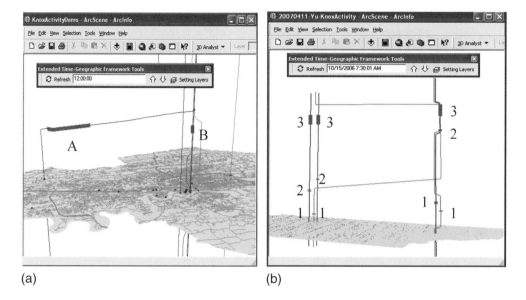

(a)   (b)

Figure 13.5 Representing relationships of activities in a space–time GIS: (a) an interaction between individuals A and B showing that A called B via cell phone while driving; and (b) a project of organizing a workshop with multiple participants and composed of three events: 1. call for participation, 2. registration, and 3. workshop participation

co-existence relationship). The identified locations and time windows reflect the opportunity space for these individuals to arrange a face-to-face meeting under their respective spatiotemporal constraints. Furthermore, as an increasing number of large individual-based tracking datasets become available, there are growing demands for a system that can help researchers comprehend the patterns and relationships hidden in these datasets. One approach is to identify spatiotemporal clusters of activities among a large number of individual space–time paths (Shaw et al., 2008). This approach can help researchers discover hidden spatiotemporal patterns among numerous individual space–time paths by deriving a small set of generalized space–time paths (Figure 13.6). Recent studies in trajectory data also report functions to identify particular spatiotemporal patterns (e.g., converging, diverging, and shrinking) among a group of moving objects (e.g., Laube et al., 2005; Huang et al., 2008). These functions represent some useful exploratory data analysis tools for large individual-based databases.

CONCLUSION

The merits of time geography in supporting the study of human activities have long been recognized in the research community. Time geography offers an elegant framework for studying individual activities and their relationships in a space–time context. While early studies used time geography mainly as a conceptual framework, recent developments of GIS offer promising opportunities to implement this framework and apply it to various application domains in today's society. There have been strong renewed interests in applying time geography to activity studies using GIS (Miller, 1991; Forer, 1998; Kwan, 2000b; Buliung and Kanaroglou, 2006; Yu, 2006; Yu and Shaw, 2008; Shaw and Yu, 2009). These studies demonstrate the capability of GIS to support the key concepts in time geography and the power of such GIS implementations to facilitate effective and efficient analysis of human activities under a space–time context. These efforts have created a solid foundation for future GIS

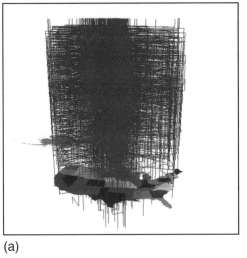

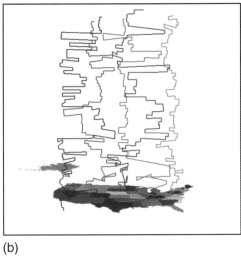

(a)   (b)

Figure 13.6 Exploring spatiotemporal patterns hidden in a large set of individual space–time paths: (a) visualization of original space–time paths; and (b) visualization of generalized space–time paths (adapted from Shaw et al., 2008)

developments in support of more advanced space–time explicit investigations of the increasingly complex and dynamic human activities in our society.

Beyond the recent progress of representing and analyzing individual activities in a space–time GIS environment, there remain some major challenges. First of all, since ICT have significantly extended human activities into a hybrid physical-virtual space, the spatial and temporal characteristics and patterns of human activities and interactions are becoming more complex than ever. What are the impacts of ICT on travel, how do people arrange their activities in physical and virtual spaces to achieve their goals, and how can GIS help investigate the patterns and relationships of activities in this hybrid environment? These are some of the critical research questions for activity studies in today's society. In order to facilitate the study of individual activities in both physical and virtual spaces, we need to revisit the classical time geography framework. Some researchers have worked on extending the classical time geography framework so that it can accom-

modate activities and interactions in a hybrid physical-virtual environment (Harvey and MacNab, 2000; Kwan, 2000a; Miller, 2005b; Yu, 2006; Yu and Shaw, 2007, 2008). Additional research efforts are needed to enhance GIS designs that can meet the needs of the research community.

Second, as suggested by the project concept in time geography, human activities and interactions are often connected and carried out in particular sequences in order to achieve specific goals. Therefore, the ability to investigate the sequential order of activities is essential for researchers to gain a better understanding of the processes behind the observed activity patterns. Although a space–time GIS is capable of representing the temporal aspect of activities and manage their sequential orders, additional analysis functions and data models are needed to develop a dynamic GIS design that can examine the processes underlying the observed human activities. What would be appropriate approaches to modeling the process of individual activity scheduling and decision making? How can we incorporate these approaches into GIS? Is the coupling of GIS with simulation models a feasible approach of extending the capability of GIS to deal with the dynamic aspect of individual activity planning and scheduling? These questions remain as unanswered challenges to the GIS research community.

Another emerging challenge is to develop efficient spatiotemporal analysis functions for large activity datasets. An increasing number of large activity datasets that are collected at the individual level are becoming available in various application fields. As data become less of an issue in activity studies, knowledge discovery from the data emerges as a new challenge. GIS should provide not only efficient data management and data representation functions but also a set of useful analysis tools to uncover the hidden information in the datasets. Miller (2005a) offers discussion of some fundamental analysis functions from a mathematical viewpoint. Some spatiotemporal analysis functions have been developed to examine the patterns and relationships among space–time paths and/or among individual space–time prisms in GIS as discussed in this chapter. However, when the size of a database becomes very large, it is difficult to analyze and comprehend the dataset because even simple visualization could be cluttered with too much information. Exploratory analysis tools are needed to uncover hidden information in a large individual-based activity dataset. The current progress in temporal GIS for representing and analyzing individual-based activity data has laid a solid foundation for future developments of a process-oriented GIS which can efficiently tackle the increasingly complex and dynamic human activities and interactions in our society.

ACKNOWLEDGMENTS

This study is partially supported by US National Science Foundation Grant #BCS-0616724. The authors would also like to thank the three anonymous reviewers for their constructive comments and suggestions.

REFERENCES

Adams, P. (2000) 'Application of a CAD-based accessibility model', in D. Janelle and D. Hodge (eds), *Information, Place and Cyberspace Issues in Accessibility*. Berlin: Springer. pp. 217–39.

Andersson, M., Gudmundsson, J., Laube, P. and Wolle, T. (2008) 'Reporting leaders and followers among trajectories of moving point objects', *Geoinformatica*, 12: 497–528.

Armstrong, M. (1988) 'Temporality in spatial databases', *Proceedings: GIS/LIS'* 88(2): 880–9.

Batty, M. and Miller, H. (2000) 'Representing and visualizing physical, virtual and hybrid information spaces'. In D. Janelle and D. Hodge (eds), *Information, Place and Cyberspace Issues in Accessibility*. Berlin: Springer. pp. 133–46.

Bian, L. (2000) 'Object-oriented representation for modeling mobile objects in an aquatic environment', *International Journal of Geographical Information Science*, 17(7): 603–23.

Brinkhoff, T. (2002) 'A framework for generating network-based moving objects', *GeoInformatica*, 6(2): 153–80.

Buliung, R. and Kanaroglou, P. (2006) 'A GIS toolkit for exploring geographies of household activity/travel behavior', *Journal of Transport Geography*, 14: 35–51.

Ellegård, K. (1999) 'A time-geographical approach to the study of everyday life of individuals – a challenge of complexity', *GeoJournal*, 48: 167–75.

Erwig, M., Güting, R., Schneider, M. and Vazirgiannis, M. (1999) 'Spatio-temporal data types: An approach to modeling and querying moving objects in databases', *GeoInformatica*, 3(3): 269–96.

Forer, P. (1998) 'Geometric approaches to the nexus of time, space and microprocess: Implementing a practical model for mundane socio-spatial systems'. In M.J. Egenhofer and R.G. Golledge (eds), *Spatial and Temporal Reasoning in Geographic Information Systems*. Oxford: Oxford University Press. pp. 171–90.

Frank, A. (2001) 'Socio-economic units: their life and motion'. In A. Frank, J. Raper and J.-P. Chylan (eds), *Life and Motion of Socio-Economic Units*. London: Taylor & Francis. pp. 21–34.

Frank, A., Raper, J. and Cheylan, J.-P. (eds) (2001) *Life and Motion of Socio-Economic Units*. London: Taylor & Francis.

Frihida, A., Marceau, D. and Thériault, M. (2002) 'Spatio-temporal object-oriented data model for disaggregate travel behavior', *Transactions in GIS*, 6(3): 277–94.

Gadia, S. and Vaishnav, J. (1985) 'A query language for a homogeneous temporal database', *Proceedings of the ACM Symposium on Principles of Database Systems*, 51–6.

Gadia, S. and Yeung, C. (1988) 'A generalized model for a relational temporal database', *Proceedings of ACM SIGMOD International Conference on Management of Data*, 251–9.

Golledge, R. and Stimson, R. (1997) *Spatial Behavior: A Geographic Perspective*. New York: Guilford Press.

Goodchild, M., May, Y. and Cova, T. (2007) 'Towards a general theory of geographic representation in GIS', *International Journal of Geographical Information Science*, 21(3): 239–60.

Güting, R., Böhlen, M., Erwig, M., Jensen, C., Lorentzos, N., Schneider, M. and Vazirgiannis, M. (2000) 'A foundation for representing and querying moving objects', *ACM Transactions on Database Systems*, 25(1): 1–42.

Hägerstrand, T. (1970) 'What about people in regional science?', *Papers of the Regional Science Association*, 24: 1–12.

Harvey, A. and Macnab, P. (2000) 'Who's up? Global interpersonal accessibility', in D. Janelle and D. Hodge (eds), *Information, Place and Cyberspace: Issues in Accessibility*. Berlin: Springer. pp. 147–70.

Huang, Y., Chen, C. and Dong, P. (2008) 'Modeling herds and their evolvements from trajectory data', in T. Cova, H. Miller, K. Beard, A. Frank and M. Goodchild (eds), *Proceedings of the 5th International Conference on Geographic Information Science (LNCS 5266)*. Berlin: Springer-Verlag. pp. 90–105.

Janelle, D. (1995) 'Metropolitan expansion, telecommuting, and transportation', in S. Hanson (ed.), *The Geography of Urban Transportation*, 2nd edn. New York: Guilford Press. pp. 407–34.

Janelle, D. (2004) 'Impact of information technologies', in S. Hanson and G. Giuliano (eds), *The Geography of Urban Transportation*, 3rd edn. New York: Guilford Press. pp. 86–112.

Janelle, D. and Hodge, D. (eds) (2000) *Information, Place and Cyberspace Issues in Accessibility*. Berlin: Springer.

Kang, H. and Scott, D.M. (2007) 'An integrated spatio-temporal GIS toolkit for exploring intra-household interactions', *86th Annual Meeting of the Transportation Research Board: Compendium of Papers CD-ROM*, Washington, DC, 21–25 January.

Kim, H.-M. and Kwan, M.-P. (2003) 'Space–time accessibility measures: A geocomputational algorithm with a focus on the feasible opportunity set and possible activity duration', *Journal of Geographical Systems*, 5(1): 71–91.

Kwan, M.-P. (1999) 'Gender and individual access to urban opportunities: A study using space–time measures', *Professional Geographer*, 51: 210–27.

Kwan, M.-P. (2000a) 'Human extensibility and individual hybrid-accessibility in space–time: A multi-scale representation using GIS', in D. Janelle and D. Hodge (eds), *Information, Place and Cyberspace: Issues in Accessibility*. Berlin: Springer-Verlag. pp. 241–56.

Kwan, M.-P. (2000b) 'Interactive geovisualization of activity-travel patterns using three-dimensional geographical information systems: A methodological exploration with a large data set', *Transportation Research Part C*, 8: 185–203.

Kwan, M.-P. and Hong, X. (1998) 'Network-based constraints-oriented choice set formation using GIS', *Geographical Systems*, 5: 139–62.

Kwan, M.-P. and Lee, J. (2004) 'Geovisualization of human activity patterns using 3D GIS: A time-geographic approach', in M. Goodchild and D. Janelle (eds), *Spatially Integrated Social Science*. New York: Oxford University Press. pp. 48–66.

Langran, G. and Chrisman, N. (1988) 'A framework for temporal geographic information', *Cartographica*, 25(3): 1–14.

Laube, P., Imfeld, S. and Weibel, R. (2005) 'Discovering relative motion patterns in groups of moving point objects', *International Journal of Geographical Information Science*, 19(6): 639–68.

Lenntorp, B. (1976) *Paths in Space-Time Environments: A Time Geographic Study of Movement Possibilities of Individuals. Lund Studies in Geography B: Human Geography*. Lund: Gleerup.

Mark, D., Egenhofer, M., Bian, L., Rogerson, P. and Vena, J. (1999) 'Spatio-temporal GIS analysis for environmental health', *2nd International Workshop on Geography and Medicine, GEOMED'99*. Paris: France.

Miller, H. (1991) 'Modeling accessibility using space–time prism concepts within geographical information systems', *International Journal of Geographical Information Systems*, 5: 287–301.

Miller, H. (1999) 'Measuring space–time accessibility benefits within transportation networks: Basic theory and computational methods', *Geographical Analysis*, 31: 187–212.

Miller, H. (2005a) 'A measurement theory for time geography', *Geographical Analysis*, 37: 17–45.

Miller, H. (2005b) 'Necessary space–time conditions for human interaction', *Environment and Planning B: Planning and Design*, 32: 381–401.

Miller, H. (2006) 'Social exclusion in space and time', in K.W. Axhausen (ed.), *Moving Through Nets: The Social and Physical Aspects of Travel*. Oxford: Elsevier. pp. 353–80.

Miller, H. and Wu, Y. (2000) 'GIS software for measuring space–time accessibility in transportation planning and analysis', *GeoInformatica*, 4: 141–59.

Neutens, T., Van de Weghe, N., Witlox, F. and De Maeyer, P. (2008) 'A three-dimensional network-based space–time prism', *Journal of Geographical Systems*, 10(1): 89–107.

Parkes, D. and Thrift, N. (1980) *Times, Spaces and Places: A Chronogeographic Perspective*. New York: John Wiley.

Peuquet, D. (2002) *Representations of Space and Time*. New York: Guilford Press.

Pipkin, J. (1995) 'Disaggregate models of travel behavior', in S. Hanson (ed.), *The Geography of Urban Transportation*, 2nd edn. New York: Guilford Press. pp. 188–218.

Porkaew, Lazaridis, K., I. and Mehrotra, S. (2001) 'Querying mobile objects in spatio-temporal databases', *SSTD 2001*, 59–78.

Raubal, M., Miller, H. and Bridwell, S. (2005) 'User-centred time geography for location-based services', *Geografiska Annaler B*, 86(4): 245–65.

Ren, F. and Kwan, M.-P. (2007) 'Geovisualization of human hybrid activity-travel patterns', *Transactions in GIS*, 11(5): 721–44.

Ren, F. and Kwan, M.-P. (2009) 'The impact of the Internet on human activity-travel patterns: Analysis of gender differences using multi-group structural equation models', *Journal of Transport Geography*, 17(6): 440–50.

Renolen, A. (2000) 'Modeling the real world: Conceptual modeling in spatiotemporal information system design', *Transactions in GIS*, 4(1): 23–42.

Rollinson, P. (1998) 'The everyday geography of the homeless in Kansas City', *Geografiska Annaler B*, 80: 101–15.

Shaw, S.-L. (2006) 'What about "time" in transportation geography?', *Journal of Transport Geography*, 14 (3): 237–40.

Shaw, S.-L and Wang, D. (2000) 'Handling disaggregate spatiotemporal travel data in GIS', *GeoInformatica*, 4(2): 161–78.

Shaw, S.-L and Yu, H. (2009) 'A GIS-based time-geographic approach of studying individual activities and interactions in a hybrid physical–virtual space', *Journal of Transport Geography*, 17(2): 141–49.

Shaw, S.-L, Yu, H. and Bombom, L. (2008) 'A space–time GIS approach to exploring large individual-based spatiotemporal datasets', *Transactions in GIS*, 12(4): 425–41.

Sinha, G. and Mark, D. (2005) 'Measuring similarity between geospatial lifelines in studies of environmental health', *Journal of Geographical Systems*, 7: 115–36.

Snodgrass, R. and Ahn, I. (1985) 'A taxonomy of time in databases', *Proceedings of ACM SIGMOD International Conference on Management of Data*, 236–64.

Spaccapietra, S. (2001) 'Editorial: Spatio-temporal data models and languages', *GeoInformatica*, 5(1): 5–9.

Tryfona, N. and Jensen, C. (1999) 'Conceptual data modeling for spatiotemporal applications', *GeoInformatica*, 3(3): 245–68.

Vazirgiannis, M. and Wolfson, O. (2001) 'A spatiotemporal model and language for moving objects on road networks', *SSTD, 200*: 20–35.

Wang, D. and Cheng, T. (2001) 'A spatio-temporal data model for activity-based transport demand modeling', *International Journal of Geographical Information Science*, 15(6): 561–85.

Weber, J. and Kwan, M.-P. (2002) 'Bringing time back in: A study on the influence of travel time variations and facility opening hours on individual accessibility', *The Professional Geographer*, 54: 226–40.

Wolfson, O., Xu, B., Chamberlain, S. and Jiang, L. (1998) 'Moving objects databases: Issues and solutions', *Proceedings of SSDB Conference*, 1998: 111–22.

Worboys, M. (1992) 'A model for spatio-temporal information', *Proceedings: The 5th International Symposium on Spatial Data Handling*, 2: 602–11.

Yu, H. (2006) 'Spatio-temporal GIS design for exploring interactions of human activities', *Cartography and Geographic Information Science*, 33(1): 3–19.

Yu, H. (2007) 'Visualizing and analyzing activities in an integrated space–time environment: Temporal GIS design and implementation', *Transportation Research Record: Journal of the Transportation Research Board*, 2024: 54–62.

Yu, H. and Shaw, S.-L. (2007) 'Revisiting Hägerstrand's time-geographic framework for individual activities in the age of instant access', in H.J. Miller (ed.), *Societies and Cities in the Age of Instant Access*. Netherlands: Springer. pp. 103–18.

Yu, H. and Shaw, S.-L. (2008) 'Exploring potential human activities in physical and virtual spaces: A spatio-temporal GIS approach', *International Journal of Geographic Information Science*, 22(4): 409–30.

Yuan, M. (1999) 'Use of three-domain representation to enhance GIS support for complex spatiotemporal queries', *Transactions in GIS*, 3(2): 137–59.

Yuan, M., Mark, D., Egenhofer, M. and Peuquet, D. (2004) 'Extensions to geographic representations', in R. McMaster and E. Usery (eds), *A Research Agenda for Geographic Information Science*. Boca Raton, FL: CRC Press. pp. 129–56.

GIS in Organisations and Institutions

14

Emerging Frameworks in the Information Age: The Spatial Data Infrastructure (SDI) Phenomenon

Ian Masser

INTRODUCTION

The development of geographic information systems (GIS) and related technologies over the last two decades has changed the way in which geographic information is handled by a wide range of public and private sector bodies throughout the world and spawned a multi-billion dollar industry. However, the full potential of these technologies is unlikely to be realised until governments throughout the world take the necessary steps to create spatial data infrastructures (SDIs) to facilitate access to the geographic information assets that are held by the various stakeholders to maximise their overall usage. As a result, governments through the world have begun to develop SDIs. The term itself was first used in 1991. Since then about half the 200 countries in the world have embarked on some form of SDI initiative. Given these circumstances, the term 'SDI phenomenon' seems to be a reasonable description of what has happened in this field over the last 15 years.

During this time the development of SDIs has been transformed by the development of new Internet-based technologies that have transformed the means of access to large volumes of digital data and also promoted the emergence of location-based services such as satellite navigation. New techniques for data collection have also been utilised such as sensors and volunteered geographic information (Craglia et al., 2008). At the same time products such as Google Earth™ have been developed that make it possible for a new generation of non-professional users to add their own data relating to the surface of the earth for their own applications (Butler, 2006).

Given these circumstances it will come as no surprise to learn that one of the distinctive features of the SDI phenomenon is the great diversity of activities that it encompasses. During its short life the concept has already been reinvented several times to respond to the changing needs of government as well as to technological innovations. As a result, a distinction can already be made between a first and second generation of SDIs and it can be argued that some of the key features of the third are already apparent (Rajabifard et al., 2006).

With these considerations in mind this chapter reviews recent developments in SDIs from the standpoint of emerging frameworks in the information age and examines some of the broader issues that are emerging from them. It is divided into three substantive sections. The first of these considers some of the main events that underlie the SDI phenomenon, describes the nature of SDIs with reference to other kinds of infrastructure and outlines some of the main economic, social and environmental benefits that are likely to be derived from their development. The second section discusses current trends in the field and the methods that have been developed to deal with SDI development with reference to key issues such as the need for multi-level structures, more inclusive models of governance and the new organisational structures that are coming into being to facilitate SDI implementation. The third considers the needs of the different levels of the SDI hierarchy with reference to some key applications at the local, national and supranational levels while some of the efforts that are being made to compare and evaluate SDI experiences as a result of the shift from SDI formulation to implementation are briefly summarised in the final section.

THE SDI PHENOMENON

Emergence

The emergence of the SDI phenomenon can best be described by reference to some of the more significant milestones that mark its path. The first milestone dates back more than 20 years to the establishment of the Australian Land Information Council (ALIC) in January 1986 as a result of an agreement between the Australian prime minister and the heads of the state governments to coordinate the collection and transfer of land-related information among the different levels of government and to promote the use of that information in decision making (ANZLIC, 1992: 1). The feature that distinguishes this body from the bodies that were set up by other governments around this time (e.g. the French Conseil National de l'Information Geographique that was set up in 1985 and the Dutch National Council for Real Estate Information that dates from 1984) is its emphasis on the need for coordination between different levels of government. In this respect it anticipates the SDI debate that began in earnest 10 years later.

The second milestone was the publication of the Report of the British Government Committee of Enquiry on Handling Geographic Information chaired by Lord Chorley in May 1987 (Department of Environment, 1987). This set the scene for much of the subsequent discussion about SDIs in the UK and elsewhere. The report reflects the committee's enthusiasm for the new technology: 'the biggest step forward in the handling of geographic information since the invention of the map' (Department of Environment, 1987: para 1.7) and also their concern that information technology in itself must be regarded as 'a necessary, though not sufficient condition for the take up of geographic information systems to increase rapidly' (Department of Environment, 1987: para 1.22). To facilitate the rapid take up of GIS the committee argued that it will be necessary to overcome a number of important barriers to effective utilisation. Of particular importance in this respect are the need for greater user awareness and the availability of data in digital form suitable for use in particular applications.

The third was the United States Office of Management and Budget's (OMB) decision to create an interagency Federal Geographic Data Committee (FGDC) to coordinate the 'development, use, sharing, and dissemination of surveying, mapping, and related spatial data' (OMB, 1990: 6). The term 'National Spatial Data Infrastructure' was not in general use at this point although a paper was presented by John McLaughlin at the 1991 Canadian Conference on Geographic Information Systems entitled 'Toward National Spatial Data Infrastructure'. The ideas contained in this paper were subsequently developed by the United States National Research Council's Mapping Science Committee in their report on 'Toward a coordinated spatial data infrastructure for the nation' (National Research Council, 1993). This recommended that effective national policies, strategies and organisational structures should be established at the federal level for the integration of national spatial data collection, use and distribution. To realise this goal it proposed that the powers of the FGDC should be strengthened to define common standards for spatial data management and to create incentives to foster data sharing particularly among federal agencies.

The next milestone was the outcome of an enquiry set up by DG XIII (now DG Information Society) of the European Commission which found that there was a strong European wide demand for an organisation that would further the interests of the European geographic information community. As a result, the first continental level SDI organisation in the world was set up in 1993. The vision of the European Umbrella Organisation for Geographic Information (EUROGI) was not to 'replace existing organisations but … catalyze effective cooperation between existing national, international and discipline-oriented bodies to bring added value in the areas of Strategy, Coordination, and Services' (Burrough et al., 1993: 31).

The turning point in the evolution of the SDI concept came in the following year with the publication of Executive Order 12906 signed by President Clinton entitled 'Coordinating Geographic Data Acquisition and Access: the National Spatial Data Infrastructure' (Executive Office of the President, 1994). This set out the main tasks to be carried out and defined time limits for each of the initial stages of the National Spatial Data Infrastructure. These included the establishment of a National Geospatial Data Clearing House and the creation of a National Digital Geospatial Data Framework. The Executive Order also gave the FGDC the task of coordinating the Federal government's development of the National Spatial Data Infrastructure and required that each member agency of that committee held a policy level position in their organisation. In this way the Executive Order significantly raised the political visibility of geospatial data collection, management and use not only among federal agencies but also nationally and internationally.

The Executive Order had an immediate impact on thinking in the European Commission. A meeting of key people representing geographic information interests in each of the member states was organised in Luxemburg in February 1995 to develop the first of what became a series of documents on 'GI2000: toward a European geographic information infrastructure'. An important by product of this debate was the decision to hold the first of what subsequently became a regular series of Global Spatial Data Infrastructure conferences at Bonn in Germany in September 1996. This conference brought together representatives from the public and private sectors and academia for the first time to discuss matters relating to SDIs at the global level.

A worldwide survey of SDIs that were operational in 1996 was carried out by Masser (1999). This showed that at least 11 SDIs were already in operation in various parts of the world. What distinguished these from other GI policy initiatives was that they were all explicitly national in scope and their titles all referred to geographic information, geospatial data or land information and included the term 'infrastructure', 'system' or 'framework'. This first generation included relatively wealthy countries such as the Australia, Canada, the Netherlands and the USA as well as a handful of relatively poor countries such as Indonesia and Malaysia.

The rapid rate of NSDI diffusion after 1996 is highlighted by the findings of another survey carried for the GSDI (http://www.gsdi.org). These show that 49 countries responded positively to his questionnaire between 1998 and 2000: 21 of these came from the Americas, 14 from Europe, 13 from Asia and the Pacific and one from Africa. The number of positive responses to this survey was more than four times the number of countries identified up to the end of 1996. Subsequent data collected by Crompvoets and Bregt (2007 on the development of clearinghouses suggests that about half the world's countries were considering SDI related projects.

These figures must be treated with some caution as they do not necessarily imply that all these countries are actively engaged in SDI formulation or implementation. Furthermore it is also likely that many of them may be engaged in some aspects of SDI development without necessarily committing themselves to a comprehensive SDI programme. Nevertheless the term 'SDI phenomenon' seems to be a reasonable description of what has happened in this field over the last 10 to 15 years.

The SDI concept

There are clear parallels between the SDI concept and other forms of infrastructure. These are typically defined as the basic facilities, services and installations needed for the effective functioning of society. They include transport and communications systems, water and electricity services as well as public institutions including hospitals, schools, post offices and prisons.

A spatial data infrastructure (sometimes called a geographic information strategy, a geospatial data infrastructure or a geo-information infrastructure) is 'the means to assemble geographic information that describes the arrangement and attributes of features and phenomena on the Earth. The infrastructure includes the materials, technology and people necessary to acquire, process and distribute such information to meet a wide variety of needs' (National Research Council, 1993: 16).

The overriding objective of SDIs is to facilitate access to the geographic information assets that are held by a wide range of stakeholders in both the public and the private sector in a nation or a region with a view to maximizing their overall usage. Coordinated action on the part of governments is required to achieve this objective.

The development of SDIs in particular countries must be user driven as their primary purpose is to support decision making for many different purposes. SDI implementation involves a wide range of activities. These include not only technical matters such as data, technologies, standards and delivery mechanisms but also institutional matters related to organisational responsibilities and overall national information policies as well as questions relating to the availability of financial and human resources. In this respect SDIs have an important role to play in capacity building for the information age.

There are some important differences between SDIs and other kind of infrastructure. SDIs are very much a product of the information age in that they are inherently digital in nature and their evolution over the last 10 to 15 years has been closely linked to the emergence of the Internet and the World Wide Web. In this respect they must be regarded as virtual rather than physical infrastructures.

Benefits and costs

It is not easy to estimate with any precision either the costs or the benefits that are associated with SDI development. Nevertheless it is clear that the tasks of SDI coordination and governance are relatively inexpensive in relation to the overall expenditure on geographic information whereas the task of core digital database development is relatively expensive. The US Office of Management and Budget has estimated that US federal agencies alone already spend at least US$4 billion annually to collect and maintain domestic geospatial data whereas the costs of supporting the FGDC and its work are less than one per cent of this amount (Masser, 2005: 47).

SDIs have economic, social and environmental benefits. The most important economic benefit of SDIs is the promotion of economic growth as a result of an expanding market for geographic information related products and services. The findings of a study carried out by PIRA International (2000: 8–9) for the European Commission give some indication of the value of public sector information in the tightly constrained European market of that time. They show that over half the economic value of public sector information in 1999 (€68 billion) came directly from geographic information sources. This is equivalent to about 1 per cent of the European GDP. They also show that the economic value of the same sector of the less constrained US market was €750 billion. As a result of the easing of these constraints through the development of SDIs it might be expected that the size of the European market would move toward that of the US market over time. More recently, a similar study in Australia (ACIL Tasman, 2008) concluded that the outputs of the spatial information industry were equivalent to between 0.6 and 1.2 per cent of GDP. Estimates of the growth of the commercial geographic information market are more readily available and have been of the order of 15 to 20 per cent per year in recent years. The impact of an expanding market of this size on job creation is also considerable. Other economic benefits of SDIs include increased efficiency and lower operating costs for both public and private sector organisations due to wider access to geographic information and information based services. These may be considerable over time.

The most important social benefits from SDIs are the extent to which they bring the key stakeholders in the public and private sectors together to create more efficient and more transparent governments at all levels as a result of the increasing availability of authoritative data to policy makers. Another important social benefit stems from the opportunities that data sharing due to SDI development creates for citizens to actively participate in the democratic process. Because of the extent to which they bring together data from many diverse sources, SDIs are also likely to lead to better arrangements for homeland security and more effective systems for emergency planning and response. There are also many operational social benefits to be obtained for social service staff, health workers, education personnel and the police from the more effective targeting of areas and groups with special needs.

There are also many environmental benefits associated with SDIs. They have an important role to play in promoting sustainable development throughout the world as a whole. At the national and local levels they provide the data that is required for the more effective management and monitoring of natural resources. They are particularly useful in coastal zones because of the extent to which they can integrate maritime and terrestrial data.

METHODS

Current trends in SDI development

The development of a second generation of SDIs began around 2000 (Rajabifard et al., 2003b). There has been an important shift in emphasis from the first to the second generation both in technological terms and also with respect to the key themes of SDI development. The shift in emphasis that has taken place in terms of the technology is particularly due to the opportunities opened up by the development of the Internet and the World Wide Web. This was recognised by the US Mapping Sciences Committee in their report on Distributed Geolibraries (National Research Council, 1999: 31). In their view 'the WWW has added a new and radically different dimension to its earlier conception of the NSDI, one that is much more user oriented, much more effective in maximizing the added value of the nation's geoinformation assets, and much more cost effective as a data dissemination mechanism.'

The most distinctive feature of the second generation of SDIs is the shift that has taken place from the product model that characterised most of the first generation to a process model of a SDI. Database creation was to a very large extent the key driver of the first generation and, as a result, most of these initiatives tended to be data producer, and often national mapping agency, led. The shift from the product to the process model is essentially a shift in emphasis from the concerns of data producers to those of data users. As a result data users have ceased to be passive partners and become more actively involved in SDI development. The main driving forces behind the data process model are data sharing and reusing data collected by a wide range of agencies for a great diversity of purposes at various times. Also associated with this change in emphasis is a shift from the centralised structures that characterised most of the first generation of national SDIs to the decentralised and distributed networks that are a basic feature of the WWW.

A shift in emphasis is also taking place from SDI formulation to implementation over time. There is a shift from single level to multi-level participation within the context of a hierarchy of SDIs. Under these circumstances it will be necessary to substantially modify the coordination models that have emerged for single level SDIs and think in

terms of more complex and inclusive models of governance. These developments are also likely to require new kinds of organisational structure to facilitate effective implementation.

There are also signs that a third generation of SDIs is emerging. The most important difference between the second and third generation is that the balance of power in the latter has moved from the national to the sub-national level (Rajabifard et al., 2006). Most large-scale, land-related data is collected at this level where it is used for collecting land taxes, land use planning, the operation of land markets, road and infrastructure development and day-to-day decision making in order to meet sustainable development objectives. Alongside these developments there has been a shift from government-led approaches to whole of industry models where the private sector operates on the same terms as its government partners. One consequence of these developments is that national SDI activities are likely to be increasingly restricted to the strategic level while most of the operational level decisions are handled at the sub-national levels by local government agencies in conjunction with the private sector.

The concept of spatially enabled government that is emerging as a result of these trends presents some important challenges for those involved. The initial development of SDIs was largely in the hands of small elite of spatially aware professionals from the fields of geography, planning, surveying, land administration and environmental science. These not only dominated the production of geographic information but were also its main users. In recent years, as a result of the development of location-based services and the expansion of e-government, the position has substantially changed to the extent that the vast majority of the public are users, either knowingly or unknowingly, of spatial information (Masser et al., 2008). As a result, traditional professional practices may need to be drastically revised to ensure that SDIs develop in such a way that they provide an enabling platform that will serve the wider needs of society in a transparent manner.

With these considerations in mind three key issues affecting emerging SDIs will be discussed in more detail in the remainder of this section. These are nature of the multilevel nature of SDI implementation, the need for more inclusive models of SDI governance and the emergence of new types of organisational structure to facilitate SDI implementation.

The multi-level nature of SDI implementation

Many existing national SDI documents seem to abide by the principle of 'one size fits all'. In other words they suggest that the outcome of SDI implementation will lead to a relatively uniform product. However, there is both a top down and a bottom up dimension to national SDI implementation. National SDI strategies drive state-wide SDI strategies and state-wide SDI strategies drive local level SDI strategies. The outcomes of such processes from the standpoint of a national SDI such as that of the USA are likely to be that the level of commitment to SDI implementation will vary considerably from state to state and from local government to local government. Consequently the SDI that emerges from this process will be like a patchwork quilt or a collage of similar, but often quite distinctive components, that reflect the commitments and aspirations of the different sub-national governmental agencies. The patchwork quilt analogy assumes that the SDI outcome will be like the product of different pieces of cloth of various colours sewn together to form a cover. This is particularly useful where the SDI participants are largely administrative regions with similar functions. The collage analogy, on the other hand, is based on the notion of a picture built up from different pieces of paper and other materials. This is most useful where the participants such as transportation and environmental agencies cover overlapping areas

(Masser, 2010: 84–6). These two categories broadly correspond to the two types of multi-level political governance identified by political scientists, such as Hooghe and Marks (2003).

These visions differ markedly from the top-down one that is implicit in much of the SDI literature. While the top-down vision emphasises the need for standardisation and uniformity, the bottom-up vision stresses the importance of diversity and heterogeneity given the very different aspirations of the various stakeholders and the resources that are at their disposal. Consequently the challenge to those involved in SDI governance and implementation will be to find ways of ensuring some measure of standardisation and uniformity while recognising the diversity and the heterogeneity of the different stakeholders. This is likely to become increasingly important as sub-national agencies take over the operational activities associated with SDI implementation.

More inclusive models of SDI governance

Many countries are moving toward more inclusive models of SDI governance to meet the requirements of a multi-level multi-stakeholder SDI (Rajabifard, et al., 2006). It must also be emphasised that the notion of 'governance' involves more than that of 'government'. According to an OECD (2001) report good governance has eight main characteristics. It is participatory, consensus oriented, accountable, transparent, responsive, effective and efficient, equitable and inclusive and it follows the rule of law. Consequently top priority must be given to the creation of appropriate SDI governance structures which are both understood and accepted by all the stakeholders. This is a daunting task given the number of organisations that are likely to be involved. In the USA, for example, there are more than 100,000 organisations engaged in SDI related GIS activities. It will not be possible in most cases to bring all the stakeholders together for decision-making purposes and structures must be devised that keep all of them informed and give them an opportunity to have their opinions heard.

One solution to this problem is to create hierarchical structures at the national, state and local levels for this purpose. The main features of these structures can be seen in the administrative arrangements that have come into being in Australia. The lead Commonwealth government agency for the Australia SDI is the Australia New Zealand Land Information Council (ANZLIC). Each of the members of ANZLIC represents a coordinating body within their jurisdiction (i.e. the Commonwealth Office for Spatial Data Management, the relevant coordination bodies at the state and territory levels and Land Information New Zealand).

Similar types of body are coming into being at the state level in Australia to perform similar functions. For example, the state of Victoria set up the Victorian Spatial Council in 2004 to oversee the implementation of the state's Spatial Information Strategy (VSIS). Its role is 'to provide a coordinated whole of industry approach to spatial information policy and development, management and utilisation in Victoria, by undertaking a spatial information management role and acting as a mechanism for cross-sectoral consultation and liaison' (Department of Sustainability and Environment, 2004: 3). Its membership is set at a maximum of 13 members drawn from state government (3), local government (2), federal government (1), academia (2), the professions (2) and the private sector (2). Each of the Council's members is responsible for briefing the members of their respective sectors on matters considered by the Council and developing their response. In this way the Council provides a mechanism for involving all the stakeholders in the State's SDI.

Federal governance structures are also beginning to emerge in other parts of the world, particularly in countries where some administrative responsibilities relating to geographic information are devolved to the state or provincial level. They are built, for example, into the German national SDI (Lenk et al., 2008) and to some extent in the US 50 states initiative that is backed by the FGDC and the National States Geographic Information Council (Robinson and Burgess, 2006).

It is important that these governance structures should be as inclusive as possible from the outset of an SDI initiative so that all those involved can develop a shared vision and feel a sense of common ownership. Otherwise it may be difficult or even impossible to bring new participants into an SDI initiative at a later stage. This is likely to be a challenging task that may slow down the progress of the work in the short term, but building up a base for future collaboration is an essential prerequisite for the long-term success of the SDI.

The emergence of new organisational structures

The multi-level nature of national SDI implementation is also likely to require the creation of new kinds of organisational structure. These can take various forms. Elsewhere I have described some of the different kinds of structures that have already emerged in the USA, Australia and Canada to facilitate national SDI implementation (Masser, 2005: Chapter 5). This shows that at least five different types of partnerships are already in operation. These range from the restructuring of existing government agencies to the establishment of joint ventures involving different combinations of the key stakeholders (Table 14.1).

The simplest case is the merger of various government departments with responsibilities for collecting geographic information. The driving force for this restructuring is the perceived administrative benefits associated with the creation of an integrated database for the agency as a whole. Land Victoria in Australia is the product of a merger of

Table 14.1 Organisational structures created to facilitate SDI implementation

Type	Status	Driver
Restructuring	Within government structures	Creation and maintenance of an integrated land information database
	External to government structures	Delivery of wide range of e-government services
Joint ventures	Consortium of data producers	Integration of datasets held by state and federal agencies
	Joint venture by key data users	Maintenance and dissemination of core datasets
	Joint ventures data producers and users	Creation and sharing of core datasets

various state government entities with responsibilities for various aspects of land administration. The objective of this merger was to establish an integrated land administration agency with a shared geographic information resource for the State of Victoria (http://www.land.vic.gov.au).

An alternative strategy is to set up a special government agency outside the existing governmental structure with a specific remit to maintain and disseminate core datasets. Service New Brunswick in Canada is a good example of such a strategy (http://www.snb.ca). It is a Crown Corporation owned by the Province of New Brunswick. It was originally set up to deal with matters relating to land transactions and topographic mapping for the Province as a whole. Since 1998 it has shifted its position to become the gateway for the delivery of a wide range of basic government services as well as national SDI implementation.

There are also some interesting examples of joint ventures between different groups of the stakeholders in SDI implementation. The simplest case is a data producer-driven joint venture such as the Australian Public Sector Mapping Agencies consortium (PSMA) that

was set up in 1993 to create an integrated national digital base map for the 1996 Census of Population (http://www.psma.com.au). The driving force behind this partnership was the recognition the whole is worth more than the sum of the parts in that there are clear benefits for the nation to be derived through the assembly of national data sets from data held by the consortium members.

The other two types of joint ventures involve more complex structures. Alberta's Spatial Data Warehouse is very much a data-user driven initiative. It is a not for profit joint venture between key data users including the State itself, the local government associations and the utility groups to facilitate the continuing maintenance and distribution of four primary provincial data sets (http://www.AltaLis.com). From the outset the partners recognised that they did not have either the expertise or the resources to maintain and disseminate the existing databases. Consequently they negotiated a long-term Joint Venture Agreement with two private sector companies in 1999 to carry out these tasks. This covers the reengineering of the databases and also makes it possible to implement new pricing and licensing options.

Finally, initiatives such as the MetroGIS collaborative in the Minneapolis-St. Paul metropolitan region of the USA that is described in the next section of this chapter bring together a large number of data producers and data users (http://www.metrogis.org). Such initiatives are both more ambitious and more open ended in their potential for development than either of the other joint ventures.

SOME SDI APPLICATIONS

The hierarchy of SDIs

The nature of SDI development varies at different levels of the administrative hierarchy. The national level occupies a central position in this hierarchy as the critical link or hinge between the higher and the lower levels (Rajabifard et al., 2003a). It is also the level at which strategic initiatives regarding the management of national geographic information assets are formulated and implemented in most countries. It must be emphasised, however, that the term 'national' is used in this context in a relative rather than an absolute sense. Consequently it may refer in some countries to comprehensive and inclusive GI strategies from the standpoint of the stakeholders involved whereas in others it may describe initiatives that are partial in their coverage and limited in stakeholder participation.

SDI development at the sub national level is closely linked to the operational needs of day to day decision making. As noted earlier there is also a top down and a bottom up dimension to the relationships between the local and national levels. Supra-national and global SDI bodies have a strong interest in strategic issues and are also actively engaged in capacity building among their members. There is also an important distinction between supranational bodies such as the European Union which have developed an institutional framework for the management of supranational activities and multinational organisations that have to operate in the absence of governmental bodies at these levels.

The three case studies described below have been chosen with a view to highlighting these characteristics. The work of MetroGIS illustrates the importance of developing procedures to facilitate data sharing at the sub-national level within the Minneapolis–St. Paul Metropolitan region in the USA. GeoConnections in Canada is a national partnership initiative which was set up to facilitate the implementation of the Canadian Geospatial Data Infrastructure while the European Union's supranational Infrastructure for Spatial InfoRmation in Europe (INSPIRE) initiative has the objective of making available relevant and harmonised geographic information to support the formulation and implementation of Community policies with a territorial dimension.

Sub-national case study – MetroGIS

MetroGIS is a multi-participant, geographic information collaborative that serves the seven-county, 7500 square kilometre, Twin Cities Metropolitan Area centered on Minneapolis-St. Paul in the USA. It was established in 1996 to provide an ongoing, stakeholder-governed, metro-wide mechanism through which participants can easily and equitably share geographically referenced graphic and associated attribute data that are accurate, current, secure, of common benefit and readily usable (Masser and Johnson, 2006).

MetroGIS provides an effective system for collaboration between the data producer and user communities to assemble, document and distribute spatial data commonly used by the more than 300 local and regional government units serving the Minneapolis–St Paul metropolitan area. It is a voluntary organisation that provides an effective forum to identify common spatial data-related needs, collectively define the organisational and technical solutions needed to address those needs and share geospatial data knowledge. MetroGIS has no legal standing and, as such, cannot own data, hire staff or finance projects. It relies on its stakeholder organisations to develop and maintain all data, develop and support data distribution tools and finance its staff and project needs. The key to MetroGIS's ability to accomplish the institutional changes needed to achieve the vision of the MetroGIS community is its unconventional organisational structure. Its Policy Board consists of 12 elected officials from its core local and regional government communities – counties, cities, school districts, watershed districts and regional government. These members are appointed by their respective communities to the Board, which has no formal legal standing.

The Policy Board is supported by a 25-member Coordinating committee. This defines goals and issues for strategic work groups, and makes recommendations to the Policy Board. Its members are drawn from a wide variety of public, academic, private, nonprofit and for-profit stakeholders in the region. MetroGIS has been successful because it focuses on both technology and building interorganisational relationships, and it raises issues to a level of public purpose. This structure ensures that 'all relevant and affected interests are involved, dominated by none'. At the outset, participants recognized that conventional hierarchical, command-and-control structures would not be capable of building and maintaining the trust relationships needed to bring all essential participants to the table or of overcoming fears of 'hidden agendas'.

The experience of the Metropolitan Mosquito Control District is a good example of the benefits that users derive from MetroGIS. Prior to access to MetroGIS data, district staff spent thousands of dollars and many hours acquiring, downloading, manipulating and reconciling parcel data from seven different counties to generate accurate and comparable field maps. The data is now free and can be downloaded from one spot and quarterly updates are available at no charge. In just two months after an updated and enhanced parcel data set was released in early 2005, nearly 50 organisations had obtained licenses for access to this data.

MetroGIS is the product of enlightened self interest on the part of its stakeholders. During the 10 years that it has been in operation it has built up a core of active users from a wide range of agencies who are able to access data that they regard as being of importance to their work. MetroGIS is also attractive to politicians and taxpayers because it saves money and makes better use of existing resources. The only direct cost of its operations is the US$200,000 that is paid annually by the Metropolitan Council to cover the costs of coordination. However, the seven counties also contribute the equivalent of 20 FTE staff time each year through the work that they carry out with respect to the core land parcel database, and the state agency and the University of Minnesota also contribute to the collaborative solutions.

National case study – GeoConnections

The Canadian Geospatial Data Infrastructure (CGDI) is made up 'of people, partners, geospatial content and technology with an aim to facilitate better policy and decision making' (GeoConnections, 2005: 1). Its main objective is to create a framework that will give decision makers access to online location based information that will help them to do their jobs better and more efficiently.

In 1999, the Canadian Government allocated 60 million Canadian dollars from its Federal budget over five years to establish a national partnership programme called GeoConnections led by Natural Resources Canada. Its mandate was to establish the foundations for such an infrastructure. During the following years GeoConnections developed a number of pilot projects involving the core elements of an operational infrastructure, thus creating in the process-standardised framework data. It also delivered a common agreement on data licensing and substantially strengthened federal, provincial territorial collaboration (Last, 2007).

On the basis of these achievements the Canadian Government decided in June 2005 to allocate a further Canadian $60 million over the next five years to enable Geo-Connections to continue its work with particular reference to four main policy areas: health, public safety, sustainable development and issues of importance for aboriginal peoples.

Key elements of the CGDI include the GeoConnections Discovery Portal (http://geodiscover.cgdi.ca), a national index and search engine that makes it possible for data providers to catalogue their data sets and also for users to find out what data exists, GeoGratis (http://geogratis.cgdi.ca), a national repository provided by the Earth Sciences Sector of Natural Resources Canada that provides geospatial data at no cost to users via their Web browsers, and GeoBase (http://www.geobase.ca), a federal, provincial and territorial initiative of the Canadian Council on Geomatics to provide a suite of framework layers that includes place names, administrative boundaries, the national road network, a national digital elevation model and a layer of satellite imagery as well as geodetic survey points. The CGDI is also the common backbone that supports a wide range of other national information systems.

A distinctive feature of GeoConnections is its governance structure. It is not only a coordinating body, as is the case with the US Federal Geographic Data Committee (FGDC), and describes itself as a national partnership initiative. According to its website 'these partners can be private companies, government agencies, at all levels, non governmental organisations, academic institutions .... We devote ample time and energy to establishing and nurturing partnerships because they anchor the success of the Canadian Geospatial Data Infrastructure as an on line resource for decision making' (http://www.geoconnections.org).

The membership of its management board includes all the main stakeholders with participation by the federal, provincial and territorial government officials, the private sector, academia, non-governmental organisations as well as advisors from each of the thematic advisory committees representing the four applications fields. Two other advisory groups are also actively involved in the work of GeoConnections. These are the Developers Network and the Policy Working Group.

GeoConnection's success owes a great deal to the degree to which it has created and built up networks of data users throughout a wide range of applications fields. A good example of the benefits that can be realised through such activities is the development of Conservation Areas Reporting and Tracking System (CARTS) that has been developed to facilitate international reporting (GeoConnections, 2006: 13–15). Before 2005 there was no consistent way of describing the nation's protected areas or assessing their protection levels. Since CARTS came into operation agencies such as the Canadian Wildlife Service and the Canadian Parks Agency are able to produce national reports more accurately and quickly than ever before. In addition, it can be expected that the data that is available from this source will be a valuable input to many other scientific activities at the national, provincial and territorial levels.

Supra-national case study – INSPIRE

The European Union's INfrastructure for Spatial InfoRmation in Europe (INSPIRE) initiative was launched in 2001 with the objective of making available relevant and harmonised geographic information to support the formulation and implementation of Community policies with a territorial dimension. INSPIRE deals with the spatial information that is required for environmental policies but can also be seen as the first step toward a broad, multi-sectoral initiative at the European level. It is a legal initiative that addresses matters such as technical standards and protocols, organisational and coordination issues, data policy issues including data access and the creation and maintenance of spatial information.

Five basic principles underlie INSPIRE:

- Data should be collected once and maintained at the level where this can be done most effectively.
- It should be possible to combine seamlessly spatial data from different sources and share it between many users and applications.
- Spatial data should be collected at one level of government and shared between all levels.
- Spatial data needed for good governance should be available on conditions that are not restricting its extensive use.
- It should be easy to discover which spatial data is available, to evaluate its fitness for purpose and to know which conditions apply for its use.

An extended impact assessment of INSPIRE was carried out which suggests that the overall costs of data harmonisation, the development of metadata services and coordination to EU, national and regional and local organisations over the first ten years of INSPIRE implementation might be somewhere between €200 and 300 million per annum (INSPIRE, 2003). These costs will be largely borne by the public sector bodies and they will be mainly incurred at the regional and local levels. It was more difficult to estimate the likely benefits associated with INSPIRE implementation but even a partial assessment of these benefits suggested that they would amount to somewhere between €1.2 and 1.8 billion a year. If this is the case the benefits of INSPIRE implementation might be of the order of six times the estimated costs.

The draft INSPIRE Directive was published by the European Commission in July 2004 (CEC, 2004). It establishes 'a legal framework for the establishment and operation of an Infrastructure for Spatial Information in Europe, for the purpose of formulating, implementing, monitoring and evaluating Community policies at all levels and providing public information.' It indicates that 'it focuses specifically on information needed to monitor and improve the state of the environment, including air, water, soil and the natural landscape' and re-assures readers that 'INSPIRE will not set off an extensive programme of new spatial data collection in the member states'. Instead 'it is designed to optimise the scope for exploiting the data that are available, by requiring the documentation of existing data, the implementation of services aimed at rendering the spatial data more accessible and interoperable, and by dealing with obstacles to the use of the spatial data'.

The draft Directive entered the co-decision process after its publication. In this procedure the European Parliament does not merely give its opinion but shares legislative power equally with the Council. In late 2006, the revised Directive was put before a conciliation committee made up of equal numbers of Council and Parliament representatives. This committee reached agreement on its contents and the Directive was formally ratified in March 2007 (CEC, 2007). As a result, the governments of all 27 European Union national member states must modify existing legislation or introduce new legislation to implement its provisions by May 2009.

Drafting teams have prepared implementation rules for the five main elements of INSPIRE that were defined in the Directive: that is metadata, spatial data specification, network services, data sharing, and monitoring and reporting. Most of these have been incorporated in legally binding regulations by the Commission. The Commission recognises that the development of implementing rules to guide subsequent work in the member states will require the participation of a large number of stakeholders from the member states. To assist in the work of the drafting teams, and to make the process as inclusive as possible, it has built up a network of Spatial Data Interest Communities (SDICs) throughout Europe. These SDICs bring together 'the human expertise of users, producers and transformers of spatial information, technical competence, financial resources and policies, with an interest to better use these resources for spatial data management and the development and operation of spatial information services' (Annoni and Craglia, 2005: 8). These SDICs are working alongside the Legally Mandated Organisations (LMOs) who are formally involved with respect to one or more elements of INSPIRE implementation.

The success of the INSPIRE initiative highlights the importance of developing an overall legal framework for a supranational SDI that ensures the commitment of the national member states to the project. It also demonstrates the need to mobilise the expertise that exists in these member states to develop implementing rules that are acceptable to users. As always, the devil is in the detail, but the prior commitment of the member states to the principle has made the task of building a consensus a more manageable one.

FUTURE DIRECTIONS

The above analysis has described the SDI phenomenon that has come into being over the last 15 years and identified some of the main trends that have emerged from this process to facilitate SDI implementation. It has also examined the different kinds of SDI that have developed at the sub-national, national and supra-national levels and illustrated their features with reference to three short case studies. The shift from SDI formulation to implementation has also been accompanied by a marked increase in the number of efforts that are being made to compare and evaluate SDI experiences. These can be broadly grouped into internal initiatives linked to overall performance measurement that are usually carried out by those directly involved, and external initiatives undertaken by the research community. For example, all three case study initiatives described above have developed their own internal structures for performance evaluation (Last, 2007; Zambon, 2007; MetroGIS, 2008). The case of INSPIRE is particularly interesting as monitoring and reporting has been identified as one of the five main elements of the initiative and work is under way to develop implementing rules for this purpose. Lance et al. (2006) provide a comprehensive review of related activities in other SDI initiatives.

A wide range of activities has also been undertaken by the research community to compare and evaluate SDI development and implementation. Some of these studies are a direct result of research undertaken for initiatives such as INSPIRE that commissioned a series of state of play studies of SDI development in all the European countries from the Spatial Applications Division of the University of Leuven (Vanderbroucke et al., 2008). However, the majority of this work stems from PhD and project-based research originating in the academic community. In addition to the generational studies quoted above, these range from questionnaire-based survey research of a sample of initiatives (Nedovic-Budic et al., 2004) to longitudinal case studies of a single country (Masser, 2005: Chapter 4). They also include detailed studies of specific topics such as SDI readiness (Delgado et al., 2005), access policies (van Loenen, 2006), data sharing partnerships (McDougall et al., 2007) and the experiences of national clearing houses (Crompvoets and Bregt, 2007). Another group of studies draws upon social science theoretical frameworks such as actor network theory (Harvey, 2001), the theory of planned behaviour (Wehn de Montalvo, 2003) and social learning processes (Rodriguez-Pabon, 2005).

It may be expected that the number and diversity of both internal and external initiatives will continue to increase as the field as a whole develops over the next few years. Nevertheless there are a number of important gaps that need to be filled in this work, particularly in the context of research in connection with the information age. In particular, the relationships between SDIs and e-government and the information society as a whole have yet to be explored in depth, particularly from the standpoint of e-government. SDI developments have also much in common with the experiences of other information infrastructures and Georgiadou et al. (2005) and de Man (2007) have already begun to explore this promising field.

ACKNOWLEDGEMENTS

Many people have helped me in the preparation of this chapter. In particular, I would like to thank Rebecca Last and Eric de Man for their very useful suggestions.

REFERENCES

ACIL Tasman (2008) *The Value of Spatial Information: The Impact of Modern Spatial Information Technologies on the Australian Economy.* Melbourne: Cooperative Research Centre for Spatial Information.

Annoni, A. and Craglia, M. (2005) 'Towards a directive establishing an infrastructure for spatial information in Europe (INSPIRE)', *Proc GSDI 8*, Cairo, Egypt (also available at www.gsdi.org).

Australia and New Zealand Land Information Council (ANZLIC) (1992) *Land Information Management in Australasia 1990–1992*. Canberra: Australia Government Publishing Service.

Burrough, P., Brand, M., Salge, F. and Schueller, K. (1993) 'The EUROGI vision', *GIS Europe*, 2(3): 30–1.

Butler, D. (2006) 'The web-wide world', *Nature*, 439: 776–8.

Commission of the European Communities, (CEC) (2004) *Proposal for a Directive of the European Parliament and the Council Establishing an Infrastructure for Spatial Information in the Community (INSPIRE)*, COM (2004) 516 final, Brussels: Commission of the European Communities.

Commission of the European Communities, (CEC) (2007) 'An Infrastructure for Spatial Information in the European Community (INSPIRE), Directive 2007/2/EC of the European Parliament and of the Council', *Official Journal of the European Union*, L108, 1–14.

Craglia, M., Goodchild, M. F., Annoni, A., Camara, G., Gould, M., Kuhn, W., Mark, D., Masser, I., Maguire, D., Liang, S. and Parsons, E. (2008) 'Next generation Digital Earth: A position paper from the Vespucci initiative for the advancement of geographic information science', *International Journal of SDI Research*, 3: 146–67.

Crompvoets, J. and Bregt, A. (2007) 'National spatial data clearinghouses 2000–2005', in H.J. Onsrud (ed.), *Research and Theory in Advancing Spatial Data Infrastructure Concepts*. Redlands: ESRI Press.

Delgado, T., Lance, K., Buck, M. and Onsrud, H.J. (2005) 'Assessing an SDI readiness index', *Proceedings GSDI 8*, Cairo, Egypt. (also available at www.gsdi.org)

De Man, E. (2007) 'Beyond spatial data infrastructures': There are no SDIs so what?', *International Journal of SDI Research*, 2: 1–23.

Department of the Environment (1987) *Handling Geographic Information: Report of the Committee of Enquiry Chaired by Lord Chorley*. London: HMSO.

Department of Sustainability and Environment (DSE) (2004) *Terms of Reference for the Victorian Spatial Council*. http://www.land.vic.gov.au (accessed 22 February 2011).

Executive Office of the President (1994) 'Coordinating geographic data acquisition and access, the National Spatial Data Infrastructure, Executive Order 12906', *Federal Register*, 59: 17671–74.

GeoConnections (2005) *The Canadian Geospatial Data Infrastructure: Better Knowledge for Better Decisions*. http://www.geoconnections.org.

GeoConnections (2006) *GeoConnections Annual Report 2005–6: Laying the Groundwork*. Ottawa: HM the Queen in Right of Canada, (also available at http://www.geoconnections.org).

Georgiadou, Y., Puri, S. and Sahay, S. (2005) 'Towards a research agenda to guide the implementation of spatial data infrastructures: A case study from India', *Int Jour of GIS* 19: 1113–30.

Harvey, F. (2001) 'Constructing GIS: Actor networks of collaboration', *URISA Journal*, 13(1): 29–37.

Hooghe, L. and Marks, G. (2003) 'Untravelling the central state, but how? Types of multi-level governance', *American Political Science Review*, 97: 233–43.

INSPIRE (2003) *Contribution to the Extended Impact Assessment of INSPIRE*, Ispra: Joint Research Centre.

Lance, K., Georgiadou T.Y. and Bregt, A. (2006) 'Understanding how and why practitioners evaluate SDI performance', *International Journal of SDI Research*, 1: 65–104.

van Loenen, B. (2006) *Developing Geographic Information Infrastructures: The Role of Information Policies*. Delft, Netherland: Delft University Press.

Last, R. (2007) *Performance evaluation for GeoConnections and the Canadian Geospatial Data Infrastructure, Paper Presented at the Multi-view Framework to Assess Spatial Data Infrastructures workshop*. Wageningen: The Netherlands, May 2007.

Lenk, M., von Doemming, A. and Mordhurst, R. (2008) 'Implementation of SDI in Germany GDI-DE technical architecture and organisation model', *Proceedings of the INSPIRE Conference*. Slovenia: Maribor.

McDougall, K., Rajabifard, A. and Williamson, I. (2007) 'A mixed method approach for evaluating spatial data sharing partnerships for spatial data infrastructure development. In H.J. Onsrud (ed.), *Research and Theory in Advancing Spatial Data Infrastructure Concepts*. Redlands: ESRI Press.

Masser, I. (1999) 'All shapes and sizes: The first generation of National Spatial Data Infrastructures', *International Journal of Geographical Information Science*, 13: 67–84.

Masser, I. (2005) *GIS Worlds: Creating Spatial Data Infrastructures*. Redlands: ESRI Press.

Masser, I. (2010) *Building European Spatial Data Infrastructures*, 2nd edn. Redlands: ESRI Press.

Masser, I. and Johnson, R. (2006) 'Implementing SDIs through effective networking: The MetroGIS Geospatial Data Collaborative', *GeoInformatics*, 9(6): 50–53.

Masser, I., Rajabifard, A. and Williamson, I. (2008) 'Spatially enabling governments through SDI implementation', *International Journal of Geographical Information Science*, 22: 5–20.

MetroGIS (2008) MetroGIS 2007 *Performance Measurement Report.* http://www.metrogis.org/benefits/perf_measure/2007_perfmeas_rept.pdf (last accessed 22 February 2011).

National Research Council (1993) *Toward a Coordinated Spatial Data Infrastructure for the Nation.* Mapping Science Committee, Washington DC: National Academy Press.

National Research Council (1999) *Distributed Geolibraries: Spatial Information Resources.* Mapping Science Committee, National Research Council, Washington D.C: National Academy Press.

Nedovic-Budic, Z., Pinto, J.K. and Warnecke, L. (2004) 'GIS database development and exchange: Interaction mechanisms and motivations', *URISA Journal,* 16(1): 15–29.

Office of Management and Budget (OMB) (1990) *Coordination of Surveying, Mapping and Related Spatial Data Activities.* Revised Circular A-16, Office of Management and Budget, Washington DC: Executive Office of the President.

Organisation for Economic Cooperation and Development (OECD) (2001) *Citizens as Partners: Information, Consultation and Public Participation in Policy Making.* Paris: OECD.

PIRA International Ltd, University of East Anglia and Knowledge Ltd. (2000) *Commercial Exploitation of Europe's Public Sector Information.* Luxembourg: EC DG INFSO.

Rajabifard, A., Feeney, M.E. and Williamson, I. (2003a) 'Spatial data infrastructures: Concept, nature and SDI hierarchy'. In I. Williamson, A. Rajabifard and M.E. Feeney, (eds), *Development of Spatial Data Infrastructures: from Concept to Reality.* London: Taylor & Francis.

Rajabifard, A., Feeney, M.E., Williamson, I. and Masser, I. (2003b) 'National spatial data infrastructures'. In I. Williamson, A. Rajabifard and M.E. Feeney, (eds), *Development of Spatial Data Infrastructures: From Concept to Reality.* London: Taylor & Francis.

Rajabifard, A., Binns, A., Masser, I. and Williamson, I. (2006) 'The role of sub-national government and the private sector in future spatial data infrastructures', *International Journal of Geographical Information Science*, 20: 727–41.

Robinson, M. and Burgess, B. (2006) 'The fifty states initiative: Building a strong NSDI', *GeoWorld*, September.

Rodriguez-Pabon, O. (2005) 'Cadre theoretique pour l'evaluation des infrastructures d'information geospatiale'. PhD thesis, Laval University, Quebec, Canada.

Vanderbroucke, D., Janssen, K. and van Osterhoven, J. (2008) 'INSPIRE State of play: Development of the NSDI in 32 European countries between 2002 and 2007', *Proc GSDI 10*, Trinidad (also available at www.gsdi.org).

Wehn de Montalvo, U. (2003) *Mapping the Determinants of Spatial Data Sharing.* Aldershot: Ashgate.

Zambon, M.L. (2007) 'INSPIRE drafting team monitoring and reporting status', 13th EC GI and GIS workshop, Porto, July 4th-6th. www.ec-gis.org/Workshops/13ec-gis/ (accessed 16 November 2008).

15

Spatial Data Infrastructure for Cadastres: Foundations and Challenges

Francis Harvey

INTRODUCTION

A key element of nearly every spatial data infrastructure (SDI) is data associated with land ownership – the cadastre. Because of its diverse and critical uses and significance the cadastre is for many the single most key element of an SDI. Cadastral information is key to connecting rights, restrictions, and responsibilities to land parcels; it is used for taxation in most countries around the world and often provides crucial ancillary information for government and private activities including flood abatement districts, soil protection areas, and countless more. For all the opportunities that cadastral information offers, the cadastre faces many challenges. Even though a major government investment in most countries it is far from a perfect system. Any cadastre is a complex and problem-laden infrastructure in its own right. Cadastres are being influenced by SDI-concepts, as the four cases taken up in this chapter evidence, but in various ways

according to existing and persisting institutions and cultures.

Indeed, around the world different approaches have developed to assure first order functions of the cadastre related to legislative mandates and second order functions arising from government policies and activities are supported at all levels of governance. Cadastres are becoming integral parts of SDI. Cadastral systems generally guarantee land title, but not necessarily the corresponding land parcel boundaries. Complex institutional, legal, and even political arrangements abound. As a result, transforming a cadastre to a SDI environment brings many challenges. The underlying issue of accuracy in its multiple facets looms large in cadastral discrepancies and continues to be an issue impacting the development of cadastral SDI. As straightforward as the underlying relationship between legalized ownership and official records of title and boundaries may seem, actual relationships can be impossibly complex resulting in the cadastral portion of any SDI facing grave challenges. This chapter engages these challenges as GIS and society issues connected to the fundamental geographical problem of formalizing land access and use, the problem of serving multiple state and private interests through the cadastral infrastructure, and the integration of the cadastral infrastructure into an SDI, especially the relationship between investments in technology and civil society–political society relationships. The discussion takes up selected examples from around the world.

The chapter reviews literature on the social role of the cadastre and its role in SDI before considering the challenges facing cadastres. The conclusion points to ongoing research and recent conceptual developments and stresses the importance of synoptically understanding the development of cadastral SDI in its historical, cultural, and political context as a means of governance.

Opportunities and challenges for cadastral spatial data infrastructure

The cadastre holds many opportunities that are quintessential to an SDI. As land availability for economical activities has been essential for all livelihoods, societies that ideologically commit to the preservation of individual land ownership have required some means of regulating, ensuring, and guaranteeing land property records. While differences in definitions abound (see later discussion), this chapter takes the assurance of these functions to be the primary and first order mandate for a cadastre in capitalist societies. One good starting point for putting the broad scope and significance of cadastral SDI in context is the recently published *National Land Parcel Data: A Vision for the Future* (National Research Council [NRC], 2007), which lays out a US perspective on opportunities for development of cadastral SDI. This publication underscores the importance of the cadastre for SDI.

Cadastral systems (including databases) describe the rights, interests, and values of property, which when systematically collected and maintained "… represent the distribution of the real property assets of a community and its ownership, form the basis for all land use and zoning decisions, and represent the location of residences, businesses and public lands. In other words, almost every aspect of government and business can be associated with a land parcel" (NRC, 2007: ix). Knowledge of land ownership is crucial to much taxation and many ongoing and planned activities. The perspective in the NLPD report emphasizes the importance of making land parcel data easily available to a host of agencies and individuals ranging from emergency response, government planning, local citizens, and investors. Cadastral data in an SDI is key to many government and private uses of geographic information in the United States and around the world. The opportunities are significant, yet the implementation of digital cadastres lags in the United States: according to the report around 30 percent of the parcels still lack digital data, mainly in rural counties. The flip side of the development is that many urban areas have multiple digitalized parcel datasets for their territories, exacerbating accuracy issues.

The Cadastre 2014 document (Kaufmann and Steudler, 1998) synthesizes a number of revised perspectives on the complexities and implementation of cadastres around the world, particularly in lower income countries. Starting from the realization among international geodesists that the cadastre with its traditional emphasis on reliable well-defined processes and guarantees of land ownership security was not up to challenges arising in the growing importance of environmental concerns and networked approaches to government organizations (see also Bogaerts, 1997), it switches focus from perfecting processes and registration and integrating the cadastre in land information systems that unify land registration and mapping. Cadastre 2014 lays out an ambitious approach to flexibly expanding the significance of the cadastre to support the broad array of applications connected to the cadastre in an SDI.

International activities have developed significant national and regional cadastral systems that support first order cadastral-related functions and support an wide-ranging variety of planning and conservation activities (Rajabifard et al., 2007). National cadastral systems are quite different (Dale, 1967), however in many countries they correspond in large degree to the cadastral system first developed (Bogaerts and Zevenbergen, 2001). The decades of these activities have led to very mixed cadastral results and sometimes quite distinct negative consequences for indigenous inhabitants (Turnbull, 1989, 1998; Barry and Fourie, 2002). Reflecting issues from Cadastre 2014, the experiences and assessment have led to a re-orientation of cadastres from a narrow focus on the organization of land title and surveying boundaries to much broader engagement with the various economical, cultural, and political relationships of people among themselves and to land. Work in this area has also drawn on anthropologically rooted studies of gender issues that are key to land use arrangement and inheritance (Arua and Okorji, 1997; Bruce, 1998; Fraser, 2007). Incorporating these dimensions of social organization into a cadastral SDI can be extremely complex. The scope and purpose of the cadastre in the SDI context is understandably wide reaching. It finds usages in matters related to rights, restrictions, registration of land and space, for example, zoning; it is also used for taxation, for a multitude of reference purposes (e.g., soil protection area's, monuments, and so on). In addition to boundaries of parcels many cadastres include other objects including factories, office buildings, agricultural structures, apartments, single family homes, infrastructure facilities, utilities, and so forth. Indeed, because of this breadth, the cadastre becomes the key and seminal reference map for government activities.

European countries have engaged the opportunities of the cadastre for some time, developing a number of applications that have been institutionally embedded, for example, the German taxation of agricultural land – the *Reichsbodenschätzung* – which began in the 1930s. In many European countries realization of the opportunities is mainly a matter of improving technology and implementing solutions within existing institutional arrangements (Hespanha et al., 2006). Many European countries have relied on cadastral data for decades to help in identifying protected areas, soil classes, and so on (Remetey-Fülöpp, 2003). Large differences in cadastres continue to persist in spite of over 20 years of attempts to reconcile differences (Bogaerts, 1997; Rajabifard et al., 2006). Newer research activities within Europe focus on developing technologies for three-dimensional cadastres (Molen, 2003; Stoter and Salzmann, 2003), improving the underlying conceptual models of the cadastre (Van Oosterom et al., 2006), and supporting new range of official mandates, particularly in the domain of agriculture (Bogaerts, Williamson and Fendel, 2002).

The many opportunities for cadastral SDI around the globe are inseparable from the challenges, which are often ancient in origin, yet modern in consequence. Both opportunities and challenges manifest themselves in vastly different ways around the world. Any published work related to the cadastre prepared for an international audience must acknowledge that major terminological, technological, and conceptual differences impair discussions (Lemmen and Van Oosterom, 2001). First, there is no common uniform terminology. For example, "deed" in the United States means something different in South Africa (Dale, 1997; Rajabifard et al., 2007). The terminological differences are exceedingly complex and tied to historical developments of national cultures and institutions (Harvey, 1998). This chapter, with examples from around the world, makes it necessary to spend an unusual amount of time on the underlying differences, although this discussion will necessarily be abbreviated compared to monographs addressing differences in international usage. One key terminological issue reflects the more recent international preference for the term land administration (Dale and McLaughlin, 1999; Van Der Molen, 2002) over surveying and cadastre, thus signaling a shift to a broader perspective on social interactions and relationships connected to land access and land tenure (Van Der Molen, 2002) than the traditional cadastral emphasis on boundaries and ownership. This distinction is significant for later discussion of the challenges for cadastral SDI.

Technologies used for the cadastre vary widely. In several countries technological innovations since World War II have created vibrant professions and institutions that produce world-wide leading technologies and organizations of cadastral information. In most countries, the effects of such innovations have left their mark in the automation and use of high-end technologies for surveying the computer-based organization, but usually co-exist side-by-side with technologies developed in 19th and early 20th centuries. Economical, political, and social factors lead to curious mixtures of the old and the new. In other countries, the impact of innovations is limited in scope and the majority of cadastral information is collected and maintained using technologies that often originate in early modern and ancient times such as plane tables.

The conceptual variations between cadastral systems likewise differ immensely. Some countries and cultures maintain a very strong connection between the administrative organization of the cadastre and peoples' identification with this official instrument of power. The governance of the cadastre in these countries is very closely connected to state policies and the roles of citizens. Other countries have variable ways to engage and support administrative and official uses of the cadastre. In a number of colonized countries the resistance to the cadastre is an integral part of resistance to state authority

(Food and Agricultural Organization of the United Nations (FAO), n.d.; Powelson, 1988; Dale, 1997; Augustinus, 2001; Barry and Fourie, 2002). In other countries, the resistance is more subvert and an official cadastre with limited relationship to actual land access may co-exist with adaptive local arrangements.

If this discussion seems to lead off the topic of cadastral SDI, it is necessary because any cadastral SDI unavoidable inherits these complexities, summarized in Table 15.1. While the cadastre's functionality in an abstract sense is a perfect and necessary element of most SDI, the reality can readily be limited by terminological, technological, and conceptual complexities before even getting to the challenges noted above (Harvey, 2006a).

The next section of this chapter turns to engage specifically the opportunities of the cadastral information for an SDI and also takes up the challenges in more detail. The key challenge of relating the cadastre's documentation to the dynamic world is it should relate to is the focus of section three. Section four then examines and contrasts different approaches to integrating cadastres into SDIs emphasizing approaches in the United States, Poland, Norway, and Western Australia. The concluding section summarizes these issues and takes up the research and methodological challenges for ongoing work on cadastral SDI.

Table 15.1 Summary of issues impacting the development of cadastral SDI

Complicating Factors for Cadastral SDI
National, professional, and cultural differences
Existing information technology implementations of the cadastre
Disagreements between concepts and laws
Complex rights, obligations, and restrictions to land
Different roles of the cadastre in governance
Political issues and factions
Institutional barriers
Older legacy technologies and bureaucracies

SDI: Complex infrastructures for data sharing and coordination

Cadastral SDI is complex due to more than the factors discussed above. The networked data sharing and coordination of activities in SDI increases, among other things, the number of participants. Other factors, notably existing institutional arrangements and inter-institutional agreements of both formal and informal nature have great impacts. Different administrative organizations, politics, and so on lead to entrenched approaches. Consequentially, as an article on formal modeling of SDI discusses, multiple perspectives on SDIs have found currency in approaches to implementing these complex infrastructures (Hjelmager et al., 2008). The authors distinguish five viewpoints:

- enterprise viewpoint;
- information viewpoint;
- computation viewpoint;
- engineering viewpoint;
- technology viewpoint.

These are drawn from the reference model for open distributed processing, which also covers different levels of abstraction and constitutes a framework for coherently connecting the parts of a SDI (ISO/TEC, 1998). As this article notes, the SDI concept is very broad, but involves a set of networked geospatial databases that can be put together in an endless variety of combinations and transformations. The actual organization and uses of an SDI support the needs of distinct spatial data communities: producers, brokers, users, mediators, and so on. By facilitating and coordinating the exchange and sharing of spatial data, an SDI becomes a key infrastructure in addressing challenges and fulfilling mandates of the multiple communities.

Reflecting this, the Global Spatial Data Infrastructure (GSDI) organization several years prior already defined a SDI as:

... the relevant base collection of technologies, policies and institutional arrangements that facilitate the availability of and access to spatial data. The SDI provides a basis for spatial data discovery, evaluation, and application for users and providers within all levels of government, the commercial sector, the non-profit sector, academia and by citizens in general. (GSDI, 2001: 8)

The GSDI Cookbook goes on to note the following key characteristics. First, an SDI is a reliable environment with theoretically unlimited access to geographical information that supports applications that "run" on its infrastructure. Second, it consists of multiple geographical information databases and methods to access the data; the need for organizational agreements is explicitly acknowledged to coordinate and administer the SDI at the relevant scales. Third, and finally, coordinating a SDI will generally lead to the creation of oversight organizations or programs.

Similarly, Groot and McLaughlin propose this definition:

The networked spatial databases and data handling facilities, the complex of institutional, organizational, technological, human, and economic resources which interact with one another and underpin the design, implementation and maintenance of mechanisms facilitating the sharing, access to and responsible use of spatial data at an affordable cost for a specific application domain or enterprise. (2000: 3)

Since their first mention in the mid-1990s has brought easier access than ever before to geographical information (see Chapter 14 by Masser). The creation of multiple SDIs with coverage of an area seem far more to be the norm (Harvey and Tulloch, 2006) than the original centralized vision of hierarchical SDIs (Federal Geographic Data Committee, 1997) in many countries. This has been established around the world and researchers have come to recognize that organizational issues are still the greatest challenge to SDI creation and maintenance (Crompvoets et al., 2004; GeorgiadouPuri and Sahay, 2005; de Man, 2006; PuriSahay and Georgiadou, 2006; Rajabifard et al., 2006). Each of the five perspectives, described for formal modeling, never stands on its own, but must be seen in connection with the social and institutional dimensions. Herein lies perhaps the greatest challenge for developing cadastral SDI.

Cadastral SDI: Core functionality for any SDI

While for many researchers and practitioners working with SDI, the cadastre is one of the key datasets, or one of the key datasets, for a SDI (Rajabifard et al., 2007). The diverse roles and organization of cadastres and the social and institutional complexity of SDIs means that cadastral SDIs are more characterized by the diversity. This is evident in a study conducted in Europe (Remetey-Fülöpp, 2003) surveying 20 countries' organization, use, and special features of their cadasters related to developments of their national SDI.

European national developments have to be seen in context of the still evolving INSPIRE program, which while focusing on environmental data, relies on cadastral data for key reporting, and a number of analysis functions required by its European Community Directive (European Commission, 2007).

Stepping back, discussions in the 1960s through 1980s are clear antecedents of more recent cadastral SDI developments. The Multi-purpose Land Information System (MPLIS) began with visionary concepts to place cadastral information among the key information used in developing GIS capacities for local government (National Oceanic and Atmospheric Administration, n.d.; NRC, 1980; McLaughlin, 1984; Tulloch, Niemann Jr and Epstein, 1996). The Framework concept of the US NSDI developed this further, including parcel-related land ownership information among the core of the NSDI architecture (Federal Geographic Data Committee, 1997), which was a conceptual configuration that was significant for SDI developments around the world (Rhind, 1997).

Cadastre: Ambiguous concepts for conflicting interests

The cadastre retains its core significance for SDIs today, but in order to begin to grasp its larger roles in SDI, we should also turn to core concepts behind the vast investments in cadastral information over millennia. Since the Roman empire, cadastral mapping has been integral to governance, especially the control of land resources and accounting of revenues in Europe (Kain and Baigent, 1992). Cadastres have always been concerned with land, law, and people (Dale, 1967), yet it is the relationship between the three and the political-economical situation that vary greatly. While the cadastre can be used for fiscal, legal, or multiple purposes, the primary motivations and organization of the cadastre constrain possible uses and indicate a great deal about a cadastre's role for government interventions in the relationships between land and people.

The cadastre's historical origins lie in the organization of territories acquired through Roman conquests (Dilke, 1985) and this usage reflects the significance of the cadastre for controlling an area and creating a territory that supports government interests. After coming to power, Napoleon implemented a cadastre in France and occupied areas with multiple objectives, one of which was the collection of tax revenue (Kain and Baigent, 1992). A long list of cadastres developed in the cause of conquest and colonization receives significant attention in post-colonial literature (Andrews, 1975; Barrett, Sahay and Walsham, 2001), but the primary goal of inventorying and mapping of land for the purpose of government territorial control is shared by all cadastres from antiquity to today (Harvey, 2006a; Kivelson, 2006; Sikor, 2006; van Oosterom et al., 2006; Masser, Rajabifard and Williamson, 2007; Permanent Committee on the Cadastre in the European Union, 2007).

What varies immensely is the institutional organization of the cadastre. The multitude of possibilities for coordinating cadastral activities through different ministries and departments, through involvement of different professions, etc. lies beyond the scope of this chapter. However these are key to the development of cadastral SDI, as recent discussions in Europe Community, related to the implementation of the INSPIRE directive at national levels, show (Permanent Committee on the Cadastre in the European Union, 2007). Focusing on the GIS and society issues connected to developing cadastres, the considerations here take up the underlying ways in which surveys of land ownership, usually via boundaries, are connected to records of land ownership and rights (deeds, title, and so forth). This relates to the relatively wide-spread problem in which formalized records of land ownership only partially correspond to actual use and when boundaries, recorded on paper or databases, only partially correspond to the actual boundaries on the ground. Discrepancies are in most countries a way of life left for the good-will among people to resolve or, failing that, the courts to resolve. Surprising is the degree to which these discrepancies persist in cadastres (Verdery, 1994, 2003; Bogaerts, Williamson and Fendel, 2002).

Important variations of cadastral SDI can be assessed by distinguishing four aspects of a cadastral infrastructure:

1 legal and organizational characteristics;
2 levels of planning and control;
3 aspects of multipurpose cadastres;
4 responsibilities of the public and the private sectors (based on Cadastre, 2014).

The legal characteristics of cadastres are usually described by a country's civil laws; in some countries they are part of legal statutes, and in several countries they are part of established common law. The majority of cadastres register ownership through titles, some rely on deeds and some use both deeds and titles. Registration is usually required, but in some countries it is optional and in several some registration is required and other is voluntary. Most countries protect people's rights by registration. Also, the

majority of cadastres use the parcel as the basic unit of the cadastre, but some use property, and at least one uses name. In most countries the cadastral infrastructure includes both land registration and land survey. Usually, cadastral maps are part of the register. A key issue for cadastre information is the type of boundary, fixed or unfixed, and the reference for legally determining the location of boundaries. Most cadastres rely on fixed boundaries, that is legally valid specifications of the location of a boundary; several cadastres use unfixed boundaries, or boundaries that can be, to put it simply, negotiated to some degree. In cadastres, the legally valid location of a boundary follows several principles. In most cadastres, monuments, measurements, and coordinates provide legal clarity about boundary location. A significant number of cadastres rely on cadastral maps to legally define boundaries (Kaufmann and Steudler, 1998).

Most cadastres are managed by one public organization, but several separate land registration from cadastral mapping. This is related to most cadastres' mandates originating in the need to support legal and/or fiscal needs of the state. Over time, the potential of cadastral data for all types of government activities has led to the cadastre becoming the keystone, enabling other government activities involving land including base mapping, assessment, land use planning, environmental and conservation activities, and so on. With this centrality, most cadastres still remain in the hands of the state (Kaufmann and Steudler, 1998). This is also tied to the strong significance of the state's guarantee of the legal security of land title in capitalist societies (de Soto, 2000).

Returning to the discrepancies, the roles of the cadastre vary distinctly. The survey reported in the Cadastre 2014 document suggests that weak links between land registration and cadastral mapping are key weaknesses. In some countries this is due to legal basis for the cadastre lacking regulations, or clear regulations and guidelines to address discrepancies. Most of these countries simply create a system to administer the title to land, there may even be no central inventory of titles, and no systematic linkage of land registration to cadastral mapping. In countries maintaining systems based on traditional rights, the overlaps between cadastre-based land registration and cadastral mapping to traditional rights can require complicated resolutions, which because of their complexity and often political nature, remain unresolved, passing on over generations and prone to abuse by local and national elites. The resulting legal ambiguity regarding land rights is marked, but reflects often less crass conflicts found in higher income countries around the world, where the clarification of legal rights is constrained by the lack of a unified system for recording these rights and connecting them to land parcels. This problem can be systematic when the land registry defines legal ownership rights, but is not connected to cadastral mapping, which usually records information about decisions made under public law and private law regarding land by different governmental organizations. This can erode owners' legal rights (Dale, 1997; Kain and Baigent, 1992; Van Dijk, 2003).

Integration of cadastres into SDI

As the preceding discussion makes evident, the integration of cadastres into SDIs varies considerably. Table 15.1 summarizes key factors influencing the cadastre developed for particular countries and areas. Social, organizational, and technological factors have noted impacts on the development. The consideration of cadastral SDI integration involves all these factors. The following section considers key factors with an emphasis on issues for GIS and society research through four case studies, Norway, Poland, the United States, and Western Australia.

Cadastres and SDIs in Norway

The Norwegian government has recently made considerable investments in developing a national SDI in which an enhanced cadastre plays a key role. In 2005, Digital Norway was established as the responsible organization. The main GeoNorge portal to cadastral data and other geographic information is to be found at http://www.geoNorge.no. GeoNorge involves public sector agencies from national, county, and municipal levels and indirectly some private sector companies. The infrastructure has been developed with the European Commission directive on INSPIRE, as well as other EU activities in mind, but the main focus is on supporting broad access to geographic information services. With e-government concepts guiding the development, a key part of GeoNorge's activities is creating and maintaining the underlying organizational structure and technological framework. All agencies participating in GeoNorge pay a yearly fee and sign a contract that they will provide data to the National Mapping Authority. The cadastre and mapping agency is the primary government body in charge of GeoNorge. It gurantees data quality and data access (Klathen, 2007).

The traditional cadastre in Norway consisted of separate a land registry and a cadastral survey maintained by different ministries. Both have been fully digitized and have been joined into an online service. A 1980 revision to the national cadastral law created a uniform system for property identification. A new register has since replaced the old registry and cadastre and adds addresses and building information. While it is administered by the Norwegian Mapping Authority it is updated by municipalities and the district courts that are responsible for the land registry (Remetey-Fülöpp, 2003).

Digital Norway has a broad social mandate and undertakes key activities to regulate interactions between partners, both administratively and technically. International and national standards are important in ensuring that regional and municipal institutions develop web services, map viewers, metadata, and portals that avoid redundancies. Both Web Mapping Services (WMS) and

Web Feature Services (WFS) are widely used by applications provided by different public institutions (Norway Digital, 2008). Following e-government concepts, Norwegian citizens can even personalize GeoNorge. The portal also allows for the inclusion of personal data as well (Klathen, 2007).

Cadastres and SDIs in Poland

While the cadastre is well established and maintained through national regulations in Poland (Ostrowski, 2000; Tanic, 2000), standardized technical procedures, and laws, the integration of the cadastre and SDI faces many challenges arising in the historical complexity of Poland (Davies, 2001). While more recent SDI developments rest on well-crafted technical and organization solutions, underlying socio-historical discrepancies impacting cadastres hinder the rapid uptake of SDI concepts and architectures.

While Poland's history is complex, key challenges for cadastre and SDI integration are also likely to arise from historical developments that are very pronounced in the territory of the modern Polish state. Particularly, the ways how the pre-World War I cadastre had been updated following World War II and the underlying organization of the cadastre are key issues. The situation is particularly complicated because from 1795 to 1918 Poland was divided into three parts by the Austro-Hungarian, German, and Russian empires. Each created its own cadastral system, although the cadastre in the Russian part is often characterized by the absence of clear boundaries (Blobaum, 1995). The German and Austro-Hungarian cadastral systems were similar in concept and provided for clearly defined parcel boundaries, but different in execution, particularly the siting of monuments, which, when physically well done, allowed later administrations to readily reconstruct the cadastral boundaries from stable monuments in the new legal and political system (Federowski, 1974). The Russian empire only registered titles (Mikoś, 1992). After World War II, the documentation for these systems, while legally invalid,

became often the source documents for new cadastres when available. Many documents were destroyed. The loss of life in World War II alone is staggering: Poland lost 20 percent of its total population. The well known near complete destruction of Warsaw is well-known. Rural areas, in general may have suffered less in the war, but the unparalleled migrations of people after the close of the war and the shift in boundaries meant that cadastral records from before both world wars, while still the best documentation, often had very little to do with actual boundaries of land ownership and use. This was noted and the socialist state, while redefining the concept of cadastre, did go on to develop and maintain cadastral records. Land consolidation programs were funded by the state under local initiative (Fedorowski, 1974). Progressive policies to assure land ownership records were in place, although frequently undercut by command economy policies and wide-spread loss of land value, both real and perceived (Palmer, Munro-Faure and Rembold, 2003).

As a consequence by 1989, when the famous round-table meetings took place in Warsaw between Solidarność and the communist government leading to a peaceful revolution and transition from a command to market economy, some areas had very accurate and well-maintained cadastres. Other areas had cadastres that were accurate to specifications and data from 1914, or earlier, but were hopelessly out of date. Because of land's marginal value in the socialist economy, many transactions were not recorded, including state taking of land for right-of-ways. Discrepancies in rural areas were as high as 40 percent between cadastral records and actual land ownership. Informal land tenure arrangements flourished. Urban areas also face high discrepancies, but the complexities surpass the political will of governing parties to make changes (World Bank, 2005; Zaręba and Zoń, 2007). In this regard, it is worth noting that Poland still has no restitution law for private property. Occasional civil cases arise, but in spite of the degree of issues, Poland has no legal framework for resolving these issues (Sikora, 2004).

For the cadastre and SDI in Poland, the 1990s were a transitional period of modest changes. What change did occur was a sweeping reform of government that strengthened county governments in various ways, including moving responsibility for the cadastre of land and buildings from local municipalities to counties (*powiaty*). Discussions with the European Commission about EU membership were accompanied by an increase in sizeable investments in the cadastre as the basis for assuring the free conveyance of property. Other notable EU related activities for the Polish cadastre include funding for the Land Parcel Information System (LPIS) required by Common Agricultural Policy (Orlińska and Jarząbek, 2004). Work on LPIS began in the 2000s and it is now operational.

By the end of the 1990s Poland had begun to develop concepts and policy frameworks for also creating SDIs through the national government to support local, regional, and national administrative activities. These concepts and policies have gone through several revisions. In 2004, the current policy and legal framework was put into place. It involves coordination among national-level ministries and the successive roll-out of standards, technical infrastructure, training, and administrative support for facilitating SDI concepts (Spatial Applications Division, 2008). The cadastral domain has been particularly significant for government-internal developments of the SDI and most counties in Poland maintain at least some data following national standards SWDE (Bydłosz and Parzych, 2007). The large number of software systems used for cadastral data has been an opportunity for SWDE and other standards to take up key roles in facilitating data sharing and coordination to fulfill administrative requirements (Knoop and Wilkowski, 2003; Zaręba and Zoń, 2007; Spatial Applications Division, 2008).

Cadastres and SDIs in the United States

While other countries and jurisdictions, including the ones considered here, seem to have leapt past recent SDI developments at the national level in the United States, the United States still has both historically and regionally some of the most significant examples of cadastral SDI development world wide. Historically, the clearest statement of the vision that becomes cadastral SDI are the publications appearing under auspices of the NRC in the early 1980s related to the Multipurpose Cadastre (NRC, 1980, 1984, 1990, 1993; National Research Council (US) Panel on a Multipurpose Cadastre, 1983). These reports lay out a framework for policy and scientific work that precedes the US NSDI and articulate the centrality of parcel data for SDIs. As developed later in policy guidelines and Federal Geographic Data Committee (FGDC) working group activities NSDI was very important. In this regard, it is also important to note that United States has no national legislation nor regulation of cadastral matters: this remains the purview of individual states. The need for a national cadastral standard has recently been discussed in great detail (NRC, 2007).

This situation reflects the devolved organization of government in the United States (Krane, 1998; Nedovic-Budic and Pinto, 2000; Putnam, 2000; Jacoby et al., 2002; Rahn and Thomas, 2002; Center for Technology in Government, 2003; Harvey, 2006b). Policy guidelines, federal laws, and federal regulations related to the NSDI have limited influence on state, tribal, regional, and local authorities. No legislation defining the NSDI, nor mandating components of the NSDI, has ever been passed by Congress (Masser, 1998), which would be the vehicle to create a legal framework for jurisdictions and private enterprises across the country. Federal government funding for pilot NSDI and ongoing projects has had significant regional impact (FGDC, 2005).

The NSDI guidelines and specifications, however, retain a key role as references and concepts for state, tribal, regional, and local jurisdictions, however flexibly in practice they may be applied. This is in fact a principle of the NSDI framework, reflecting the devolved and in many instances fractured nature of territorial governance in the United States (FGDC, 1997). Numerous, far too many to list or summarize here, STRL SDI activities create a multitude of marked successful integration of cadastral and SDI activities. State-supported activities in Wisconsin, regional activities in the Minnesotan Twin Cities metropolitan area, ongoing San Diego county and municipality collaboration, Lexington Fayetter Urban County government work, and Portland, Oregon regional planning activities would belong on any list of successful regional activities that integrate cadastral information into an SDI. Given alone the over 3200 counties and 59,000 units of local government, there are also a good number of cadastral SDI developments that have struggled, or even failed, before being abandoned (Tulloch et al., 1997; Nedovic-Budic and Pinto, 2000; Johnson, Nedovic-Budic and Covert, 2001; Harvey and Tulloch, 2003; Nedovic-Budic, Pinto and Warnecke, 2004; Harvey and Tulloch, 2006; Tulloch, 2008).

Cadastres and SDIs in Australia

Mandated under state laws, and an intrinsic part of the country's development (Williamson, 1994), Australia's cadastre has evolved to become an integral part of the Australian SDI (ASDI) to support multipurpose needs of citizens, government, and industry. A federation with a parliamentary democracy, the nine states and territories of Australia carry responsibility for the cadastre. The earlier division of cadastral surveys and land title in two separate systems has largely been replaced by one government department responsible for both. In Western Australia, for example, a project was begun by DOLA in the 1990s to redevelop the existing cadastral database and replace the paper cadastral map system. Known as Smart Plan, the new cadastral system included an online viewer application that is integrated into the Australian SDI. Since then, cadastral approaches across Australia have also undergone a transformation to become a multipurpose register of interests integrated into an SDI.

Overall, the Australian SDI follows a hierarchical organization model and is connected to state policies and national-level discussions and coordination. At the top, an inter-governmental council (ANZLIC – Australian New Zealand Land Information Council) leads development of the ASDI. In the Commonwealth of Australia, the Commonwealth Office of Spatial Data Management (OSDM) administrates under guidance of an executive policy group and a management group.

The most significant aspect of Australian cadastral SDI integration of relevance to GIS and society research is the great significance recent policies have embraced in broadly situating the cadastre and taking up diverse concepts of land access and rights in reformulating the cadastre as a key part of a land administration focused strategy. Embracing a broad concept of the multiple roles of the cadastre for citizens, government, and industry, land administration has become in Australia the emphasis for integrating existing cadastral information into the SDI. This concept is connected to increasing recognition in Australia that the traditional cadastral administration is facing its limits given a broad set of changes. In using cadastral information in the growing complex administration of land and property rights, implicit property rights are being separated in order to allow laws and regulations to deal with them independently. For example, in wetland regulations, the concept of ownership is undergoing evolution (Lyons, Cottrell, and Davies, 2004). In Western Australia, work on a framework to include all relevant information for an area that appears on the title or supplementary documents is called the Register of Interests (ROI), which will provide a single source of information on interests in land, sea, or air when completed (Department of Land Administration, 2006).

Through the Landgate SDI, the Western Australian Shared Land Information Platform (SLIP) supports cross-governmental access to information from DOLA and other agencies on active land market activities, the assessment of land, land taxation, planning, development, local government and utilities management, emergency management, and other functions. The broad audience for these applications and re-consideration of the cadastre in an SDI-based approach stand out.

CONCLUSION

As all cases make clear, SDI concepts serve as the foundation for re-visioning a new organization of the cadastre part of each nation's evolving understanding of key land related issues. Cadastres in the four regions taken up in this chapter are being influenced by SDI-concepts, but in various ways according to existing and persisting institutions and cultures. In each region, SDI-concepts serve to enable a new institutional platform for moving beyond the traditional cadastre's emphasis on parcel boundaries and management of land transactions to approaching these records as part of society's mandates for evolving concepts of land administration. In the case of Norway, the centralization of cadastral records has gone hand-in-hand with facilitation of multi-agency projects and collaboration. Parallel to these developments, the cadastral records have also been made accessible for Norwegians. In Poland, progress has been made on facilitating inter-agency collaboration in an SDI framework and regional SDI, although historically rooted factors still impede the integration of cadastral SDI. In contrast, the devolved nature of US government organization has been the fertile grounds for 1000s of cadastral SDIs, some of which are unparalleled for their successes, although failures and partial successes bear witness to the complexities of creating sustainable governance

arrangements to guide cadastral SDI development and integration. Australia stands out for the many dynamic e-government-based approaches to integrating cadastral SDI in new arrangements that take up the challenges arising from changing societal concepts of how land administration should be taking place. Support for first and second order cadastral functions is evolving in different ways.

Table 15.2 summarizes how complicating factors show themselves in each case taken up in this chapter. The distinct paths taken by each region or country to develop a cadastral SDI are quite evident, even in this very simplified abstraction of the complex issues. Certainly, on the ground, the complexity of cadastral issues means that the simplifications of Table 15.2 reflect only generalities for these factors. From the resources consulted in the preparation of this paper, it was not possible to provide reliable entries for the evaluation of political issues and factions in the cases of Norway and Australia. Even without this information, the complexity of the arrangements across agencies, institutions, political groups, technologies, and so forth remain vastly complex. Modeling SDIs following the five system development perspectives in a holistic fashion that adequately accounts for these complications remains an enormous challenge for practitioners and researchers.

In all of these developments, it is evident that distinct factors complicate the development of cadastral SDI in each county. Cultural differences stand out here, evidenced in Australia by the engagement with aboriginal rights or in Poland shown through the different historical organizations of local cadastre. Also, information technology implementations vary. Governments in the United States have rich experiences with 1990s data sharing approaches and the transition to cloud-computing approaches and mobile systems has taken place on top of these established approaches to information technology. In comparison, countries that took up SDI-concepts somewhat later, such as Norway,

Table 15.2 Issues impacting the development of cadastral SDI identified in each case

Complicating Factors for Cadastral SDI	Norway	Poland	United States	Australia
National, professional, and cultural differences	Local and national administrations	Cadastre from other professional fields	Devolution leads to distinct regional administrative cultures	Indigenous and other rights from European-based cadastre
Existing information technology implementations of the cadastre	Integrated within national e-government framework	Emphasis on administrative activities	Disparate projects on widely established commercial software platforms	Integration of cadastre into state and national approaches to SDI
Disagreements between concepts and laws	Challenges of bureaucracy in a centralized approach	Historically grounded disparities	Flexibility of local approaches reflect regional and local politics	Merging European-based concepts with indigenous and other rights
Complex rights, obligations, and restrictions to land	Systematized in nationally codified cadastre	Discrepancies enhanced by flexible interpretation of statutes	Title insurance system provides assurances	Changing conceptual understanding of land title and ownership
Different roles of the cadastre in governance	Centralized coordination	Mandatory procedures for administration	Title has a key role in taxation; maps more limited	National coordination connected to regional flexibility
Political issues, factions, institutional barriers, older legacy technologies, and bureaucracies	No assessment established bureaucracies	Populist challenges to altering the status quo bureaucratic barriers and hierarchies	Disparaged under populist sentiment towards taxation fragmentation of local governance	No assessment part of new governance policies

have been able to forge full speed ahead in following e-government concepts and create new infrastructure. Of special importance to each country's cadastral SDI integration activities is accounting for institutional boundaries. Further research on how each country addresses these issues will be significant for GIS and society scholarship on the relationship between geographic information technologies and evolving concepts and practices of governance. As SDI-concepts change, the cadastre evolves, but its centrality for many aspects of government and private economic life remain un-eclipsed. In comparing these four countries' developments, the importance of changing social values points to the continued importance

of GIS and society research for SDI and cadastres alike.

ACKNOWLEDGEMENTS

Thanks are due the three anonymous reviewers of an earlier version for their insightful and thorough comments. I would also like to acknowledge comments offered by Dr Gianluca Miscione and Dr Yola Georgiadou, who offered helpful remarks on this version, which I believe add to the chapter's clarity. Portions of this work have been supported by NSF Geography and Spatial Sciences award 0522257 and by a Marie

Curie International Reintegration Grant within the 6th European Community Framework Programme.

REFERENCES

Andrews, J.H. (1975) *A Paper Landscape. The Ordnance Survey in Nineteenth-Century Ireland*. Oxford: Clarendon Press.

Arua, E.O. and Okorji, E.C. (1997) *Multidimensional Analysis of Land Tenure Systems in Eastern Nigeria*, http://www.fao.org/sd/LTdirect/LR972/w6728t14.htm (accessed 9 June 2004).

Augustinus, C. (2001) *The Use of new Forms of Spatial Information, not the Cadastre, to Provide Tenure Security in Informal Settlements*, http://users.iafrica.com/a/au/augusart/online_nairobi.html (accessed 31August 2005).

Barrett, M., Sahay, S. and Walsham, G. (2001) 'Information technology and social transformation: GIS for forestry management in India', *The Information Society*, 17: 5–20.

Barry, M. and Fourie, C. (2002) 'Analysing cadastral systems in uncertain situations: A conceptual framework based on soft systems theory', *International Journal of Geographical Information Science*, 16(1): 23–40.

Blobaum, R.E. (1995) *Rewolucja: Russian Poland 1904–1907*. Ithaca, NY: Cornell University Press.

Bogaerts, T. (1997) 'Cadastral reform: An overview', in M. Craglia (ed.), *Geographic Information Research at the Milennium: GISDATA Final Conference*. Le Bischenburg: ESF.

Bogaerts, T. and Zevenbergen, J. (2001) 'Cadastral systems – alternatives', *Computers, Environment and Urban Systems*, 25: 325–37.

Bogaerts, T., Williamson, I.P and Fendel, E.M. (2002) 'The role of land administration in the accession of central European countries to the European Union', *Land Use Policy*, 1929–46.

Bruce, J. (1998) *Review of Tenure Terminology*, http://www.ies.wisc.edu/ (accessed 25 September 2006).

Bydłosz, J.A. and Parzych, P. (2007) 'The cadastral data exchange standards in Poland'. In Anon. (ed.), *Strategic Integration of Surveying Services, FIG Working Week 2007*. NA, Hong Kong SAR, China.

Center for Technology in Government (2003) *Some Assembly Required: Building a Digital Government for the 21st Century*, http://www.ctg.albany.edu/publications/reports/some_assembly?chapter=4&PrintVersion=2 (accessed 17 May 2004).

Crompvoets, J., Bregt, A., Rajabifard, A. and Williamson, I.P. (2004) 'Assessing the worldwide developments of national spatial data clearinghouses', *International Journal of Geographical Information Science*, 18(7): 665–89.

Dale, P.F. (1967) *Cadastral Surveys within the Commonwealth*. London: HMSO.

Dale, P.F. (1997) 'Land tenure issues in economic development', *Urban Studies*, 34(10): 1621–33.

Dale, P.F. and Mclaughlin, J.D. (1999) *Land Administration*. Oxford: Oxford University Press.

Davies, N. (2001) *Heart of Europe. The Past in Poland's Present*. Oxford: Oxford University Press.

De Man, W.H.E. (2006) 'Understanding SDI: Complexity and institionalization', *International Journal of Geographical Information Science*, 20(3): 329–43.

De Soto, H. (2000) *The Mystery of Capital: Why Capitalism Triumphs in the West and Fails Everywhere Else*. New York: Black Swan.

Department of Land Administration (2006) *Registration Services Customer Information Bulletin*. Midland, Department of Land Administration.

Dilke, O.A.W. (1985) *Greek and Roman Maps*. London: Eastern Press.

European Commission (2007) Directive 2007/2/Ec of the European Parliament and of the Council of 14 March 2007 establishing an Infrastructure for Spatial Information in the European Community (INSPIRE). Official Journal of the European Union.

Federal Geographic Data Committee (1997) *Framework Introduction and Guide*. Washington, DC: Federal Geographic Data Committee.

Federal Geographic Data Committee (2005) *FGDC Geospatial Grant Guidance To Federal Agencies*. Washington, DC: Federal Geographic Data Committee.

Federowski, W. (1974) *Ewidencja Gruntów*. Warszawa: Panstwowe Przedsiębiorstwo Wydawnictw Kartograficznych.

Food and Agricultural Organization of the United Nations (Fao) (no date) *What is Land Tenure?*, http://www.fao.org/documents/show_cdr.asp?url_file=/DOCREP/005/Y4307E/y4307e05.htm (accessed 28 May 2005).

Fraser, A. (2007) 'Land reform in South Africa and the colonial present', *Social and Cultural Geography*, 8(6): 835–51.

Georgiadou, Y., Puri, S.K. and Sahay, S. (2005) 'Towards a potential research agenda to guide the implementation of Spatial Data Infrastructures – A case study from India', *International Journal of Geographical Information Science*, 19(10): 1113–30.

Groot, R. and Mclaughlin, J. (eds) (2000) *Geospatial Data Infrastructure: Concepts, Cases and Good Practice.* Oxford: Oxford University Press.

GSDI (2001) 'The SDI Cookbook', Version 2, in D. Nebert. (ed.), Washington, DC: GSDI.

Harvey, F. (1998) 'National cultural influences on GIS design'. In M. Craglia and H. Onsrud (eds), *Geographic Information Research: Trans-Atlantic Perspectives.* London: Taylor & Francis. pp. 55–68.

Harvey, F. (2006a) 'Elasticity between the cadastre and land tenure: Balancing civil and political society interests in Poland', *Information Technology for Development,* 12(4): 291–310.

Harvey, F. (2006b) 'Reconfiguring administrative geographies in the United States', *ACME: An International E-Journal for Critical Geographies,* 4(1): 57–79.

Harvey, F. and Tulloch, D. (2003) 'Building the NSDI at the base: Establishing best sharing and coordination practices among local governments', http://www.tc.umn.edu/~fharvey/research/BestPrac4-03.pdf.

Harvey, F. and Tulloch, D.L. (2006) 'Local government data sharing: Evaluating the foundations of spatial data infrastructures', *International Journal of Geographical Information Science,* 20(7): 743–68.

Hespanha, J.P., Van Oosterom, P., Zevenbergen, J. and Paiva, D.G. (2006) 'A modular standard for the cadastral domain: Application to the Portuguese Cadastre', *Computers, Environment and Urban Systems,* 30: 562–584.

Hjelmager, J., Moellering, H., Cooper, A., Delgado, T., Rajabifard, A., Rapant, P., Düren, U., Huet, M., Laurent, D., Iwaniak, A., Abad, P. and Martynenko (2008) 'An initial formal model for spatial data infrastructures', *International Journal of Geographical Information Science,* 22(11): 1295–309.

ISO/TEC (1998) 'Information technology'. *Open Distributed Processing. Reference Model.* ISO/TEC.

Jacoby, S., Smith, J., Ting, L. and Williamson, I. (2002) 'Developing a common spatial data infrastructure between state and local government-an Australian case study', *IJGISci,* 16(4): 305–22.

Johnson, R., Nedovic-Budic, Z. and Covert, K. (2001) 'Lessons from Practice'. In V.A. Reston (ed.), *A Guidebook to Organizing and Sustaining Geodata Collaboratives.* GeoData Alliance.

Kain, R.J.P. and Baigent, E. (1992) *The Cadastral Map in the Service of the State: A History of Property Mapping.* Chicago, IL: University of Chicago Press.

Kaufmann, J. and Steudler, D. (1998) *Cadastre 2014. A Vision for a Future Cadastral System,* http://www.fig.net/cadastre2014/translation/c2014-english.pdf (accessed 5 August 2008).

Kivelson, V. (2006) *Cartographies of Tsardom: The Land and Its Meanings in Seventeenth-Century Russia.* Ithaca, NY: Cornell University Press.

Klathen, K. (2007) 'Norway SDI: Building sustatinability through strategic alliances'. In *Współpraca i Koordynacja w Zakresie Geoinformacji.* Warsaw: PTIP.

Knoop, H. and Wilkowski, W. (2003) *Integrating Electronic Platform (IPE) as a Basic Component of Cadastral System in Poland,* http://www.eurocadastre.org/eng/documentseng.html (accessed 6 April 2004).

Krane, D. (1998) *Local Government Autonomy and Discretion in the USA.* http://www.napawash.org/aa_federal_system/98_national_local.html (accessed 6 August 2005).

Lemmen, C. and Van Oosterom, P. (2001) 'Editorial: cadastral systems', *Computers, Environment and Urban Systems,* 25: 319–324.

Lyons, K., Cottrell, E. and Davies, K. (2004) *A Summary of the Paper 'On the Efficiency of Property Rights Administration',* http://www.anzlic.org.au/get/2403299376.pdf (accessed 14 April 2009).

Masser, I. (1998) *Governments and Geographic Information.* London: Taylor and Francis.

Masser, I., Rajabifard, A. and Williamson, I. (2007) 'Spatially enabling governments through SDI implementation', *International Journal of Geographic Information Science,* pp. 1–16.

Mclaughlin, J.D. (1984) 'The multipurpose cadastre concept: Current status, future prospects', in B.J.J. Niemann (ed.), *Seminar on the Multipurpose Cadastre: Modernizing Land Information Systems in North America.* Madison: Institue for Environmental Studies, University of Wisconsin-Madison. pp. 82–93.

Mikoś, M.J. (1992) 'Monarchs and magnates: Maps of Poland in the sixteenth and eighteenth centuries'. In D. Buissert (ed.), *Monarchs, Minister and Maps, The Emergence of Cartography as a Tool of Government in Early Modern Europe.* Chicago, IL: University of Chicago Press. pp. 168–82.

Molen, P.V.D. (2003) 'Institutional aspects of 3D cadastres', *Computers, Environment and Urban Systems,* 27: 383–94.

National Oceanic and Atmospheric Administration (NOAA). *The MPC: Multipurpose Cadastre.*

National Research Council (NRC) (1980) *Need for a Multipurpose Cadastre.* Washington, DC: National Academy Press.

NRC (1984) *Modernization of the Public Land Survey System.* Washington, DC: National Academy Press.

NRC (1990) *Spatial Data Needs: The Future of the National Mapping Program*. Washington, DC: National Academy Press.

NRC (1993) *Toward a Coordinated Spatial Data Infrastructure*. Washington, DC: National Academy Press.

NRC (2007) *National Land Parcel Data: A Vision for the Future*. Washington, DC: The National Academies Press.

NRC (US). Panel on a Multipurpose Cadastre (1983) *Procedures and Standards for a Multipurpose Cadastre*. Washington, DC: National Academy Press.

Nedovic-Budic, Z. and Pinto, J.K. (2000) 'Information sharing in an interorganizational GIS environment', *Environment and Planning B: Planning and Design*, 27(3): 455–74.

Nedovic-Budic, Z., Pinto, J.K. and Warnecke, L. (2004) 'GIS database development and exchange: Interaction mechanisms and motivations', *URISA Journal*, 16(1): 16–29.

Norway Digital (2008) General Terms and Conditions for Norway Digital Cooperation. Oslo: Norway Digital.

Orlińska, J. and Jarząbek, J. (2004) 'LPIS – the core of IACS', *In Geodeta*, 2–7, Warsaw: Geodeta Sp. z o. o.

Ostrowski, L. (2000) 'Selected problems of Polish agricultural land policy in the process of accession to the European Union'. In Institute of Agricultural Development in Central and Eastern Europe (Iamo) (ed.), *Studies on the Agricultural and Food Sector in Central and Eastern Europe*. Kiel: Wissenschaftsverlag Vauk Kiel KG. pp. 308–19.

Palmer, D., Munro-Faure, P. and Rembold, F. (2003) *Land Consolidation and Rural Development in Central and Eastern Europe*, http://www.eurocadastre.org/eng/2congress.html (accessed 5 January 2005).

Permanent Committee on the Cadastre in the European Union (2007) *The Cadastral parcel in NSDI's and in INSPIRE*. Brussels, Belgium: Eurographics.

Powelson, J.P. (1988) *The Story of Land*. Lincoln, NE: The Lincoln Institute of Land Policy.

Puri, S.K., Sahay, S. and Georgiadou, Y. (2006) 'A metaphor-based socio-technical perspective of SDI implementations: Some lessons from India. *GSDI-9 Conference Proceedings*. Santiago, Chile.

Putnam, R. (2000) *Bowling Alone. The Collapse and Revival of American Community*. New York: Simon and Schuster.

Rahn, W. and Thomas, R. (2002) 'Trust in local governments'. In B. Norrander and C. Wilcox (ed.), *Understanding Public Opinion*. Washington, DC: CQ Press. pp. 281–300.

Rajabifard, A., Binns, A., Masser, I. and Williamson, I. (2006) 'The role of sub-national government and the private sector in future spatial data infrastructures', *International Journal of Geographical Information Science*, 20(7): 727–42.

Rajabifard, A., Williamson, I. Steudler, D., Binns, A. and King, M. (2007) 'Assessing the worldwide comparison of cadastral systems', *Land Use Policy*, 24(1): 275–88.

Remetey-Fülöpp, G. (2003) *Cadastral GI Systems in Europe*. Granada: EUROGI.

Rhind, D. (ed) (1997) *Framework for the World*. Cambridge: GeoInformation International.

Sikor, T. (2006) 'Land as asset, land as liability: property politics in rural central and eastern Europe'. in F. Von Benda-Beckmann, K. Von Benda-Beckmann and M. Wiber (eds), *Changing Properties of Property*. New York: Berghahn. pp. 175–204.

Sikora, A. (2004) *Vademecum Prawne Geodety*. Warszawa: Gall.

Spatial Applications Division (2008). *Spatial data infrastructures in Poland: State of play Spring 2007*. Leuven, Belgium, K.U. Leuven Research and Development.

Stoter, J. and Salzmann, M. (2003) 'Towards a 3D cadastre: Where do cadastral needs and technical possibilities meet?', *Computers, Environment and Urban Systems*, 27: 395–410.

Tanic, S. (2000) 'The impact of land laws and legal institutions on the development of land markets and farm restructuring in Hungary, Lithuania, Poland and Romania', in C. Csaki and Z. Lerman (ed.), *Structural Change in the Farming Sectors in Central and Eastern Europe*. Washington, DC: The World Bank. pp. 150–4.

Tulloch, D.L. (2008) 'Institutional geographic information systems and geographic information partnering'. In J. P. Wilson and A. S. Fotheringham (ed.), *The Handbook of Geographic Information Science*. Oxford: Blackwell Publishing. pp. 449–65.

Tulloch, D.L., Niemann Jr., B.J. and Epstein, E.F. (1996) 'A model of multipurpose land information systems development in communities: Forces, factors, stages, indicators and benefits'. In Denver (ed.), *GIS/LIS '96*, Co, ASPRS/AAG/URISA/AM-FM. pp. 325–48.

Tulloch, D.L., Barnes, D., Bartholomew, D., Danielson, D. and Von Meyer, N. (1997) 'The Wisconsin land information program: supporting community land information system development', *Surveying and Land Information Systems*, 57(4): 241–48.

Turnbull, D. (1989) *Maps are Territories. Science is an Atlas.* Chicago, IL: University of Chicago Press.

Turnbull, D. (1998) 'Mapping encounters and (en)countering maps: A critical examination of cartographic resistance'. In *Knowledge and Society.* London: JAI Press. pp. 15–43.

Van Der Molen, P. (2002) 'The dynamic aspect of land administration: An often-forgotten component in system design', *CEUS*, pp. 26361–81.

Van Dijk, T. (2003) *Dealing with Central European Land Fragmentation. A Critical Assessment on the Use of Western European Instruments.* Delft: Eburon.

Van Oosterom, P., Lemmen, C., Ingvarssona, T., Van Der Molen, P., Ploegera, H., Quaka, W., Stoterc, J. and Zevenbergen, J. (2006) 'The core cadastral domain model', *Computers, Environment and Urban Systems*, 30: 627–60.

Verdery, K. (1994) 'The elasticity of land: Problems of property restitution in Transylvania', *Slavic Review*, 53(4): 1071–109.

Verdery, K. (2003) *The Vanishing Hectare: Property and Value in Postsocialist Transylvania.* Ithaca, NY: Cornell University Press.

Williamson, I. (1994) *The Australian Cadastre System*, http://www.sli.unimelb.edu.au/research/publications/IPW/AustCadSystem.htm (accessed 14 April 2009).

Worldbank (2005) *Registering Property in Poland*, http://www.doingbusiness.org/ExploreTopics/RegisteringProperty/Details.aspx?economyid=154 (accessed 26 July 2006).

Zaręba, S. and Zoń, J. (2007) 'Założenia technologiczne tworzenia bazy danych wektorowej mapy ewidencyjnej LPIS z wykorzystaniem dotychczasowych materiałów ewidencyjnych', *Roczniki Geomatyki*, 5(4): 63–80.

16

A GIS-based Computer-supported Collaborative Work Flow System in Urban Planning

Anthony G.O. Yeh and Kenneth S.S. Tang

INTRODUCTION

GIS can be used in different stages and functions of urban planning. General administration, development control and plan making are the three major applications of GIS in urban planning (Yeh, 1999). Most applications of GIS in urban planning are to support plan making in land-use planning. GIS is commonly used to assess whether the land is suitable for the proposed development and whether there are any effects on the natural, social, traffic and visual environment of the neighbourhood. Land suitability analysis through GIS overlay analysis is the most common use of GIS in assessing whether land is suitable for the proposed development. Buffer analysis is often used to assess the environmental and traffic impact of the proposed development. A GIS model or 3D CAD is often used to assess the visual impact of the proposed development on the surrounding environment. Instead of focusing on the above commonly used applications of GIS, this chapter will discuss the use of GIS

in office automation for facilitating the decision-making process in development control as well as public participation.

Similar to the planning process, there are different stages in the development control process. Most planning applications in development control have a statutory time period in which a decision on the proposed development must be made. In most cities, decisions on development control are made by a committee, such as planning commission, town planning board and planning committee, with representatives from the community. Government planning officials may or may not be members of the committee, but the role of the planning officials is to make sure that the statutory time period of the planning application is strictly adhered to, and that relevant government departments and the community have been consulted before the meeting of the planning committee. They will compile all the inputs and decisions of similar past cases for members of the planning committee to consider. A GIS-based computer-supported collaborative work flow

(CSCWF) system can facilitate the tracking of different stages of the planning applications (Chen et al., 2004).

In addition to plan making and development control, public consultation plays an important role in the planning process. Traditional public consultation or engagement methods are commonly conducted through face-to-face encounters. However, this type of public consultation method may not be efficient and effective enough. In most cases, it is not easy to gather stakeholders to attend pre-scheduled meetings as the participants are physically separated. Travelling time and cost are also major concern. Most important of all, the quality and quantity of information collected from the participants is often constrained by the limited duration of these meetings. Under such circumstances, new and innovative methods for achieving better democratic decision making emerge.

In its *2006 Planning and Urban Design Standards Handbook*, the American Planning Association (APA) indicates that planners are increasingly recognizing the potential of computer-based participation as a key element in developing appropriate and effective solutions to community design and planning problems (APA, 2006). Advancement in IT brings more and new technologies, which are highly communicative and collaborative in nature and are uniquely designed to enable planning processes and ideologies (Al Kodmany, 2002). As a result of these trends, computerized tools have fundamentally changed the way planners communicate ideas to the public. These represent a paradigm shift in the planning and design process (APA, 2006).

GIS-BASED COMPUTER-SUPPORTED COLLABORATIVE WORK FLOW SYSTEMS

Development control is a collaborative decision-making process that involves urban planners and related government officials located in different rooms, buildings or departments. They have to review and process planning applications submitted by a developer or citizen according to the predefined regulations and workflow. The output of planning applications is either a legal permit describing both the geometric and thematic states of the land parcel or a notice explaining to the applicant why the application is rejected. In the past, this was done mainly by circulating the hard copies among different actors in the planning application process. This can be automated and made more efficient through the application of information technology. The application files and related plans, maps and photos can be processed electronically through the Planning Department's internal computer system (LAN or intranet).

From the point of view of behavioural modelling, agents, events and states are the three major components in the collaborative process of development control as illustrated in Figure 16.1. The staff in different departments (or levels) can be viewed as agents who have the responsibility to make decisions in the development control process. Each decision made by the agent(s) triggers one or more reviewing events, such as site evaluation, land-use approval and title registration. The results of these reviewing events are states, such as site location, boundary delineation and property registration. The state of a land parcel is comprised of its geometry, thematic attributes and topological relations with other parcels.

The relations between these agents, events and states include sequential order and hierarchical relations between two agents, relations between agent(s) and event(s), relations between events, causal relations between events and states, and relations between states (Jiang, 2000; Jiang et al., 2000). For example, site evaluation event E1 occurs before land-use approval event E2, and title registration event E3 cannot begin until E2 is finished. The entire development control process can be represented by a composite

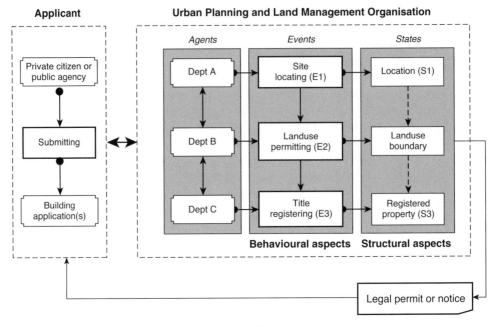

Figure 16.1   Collaborative development control process

event, such as E1, E2 and E3 in Figure 16.1. Each of these three events can be further divided into sub-events. The causal relations between events and states of land parcels reflect the geometrical and thematic changes in the land parcels. In general, any change of states would be driven or caused by a specific event. Let S0 be the initial state of a land parcel. After the execution of the event site evaluation E1, the site location of land parcel S1 is created. S1 is modified after executing E2 and land boundary S2 is delineated. The boundary of the property S3 is further registered by following event E3. There are relations between different states of the same land parcel. S1 is created on the basis of S0, and S1 is modified and transformed into S2. The one-to-one relation between sequential states of the same land parcel needs to be considered in the entity–relation modelling of development control.

In the earlier applications of urban GIS, emphasis was placed on the representation of the states of spatial objects. The attributes of the states of the spatial system were modelled with the cartographic layers, features

attribute tables, lookup tables, annotation and the map library (using an ARC/INFO database). Modelling both the structural and behavioural aspects is not new in computer science (Pernici, 1990; Quer and Olive, 1993). For example, Teisseire et al. (1994) extended the semantic IFO (Is-a-relationships, Functional relationships, complex Objects) model to integrate both the structural and behavioural representation of applications in a consistent and uniform manner in terms of both the formalization and the associated graphic representation. Snoeck and Dedene (1998) tried to express the semantic integrity of structural and behavioural schema with an existence dependency graph. Yet, the task had never been an easy one especially for the design of event-based non-spatial databases (Scheer, 1992).

There were some initial attempts to represent both structural aspects and behavioural aspects in GIS applications. Peuquet and Duan (1995) proposed an event-based spatiotemporal data model whereby the sequence of events through time was organized in an increasing order along a time line.

Claramunt and Theriault (1995, 1996) presented another event-oriented approach that modelled changes among a set of entities. Spatial entities and their temporal versions were associated through intermediary logical tables (past events, present events and future events) that permit the description of complex succession, production, reproduction and transmission processes. Time, however, was treated as a complementary facet of spatial and thematic domains that are separated into distinct structures and unified by domain links. Allen et al. (1995) tried to develop a generic model for explicitly representing causal links within a spatiotemporal GIS. A small number of elements were presented in that model using an extended entity–relationship formalism, including objects and their states, events, agents and conditions, as well as the relations (Produces, Is Part Of, Conditions). However, these initial efforts gave priority to some local or partial behaviour of the applications rather than an overview of the system behaviour. In the case of the development control reviewing system, both the structural and behavioural aspects of the overall system need to be modelled. In other words, the agents, events and states, as well as the relations between them, should be taken into consideration in designing and developing the GIS-based CSCWF system for development control.

Hierarchical representation of the relations between events, agents and states

Instead of using one large diagram, a hierarchical representation of agents, events and states as well as their relations was proposed. A first-level diagram of the development control process is shown on the left-hand side of Figure 16.2, and each of its blocks can be detailed out on the second-level diagram. For instance, the block Department B was detailed out on the right-hand side of Figure 16.2 with the sub-agents, sub-events and sub-states at the next level. The whole process is represented by a hierarchical set of diagrams.

Among the relations represented in the hierarchical set of diagrams, there exist the collaborative relations between agents, sequential relations between events, transitional relations between states and executive relations between an agent and an event, triggering relations between an event and a state (Jiang, 2000). The collaborative relation

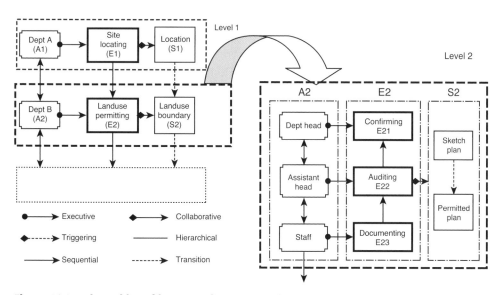

Figure 16.2 Hierarchies of integrated representation of agents, events and states

between agents is a dynamic process involving actions such as enquire, reject, accept and inform. The transitional relation between states reflects the transition from an intermediate result (such as a sketch map) to a final result (legally permitted map). It is quite possible that several events in conjunction initiate an event, or that a state is the result of several events. Moreover, one agent might execute more than one event. Communication to other parts of the system can be shown within an upper-level diagram at the appropriate level.

Formal representation of events and their relations with states can be modelled with the event pattern language (EPL) (Gehani et al., 1992a, 1992b). An event can be described with a tuple (Eid, Ea, Epro, Es), where Eid is an identifier of the event, Ea represents the attributes of the event, Epro is the pre-condition of the event occurrence and Es is the sub-sequential effects of the event occurrence. The Eid is a character string representing hierarchy and generalization. For instance, E2 in Figure 16.2 is a composite event with E21, E22 and E23 as its sub-events. A state of a spatial object can be described by a tuple (Sid, Sec, See, Spro, Spost), where Sid is the identifier of the state, Sec is the event that creates the state, See is the event that ends the state, Spro is the previous state and Spost is the post state. With these expressions, the delineation of a land boundary in Figure 16.2

can be represented as (S2, E22, E3, S1, S3). This tuple describes not only the relation between spatial objects and the related events but also the corresponding relations between different states (Chen and Jiang, 2000).

Integration of heterogeneous and disparate spatial and non-spatial data

It is essential to have easy access to existing or newly created spatial and non-spatial data during the process of development control, which generally includes various plans, topographic maps, facility maps, administrative boundaries, cadastral maps, decision-related documents, various permits, ordinances and regulations. These heterogeneous and disparate sources of data within an urban planning and land management bureau need to be assembled into an integrated database (Jiang et al., 2002). To integrate these multi-scale, multi-type data, a unique identification code (called Feature ID [FID]) is assigned to each spatial object. The linkage between different spatial objects and that between a spatial object and the related attribute tables can be executed using the FID as shown in Figure 16.3.

The successive spatial states in the development control process are defined as

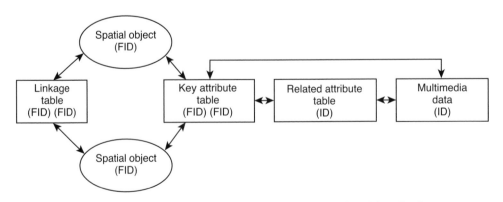

Figure 16.3   Links between spatial objects, attribute tables and multimedia data

composite spatial objects, such as planned site location, delineated land-use boundary, permitted building area and registered property. The causal linkages between these states are represented explicitly with an entity–relation diagram as shown in Figure 16.4. Each state might be composed of a set of primitive spatial objects that are represented in the federated database.

A node-link structure was also used for the associative linking of a variety of multimedia information (Shiffer, 1995). The aerial images, ground photos, 3D landscape, narrative descriptions and digital video and sound can be encapsulated by nodes and associated with spatial object(s) on digital maps. The maps are used as the spatial reference attached by other document nodes. Users can navigate in or through geographic space to retrieve the multimedia information about the past and existing conditions of a particular location. With the support of this hypermedia information, planners are able to show people explicit photo-textured information of what their city will look like after a proposed change, instead of presenting citizens with only abstract maps and descriptive text to explain, analyse and debate design ideas and urban processes.

Specific functions for day-to-day routine work

Once a planning application is submitted, a sequence of legally defined events will be executed by planning staff and land managers according to the nature of the applied case, such as application registering, outline (of land use and construction) delineating, opinion giving, permits printing and documents filing. In order to automate such manual process with networked communication and spatial data handling capabilities, three kinds of functionalities were developed for urban planners and land managers, that is, office automation for paperwork, desktop boundaries mapping and network-based generic queries.

Office automation functionalities

Each planning application is considered as a case and assigned a unique code as the identifier. A series of office automation functions are developed within the Oracle environment, including application registering, documents checking, opinions giving and transferring legal permits, as well as preparation and issue of associated graphic documents. While each of these functions is

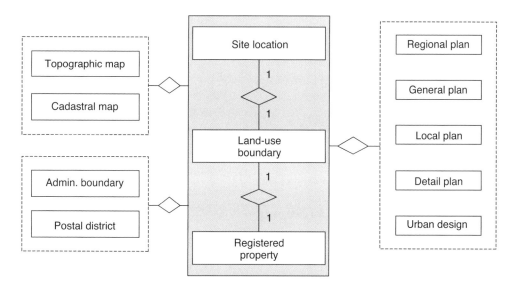

Figure 16.4   An entity-relation diagram of states in development control

executed, the results are processed and transferred immediately to the next stage.

Desktop spatial data handling tools

Delineating new land lots and locating new buildings on large-scale digital maps is one of the key desktop spatial data handling tasks. A specific toolkit has been developed. Some of the toolbars are shown in Figure 16.5, such as road arc generating, coordinates and areas measuring, legend labelling, official stamp mapping and so on.

Network-based generic queries

Process-query, facts-query, map-query and law-query are the four major generic queries developed on the basis of the classification of data and the integrated structure. For a given development application, it is possible to access its current, previous and following reviewing steps with the integrated agent-event-and-state structure. In other words, it is possible to know how many steps the development application has gone through, and what the current and other remaining reviewing stages are. An example is given in Figure 16.6. In order to provide easy access by content and in a natural way, visual interfaces are designed by integrating the workflow charts, fancy icons

and tip wizard. Differences in technical languages of different application areas are also taken into consideration. In fact, the end users do not always know the terms adopted by 'experts' in charge of the application. One example is that the term 'project' is used in the interface instead of 'record' which is used by the system developers.

It is also possible to know for a given step how many application cases have been reviewed in a given period of time, and what applications are under review (Figure 16.6). The administrators, planning staff and land managers at different levels can use this query to track the progress of different stages of the development control process and speed them up if there are delays.

The relevant states and other documents can also be retrieved with the help of the linkages between events and states. For instance, tracking permits that have been issued is routine work in development control. Based on the records related to the parcels approved, or building occupancy permitted, all the changes that have taken place since a specific timeframe can be retrieved from the federated database. Maps, remote sensing images, aerial photographs and pictures related to the site can also be

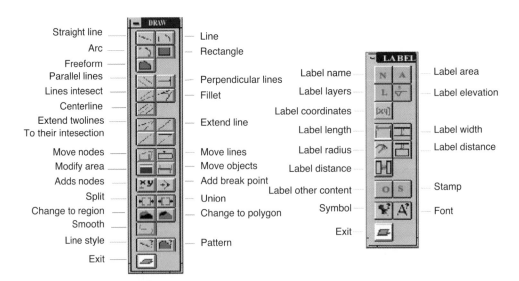

Figure 16.5   Some toolbars for producing development control maps

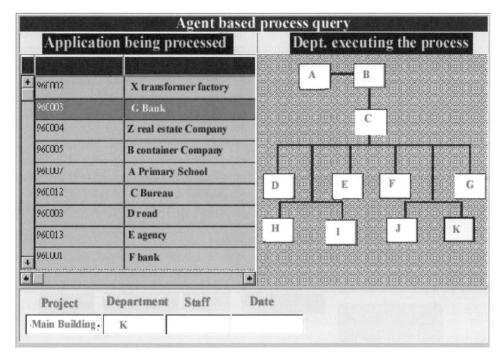

Figure 16.6   Agent-based process query about a development application

retrieved and displayed through the system (Chen et al., 1998).

Design of a collaborative system in an organisation

As pointed out by Nunamarker and Briggs (1997), in the design of collaborative system, there are three possible levels, namely individual level, coordinated level and concerted level. The individual level involves uncoordinated individual effort towards a common goal. This type of collaboration is considered not desirable in terms of efficiency and effectiveness. Coordinated level requires coordinated but independent effort while collaborative effort at the concerted level involves a number of agents working simultaneously towards a common goal. It is apparent that coordinated and concerted level of collaboration can save a lot time and resources in completing a complicated task. As these two levels of collaboration are more structured than collaboration at the individual

level, the adoption of CSCWF for its implementation is more feasible.

Michelis and Ellis (1998) proposed that an important facet that is required to be taken into account in the design of a collaborative information system should be the independence between the group collaboration support model and the organisational model. Due to the above reason, the system should be designed in such a way that these two models are able to self-modify according to the 'lesson learnt' during the collaborative process. It is evident that with this automated feedback mechanism built up in a CSCWF system, its performance can be progressively enhanced.

Use of GIS-based computer-supported collaborative work flow systems as public participatory GIS

In the past two decades, GIS technologies that are originally designed for spatial query and analysis have been adopted for public consultation in planning. One of the reasons for this trend is that information on planning proposals and statutory land-use plans contains a spatial component. Another reason is that extending the use of spatial information to all relevant stakeholders will not only lead to better policy but will also enhance the ability to convey ideas persuasively and convince people of the importance of these ideas (Wood, 1992). Hence, in addition to decision support in development control, GIS has been widely used for public consultation through the Internet. There have been government organisations successfully integrating GIS with workflow systems for improving efficiency and disseminating information to the public.

Many planners share the view that Public Participatory GIS (PPGIS) has added value at several stages of the decision-making process as follows: improving the articulation of stakeholders' views, increasing individual or group understanding of technology, making more complex decisions more transparent and objective, augmenting deliberation and consensus, furthering communication and linkage among internal and external parties, disseminating or sharing information, resolving conflicts and enabling greater exploration of ideas (Drew, 2003). Due to this distinct value of GIS for public consultation, PPGIS has been developed by many government organisations to broaden public involvement in public policy making (Sieber, 2006). As a result, PPGIS has also become one of the key components of integrated collaborative systems serving planning authorities.

A CASE STUDY ON A COLLABORATIVE WORKFLOW SYSTEM INTEGRATED WITH GIS

Since 1997, workflow systems integrated with GIS and other IT have been widely used by many planning authorities in China, including the regions of Guangzhou, Changzhou and Liuzhou. These systems have largely improved the efficiency of the collaborative decision making of development control by reducing duplication of effort, minimising redundant data collection and analysis, maximising the sharing of information and coordinating and keeping track of the development control process. Planning staff and land managers as well as other related government officials of these cities can perform the development control steps in a logical order instead of some ad hoc sequences. Apart from China, other cities in Asia, such as Kuala Lumpur (Yaakup, 2004), are also using such CSCWF system in development control.

Since the 1990s, the Planning Department in Hong Kong, an executive arm of the Town Planning Board (TPB), has effectively deployed office automation and GIS technologies in preparing various types of plans, including the statutory Outline Zoning Plans (OZPs) for development control, facilitating professional planners to conduct spatial analysis such as land suitability and buffer analysis during various stages of the planning process. Most important of all, web-based GIS technologies have also been adopted for the purpose of facilitating public engagement and participation.

The 2004 Town Planning Amendment Ordinance of Hong Kong came into operation in June 2005. This Ordinance has three main objectives: (1) to enhance transparency and public participation in the planning process; (2) to streamline planning procedures and (3) to enhance the efficiency and effectiveness of planning enforcement control in the rural areas of the New Territories. Upon its enactment, the planning system of Hong Kong has become more open, transparent, efficient and effective.

To cope with the new measures and additional procedures brought about by the Amendment Ordinance and to deliver quality services to the public, a workflow system integrated with GIS, CAD and office automation technologies with the support of a central planning data hub (CPDH) at the backend has been developed to facilitate the collaboration of planning staff in processing of planning applications for the consideration of the board within the statutory time period.

Information flow of the integrated collaborative workflow system

One of the key features of the collaborative workflow system is that information (both spatial and non-spatial) collected during different stages of the workflow is captured and stored in the CPDH for subsequent use by different categories of staff and dissemination of relevant information to the public during the consultation process.

The example below demonstrates how the same set of information on 'recommended approval conditions' captured during the workflow processes is used for various purposes at different stages of the workflow.

Under the current planning application system of Hong Kong, approval conditions are imposed on most approved planning applications to ensure that the proposed developments put forward by the applicants will not cause adverse effects on the surrounding environment. For short-term development applications such as open storage use, it is quite common that time clauses for compliance are attached to approval conditions. This measure can ensure compliance of the approval conditions within a short period of time for the benefit of the public.

In accordance with the prevailing town planning ordinance, when approval conditions of a planning permission are not satisfied on time, the planning approval granted by the board will lapse and the development will then be subject to enforcement actions unless the applicant can obtain approval for extension of time before the due date. Due to this reason, all the approval conditions will be put under close monitoring by the planning authority.

Recommended approval conditions to be imposed on a planning application is first prepared by the town planners responsible

for the case and incorporated into the TPB paper for consideration of the board. This set of approval conditions, if agreed by the board, will appear in the minutes of the TPB meeting, approval letter issued to the applicant, geo-database for monitoring compliance of approval conditions and textual attributes attached to the 'planning application' polygon of the GIS. Under this design, information will only be captured once and it can then be used and displayed again in different formats at subsequent stages of the process by extracting relevant information from the geo-database.

Time and resource saving aside, another major advantage of this system design is that it can enable timely completion of all tasks involved in the workflow. As data entry is captured under a controlled environment, data/information integrity can be maintained.

Actors, events and states of the integrated system

The framework of this integrated workflow system is shown in Figure 16.7. The agents are comprised of three categories of staff, including the town planners, survey officers and technical officers. The town planners oversee the processing of the applications and present analytical findings and make recommendations to the TPB. The survey officer's main duty is to assist the planners in conducting site survey, gathering relevant planning information and compiling analytical reports, while the technical officers are responsible for producing plans for public consultation and for incorporation into the TPB paper.

The major events of the integrated system are monitoring, planning information dissemination, planning analysis and plan production.

Monitoring

Once an application is received and confirmed valid, a case is created by the system

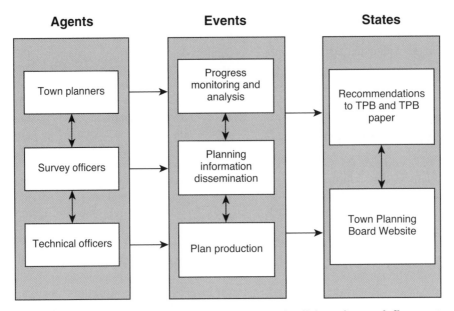

Figure 16.7   Framework of the computer-supported collaborative work flow system integrated with GIS technologies for processing planning applications

and it will be subject to close monitoring by the system. In processing the application, the workflow is not entirely linear. During certain stages, parallel processing is also required. When an agent has completed his/her task, the case will be passed on to the next agent and a new task for that case is created in the inbox of the next agent. If the task is not completed on time, an email alerting the responsible agent will be issued by the system.

With appropriate 'right control', the agents concerned are able to query the current status of each case under processing. It is also possible to find out what cases are currently being processed by a particular agent. With the operation of this case-based and agent-based monitoring mechanism, timely completion of all planning application cases within the statutory time period can be guaranteed.

Planning information dissemination
Planning information disseminated to the public is carried out at different stages of the

process, namely after the receipt of the planning application, during the processing of the application and after the TPB's consideration of the case.

Once an application is received and confirmed to be valid, the public will be informed through posting of site notices and newspaper publication. The gist of the application (including relevant textual and graphical information of the application) will be sent to the district board, rural committee and owners' corporation (OC) of buildings within 100 feet from the application site. Buffer analysis is carried out to identify the OCs that can meet this criterion. The location plan of the application site is disseminated by extracting appropriate thematic layers from the CPDH (including the survey base and zoning on the OZP). The gist is uploaded onto the TPB website by an automated web-content management system (Figure 16.8).

During the processing of the application, the public can enter comments on these planning applications through the TPB website

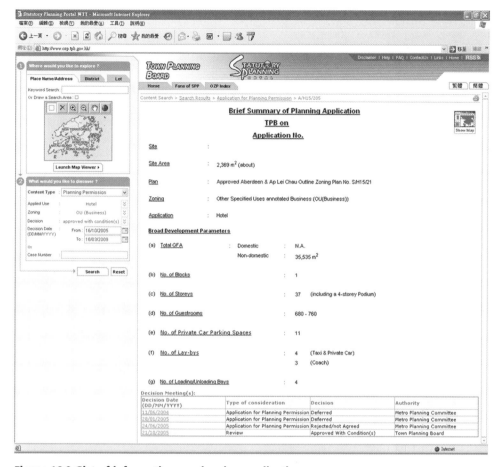

Figure 16.8 Gist of information on planning applications

Source: Town Planning Board, Statutory Planning Portal, 18 November 2009.

(Figure 16.9). Online comments provided by the public through the Internet within the consultation period are stored in the CPDH, which can be accessible to planners for subsequent processing and analysis. Results of analysis on comments received either online or from other sources will be incorporated into the TPB paper for the board's consideration.

On the day the planning application is considered by the TPB, the gist of the decision of the TPB will be disseminated through the TPB website right after the meeting while the detailed decision of the application, including the approval conditions imposed on each approved case stored in the

CPDH, will be disseminated to the public through the TPB website upon confirmation of the meeting minutes (Figures 16.10 and 16.11).

Planning analysis and plan production

The relevant information including previous applications and applications of similar nature in close proximity to the subject application site, lot boundaries, aerial photos and survey base plans will all be incorporated into the plans for presentation to the TPB. Textual and spatial information required for generating these plans are extracted from the geo-database stored in the CPDH.

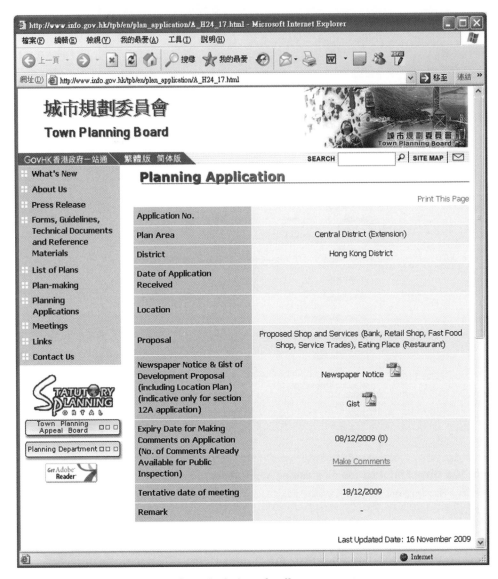

Figure 16.9 Website of the TPB for submission of online comments

Source: Town Planning Board, Town Planning Board Website, 18 November 2009.

Potential areas of enhancement

The workflow system integrated with GIS technologies developed by PlanD has found to be an efficient and effective tool for handling planning applications, involving the collaboration of a number of agents working on different tasks and physically located at different offices.

The Hong Kong planning system has become more open and transparent. In response to calls for providing more detailed spatial and textual information on the planning applications, the planning authority may

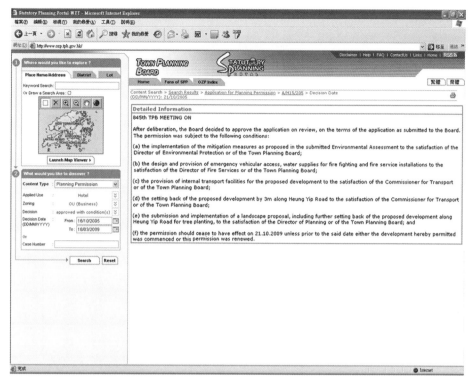

Figure 16.10 Detailed decisions of the TPB on planning applications
Source: Town Planning Board, Statutory Planning Portal, 18 November 2009.

need to take appropriate steps to meet these public aspirations.

Following technological advancement and gradual upgrading of the government IT infrastructure, the following aspects of work to further improve staff efficiency and services to the public can be considered:

- Scope of the workflow system – in processing planning applications by the workflow system, inputs from officers of other relevant government departments are required. However, the existing workflow system can only accommodate intra-departmental collaboration. If the scope of the system can be extended to cover other relevant government departments, inter-departmental collaboration becomes possible and higher levels of efficiency and information integrity can be achieved.
- Level of collaboration – the existing workflow system is designed in such a way that it enables a coordinated level of collaboration. Under this

level of collaboration, the actor takes on a particular task in a workflow process and passes on the finished task to the next actor on the flow. To further improve collaboration, a concerted level of collaboration can be considered under which the same task may be worked on by a number of actors simultaneously. By incorporating this level of collaboration into the system, efficiency can be further enhanced.
- Case-base reasoning (CBR) algorithm – in identifying similar applications, the current integrated system enables the planners to carry out a spatial or textual search and to find and display cases belonging to the same type of application in close proximity to the subject application site. With the adoption of the CBR algorithm, the integrated system can assess the extent of similarity between cases and this can help to provide additional information to the planners in making recommendations to the Board (Shi and Yeh, 1999).
- Application of MASHUP technology – with the advancement of GIS technologies in web

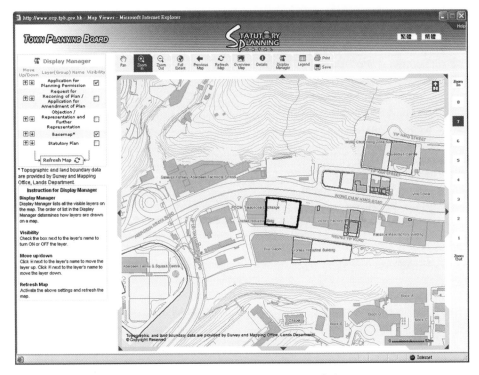

Figure 16.11 Location of application sites shown on TPB website

Source: Town Planning Board, Statutory Planning Portal, 18 November 2009.

applications, it is considered that MASHUP technology be incorporated into the integrated system so that more distributed web applications or web functions, preferred by the public and stakeholders such as spatial analysis, can be combined into a single web application deployed to the public through the Internet.

CONCLUSION

An event-based workflow collaborative system integrated with GIS technologies can help to keep track of decision and comments of different actors in the development control process as well as dissemination of information and collection of views during the public consultation process through the operation of an effective PPGIS.

Nevertheless, as pointed out by Ghose (2001), in the development of a PPGIS, it is essential to ensure that it is not implemented in a void but rather is conditioned by the law, culture, politics and history of the community, city, regions or nations in which it is applied. Otherwise, the PPGIS developed may not be able to meet the objectives of the government organisations and the need of the public at large.

It is anticipated that with the advancement of web-based GIS technologies such as MASHUP and stronger aspirations towards public participation in the planning process, the planning authorities should be prepared to deliver more complex online planning services to the public in the years to come.

It has been shown by a number of studies that staff and organisational factors are more important than technology in the successful application of GIS (Campbell, 1994; Campbell and Masser, 1995). To ensure the effective and efficiency application of information technologies in particular GIS, the management of planning authorities should not only focus on exploring new and powerful technologies but should devote considerable amount of effort to formulating appropriate information management strategies, participation in implementation of information technologies at all levels and maintaining a high degree of organisational and environmental stability (Masser and Campbell, 1991; Campbell, 1994). These aspects of the organisation that are likely to be neglected are believed to be essential prerequisites for establishing a favourable environment for the nurturing of effective information.

REFERENCES

Al Kodmany, K. (2002) 'Visualization tools and methods in community planning: From freehand sketches to virtual reality', *Journal of Planning Literatures*, 17 (2): 189–211.

Allen, A., Edwards, G. and Bedard, Y. (1995) 'Qualitative causal modeling in temporal GIS', in A.U. Frank and W. Kuhn (eds), *Spatial Information Theory: A Theoretical Basis for GIS*. New York: Springer. pp. 397–417.

American Planning Association (2006) *Planning and Design Standards*. New York: John Wiley. pp. 63–4.

Campbell, H. (1994) 'How effective are GIS in practice? A case study of British local government', *International Journal of Geographical Information Systems*, 8(3): 309–25.

Campbell, H. and Masser, I. (1995) *GIS and Organizations: How Effective Are GIS in Practice?* London: Taylor & Francis.

Chen, J. and Jiang, J. (2000) 'An event-based approach to spatio-temporal data modeling in land subdivision system for spatio-temporal process of land subdivision', *Geoinformatica*, 4(4): 387–402.

Chen, J., Jiang, J., Jin, S.P. and Yan, R.H. (1998) 'Developing an office GIS by Integrating GIS with OA', *Journal of Remote Sensing* 2(3): 59–64. [In Chinese.]

Chen, J., Jiang, J. and Yeh, A.G.O. (2004) 'Designing a GIS-based CSCW system for development control with an event-driven approach', *Photogrammetric Engineering and Remote Sensing*, 70(2): 225–33.

Claramunt, C. and Theriault, M. (1995) 'Management time in GIS, an event-orient approach', in J. Clifford and A. Tuzhilin (eds), *Recent Advances in Temporal Databases*. Berlin: Springer. pp. 23–42.

Claramunt, C. and Theriault, M. (1996) 'Toward semantics for modeling spatio-temporal processes within GIS', in M.J. Kraak and M. Molenaar (eds), *Advances in GIS Research II (Proceedings of the 7th International Symposium on Spatial Data Handling)*. London: Taylor and Francis. pp. 47–64.

Dew, C.H. (2003) 'Transparency – Considerations for PPGIS research and development', *Urban and Regional Information Systems Association (URISA) Journal*, 15 APAI, 73–8.

Gehani, N.H., Jagadish, H.V. and Shmueli, O. (1992a) 'Event specification in an active object-oriented database', *ACM SIGMOD Record*, 21(2): 81–90.

Gehani, N.H., Jagadish, H.V. and Shmueli, O. (1992b) 'Composite event specification in active databases: Model and implementation', in Yuan, L.-Y. (ed.), *Proceedings of 18th International Conference on Very Large Databases*, 23–27 August, Vancouver, British Columbia, Canada. San Francisco: Morgan Kufmann. pp. 327–38.

Ghose, R. (2001) 'Use of information technology for community empowerment: Transforming Geographic Information Systems into community information systems', *Transaction in GIS*, 5(2): 141–63.

Jiang, J. (2000) 'Research on event based spatio-temporal database', PhD dissertation, China University of Mining and Technology, Beijing, China. [In Chinese.]

Jiang, J., Chen, J., Yan, R.H. and Xu, L.L. (2000) 'A CSCW system for building reviewing by integrating GIS with OA', *Geo-Spatial Information Science*, 3(1): 45–9.

Jiang, J., Chen, J. and Yeh, A.G.O. (2002) 'A GIS-based computer supported collaborative work (CSCW) system for urban planning and land management', *Photogrammetric Engineering and Remote Sensing*, 68(4): 353–9.

Michelis, G.D. and Ellis, C.A. (1998) *Lecture Notes in Computer Science: Computer Supported Cooperative Work and Petri Nets*. Berlin: Springer.

Masser, I. and Campbell, H. (1991) 'Conditions for effective utilization of computers in urban planning in developing countries', *Computers, Environment and Urban Systems*, 15(1–2): 55–67.

Nunamarker, J.F. and Briggs, R.O. (1997) 'Lessons from a dozen years of group support systems research: A discussion of lab and field findings', *Journal of Management Information System* 13 (3): 163–207.

Pernici, B. (1990) 'Objects with roles', in F.H. Lochovsky and R.B. Allen (eds), *Proceedings of the Conference on Office Information System*, 25–27 April, MIT, Cambridge, Massachusetts: ACM Press. pp. 205–15.

Peuquet, D.J. and Duan, N. (1995) 'An event-based spatiotemporal data model (ESTDM) for temporal analysis of geographical data', *International Journal of Geographical Information Systems*, 9(1): 7–24.

Quer, C. and Olive, A. (1993) 'Object interaction in object-oriented deductive conceptual models', in C. Rolland, F. Bodart and C. Cauvet (eds), *Proceedings of 5th International Conference on Advanced Information Systems Engineering*, 8–11 June, Paris. (*Lecture Notes in Computer Science [LNCS]*) Heidelberg: Springer-Verlag. 685: 374–96.

Scheer, A.W. (1992) *Architecture of Integrated Information Systems*. New York: Springer-Verlag.

Shiffer, M.J. (1995) 'Geographic integration in the city planning context: beyond the multimedia prototype', in T.L. Nyerges, D.M. Mark, R. Laurini and M.J. Egenhofer (eds), *Cognitive Aspects of Human-computer Interaction for Geographic Information Systems*. New York: Kluwer. pp. 295–310.

Sieber, R. (2006) 'Public participation geographic information systems: a literature review and framework', *Annals of the American Association of Geographers*, 96(3): 491–507.

Snoeck, M. and Dedene, G. (1998) 'Existence dependency: The key to semantic integrity between structural and behavioral aspects of object types', *IEEE Transactions on Software Engineering*, 24 (4): 233–51.

Teisseire, M., Poncelet, P. and Cicchetti, R. (1994) 'Towards event-driven modeling for database design', in J.B. Bocca, M. Jarke and C. Zaniolo (eds), *Proceedings of 20th International Conference on Very Large Databases*, 12–15 September, Santiago de Chile. San Francisco, CA: Morgan Kufmann. pp. 285–96.

Wood, D. (1992) *The Power of Maps*. New York: Guilford Press.

Yaakup, A. et al. (2004) 'Computerised development control and approval system for city hall of Kuala Lumpur', *Geo-Spatial Information Science*, 7(1): 39–49.

Yeh, A.G.O. (1999) 'Urban planning and GIS', in P.A. Longley, M. Goodchild, D. Maguire and D. Rhind (eds), *Geographical Information Systems: Principles, Techniques, Applications and Management*, 2nd edn. New York: John Wiley. pp. 877–88.

Yeh, A.G.O. and Shi, X. (1999) 'Applying case-based reasoning to urban planning: a new planning-support system tool', *Environment and Planning B, Planning and Design*. 26: 101–115.

17

GIS and Emergency Management

Christopher T. Emrich, Susan L. Cutter
and Paul J. Weschler

The use of geographic information systems (GIS) within emergency management (EM) has enhanced the ability of practitioners to plan for, respond to, and aid in recovery from natural- and human-induced hazards in a more comprehensive fashion than ever before (Gunes and Kovel, 2000; Cutter et al., 2007). Current and future developments in geospatial technology promise to strengthen the use of geographic data in disaster response and recovery to save lives, protect property, and reduce the economic impacts of hazards (Brown, 2008; Mills et al. 2008). This chapter describes the applications of GIS for emergency management and the future directions of the field in both research and practice. We first provide a historical perspective on GIS and emergency management including a brief description of the four phases – preparedness, response, recovery, and mitigation. The remainder of the chapter provides a detailed discussion on research and the practical use of GIS in each phase, with particular emphasis on applications since 2000. We then provide a short discussion on strengths, weaknesses, and constraints of the current practice and research

and identify future opportunities to improve the science and practice of GIS and emergency management.

EMERGENCY MANAGEMENT FUNCTIONS

The emergency management cycle (Figure 17.1) shows the primary functions of emergency management. Each phase of the cycle represents a different suite of issues, information requirements, and professional expertise. Some of the phases are time dependent (happen quickly and require real time information and data flows for decision makers – such as the response phase), while others are more protracted, where data gathering, analytical modeling, and decision support tools are developed over longer time frames using an iterative process. Emergency support functions (ESF) prescribed in the national response framework (NRF) provides detail on the specific roles and responsibilities of federal agency partners during times of crisis. While each of these functions are

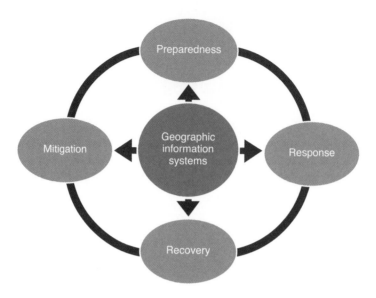

Figure 17.1   Conceptual model of GIS interaction with each phase of the emergency management cycle

primarily focused on different aspects of the disaster impact, the implementation of geospatial technologies has provided for and fostered cross-pollination of ideas, theories, metrics, and methods within and between ESFs at all levels of government.

A SHORT HISTORY OF GIS AND EMERGENCY MANAGEMENT

Prior to the formulation of the Federal Response Plan (FRP) for catastrophic earthquakes in 1987, the Stafford Disaster Relief Act 1988, and the FRP for natural hazards in 1989, the need for a unified response and recovery plans and procedures was not a high priority for federal, state, or local governments (Rubin, 2007). Moreover, the application of GIS techniques and methods in this newly established field of emergency management resided more in post-event research and analysis and did not begin to take a consistent operational role until the 1990s. There are, of course, exceptions to nearly every trend – rudimentary GIS

procedures were used in the evacuation of coastal populations during the pre-event phase of Hurricane Hugo in 1989 (Chan et al., 2004). However, the devastating impact of Hurricane Andrew on southern Florida provided fertile ground for incorporating research-driven geospatial technologies into disaster response (Wakimoto and Black, 1994; Jensen and Hodgson, 2006) and ushered in a higher level of appreciation for the use of GIS in disaster response, recovery, mitigation, and preparedness at both federal and state levels. Since that time, the use of GIS/RS technologies in emergency management has grown, in breadth and scope, into a field of research, application, and development that is unparalleled in comparison to other fields of similar maturity levels (Tobin and Montz, 2004).

A comprehensive review of GIS implementations related to EM research and practice is an enormous task. There have been many different overviews of the evolution of geospatial technologies and their use in EM (Waugh, 1995; Cova, 1999; Jensen and Hodgson, 2006; Cutter et al., 2007). There are also significant scholarly articles, government reports, and practitioner studies from the early 1970s to the present, which provide a bellwether for the types of geospatial research conducted in each of the four decades that GIS was utilized in EM that are worth noting.

A review of such studies is useful and illustrates the trends in research and practice. We briefly examined the published research found in two digital libraries – one located at the Hazards Research Center at the University of Colorado (http://www.colorado.edu/hazards/library/), and the other based on the holdings of the Hazards and Vulnerability Research Institute at the University of South Carolina. Figure 17.2 provides the temporal trend in the research, based on a simple classification of the implementation of either Geographic Information Systems or Remote Sensing technologies, while Figure 17.3 illustrates the general topical areas addressed by the research studies. Both figures reveal fundamental shifts in the focus of geospatial related research and applications for EM. The first transition relates to general technological changes and improvements in hardware,

software, and applications. Remote sensing research provided the primary focus in the 1970s and 1980s and then segued to a mixture of remote sensing and GIS in the mid 1990s (Figure 17.2). This trend continues into the late twentieth century and begins to reverse as we move toward the second decade of the twenty-first century. The second transition (Figure 17.3) illustrates a shift in the hazard research paradigm from an initial interest in the use of GIS for characterizing the physical hazard to a broader focus on using GIS to understand all phases of EM, including the human–environment interactions. The earlier years of hazard research and EM focused mainly on understanding physical processes and managing the threat source itself, while the later part of the time period showed a strong concentration on multi-hazard management, response, preparedness, and mitigation.

To examine some of the reasons for these shifts, we examined major disaster events. The Public Entity Risk Institute (PERI) provides a disaster timeline (http://www.disaster-timeline.com/DTL09_Sept26_2009-secure.pdf), and we adapted this framework

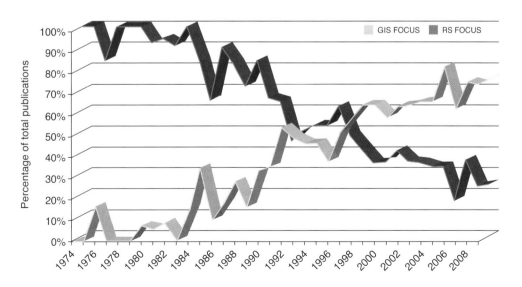

Figure 17.2 Graph depicting main focus of publications pertaining to spatial technologies and emergency management over the past 20 years

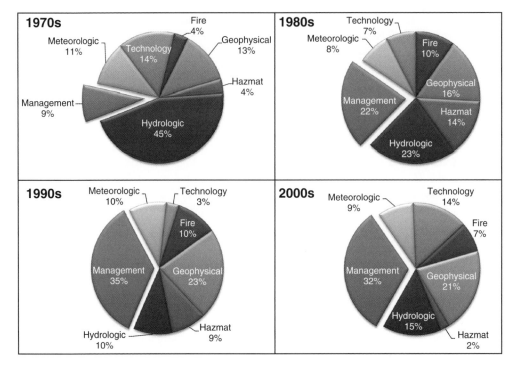

Figure 17.3 Breakdown of Topical areas addressed by GIS and RS research related to emergency management and natural hazards during each of the past 4 decades

to pinpoint some major advancement in the utilization of geospatial technologies. It is worth noting that in each time-period there were specific concentrations of research that roughly parallel disaster events in the PERI disaster timeline. Figure 17.4 illustrates the lag effect from the occurrence of major disaster events to the publication date of research utilizing geospatial technologies. While an imperfect metric, it does illustrate that some of the stimuli for research is the event itself, especially if the event was large (Northridge earthquake) or unprecedented (11 September).

The remainder of the chapter describes the utilization of GIS in each phase of the EM cycle starting with the practical experience and then describing the specific research contributions, especially those published since 2000. As will be shown, the use of GIS varies both in practice and in research contributions between each phase in the cycle.

GIS IN THE PREPAREDNESS PHASE

Most often viewed as down time in EM circles, the preparedness phase allows emergency personnel time to reflect on past events, evaluate practices and procedures, and create new applications and technologies to aid in the next emergency event. It is during this phase of the EM cycle that many of the geospatial tools and technologies move from "band-aid" patches applied in the field into full-fledged operational solutions designed to reduce future loss while enhancing the overall ability to react quickly and efficiently in future disasters. The process of preparing for natural disasters, accidental and intentional events, and public health emergencies gives GIS personnel the necessary time to complete development and deployment of useful products and solutions initially conceived during previous emergencies. These steps in

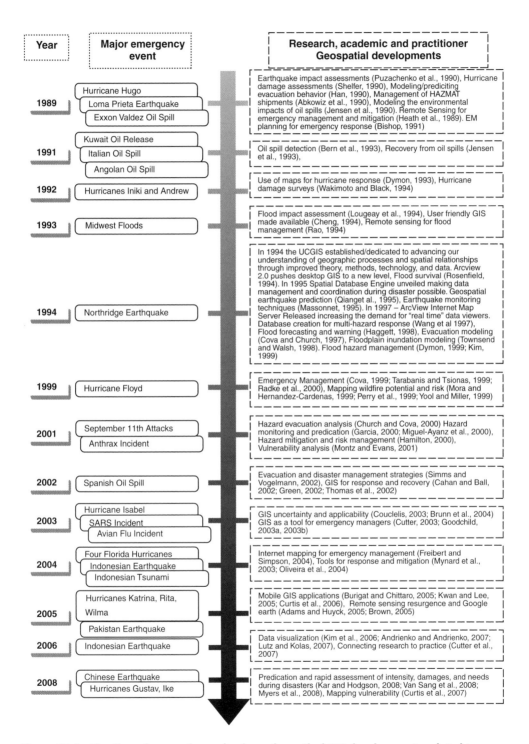

Figure 17.4 Timeline of research, academic, and practical GIS developments related to emergency management

the technological development process include improvements in post-event damage assessment techniques; procedures for baseline data collection; and the creation of deployable tools for field assessment of damages. This "down time" also affords an opportunity for practitioners to address issues surrounding the standardization of map templates, symbology, and vocabulary. Research in the preparedness phase supports all aspects of planning including protective actions such as sheltering or evacuation.

Practice

Preparedness involves partnerships between local, state, and federal agencies as well as the private sector, non-governmental organizations, and academe. Pre-impact planning is a large part of the preparedness effort. The National Research Council (NRC, 2007) recently evaluated the current use of geospatial data and tools in EM and made an important series of recommendations to enhance geospatial preparedness for the nation. Foremost among their dozen recommendations was the need to develop geospatial plans, procedures, and policies that were multi-agency, multi-jurisdictional (local to federal), and involved non-governmental organizations and local stakeholders. They also prepared a detailed checklist for gauging the community or agency's ability to use geospatial information in EM. This preparedness checklist covered nine thematic areas (integration, human resources, training, data access, data quality, data gathering, data improvement, information delivery, and equipment and infrastructure [NRC, 2007: Appendix C]). The creation and maintenance of baseline data is a crucial part of geospatial preparedness activities. Such data on populations, critical facilities, weather, land and property ownership, flood zones, jurisdictions, transportation networks, and businesses provide the foundational information needed by emergency managers and first responders.

There are a number of excellent examples of the current use of GIS in providing such baseline data at the state level. Notably, the State of Alabama's Department of Homeland Security has created a spatial decision support system (http://www.dhs.alabama.gov/virtual_alabama/home.aspx) for use by state, county, and local EM personnel and any other entity interested in leveraging geospatial data from a broad suite of practitioners. This free Google Enterprise-based system supports mapping, analytics, geospatial data acquisition, visualization, and provides a common operating picture (COP) for more than 4000 users and 1100 agencies within the state. Built in the field, by and for the support of field operations, Virtual Alabama (VA) has revolutionized the idea of enterprise-level data and analysis structures in a low cost, collaborative, technically maintainable, scalable, and extendable platform. North Carolina provides a GIS-based (http://www.ncfloodmaps. com/default_swf. asp) online – flood mapping tool that enables users to interactively view flood data, download current data, maps, and reports, and see the status of DFIRM adoption and vector data and metadata. The State of California Resource Agency's CERES – California Environmental Resources Evaluation System – Program (http://ceres.ca.gov/) utilizes geospatial technologies to empower local government provision of information on sensitive natural areas and natural hazards. South Carolina maintains a web-based geospatial application for mapping of baseline historic hazards and impact zones, and infrastructure data (transportation, critical facilities) that is readily accessible to both researchers and practitioners (http://webra.cas.sc.edu/hvri/quicklinks/scemdmain.aspx).

Research

Most of the GIS-based research in the preparedness arena focuses on evacuation plans and models, the development of spatially enabled databases for EM applications, or the construction of spatial decision support systems. An example of the latter is the remote sensing hazard guidance system (RSHGS) developed by Hodgson, Davis, and Chen (http://www.rshgs.sc.edu/). The RSHGS assists emergency managers in acquiring and analyzing remote sensing imagery for a particular unfolding hazard event. The system provides information to users of geospatial technologies on the most appropriate satellite sensors for data pertaining to particular locale, including when and where specific satellites will pass overhead. Additional functions of the RSHGS include a modeling component, which predicts impact area from specific events based on user-defined input, and an image collection plan interface, which aids the user in identifying appropriate systems, data components, period, and image processing plans for unclassified image collection.

Evacuation route modeling is another research area heavily invested in GIS and GIS-based modeling. Lindell (2008) and Lindell and Prater (2007) have developed an evacuation time estimate model incorporating both GIS-based routing and behavioral assumptions in planning egress routes from the Texas coast during hurricanes. The site selection of evacuation shelters for people (Kar and Hodgson, 2008) and pets (Edmonds and Cutter, 2008) has received research attention as well. The most significant research on evacuation modeling using GIS is by Cova and colleagues (Cova and Church, 1997; Church and Cova, 2000; Cova and Johnson, 2002, 2003). The utilization of spatial models for wildfire evacuation preparedness and response (see next section) illustrates the power of the geospatial models and their application to real time EM.

There is a significant research base on the use of GIS to delineate potential hazard zones and to model such zones, especially related to hazards with root causes in geophysical or hydrological processes. Temesgen et al. (2001) focus on the broad application of GIS and RS technologies for the assessment of natural hazards, while in

the case of flood zone delineations, Gall et al. (2007) used GIS-modeling to replicate 100-year flood plains for the state of South Carolina in those counties where flood data were not available. Gritzner et al. (2001) and Perotto-Baldiviezo et al. (2004) focus on the implemented geospatial modeling techniques for the prediction of landslide hazards determining that the science of geospatial modeling of earth movement events is more dependent on data than specific model elements. Petersen et al. (2002), He et al. (2003) and Chau and Lo (2004) have implemented geospatial modeling techniques both in the United States and abroad for seismicity, seismic zone delineation, and debris flow modeling using spatial analysis functions. Using these types of geospatial models to understand the dynamics of geophysical events during the pre-event or preparedness phase of the EM cycle creates useful scenario-based information for all levels of government--information that can mean the difference between life and death during an actual event.

GIS IN THE RESPONSE PHASE

The ability to mount an effective response effort in an immediate post-disaster timeframe is critical to life saving efforts. The Federal role as outlined in the NRF provides roles, responsibilities, and lead federal agency contacts for 15 emergency support functions (ESFs) activated during the response phase. Table 17.1 describes each ESF and provides a small set of research-based geospatoial applications, advancements, and implementations related to each specific function. Accompanying this need for a rapid deployment of teams, supplies, emergency response vehicles, and health care providers, is a whole suite of operational questions, many of which can be easily answered and logically solved using the latest geospatial tools and techniques. Because most response-related operations contain spatial components, this phase of the EM cycle lends

Table 17.1 GIS tools and techniques for specific emergency support functions (ESFs)

ESF	Current Geospatial Tools and Techniques
ESF 1 – Transportation	Evacuation planning, routing disaster aid, remote sensing damage assessment of bridges and roads (Pal and Graettinger, 2003)
ESF 2 – Communications	Deploying wireless networks (Midkiff and Bostian, 2002)
ESF 3 – Public Works and Engineering	SAR and Optical Remote Sensing for damage detection (Huyck et al., 2004; Jensen and Hodgson ,2005; Womble et al., 2006)
ESF 4 – Firefighting	Mapping fire perimeters, GIS, SPD, and GSM technologies for management of emergency vehicles (Derekenaris et al., 2001)
ESF 5 – Emergency Management	Mapping emergency facilities, decision support systems (O'Looney, 1997; Cahan and Ball, 2002; Zerger and Smith, 2003; Chiroiu, 2005)
ESF 6 – Mass Care, Emergency Assistance, Housing, and Human Services	Determine optimal placement of feeding stations, shelters, emergency assistance centers, and temporary housing sites. Field incident command and field care technologies (Chan et al., 2004)
ESF 7 – Logistics Management and Resource Support	Track food, water, blankets, tarps, and other emergency relief commodities. GPS-GIS fleet management (Prakash and Kulkarni, 2003)
ESF 8 – Public Health and Medical Services	Identify "special need" medical populations. Locational assessment for emergency services (Hanson, 2000)
ESF 9 – Search and Rescue	Prepare and print maps for field personnel. USAR mobile technologies and remote damage assessment techniques (Chiroiu and Andre, 2001; Huyck and Adams, 2002)
ESF 10 – Oil and Hazardous Materials Response	Plume modeling, analyzing environmental impact of oil spills (Knudsen and Anderson, 2006)
ESF 11 – Agriculture and Natural Resources	Mapping impact on natural and cultural resources. Analyzing hurricane timber blow down (Mynard et al., 2003)
ESF 12 – Energy	Mapping electricity outages and oil and gas pipeline ruptures (Johnston, 2001)
ESF 13 – Public Safety and Security	Determining facility perimeter buffers, securing sites of prominent events with view shed analysis (Leitinger, 2004)
ESF 14 – Long-Term Community Recovery	Geospatial analysis supporting economic impact and development planning (Cheng et al., 2006)
ESF 15 – External Affairs	Web maps giving public emergency information (Croner, 2003)

itself particularly well to the processes, metrics, and functionality of geospatial solutions. However, much of the geospatial activity during this phase is borne out of necessity in the field rather than the controlled environment of an academic or research institution.

Practice

Nearly every question related to emergency response is rooted in two main planning principles related to the location and placement of tangible and intangible items. These spatial questions include the following.

- Where are the access points to the disaster area?
- Where are the hardest hit areas?

- Are there immediate "secondary" disasters (fire, downed electric lines, flood victims) and where are they located?
- Which sectors of the area are without power, heat, potable water; and where are medical, and search and rescue assets located in relation to need?

These questions, and many others related to emergency response, lend themselves well to the implementation of geospatial strategies, metrics, and technologies, and the analytical power of spatial analysis may be the difference between life and death during disaster situations. No other phase of the EM cycle presents a forum as rich in cutting edge – in situ development and creative geospatial development as disaster response.

Ahearn (2003) provides a useful synopsis focused on the use of GIS and RS technologies during the response phase of the World Trade Center attack in 2001. The unique ways in which remotely sensed data were utilized during the immediate emergency response to this disaster and the tools and technologies brought to bear on the city of New York created the most intensive collaboration between GI scientists, researchers, and practitioners of the early twenty-first century.

The response phase creates innovations and true advancements in the field, often out of sheer necessity. It is these breakthroughs and connections between science, technology, and practice that provide a window into the truly universal nature of geospatial applications related to disaster management (see Box 17.1). Many of these innovative applications never make it through the disaster response phase to become a regular component of emergency response, yet this type of experimentation leads to new geospatial applications, such as those described in the Columbia disaster.

Access to dynamic, extendable, and multi-purpose GIS software is critical to any EM initiative. Large-scale emergencies with responders from multiple agencies and organizations (such as the seemingly every-present California wildfires) create an environment conducive to the implementation of large-scale GIS software solutions such as ESRI ArcGIS Desktop or technologies leveraging the internet such as ArcIMS or ArcGIS Server mapping software. The GeoMac project (Box 17.2) is one example of the application of technology across a broad array of stakeholders at the federal, state, and local levels that provides geospatial information in an easily accessible manner.

However, recent "smaller" disasters such as the Florida Christmas and Groundhog Day tornado outbreaks in 2007, Hurricane Gustav in 2008, and the numerous flooding events of 2009 provided a fertile environment for the adaptation and implementation of mapping and spatial analysis tools from the large suite of available low cost and free "open source" GIS applications and organizations. These "free" tools and applications have grown to rival mainstream geospatial products in their use within the different phases of EM. Perhaps the most well known of these is the set of Google-based mapping and visualization tools found in Google Maps™ and Google Earth™ as well as Microsoft®'s Virtual Earth® – however, there are many other open-source GIS applications available for users to leverage within a variety of operating platforms (Table 17.2). These free, broadly accessible tools provided user friendly alternatives to the often

---

Box 17.1   GIS modeling in support of the Columbia disaster

There was an outpouring of support and coordination between more than 130 federal, state, and local organizations responding to the Columbia Disaster in early 2003. Although the Federal Emergency Management Agency was footing the bill for the search and recovery operation (more than US$1 million per day), much of the geospatial support came from organizations outside of the DHS umbrella, and included the coordination of academic expertise and field based practical knowledge.

The shuttle recovery operation, built pragmatically upon a gridded pattern, allowed for the systematic search of the debris field distributed across a 2,400 square mile disaster area. The search for remnants of the shuttle was originally confined to a specified area around the trajectory of the orbiter as plotted by NASA, and resulted in X and Y ground locations for each recovered piece. Skilled engineers identified and cataloged each piece of recovered shuttle material based on the location from which it originated on the shuttle, and assigned an X and Y grid location associated with its "as-built" position on the orbiter. These two "geographic" locations enabled a geographer, deployed by the US Forest Service, to dynamically link ground recovery location with original part location.

The orbiter location grid depicts the original location of recovered shuttle parts and is correlated with the geographic location of each piece recovered from the field). The discovery of this correlation aided in the response and recovery efforts and provided a new geospatial tool to emergency managers and decision makers.

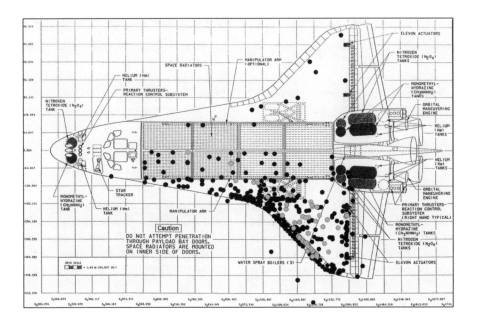

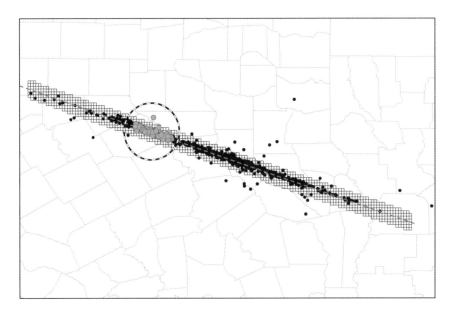

This spatial association was the impetus leading to the development of a GIS analysis and visualization tool that revolutionized the shuttle search and recovery process and aided in the reconstruction of the final timeline of disintegration.

The initial theory that items of comparable weight, material construction, trajectories, and ballistic coefficients, as they broke free from the orbiter, should have landed on the ground near each other provided GIS specialists with the details needed to construct a spatial-temporal representation of the shuttle debris field. The use of this newly identified correlation between original locations on the Orbiter Grid vs. ground search locations yielded a cutting-edge breakthrough intersecting GIS technology and NASA engineering expertise. It also generated revisions in the general response plan by expanding the overall search pattern of the crash site, adjusting the trajectory-based search area in specific zones, shifting the grid search priority, and including one additional nautical mile in the overall search radius from the originally identified shuttle debris cloud trajectory.

Source: Personal communication and graphics from Dr. Tara Plewa, Geographic Information Officer, South Carolina Army National Guard, January 24, 2008.

Box 17.2   Cooperative GIS for emergency management

The need for real-time, integrated, multi-functional, and accessible geospatial information for both situational awareness and response activities became apparent in September of 2000 when nearly 80,000 fires in the Western United States began burning some 6.5 million acres of land containing not only structures, but also valuable natural resources. More than 25,000 firefighters, nearly 1,000 fire engines, 200 helicopters, and every available air tanker were deployed on the fire-lines resulting in one of the largest coordinated emergency management efforts to date. Response priorities for the entire area of impact were set at diffuse and dis-jointed (off site) geographic fire coordination sites which were focused primarily on human safety and the protection of property and natural resources. While past efforts had relied heavily on printed map documents, this event quickly set the need for integrated, real-time, geospatial products and analysis for emergency management. The result was GEOMAC, Wildland Fire Support System, an internet-based mapping application used to visually represent active fires. Supported by a multi-agency group comprised of the Bureau of Land Management, the US Forest Service, the National Park Service, the National Interagency Fire Center, the National Weather Service, the Bureau of Indian Affairs, the US Fish and Wildlife Service, the US Geological Survey, the California Fire Geospatial Task Group, and the Office of Wildland Fire Coordination, data from GEOMAC can be incorporated into many desktop and internet-based mapping applications and combined with other spatial data such as deployed resources, forecasted fire-weather, critical infrastructure, and population information to create a more realistic idea of where to focus resources in the present as well as where to stage for future deployment. More information about GEOMAC can be found at http://www.geomac.gov.

---

programming intensive web-based GIS solutions found in other geospatial software and have become essential in the response and recovery efforts for many disaster events. The use of these tools became paramount for the communication of data and analytics along the Gulf Coast during and immediately following the impact of Hurricanes Katrina and Rita in 2005, Southern California wildfires in 2007, and Hurricanes Gustav and Ike in 2008 (Luccio, 2005; McKee, 2005; California Daily News, 2007). The quote in Box 17.3 provides insight into the dynamic nature of open-source web GIS as a means to communicate data and information in the aftermath of a disaster. A complete list of open source geospatial applications and technologies can be found at http://opensourcegis.org.

Table 17.2 Open source GIS software solutions

Software name	URL
Tools and Applications for Analysis and Display	
GRASS	http://grass.osgeo.org/
HidroSIG	http://poseidon.medellin.unal.edu.co/~hidrosig/
JUMP	http://www.vividsolutions.com/jump/
QGIS	http://qgis.org/
FMaps	http://sourceforge.net/projects/fmaps/
OpenEV	http://openev.sourceforge.net/
MapWindow	http://www.mapwindow.org/
Tools and Applications for Analysis and Modelling	
BASINS	http://www.epa.gov/waterscience/ftp/basins/system/BASINS4/
SAMT	http://www.samt-lsa.org/
Tools and Applications for Spatial Database Development	
GDAL	http://www.gdal.org/
Deegree	http://www.deegree.org/
Map Bender	http://www.mapbender.org/Main_Page
PostGIS	http://postgis.refractions.net/
PostgreSQL	http://www.postgresql.org/
Tools and Applications for Web Mapping	
Chameleon	http://chameleon.maptools.org/index.phtml
FIST	http://fist-mapping.org/
InterMap	http://sourceforge.net/projects/intermap/
Ka-Map	http://ka-map.maptools.org/
Majas	http://www.geomajas.org/
Mapbuilder	http://communitymapbuilder.org/
MapGuide	http://mapguide.osgeo.org/
MapJunction	http://www.mapjunction.com/bra/
MapServer	http://mapserver.gis.umn.edu/index.html

Box 17.3   Open source GIS for emergency management

More missions have been flown, data moved and mosaics generated. There are now many different types of data sets and over 5000 high-resolution images geocoded and mosaicked online...Along the way members from NGA, NRO, USGS, NRL have been very supportive and interested. The site is now on the master list of resources for disaster response for Katrina and has briefed to decision makers within the various government agencies. It has been one of the finest collaborations between government, academia, research, and open source software developers that I have ever witnessed.-M. Lucas (L3-Titan) discussing the collaborative efforts taking place during the immediate response phase for Hurricane Katrina (Mitchell, 2005).

Research

Although generally not implemented at the same temporal speed or under the same type of critical need as those applications developed during disaster response itself, the academic and research focused on this phase includes the near real time implementation of geospatial models to highlight impacted areas or to provide inputs into spatial decision support systems. Findings from research related to response initiatives generally relate to two broad topical categories – issues involving the location of and movement of people out of the impact area and those focused on movement of emergency goods and services into the disaster area following an event. For example, Mitchell et al. (2007) identified a larger behavioral response than expected in the aftermath of a chemical spill, thus producing an "evacuation shadow." This over-response led to management difficulties as more people than anticipated evacuated the area, putting stress on the local response resources. Other research examined optimal response models for routing of emergency vehicles, goods, and services into an area (Huyuk and Adams, 2002) and barriers to real-time GIS in response (Zerger and Smith, 2003).

GIS IN THE RECOVERY PHASE

The recovery phase of a disaster is the most time and resource consuming of all the phases in the EM cycle (Kates and Pijawka, 1977). In reality, the GIS component of disaster recovery provides paper maps as overviews for decision makers and planners as more of a "rearview mirror" approach than as a proactive management tool. However, advances in technologies, data quality and availability, and better visibility into the effectiveness and efficiency of GIS as a planning and management tool have lead to some minor breakthroughs in the application of geospatial techniques in the recovery phase. Specifically, the need to respond to increasing public scrutiny of state and federal government actions spawned a new subfield of GIS applications in EM tracking recovery processes and fostering greater public awareness. FEMA, the US Army Corps of Engineers, state and local governments, and the public have become entranced with the ability to see "real time" recovery data on the web, whether through a publicly edited WIKI or a more stringently controlled geospatial server application. The use of the internet and geospatial technologies for use within EM is not a new concept, but rather one that has been steadily developing since the late 1980s as a useful

technology with potentially far-reaching EM applications (Newsom et al., 1999). However, the surge in internet and information technologies over the past decade has proven that while successful response does indeed start with a map, the dynamic processes of recovery lend themselves well to interactive, flexible, and reactive technologies (i.e., the Internet and real-time geospatial analytics). Unfortunately, the need for real-time information means that hard copy cartographic representations (e.g., paper maps) are becoming obsolete, replaced by digital geo-visualization tools and processes (Hanson, 2000; NRC, 2007).

Practice

The recovery phase has become more than simply "a return to normalcy." This step of the EM cycle is one of the main focal points of public interest, academic research, and EM. Geospatial tools help decision makers and stakeholders to quickly analyze and view spatial data related to the many intricate issues associated with the recovery process, and requires much more insight, investigation, and analysis than simply displaying progress to the public in the form of flat or hard copy maps (Babcock, 2005). Technological innovations in both hardware (smart phones), and software (Enterprise level Solutions) provide the means to view and query vast amounts of data (in near real time) and have created a consumer culture in constant need of more information, more useful tools, and faster answers.

Breakthroughs in the application of geospatial technologies like the United Nations Office for the Coordination of Humanitarian Affairs' (UNOCHA) Humanitarian Information Center (HIC) deployment of a web-enabled mapping application, identified "who was doing what and where" within the impact zone of the 2004 Indian Ocean tsunami. This application provided valuable information to relief workers about which organizations were aiding in recovery efforts in which parts of the impact area. Additionally, geospatial solutions such as FEMA's implementation of a publicly available ArcGIS Server application used to provide consistent, detailed information about the infrastructure repair and rebuilding projects across the Gulf Coast (http://www.femarecovery.gov/) informs not only decision makers, but also the public in need of answers about recovery progress. Increasingly, advances in mobile GIS applications for data capture, update, and on-the-fly assessment and analysis have made it possible for the recovery process to speed up in areas historically burdened with countless hours of research and analysis (Accela, 2005; Wilson and Cretini, 2007). Geo-spatial visualizations, representations, and analysis tools linked to recovery operations provide much-needed monitoring information on the pace and progression of the recovery process at the local level.

Research

All disasters are local, and recovery for disaster events is intricately woven into the context of place. This means that the operationalization of spatial models of recovery has been a difficult undertaking and from a research perspective, often the most neglected sector of the EM cycle (Mills, 2008). The need for a clearer understanding of the interactions between humans and the environment lends itself well to geospatial analysis, visualization, and validation. However, theory-based geospatial models of recovery have been slow to materialize and have often been too site specific. Nevertheless, geographically based and specific geospatial research on different aspects of recovery (Godschalk, 2003; Vest et al., 2007), indications of a propensity to recovery (Cutter et al., 2008), and spatial frameworks and models aimed at understanding differential recovery (Liu and Plyer, 2007; Ross et al., 2008) from disasters continue to be developed. Since Hurricane Katrina, the application

of RS and GIS technologies in academic research into recovery (Curtis et al., 2007; Laituri and Kodrich, 2008; Pais and Elliott, 2008) have seen a dramatic increase and it is only a matter of time until these research-oriented projects migrate into the realm of user-friendly practical applications for disaster recovery.

GIS IN THE MITIGATION PHASE

The Disaster Mitigation Act (DMA) 2000 was perhaps the most influential event in the history of GIS and EM operations (Rubin, 2007). The passage of this act resulted in the implementation of geospatial data, tools, and techniques in the assessment of hazard vulnerability and in the (federally required) formulation of disaster management and mitigation plans. In many ways, DMA 2000 fostered the technological revolution within EM. This fundamental shift from theory to practice is seen most clearly in disaster mitigation. Nearly every state in the nation has become compliant with the policies and procedures put forth by DMA 2000 – each utilizing geospatial tools and techniques in diverse and powerful ways.

Practice

The implementation of GIS applications within the mitigation phase of the EM cycle occurs in three main areas: analysis of risks and vulnerabilities; risk reduction; and insurance analysis. Unfortunately, many of the geospatial techniques employed under the broad brush of mitigation are fraught with obstacles stemming from both a lack of conceptual development and the need to have public buy-in and cooperation in order to implement plans and policies. There are two good examples of practitioner use of GIS in hazard mitigation stemming from DMA 2000. The first is the development of a GIS-based methodology for hazard vulnerability assessment, first implemented by the State of South Carolina (State of South Carolina, 2005). This GIS-based product integrates socio-demographic and hazard information to illustrate those counties with the greater degree of hazard vulnerability as well as the source of the vulnerability (e.g., vulnerable populations or high-risk hazard zones, or some combination of the two). The state hazard assessment plan, revised very three years using geospatial data and tools, is the basis for the state mitigation plan under the requirements of DMA 2000. A more recent development is the movement of all the geospatial data for the statewide hazard assessment to a web-based product, easily available to the emergency planner through an Integrated Hazard Assessment Tool (IHAT) (http://mapra.cas.sc.edu/ihat/index. html). Once the counties determine their level of hazard vulnerability, the development of mitigation plans ensues. In fact, under DMA 2000 all counties in the USA must have mitigation plans derived from hazard vulnerability assessments. If these are lacking, the mitigation plans will not have federal approval and counties and states run the risk of not receiving federal disaster relief if they are not in compliance.

The second example is the loss-estimation tool, HAZUS-MH, developed by FEMA. Modeling the effects of potential events and disasters is an important tool for assessing the value of mitigation measures. HAZUS-MH models physical damage, economic loss, and social impacts from earthquakes, floods, and hurricanes. The software comes with its own population, building, and critical facility data, with locally generated data by the end-users easily incorporated into the software. Results are generated based upon varying natural disaster scenarios, geography, and mitigation measures. These "what if" scenarios can help evaluate the effectiveness of potential mitigation measures for communities and aid in their decision-making. This no-cost spatial decision support tool is readily available to practitioners (http://www.fema.gov/plan/prevent/hazus/).

Research

The mitigation phase of the EM cycle has all of the crucial elements that classic academic research uses to frame theory, extend concepts, and generate process models. Since the idea of mitigation is to reduce future impacts of disaster events, most mitigation research focuses on past events using the "rearview mirror" approach and provides statistically sound exemplars of costs savings, reduction of human and monetary impacts, and improved capacities to bounce back after disasters. Recently, the term hazard vulnerability (although not new within the field of hazard research) has gained popularity within the practitioner community. This re-enlightenment of federal, state, and local officials has provided a constant flow of research focused on identifying and decreasing vulnerability while increasing resiliency (Montz and Evans, 2001; Cutter et al., 2003; Rashed and Weeks, 2003; Dow, 2005; Cutter, 2005; Cutter and Emrich, 2006; Schmidtlein et al., 2008). Many of these conceptual and theoretical models employ the analytical techniques available in state-of-the-art GISs (Cutter, 2003, 2006, 2008; Boruff et al., 2005; Colten, 2006; Cutter et al., 2006; Piegorsch et al., 2007). The ability to integrate social and environmental data for places, scale differences, and temporal variations into the equation of vulnerability has produced an entirely new avenue of research inquiry that links mitigation to preparedness, and ultimately to response and recovery (Puszkin-Chevlin et al., 2006; Burton and Cutter, 2008; Cutter and Finch, 2008).

The mitigation phase of the cycle also provides a unique opportunity to engage research interest in the communication of risk and cooperative mitigation with the public. Not only does the public need to become more aware of the type and magnitude of hazard events but the need for progressive collaborative efforts among policy makers, planners, emergency managers, and the general public is crucial to curtailing future losses (Beer et al., 2004).

One example is the availability of research-based online interactive hazards atlases. These include coverage of Pacific Realm disasters (http://www.pdc.org/atlas), Hawaiian hazards (http://pubs.usgs.gov/imap/i2761/), Texas coastal hazards (http://www.beg.utexas.edu/coastal/hazard_atlas1.htm), and international hazards (http://esri.com/news/arcuser/0402/swissre.html). These sites, among others, provide users with place-based, geospatial understanding of hazards, thus allowing the communication of hazard risk and mitigation strategies to become a more significant part of the decision-making process. The spatial analysis tools and technologies are infinitely useful for taking into account stakeholder ideas, thoughts, and concerns related to hazard mitigation, risk, and vulnerability (Craig et al., 2002; Chiwaka, 2005; Pelling, 2007).

OUTLOOK FOR THE FUTURE

The efficiency and effectiveness of GIScience within the broader EM community is well established. Yet, this has only occurred during the past decade, as the EM community has been able to capitalize on the vast array of geospatial functionality that is available to end users, ranging from desktop products, to mobile applications, and web-based query and analysis tools. The full utilization of geospatial technologies is a positive trend, but institutional barriers exist, including a trained workforce. The use of geospatial technologies in EM needs to be extended into all aspects of the disaster cycle, systematically implemented in future disasters, and provided to all citizens and levels of government for transparency of operations and unified decision making.

There has been a general trend toward the development of regional or multi-jurisdictional GISs centered near major metropolitan areas and large urban counties, such as VA and Virigina's VIPER (Virginia Interoperability Picture for Emergency Response) system. Federal, state, and local governments recognize that emergencies and disasters do not fall neatly within individual administrative areas and that effective response and recovery operations requires multi-jurisdictional organization (Public Technology Institute [PTI], 2006). This includes geospatial assets.

A third trend has been the increased demand for GIS specialists within EM. Our colleges and universities are not meeting the demand for the next generation of skilled EM practitioners. This is due to two reasons. First, students must be conversant with hazards and disasters generally, and the principles of EM more specifically in order to be effective during disaster events. Disciplinary programs in geography, sociology, political science, public administration, or through interdisciplinary programs focused on disasters, EM, or homeland security provide such knowledge. Second, students must have expertise in geospatial thinking, geospatial techniques, and in information technology (including databases and programming). This knowledge is found most often within geography curricula and to a lesser extent through computer science programs. To be successful, the next generation of EM personnel needs strong backgrounds in both GIScience and hazards/EM concepts and theory. Currently, however, there are very few academic programs nationally that offer such expertise in one major or within one university.

Successful EM begins with geospatial information. There are two avenues for the integration of research and practice that merit discussion. The first is the systematic implementation of some type of a distributed network for GIS-based support for emergency response to supplement local, state, and federal efforts. In many instances, the disaster itself (11 September, Hurricane Katrina) simply overwhelmed the local expertise, both of the practitioners as well as the local research community. Volunteers descended into the affected regions to assist, but the efforts were not coordinated and thus underutilized. In the extreme cases, EM staff had to reorganize the volunteer efforts to meet agency standards for quality. The establishment of a pre-selected, regionally based GIS hazard corps, with nodes off site, could ably assist in the analysis of data and production of visual materials in real time and provide the requisite 24/7 access to information. Using web technology and IT these teams, activated when needed, would assist local efforts, not supplant them.

The second area is the development of a standardized archiving system for the data and products generated during a disaster response, including analytical tools, research products, and the suite of geospatial solutions created during the event itself. This information is extremely valuable to advancing theoretical constructs within research and is normally not archived (in the field) in a systematic fashion. Such an archiving system will capture perishable data, facilitate future research, and improve current practice through lessons learned. There is limited experience with just such an archive (Mills et al., 2008), but clearly more needs to be done.

CONCLUSION

It is clear that any application (or suite of applications) that is able to model, predict, or spatially comprehend the interaction between physical processes and the human use system can be applied in many EM applications. The real question is to what extent and how much will it cost? Federal, state, and local agencies often must leverage their resources to achieve multiple uses. Geospatial tools have an advantage in that they are useful for municipal planning and taxation, growth management, or emergency preparedness and response. More importantly, if one considers the increasing monetary impacts of disasters, the investment in equipment, training, and personnel is obvious. Yet, the NRC (2007) committee found that "… funding for

geospatial preparedness is insufficient and the funding that exists is often used ineffectively' (p. 7)." The future of GIS in EM is here, yet the nation is not taking advantage of this rich resource. Institutional barriers (data sharing, confidentiality, proprietary data), inadequate funding, lack of relevant data, human resources, and unequal access all contribute to the problem. The real issue for research and practice is determining how to build capacity and bring GIS skills to emergency managers in communities, especially those that are disadvantaged, before, during, and after the disaster.

REFERENCES

Abkowiz, M., Cheng, P.D. and Lepofsky, M. (1990) 'The use of geographic information systems (GIS) in managing hazardous materials shipment', *Transportation Research Record*, 1261: 35–43.

Accela. (2005) *New Orleans Leverages Web-based and Mobile Technology to aid in Response and Recovery: Accela Case Study.* http://www.accela.com/products/includes/assets/casestudy_NOLA.pdf (accessed 1 November 2008).

Adams, B.J. and Huyck, C.K. (2005) 'The emerging role of remote sensing technology in emergency management', in C. Taylor and E. VanMarcke (eds), *Infrastructure Risk Management Processes: Natural, Accidental, and Deliberate Hazards.* Reston, VA: American Society For Civil Engineers. pp. 95–117.

Ahearn, S.C. (2003) 'Case study: Response to the WTC disaster', in K. C. Clarke (ed.), *Getting Started with Geographic Information Systems*, 4th edn., Prentice Hall.

Andrienko, N. and Andrienko, G. (2007) 'Intelligent visualization and information presentation for civil crisis management', *Transactions in GIS*, 11 (6): 889–909.

Babcock, C. (2005). *New Orleans Residents Want Homes, but Data is a Start – Since Katrina, City Inspectors have Scrambled to Get Information Posted Online. Information Week*, December. http://www.informationweek.com/news/ global-cio/showArticle.jhtml?articleID=174910729&queryText=Katrina (accessed 2 December 2009).

Beer, T., Bobrowsky, P., Canuti, P., Cutter, S. and Marsh, S. (2004) 'Hazards – minimising risk, maximizing awareness, prospectus for a key theme for the International Year of the Planet Earth 2005–2007', *Earth Sciences for Society, International Union of Geological Sciences, UNESCO*. Leiden, The Netherlands: Earth Sciences for Society Foundation. p. 16. Available online from http://www.esfs.org.

Bern, T.I., Wahl, T., Anderssen, T. and Olsen, R. (1993) 'Oil spill detection using satellite based sar: Experience from a field experiment', *Photogrammetric Engineering and Remote Sensing*, 59 (3): 423–28.

Bishop, J. (1991) 'ER planning – computer systems allowing integrated planning, real-time aid in emergency response', *HAZMAT World*, 4(7): 48–52.

Boruff, B.J., Emrich, C. and Cutter, S.L. (2005) 'Erosion hazard vulnerability of U.S. coastal counties', *Journal of Coastal Research*, 21(5): 932–42.

Brown, P.J. (2005) 'Hurricane Katrina: Satellite technology stands tall', *Journal of Emergency Management*, 3: 22–6.

Brown, P.J. (2008) 'Expanding role of satellites in preparedness, surveillance and response', *Disaster Medicine and Public Health Preparedness*, 2(3): 200–3.

Brunn, S.D., Cutter, S.L. and Harrington, J.W. Jr. (eds) (2004) *Geography and Technology*. Dordrecht, Boston and London: Kluwer Academic Publishers.

Burigat, S. and Chittaro, L. (2005) 'Visualizing the results of interactive queries for geographic data on mobile devices', *Proceedings of the 13th ACM International Symposium on Advances in Geographic Information Systems*. Bremen, Germany. 11: 4–5.

Burton, C. and Cutter, S.L. (2008) 'Levee failures and social vulnerability in the sacramento – San Joaquin Delta area, California', *Natural Hazards Review* 9(3):136–49.

Cahan, B. and Ball, M. (2002) 'GIS at ground zero: Spatial technology bolsters world trade center response and recovery', *GEO World*, 15(1): 26–9.

California Daily News (2007) *Google Map and Evacuation List*. http://www.dailynews.com/breakingnews/ci_7243279 (accessed 2 December 2009).

Chan, T.C., Killeen, J., Griswold, W. and Lenert, L. (2004) 'Information technology and emergency medical care during disasters', *ACAD Emergency Medicine*, 11(11): 1229–36.

Chau, K.T. and Lo, K.H. (2004) 'Hazard assessment of debris flows for Leung king estate of Hong Kong by incorporating GIS with numerical simulations', *Natural Hazards and Earth System Sciences*, 4: 103–16.

Cheng, M. (1994) 'User-friendly GIS aids in flood management', *Water Environment and Technology*, 4(4): 34.

Cheng, S., Stough, R.R. and Kocornick Mina, A. (2006) 'Estimating the economic consequences of terrorist disruptions in the national capital region: An application of input – output analysis', *Journal of Homeland Security and Emergency Management*, 3(3): 1–19.

Chiroiu, L. (2005) 'Damage assessment of 2003 Bam, Iran, Earthquake using Ikonos imagery', *Earthquake Spectra*, 21(S1): S219–S224.

Chiroiu, L. and André, G. (2001) *Damage Assessment Using High Resolution Satellite Imagery: Application to 2001 Bhuj, India Earthquake, RiskWorld*. http://www.riskworld.com/Nreports/2001/Bhuj,India,earthquake2001.PDF (accessed 4 February 2008).

Chiwaka, E. (2005) *Mainstream Participatory Vulnerability Analysis in Action Aid International*. Benefield Research Centre. Disaster Studies Working Paper No. 13.

Church, R.L. and Cova, T.J. (2000) 'Mapping evacuation risk on transportation networks using a spatial optimization approach', *Transportation Research* 8C(1–6): 321–36.

Colten, C.E. (2006) 'Vulnerability and place: Flat land and uneven risk in New Orleans', *American Anthropologist*, 108(4): 731–4.

Couclelis, H. (2003) 'The certainty of uncertainty: GIS and the limits of geographic knowledge', *Transactions in GIS*, 7(2): 165–75.

Cova, T.J. and Church, R.L. (1997) 'Modeling community evacuation Culnerability using GIS', *International Journal of Geographic Information Science*, 11(8): 763–84.

Cova, T.J. (1999) 'GIS in emergency management', in P. A. Longley, M. F. Goodchild, D. J. Maguire and D. W. Rhind (eds), *Geographic Information Systems: Principles, Techniques, Applications, and Management*, New York: John Wiley and Sons. pp. 845–58.

Cova, T.J. and Johnson, J.P. (2002) 'Microsimulation of neighborhood evacuations in the urban-wildland interface', *Environment and Planning A*, 34: 2211–29.

Cova, T.J. and Johnson, J.P. (2003) 'A network flow model for lane – based evacuation routing', *Transportation Research A*, 37: 579–604.

Craig, W.J., Harris, T.M. and Weiner, D. (2002) *Community Participation and Geographic Information Systems*. London: Routledge.

Croner, C.M. (2003) 'Public health GIS and the internet', *Annual Review of Public Health*, 24: 57–82.

Curtis, A., Mills, J.W. and Leitner, M. (2006) 'Spatial confidentiality and GIS: Re – engineering mortality locations from published maps about hurricane Katrina', *International Journal of Health Geographics,* 5(44): 12.

Curtis, A., Mills, J.W. and Leitner, M. (2007) 'Katrina and vulnerability: The geography of stress', *Journal of Health Care for the Poor and Underserved,* 18(2): 315–30.

Curtis, A., Mills, J.W., Kennedy, B., Fotheringham, S. and McCarthy, T. (2007) 'Incorporating a spatial video acquisition system into disaster response and recovery: A case study of the lower 9th Ward', *Journal of Contingencies and Crisis Management,* 15(4): 208–19.

Cutter, S.L. (2003) 'GI science, disasters and emergency management', *Transactions in GIS* 7(4): 439–45.

Cutter, S.L. (2005) 'The geography of social vulnerability: Race, class, and catastrophe, social science research council', Understanding Katrina: Perspectives from the Social Sciences. Available from http://understandingkatrina.ssrc.org/Cutter/.

Cutter, S.L. (2005) 'The role of vulnerability Science in disaster preparedness and response research'. Testimony provided to the Subcommittee of the U.S. House of Representatives' Committee on Science, 'The Role of Social Science Research in Disaster Preparedness and Response'. Available from http://science.house.gov/publications/hearings_markups_details.aspx?NewsID=976 (accessed 10 November 2005).

Cutter, S.L. (2006) *Hazards, Vulnerability, and Environmental Justice.* London and Sterling, VA: Earthscan. p. 418.

Cutter, S.L. (2008) 'Vulnerability analysis, environmental hazards', in E. Melnick and B. Everitt (eds), *Encyclopedia of Quantitative Risk Assessment.* John Wiley and Sons Ltd. pp. 1845–48.

Cutter, S.L., Boruff, B.J. and Shirley, W.L. (2003) 'Social vulnerability to environmental Hazards', *Social Science Quarterly,* 84(1): 242–61.

Cutter, S.L. and Emrich, C.T. (2006) 'Moral Hazard, social catastrophe: The changing face of vulnerability along the Hurricane coasts', *Annals of the American Academy of Political and Social Science,* 604: 102–12.

Cutter, S.L., Emrich, C.T., Mitchell, J.T., Boruff, B.J., Gall, M., Schmidtlein, M.C., Burton, C.G. and Melton, G. (2006) 'The long road home: Race, class and recovery from hurricane Katrina', *Environment,* 48(2): 8–20.

Cutter, S.L., Emrich, C.T., Adams, B.J., Huyck, C.K. and Eguchi, R.T. (2007) 'New information technologies in emergency management', in W. Waugh and K. Tierney (eds), *Emergency Management: Principles and Practice for Local Government,* 2nd edn.

Washington DC: International City/County Management Association (ICMA) Press. pp. 279–97.

Cutter, S.L. and Finch, C. (2008) 'Temporal and spatial changes in social vulnerability to natural Hazards', *Proceedings of the National Academy of Sciences,* 105(7): 2301–6.

Cutter, S.L., Barnes, L., Berrry, M., Burton, C., Evans, E., Tate, E. and Webb, J. (2008) 'A place – based model for understanding community resilience to natural disasters', *Global Environmental Change,* 18(4): 598–606.

Derekenaris, G., Garofalakis, J., Makris, C., Prentzas, J., Sioutas, S. and Tsakalidis, A. (2001) 'Integrating GIS, GPS and GSM technologies for the effective management of ambulances', *Computers, Environment and Urban Systems,* 25: 267–78.

Dow, K. (2005) *Steps Toward Mapping Vulnerability to Climate Change. Directions Magazine.* July. http://www.directionsmag.com/article.php?article_id=901&trv=1 (accessed 23 June 2008).

Dymon, U.J. (1993) *Map Use During and After Hurricane Andrew. Natural Hazards Research and Applications Information Center.* March: 10.

Dymon, U.J. (1999) 'Effectiveness of Geographic Information Systems (GIS) applications in flood management during and after Hurricane Fran', *Quick Response Report No. 114.* http://www.colorado.edu/hazards/research/qr/qr114/qr114.html (accessed 1 October 2008).

Edmonds, A.E. and Cutter, S.L. (2008) 'Planning for pet evacuations during disasters', *J. Homeland Security and Emergency Management* 5(1): Article 33 (p. 18). Available at: http://www.bepress.com/jhsem/vol5/iss1/33 (accessed 5 January 2009)

Freibert, P. and Simpson, D.M. (2004) 'The role of the Internet Map Servers (IMS) in emergency management', *Journal of the American Society of Professional Emergency Planners,* 11: 92–8.

Gall, M., Boruff, B.J. and Cutter, S.L. (2007) 'Assessing flood hazard zones in the absence of digital floodplain maps: A comparison of alternative approaches', *Natural Hazards Review,* 8(1): 1–12.

Garcia, S.G. (2000) 'A real-time flood forecasting system based on GIS and DEM', *International Association of Hydrological Sciences – Association Iinternationale des Sciences Hydrologiques,* 267: 439–45.

Godschalk, D.R. (2003) 'Urban hazard mitigation: Creating resilient cities', *Natural Hazards Review,* 4: 136–43.

Goodchild, M.F. (2003a) 'Geospatial data in emergencies', in. S. L. Cutter, D. B. Richardson and T. J. Wilbanks (eds), *Geographical Dimensions of Terrorism,* New York: Routledge. pp. 99–104.

Goodchild, M.F. (2003b) 'Data modeling for emergencies', in S.L. Cutter, D.B. Richardson and T.J. Wilbanks (eds), *Geographical Dimensions of Terrorism*. New York: Routledge. pp. 105–9.

Green, R.W. (2002) *Confronting Catastrophe: A GIS Handbook*. Redlands CA.: ESRI Press.

Gritzner, M.L., Marcus, W.A., Aspinall, R. and Custer, S.G. (2001) 'Assessing landslide potential using GIS, soil wetness modeling and topographic attributes, Payette river, Idaho', *Geomorphology*, 37: 149–65.

Grunes, A.E., and Kovel, L.P. (2000) 'Using GIS in emergency management operations', *Journal of Urban Planning and Development*, 126(3): 136–49.

Heath, G., Hovmork, G., Sax, H. and Carter, D. (1989) '"Space applications for disaster mitigation and management"', *Acta Astronautica*, 19(3): 229–49.

Haggett, C. (1998) 'An integrated approach to flood forecasting and warning in England and Wales', *Journal of the Chartered Institution of Water and Environmental Management*, 12(6): 425–32.

Hamilton, R.M. (2000) 'Science and technology for natural hazard reduction', *Natural Hazards Review*, 1(1): 55–60.

Han, A. (1990) 'Tevacs: Decision support system for evacuation planning in Tiawan', *ASCE Journal of Transportation Engineering*, 116: 821–30.

Hanson, M. (2000) 'Beyond first aid: Emergency response teams turn to graphics', *IEEE Computer Graphics and Applications*, 20(6): 12–18. http://csdl2.computer.org/persagen/DLAbsToc.jsp?resourcePath=/dl/mags/cg/& toc=comp/mags/cg/2000/06/g6toc.xml (accessed 20 January 2008).

He, Y.P., Xie, H., Cui, P., Wei, F.Q., Shong, D.L. and Gardner, J.S. (2003) 'GIS-based Hazard mapping and Zonation of debris flows in Xiaojiang basin, Southwestern China', *Environmental Geology*, 45(2): 286–93.

Huyck, C. and Adams, B.J. (2002) 'Emergency response in the wake of the World Trade Center attack: The remote sensing perspective', *MCEER Special Report Series*, Vol. 3 of Engineering and Organizational Issues Related to the World Trade Center Terrorist Attack. Buffalo, NY: Multidisciplinary Center for Earthquake Engineering Research (MCEER).

Huyck, C.K., Adams, B.J., Cho, S. Eguchi, R.T., Mansouri, B. and Houshmand, B. (2004) 'Methodologies for Post-Earthquake building damage detection using SAR and optical remote sensing: Application to the 17 August 1999, Marmara, Turkey Earthquake', *Multidisciplinary Center for Earthquake Engineering Research*, Technical Report MCEER-04–0004, June 15.

Jensen, J.R., Ramsey, E. W., Holmes, J.M., Michel, J.E., Savitsky, B. and Davis, B. (1990) 'Environmental Sensitivity Index (ESI) Mapping for oil spills using remote sensing and geographic information system technology', *International Journal of Geographic Information Systems*, 4 (2): 181–201.

Jensen, J.R., Narumalani, S., Weatherbee, O., Murday, M., Sexton, W.J. and Green, C.J. (1993) 'Coastal environmental sensitivity mapping for oil spills in the United Arab emirates using remote sensing and GIS technology', *Geocarto International*, 8(2): 5–13.

Jensen, J.R. and Hodgson, M.E. (2006) 'Remote sensing of natural and man-made hazards and disasters', in M.K. Ridd and J.D. Hipple (eds), *Manual of Remote Sensing: Remote Sensing of Human Settlements*. American Society for Photogrammetry and Remote Sensing. pp. 401–29.

Johnston, R.B. (2001) 'AM/FM/GIS Moves to the Web', *Transmission and Distribution World*. October.http://www.tdworld.com/mag/power_ amfmgis_moves_web/index.html (accessed 5 February 2008).

Kar, B. and Hodgson, M.E. (2008) 'A GIS-based model to determine site suitability of emergency evacuation shelters', *Transactions in GIS*, 12(2): 227–48.

Kates, R.W. and Pijawka, D. (1977) 'From rubble to monument: The pace of recovery', in J. E. Haas, R. W. Kates and M. J. Bowden (eds), *Reconstruction Following Disaster*. Cambridge, MA: The MIT Press. pp. 1–23.

Kim, C. (1999) *Flood Damage Mapping in North Korea using JERS-1 data*. International Geoscience and Remote Sensing Symposium (IGARSS'99), Piscataway, NJ: Institute of Electrical and Electronics Engineers (IEEE).

Kim, T.H., Cova, T.J. and Brunelle, A. (2006) 'Exploring map animation for post – event analysis of wildfire protective action recommendations', *Natural Hazards Review*, 7 (1): 1–11.

Knudsen, R. and Anderson, C. (2006) 'Using ArcGIS 'on-the-fly' for Coastal Disaster Response Following Hurricane Katrina.' ESRI Professional Papers. http://gis.esri.com/library/userconf/proc06/papers/papers/pap_1714.pdf (accessed 5 February 2008).

Kwan, M. and Lee, J. (2005) 'Emergency response after 9/11: the Potential of real – time 3D GIS for quick emergency response in micro-spatial environments', *Computers, Environment and Urban Systems*, 29: 93–113.

Laituri, M. and Kodrich, K. (2008.) 'On line disaster response community: People as sensors of high magnitude disasters using internet GIS', *Sensors*, 8(5): 3037–55.

Leitinger, S.H. (2004) *Comparison of GIS – Based Public Safety Systems for Emergency Management.* Austria: Salzburg Research Forschungsgesellschaft. http://www.salzburgresearch.at/research/gfx/udms2004_final_paper_leitinger.pdf (accessed 2 February 2008).

Lindell, M.K. and Prater, C.S. (2007) 'Critical behavioral assumptions in evacuation – time estimate analysis for private vehicles: Examples from hurricane research and planning', *Journal of Urban Planning and Development*, 133(1): 18–29.

Lindell, M.K. (2008) 'An empirically based large scale evacuation time estimate model', *Transportation Research A*, 42: 140–54.

Liu, A. and Plyer, A. (2007) *The New Orleans Index*. Greater New Orleans Community Data Center. http://www.gnocdc.org/KI/KatrinaIndex.pdf (accessed 4 November 2008).

Lougeay, R., Baumann, P. and Nellis, M.D. (1994) 'Two digital approaches for calculating the area of regions affected by the great American flood of 1993', *Geocarto International*, 9(4): 53–9.

Luccio, M. (2005) 'Imagery for the Katrina Relief Effort', *GIS Monitor*, 13 October http://www.profsurv.com/magazine/article.aspx?i=70445 (accessed 30 November 2009).

Lutz, M. and Kolas, D. (2007) 'Rule-based discovery in spatial data infrastructure', *Transactions in GIS*, 11(3): 317–36.

Massonnet, D. (1995) 'Application of remote sensing data in earthquake monitoring', *Advances in Space Research*, 15(11): 37–44.

MCKee, L. (2005) 'Katrina Maps and Photos Delivered Using OGC Web Service Interface Standards', *Open Geospatial Consortium, Inc*, December Vol. 4. http://ogcuser.opengeospatial.org/comment/reply/123 (accessed 23 November 2009).

Midkiff, S.F. and Bostian, C.W. (2002) 'Rapidly deployable broadband wireless networks for disaster and emergency response', *Proceedings of the First IEEE Workshop on Disaster Recover Networks*. New York, NY; June. www.cwt.vt.edu/research/detail/disaster_response/Midkiff_Bostian _DIREN02.pdf (accessed 25 January 2008).

Miguel-Ayanz, J.S., Vogt, J.V., De Roo, A.P.J. and Schmuck, G. (2000) 'Natural hazards monitoring: forest fires, droughts and floods – the example of European pilot projects', *Surveys in Geophysics*, 21(2–3): 291–305.

Mills, J.W. (2008) 'Understanding disaster: GI science contributions in the ongoing recovery from Katrina', *Transactions in GIS*, 12(1): 1–4.

Mills, J.W., Curtis, A., Pine, J.C., Kennedy, B., Jones, F., Ramani, R. and Bausch, D. (2008) 'The clearinghouse concept: A model for geospatial centralization an dissemination in a disaster', *Disasters*, 32(3): 467–79.

Mitchell, J.T., Cutter, S.L. and Edmonds, A.S. (2007) 'Improving shadow evacuation management: Case study of the Graniteville, South Carolina chlorine spill', *Journal of Emergency Management*, 5(1): 28–34.

Montz, B.E. and Evans, T.A. (2001) 'GIS and Vulnerability Analysis', in E. Gruntfest and J. Handmer (eds), *Coping with Flash Floods*. Dordrecht, The Netherlands: Kluwer Academic Publishers. pp. 37–48.

Mora, F. and Hernandez-Cardenas, G. (1999) *Modeling and Mapping Wildfire Potential in Mexico Based on Vegetation and Drought Conditions Using Remote Sensing and GIS Technology*. Joint Fire Science Conference and Workshop, National Interagency Fire Center. http://jfsp.nifc.gov/conferenceproc/Mo-03Moraetal. pdf (accessed 6 June 2008).

Myers, C.A., Slack, T. and Singelmann, J. (2008) 'Social vulnerability and migration in the wake of disaster: The case of hurricanes Katrina and Rita', *Population and Environment*, 29: 271–91.

Mynard. C.R., Keating, G.N., Rich, P.M. and Bleakly, D.R. (2003) *Geographic Information System (GIS) Emergency Support for the May 2000 Cerro Grande Wildfire, Los Alamos, New Mexico, USA*. Los Alamos National Laboratory report LA-14007-MS Issued: May 2003. http://www.osti.gov/bridge/purl.cover.jsp;jsessionid=9C6BF8C2458C60133B4A5FCA05AB438A?purl=/812177-bHdm0H/native/ (accessed 4 February 2008).

National Research Council (2007) *Successful Response Starts with a Map: Improving Geospatial Technologies for Disaster Management*. Washington DC: National Academies Press.

Newsom, D.E., Herzberg, C.L. and Swietlik, C.E. (1999) 'Value of the internet in emergency response', *Proceedings, 1999 IEEE International*. New Orleans, LA, USA. September 7–10, 1999.

Oliveira, C.S., Ferreira, M.A., Oliveira, M. and Sá, F.M. (2004) 'Planning in Seismic Risk Areas –The Case of Faro – Algarve: A First Approach', *Proceedings XI ANIDIS*, Jan 2004, CD Rom B4–05. Génova.

O'Looney, J. (1997) *Beyond Maps: GIS and Decision Making in Local Government*. Washington, DC: ICMA, 4.

Pais, J.F. and Elliott, J.R. (2008) 'Places as recovery machines: Vulnerability and neighborhood change after major hurricanes', *Social Forces*, 86(4): 1415–53.

Pal, A. and Graettinger, A.J. (2003) *Emergency Evacuation Modeling Based On Geographical Information System Data*, CD-ROM Proceedings of the 2003 TRB Annual Meeting, Washington D.C.

Pelling, M. (2007) 'Learning from others: The scope and challenges for participatory disaster risk assessment', *Disasters*, 31(4): 373–85.

Perotto-Baliviezo, H.L., Thurow, T.L., Smith, C.T., Fisher, R.F. and Wu, X.B. (2004) 'GIS-based spatial analysis and modeling for landslide Hazard assessment in steep lands, southern Honduras', *Agriculture, Ecosystems and Environment*, 103: 165–76.

Perry, G.L.W., Sparrow, A.D. and Owens, I.F. (1999) 'A GIS-supported model for the simulation of the spatial structure of wildland fire, Cass basin, New Zealand', *Journal of Applied Ecology*, 36(4): 502–18.

Petersen, M.D., Cramer, C.H. and Frankel, A.D. (2002) 'Simulations of seismic hazard for the pacific northwest of the United States from earthquakes associated with the cascadia subduction zone', *Pure and Applied Geophysics*, 159: 2147–68.

Piegorsch, W.W., Cutter, S.L. and Hardisty, F. (2007) 'Benchmark analysis for quantifying urban vulnerability to terrorist incidents', *Risk Analysis*, 27(6): 1411–25.

Prakash, S.S.S. and Kulkarni, M.N. (2003) 'Fleet management: A GPS – GIS integrated approach', *Proceedings of the Map India Conference 2003*. http://www.gisdevelopment.net/technology/gps/pdf/159.pdf (accessed 4 February 2008).

Public Technology Institute (2006) *Using GIS to Support Emergency Management and Homeland Security*. https://www.netforumondemand.com/eweb/shopping/shopping.aspx?site=pti&prd_key=870d1834–1634–4737–981d-c219a5f031ee. (accessed 5 February 2008).

Puszkin-Chevlin, A., Hernandez, D., and Murley, J. (2006) 'Land use planning and its potential to reduce hazard vulnerability: Current practices and future responsibilities', *Marine Technological Society Journal*, 40(4): 7–15.

Puzachenko, Y.G., Borunov, A.K., Koshkarev, A.V., Skulkin, V.S. and Sysuyev, V.V. (1990) 'Use of remote sensing Imagery in analysis of consequences of the Armenian earthquake', *Mapping Sciences and Remote Sensing*, 27(2): 89–102.

Qiang, Z., Changgong, D., Yong, Z. and Guo, M. (1995) 'Satellite thermal infrared temperature increase precursor-short term and impending earthquake prediction', *Proceedings of the Space Congress on Environmental Assessment of Geological Hazards*. Germany: Munich. pp. 53–7.

Radke, J., Cova, T., Sheridan, M.F., Troy, A., Mu, L. and Johnson, R. (2000) 'Application challenges for geographic information science: Implication for research, education and policy for emergency preparedness and response', *URISA Journal*, 12(2): 15–30.

Rao, R.S. (1994) 'Role of remote sensing in flood management: The May 1990 cyclone', *International Journal of Remote Sensing*, 15(8): 1557–58.

Rashed, T. and Weeks, J. (2003) 'Assessing vulnerability to earthquake hazards through spatial multicriteria analysis of urban areas', *International Journal of Geographical Information Science*, 17(6): 547–76.

Rosenfeld, C.L. (1994) 'Flood Hazard reduction: GIS maps survival strategies in Bangladesh', *Geographical Information Systems*, 4 (5): 29–37.

Ross, D.W., Ortiz, E. and Bonaguro, J. (2008) *Postal Data and Google Maps Shine Light on New Orleans Recovery*. Presentation at the 2008 URISA Annual Conference and Exposition, 7–10 October 2008 – New Orleans, LA.

Rubin, C.B. (ed.) (2007) *Emergency Management: The American Experience 1900–2005*. Washington D.C.: Public Entity Risk Institute (PERI).

Shelfer, R.B. (1990) *Hurricane Hugo Damage Assessment on the Francis – Marion National Forest*. Third Biennial Conference on Remote Sensing Applications, Evans City, PA, American Society for Photogrammetry and Remote Sensing.

Schmidtlein, M.C., Deutsch, R.C., Piegorsch, W.W. and Cutter, S.L. (2008) 'Building indexes of vulnerability: A sensitivity analysis of the social vulnerability index', *Risk Analysis*, 28(4): 1099–114.

Sims, H. and Vogelmann, K. (2002) 'Popular mobilization and disaster management in Cuba', *Public Administration and Development*, 22: 389–400.

State of South Carolina. (2005) *State of South Carolina Hazard Assessment*. Columbia, SC: Emergency Management Division. http://www.scemd.org/Library/SCEMD_Hazards_Assessment_Final_Report_2005–1.pdf (accessed 24 October 2008).

Tarabanis, K. and Tsionas, I. (1999) 'Using network analysis for emergency planning in case of an earthquake', *Transactions in GIS*, 3(2): 187–97.

Temesgen, B., Mohammed, M.U. and Korme, T. (2001) 'Natural Hazard assessment using GIS and remote sensing methods, with particular reference to the landslides in the Wondogenet Area, Ethiopia', *Physics and Chemistry of the Earth*, 26(9): 665–75.

Thomas, D.S.K., Cutter, S.L., Hodgson, M.E., Gutekunst, M. and Jones, S. (2002) *Use of Spatial Data and Technologies in Response to the September 11 Terrorist Attack*. Boulder, CO,

University of Colorado, Natural Hazards Research and Applications Information Center.

Tobin, G.A. and Montz, B.E. (2004) 'Natural Hazards and technology: Vulnerability, risk and community response in Hazardous environments', in S. D. Brunn, S. L. Cutter and J. W. Harrington Jr. (eds), *Geography and Technology.* Dordrecht: Kluwer. pp. 547–70.

Townsend, P.A. and Walsh, S.J. (1998) 'Modeling floodplain inundation using an integrated GIS with radar and optical remote sensing', *Geomorphology*, 21(3–4): 295–312.

Van Sang, N., Smith, R.K. and Montgomery, M.T. (2008) 'Tropical-cyclone intensification and predictability in three dimensions', *Quarterly Journal of the Royal Meteorological Society*, 134: 563–82.

Vest, J.R., Patton-Levine, J. and Valadez, A.M. (2007) 'Geocoding and GIS analysis of displaced populations', *Journal of Emergency Management*, 5(4): 57–63.

Wakimoto, R.M. and Black, P.G. (1994) 'Damage survey of hurricane Andrew and its relationship to the eyewall', *Bulletin of the American Meteorological Society*, 75 (2): 189–200.

Wang, J., Wise, S. and Haining, R. (1997) 'An integrated regionalization of earthquake, flood and drought hazards in China', *Transactions in GIS*, 2(1): 25–44.

Waugh, W.L. (1995) 'Geographic information systems: The case of disaster management', *Social Science Computer Review*, 13(4): 422–31.

Wilson, S. and Cretini, C. (2007) 'Data access and dissemination for emergency response and long-term recovery efforts related to hurricanes Katrina and Rita', in G. S. Farris, G. J. Smith, M. P. Crane, C. R. Demas, L. L. Robbins and D. L. Lavorie (eds), *Science and the Storms: The USGS Response to the Hurricanes of 2005: U.S. Geological Survey Circular*, 1306: 283.

Womble, J.A., Ghosh, S. and Adams, B. (2006) Engineering and Organizational Issues Before, During and After Hurricane Katrina, vol. 2, Advanced Damage Detection for Hurricane Katrina: Integrating Remote Sensing and VIEWSTM Field Reconnaissance, MCEER Special Report Series, MCEER-06-SP02 (Buffalo, N.Y.: MCEER, March 2006). http://www.mceer.buffalo.edu/publications/Katrina/06SP02-web.pdf (accessed 4 February 2008).

Yool, S.R. and Miller, J.D. (1999) *Mapping Risk at the Los Alamos Urban-Wildland Interface*. Proceedings from the Joint Fire Science Conference and Workshop: "Crossing the Millennium: Integrating Spatial Technologies and Ecological Principles for a New Age in Fire Management" http://jfsp.nifc.gov/conferenceproc/Ma-10Yooletal.pdf (accessed 28 October 2008).

Zerger, A. and Smith, D.I. (2003) 'Impediments to using GIS for real-time disaster decision support', *Computers, Environment and Urban Systems*, 27(2): 123–41.

GIS in Public Participation and Community Development

18

Designing Public Participation Geographic Information Systems

Piotr Jankowski

INTRODUCTION

The concept of public participation geographic information systems (PPGIS) traces back to the supposition that geographical data stored in GIS and spatial analysis tools might empower different groups of the public, including marginalized communities, to represent their interests in democratic decision-making processes concerning land-based resource allocations (Harris et al., 1995). The emergence of PPGIS has also been a reaction to the perception of GIS technology as being top-down, technocratic, and non-inclusive of the interests of communities affected by planning and decision-making processes. In that context, PPGIS was conceptualized as a bottom-up, technology-facilitated, social process allowing users to combine their informal and often qualitative knowledge, impressions, and ideas with formalized knowledge about real world objects, their locations, and properties stored in GIS database (Talen, 2000). Since its introduction in the mid-1990s, the idea of PPGIS has grown and today it comprises a prominent area of

research in geographic information science (GIS) using different, but related names such as Participatory GIS (PGIS), Collaborative GIS (CGIS), and Group Spatial Decision Support Systems (GSDSS). Nyerges et al. (2006a) trace the roots of PPGIS and PGIS to 'community-integrated GIS' where the technology is as important as the context, process, and people who use it. Sieber (2006) sees PPGIS as the overarching paradigm that developed in the mid-1990s out of an interest in social implications of GIS and later became a part of Critical GIS, which is structured around social-theory motivated research on uses of GIS in social, political, organizational, and technological contexts. Balrm and Dragicevic (2006) use PGIS as an aggregate term for GIS-based technologies supporting participatory planning and decision making. In their view, PGIS includes PPGIS, which deals with the use of GIS by the general public and community groups. PGIS also includes group spatial decision support systems (GSDSS). GSDSS focuses on the use of GIS-based tools by more homogenous (than the general public) groups of stakeholders or experts. Kingston presents elsewhere in this book a more nuanced distinction, according to which PGIS is aligned predominantly with bottom-up approaches ascribed to community driven processes whereas PPGIS is more characteristic of top-down approaches driven by governmental agencies. He then concludes that the differences between PPGIS and PGIS are mostly ontological focusing on the issue of participation (who participates, why, and for what purpose) and that in practice there is a very little difference between PPGIS and PGIS. Ramsey (2010) organizes the terminology into three approaches comprising PPGIS: participatory GIS, collaborative decision support GIS, and web-based grassroots GIS. Participatory GIS involves empowering marginalized groups at the community level and is often characteristic of, as Kingston points out, bottom-up approaches to public participation supported by GIS. Collaborative decision support GIS, rooted in SDSS concepts and methods, often enables sophisticated analytical capabilities exceeding by far those found in most PGIS. These capabilities, however, constrain the participation to analytically and technologically savvy groups. Web-based grassroots GIS relies on advances in "Web 2.0" technologies enabling the creation of web mapping applications which are freely available to anyone with an Internet connection, a web browser, and basic surfing skills.

The vast literature on the conceptual underpinnings, social theory driven critiques, and application examples of PPGIS in various domains and diverse cultural settings provides plenty of empirical and theoretical fabric but offers surprisingly little in terms of systematic evaluation of PPGIS in practice and resulting PPGIS design methodologies. In a broad sense, the concept of "PPGIS evaluation" can be understood as assessing the social and political outcomes of using GIS technology. This conceptualization led Jordan (2002) to caution against the lack of systematic evaluations of PPGIS resulting in potentially poor uses of GIS technology

combined with socially and politically irrelevant results. Barndt (2002) offered three evaluation criteria for assessing the utility of PPGIS projects: (1) value of PPGIS results as the bases for decision making; (2) sustainability of PPGIS activities over the longer term; and (3) the level of acceptance and support for PPGIS in a local community. Other studies focused on the usability, human–computer–human interactions, tool and process evaluation, and comparative analysis of PPGIS applications (Carver et al., 2001; Sawicki and Peterman, 2002; Haklay and Tobón, 2003; Steinmann et al., 2005; Aggett and McColl, 2006; Jankowski et al., 2006; Nyerges et al., 2006b). Despite these efforts more work is needed to develop a methodology for evaluating and designing PPGIS that fit participatory processes, information needs of participants, and political/institutional context for intended PPGIS use. This chapter takes a step toward this goal by focusing on one systematic and on-going effort to develop a design methodology for PPGIS undertaken by Nyerges, Jankowski, and their colleagues (Nyerges and Jankowski, 1997; Jankowski and Nyerges, 2001; Nyerges et al., 2006b). In the remainder of the chapter I discuss enhanced adaptive structuration theory (EAST) – an assessment framework for scoping the designs of PPGIS. I focus on the relationship between participants and their information needs, and process dynamics involving the people–technology interaction. I then show how these information needs link with other components of PPGIS and how they factor into the design considerations. These components, including participants and their characteristics, participation setting, information and communication technologies, as well as system architecture are based on the acknowledgment that the key drivers of PPGIS are participants, participatory processes, and the technology used in support of these processes (Schlossberg and Shuford, 2005). I close the chapter with a brief account of current challenges and opportunities for developing future PPGIS designs.

DESIGN CONSIDERATIONS FOR PPGIS

Research concerning models and the practice of public participation shows that meaningful public participation can be achieved by providing access to voice and competence of knowledge that foster shared understanding of facts, data, cultural values, interests, and concerns (National Research Council, 1996; Renn et al., 1997). The notion of meaningful public participation is situated in the context of Habermas's theory of communicative rationality, which according to Wilson "… is the working out of claims, the interpretation of knowledge and values, and the sharing of facts and stories, while maintaining a critical self awareness of the ground rules for communication" (Wilson, 2001: 12). Such a broad-based definition of communication is open both to analysis and deliberation and hence, it can be conducted in a form that the authors of the book *Understanding Risk* (National Research Council, 1996) call *deliberative-analytic* participation process. In the analytic-deliberative process, deliberation is used to elicit concerns and ideas from participants. The concerns and ideas help in turn to guide and motivate analysis, which provides fact and data-based information in order to inform deliberation. In a model of analytic-deliberative participation applied to environmental decision making called *cooperative discourse* (Renn et al., 1997), technical experts perform the analysis while the representatives of the public deliberate on the bases of information presented by the experts.

The cooperative discourse and other deliberative-analytic models conceptualize public participation as structured activity. Accordingly, public participation is a process that has defined objectives, a sequence of steps leading to the achievement of objectives, rules of participation, means of supporting the steps of the process, and measures (qualitative or quantitative) of gauging progress made toward achieving the objectives. Objectives may be any given goal set forth by the individuals participating, be they an improved understanding of an issue by the public or a collective preference statement for a particular solution to a problem. Consequently, the central questions for the design of PPGIS aimed at supporting deliberative-analytic processes include: (1) what is the nature of participatory process to be supported by PPGIS; (2) what is the nature of the public participating in the process; and (3) what analytic-deliberative system capabilities are necessary to foster public participation? I address these questions, beginning with the nature of PPGIS-supported, analytic-deliberative process, in the following section.

Characterizing public, process, and outcomes in PPGIS

Any analytic-deliberative process involving a group of participants can be considered as an information exchange process. Through the exchange process, the participants pool together different types of information (e.g., ideas, evaluations, facts, questions, interpretations) in order to gain a shared understanding of the problem at hand, and to arrive at a solution. The information is continuously integrated and assessed as the participants move toward a recommendation(s) on how to solve a decision problem. The information exchange involves both a task process and a social process. A number of normative approaches exist for structuring the information exchange involving both the task and social processes. Nyerges et al. (2006b) identified four methods of structured participation based on extensive review of planning and management literature. These methods include nominal group technique, Delphi process, technology of participation, and citizen panel/jury. Each technique offers steps transitioning a group of participants from the initial stage of a group process involving setting an agenda and stating a goal, through idea generation and synthesis, to negotiation

Table 18.1 Synthesis of participatory activity steps shared by two or more structured participation methods

NGT	DP	CPJ	ToP	Participatory activities
X	X		X	Goal statement (context setting)
X	X		X	Brainstorm items
X		X	X	Negotiate (clarify) items
	X		X	Synthesize clusters and label items
X		X	X	Vote/poll
	X	X		Review/evaluation

Notes: NGT – nominal group technique, DP – Delphi process, CPJ – citizen panel/jury, ToP – technology of participation (Adapted from Nyerges et al. 2006b)

and solution recommendation. There are commonalities among the methods and many steps are shared by two or there of them (see Table 18.1). It is not immediately clear how the steps listed in Table 18.1 might be implemented in a specific participatory process nor is it obvious what facts, data, and information tools might be fitting the task at hand. In order to answer this question and to provide a more in-depth articulation of what can transpire during a participatory decision-making process, Nyerges and Jankowski (1997) developed EAST, which is now in a second version as EAST2 (Jankowski and Nyerges, 2001).

EAST2 is a network of constructs and their relationships providing a theoretical framework to consider and subsequently help plan the steps comprising a structured analytic-deliberative process (see Figure 18.1). In the simplest terms, EAST2 can be viewed as a check-list that a PPGIS designer might want to go through in order to articulate the conditions leading to the deployment of PPGIS, use of PPGIS during an actual participatory process, and the expected outcomes of the process. In a more sophisticated view, EAST2 is a framework for envisioning a future participatory interaction including both task and social processes. From the practical/application perspective EAST2 helps to set up PPGIS for specific participatory decision situations. From the research perspective,

EAST2 helps to explain the expected and observed realizations of participatory decision processes involving human interactions mediated by information technology.

EAST2 provides the basis for developing PPGIS and selecting tools appropriate for a given task due to its comprehensive character. In Figure 18.1, the EAST2 framework consists of a set of eight constructs, with 25 *aspects* as the basic elements (bulleted items) characterizing participatory decision making, and a set of seven premises (the Ps) that represent our expectations about the *relations* between the eight constructs. The 25 aspects, taken as a whole or as a subset, can represent different conditions and relationships, which may occur during group interactions. The aspects in conjunction with the premises help us assess which methods and decision support tools will likely address information exchange needs.

The structuration process of what/who influences what/who is the embedding context for EAST2. Neither technological nor social constructs predominate, but rather they work together to structure, and therefore reconstruct each other. This is the fundamental idea underlying "adaptive structuration." The organization of constructs in EAST2 reflects an organization of analytic-deliberative participatory process. The constructs are grouped into convening, process, and outcome categories. Jankowski and Nyerges (2003) provide a detailed explanation of each of the eight constructs, their 25 aspects, and accompanying seven premises. Subsequently, Nyerges at al. (2006a) give an example of using EAST2 for the planning of a participatory decision-making process involving conjunctive water administration and the representatives of major ground and surface water users. In the context of PPGIS design, the aspects of EAST2 can be posed as questions and answered by examining the conditions prior to the participatory process (aspects of the convening constructs), envisioned task and social process interactions (aspects of the process constructs), and their outcomes (aspects of the outcome constructs).

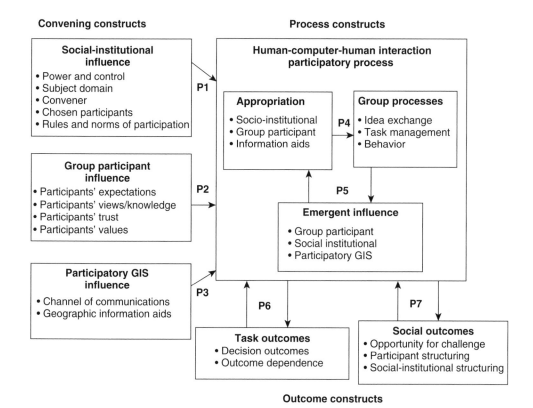

Figure 18.1   Diagram representing constructs, aspects, premises, and relations (arrows) between the constructs comprising Enhanced Adaptive Structuration Theory 2 (EAST2) framework

Source: Jankowski, P. and Nyerges, T. (2003) Toward a framework for research on geographic information-supported participatory decision-making, *URISA Journal Online,* 15(1).

One of the crucial convening constructs, from the perspective of PPGIS design, is "Group Participants Influence." The examination of the aspects comprising this construct can help the PPGIS designers understand who the future participants are, what are their expectations vis-à-vis the participatory process, as well as what values, knowledge about the problem domain, and trust in the process they have. Taking into account participants information needs is essential for creating a PPGIS capable of providing real answers to questions asked during a participatory process. I now turn to discussing approaches of eliciting participant information needs.

Anticipating the participant information needs

One of the key issues in designing an effective PPGIS is the anticipation of participant information needs. Knowledge of participant information needs can guide designers in creating a system that fits the participatory process. One approach to learning about information needs is to find out about participants' concerns. This approach is based on a theoretically founded relationship between fundamental values (moral, religious, economic, environmental) that the members of the society have, and the concerns that they experience and share in relation to a specific problem situation. The work of Keeney (1992) and his colleagues (Edwards and von Winterfeldt, 1987) suggest that participant information needs during a decision process are derived from deeply held values and beliefs. The practical question facing a PPGIS designer is then how to elicit participant values. Edwards and von Winterfeld (1987) demonstrated that values can be linked to decision objectives, which in turn can be linked to criteria used to evaluate progress toward achieving the objectives. Jankowski et al. (2006) suggested that user concerns are good proxies for values relevant to a given decision problem. The term "concern" is used here as the everyday proxy word (concept) to engage people in unpacking their values, which otherwise might be difficult to elicit. The difference between values and concerns is that the former represent a fundamental basis for judging whether something is good, bad, or neutral, and hence motivates a potential choice whereas the latter are participants' manifestations in reaction to a specific problem situation. Values derive from cultural traditions, social, and religious norms but are rarely invoked during a deliberative discourse. Instead, people commonly voice their concerns, which derive from values.

The difference between value and concern can be illustrated on the example of one particular study involving water administration planning. In the study, described by Nyerges et al. (2006a: 710-712), stakeholders did not state their positions in terms of value-laden phrases such as "preservation of one's way of life" or "equal access to water for everyone." Instead, they stated their positions in terms of value-derived concerns such as "impact of ground water pumping on surface water availability," which represented a concern of surface water users, or "hydraulic connection between ground and surface water," which represented a concern of ground water users. The concerns voiced by stakeholders are indicative of how user information needs are likely to surface in the form of data-specific questions during a participatory process. Once these needs are anticipated, they can be

provided for during the design process. A PPGIS design process that is based on real user information needs is much more likely to lead to a final product that works in a specific participatory context than PPGIS that is based only on assumptions and expectations about user information needs.

In the case of the stakeholder-driven process of water administration planning, anticipation of stakeholders' questions about the flow capacity of wells, cumulative impact of wells water pumping, flows in the Boise River, and the impact of ground water pumping on surface water flows was possible due to finding out about the stakeholder information needs in the course of structured group interviews (Jankowski et al., 2006). The interviews followed the steps of structured participation methods listed in Table 18.1. The anticipated questions, which represent the participant information needs, guided the development of PPGIS' database. Had the user information needs been not identified and the corresponding data not compiled and stored in the PPGIS database, the participatory process involving the stakeholders would have been much less effective. Hence, the identification of users, information needs can be considered as an important step in guiding the design and implementation of the PPGIS' database.

What specific techniques can be used to guide the elicitation of users' information needs? The answer depends on: (1) the number of participants; and (2) whether or not PPGIS designers can meet with the participants before the actual system design begins. In the case of a small group (on the order of 10 participants) depending on the group member availability, the information needs can be elicited in the course of a meeting led by an impartial facilitator who leads a discussion about issues surrounding the decision problem. In the case of a large group (on the order of hundreds of participants), with access available only to a small sample of participants, Nyerges et al. (2006b) recommend the use of *personas* and *decision scenarios* in order to learn about users' information needs. Personas are narratives describing fictional but realistic participants developed from interviews with real potential software users. The motivation behind developing personas for PPGIS design is to help system designers understand the perspectives, information needs, and anticipated behaviors of potential participants. It is important to note that personas should not be reduced to generic user types representing specific user groups. The whole point of developing personas is to generate a set of unique and richly described fictional participants. Personas should include the multiplicity of subject positions that can help the designers to imagine how the real participants would respond to different scenarios of PPGIS use. Creative explorations of scenarios may help to imagine what data and software functions a persona(s) would find useful in a given context. This approach to eliciting users information needs helps the designers not only to anticipate future data use patterns but also the user demand for specific system functionalities involving database access, data analysis and visualization, communication, and reporting.

Considering group size, setting, and technology

So far, I have explained the conceptual link between the aspects of "Group Participant Influence" construct (Figure 18.1) and participants' information needs identified as an important element of PPGIS design. The assessment of aspects comprising the other two convening constructs, "social-institutional influence" and "participatory GIS influence," can help illuminate elements of PPGIS design such as group size, setting, and the choice of technology. Specifically, three aspects, "chosen participants," "channel of communications," and "geographic information aids," relate to group size, participation setting, and GIS technology. These three design considerations (group size, setting, and technology) can be conceptualized as a

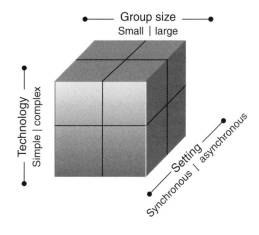

Figure 18.2 Design cube with axes representing three dimensions of PGIS design: group size, setting, and technology

cube with three axes represented by dichotomous, categorical variables (Figure 18.2).

The three dimensions of the cube, with each dimension having two different categories, represent eight potential design combinations (e.g., small group, synchronous setting, and simple technology, or large group, asynchronous setting, and complex technology). The question of which specific combination(s) should be incorporated into the PPGIS design can be answered by considering who the likely participants are and what their potential number will be, ways in which they will exchange information, and tools/functions that are likely to use (appropriate). Not all of the eight combinations are suitable and a careful assessment of the aspects leading to a participatory process should reveal them. For example, a large number of expected participants and the need to visualize information using 3D models may require a synchronous setting. Hence, a large group and a synchronous setting would require complex technology. In a different situation involving a small group, the use of an asynchronous setting may be counterproductive, and hence, the combination small group, asynchronous setting would be unsuitable.

Participatory process dynamics

The dynamics of the participatory decision-making process is influenced by a feedback loop called "Process Constructs" shown in Figure 18.1. The loop presents its own internal dynamics in which the appropriations of social-institutional mandates and group member status influence the quality of communication that can be measured by the quality of generated ideas. The communication within a group leads to the emergence of new structures and communicative behavior at a group and institutional level, which in turn, shapes appropriations of social-institutional mandates and group member influence. The dynamics of the described feedback loop can be altered intentionally or unintentionally by the introduction of information aids, including spatial data visualization and analysis tools of GIS, and by managing participatory process tasks. The chief reason for managing the dynamics of the participatory process is to improve the quality of the process and subsequently to achieve a better quality of process outcomes than what may be expected from an unmanaged or poorly managed group process.

The importance of skillful management of group/participatory processes derives from a recognition that biases in communication, called also "process losses," undermine the group productivity measured in terms of the quality and quantity of generated new ideas. The process losses, which are attributed to social loafing (waiting for others to contribute), groupthink (getting too quickly to a consensus without considering the consequences of decision), and social dominance (constraining the communication in the group), are symptomatic of the Ringlemann Effect. The effect described first by Ringlemannn (1912) can be observed by comparing potential group productivity to observed group productivity (Figure 18.3). The evidence from experiments with groups working in same-place, same-time settings shows that the maximum observed productivity is achieved for groups numbering 10–11 members (Troyer, 2003).

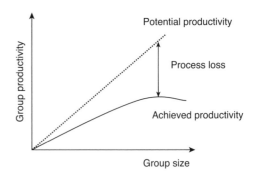

Figure 18.3 Divergence between the potential and achieved group productivity according to the Ringlemann Effect

In addition to the above-mentioned factors contributing to process losses, researchers in the field of group decision support systems, recognized hierarchy and social status in groups as additional factors influencing communication and idea generation (Silver and Troyer, 1994; Troyer, 2003). In analytic-deliberative participatory processes, similar to other group communication processes, the participants are frequently concerned with maintaining their status and social position in a group. This concern can have a negative effect on the quality of information exchange and process outcomes, as some participants may shy away from proposing innovative ideas for the fear of receiving negative evaluations from other group members and eroding their status position in a group. Experimental studies showed that the negative effects on the quality of information/ ideas created by group members concerned with preserving their social status was not a problem in anonymous groups (Connolly et al., 1990; Poole et al., 1991). The anonymous groups, however, took up to four times as long to generate the same number of ideas as the groups in which the identities of participants were known. These findings present an interesting dilemma as well as an opportunity to PPGIS designers. For example, in the decision situations calling for public involvement, should participation be anonymous or based on revealed identities of participants?

Or perhaps, should both models of participation be supported? What functions and tools should be built into PPGIS to reduce process losses associated with the negative effects of "groupthink," and the fear of negative evaluations? Are findings from the early group-work experiments in the 90s concerning the slow pace of generating ideas in anonymous groups still valid now under the conditions of on-line PPGIS systems? What software architectures should be used for different combinations of group size and setting (see Figure 18.2), and how do they restrict/support two different modes of participation: named and anonymous? While I leave most of the above questions as "food for thought" I discuss the question of software architectures for PPGIS in the next section.

SOFTWARE ARCHITECTURES FOR PPGIS

A list of considerations that should be taken into account prior to designing and subsequently implementing PPGIS software is potentially long. Some of the essential elements on the list include: the number of participants, their knowledge and skills, the time horizon of the participatory process, political and institutional constraints, task difficulty, desirable level of participation, available resources, and skills of developers. These elements can be treated as PPGIS design constraints. The reader should observe that the initial five elements listed above comprise some of the aspects of the convening constructs in the EAST2 framework (Figure 18.1).

The design constraints influence the choice of software structural arrangements, which dictates communication among the software components. This association is referred to as software architecture. Assuming that each of eight aforementioned constraints can take on two values only (e.g., knowledge and skills: high, low), which is clearly a simplification, one could theoretically consider $2^8 = 256$ combinations of constraining factors that potentially can influence the design choices. In reality, only a few combinations will be feasible in light of the participatory decision problem under consideration. For example, a complex participatory task(s) requiring interpretations of analytical results may limit the number of interesting members of the public to a small group. The convener of the participatory decision-making process may require that the meetings take place at a specific physical location (e.g., a conference room), and that they include the testimonies of experts explaining the meaning of data and scientific facts. This constraint may restrict the setting to a few, full-day meetings organized over an extended period of time. Under this setting, depending on the resources at the disposal of the process convener and skills of PPGIS designers/developers, different architectures can be considered. Fundamentally, two different types of architectures for PPGIS can be considered; *a tightly integrated architecture*, in which data management, analysis, and communication support, including visualization, reside on one physical computer platform, and *a distributed architecture*, which allows for a physical separation of data management and analytical processing from participant communication support.

An example of a tightly integrated architecture for PPGIS software is described in Jankowski et al. (2006) and depicted here in Figure 18.4.

The participants communicate from their own desktops with the facilitator. Both software versions, the participant's and the facilitator's, share the same architecture. The main program, which contains analytical functions, communicates through data exchange protocols with other software programs. In the example presented in Figure 18.4 the program provides 2D/3D map and imagery display, charting, and database management capabilities. This type of architecture is well suited for small groups involved in focused, analytic-deliberative decision processes where a participatory process can

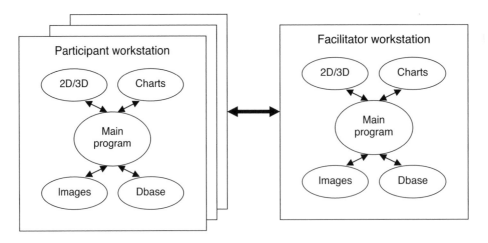

Figure 18.4   An example of tightly integrated architecture

be either fully named or fully anonymous, or take turns between named and anonymous. Software based on a tightly integrated architecture can be useful in supporting higher levels of participation requiring focused work during which the members of the public participate in developing decision options. The implementation of such architecture is labor-intensive and requires substantial software engineering skills. The tightly integrated architecture is unsuitable for distributed systems and hence, does not lend itself well for software intended to support more flexible participation settings (e.g., different place/ different time).

There are numerous examples of distributed architectures described in the PPGIS literature (Carver, 2001; Peng, 2001; Han and Peng, 2003). All of them follow a client-server type of distributed software architecture taking the advantage of wide area network communication protocols. The capability to communicate over a wide area network and distribute system functions between a client and a server makes the distributed software architecture an attractive choice for different place – different time or different place – same time participatory settings. A popular version of the client-server architecture for Web-based PPGIS is a three-tier architecture depicted in Figure 18.5.

The first tier of the architecture, called the *client tier*, includes the web browser and browser-resident Java applets/HTML documents. The client tier accepts participants' data requests and communications, and then displays the results. The participants interact with the client tier via a graphical user interface (GUI) to communicate among each other and to carry out analytical tasks involving visualization, spatial and attribute data query, and spatial analysis. The second tier, called the *middleware tier*, includes the Web Server and the Server Connectors. The connectors may include Java Servlets or Active Server Pages (ASP connectors), and their function is to bridge the communication between clients and the map server. The application server (e.g., a map server) and the spatial database server comprise the third tier, called the *data storage tier*. The client tier communicates with the database through the Web server, and the communication between the application server and the database takes places through either open database connectivity (ODCP) interface or through a newer Java database connectivity (JDBC) interface. Zhong et al. (2008) describe a specific implementation of three-tier architecture for a participatory GIS for transportation (PGIST) decision making (http://www.pgist.org). PGIST architecture

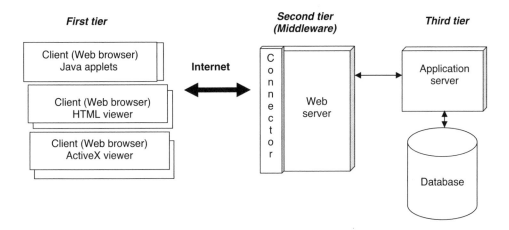

Figure 18.5   A three-tier architecture for Web-based PGIS

Source: Adapted from Jankowski et al. 2007.

emphasizes a robust application server supporting structured discourse and analytical functions, allowing the participating public to develop decision options comprised of transportation improvement projects, evaluate, and vote on alternative decision options. The users of PGIST communicate with each other through a standard Web-browser. They also use a Web browser to access tools and functions of the application server, which communicates with the data server.

The distributed architectures, such as the three-tier architecture, are potentially attractive for larger groups comprised of Internet-aware citizens who support in principle the idea of participative democracy and want to get involved but find the fixed place and time setting as too limiting, or simply feel more comfortable when participating as anonymous individuals. The distributed architecture does not limit the format of participation to one-way (suggestion/complaint box style) communication between the convener and the public, or a simple two-way communication, in which the public makes suggestions and submits questions and the convener posts answers. In their review of 12 on-line PPGIS applications in the USA, UK, and Germany, Steinman et al. (2005) found out that some of the applications enabled the participating

citizens to engage actively in city and regional planning projects. At the same time, however, the authors also noticed that by 2004 only a small number of PPGIS applications existed. They blamed it on the shortcomings of online PPGIS including the need for highly skilled personnel who can first develop and later maintain Web-based PPGIS applications, and on the limited awareness of conveners of public participation (planners and local government agencies) about the possibilities that come with online PPGIS. More recent developments involving geographically enabled technologies such as virtual globes, open application programming interfaces (APIs) and associated tools enabling various forms of communication by, for example, geo-tagging using structured text, images, and symbols, have opened up new opportunities for online PPGIS that can become accessible to wider groups of society (Sidlar and Rinner, 2007).

NEW OPPORTUNITIES FOR PPGIS

The promise of ubiquitous access to spatial data and information enabling citizens not only to become better informed but also more involved in governance, planning, and local decision making is today much closer to become the reality than ever before. For example, in the area of location-based services (LBS) including mobile phone applications and car navigation systems, the projections for the next 5 years forecast 50 percent growth compared to only 9 percent growth in GIS/Mapping software (Vincent Tao, Microsoft Corporation, pers. comm.). The same source projects the growth of online mapping and local search applications by 30 percent. Much of the projected growth rests on new Web-based geovisualization technologies, which have enabled an unprecedented access to georeferenced data by millions of people who have used the Internet and Web-browsers but have never heard about GIS. At the forefront of the applications driven by these technologies are virtual globes such as Google Earth™, NASA's World Wind, or Microsoft® Virtual World®. Tuttle et al. (2008: 1484) list seven features, to which virtual globes owe their popularity with millions of users including "pseudo-3D nature of virtual globes, which allows people to interact in an environment that they naturally comprehend and that makes the data and information presented easier to understand." Another important feature is the client-side nature of virtual globes, which gives their users direct control over the tool and opens up a possibility for creating, posting, and distributing user-collected data. More importantly, however, virtual globes can be combined with web services, which utilize standardized data description formats and input–output interfaces, and thus are able to interoperate with other services. The combination of virtual globes, large geospatial data depositories, and interoperable services opens up a real possibility for creating powerful tools for geographical data access, analysis, and geo-enabled communication enhanced by 3D metaphor of terrestrial space and familiar user interface. An important factor that makes virtual globes an important technological medium for PPGIS is a very low entry barrier as compared with traditional GIS/mapping software or Internet-based GIS. At the expense of data manipulation functionalities, which incorporate only navigation, search, and data-posting tools, the current generation of virtual globes can be used by a novice user in a matter of minutes without training, which is required by traditional GIS/mapping software.

Virtual globes and associated Web mapping tools have been viewed as the new enablers of public participation. The ease of use coupled with the possibility of technically uncomplicated ways of sharing user-collected data (volunteered geographic information or VGI) are undoubtedly attractive for supporting bottom-up participation. New open-source analytical tools are being developed that one will be able to easily embed into virtual globes and thus, extend data exploration capabilities on the need bases without the necessity of providing such functions up-front in PPGIS software. Needless to say, these developments will influence our approach to future designs of PPGIS. There are also challenges associated with user-collected data such as data quality, integration, privacy, and fitness for use in various participatory application contexts. These issues will need to be resolved before VGI can adopted for planning and decision making.

CONCLUSION

PPGIS needs reliable, inexpensive, scalable, and easy to deploy and maintain geographic information and communication technologies if it is to become adopted by planners, local government agencies, and citizen groups for public participation in local and regional decision making. However, since PPGIS is not only a technology, but also a social process in which participants interact with each other and with technology, a sound methodology for PPGIS design is needed. In this chapter I have advocated the need to assess conditions that precede a participatory process, structure and influence the process, and are structured and influenced by the process itself. I discussed a number of PPGIS design-pertinent considerations including participant information needs, setting of participation, group size, technology, and software architectures. What I did not offer, however, is a comprehensive methodology for designing PPGIS. I did not offer it for a simple reason: such a methodology does not exist. What exists is a loosely knit collection of frameworks, heuristics, rules of thumb, and examples of implementing PPGIS. Hence, there is a need and opportunity for future research, which should work toward developing a comprehensive body of knowledge on how to design PPGIS. Such research might lead to developing a knowledge base of "best practices" for PPGIS design, which would take much of the guesswork out of creating PPGIS. It might also persuade those professionals in the planning community who are skeptical about potential benefits coming out of participatory planning/decision making processes outweighing their costs. The first step toward the advocated research agenda could be cataloguing the implemented PPGIS projects including their design solutions. Kingston (Chapter 19, this handbook) reports on such an effort at the University of Manchester (http://www.pgis.manchester.ac.uk/). A further extension of the catalog of PPGIS projects could include evaluation of specific projects in terms of their designs promoting or hindering the achievement of participation objective(s). The EAST2 framework, presented in this chapter, might be a starting point for such an evaluation. The results of such an evaluation may help to discover a set of factors and relationships comprising the building blocks of PPGIS design knowledge.

REFERENCES

Aggett, G. and McColl, C. (2006) 'Evaluating decision support systems for PPGIS applications', *Cartography and Geographic Information Systems*, 33(1): 77–92.

Balrm, S. and Dragicevic, S. (eds) (2006) *Collaborative Geographic Information Systems: Origins, Boundaries and Structures*. Hershey, PA: Idea Group Inc.

Barndt, M. (2002) 'A model for evaluating public participation GIS'. In W.J. Craig, T.M. Harris, and D. Weiner (eds) *Community Participation and Geographic Information Systems*. London: Taylor & Francis, pp. 346–56.

Carver, S. (2001) 'Public participation using web-based GIS', *Environment and Planning B*, 28(6): 803–4.

Carver, S., Evans, A., Kingston, R. and Turton I. (2001) 'Public participation, GIS, and cyberdemocracy: evaluating on-line spatial decision support systems', *Environment and Planning B*, 28(6): 907–21.

Connolly, T., Jessup, L.M. and Valacich, J.S. (1990) 'Effects of anonymity and evaluative tone on idea generation in computer mediated groups', *Management Science*, 44: 589–609.

Edwards, W. and von Winterfeldt, D. (1987) 'Public values in risk debates', *Risk Analysis*, 7(2): 141–58.

Haklay, M.E. and Tobón, C. (2003) 'Usability evaluation and PPGIS: towards a user-centered design approach', *International Journal of Geographical Information Science*, 17(6): 577–92.

Han, S. and Peng, Z. (2003) 'Public participation GIS (PPGIS) for town council management in Singapore', *Environment and Planning B*, 30: 89–111.

Harris, T. Weiner, D. Warner, T. and Levin, R. (1995) 'Pursuing social goals through participatory geographic information systems: redressing South Africa's historical political ecology'. In J. Pickles (ed.), *Ground Truth: The Social Implications of Geographic Information Systems*. New York: Guilford Press. pp. 196–222.

Jankowski, P. and Nyerges, T. (2001) *Geographic Information Systems for Group Decision Making: Towards a Participatory, Geographic Information Science*. New York: Taylor & Francis.

Jankowski, P. and Nyerges, T. (2003) 'Toward a framework for research on geographic information-supported participatory decision-making', *URISA Journal Online*, 15(1). http://www.urisa.org/Journal/APANo1/jankowski.pdf (accessed 24 February 2008).

Jankowski, P., Nyerges, T., Robischon, S., Ramsey, K. and Tuthill, D. (2006) 'Design considerations and evaluation of a collaborative, spatio-temporal decision support system', *Transactions in GIS*, 10(3): 335–54.

Jankowski, P., Tsou, M.-H. and Wright, R. D. (2007) 'Applying internet geographic information system for water quality monitoring', *Geography Compass*, 1(6): 1315–37, online version: http://www.

blackwell-compass.com/subject/geography/section_ home? section=geco-gis (accessed 6 October 2010).

Jordan, G. (2002) 'GIS for community forestry user groups in Nepal: putting people before technology'. In W.J. Craig, T.M. Harris and D. Weiner (eds), *Community Participation and Geographic Information Systems.* London: Tylor and Francis. pp. 232–45.

Keeney, R.L. (1992) *Value-Focused Thinking: A Path to Creative Decision-making.* Cambridge, MA: Harvard University Press.

National Research Council (1996) *Understanding Risk: Informing Decisions in a Democratic Society.* Washington, DC: National Academy Press.

Nyerges, T., Jankowski, P., Ramsey, K. and Tuthill, D. (2006a) 'Collaborative water resource decision support: results of a field experiment', *Annals of the Association of American Geographers,* 96(4): 699–725.

Nyerges, T., Ramsey, K. and Wilson, M. (2006b) 'Design considerations for an internet portal to support public participation in transportation improvement decision making'. In S. Balram and S. Dragicevic (eds), *Collaborative Geographic Information Systems.* Hershey, PA: Idea Group. pp. 207–35.

Nyerges, T. and Jankowski, P. (1997) 'Enhanced adaptive structuration theory: a theory of GIS-supported collaborative decision making', *Journal of Geographical Systems,* 4(3): 225–59.

Peng, Z.R. (2001) 'Internet GIS for public participation', *Environment and Planning B,* 28(6): 889–905.

Poole, M.S., Holmes, M. and DeSanctis, G. (1991) 'Conflict management in a computer-supported meeting environment', *Management Science,* 27: 926–53.

Ramsey, K. (2010) 'Public participation GIS', *Encyclopedia of Geography.* SAGE: in press.

Renn, O., Blattel-Mink, B. and Kastenholz, H. (1997) 'Discursive methods in environmental decision making', *Business Strategy and the Environment,* 6(4): 218–31.

Ringlemann, M. (1913) 'Research on animate sources of power: the work of man', *Annales de l'institute National Agronomique,* 12: 1–40.

Sawicki, D.D. and Peterman, D.R. (2002) 'Surveying the extent of PPGIS practice in the United States'.

In W. Craig, T. Harris and D. Weiner (eds), *Community Participation and GIS.* London: Taylor & Francis. pp. 17–37.

Sidlar, C. and Rinner, C. (2007) 'Analyzing the usability of an argumentation map as a participatory spatial decision support tool', *URISA Journal,* 19(1): 47–55.

Sieber, R. (2006) 'Public participation geographic information systems: a literature review and framework', *Annals of the Association of American Geographers,* 96(3): 491–507.

Silver, S.D. and Troyer, L. (1994) 'Managing information exchange to increase the quality of group decisions: conceptual foundations for an event-sensitive GDSS', *Proceedings of the 23rd Annual Meeting of the Western Decision Sciences Institute.*

Schlossberg, M. and Shuford, E. (2005) 'Delineating "public" and "participation" in PPGIS', *URISA Journal,* 16(2): 15–26.

Steinmann, R., Krek, A. and Blaschke, T. (2005) 'Can online map-based applications improve citizen participation?', *Lecture Notes in Computer Science.* Springer Verlag: Berlin/Heidelberg, 3416: 25–35.

Talen, E. (2000) 'Bottom-up GIS: a new tool for individual and group expression in participatory planning', *Journal of the American Planning Association,* 66(3): 279–94.

Troyer, L. (2003) 'Incorporating theories of group dynamics in group decision support system (GDSS) design', *Proceedings of the International Parallel and Distributed Processing Symposium* (IPDPS'03), IEEE Computer Society.

Tuttle, B.T., Anderson, S. and Huff, R. (2008) 'Virtual Globes: an overview of their history, uses, and future challenges', *Geography Compass,* 2(5): 1478–505, on-line version: http://www.blackwell-compass.com/ subject/geography/section_home?section=geco-gis (accessed 6 October 2010).

Wilson, R. (2001) 'Assessing communicative rationality as a transportation planning paradigm', *Transportation,* 28: 1–31.

Zhong, T., Young, B.K., Lowry, M. and Rutheford, G.S. (2008) 'A model for public involvement in transportation improvement programming using participatory geographic informatn systems', *Computers, Environment and Urban Systems,* 32(2): 123–133.

19

Online Public Participation GIS for Spatial Planning

Richard Kingston

INTRODUCTION

The emergence of GIS as a tool to assist interactive participatory planning since the mid 1990s has created numerous opportunities to improve decision-making processes but at the same time has led to a number of interesting challenges. This chapter focuses on the role of information and communication technologies (ICT) and in particular GIS, to improve access to and participation in environmental decision making at local, regional and national scales. Early research in this area focused on overcoming some of the criticisms levied at GIS (Pickles, 1995) with the focus on a range of technical challenges in enabling GIS to operate over the Internet (Craig, 1998; Kingston et al., 2000; Kingston, 2002; Plewe, 1997) closely followed by socio-technical concerns in relation to equitable access and understanding of the decision making-process using the tools and methods of GIS (Obermeyer, 1998; Sieber, 2004).

Using a series of case studies this chapter plots the relatively youthful history of Internet-based public participation GIS (PPGIS)

applications and focuses on the key issues of concern in relation to the rationale for this approach for supposedly enhancing public participation. Drawing on past and current research, the chapter will highlight prominent examples of web-based PPGIS and draw out the key strengths, weaknesses, opportunities and challenges that they offer. This includes early examples at a range of spatial scales and also addresses a series of key issues relating to the questions of *why*, *who* and *for what purpose* do we develop PPGIS and examines some of the inherent problems of public participation using ICTs.

Since the emergence of web-based PPGIS in the mid-1990s, governments around the world have developed e-government policies and a range of technical tools to support their decision making. It is therefore important to briefly discuss the government policymaking machine in an attempt to assess the methods and models of technological implementation within decision-making frameworks. Recent research by the author into the concept of the Intelligent City will be used to investigate the future of PPGIS applications and how citizens can engage in decision-making processes.

Finally the chapter focuses on the future direction of web-based PPGIS in relation to new technological developments such as, mashups and the implications of Web 2.0 technology.

PUBLIC PARTICIPATION IN DECISION MAKING ON THE WEB

The recognition that the Internet offers immense opportunities for public participation is reflected in the literature (Kellog, 1997) with the transformation of public services around the needs of the citizen: 'Electronic service delivery will transform public services to focus on the citizen' (PIU, 2000: 17). Since the mid-1990s it has been recognised that the Internet and its associated technologies (email, web browsers, ftp servers, blogs and so on) has gradually grown into a medium which provides a powerful mechanism for different sectors of society, in its widest sense, to engage in a range of activities at local, regional, national and international scales. From its early development as a military communications tool (Salus, 1995) to the emergence of Tim Berners-Lee's first-ever web browser at the end of the 1980s the Internet has encroached upon society arguably much quicker than any

other technology before it. It took the telephone and the television a number of decades to permeate into peoples' everyday lives unlike the breakneck speed at which the Internet has, as can be seen from the penultimate column of Table 19.1 below.

For over a decade now ICTs have and remain to be proclaimed by many academics, governments and policymakers as one of the major contributors to providing better, more efficient and joined-up public services. Increasingly, decision makers in Europe accept that digital technologies are an intrinsic part of the fabric of modern society and are thus assuming an active role in the 'digital development' of their towns, cities and regions. The spatial scale at which the majority of the public participate in decision making tends to be at the local level. The role of ICT in local level decision making is a relatively new concept in both policy and research terms. Many governments appear to have adopted the view that the deployment of information technology will deliver wider social, economic and even environmental benefits to communities and neighbourhoods: 'Technology is one of the most important tools for transformation. It can improve the life chances of socially excluded people by increasing opportunities to intervene and tackle emerging problems …' (DCLG, 2006: 139).

Table 19.1   World Internet Usage (March 2009)

	Population (2008 Estimate)	Internet Users Dec 2001	Internet Users March 2009	Penetration (% population)	Users Growth 2000–08	Users (% of table)
Africa	975,330,899	4,514,400	54,171,500	5.6%	1100.0%	3.4%
Asia	3,780,819,792	114,304,000	657,170,816	17.4%	474.9%	41.2%
Europe	803,903,540	105,096,093	393,373,398	48.9%	274.3%	24.6%
Middle East	196,767,614	3,284,800	45,861,346	23.3%	1296.2%	2.9%
North America	337,572,949	108,096,800	251,290,489	74.4%	132.5%	15.7%
Latin America/ Caribbean	581,249,892	18,068,919	173,619,140	29.9%	860.9%	10.9%
Oceania / Australia	34,384,384	7,620,480	20,783,419	60.4%	172.7%	1.3%
World Total	6,710,029,070	360,985,492	1,596,270,108	23.8%	342.2%	100.0%

Source: http://www.internetworldstats.com/

Academics however are divided over the issue of whether these benefits will materialise, especially in deprived urban neighbourhoods (see for example, Graham, 2002; Southern, 2002; van den Berg and van Winden, 2002). The role of ICT is not contested only in terms of the outcomes with urban revitalisation; many commentators suggest that there is a 'gap between vision and delivery' in the use of ICT in government generally (Kolsaker and Lee-Kelley, 2007: 247). Recent research shows that the so-called 'transformation', which ICTs are meant to be responsible for has been slower and more difficult than anticipated and that citizen empowerment has not made the transition from rhetoric to reality (Eynon and Dutton, 2007; King and Cotterill, 2007). Despite this pessimism the Internet has offered many opportunities to improve participation in decision-making processes. Many local government authorities and municipalities have allowed members of the public to choose between different spending priorities and there are increasing opportunities to use the Internet to vote in elections (Svensson and Leenes, 2003) and take part in the policy-making process (Macintosh, 2006).

It has been recognised that over 80 per cent of local government data has a spatial element (Department of Environment, 1987) making GIS a key support tool in decision making at all levels of government. This is particularly true within the urban and regional planning domain of local government whether that relates to forward planning over the longer term, dealing with current developments or dealing with the regeneration of deprived areas of a city or neighbourhood. Traditional methods of public participation in planning in many countries focuses on two aspects of the planning system; the permitting of development subject to a number of controls, and dealing with planning in the medium to long term over a 5–20 year timeframe. The degree to which the public are provided with the opportunity to become actively involved in either of these processes is debatable (Thomas, 1995).

Public involvement in the planning system is often perceived as a them and us situation with authoritative decision makers holding all the knowledge, expertise and power. Other participants in the process are primarily large organisations or pressure groups with vested interests as opposed to individuals or small community groups. This can often lead to the vocal minority dominating the debate at the expense of the general population leaving those with equally valid and possibly more important points to make resisting from expressing their concerns, opinions and viewpoints (Healey et al., 1988). The ability of the public to effectively participate in this type of planning process depends on a variety of circumstances and access to resources. In order to participate in such events takes a lot of time, familiarity and confidence with the relevant bureaucratic procedures, quite often money for campaigns is required and private transport in order to attend meetings and so on (Parry et al., 1992). All these factors play a key role in whether the public can be involved in the participatory process. While this situation may not appear to be encouraging for participatory democracy, evidence suggests that technology and in particular the Internet (Craig, 1998; Howard, 1998; Kingston, 2002) may have a leading role to play in the way the public participate in how their neighbourhoods are planned in the immediate and longer term and also on a day-to-day basis (Kingston, 2007). 'Participation often involves the sorts of interactive meetings which can be alien and intimidating to people unaccustomed to such environments' (Involve, 2005: 25) but the use of certain types of technology can overcome this by allowing individuals to participate in a less confrontational manner. The EU's Kronberg Declaration sees the Internet playing an increasingly crucial role for citizens:

> Knowledge acquisition and sharing will increasingly be technology mediated [through the Internet] … the importance of acquiring factual knowledge will decrease, whereas the ability to find one's way in complex systems and to find, judge, organise

and creatively use relevant information, as well as the capability to learn, will become crucially important. (Kronberg Declaration, 2007: 2)

PUBLIC PARTICIPATION GIS AND THE WEB

With the emergence of the Internet as a tool to enhance participation in decision making the merging of the Internet with GIS started to occur in the mid-1990s when a number of software vendors developed Web Map Servers to deliver spatial data over the web (Plewe, 1997). ESRI's ArcIMS and Auto-Desk's MapGuide both appeared in the latter part of the 1990s while at the same time a number of open source solutions were developed including MapServer and GeoTools among many others. Since the emergence of Google Maps™ in 2005 and Yahoo Maps both with an accessible application programming interface (API), the ability to display spatial data on the Internet has now become widespread and is providing many opportunities for non-experts to display their own data. This is leading to the concept of Volunteered Geographic Information (Goodchild, 2007) and Neogeography (Turner, 2006). While these technologies are not PPGIS as such, they are the enabling technologies with which it is possible to deliver PPGIS processes.

PPGIS as a term was first suggested at a meeting organised by the National Center for Geographic Information and Analysis (NCGIA, 1998) to cover a specific geographical context predominantly within North America, although it equally applies to Europe, and other westernised nations (Kingston, 2002). Its initial definition, if one can call it that, was to encapsulate the various functions of public participation within a spatial planning context, which has a rich and historical literature in terms of conceptualising and applying public participation processes. This is most famously represented in Arnstein's (1969) Ladder of Participation. In this context PPGIS is viewed as how GIS

technology could support public participation for a variety of possible applications mainly within a public sector setting from local community planning (Kingston et al., 2000) through regional to national issues (Evans et al., 2004). Its early development has been documented by Obermeyer (1998:1) who noted that the 'evolution of public participation GIS is a direct outgrowth of the research on societal issues related to implementation of the technology' and was also a response to criticisms levied at the GIS community in the mid-1990s in a seminal book by Pickles (1995). At the heart of PPGIS should be the recognition that 'the development of GIS, or any other, technology is a social process' (Sheppard, 1995: 6).

Others see PPGIS as making use of increasingly sophisticated approaches to public participation particularly in western societies and through the use of ICTs. For early examples of such approaches see Shiffer (1995) who developed innovative applications of multimedia GIS to assist spatial decision making. Such applications range from working with deprived inner-city neighbourhoods and indigenous communities where technical competency and cost have been barriers to GIS implementation to more affluent, socially aware and technically informed neighbourhoods. Such PPGIS applications occur within a range of organisational arrangements including: community – university partnerships with inner city communities (Craig and Elwood, 1998; Ghose, 2001; Kingston, 2007, Ramasubramanian, 1999); grassroots social organisations (Sieber, 2000) and web-based PPGIS (Craig et al., 2002; Kingston et al., 2000). These organisations combine GIS with a host of modern communication technologies to facilitate dialogue and data usage among local groups and this is increasingly becoming web-based. Sieber (2006: 503) makes an excellent attempt in a review of the PPGIS literature stating that: 'PPGIS provides a unique approach for engaging the public in decision making through its goal to incorporate local knowledge, integrate and contextualise complex spatial information, allow participants to dynamically interact with input, analyse alternatives and empower individuals and groups.

This chapter focuses mainly on PPGIS but sits within the wider concept of *Participatory GIS* (PGIS) that is, GIS-based techniques and technologies that support participation in decision making incorporating a wide range of stakeholder groups (Weiner and Rambaldi, 2004). PGIS facilitates the representation of local people's spatial knowledge using two or three-dimensional maps which are initially usually physical constructs rather than digital representations in a computer-based GIS. These map products are used to facilitate decision-making processes, as well as supporting communication and community advocacy. In many ways this is very similar to the Planning for Real approach developed in the UK in the 1970s and discussed later. Possibly the most important distinction between PGIS and

traditional GIS tools and applications such as ESRI's ArcGIS or MapInfo, is that PGIS places the control of access to and use of, often culturally sensitive spatial data, in the hands of those communities who generated it (Rambaldi et al., 2006). In a traditional GIS setting the data is nearly always owned and predominantly controlled by government or one of its agents making it difficult for the public or other stakeholders to re-present their own knowledge within a GIS framework.

A grass-roots participatory approach by its very nature can be viewed as being *bottom-up* where as more traditional government-led approaches are viewed as *top-down*. A top-down approach is often set within current public participation practices within a government setting. This approach is one whereby an authoritative decision maker, or some formal body is making the decisions. This approach to public participation often occurs on the lower rungs of Arnstein's ladder and in types 1–3 in the OECD's typology (Figure 19.1).

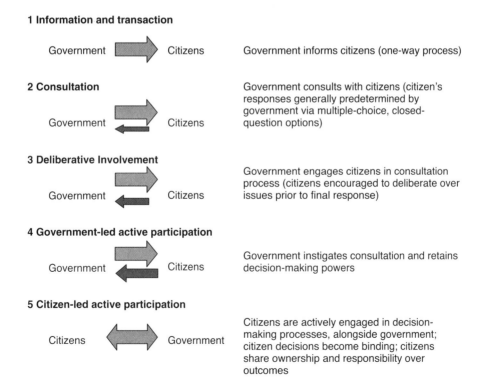

1 Information and transaction

Government ⟹ Citizens   Government informs citizens (one-way process)

2 Consultation

Government ⇄ Citizens   Government consults with citizens (citizen's responses generally predetermined by government via multiple-choice, closed-question options)

3 Deliberative Involvement

Government ⇄ Citizens   Government engages citizens in consultation process (citizens encouraged to deliberate over issues prior to final response)

4 Government-led active participation

Government ⇄ Citizens   Government instigates consultation and retains decision-making powers

5 Citizen-led active participation

Citizens ⟺ Government   Citizens are actively engaged in decision-making processes, alongside government; citizen decisions become binding; citizens share ownership and responsibility over outcomes

Figure 19.1   OECDs typology of public involvement in government decision making

The top-down approach more often than not involves the concept of *Decide – Announce – Defend* (Renn et al., 1995) on the decision makers' part whereby those in power decide what they are going to do in terms of their policy or decision, announce it to the wider public and defend their decision through 'consultation'. Conversely, though PPGIS can originate from the grass roots with a bottom-up approach (Talen, 1999) and it is argued that PGIS is always approached from this stance. A bottom-up approach is always one that originates from the grassroots (Sieber, 2000). Typically this involves a large number of people resolving issues together and leading to decisions being taken from within the community and maps onto the OECD's notion of citizen-led active participation. The urban planning literature has recognised since the 1960s that an approach to participation which involves the grass roots leads to better spatial planning decisions being taken (Arnstein, 1969; Healey, 2005).

Why, who and for what purpose do we develop PPGIS

So why do we develop PPGIS? Part of this answer goes back to the previous section in terms of addressing some of the criticism laid at the door of GIS in the 1990s as being an elitist technology. Much of this criticism is still true today: the majority of spatial data is still in the hands of those in positions of power; you still need to be technically savvy to use the tools; the technology itself is still very expensive; and the participation process is controlled from a top-down perspective. When GIS is made publicly accessible it is predominantly controlled by government organisations and not by the public. It also tends to be about disseminating data and not about participation – it is a very one-way, top-down process. However, PPGIS does offer opportunities to overcome some of these problems. What is important is that systems are put in place to allow the public to easily engage fully and properly in

the decision-making process. It is also the simple fact that we can develop GIS which is simple to use (Innes and Simpson, 1993) and it can be designed in such a way that it can become an extremely useful tool to allow people to engage in decision making about their community at whatever spatial scale is relevant to them.

Policy- and decision makers, and in particular town planners, have historically used ICTs to assist them in their day to day task. Indeed, Klosterman (1997) has argued that there has been a parallel progression with respect to the planning professions' view of their own role and purpose, and the evolving concerns of ICT within planning. Here the view of ICTs has changed from being a simple provider of data through to being a medium for the transferral of knowledge and intelligence. This has coincided with the realisation that the communication of ideas to others and the process of 'collaborative planning' or 'planning through debate' (Healey, 2005) to create jointly derived knowledge are just as important in planning as the collection and provision of information. The connectivity provided by the Internet is very much in keeping with this current view of planning, and increasingly the use of PPGIS will help support planners and other policy makers in reaching consensus on important spatial issues within their communities in a geographical sense. With this in mind one might rightfully ask what would we imagine a web-based PPGIS to include? Ideally such a system should include the following.

- Quality, unbiased information that is structured in a manner that allows the public to gain both a rapid understanding of complex problems and explore topics in depth if they wish. Meta-information should also be included. Such information schemes are much easier to implement on the web than in traditional media, which are usually aimed at exclusive audiences with different prior levels of understanding (public pamphlets versus expert documents, for example).
- The ability for the public to add their own information to the above knowledge, discuss

problems with others, and form a consensus. On the web such material can be in a wide set of formats: text, video and pictures, audio, 3D worlds.

- The opportunity for the public to examine relevant spatial data involved in the decisions being taken. And further to this, for them to manipulate the data to examine a number of complex 'What if?' scenarios and to examine how these complexities develop.
- The ability for the public to reach an informed decision on the given problem, submit this decision to those responsible for implementing it, see the results, and gain feedback as to the reasons for the final choice.

In addition the web provides the following advantages.

- It is not time-limited in the same way as public meetings are, although they should be limited to a specified period to maintain community and organiser interest, and to fit with a planned schedule.
- It provides access to groups that can not reach public participation meetings: the blind, deaf and those with mobility difficulties and so on.
- It allows for broader public involvement. Frequently public participation meetings are dominated by small, disproportionately vocal groups. Many individuals hesitate to express their concerns and opinions. The web allows increased potential anonymity between members of the public putting forward their views, and gives everyone involved a potential voice.
- Ease of data processing – the data contributed by the public can be tailored around processing needs, the information is already in electronic format, and it can often be displayed back to the public instantaneously in terms of a developing group consensus.
- Allows for an understanding of the public's understanding of a problem. Those who wish to provide information to the public can track what their pre-informed decisions are, how they alter, what paths they take through the provided and public-supplied knowledge, thus allowing such systems to be improved. (Adapted from Evans et al., 1999)

One of the main reasons for developing and using PPGIS is to allow the public to have a greater degree of participation in the decision-making process. Many public participation exercises which starting off from a top-down approach lay claim to offering a high degree of citizen interaction in the decision making process. Quite often the extent to which real participation is taking place is rather limited and often takes place in an environment whereby those in control are merely defending a decision they have already taken. Arnstein's (1969) ladder of participation developed a typology of eight levels of participation with the suggestion that as one moves up the ladder the degree of participation becomes more legitimate. The rungs of the ladder range move from: manipulation; therapy; informing; consultation; placation; partnership; delegated power and citizen control. While the ladder still has some relevance to participation in planning today the notion whereby the further up the ladder one gets the better the level of participation becomes for everyone is not always true. Moving up the ladder may not be the best analogy and there are more appropriate methods of conceptualising the processes by which communities become involved in decision making. While the ladder metaphor may help to clarify the difference between active engagement and passive information sharing, some practitioners have challenged the metaphor of the ladder as leading to the view that the top of the ladder is the ultimate aim of all participation exercises when this may not always be the case. Further criticisms stem from a suggestion that this notion proposes a simplistic view of power, and with the suggestion that manipulation can occur at each rung of the ladder (Abbott, 1996). There maybe legitimate reasons why a particular exercise may only require participants to be engaged at particular levels for example, in informing and consulting on issues or options. Others over the decades have attempted to come up with alternatives such as the Wheel of Participation (Davidson, 1998) to avoid the notion of hierarchy. The OECD (2001) split participation into five types (Figure 19.1) of public involvement in government decision-making. In far too many cases citizens' interaction with public bodies tends to be focused on types 1 and 2, but web-based PPGIS has the potential to, and in some cases is, moving participation into types 3, 4 and 5 as will be shown in some of the examples in the next section of this chapter.

PPGIS in practice

Some of the examples outlined in this section show how by providing the necessary tools, skills, knowledge and understanding to allow citizens to fully engage in the decision-making process it is possible to develop public involvement focused on OECDs types 3–5 using web-based PPGIS. Although many municipalities make use of GIS to support many of their functions there are still limited examples in many countries of them using PPGIS within their decision-making

procedures. In a major review of technology for urban e-governance, researchers found that 'Several cities provide fully functional GIS. Visitors to these sites can obtain a variety of information, depending on the site. Some allow address look-up. Others provide maps of proposed city projects. Several cities offer slightly less functional GIS or as-built GIS images that are available for download (Christodoulou et al., 2004: 27).

LOCAL PLANNING

One of the earliest web-based PPGIS systems (Figure 19.2) was developed in the UK to test the potential of such an approach in a local neighbourhood planning exercise mirroring a traditional community planning

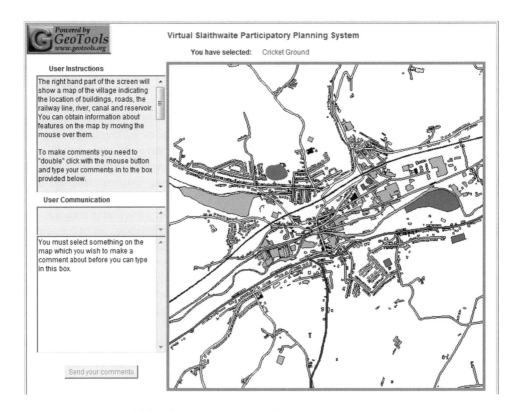

Figure 19.2   Virtual Slaithwaite: main map interface
Source: http://www.ppgis.manchester.ac.uk/

process called 'Planning for Real©' (PfR). This approach was first developed and patented by the Neighbourhood Initiatives Foundation (http://www.planningforreal.org.uk/) as a means of involving people more closely in local environmental planning problems and decision making. This involves the local community creating a large-scale map or three dimensional model of the area, into which local people place flags of various colours. Written on each flag are their ideas and suggestions for the locations where they place the flag. The colours represent different classes of problems (such as crime, employment, environment, health, housing, shopping, transport and so on). In this instance, the map was built by local schoolchildren at a 1:1000 scale as part of a community planning event taking place on the day of the village fair, making it well attended by a broad range of the community (Carver et al., 2001; Kingston et al., 2000). While by today's standards this was a fairly rudimentary system, many lessons were learnt about using a web-based PPGIS in a real local planning exercise (Kingston et al., 2002).

Unlike the PfR physical model, it was decided not to allow users to view other people's comments to encourage individual and imaginative responses. However, at the end of the consultation period the system was updated to allow the public to query a map containing all the comments made during the consultation period and these comments were fed into the PfR process. The final outcome of the PfR process was a new village plan taking on board the many comments made by people living and working in the local community.

The potential role of PPGIS within planning should be to help minimise conflict and arrive at decisions that are acceptable to the majority of stakeholders through consensus building approaches based on awareness of the spatial implications of a decision problem. An important aspect is the provision of and access to better data and information for public consumption (Laituri, 2003) to assist them in forming a considered opinion in a decision-making problem. Therefore 'GIS-based decision tools should provide the means by which stakeholders can explore a decision problem using existing information, experiment with possible solutions, view other people's ideas, formulate their own views and share these with the wider community' (Carver, 2001: 64). It is argued that the increased use of the PPGIS approach offers opportunities for citizen empowerment through greater involvement and openness and accountability on behalf of decision makers. With this in mind recent research has been focusing on what type of system should be developed and how it can enhance participation in the planning and regeneration process.

Another PPGIS was developed as part of an EU funded project, IntelCities (Kingston, 2007), aimed at supporting and improving open and transparent dialogue which has a spatial planning focus. The system allows citizens to discuss new proposals or identify issues relating to space and place within their community. The PPGIS can fulfil the tasks set out by the processes categorised as providing 'Citizen-led Active Participation' outlined in Figure 19.1. While this tool can be used to facilitate all the different types of public participation processes, it can be used to assist citizen-led active participation in the spatial policymaking process. In this scenario, citizens start discussions and debate issues and thereby, in a sense, create their own geo-referenced community database of issues which are of concern to them in their local neighbourhood rather than the process being local government top-down led.

The PPGIS tool uses the same base technology as the other systems developed for reporting environmental problems in cities (Kingston, 2007) and is therefore easily replicated in other locations. The system is based on the OGC compliant Web Map Server (WMS) technology and supports a range of spatial data formats including ESRI Shape files, MapInfo and various raster data formats such as geoTIFF. It also has functions for the inclusion of further geospatial layers to show relevant spatial policy data and information. It makes use of CGI executable files for the processing and management of citizen comments and feedback using PHP. The system also incorporates a geo-referenced discussion forum written in PHP and uses a mySQL database to store citizen discussions as shown in Figure 19.3. The latest version now works with the Google Maps API allowing users to choose between the standard map bases. Citizens can navigate the map by zooming and panning into an appropriate location or searching by street name or postal code. They can also turn relevant GIS layers on or off and query these for appropriate attribute information from the spatial plan such as proposed policies. Citizens can overlay proposed policies and make informed comments and judgements. A discussion can be started by switching to the appropriate mode and clicking on a specific location. The citizen activates the discussion forum by creating a topic and initiating a discussion based on either a particular location or policy. Other citizens can search the map for discussions based on a specific topic, keyword or click on point locations on the map to view previous citizens' comments and make appropriate comments themselves. Over time the PPGIS develops into a deliberative discussion about particular planning policy proposals or options in ways similar to Rinner's (2001) and Rinner et al. (2008) augmentation maps.

In this example planning officials can initiate discussions on specific issues at specific time intervals as and when the policy process dictates in parallel with community-led initiatives. The discussion forum can syndicate the latest discussions to other web sites/pages to highlight the latest activity. There are still a number of key operational issues to be overcome with a PPGIS of this nature such as the following.

- Should a moderator be present for discussions and if so who should appoint them?

Figure 19.3   PPGIS with a geo-referenced threaded discussion list
Source: **http://www.ppgis.manchester.ac.uk/**

- What spatial data layers should be/not be included? (Updating the system to use the Google Maps™ API allows users to overlay their own KML data.)
- An evaluation system is required to provide questionnaires and interactive weighting and priority setting for citizens to give feedback on plans and programmes.
- A layer for information providing access to photos, text, 3D environments and so forth is under development.
- A facility for citizens to link to their own text and graphics allowing them to provide their own material is also under development.
- If citizens are able to upload their own spatial data how do officials decide what is legitimate data?

As these tools are being developed within a UK local government setting they must meet a set of standards called the Electronic Government Interoperability Framework (e-GIF, 2006) which is a requirement for public sector websites in the UK and Europe. While the systems developed here are focused on Manchester, they are scalable and can be expanded to include the whole of the Manchester Metropolitan district and the wider city-region. Indeed the system can work in any place by changing the spatial data to the appropriate location which is fairly easy if implemented with the Google Maps™ API.

REGIONAL PLANNING

At a regional scale the Yorkshire Dales National Park Authority (YDNP) in northern England proposed a 50 per cent increase in the 'native' woodland in the National Park over a 25 years period up to 2020 (YDNPA, 1995). Many PPGIS are limited in their ability to perform spatial analysis 'on the fly' but this example allows the public to undertake multi-criteria evaluation using a range of spatial data pertinent to the woodland planting issue. The National Park did not have any fixed idea over the locations at which new

trees would be planted and clearly such a planning problem leant itself to involving the use of GIS modelling and the participation of both local communities and tourists in the decision-making process. To involve these groups in the planning process a web-based PPGIS was developed (Figure 19.4), centred on an easy-to-use GIS which allowed the public to model a number of possible tree planting scenarios.

The public is first shown information relevant to the problem such as the factors that might constrain possible planting locations. They are asked which factors are relevant and how important they feel their specific influences should be. For example, how important, on a sliding scale between important and unimportant, are protected grassland or meadow areas? A map of suitability for woodland regeneration is generated from these inputs, and stored as an example of the user's opinion prior to exposure to the GIS. The user is allowed to regenerate the map on the fly by changing their factor choices and/ or changing the weighting of the factors included. A further facility allows users to 'top slice' the suitability map to identify the best areas for woodland planting. This allows the users to experiment with different scenarios, and see the implications of their choices. Finally both the initial and the final set of factor choices and weights are recorded allowing decision maps for each user to be recreated as required at a later date.

An information system that allows users to browse in-depth information relevant to the problem is also provided. Access to this is through a menu hierarchy, with more detailed information on each subject further down each branch of the menu. The menu system was designed to encourage the exploration of information to a level of detail the user felt comfortable with. Should the user be interested, meta-information is also provided on how the spatial data has been derived, its quality, and how the system works from a GIS modelling perspective.

With the development of open APIs by the likes of Google, Yahoo and Open Street Map

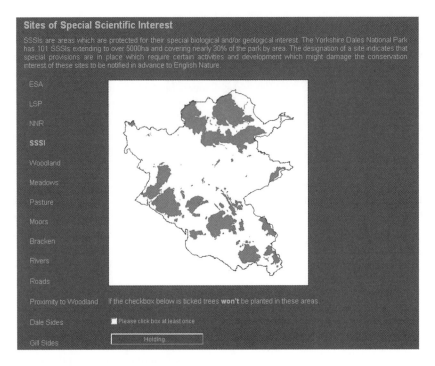

Figure 19.4   Factor map selection and information interface
Source: http://www.ccg.leeds.ac.uk/projects/dales/

the concept of web-based mapping and volunteered geographic information has become more widespread than when some of the first web-based PPGIS were developed. This has offered access to spatial data and aerial photography to those who have not used this type of data until very recently and is providing some interesting opportunities for creating what are known as mash-ups or ways of combining data from more than one source into a single integrated tool. This has provided the opportunity to implement a PPGIS for shoreline management planning (SMP). Continuing concerns over sea-level rise and associated flood risk within coastal areas in the UK has led the government to recognise that the adoption of integrated approaches to environmental management will be fundamental to countering the negative impacts of coastal hazards (O'Riordan and Ward, 1997). This recognition has been coupled with awareness that one of the main impediments to achieving

integrated management is the fragmented nature of current formal arrangements. Statutory approaches to coastal management in England and Wales are characterised by sectoral responses to site specific problems. The result of this has been the limited consideration of environmental and socio-economic issues, a lack of spatial awareness and limited stakeholder participation in managing the coastline (Potts, 1999).

As a response to this, local districts along the UK's coastline have been issued with government guidance (DEFRA 2006) and one of the central components of the guidance is an attempt to account for a broad spectrum of stakeholders ranging from government agencies through to the wider public. The guidance emphasises the importance of continual public engagement and highlights the significance of negotiation and dialogue rather than the receipt and dissemination of information. This can be a challenging task, particularly when you are dealing with a wide range of interested parties with both specific issues to be addressed and spread over a large geographical area – in this case 16 local, three county and two regions/countries are involved in North Wales and NW England along a 500 mile stretch of coastline. The very nature of SMP means that that they cut across traditional administrative boundaries making it a more demanding task in terms of engaging the public in deliberative and inclusionary dialogue and managing such a process. One possible solution to this dilemma has been to make use of a PPGIS to offer particularly innovative opportunities for participatory dialogue. The main aim of the Shoreline Management PPGIS (SM-PPGIS) in Figure 19.5 is to *consult* on a range of coastal flood prevention issues, *involve* as many members of the public and stakeholders through examining different scenarios and allow them to *collaborate* in the different management options (White et al., 2010).

The primary method of engaging the public and stakeholders in the SMP process has been to develop an interactive geospatial website providing facilities to:

- inform and build a knowledge base on SMP processes and decision making;
- provide access to relevant and accurate information at a variety of spatial scales;
- provide a forum for views, issues and further information to be gathered and considered linked to specific spatial locations identified by users;
- provide a platform for participation and empowerment through network working at a variety of spatial scales; and
- provide a mechanism to share decisions and outcomes with auditable routes to how these decisions were made.

The SM-PPGIS uses the Google Maps API dynamically linked to a backend database containing XML-formatted spatial data layers of different costal scenarios. The reasoning behind using Google Maps is threefold: it is

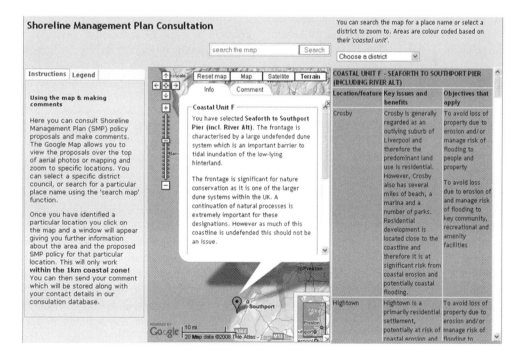

Figure 19.5   Shoreline management planning PPGIS
Source: http://www.ppgis.manchester.ac.uk/

free (spatial data in the UK is very costly, particularly if you wish to put it online and heavily restricted in terms of its manipulation); it is highly customisable; and probably most importantly from a users' perspective it is very simple to use and navigate. Many proprietary online mapping systems make an assumption that the user has a certain degree of GIS knowledge and an understanding of relevant terminology when, most likely, they do not (Kingston et al., 2000). Considering the public, stakeholder, policy- and decision-making audience that will be making use of such a tool, creating a website which is intuitive and simple to use is the key to its success. The spatial nature of SMP means that a PPGIS-based approach to participation offers a pioneering solution to engaging people. By providing interactive access to the SMP process users can obtain information (by turning layers of data on/off), formulate opinions (by reading attribute information about data/policy) and make informed judgments on proposals which goes far beyond more standard methods of consultation which tend to focus just on dissemination and the receipt of static information that is, the lower rungs of the ladder and OECD's typologies 1 and 2. The system allows users to make comments or offer opinions based on particular locations or more general areas through the use of the SM-PPGIS.

This approach offers opportunities to collate information about specific locations within the SMP relating to objectives of the plan, aspirations for the shoreline, the value of elements of the shoreline and many other aspects identified in the DEFRA guidance documentation. The SM-PPGIS stores all responses in a geo-referenced database. This information can be disseminated for review later in the process by stakeholders with possibilities for viewing other comments and for developing understandings of competing viewpoints. Updated policies can be displayed within the system as policy proposals and decisions are finalised throughout the SMP process which allows full and open

deliberation by the public and the coastal community through considered social debate and interaction.

NATIONAL PLANNING

At a national scale a PPGIS which allows public participation in the siting of facilities for Britain's low and intermediate level radioactive waste was first developed in 1996 (Carver et al., 1997) and re-designed in 2000 using Java (Evans et al., 2004). At present the responsibility for identifying solutions to this problem lies with the Nuclear Decommissioning Authority. At present most of the waste is stored at various nuclear sites around the country or disposed of at Drigg, near Sellafield in Cumbria. The system developed here is broadly based around that developed in the Yorkshire Dales National Park study and allows users to specify factors and apply weights before top-slicing to find the optimum locations.

While this example is not used by the government to assist their decision making it is widely used as a teaching aid by students to understand the complexities of spatial data to support decision making. The case studies discussed above only offer a glimpse of some of the possibilities web-PPGIS offer and it has been impossible here to discuss all those excellent PPGIS that are out there. Table 19.2 summarises those that have been discussed in this chapter and provides information of two further PPGIS under development. To assist the GIS and society community a PPGIS inventory is under development at http://www.ppgis.manchester.ac.uk/ and this contains a live listing of web-based PPGIS. Readers are encouraged to add their own PPGIS examples using an interactive online map. These will be categorised by geographical location and application type and it is hoped this will become a useful resource for disseminating good and possibly poor practice.

Table 19.2   Summary of case studies

Name	Geographical Scale	OECD Type	Date	Notes
Virtual Slaithwaite	Local	Citizen-led active participation	1998	Research project but linked to real decision-making problem
URL	http://www.ppgis.manchester.ac.uk/projects/slaithwaite/			
IntelCities	Local	Government-led active participation	2004	Research project
Woodland Planning	Regional	Deliberative involvement	1999	Research project but linked to real decision-making problem
URL	http://www.ccg.leeds.ac.uk/projects/dales/			
Shoreline Management Planning	Regional	Deliberative involvement	2008–9	Linked to actual decision/policy making
URL	http://www.ppgis.manchester.ac.uk/sm-ppgis/			
Nuclear Waste	National	Deliberative involvement	On-going	Demonstrator project
URL	http://www.ccg.leeds.ac.uk/teaching/nuclearwaste/			
PPGIS under development:				
GRaBS Climate Change Adaptation	10 European region and/or city wide	Government-led active participation	2010–11	EU Interreg IVC Project
URL	http://www.ppgis.manchester.ac.uk/grabs/			
SURegen	Local	Citizen-led active participation	2010–11	Research project but linked to real decision-making problem
URL	http://www.ppgis.manchester.ac.uk/suregen/			

Key challenges

In light of research in real decision-making problems, a set of PPGIS principles have begun to emerge which could be used as a guide to implementing a web-based PPGIS strategy. It is suggested that a web based system should:

- allow the public to explore and experiment with the data and information sources which are available and provide the opportunity to formulate different scenarios and solutions to decision problems;
- be understandable by all sectors of the community who wish to be involved and not tied up in technical jargon;
- provide information and data that are both explicit and bipartisan; and
- foster a high degree of trust and transparency that can be maintained within the public realm to give the process legitimacy and accountability.

One way of addressing the final principle is through maintaining web-based PPGIS by publishing summaries of public inputs and demonstrating how these have been used to develop policy and to make decisions which themselves are available for public scrutiny and comment. Such 'living systems' may well go a long way to fostering continued participation and wider acceptance of planning decisions. That is why PPGIS should always work in parallel and as a compliment to other participatory approaches.

There are of course many problems associated with web-based participation ranging from issues of social access to how you develop a sense of community cohesion around decisions made. The vast majority of Internet activity takes place at the individual level rather than in a group situation unlike the vast majority of current consensus building.

The issue of data quality in terms of its accuracy and resolution is also a key challenge – whose data is correct and how was it collated are key questions when designing a PPGIS. This is best illustrated by using the example of siting a windfarm using GIS. In most cases for identifying suitable locations for a windfarm a developer more than likely will have used various functions within a GIS such as viewshed analysis to identify those areas of the landscape most suitable. The PPGIS may highlight these potential locations on a map and people can visualise the windfarm and make comments (Berry et al., 2007). The critical issue in this whole process is the calculation of the viewshed which is dependent upon the contour intervals originally used as this will affect the detail in the TIN and the digital elevation model it produces. And here lies one of the most important issues within PPGIS. Whose data is used within a PPGIS can have profound effects on the outcomes, leading to questions of whose data is correct? A TIN generated using 10 m contour intervals will produce a very different viewshed analysis to one using 50 m intervals.

E-GOVERNMENT AND THE MAINSTREAMING OF PPGIS

Since the emergence of web based PPGIS, governments around the world have been developing e-Government policies and a range of technical tools. One of the distinguishing factors of web-based PPGIS is that they are predominantly institutionalised within democratic decision making processes. Electronic communication technologies deliver both immense opportunities and challenges for the *active citizen* as well as the *consumer-citizen*. These two conceptions of citizenship could also be described as being motivated either by self-interest in a consumer/marketplace democracy or participation in communal affairs and self-governance in a participatory democracy. These approaches are often seen to be in conflict with one another and some critics of the consumerist notion label it as undemocratic. The dichotomy between the active citizen and the consumer-citizen has a distinct dimension in the field of e-government.

The dilemma around the promise and problems of ICT revolves around the expectations brought about by modern technology for speedy responses the consumer-citizen would expect based on the potential of ICT. This is in conflict with a more participatory/deliberative process of engagement that is 'complex, costly and time-consuming' (Andrews and Turner, 2006: 388; also Fagan et al., 2006) but, PPGIS can offer a useful method for engagement as examined earlier in this chapter. PPGIS also provides opportunities for improving the management of towns, cities and neighbourhoods and helping achieve long-term physical, social and economic sustainability (Viitanen and Kingston, 2009).

While many web-based PPGIS examples have been part of research projects, particularly within universities, there are emerging examples where it is being used in *real* decision-making environments. The main focus should always be on improving public participation and not be technology driven. When putting together such systems it is important to remember that PPGIS in principle is much more about how one approaches the project, whose interests are being served, and who is involved in it than it is with the underlying technology. As Rambaldi et al. (2005, p.109) put it 'Consider using spatial information technologies that can be mastered by local people (or local technology intermediaries) after being provided sufficient training – The use of GIS is not a must: it is an option. As technology complexity increases, community access to the technology decreases.

Always ask yourself is a GIS really necessary? Would GIS add anything that cannot better be achieved through other participatory mapping methods? What is apparent is that many web-based participation tools developed merely replicate old participatory practices in digital form with the main focus on making efficiency gains in terms of time and money rather than improving participation. Many current examples from practice are not particularly clear in showing how they actually improve the level of participatory dialogue between citizens and the decision and policymakers from a citizen-led active participation perspective.

CONCLUSION

PPGIS is not a panacea to resolve the complex issues that communities and municipalities face when delivering twenty-first-century services. However, it is one possible approach beginning to unpack the theories and assumptions about e-government into a practical solution that allows active citizens to contribute and participate in decision making in their locality of interest while also fulfilling the transparency and efficiency requirements of good decision making. Web-based PPGIS should not be about technical gimmicks; instead it should be about building an online presence and hopefully an enhanced sense of place and trust in the long run.

Finally, this chapter began by examining some of the criticisms of GIS in the 1990s and to some extent PPGIS has overcome some of this criticism but in other ways it has not. GIS is still expensive and relatively difficult to access with problems (particularly in UK/EU) due to uneven spatial data access and uneven access to technology. There is also the question of political apathy. Until the lack of public trust in the political process is overcome no amount of technology will re-engage them in participatory spatial planning or any other democratic process. On the other hand the emergence of open APIs such as Google and Yahoo Maps and Open Street Map is offering improved public access to the technology to develop PPGIS. While many of the systems out there are example projects there are emerging cases which are beginning to be used in real decision-making situations offering new and enhanced opportunities to participate in decision making from a bottom-up perspective. What most web-based PPGIS are about though is accessing, displaying, querying and commenting on spatial data rather than being full-blown GIS with access to the types of spatial analysis tools available within desktop GIS. They are thus still not without their critics. Declining public trust and general disenchantment with politics often create a hostile, or at best disengaged, community of citizens and stakeholders. The direction from the centre demands that local councils engage their residents and transform their business into a slicker and more efficient citizen-centric ventures while also delivering efficiency savings to the public purse. As Web 2.0 begins to take hold, coupled with societal and technological change web-based PPGIS offers real opportunities to improve decision making and participation in a new form of spatial planning.

ACKNOWLEDGEMENTS

Much of the on-going research discussed in this chapter would not have come about if it was not for the author's collaboration with Steve Carver and Andrew Evans in the School of Geography at the University of Leeds and their collaboration on a number of PPGIS projects is greatly appreciated. Parts of this research were funded by ESRC's Virtual Society? Programme award No. L132 25 1014 and the EU FP6 IST IntelCities project No. 507860.

REFERENCES

Abbott, J. (1996) *Sharing the City: Community Participation in Urban Management.* London: Earthscan.

Andrews and Turner (2006) 'Modelling the impact of community engagement on local democracy', *Local Economy*, 21(4): 378–90.

Arnstein, A. (1969) 'A ladder of citizen participation', *Journal of the American Planning Association*, 35(4): 216–24.

Berry, R., Higgs, G., Kidner, D. and Langford, M. (2007) 'Examining the potential of Internet-based geographical information systems for promoting public participation in wind farm planning in the UK', *Proceedings of GISRUK NUI Maynooth*, Ireland, 11–13 April.

Carver, S., Blake, M., Turton, I. and Duke-Williams, O. (1997) 'Open spatial decision-making: Evaluating the potential of the World Wide Web', in Z. Kemp (ed.), *Innovations in GIS 4*, London: Taylor and Francis.

Carver, S. (2001) The future of participatory approaches using geographic information: Developing a research agenda for the 21st century. *URISA Journal*, 15(1), 61–71.

Carver, S., Evans, A., Kingston, R. and Turton, I. (2001) 'Public participation, GIS and cyberdemocracy: Evaluating on-line spatial decision support systems', *Environment and Planning B: Planning and Design*, 28(6): 907–21.

Christodoulou, E., Samaras, G. and Germanakos, P. (2004) 'Technologies for Urban eGovernance Currently in Use: Review and Classification', *IntelCities WP11 Deliverable 3.2*. http://intelcities.iti.gr/intelcities (accessed 12 December 2007).

Craig, W. (1998) 'The internet aids community participation in the planning process', *Computers, Environment and Urban Planning*, 22(4): 393–404.

Craig, W., Harris, T. and Weiner, D. (eds.) (2002) *Community Empowerment, Public Participation and Geographic Information Science*. London: Taylor and Francis.

Davidson, S. (1998) 'Spinning the wheel', *Planning*, 1262: 14–5.

Department for Communities and Local Government (2006) Strong and Prosperous Communities: The Local Government White Paper. *Cm6939-1*.

DEFRA (2006) *Shoreline Management Plan Guidance*, vol. 1 and 2. London: DEFRA.

Department of Environment (1987) *Handling Geographic Information*. London: Her Majesty's Stationery Office.

e-GIF (2006) *GovTalk Information on Policies and Standards for e-Government*. http://www.govtalk.gov.uk/ (accessed 17 November 2007).

Evans, A., Kingston, R. and Carver, S. (2004) 'Democratic input into the nuclear waste disposal problem: The influence of geographical data on decision making examined through a web-based GIS', *Journal of Geographical Systems*, 6(2): 117–32.

Evans, A., Kingston, R., Carver, S. and Turton, I. (1999) 'Web-based GIS to enhance public democratic involvement', *Proceedings of Geocomputation '99*, Mary Washington College, Virginia, USA, 25–28 July.

Eynon, R. and Dutton, W.H. (2007) 'Barriers to networked governments: Evidence from Europe', *Prometheus*, 25(3): 225–42.

Fagan, G., Newman, P., McCusker, P., Murray, M. (2006) *E-consultation: Evaluating Appropriate Technologies and Processes for Citizens' Participation in Public Policy*. http://www-econsultation.org/ (accessed 2 December 2007).

Goodchild, M.F. (2007) *Citizens as Sensors: The World of Volunteered Geography. Position Paper, Workshop on Volunteered Geographic Information*, 13–14 December, NCGIA, Santa Barbara. http://www.ncgia.ucsb.edu/projects/vgi/docs/position/Goodchild_VGI2007.pdf (accessed 8 January 2008).

Ghose, R (2001) Use of information technology for community empowerment: Transforming geographic information systems into community information systems. *Transactions in GIS* Vol. 5, No. 2 pp. 141–63.

Graham, S. (2002) 'Bridging urban digital divides? Urban polarisation and information and communications technologies (ICTs)', *Urban Studies*, 39(1): 33–56.

Healey, P. (2005) *Collaborative Planning: Shaping Places in Fragmented Societies*. London: Palgrave Macmillan.

Healey, P., McNamara, P., Elson, M. and Doak, A. (1988) *Land Use Planning and the Mediation of Urban Change*. Cambridge: Cambridge University Press.

Howard, D. (1998) 'Geographic Information Technologies and Community Planning: Spatial Empowerment and Public Participation. Paper presented at the NCGIA's', *Empowerment, Marginalisation and Public Participation GIS meeting*. 15–17 October 1998, Santa Barbara, California.

Innes, J.E. and Simpson, D.M. (1993) 'Implementing GIS for planning', *Journal of the American Planning Association*, 59: 230–36.

Involve (2005) People & participation: How to put citizens at the heart of decision-making. http://www.involve.org.uk/assets/Uploads/People-and-Participation.pdf (accessed 8 January 2008).

Kellog, N.R. (1997) 'The Internet, Conversational Communities, and the Future of Planning'. Proceedings of the American Planning Association Conference, San Diego.

King, S. and Cotterill, S. (2007) 'Transformational government? The role of information technology in delivering citizen-centric local public services', *Local Government Studies*, 33(3): 333–54.

Kingston, R. (2002) 'Web based PPGIS in the UK', in W. Craig (ed.), *Community Participation and*

Geographic Information Science. London: Taylor & Francis.

Kingston, R. (2007) 'Public participation in local policy decision-making: The role of web-based mapping', *The Cartographic Journal*, 44(2): 138–44.

Kingston, R., Carver, S., Evans, A. and Turton, I. (2000) 'Web-based public participation geographical information systems: An aid to local environmental decision-making', *Computers, Environment and Urban Systems*, 24(2): 109–25.

Klosterman, R.E. (1997) 'Planning support systems: A new perspective on computer-aided planning', *Journal of Planning Education and Research*, 17: 55–62.

Kolsaker, A. and Lee-Kelley, L. (2007) 'G2C e-government: Modernisation or transformation?', *Electronic Government, an International Journal*, 4(1): 68–75.

Kronberg Declaration (2007) *The Future of Knowledge Acquisition and Sharing*. UNESCO 22–23 June 2007, Kronberg, Germany.

Laituri, M. (2003) 'The issue of access: An assessment guide for evaluating public participation geographic information science case studies. Ensuring access to GIS for marginal societies', *The URISA Journal*, 15 (APA 2): 25–32.

Macintosh, A. (2006) 'eParticipation in policy-making: The research and the challenges', in P. Cunningham and M. Cunningham (eds), *Exploiting the Knowledge Economy: Issues, Applications and Case Studies*, Amsterdam: IOS Press. pp. 364–69.

NCGIA (1998) Empowerment, Marginalization and Public Participation GIS. http://www.ncgia.ucsb.edu/varenius/ppgis/ (accessed 8 January 2008).

O'Riordan, T. and Ward, R. (1997) 'Building trust in shoreline management: Creating participatory consultation on shoreline management plans', *Land Use Policy*, 14(4): 257–76.

Obermeyer, N. (1998) 'The evolution of public participation GIS', *Cartography and Geographic Information Systems*, 25(2): 65–6.

OECD (2001) *Citizens as Partners: Information, Consultation and Public participation in Policy-Making*. Paris: OECD.

Parry, G., Moyser, G. and Day, N. (1992) *Political Participation and Democracy in Britain*. Cambridge: Cambridge University Press.

Pickles, J. (ed.) (1995) *Ground Truth: The Social Implications of Geographical Information Systems*. London: Guilford Press.

PIU (2000) *Electronic Government Services for the 21st Century*. London: Stationery Office.

Plewe, B. (1997) *GIS Online: Information Retrieval, Mapping, and the Internet*. Santa Fe, NM: Onword Press.

Potts, J.S. (1999) 'The non-statutory approach to coastal defence in England and Wales: Coastal defence groups and shoreline management plans', *Marine Policy*, 23(4/5): 479–500.

Ramasubramanian, L. (1999) 'Nurturing community empowerment: Participatory decision making and community based problem solving using GIS', in M. Craglia and H. Onsrud (eds), *Geographic Information Research: Trans-Atlantic Perspectives*. London: Taylor & Francis.

Rambaldi, G., Kwaku Kyem, A.P., Mbile, P., McCall, M. and Weiner, D. (2005) 'Participatory spatial information management and communication in developing countries', *Mapping for Change International Conference* (PGIS'05), Nairobi, Kenya, 7–10 September 2005.

Rambaldi, G., Kwaku Kyem, A.P., McCall, M. and Weiner, D. (2006) 'Participatory spatial information management and communication in developing countries', *Electronic Journal of Information Systems in Developing Countries*, 25(1): 1–9.

Rambaldi, G., Chambers, R., McCall, M. and Fox, J. (2006) 'Practical ethics for PGIS practitioners, facilitators, technology intermediaries and researchers', *Participatory Learning and Action*, 54: 106–13.

Renn, O., Webler, T. and Wiedemann, P. (eds) (1995) *Fairness and Competence in Citizen Participation: Evaluating Models for Environmental Discourse*. London: Klewer.

Rinner, C. (2001) 'Argumentation maps – GIS-based discussion support for online planning', *Environment and Planning B*, 28(6): 847–63.

Rinner, C., Kebler, C. and Andrulis, S. (2008) 'The use of Web 2.0 concepts to support deliberation in spatial decision-making', *Computers, Environment and Urban Systems*, 32: 386–95.

Salus, P.H. (1995) *Casting the Net: From ARPANET to Internet and Beyond*. London: Addison-Wesley.

Sheppard, E. (1995) 'GIS and society: Toward a research agenda', *Cartography and Geographic Information Science*, 22, 5–16.

Shiffer, M. (1995) 'Interactive multimedia planning support: Moving from stand alone systems to the Web', *Environment and Planning B: Planning and Design*, 22(6): 649–64.

Sieber R.E. (2000) 'GIS implementation in the grass-roots' *Urban and Regional Information Systems Association Journal*, 12(1): 15–29.

Sieber, R.E. (2004) 'Conforming (to) the opposition: The social construction of geographical information systems in social movements', *International Journal of Geographical Information Science*, 14(8): 775–93.

Sieber, R.E. (2006) 'Public participation geographic information systems: A literature review and framework', *Annals of the Association of American Geographers*, 96(3): 491–507.

Southern, A. (2002) 'Can information and communication technologies support regeneration?', *Regional Studies*, 36(6): 697–702.

Svensson, J. and Leenes, R. (2003) 'E-voting in Europe: Divergent democratic practice', *Information Polity*, 8(1–2): 3–15.

Talen, E. (1999) 'Constructing neighborhoods from the bottom up: The case for resident-generated GIS', *Environment and Planning B: Planning and Design*, 26(4): 533–54.

Thomas, H. (1995) 'Public participation in planning', in M. Tewdwr-Jones (ed.), *British Planning Policy in Transition*. London: UCL Press, pp. 168–88.

Turner, A. (2006) *Introduction to Neogeography*. Sebastopol, CA: O'Reilly Media.

van den Berg, L. and van Winden, W. (2002) 'Should cities help their citizens to adopt ICTs? On ICT-adoption policies in European cities', *Environment and Planning C: Government and Policy*, 20(2): 263–79.

Viitanen, J. and Kingston, R. (2009) 'The role of public participation GIS in local service delivery', in C. Reddick (ed.), *Strategies for Local E-Government Adoption and Implementation: Comparative Studies*. Hershey, PA: IGI Global. pp. 611–30.

Weiner, D. and Rambaldi, G. (2004) *International Perspectives: Summary Proceedings*. 3rd International Conference on Public Participation GIS, University of Wisconsin-Madison, 18–20 July Madison, Wisconsin. http://www.iapad.org/publications/ppgis/PPGIS_2004_Intl_track_summary.pdf (accessed 17 November 2007).

White, I., Kingston, R. and Barker, A. (2010) 'Participatory GIS for developing flood risk management policy options', *Journal of Flood Risk Management, 3(4), 337–346. DOI:10.1111/j.1753-318X.2010.01083.x.*

YDNPA (1995) *The Dales Woodland Strategy*. Leyburn: Yorkshire Dales National Park Authority.

20

Participatory Approaches in GIS and Society Research: Foundations, Practices, and Future Directions

Sarah Elwood

INTRODUCTION

Geographers and other social scientists have studied cartography and GIS as social and political processes for many years, but the late 1980s and early 1990s saw a surge of interest in how social, political, and economic power are negotiated in and through GIS and cartography (Harley, 1988; Harley, 1989; Pickles, 1991; Wood, 1992; Abler, 1993; Lake, 1993; Sheppard, 1993). These efforts to understand the social production and impacts of GIS later coalesced into the GIS and society research agenda. A central concern in these early discussions was differential access to resources and tools for using GIS, and the potential for disenfranchisement in planning and decision-making processes where maps and geospatial technologies are used. But simultaneously diminishing hardware and software costs and more

user-friendly interfaces were making cartography, and to a certain extent GIS, more accessible to those without specialized training. In spite of financial, time, and training limitations, a growing number of activists, community organizations, and non-profit agencies turned to cartography and GIS to support their activities (Yapa, 1991; Aberley, 1993; Peluso, 1995).

From these early concerns with equity and access in the production and use of maps, spatial data and GIS, questions of participation have long been a part of the GIS and society research agenda. Researchers have questioned who is most likely to be involved in the creation and use of spatial data and GIS, and how will they be involved? Whose knowledge might be systematically excluded and why? Could a more participatory process of producing and using GIS disrupt these potential exclusions? Might participatory research methods help us better understand the genesis of these processes of inclusion and exclusion (Aitken and Michel, 1995; Harris et al., 1995; Pickles, 1995; Sheppard, 1995)?

This chapter examines a diverse range of substantive and methodological engagement with participation that have emerged as GIS and society research has sought to answer these questions, with specific attention to how participation has been differently theorized, facilitated, and investigated. In referring to "participatory approaches" in GIS and society, I mean research about participatory decision making or approaches for participatory knowledge creation in a GIS context, as well as research that integrates GIS into participatory action research (PAR). This definition allows for a more expansive examination of the ways in which participation has been embedded in GIS and society research. My purpose in this chapter is not to provide a review of methodologies used in public participation GIS research and practice, nor to revisit debates about how to differentiate public participation GIS (PPGIS) and participatory GIS (PGIS).[1] Instead, in the following section I examine the intellectual and societal foundations of GIS and society research's commitment to participatory approaches. Then I discuss in more detail substantive and methodological engagements with participation that are part of this research agenda, further considering what these different approaches share in their epistemological underpinnings and research practices, as well as how they are different. The final section examines some key questions in participation and spatial technologies that face future GIS and society research.

FOUNDATIONS OF PARTICIPATORY APPROACHES IN GIS AND SOCIETY RESEARCH

GIS and society research has engaged participation as an "object of research" *and* as a component of many of its research methodologies. Both of these engagements with participation have roots in the social, political, and epistemological critiques around which the GIS and society research agenda originally coalesced; and in the epistemological foundations of some of its earliest empirically grounded research. Shifts in governmental structures and practices in the 1990s toward so-called collaborative governance have also fostered GIS and society researchers' strong focus upon participation.

The sustained focus upon participation and presence of participatory methods in GIS and society research is rooted most directly in critiques of GIS from which this research agenda emerged. Among other things, these critiques were concerned about the difficulty of incorporating multiple, contradictory, or non-cartographic forms of spatial knowledge into then-current forms of the technology, and questioned whether the greater ease of incorporating quantitative or cartographic data would exclude other forms of knowing and reasoning. Scholars were concerned about whether GIS would tend to promote positivism in research and rationalist approaches to planning and policymaking because of its reliance on quantitative techniques and computerized analytical tools, potentially inhibiting other forms of academic inquiry or political projects (Pickles, 1995; Sheppard and Poiker, 1995; Harris and Weiner, 1996). While these critiques raise different issues, and the validity of their claims has been debated (Schuurman, 2000), they frame a common interest in the inclusion of diverse individuals, social groups, priorities, and epistemologies in GIS application.

Concerns with the intellectual and sociopolitical implications of GIS are also strongly informed by feminist critiques of science. Early GIS and society research shared a great deal in common with the feminist research methodologies that have sought to respond to them.[2] Feminist critiques of science challenge the notion of scientific objectivity and assert that all knowledge is incomplete, shaped by the particular context in which it is developed, and by the identity and experiences of those developing it (Harding, 1986; Haraway, 1991). Several propositions follow from this notion. If all knowledge is partial, then incorporating multiple forms of knowledge is a fundamental practice of good science. So-called "expert knowledge" is but one of many valid forms of knowledge that may be brought to bear upon a research question, and experiential forms of knowledge may be equally appropriate. These same arguments about the necessity of incorporating multiple forms of knowledge in a GIS were at the heart of many of the early critiques of GIS (Lake, 1993; Sheppard, 1995).

While characterizations of feminist research methodologies vary considerably,[3] a number of specific practices have tended to follow from feminist critiques of science. Researchers are encouraged to be attentive to how their own social and political positions and those of other people involved in the research affect specific research practices, interpretations and conclusions, or the actual and potential impacts of research findings (Nast, 1994). Other responses include involving research "subjects" as co-researchers directly involved in formulating research questions and methodologies, interpretation, analysis, and findings, with particular emphasis on bringing multiple forms of knowledge to bear upon research questions (Moss, 2002). These responses share a strong commitment to participation, self-representation in research, and self-determination in formulating research goals.

Parallel concerns about multiple knowledge, diverse expertise, and situated knowledge have fostered a strong commitment to participatory research practices in GIS and society research. Early agenda setting statements, such as reports on the National Center for Geographic Information and Analysis' Initiative 19, posed questions about how people, place, and the environment are represented in GIS, with the strong suggestion that externally created representations of marginalized people and places are potentially problematic (Harris and Weiner, 1996).

This perspective emphasizes self-representation, self-authorship, and direct involvement of affected individuals and groups. Perhaps unsurprisingly then, empirically informed GIS and society research incorporated participatory research methodologies from the outset. Examples include participatory research on the impacts of GIS use upon the politics and processes of land reform in post-apartheid South Africa (Harris et al., 1995), or university–community collaboration in development of GIS-based spatial data resources for community-based environmental research and activism (Kurtz et al., 2001).

The sustained presence of participatory methodologies in GIS and society research can also be linked to a resurgence of such methodologies across geography over the past decade. Pain (2003) roots these developments in calls for "rematerializing" human geography (Lees, 2002), and charts the growth of action-oriented approaches such as critical policy research or PAR. PAR is a diverse collection of research approaches that share a commitment to research that is undertaken and guided by the people who will be affected by its findings and the application of those findings. Such research projects are often initiated by citizens or community organizations, sometimes working in collaboration with academic researchers (Pain, 2003; Kindon and Elwood, 2009). As Weiner and Harris (2003) have shown, the use of a complicated technology such as GIS may necessitate guided or chauffeured approaches in which one participant operates the technology with input from others. They emphasize that participatory research is not defined by every participant directly using every tool, but rather, by the collaborative negotiation of research questions, design, analysis, and outcomes among all participants. PAR is rooted in the notion that greater access to information, knowledge production processes, and research tools and techniques may have the potential to empower marginalized groups, a set of assumptions that no doubt further fuels the strong presence of these approaches in GIS and society research.

GIS and society researchers' engagement with participation is also closely linked to changes in governmental structures and practices around the world that have fostered an explosion in so-called participatory or collaborative governance (Smock, 2004). Sometimes associated with neoliberal policy shifts and devolution of governmental responsibilities to ever-lower administrative levels, collaborative governance has been justified through arguments that involving immediately affected stakeholders will lead to more efficient and effective decision making and higher levels of public satisfaction (Fung and Wright, 2003). These claims are hotly debated, with many scholars arguing that collaborative governance does not in fact foster robust public deliberation nor the transfer of significant planning and decision-making power to these stakeholders (Cooke and Kothari, 2001; Lake, 2002).

Many different forums for facilitating collaboration are used in these participatory governance initiatives, with new practices emerging rapidly. Techniques include planning charrettes in which members of the public work together with professional planners to create community designs, neighborhood planning processes where revitalization plans are researched and authored by residents and community organizations, and online public deliberation informing planning and decision making (Brody et al., 2003; Burby, 2003). GIS and other geospatial technologies are used in growing number of these forums to incorporate, collect, analyze, and represent spatial data (McCann, 2001; Elwood and Leitner, 2003). The ongoing expansion of participatory planning and governance practices, and diversifying ways that geospatial data and technologies are integrated in these processes, will no doubt continue to inform GIS and society research.

Thus, participatory approaches have come to occupy a prominent position in GIS and society research through diverse pathways. Critiques of GIS in the mid-1990s framed participation as a central mechanism through which the social and political implications of

the technology are wrought. Epistemological and political commitments shared in common with feminist methodologies and critiques of science have fostered an ongoing commitment to self-representation and self-determination of traditionally excluded social groups in geospatial data, GIS applications, and spatial decision making. Coinciding trends in academia and society, such as the growing popularity of PAR in the social sciences and the rising adoption of participatory governance practices, also underlie GIS and society's strong focus upon participation. The following section examines in more detail the diversity of ways that GIS and society research has developed from these foundational commitments.

FRAMING THE DIVERSITY OF PARTICIPATORY APPROACHES IN GIS AND SOCIETY RESEARCH

Substantive and methodological engagements with participation in GIS and society research over the past 10 to 15 years have largely occurred under the auspices of PPGIS or PGIS research and practice. Some scholars use the identifications "PPGIS" and "PGIS" interchangeably. But for others, PGIS refers to the development of geospatial technologies that is initiated and directed by participants, usually in participatory development processes in the Global South, while PPGIS refers to projects initiated and directed by government or other powerful actors, with relatively little direct input from local participants (Rambaldi et al., 2004). However the use of these terms in the literature is variable and it is often difficult to precisely divide specific research initiatives into one category or the other. I use "PPGIS/PGIS" here to refer to the research questions and practices that they encompass together.[4]

PPGIS/PGIS research and practice include those inquiries that are concerned with explaining the socio-political, economic, or behavioral factors that affect access to GIS and digital spatial data; understanding how GIS use influences participation in collaborative decision-making processes (and identifying mechanisms through which these impacts occur); and developing strategies to incorporate GIS into social and political processes in ways that promote inclusion and recognize diverse forms of knowledge. I characterize PPGIS/PGIS as including research *and* practice because of its commitment to explaining relationships between participation and GIS, while also seeking ways to facilitate participation through the use of spatial technologies or expand access to spatial data and technologies for traditionally marginalized groups. Thus, PPGIS/PGIS research and practice respond to at least three dimensions of the GIS and society agenda: Concerns about uneven access to GIS and digital spatial data, focus on the social and political implications of GIS, and focus on the capacity of GIS to include and represent diverse forms of spatial knowledge.

Participation has come to occupy multiple positions in PPGIS/PGIS research and practice. In some instances, participation is an object of inquiry, as in research that assesses how spatial technologies may affect participation in decision making, or considers how knowledge, identity, and power are produced in participation processes that use GIS (Elwood, 2006c; Ghose, 2006). In other instances, participation is constituted as a desired outcome in PPGIS/PGIS practice, something researchers and practitioners intend to facilitate through the deployment of spatial technologies (Jankowski and Nyerges, 2001a; Nyerges et al., 2006). Finally, participation can also function as part of methodology, as in research that adopts a participatory action research framework (Weiner and Harris, 2003; Pain et al., 2006). Within this diversity, participation has been theorized, facilitated, and investigated somewhat differently in different arenas of PPGIS/PGIS. In the remainder of this section, I characterize participation in two broad groupings of PPGIS/PGIS research, one which I will term grassroots GIS and another which I identify as group decision and collaborative GIS research.

'Grassroots GIS' (and PAR with geospatial technologies)

A great deal of PPGIS/PGIS research has focused on GIS use by social movement groups, non-profit and community-based organizations, and activists, usually for their own planning, decision-making, activism/advocacy, or resource management; often at highly localized levels. This work, which I refer to here as "grassroots GIS" research has sought to understand how participation and GIS technologies are produced from and contribute to unequal power relations, differential forms of knowledge, and diverse social and political identities. In using the term "grassroots," I do not mean to imply a particular social or political scale of action. Rather, I use the term to characterize the focus in this arena of PPGIS/PGIS research upon self-directed GIS development and application by traditionally marginalized groups, institutions of civil society, and non-governmental organizations.

In this context, grassroots GIS research has studied uneven access to spatial data and technologies, the challenges of integrating diverse forms of spatial knowledge into a GIS, and its empowerment potential. It has generally been concerned with participation in two arenas of GIS development and application: the involvement of individuals and groups in decision-making processes in which spatial data and technologies are used, and the inclusion of their knowledge, needs, and priorities within GIS-based spatial data and analyses. Most grassroots GIS research has conceived of participation as a process that is simultaneously constitutive of and constituted by representation, knowledge, and power; and has identified the representational capabilities of GIS, organizational and political structures and relationships, and social identities as particularly significant in structuring this nexus (Harris and Weiner, 1998; Ghose, 2001; Elwood, 2002).

Some grassroots GIS research has focused upon the interplay between participation and the representational capabilities of GIS, noting that the forms of knowledge that can be included in a GIS, as well as the forms of analysis and display that are supported affect whose knowledge and needs are included. An important contribution in this arena has been those efforts to demonstrate how GIS might be adapted to support more diverse forms of knowledge and analysis. Multimedia GIS, for example, offer ways of incorporating non-cartographic representations of spatial knowledge, such as oral narrative, sketches, or photographs (Al-Kodmany, 2001; Shiffer, 2002; Elmes et al., 2004). Other researchers have adapted spatial data structures to expand their flexibility, as in the case of Sieber's (2004) strategies for encoding spatial data that may be fuzzy, multiple, or indeterminate. And other researchers have sought to diversify the ways in which knowledge may be generated in GIS, as in Jung's (2009) strategy for incorporating qualitative coding of spatial data directly into a GIS, to support qualitative analysis techniques within GIS software. The shared assumption underlying these contributions is that participation is mediated through knowledge and strategies for producing knowledge (such as specific analytic techniques), and the way these are incorporated into GIS. By extension, expanding the forms of spatial knowledge that can be incorporated may enable a decision-making process to take into account the knowledge or needs of a more diverse range of individuals or social groups.

Other researchers have illustrated ways that participation is also mediated by organizational and political structures and practices, demonstrating how these mechanisms affect spatial data sharing, and the access of particular individuals and groups to information, material resources, or decision-making forums. Leitner et al. (2000) show how the institutional arrangements through which non-governmental organizations gain access to spatial data and technologies create uneven access, ultimately differentiating these organizations'

participation in decision making, while Ghose (2006) and Sieber (2000a, 2000b) demonstrate how networks among non-governmental organizations can create similarly uneven outcomes. Other researchers note the capacity of political cultures and structures to facilitate or impede citizens' and civic institutions' access to spatial data and opportunities for them to play an active role in key societal decisions (Craglia and Masser, 2003; Tulloch and Shapiro, 2003; Elwood and Ghose, 2004). The shared assumption in these studies is that participation is mediated through the larger institutional and political contexts in which it is situated, by way of the knowledge, political strategies, skills, and material resources that are enabled or constrained by various aspects of these contexts.

The emphasis in grassroots GIS upon the relationship between knowledge and participation is also demonstrated in accounts of the important role that social identities play in shaping what individuals know, the kinds of knowledge claims they can and do make, and the power relations of any social situation in which a GIS is embedded. Harris and Weiner's (1998) work highlights how gender, age, community status, and race affect access to land and resources, thereby differentiating individuals' experiences and spatial knowledge. They further show that these differentiations in knowledge and experience affect what and how people contribute to a participatory process of land reallocation. Elwood (2002, 2006a) illustrates how some of these same axes of identity shape the kinds of knowledge claims that people make, and notes how participatory governance schemes tend to prioritize knowledge that is expressed in cartographic or quantitative terms over experiential or narrative knowledge claims. This hierarchy of knowledge claims gives some groups greater influence in participatory forums. Other studies have reinforced these explanations of the relationship between identity, knowledge, and participation in GIS-based decision-making processes and geographic contexts (Ghose and Huxhold, 2002; Weiner and Harris, 2003; Kyem, 2004).

Given the emphasis in grassroots GIS research upon self-representation in GIS-based spatial knowledge production, participatory action research strongly informs its methodologies. In Weiner and Harris's (2003) extended research in South Africa, rural residents used mental mapping workshops and participatory land use planning activities to compile diverse local knowledge about the history and politics of land access, as well as to develop specific goals for post-apartheid land reform. Gilbert and Masucci's (2006) collaborative project in Philadelphia has worked closely with women on low incomes to develop spatial data resources and technological infrastructures supporting the women's access to these data. In particular this project has emphasized participants' development of skills with computer technologies, as well as their role in determining how these geospatial technology resources will be applied, whether in employment efforts, education access, public health outreach, or other activities. Elwood's (2006b) work with community development organizations in Chicago follows a similar path, with community residents and staff determining how and for what purposes they will use their GIS and data resources, and university-based researchers playing a supporting role of assisting in spatial data development and GIS skill building.[5]

Closely related to these projects, a growing number of action research and participatory development projects have begun to incorporate GIS and geovisualization techniques. While much of this work does not self-identify as PPGIS/PGIS, it is nonetheless another instance of participatory engagements with spatial technologies inspired through GIS and society research. Pain et al. (2006) for example, profile a participatory research project that explores relationships between street lighting, crime, and residents' perceptions of safety, using a multi-method integration of GIS and ethnographic interviews. Williams and Dunn (2003) use participatory sketch mapping, GPS-based data collection by local residents, and community

meetings to understand the relationship between people's social and economic lives and their exposure to risk from land mines in rural Southeast Asia. Dennis's (2006) multimedia GIS methodologies rely on participatory development with urban teens, allowing them to incorporate their narratives, sketches, and photographs into geovisual representations of their own neighborhood designs. A growing number of participatory development projects in the Global South that integrate participatory rural assessment techniques with three-dimensional modeling, GPS data collection, sketch mapping, and other geovisualization techniques (Rambaldi, 2005).[6]

Many of these PAR–GIS intersections focus upon substantive research questions outside of PPGIS/PGIS. For example, the Pain et al. (2006) project described above studied the relationships between material infrastructural conditions in urban neighborhoods and residents' perceptions of their personal safety. Nonetheless, because these initiatives integrate geospatial technologies as part of participatory research, they can be understood as part of GIS and society research's engagement with participation. PAR–GIS intersection projects are closely related to grassroots GIS research in PPGIS/PGIS, because their shared commitment that data sources, research methodologies, and research outputs must be multi-vocal, inclusive, and accessible to diverse participants. PAR–GIS projects have served as a productive sort of practical laboratory for adapting geospatial technologies to better suit these diverse settings and constituencies. While some scholars take the position that efforts to produce "alternative" GIS have not changed traditional GIS software and geospatial data (Miller, 2006), PAR–GIS projects suggest otherwise. They develop creative mixed methods GIS practices and strategies for incorporating diverse forms of knowledge and spatial reasoning, and make important contributions to the GIS and society agenda's innovations in technologies and participatory processes.

In sum, grassroots GIS research has explored the mutually constitutive interplay between participation and GIS. This engagement with participation has been both substantive, as in research that has sought to explain how structures such as representation, knowledge, and identity are co-produced with participation, and also methodological, as in those projects that use a PAR framework to investigate social and political impacts of GIS. A key contribution from this area of PPGIS/PGIS research is its particular attention to inequality and difference, seeking to explain how unequal power relations, diverse forms of knowledge, or uneven access to material, political, or informational resources may differentiate participatory practices and outcomes.

Group decision making and collaborative GIS

Participation is also a central element of research examining the development and use of GIS for collaborative or group decision making, such as the growing number of deliberative decision-making forums that seek to involve members of the public in planning and policymaking.[7] Examples of these forums include large public meetings convened to gain citizens' input on design or routing of major infrastructure projects, urban revitalization programs in which residents create neighborhood strategic plans, or even large regional planning projects in which residents contribute to multi-decade 'visioning' of regional transit, housing, and economic development goals (Bright, 2003; Burby, 2003; Dieber, 2003). GIS, geospatial data, and geovisual methods are used in these forums in many ways, including online deliberation, model building by stakeholder groups, digital sketch mapping, and electronic polling by large groups to express their preferences for different designs or spatial characteristics.

Group decision making and collaborative GIS research takes up the GIS and society agenda's concerns with the accessibility of important societal decisions in which geospatial technologies are engaged. In particular it has examined how and whether these technologies might be used to support richer deliberation, expanded access, and effective communication in these settings. This research shares in common with grassroots GIS research a commitment to actively embedding GIS in participatory processes and understanding the implications of different technological interfaces, forms of spatial data, and deliberation processes upon participation and influence of individuals and groups in decision making.

A key contribution from group decision and collaborative GIS research is its efforts to theorize group decision-making processes, with a specific focus on understanding types of participation, stages in decision processes, and how spatial information and knowledge are constructed and used in different modes of participation or stages in a decision process (Hamilton et al., 2001; Jankowski and Nyerges, 2001a, Peng, 2001; Rinner, 2001; Balram et al., 2003). Jankowski and Nyerges (2001a), for example, conceptualize participation as involving four kinds of interactions: Communication, cooperation, coordination, and collaboration. In group decision and collaborative GIS research, scholars have focused upon several mechanisms or interactions as key mediators affecting how participants use information in decision making, how deliberation occurs, how conflict is mediated and outcomes reached, or how diverse knowledge can be incorporated. Jankowksi and Nyerges (2001a,b) focus on human–computer–human interaction processes as central mediators of participation, access, and outcomes in group decision making with GIS, and use enhanced adaptive structuration theory (EAST) (Nyerges and Jankowski, 1997) to theorize different aspects of these interactions. Rinner (2001) focuses upon participants' framing of their positions or arguments as central to understanding collaborative decision making, and uses argumentation models from communication to theorize this process. Hamilton et al. (2001) focus on participants' learning, arguing that participatory decision making is most effectively understood through learning models such as Kolb's (1984) experiential learning cycle. Balram et al. (2003) begin with a model that divides participatory processes into consecutive stages, and explore the extent to which different stages can incorporate geospatial technologies, as well as diverse forms of spatial knowledge.

Though quite different in their empirical and conceptual bases, these varied projects in group decision and collaborative GIS share a similar approach. Each seeks to create a theoretically grounded but empirically informed account of participatory decision making with geospatial technologies. This approach is aimed at systematically comparing different technological or procedural practices, to understand how these practices affect participants' access to information and deliberation, the incorporation of diverse stakeholder knowledge in a decision, or participants' satisfaction with a process or decision.

Researchers in this arena have created a variety of innovative technological interfaces and deliberative processes for supporting collaborative decision making. They draw upon many of the theoretical frameworks noted above to try to create technology-mediated decision processes that are more inclusive of individuals and forms of spatial knowledge. Some of this work is quasi-experimental in design, creating controlled decision environments where geospatial technologies and decision tools are used by participants (Jankowski and Stasik, 1997; Jankowski and Nyerges, 2001b). Other scholars have developed geospatial decision tools and methodologies, facilitated the deployment of these approaches in actual collaborative planning processes, and assessed their impacts (Grossardt et al., 2001; Bailey and Grossardt, 2006; Bailey et al., 2007). Hall and Leahy's (2006) and Nyerges et al. (2007) web-based GIS tools, for example, are intended to structure and facilitate participants' contributions to collaborative decision

making, with many functions carried out by the participants using the web interface. Other web-based tools do not facilitate group deliberation directly, but enable participants to explore scenarios and build their own knowledge to support their participation in face-to-face deliberations. Peng's (2001) web-based GIS allows participants to explore the consequence of different urban policy designs and create their own alternatives, while the online wildfire alternatives model profiled in Orr (2003) allows stakeholders to adjust the parameters of a wildfire risk model to explore the possible consequences of different actions or scenarios, intended to inform their participation in decisions about land and water use.

Other researchers in group decision and collaborative GIS research have developed geospatial tools that support the incorporation of stakeholders' diverse priorities and preferences expressed in collaborative planning forums. Grossardt et al. (2001) and Bailey et al. (2007) for instance, focus on large-group, face-to-face deliberative processes that incorporate decision-support models and visualization techniques to try to increase participants' understanding of a project, strengthen their contributions to a final design or policy decision, and increase their satisfaction with the process and outcomes. In this context, Bailey and Grossardt's (2006) structured public involvement techniques rely on large group polling in response to sketches and photographs of different design elements or spatial decisions (such as routing of a power line), and use statistical and geovisualization techniques to propose a decision or design based upon expressed preferences.

Group decision and collaborative GIS research has also sought to evaluate its tools and techniques. Evaluation efforts typically consider the efficacy of different approaches to facilitating participants' access, learning, and ability to be informed and active contributors. They may assess the impact of geospatial tools upon various characteristics of participatory decision making, such as the likelihood of reaching a decision, time needed to do so, or level of participants' satisfaction with the deliberative process and its outcomes (Carver et al., 2001; Hamilton et al., 2001; Jankowksi and Nyerges, 2001b; Jankowski et al., 2006). Other evaluation efforts, such as Ramsey and Wilson (2007) examine how different geospatial participation tools produce different kinds of "informed participants," such as those who have information access versus those who have the ability to critically assess the limitations or usefulness of the information they have.

With these conceptual, technological, and procedural contributions, group decision making and collaborative GIS research responds to the GIS and society agenda's call for research investigating the role and impact of geographic information technologies and digital spatial data in important societal decision making. They employ several different perspectives on participation than the grassroots GIS approaches described earlier. Below, I explore some key areas of theoretical and methodological similarity and difference between these engagements with participation in GIS and Society research.

Shared territory and points of departure in PPGIS/PGIS research

There is a great deal of shared territory between grassroots GIS and group decision and collaborative GIS research, as well as a number of key differences. As with any such rubric for differentiating two large bodies of research, readers will inevitably find exceptions to the trends I outline here. My goal is to identify central areas of similarity and difference as a means of highlighting the unique contributions made by these different approaches. One especially important commonality bears comment at the outset. These two arenas of GIS and society research share a commitment to exploring how and under what conditions cartography, visualization, and GIS might enhance participatory practices. They vary widely in their accounts of

the extent to which these outcomes are possible, or how they might be achieved, but nonetheless each is motivated by this possibility.

Grassroots GIS and group decision and collaborative GIS research share some key epistemological underpinnings and methodologies. Both are informed by a realist emphasis upon the important role of structure in shaping events, assuming for instance that participation is more than just what we can observe; that participation is situated within and affected by social and political structures, as are the knowledge and experience of participants. The focus on process that pervades PPGIS/PGIS research is also strongly realist in orientation, evident in the common goal of explaining how participation processes work, or illustrating the processes through which particular outcomes come to be. As well, both approaches emphasize validating knowledge by examining its explanatory power in practice, a commitment rooted in pragmatist philosophies. These shared tendencies to focus on process and see participation as contextually mediated have fostered a strong mixed methods tradition across PPGIS/PGIS, as researchers rely on multiple sources of evidence or analysis techniques to examine different elements of participatory processes and their social, institutional, and organizational contexts.

But there are also several key differences in how grassroots GIS and group decision and collaborative GIS research have approached participation. One arena of difference is the role that participants tend to play in the research process, specifically their role in scripting the process and what substantive contribution their participation makes in answering the driving questions of the research. In group decision and collaborative GIS, research projects tend to involve participants in navigating participation procedures, using software, or engaging in deliberative practices that have been structured by the academic researchers.[8] These activities tend to occur in more controlled settings, such as the decision experiments that are employed in several of the studies cited previously, or in a "real world" deliberation process, as in Bailey and Grossardt's (2006) structured public involvement method. The behaviors, actions, or statements of the participants constitute data which can be analyzed to understand how different elements of a participatory process function, what kind of participation are promoted or inhibited by a particular process, how characteristics of a decision software tool will promote different types of actions or interactions, such as information gathering, deliberation, or conflict resolution.

In grassroots GIS research, researchers have tended to study already-existing participatory processes and the use of spatial technologies in these settings. Ghose (2006) and Sieber (2000a), for example, consider how non-governmental organization utilize GIS in decision-making processes that were developed and structured by those organizations themselves. Participants may be involved in a process that neither they nor academic researchers set up, as in the case of local residents participating in a community-based planning process convened by a community organization. Or participants may be co-developing the process, as in PAR research and other forums in which participants are creating their own process for using GIS to work together toward a plan, decision, or action. The social interactions and technological practices produced by the participants constitute data that are analyzed to better understand their meanings, the knowledge they create, or the kinds of participation they foster or impede.

Grassroots GIS and group decision and collaborative GIS research also differ with respect to the main theorizations or models that tend to be used to structure research projects, particularly research design, sources of evidence, and ways of developing theoretical contributions. Group decision and collaborative GIS research has tended to draw on socio-behavioral theories for understanding participation, human–computer interaction, decision making, or communication. A great

deal of explanatory weight is placed upon different components of participation processes or different aspects of human–computer interactions, to understand or explain why they may tend to generate certain behaviors or outcomes. These socio-behavioral theorizations are often used to structure a participation process or inform development of software supporting GIS-based decision making. For example, Rinner (2001) used argumentation models from communication, sociology, and philosophy to conceptualize how groups make decisions, and created decision support software that embedded this model of decision making in the design of the software. An argumentation model conceives of communication as several logical types of "speech acts" that are part of a structured grammar defining certain rhetorical practices, such as "answers" that respond to "questions."

These socio-behavioral theorizations are also used to understand and explain the behaviors or interactions that are observed. A researcher interested in developing collaborative GIS interface to support group decision making might, for example, use an argumentation model to characterize the speech acts and rhetorical practices that are likely to be part of a decision process, and then attempt to accommodate these in the software design. Or, a researcher might observe a group using GIS, and employ the argumentation model as a rubric for analysis, to characterize the different speech acts and rhetorical moves, to better understand the kinds of outcomes that particular modes of communication are likely to produce. In these approaches, analysis often involves manifest content analysis (Babbie, 2008), focused upon the content of behaviors directly observed, actions taken, or information spoken, written, or otherwise communicated by participants.

In contrast, a great deal of grassroots GIS research draws on political economic and social theory, with particularly strong emphasis on the role of structures such as identity, political systems, or economic relationships in shaping knowledge, power, and meaning, with implications for participation. Thus, the motivating theories here are theorizations of society, not theories of specific social interactions. So, for example, Weiner and Harris' (2003) participatory GIS with community-based land reform in South Africa draws in part on social theories of post-colonialism and gender to explain how particular historically and geographically embedded structures affect participatory processes. The uneven access of different individuals to community mapping processes undertaken within government-initiated land reform planning can be understood as resulting in part from the differential economic, political, and social power that of white landowners or black farm laborers, based on the history and structures of apartheid colonialism. In the same study, the different forms of geographic information contributed by men and women are explained by way of theories of gender, and how it prescribes particular social roles to women and men, with implications for their experiences and knowledge in place. These theoretical foundations inform the tendency in grassroots GIS to study participation and spatial technologies "in situ" – as they are present in already-existing processes. Such approaches tend to rely on ethnographic research designs and the use of grounded theory or extended case method to generate theoretical contributions. As well, their analysis tends to be a latent content analysis (Babbie, 2008), focused upon interpreting the underlying meaning of actions observed, statements made, or artifacts produced by the participants.

These different approaches to studying participation in PPGIS/PGIS research lend themselves to developing different types of findings and contributions. For example, in a grassroots GIS project that uses a PAR orientation, the negotiated nature of the research process may make it more difficult for an academic researcher to isolate focus upon a specific set of explanatory variables than in the researcher-controlled designs that are more evident in group decision and collaborative GIS research. The ethnographic approach that has dominated grassroots GIS is quite effective for investigating the situated production of meaning, or detailed negotiation of social and political process. The field experiments and other more controlled participation forums of some group decision and collaborative GIS research can be useful for examining very specific mechanisms or constructs within a decision process. These approaches also vary in their temporal and geographic extensibility. A great deal of grassroots GIS research has been single case or small comparative case studies, because the intensive qualitative methods used have practical limits to the scale and scope of research that can be undertaken. Group decision and collaborative GIS research shows a wider range of research designs and scopes. In sum, the different methodological, substantive, and political engagements with participation in PPGIS/PGIS research are useful for asking and answering different kinds of questions.

FUTURE DEVELOPMENTS AND RESEARCH DIRECTIONS

Ongoing changes in digital spatial data availability, the structure and functioning of geospatial technologies, and the ways these data and technologies are embedded in societal processes continue to generate questions for GIS and Society research. Here, I outline several important issues that could be part of future work on participation and geospatial technologies. My goal is not to frame a comprehensive agenda, but rather to outline several current developments that raise key issues for GIS and society's engagements with participation and to discuss some of their implications.

First, in spite of the diversity of GIS and society work that engages participation in substantive or methodological ways, there has been relatively little cross-fertilization between the two broad research groupings outlined in this chapter – grassroots GIS and group decision and collaborative GIS research. Some scholars do note that both literatures inform the conceptual foundations of their work (Nyerges et al., 2006), and there are some conceptualizations that have been taken up in both arenas. For example, researchers across PPGIS/PGIS research have used Arnstein's (1969) notion of a 'ladder' of participation, using it to inform their efforts to examine the practices and implications of different forms of participation that may be present in or promoted by particular GIS-based collaborations.[9] But there are many other productive possibilities that could accrue from a stronger exchange of conceptual frameworks and research practices across this gap.

Group decision and collaborative GIS research, for example, has conceptualized deliberation and decision-making processes as having multiple stages, in which different activities are performed and different forms of information are needed, used, or created. In contrast, relatively little has been done in grassroots GIS research to interrogate different elements of participatory processes within these initiatives, or what may be happening within them in terms of inclusion, exclusion, and knowledge production. Wilson (2005) and Schlossberg and Shuford (2005) have pointed to this kind of under-examination of participation processes. While many researchers involved in grassroots GIS research and practice would resist the notion that different stages of deliberation and decision making can be identified in advance or controlled in practice, adopting a conceptualization of these processes as having multiple stages in which different actions or relationships are negotiated could greatly refine and strengthen theorizations of participation in this research.

In addition to this sort of conceptual interchange, future grassroots GIS and group decision and collaborative GIS research could also benefit from expanding their engagement with mixed methods. Already there exists a longstanding tradition of multiple methods research. Scholars in all areas

of PPGIS/PGIS have used research designs that incorporate multiple techniques or sources of evidence, often using their techniques to complement one another or to create new insights that neither could create separately. But I would argue that many of the currently pressing questions in PPGIS/PGIS demand an integration at epistemological levels – incorporating very different approaches to conceptualizing and studying participation in order to more fully understand it. For example, both Nyerges (2005) and Sieber (2006) note the growing need in PPGIS/PGIS research to theorize across the many richly contextualized case studies in this area. The multiple case designs more commonly seen in group decision and collaborative GIS research may be useful in doing just that. Conversely, the ethnographic approaches more common in grassroots GIS have tremendous potential for group decision and collaborative GIS research, particularly for developing more detailed understandings of how participants create knowledge and meaning as they interact with spatial technologies or participatory decision activities.

Future methodological and substantive engagement with participation in GIS and Society research will also need to investigate the significance and impacts of the ever-expanding host of new spatial technologies that are altering our understanding of what constitutes a geographic information system. Of particular significance are wireless technologies and those that use the Internet. Wireless or remote technologies such as handheld GPS-enabled data-collection devices are changing how potential participants are able to produce, contribute, and receive spatial information, and altering who is able to do so and when (Rambaldi, 2005; Parikh and Lazowska, 2006). As well, there are a number of intersections between GIS and the user-mediated web services known as "Web 2.0" that are altering participation and geospatial technology access and use. In the past several years, new Web 2.0–GIS intersections have included Web sites that enable user editing where users can add their own data, annotate features, comment on others' data, or provide information about locations on the map. As well, open source programming code is being used to support "map hacking" in which users incorporate mapping functionality on their own websites using this code (Crampton and Krygier, 2005; Miller, 2006).

There are countless other examples of new technological developments in GIS, and they raise a number of substantive and methodological implications for participatory approaches in GIS and society research. These new spatial technologies are substantially changing the kinds of GIS applications that are part of PPGIS/PGIS. GPS-enabled handheld devices, for instance, have dramatically altered the ability of under-resourced PPGIS/PGIS initiatives in remote locations to create their own digital data. Web interfaces developed to facilitate public input upon extremely large planning initiatives are now able to support new forms of interaction and information exchange, such as participants adding their comments or sketches to a map, or responding to those added by others. Future research must continue to investigate how these new practices are incorporated into different types of participatory decision making, ranging from grassroots activism to structured public involvement settings, and examine their implications for participation, power relations, and outcomes. Much as in the early GIS and society debates, a great deal of frenetic discussion has centered on Web 2.0–GIS intersections such as Google's mapping application programming interface and provision of high-resolution satellite images and aerial photographs. But there remains a need for systematic empirically grounded research on how and with what impacts such new technologies are actually taken up in activism, collaborative planning, and other contexts.

In the context of PPGIS/PGIS, researchers must examine how these new technologies alter existing dynamics of inclusion and exclusion. For instance, in participatory action research that uses GIS, introducing a new computer-based technology into the research process often inhibits the contributions of participants with the least computer expertise. While emerging Web 2.0/GIS intersections might have this same affect, it is possible as well that novice computer users who are nonetheless familiar with the Internet may find these interfaces more accessible than traditional GIS software. As well, PPGIS/PGIS research needs to systematically examine the appropriateness of different data collection techniques for studying participation that occurs online, as much of it does through these new technologies. As Wong and Chua (2001) note, designing appropriate data methodologies for studying participation in web-mediated GIS activities is challenging because of the often asynchronous nature of participants' contributions, difficulty in identifying precisely who is participating, and an often-limited capacity to create face-to-face forums with these participants for research purposes.

CONCLUSION

In its first two decades, GIS and society research has had a sustained methodological and substantive commitment to understanding and practicing participation in the use of geospatial technologies. This commitment was initially motivated by concerns raised in early GIS and society critiques about the potential exclusion of people, information, and ways of knowing from geospatial technologies and from processes in which they are used. As well, is has been sustained by parallel growth in the adoption of geospatial technologies and participatory decision-making processes in planning, problem solving, and policymaking settings around the world. These commitments have fostered a diverse array of interventions and research projects, promoting and studying the use of GIS and other geographic information technologies in participatory forums ranging from grassroots activism to highly structured collaborative planning initiatives.

In this discussion, I have framed participatory approaches in GIS and society research as encompassing substantive and methodological engagement with participation in grassroots GIS research, participatory action research that incorporates GIS, and group decision and collaborative GIS research. As I have developed in the preceding sections, these research areas share some foundational assumptions and research questions, but are also characterized by differences in their objects and subjects of study, and their approaches to creating and validating knowledge. My motivations in framing these similarities and differences as part of a broader discussion of participatory approaches in GIS and society research are twofold. First, I have sought to trace some of the theoretical and political foundations that inform the longstanding focus upon participation that was inspired by the GIS and society critiques of the mid-1990s, and to characterize the diversity of substantive and methodological encounters with participation that have developed from these foundations. Second, I have tried to systematically set out some of the key points of departure between these two groups of work as a way toward fostering greater engagement between them. Researchers working in both areas are motivated by some of same goals of promoting equitable access to important societal processes *through* the use of geospatial technologies and *in* the use of geospatial technologies. Unpacking some of the key differences between these research areas is useful starting place from which to consider possibilities for productive engagements with one another in future GIS and Society research.

NOTES

1 The terms PGIS and PPGIS are used variably in the literature, but emerge from efforts to differentiate the modes of participation that are present in citizen-initiated and citizen-controlled forums, versus structured planning processes in which citizens are invited by others to participate. See Rambaldi et al. (2004) and Sieber (2006) for further discussion.

2 Feminist GIS research has explored these connections in more detail that space in this chapter allows. See Kwan (2002a and 2002b), Pavlovskaya (2006), and Pavlovskaya and St. Martin (2007).

3 For instance, papers in a 1995 collection in *The Professional Geographer* (Vol. 47, No. 4) debate the role of quantitative techniques in feminist methodologies, and papers in a 2002 collection of *Gender, Place and Culture* (Vol. 9, No. 3) take up similar issues with respect to GIS-based methods.

4 An important facet of debates about the difference between PGIS and PPGIS has been discussions about how "the public" should be defined and what sorts of practices should be considered "participation." These questions are of course central to key issues in GIS & Society research, especially those to do with inequity, diverse knowledge, and the empowerment/disempowerment potential of GIS, but a full discussion is beyond the scope of this paper. See Nyerges (2005) and Schlossberg and Shuford (2005) for detailed discussion of these issues.

5 Other examples of grassroots GIS research that uses participatory research methods are discussed in Warren (2004) and McLafferty (2002). As well, bibliographic resources included in Sieber (2006) and the Integrated Approaches for Participatory Avenues in Development website (http://www.iapad.org) provide access to a host of other projects employing similar methods.

6 Participatory rural assessment (PRA) techniques involve local people in development of their communities, responding to critiques of the top-down nature of many (failed) development initiatives that relied on outside "experts." PRA instead involves these experts as facilitators and encourages residents' own information collection and proposals for action and change (Chambers, 1994).

7 I focus on only one part of collaborative GIS research here – that which focuses on use of GIS in collaborative decision making outside of academia. I do not consider studies of how GIS and other geospatial technologies might be used to help researchers collaborate with one another such as MacEachren (2000) or Matthews et al. (2006).

8 This is not to say that participants do not have any input. Nearly all of the group decision or collaborative GIS research cited in this chapter consulted in some manner with stakeholders or potential users to gather information about the necessary functionalities to be in included in such tools, or to evaluate preliminary versions.

9 Arnstein (1969) was one of the first scholars in planning to argue, amidst a rush toward purportedly "participatory" planning, that not all forms of participation were created equal. Her ladder of participation is a heuristic that outlines a hierarchy of levels of self-determination that are afforded to "participants," ranging from simply being informed to having an opportunity to produce plans and actions themselves.

REFERENCES

Aberley, D. (ed.) (1993) *Boundaries of Home: Mapping for Local Empowerment.* Philadelphia, PA: New Society Publishers.

Abler, R. (1993) 'Everything in its place: GPS, GIS, and geography in the 1990s', *The Professional Geographer*, 45(2): 131–39.

Aitken, S. and Michel, M. (1995) 'Who contrives the "real" in GIS? Geographic information, planning, and critical theory', *Cartography and Geographic Information Systems*, 22(1): 17–29.

Al-Kodmany, K. (2001) 'Supporting imageability on the World Wide Web: Lynch's five elements of the city in community planning', *Environment and Planning B: Planning and Design*, 28(6): 805–32.

Arnstein, S. (1969) 'A ladder of citizen participation', *American Institute of Planners Journal*, 35: 216–34.

Babbie, E. (2008) *The Basics of Social Research*, 4th edn. Belmont, CA: Thomson.

Bailey, K., Grossardt, T. and Pride-Wells, M. (2007) 'Community design of a light rail transit-oriented development using casewise visual evaluation (CAVE)', *Socio-Economic Planning Sciences*, 41(3): 235–54.

Bailey, K. and Grossardt, T. (2006) 'Addressing the Arnstein gap: improving public confidence in transportation planning and design through Structured Public Involvement (SPI)', in M. Schrenk (ed.), *Proceedings of the 11th International GeoMultimedia Symposium.* CORP2005. Vienna, Austria. pp. 337–41.

Balram, S., Dragicevic, S. and Thomas, M. (2003) 'Achieving effectiveness in stakeholder participation using the GIS-based Collaborative Spatial Delphi methodology', *Journal of Environmental Assessment Policy and Management*, 5(3): 365–94.

Bright, E. (2003) *Reviving America's Forgotten Neighborhoods: An investigation of Inner City Revitalization Efforts.* New York: Routledge.

Brody, S., Godschalk, D. and Burby, R. (2003) 'Mandating citizen participation in plan making', *Journal of the American Planning Association*, 69(3): 245–64.

Burby, R. (2003) 'Making plans that matter', *Journal of the American Planning Association*, (1): 33–49.

Carver, S., Evans, A., Kingston, R. and Turton, I. (2001) 'Public participation, GIS and cyberdemocracy: evaluating on-line spatial decision support systems', *Environment and Planning B: Planning and Design*, 28(6): 907–21.

Chambers, R. (1994) 'The origins and practice of participatory rural appraisal', *World Development*, 22(9): 1253–68.

Cooke, B. and Kothari, U. (eds) (2001) *Participation: The New Tyranny?* London: Zed Books.

Craglia, M. and Masser, I. (2003) 'Access to geographic information: a European perspective', *The URISA Journal*, 15 (APAI): 51–60.

Crampton, J. and Krygier, J. (2005) 'An introduction to critical cartography', *ACME*, 4(1): 11–33.

Dennis, S. (2006) 'Prospects for qualitative GIS at the intersection of youth development and participatory urban planning', *Environment and Planning A*, 38(11): 2039–54.

Dieber, M. (2003) 'Paint the town: lessons learned', *Paper presented at the 2nd Annual Public Participation GIS Conference, July 20–22, 2003. Portland, OR.* http://www.urisa.org/PPGIS/2003/papers/Dieber.pdf:3/15/2005 (accessed October 20, 2008.

Elmes, G., Dougherty, M., Callig, H., Karigomba, W., McCusker, B. and Weiner, D. (2004) 'Local knowledge doesn't grow on trees: community-integrated geographic information systems and rural community self definition', in P. Fisher (ed.), *Developments in Spatial Data Handling.* Berlin: Springer-Verlag. pp. 29–39.

Elwood, S. (2002) 'GIS and collaborative urban governance: understanding their implications for community action and power', *Urban Geography*, 22(8): 737–59.

Elwood, S. (2006a) 'Beyond cooptation or resistance: urban spatial politics, community organizations, and GIS-based spatial narratives', *Annals of the Association of American Geographers*, 96: 2.

Elwood, S. (2006b) 'Critical issues in participatory GIS: deconstructions, reconstructions and new research directions', *Transactions in GIS*, 10(5): 693–708.

Elwood, S. (2006c) 'Negotiating knowledge production: the everyday inclusions, exclusions, and contradictions of participatory GIS research', *The Professional Geographer*, 58(2): 197–208.

Elwood, S. and Ghose, R. (2004) 'PPGIS in community development planning: framing the organizational context', *Cartographica*, 38(3/4): 19–33.

Elwood, S. and Leitner, H. (2003) 'GIS and spatial knowledge production for neighborhood revitalization: negotiating state priorities and neighborhood visions', *Journal of Urban Affairs*, 25(2): 139–57.

Fung, A. and Wright, E. (2003) *Deepening Democracy: Institutional Innovations in Empowered Participatory Governance.* London: Verso.

Ghose, R. (2001) 'Use of information technology for community empowerment: transforming geographic information system into community information systems', *Transactions in GIS*, 5(2):141–63.

Ghose, R. and Huxhold, W. (2002) 'Role of multi-scalar GIS-based indicators studies in formulating neighborhood planning policy', *The URISA Journal*, 14(2): 3–16.

Ghose, R. (2006) 'Politics of scale and networks of association in public participation GIS', *Environment and Planning A*, 39(8): 1961–80.

Gilbert, M. and Masucci, M. (2006) 'The implications of including women's daily lives in a feminist GIScience', *Transactions in GIS*, 10(5): 751–61.

Grossardt, T., Bailey, K. and Brumm, J. (2001) 'AMIS: geographic information system-based corridor planning methodology', *Transportation Research Record*, 1768: 224–32. Washington, DC: National Academies.

Hall, B. and Leahy, M. (2006) 'Internet-based spatial decision support using open source tools', in S. Balram and S. Dragicevic (eds), *Collaborative Geographic Information Systems*. Hershey, PA: Idea Group. pp. 237–62.

Hamilton, A., Trodd, N., Zhang, X., Fernando, T. and Watson, K. (2001) 'Learning through visual systems to enhance the urban planning process', *Environment and Planning B: Planning and Design*, 28(6): 833–45.

Haraway, D. (1991) *Simians, Cyborgs, and Women: The Reinvention of Nature*. New York: Routledge.

Harding, S. (1986) *The Science Question in Feminism*. Ithaca, NY: Cornell University Press.

Harley, J. (1988) 'Maps, knowledge, and power', in D. Cosgrove and S. Daniels (eds), *The Iconography of Landscape: Essays on the Symbolic Representation, Design, and use of Past Environments*. Cambridge: Cambridge University Press. pp. 277–312.

Harley, J. (1989) 'Deconstructing the map', *Cartographica*, 26(1): 1–20.

Harris, T. and Weiner, D. (1996) 'Initiative 19 – GIS and society: the social implications of how people, space and environment are represented in GIS', *National Center for Geographic Information and Analysis Report #96–7*. http://www.geo.wvu.edu/i19/report/report.html

Harris, T. and Weiner, D. (1998) 'Empowerment, marginalization, and community-integrated GIS', *Cartography and Geographic Information Systems*, 25(2): 67–76.

Harris, T., Weiner, D., Warner, T. and Levin, R. (1995) 'Pursuing social goals through participatory GIS: Redressing South Africa's historical political ecology', in J. Pickles (ed.), *Ground Truth: The Social Implications of Geographic Information Systems*. London: Guilford Press. pp. 196–222.

Jankowski, P. and Nyerges, T. (2001a) *Geographic Information Systems for Group Decision Making*. London: Taylor & Francis.

Jankowski, P. and Nyerges, T. (2001b) 'GIS-supported collaborative decision-making: results of an experiment', *Annals of the Association of American Geographers*, 91(1): 48–70.

Jankowski, P. and Stasik, M. (1997) 'Spatial understanding and decision support system: a prototype for public GIS', *Transactions in GIS*, 2(1): 73–84.

Jankowski, P., Robischon, S., Tuthill, D., Nyerges, T. and Ramsey, K. (2006) 'Design considerations and evaluation of a collaborative, spatio-temporal decision support system', *Transactions in GIS*, 10(3): 335–54.

Jung, J. (2009) 'Computer-aided qualitative GIS: A software-level integration of qualitative research and GIS', in M. Cope and S. Elwood (eds), *Qualitative GIS: A Mixed Methods Approach*. London: Sage Publications. pp. 115–35.

Kindon, S. and Elwood, S. (2009) 'Introduction: more than methods – reflections on participatory action research in geographic teaching, learning and research', *The Journal of Geography in Higher Education*, 33(1): 19–32.

Kolb, D. (1984) *Experiential Learning: Experience as a Source of Learning and Development*. Inglewood Cliffs, CA: Prentice-Hall.

Kwan, M. (2002a) 'Is GIS for women? Reflections on the critical discourse in the 1990s', *Gender, Place and Culture*, 9(3): 271–79.

Kwan, M. (2002b) 'Feminist visualization: re-envisioning GIS as a method in feminist geographic research', *Annals of the Association of American Geographers*, 92(2): 656–61.

Kurtz, H., Leitner, H., Sheppard, E. and McMaster, R. (2001) 'Neighborhood environmental inventories on the Internet: creating a new kind of community resource for Phillips Neighborhood', *CURA Reporter*, 31(2): 20–6.

Kyem, K. (2004) 'Of intractable conflicts and participatory GIS applications: the search for consensus amidst competing claims and institutional demands', *Annals of the Association of American Geographers*, 94(1): 37–57.

Lake, R. (1993) 'Planning and applied geography: positivism, ethics, and geographic information systems', *Progress in Human Geography*, 17(3): 404–13.

Lake, R. (2002) 'Bring back big government', *International Journal of Urban and Regional Research*, 26(4): 815–22.

Lees, L. (2002) 'Rematerializing urban geography: "new" urban geography and the ethnographic void', *Progress in Human Geography*, 26(1): 101–12.

Leitner, H., Elwood, S., Sheppard, E., McMaster, S. and McMaster R. (2000) 'Modes of GIS provision and their appropriateness for neighborhood organizations: examples from Minneapolis and St. Paul, Minnesota', *The URISA Journal*, 12(4): 43–56.

MacEachren, A. (2000) 'Cartography and GIS: facilitating collaboration', *Progress in Human Geography*, 24(3): 445–56.

Matthews, S., Detwiler, J. and Burton, L. (2006) 'Geo-ethnography: coupling geographic information analysis techniques with ethnographic methods in urban research', *Cartographica*, 40(4): 75–90.

McCann, E. (2001) '"Doctors of space?" Geographic information in the politics of urban and regional planning', *Studies in Regional and Urban Planning*, 9: 3–20.

McLafferty, S. (2002) 'Mapping women's worlds: knowledge, power, and the bounds of GIS', *Gender, Place and Culture*, 9(3): 263–69.

Miller, C. (2006) 'A beast in the field: the Google Maps mashup as GIS', *Cartographica*, 41(3): 187–99.

Moss, P. (ed.) (2002) *Feminist Geography in Practice: Research and Methods*. London: Blackwell.

Nast, H. (1994) 'Opening remarks on "Women in the field"', *The Professional Geographer*, 46(1): 54–66.

Nyerges, T. (2005) 'Scaling-up as a grand challenge for public participation GIS', *Directions Magainze*, 20 September 2005. http://www.directionsmag.com/article.php?article_id=1965&trv=1.

Nyerges, T. and Jankowski, P. (1997) 'Enhanced adaptive structuration theory: a theory of GIS-supported collaborative decision making', *Geographical Systems*, 4(3): 225–59.

Nyerges, T., Jankowski, P., Tuthill, D. and Ramsey, K. (2006) 'Collaborative water resource decision support: results of a field experiment', *Annals of the Association of American Geographers*, 96(4): 699–725.

Nyerges, T., Ramsey, K. and Wilson, M. (2007) 'Design considerations for an Internet portal to support public participation in transportation improvement decision making', in S. Balram and S. Dragicevic (eds), *Collaborative Geographic Information Systems*. Hershey, PA: Idea Group. pp. 208–36.

Orr, B. (2003) 'WALTER: a model for wildfire alternatives', *Southwest Fire Initiative Conference*. 29 April 2003. Northern Arizona University. Flagstaff, Arizona. http://www.for.nau.edu/research/pzf/swfi/Abstracts.htm#Orr.

Pain, R. (2003) 'Social geography: on action orientated research', *Progress in Human Geography*, 27(5): 649–57.

Pain, R., MacFarlane, R., Turner, K. and Gill, S. (2006) '"When, where, if and but": qualifying GIS and the effect of streetlighting on crime and fear', *Environment and Planning A*, 38(11): 2055–74.

Parikh, T. and Lazowska, E. (2006) 'Designing an architecture for delivering mobile information services to the rural developing world., International World Wide Web Conference 2006, 23–26 May 2006, Edinburgh, Scotland.

Pavlovskaya, M. (2006) 'Theorizing with GIS: a tool for critical geographies?', *Environment and Planning A*, 38(11): 2003–20.

Pavlovskaya, M. and St. Martin, K. (2007) 'Feminism and GIS: from a missing object to a mapping subject', *Geography Compass*, 1(3): 583–606.

Peluso, N. (1995) 'Whose woods are these? Counter-mapping forest territories in Kalimantan, Indonesia', *Antipode*, 27(4): 383–406.

Peng, Z. (2001) 'Internet GIS for public participation', *Environment and Planning B: Planning and Design*, 28(6): 889–905.

Pickles, J. (1991) 'Geography, GIS and the surveillant society', *Papers and Proceedings of Applied Geography Conferences*, 14: 80–91.

Pickles, J. (ed.) (1995) *Ground Truth: The Social Implications of Geographic Information Systems*. London: Guilford Press.

Rambaldi, G. (2005) 'Who owns the map legend?', *The URISA Journal*, 17(1): 5–13.

Rambaldi, G., McCall, M., Weiner, D., Mbile, P. and Kyem, P. (2004) *Participatory GIS*. http://www.iapad.org/participatory_gis.htm (accessed 20 October 20 2008).

Ramsey, K. and Wilson, M. (2007) 'Rethinking the "informed participant": precautions and recommendations for the design of online deliberation', in T. Davies (ed.), *Online Deliberation*. Stanford: CSLI Publications.

Rinner, C. (2001) 'Argumentation maps: GIS-based discussion support for on-line planning', *Environment and Planning B: Planning and Design*, 28(6): 847–63.

Schlossberg, M. and Shuford, E. (2005) 'Delineating "public" and "participation" in PPGIS', *The URISA Journal*, 16(2): 15–26.

Schuurman, N. (2000) 'Trouble in the heartland: GIS and its critics in the 1990s', *Progress in Human Geography*, 24(4): 564–90.

Sheppard, E. (1993) 'Automated geography: what kind of geography for what kind of society?', *The Professional Geographer*, 45(4): 457–60.

Sheppard, E. (1995) 'GIS and society: towards a research agenda', *Cartography and Geographic Information Systems*, 22(2): 5–16.

Shiffer, M. (2002) 'Spatial multimedia representations to support community participation', in W. Craig,

T. Harris and D. Weiner (eds), *Community Participation and Geographic Information Systems.* London: Taylor & Francis.

Sieber, R. (2000a) 'Conforming (to) the opposition: the social construction of geographical information systems in social movements', *International Journal of Geographic Information Systems*, 14(8): 775–93.

Sieber, R. (2000b) 'GIS implementation in the grassroots', *URISA Journal*, 12(1): 15–51.

Sieber, R. (2004) 'Rewiring for a GIS/2', *Cartographica*, 39(1): 25–40.

Sieber, R. (2006) 'Public participation geographic information systems: a literature review and framework', *Annals of the Association of American Geographers*, 96(3): 491–507.

Smock, K. (2004) *Democracy in Action: Community Organizing and Urban Change.* New York: Columbia University Press.

Tulloch, D. and Shapiro, T. (2003) 'The intersection of data access and public participation: impacting GIS users' success?', *The URISA Journal*, 15(APAII): 55–60.

Warren, S. (2004) 'The utopian potential of GIS', *Cartographica*, 39(1): 5–15.

Weiner, D. and Harris, T. (2003) 'Community-integrated GIS for land reform in South Africa', *The URISA Journal*, 15(APAII): 61–73.

Williams, C. and Dunn, C. (2003) 'GIS in participatory research: assessing the impacts of landmines on communities in Northwest Cambodia', *Transactions in GIS*, 7(3): 393–410.

Wilson, M. (2005) 'Implications for a public participation geographic information science: analyzing trends in research and practice', MA Thesis, Department of Geography, University of Washington, Seattle.

Wong, S. and Chua, Y. (2001) 'Data intermediation and beyond: issues for web-based PPGIS', *Cartographica*, 38(3/4): 63–79.

Wood, D. (1992) *The Power of Maps.* New York: Guilford Press.

Yapa, L. (1991) 'Is GIS appropriate technology?' *International Journal of Geographical Information Systems*, 5(1): 41–58.

21

PPGIS Implementation and the Transformation of US Planning Practice

Laxmi Ramasubramanian

INTRODUCTION

This chapter reflects on the changing nature of planning practice in the USA in order to make the argument that the use of geo-spatial technologies can contribute to make the day-to-day planning practice more efficient, inclusive, transparent, and accountable only when coupled with credible participatory processes. Planning is often accused of serving the power elite exclusively. However, since the 1960s new planning frameworks[1] that explicitly create opportunities for public scrutiny, emphasize transparency and account-ability, and invite public involvement have emerged in the USA. In the last two decades, GIS and other digital technologies have been credited with "giving teeth" to these pro-cesses. However, it is instructive to note that these positive gains have not come easily or quickly. Consequently, it is worthwhile for the reader seeking to understand participa-tory GIS implementation to carefully consider how participatory and advocacy planning

practitioners have adopted and adapted GIS to effect social change. There is a synergistic relationship between successful technology adoption and use by community groups and changes in conventional planning practice in the USA.

The next section provides an overview of planning practice in the USA. Lacking a clear mandate for planning (in contrast to many other democratic societies), planning as practiced in the USA constantly wrestles with four major dilemmas; the framing of planning problems, identifying the locus of planning authority, defining the public inter-est, and the management of public participa-tion within formal planning processes. I have previously argued that these ideological, con-ceptual, and methodological understandings about the nature of participation shape insti-tutional resolutions to these dilemmas. Where GIS and related technologies have been adopted by organizations or government agencies, the technologies are used in ways that reify pre-established understandings of the benefits and limits of participation (Ramasubramanian, 1995, 1999, 2004).

Authors such as Pickles (1995), Graham and Marvin (1996), and Carver (2003) have proposed that technology adoption must be examined in the context of causal events and resulting socio-political transformations. In keeping with this rationale, I discuss the converging trends and dynamics of GIS adoption by grassroots advocacy groups. The results of technology adoption to address a range of social issues are clear – in advocacy and participatory planning work, GIS is now part of the organizing arsenal required to challenge "official" planning decisions and policies, often generating new data and information. These new forms of evidence have served well to energize citizen activism at the neighborhood scale. Yet, the results are not as clear when we seek to understand the transformative and collective impacts of participatory projects that used GIS, perhaps because published narratives of public participation GIS (PPGIS) adoption and use often focus on the particular case (Craig et al., 2002), that place little or no emphasis on the larger planning frameworks that govern technology adoption and use.

An evaluation framework to understand participatory GIS implementation as a part of larger planning and decision-making frameworks is presented in the next section. The framework highlights the unique ways in which mainstream US planning practice simultaneously creates opportunities and obstacles to long-term sustainability of PPGIS initiatives. I focus my attention on three case studies where GI technologies were implemented to address a wide variety of citizen concerns. I selected these case studies quite deliberately because I am able to discuss details about the socio-political and institutional context of implementation. In addition, I am also able to describe the planning process (as designed and in practice) because of my contributions as a researcher/practitioner to the development and implementation of these projects. This is a reflective exercise of documenting evidence about what happened

after the project concluded. The evaluation framework organizes the three separate narratives in order to better understand (1) process, (2) outcomes, and (3) impacts.

The conclusions summarize and synthesize findings from the case studies to reflect on the transformation of planning practice, the ways in which GIS technologies are now deployed and used effectively, and where the use of digital technologies are having a significant impact.

PLANNING PRACTICE IN THE USA

"Planning" is simultaneously an everyday word that communicates a systematic and reasoned approach to problem solving and a discipline with its own set of tools, methods, and processes all of which are designed to guide future action (Dalton et al., 2000). Twentieth-century planning is intricately linked with the development, growth, and management of cities (Hall, 1996). Contemporary planning practice in the USA is also unashamedly normative; where individuals and organized groups have sought to establish their own visions of a preferred future and are working towards that goal.

In the early part of the twentieth century, planning was dominated by social reformers who sought to redress the negative consequences of the nineteenth century industrial city. The earliest planning efforts in some of the most populous and polluted cities of the day including London, New York, and Chicago were directed towards ensuring the health and well-being of all citizens, although the reformers placed greater emphasis on meeting the needs of economically and socially vulnerable populations (Hall, 1996). During the depression and the 1920s and 1930s, planning became identified with integrated management of capital and resources. The Tennessee Valley Authority (TVA) was created in 1933 to develop and implement an integrated plan to meet the needs of a poor region. Its establishment was supported across traditional rural–urban divisions and across party lines (Neuse, 1983). Viewed as a model of "good" planning (Berke et al., 2000), the TVA model was expanded and exported to other countries such as Brazil and India post World War II, where the focus of planning was the creation and management of large-scale infrastructure projects designed to support regional planning.

In order to meet the needs of returning war veterans, the US government took on an activist role and put in place policies and programs to create affordable housing, educational and work opportunities. These initiatives contributed to, and expanded the growth of suburbs (Jackson, 1985). Subsequently, as suburban populations continued to grow, planning began to focus on the development of a robust transport infrastructure to assist in the safe movement of goods and people between cities and suburbs (Hall, 1996). Comprehensive planning and investment in infrastructure improvements also resulted in the establishment of the Interstate Highway System in 1956 (Federal Highway Administration, United States Department of Transportation, 2006). The Great Society programs of the 1960s championed by President Johnson can be seen as continuation of the social reform movements of an earlier era.

The range of activities subsumed under the word "planning" described briefly above can provide some useful insights and move us towards the creation of a working definition of planning practice. To offer a working definition, planning is a set of frameworks and processes designed to address novel problems in complex contexts, supported through institutional and political power structures in order to accomplish agreed upon goals (based on Alexander, 1992). Planning seeks to create 'better' futures for all citizens (typically considering quality of life issues such as housing affordability, safe and well-paying jobs, safe neighborhoods, and so on), by creating a range of mechanisms (e.g., legislation, guidelines, and new institutions with authority to review and

evaluate both processes and outcomes) to ensure that plans are implemented, monitored, and evaluated systematically.

While planning and policymaking are intricately linked, *planning practice*, the subject and focus of this chapter, is bounded by institutional and political norms, protocols, methods, and systems (e.g., demographic analyses, cost-benefit studies, interviews, urban design analyses, consultations, and so on), by spatial references (such as city, town, region, watershed), and by a series of well defined types of plans intended to serve specific purposes at different spatial scales.

The USA is unique among other industrialized and modern nations in that it has no federal department of planning. Planning activities are split across a plethora of agencies and branches of government. At the local government level, planning includes: comprehensive planning, planning for affordable housing, economic development planning, urban design, zoning, and growth management. It is important to observe that land use planning continues to be in the control of towns and municipalities, emphasizing local control of land planning decisions. At the county and regional government level, natural resource management, investments in infrastructure and transportation, economic development, and growth management are dominant planning themes. The federal government has created a variety of agencies (e.g., Environmental Protection Agency), and has passed legislation (establishment of Metropolitan Planning Organizations)[2] to encourage municipalities to work collaboratively across regions.

Reviewing two centuries of planning thought, John Friedmann (1987) notes that there are four dominant intellectual traditions that shape contemporary planning discourse – policy analysis, social reform, social learning, and social mobilization. The social learning and social mobilization traditions, although they emerge from the right and left of the political spectrum respectively, believe that societal transformation is at the heart of the planning enterprise. Thus, it should come as no surprise that the notion of participation is championed extensively within these two traditions. Within the social learning tradition, John Dewey's scientific epistemology emphasizing "learning by doing" creates room for public engagement in problem framing. In the social mobilization tradition, the Marxian ideology of class struggle and the neo-Marxian endorsement of emancipatory social movements both emphasize the centrality of collective action at the grassroots. It is within these intellectual traditions that we must situate contemporary participatory planning initiatives.

Public participation in planning

Public participation (taking account of the views of the citizenry) in planning decisions was limited to the power elite during the first half of the twentieth century, although the generally reform-minded planners of this era believed that they were acting in the public's interest (Hall, 1998). Public participation is a slippery term, with no agreed upon definition. At the very minimum, public participation is understood to mean information dissemination and transparency about proposed plans for an area. In ideal circumstances, genuine public participation includes interactive strategies that allow officials and citizens to articulate a shared vision or plan and a process for monitoring plan implementation.

Despite these good intentions, the planning profession has had a long trajectory of developing and supporting large-scale, comprehensive planning initiatives that have gone terribly awry. The destruction of neighborhoods and communities unleashed by the highway building programs and the urban removal programs of the 1950s and 1960s created a justifiable mistrust about professional planning initiatives. The backlash against comprehensive top-down planning of the 1960s and 1970s helped spur the development and acceptance of the culture of citizen participation in planning (Davidoff, 1965).

The apparent arrogance of professional planners who sought to define vibrant neighborhoods and communities in bricks and mortar terms alone angered citizens already energized by the *zeitgeist* of the civil rights struggle (Arnstein, 1969; Gans, 1969). The 1960s were a period when ordinary citizens organized and mobilized to challenge the professional wisdom of significant planning decisions (King, 1981; Medoff and Sklar, 1994).

Since the 1960s, when the federal government included "citizen participation" as a requirement in antipoverty programs, citizen involvement in professional planning efforts has been *de rigueur* (Hoch et al., 2000). Furthermore, direct participation in governmental decision-making is viewed as the cornerstone of a vibrant democracy (e.g., Barber, 2004). Yet, it is a concept that seems to have been accepted more in theory than practice. Planning practice interweaves conceptual ideals of public participation within existing decision-making structures, thus resulting in some enduring dilemmas for practicing planners.

Dilemmas in implementing public participation in planning practice

As a practice-oriented discipline, planning is incredibly self-conscious and analytical about its role and purpose. A large body of theory, often called "theory in practice" has been assembled to discuss the core dilemmas that affect all planning endeavors (Schön, 1983). Each dilemma discussed below is linked to some aspect of public participation.

Framing planning problems
Framing a problem has a powerful impact on the solutions that are proposed. Schön and Rein propose that institutional action frames are "beliefs, values, and perspectives held by particular institutions and interest groups from which particular policy positions are derived" (1994: xii). While rational planning is successful, in part, because it helps

integrate data and analysis to establish causal chains, it also is spectacularly unsuccessful when it is required to integrate non-quantifiable, non-economic models of cause and effect, often hidden within institutional action frames.

Community activists, in particular, have long known that it is near impossible to shape outcomes of particular planning studies, because they are framed in ways that can only result in outcomes suitable to the framers. For example, in 1960s, when urban renewal was at its peak, the discussions about the need for urban renewal were cast (framed) as problems of poor housing and living conditions (sub-standard and dangerous structures, health and safety of residents was at risk because of living in over-crowded conditions), wherein the only plausible solution was to remove the decrepit housing stock and replace it with new, presumably, better quality housing. However, intangible qualities such as sense of community could not be factored into any analyses, given that the problem focused exclusively on the built environment.

Determining the locus of planning authority

It is often argued that the rational planning model survives because it "appears to provide a strong rationale for professional expertise" (Hoch, 2000: 23). In the USA, community activists and citizens have consistently challenged the authority of professional planners resisting the dictates of expert-driven, institutionally mandated planning. Advocacy planning, in particular recognized that professional expertise was often used to thwart the challenges posed by average citizens. As a response, advocacy planning as practiced in the 1960s championed a legalistic approach (akin to providing poor/indigent citizens with the services of a public defender). In this model, "progressive" expert-planners argued against other planners working for city government on behalf of beleaguered "naïve" members of the public (Davidoff, 1965). Advocacy planners used the

language of expertise to challenge unspoken assumptions, revealed inaccurate and sloppy analyses, and drew attention to the social issues that were being ignored because of the emphasis on physical planning. Planning theorists such as Forester (1989), Healy (1996), Hoch (1994), Innes (1996) have further articulated planning approaches such as collaborative planning and communicative planning to further articulate how planning practice actually occurs within the limits set up the rational planning ethos. Participatory planning, as it has evolved in the 1980s and 1990s validated the voices of experience, that is to say, the voices of those who were directly affected by particular planning decisions (Freire, 1970; Gaventa, 1993). Both participatory and advocacy planning have made some significant inroads in shaping conventional planning processes. Presently, even rational planning models such as the federal transportation planning process have specific opportunities for citizen input and citizen scrutiny. However, the essential dilemma remains – the legitimacy of professional planning continues to be contested terrain.

Defining the public interest

The USA, because of its unique history, and as a relatively young nation, has always been reluctant to subsume individual rights and primacy of private property ownership under law or legislation. Land use (a designation determining the type of use such as residential or commercial) and zoning (a designation determining the height and mass of a building) are often the legal instruments used to implement planning decisions. For the early social planners, zoning was an instrument necessary to protect the general public (ensuring light and air, safe working conditions, reduction of overcrowded housing conditions, and so on) against unscrupulous profiteers. The roots of zoning law, first established in New York[3] were designed to prevent one property developer from designing a building that would block access to natural light and air, thereby affecting the quality of life of residents in adjoining properties.

Later on, these laws were expanded when the Village of Euclid, Ohio, zoned land to preserve community character by imposing height and density restrictions. The ensuing 1926 Supreme Court Case (*Euclid* v. *Ambler*)[4] which upheld the rights of the Village of Euclid established the need to protect the public interest against individual owners or developers who, in their desire to maximize profits, were likely to ignore concerns about health, safety, and quality of life concerns. Eminent domain, the taking of private land for public purposes by government is highly controversial. It has often been used for the development of large-scale infrastructure or transportation projects which require large-scale assemblages of contiguous land. More recently, in the 2005 Kelo case (*Kelo* v. *City of New London*)[5], the US Supreme Court ruled that the community's desire to support economic development justified the taking of private land using the principle of eminent domain. As planners strive to represent the needs of the many, including those who are not present (under-represented populations and future generations), the concept of the "public interest" continues to be negotiated and re-defined to suit particular situations and contexts.

Management of participation within formal processes

While citizen activists and special interest groups vociferously clamor for increased opportunities for participation, there is a growing and uncomfortable realization that citizen participation has become a series of formalized bureaucratic rituals (e.g., designated periods for public comment) that are ineffective and sometimes counter-productive (Innes and Booher, 2004). Many professional planners are beginning to observe that public participation as currently managed undermines their professional expertise, reducing them to "glorified event planners".[6] Planners working in public agencies continue to be uneasy about opening up professional planning processes to the general public. Carp (2004: 242) explains these attitudes thus;

"public participation costs time and attention; and to the extent that it introduces political and interpersonal complexities into decisions, it compromises planners' autonomy and efficiency." In addition, planners are also concerned about raising expectations among citizenry by promising more control over a project that can realistically be delivered.[7] Finally, planners working for government agencies are also ambivalent about citizen participation because their counterparts in the community (advocacy planners working with/for communities) continue to maintain an adversarial relationship with them.[8]

USING GEOSPATIAL TECHNOLOGIES FOR PUBLIC PARTICIPATION

The adoption and use of geo-spatial technologies (ranging from early desktop GIS applications to contemporary sophisticated web services that define the contemporary trend) are best understood when they are embedded within the larger context of the digital revolution.

The digital revolution and the digital divide

While the emergence of the Internet and the World Wide Web is often credited with increasing public participation (Mitchell, 1995; Negroponte, 1995; Toffler and Toffler, 1995), many others have argued that the digital revolution has contributed to the isolation and marginalization of individuals and communities (Shenk, 1997). From the beginning these debates have been polarized because of competing ideologies. Unsurprisingly, the reality of technology adoption and its use has been far more complex. On the positive side, Rheingold (1993) argues that digital communities provide *social network capital* (the capacity to meet others with similar interests), *knowledge capital* (the capacity to get on the network and ask for help on a range of subjects from a gathered group with diverse experience and expertise), and a sense of *communion* (being supported emotionally by an invisible community). To some extent, the Internet also leveled the playing field between "information haves" and "have nots" by democratizing access to data and information.

Access to the Internet is not evenly distributed. The so-called "digital divide" has been identified in terms of a lack of access to technology (Norris, 2001) and the skills to use the technology (Mossberger et al., 2003). Based on data from the Pew Internet and American Life Project, Mossberger et al. (2008) report that "twenty-seven percent of Americans still do not go online at all and are therefore completely excluded from participation in society online." These revelations have broadened discussions about access to consider the social and institutional contexts that can either provide or impede access to information. Likewise, the ability of the individual or group to be able to interpret and thereby use the information they have managed to obtain (sometimes discussed under the rubrics of digital literacy or digital citizenship) are also topics that concern practitioners and policymakers who want to promote easy access to planning-related information. Presently, discussions about access includes topics such as freedom of information, individual privacy rights, the commodification of information, data quality, data sharing standards, spatial literacy, and the role of intermediaries (e.g., non-governmental organizations) in assisting the public to gain access to information (Craglia and Masser, 2003; Ramasubramanian, 2007).

The history and evolution PPGIS practice in the USA

Public participation GIS is an awkward phrase that came to encapsulate the intersection of community interests and the widespread adoption of GIS technology. As one reviews the social history of the field, it is interesting to note that the name choice PP+GIS emerged from the planning field[9] (Obermeyer, 1998). The early origins of PPGIS were focused on harnessing the capacities of GIS to serve community interests, while remaining cognizant of the potential limits of the technologies themselves. Even an exhaustive review of the field (Sieber, 2006) failed to provide a clear definition of PPGIS, opting instead to characterize PPGIS as a field or a broad umbrella of practice activities, emerging from various disciplines and driven by disparate agendas.

Despite ambiguity about its nomenclature (fortunately limited to the academic enterprise), PPGIS adoption, or in other words, community-focused GIS adoption grew rapidly in the early 1990s benefiting from the larger technology growth trends of the 1990s and was supported by the investments made by the federal government in the areas of education, health care, business, commerce, and environmental management, and in community development.[10] For example, between 1995 and 2000, US Department of Commerce[11] funded over a hundred projects including demonstration projects, community networking projects, and infrastructure development projects all designed to improve electronic telecommunications and showcase the advantages of connectivity.

One of the earliest descriptions of IT applications designed to serve "low income" communities came from Richard Krieg (1995). Although the "PPGIS" terminology was not used in his survey, many of the applications and functions listed are examples of community-oriented spatially referenced information systems. At the time of Krieg's survey, many providers and consumers of information strove to bridge the digital divide by providing free or low-cost access to e-mail and the Internet. Other applications required users to be at particular physical locations to access services (e.g., the offices of community agencies, public libraries, and other high-volume access points). While technology (the hardware) was seen as a primary barrier to bridging the digital divide, other barriers such as software, technical, and literacy skills, as well as access to data were beginning to be recognized. The federal government's investment in technology access projects during this period cannot be underestimated. At the same time, community-based organizations in the USA were being challenged to take on additional service provision and advocacy responsibilities with limited resources. Creative community-based organizations were quick to explore the potential of emerging technologies to help achieve organizational goals. In some instances the traditional funders of community-based organizing and development provided funding for technology-related projects while industry provided hardware and software donations.

By 1995, the US Department of Housing and Urban Development was requiring community-based organizations to develop applications to demonstrate community need in order to be eligible to receive block grant funding. Community organizers discovered that by mapping census data and integrating it with additional information gathered from other city and county sources, they could begin to create a narrative that better described neighborhoods in need. Thus, the mid-1990s efforts tended to map misery (e.g., crime, socioeconomic deprivation) quite effectively with the goal of drawing precise geographic boundaries to target areas of greatest need. However, they spurred a culture of data-driven analysis of social issues that facilitated data gathering and data integration. Many of the nation's smaller cities also received support for these efforts from philanthropic institutions. The planning literature cites a plethora of small community-focused GIS activities (e.g., Myers et al., 1995; Talen, 2000). Many of these case studies including PPGIS work with community-based organizations in several US cities are found in a compendium of community participation and GIS edited by Craig et al. (2002).

In the nation's larger cities, comprehensive community building initiatives also encouraged data collection, integration, and a managerial approach to social problem solving.

Community-based organizations began providing access to real property and infrastructure inventories on stand-alone computer to better understand the dynamics of neighborhood change. Using an indicators-based approach, community groups were able to target physical interventions that were intended to address social problems (e.g., removing abandoned/boarded up houses to reduce risk of arson or drug crime). These systems eventually evolved into Neighborhood Early Warning Systems which were adopted in many cities such as Minneapolis, Chicago, Philadelphia, and Los Angeles among others (Snow et al., 2004).

Sawicki and Peterman (2002) using data from a 1998 national survey designed to assess the extent of PPGIS practice report that a wide range of nonprofits, some affiliated with universities, as well as some government agencies were engaged in some kind of PPGIS activity. The 18 university-affiliated projects identified in the Sawicki/ Peterman study included centers that provided mapping and technical assistance services such as the East St. Louis Action Research Project[12] (ESLARP), and Neighborhood Knowledge Los Angeles[13] (NKLA). By this time, the web had matured to support Internet-based data delivery and city agencies were just beginning to get involved in data provision and dissemination via the web, with the lead being taken by federal departments and agencies such as the US Census Bureau, the US Department of Housing and Urban Development, and the Environmental Protection Agency.

Nonprofit organizations such as community-based service providers and advocacy groups now play an important role in facilitating PPGIS efforts. Local data providers often create customized data sets that organize information relevant to a particular population subgroup (e.g., caregivers of young children) or by geographic boundaries that are more easily understood by ordinary citizens (e.g., neighborhood areas rather than census tracts). Community data centers are also repositories of rich local and contextual knowledge.

Community archives often include geo-referenced information not available in official records through oral histories, drawings, sketches, photographs, as well as video and film clips.

In 2007, the trend documented by Sawicki and Peterman continues; PPGIS projects continue to be linked to academia; the London Air Quality Network[14] and Living Independently in Los Angeles[15] are but two examples of this trend. However, there are a whole range of PPGIS applications that are the result of innovative work by individuals who have integrated two or more disparate sources of data to create new web-based services. These applications, often called mashups[16] address specific community aspirations. Examples include Chicago Crime Map[17], Trailhead Finder[18], and HotSpotr[19], and their number continues to grow. In some of these instances, the data is provided from existing public sources. For example, the Chicago Crime Map data comes from the Chicago Police department, although the Chicago Crime Map is not an official source of crime information. In other instances, data is willingly provided by individuals who participate in the initiative by entering information into an online database (e.g., where users enter data about wifi hotspots). There is great interest in the use of such volunteered geographic information to energize and foster PPGIS activities.[20]

ESTABLISHING AN EVALUATION FRAMEWORK

Goals and purpose

In everyday terms, evaluation consists of systematic and careful assessments of individuals, projects, programs, and/or policies. Evaluation research emphasizes rigor, integrity, transparency, and systematic gathering of evidence to support conclusions. Evaluations are always purposeful; therefore evaluation methods must be appropriate to meeting stated goals. Evaluation research emphasizes respect for people and institutions participating in the evaluation process. Evaluation can be formative (with a goal of assisting participants refine and develop a better process) or summative (with a goal of assessing impacts and outcomes of a particular program or programs) (Werner, 2004).

During the 15-year time frame that participatory planning using digital technologies have been in vogue, the overt goal has always been individual and community empowerment. However, the empowering qualities of PPGIS work are difficult to evaluate, in large part, because PPGIS activities are often embedded within larger initiatives with broader organizational goals. In addition, it is difficult to document intangible benefits that accrue from a particular project and develop a causal linkage with a specific PPGIS activity. In addition, there appears to be resistance in subjecting PPGIS case studies to a uniform evaluation framework, because it is argued that the situational context and goals of each PPGIS project are unique enough to limit any generalizability. There is some truth to this position, for instance, it would be unproductive to compare PPGIS activities in small fishing villages in Indonesia with the work of community boards in New York City. Despite these limitations, I propose that it is reasonable to compare and evaluate PPGIS projects in the USA using a common framework because we share a common spatial data and technological infrastructure and are united under the planning paradigms discussed previously.

There are many activities that are labeled PPGIS and there is great confusion among practitioners about what constitutes a PPGIS activity. While there are many researchers developing tools and methods to support PPGIS work (e.g., Lowry et al., 2009) that may or may not involve active public participation, an ideal PPGIS project is a participatory planning project that is supported with digital technologies. At a minimum, it should include the following ingredients:

1   develop the capacity of the participants to organize, analyze, and discuss planning concepts to

the level required by the particular endeavor they are involved;

2   engage participants in every aspect of the planning process, that is, in framing the project goals and the methods that are selected to examine and investigate these goals, in project implementation, and assessment;

3   develop techniques to carefully incorporate participants' views and participant-generated data into formal planning processes, and;

4   provide clear and transparent strategies for data generated from the project to be available to the participants.

Akin to Arnstein's (1969) ladder of political participation, and Voogd and Woltjer's (1999) guidelines for ethical planning, the definition of the ideal PPGIS project stated above, are a set of goals that all projects/programs can aspire to meet. Using this definition, the purpose of the evaluation is to capture the unique as well as the ubiquitous ways in which PPGIS-based advocacy work has transformed the day-to-day planning practice in the USA. By examining if and how neighborhood and community institutions have altered or changed their established practices because of their exposure to, and use of geospatial technologies, I seek to highlight both positive and negative impacts of PPGIS adoption and use. Furthermore, by examining the extent to which PPGIS practices are successfully established within the day-to-day vernacular of institutionalized planning practice, I hope to stimulate a more robust debate about the best ways to better embed the use of participatory planning methods and geospatial technologies within planning and decision-making processes.

Framework

There are three main components that anchor the evaluation framework: first, I ask, what is the *process design* that was used to introduce geospatial technologies within a specific organizational or institutional context? In other words, how was the program planned and developed? Second, I ask, what is the

range of *short-term outcomes* that emerged immediately after the program or PPGIS implementation effort concluded? Were these gains and losses planned for/anticipated or were there unintended consequences? Finally, I ask, what are the *long-term impacts* of these efforts after some time has elapsed? Are there lasting, observable changes in planning practice that can be attributed to the adoption and use of a participatory process using geospatial technologies?

Process

Planning that precedes introduction of geo-spatial technologies to a community is critical to the success or failure of the implementation, an observation extensively supported by researchers (Rogers, 1983; Onsrud and Pinto, 1993; Obermeyer and Pinto, 1994; Campbell and Masser, 1995; Huxhold and Levinsohn, 1995; Harris and Weiner, 1998 among others). Non-technical factors including the presence of GIS champions, skills and motivation of users, technological congruence with organizational needs, leadership support for information-driven solutions, and political imperatives all affect implementation efforts. The challenges are far greater for PPGIS adoption and use, because PPGIS practice includes the additional obligation/burden to include credible participatory processes within the implementation effort. Thus a PPGIS implementation must be preceded by careful and conscious attention to process, in which the roles and mandates of participants are clearly defined. In the USA, good PPGIS practice is modeled after good community development practice, wherein PPGIS advocates can serve as community organizers (Rivera and Erlich, 1992). In addition, PPGIS advocates concerned about long-term sustainability will attempt to link and integrate their work to on-going planning initiatives that are underway.

Short-term outcomes

The introduction of new technologies and innovations often promises efficiencies – in terms of use of staff time and resources. More significantly, GIS has been most productive in routine task automation, a feature used effectively in the day-to-day business of planning (Huxhold, 1991; Ramasubramanian, 1999). Evidence of these efficiencies can be observed in customized map production using data that has been assembled and organized from data providers. These efficiencies are increased with the advent of the Internet, a transformation which has moved PPGIS away from individual desktops to the interactive public realm. Examples of such Internet-based data providers include the US Census American FactFinder (for socio-demographic information) and DataPlace™ (for housing and community development information). Localized community-based data providers abound, although data quality is variable. Even if one assumes that PPGIS advocates may be able to achieve efficiencies in some routine tasks, benefits are gained only if they redeploy time and resources to meet other needs (like reaching under-served populations or conducting more thorough analyses). Information dissemination is another short term goal that most PPGIS advocates should seek, specifically to get their issue heard by a wider audience; to engage multiple publics; to foster conversations and debates about the issues. A third short-term outcome would be an immediate successful resolution of a problem or controversy. In policy controversies such as the need to achieve social equity goals, data-driven analyses can result in "quick wins." In this context, the creative use of digital technologies to support multiple or alternative representations of the issues would be a short-term impact. Negative impacts too must be considered in analysing short-term outcomes. Project cost overruns, technical problems, staff burnout, exacerbation of existing tensions within communities are examples of likely short-term outcomes that PPGIS advocates must strive to avoid.

Long-term impacts

Essentially, long-term impacts can be grouped into two categories – impacts/changes to process (the ways in which planning takes place), and impacts/changes in policies and programs. These long-term impacts are those gains that inspired the initiative in the first place, but may not have been accomplished when the initiative was concluded. Thus, if the goal was to create a more transparent and inclusive planning process, then a long-term impact would be the creation of mechanisms and processes that support such inclusive planning. Examples of such impacts include the creation of community councils to monitor planning initiatives or the inclusion of a review/comment phase in a process that formerly did not include that component. Likewise, long-term impacts are the establishment of policies and programs that were deemed desirable goals when participatory initiatives were initiated. Examples can include changes in policy to achieve social equity/ social justice goals, or the creation and support of programs to monitor such goals. With this framework, a review and analysis of three case studies will provide the much needed context to anchor discussion and synthesis.

THE CASE STUDIES

Overview of cases

Three case studies are introduced and described briefly in this section. In each case study, geo-spatial technologies were adopted and used to achieve specific planning objectives. These cases were chosen strategically to illustrate and explicate the usefulness of the framework discussed earlier. Since the framework requires that attention be paid to process, short- and long-term impacts, I selected cases where I have extensive in-depth knowledge about the context of the case and personal familiarity with many of the activities undertaken to achieve project goals, as a participant-observer, or as an architect engaged in implementing the PPGIS initiative. I have elaborated on the

South End Community Organization case in Ramasubramanian (2004) and the Oak Park case is discussed in greater detail in a book chapter by Ramasubramanian and Quinn (2006). One of the shortcomings of using familiar cases is the possibility of bias, of reading into the situation, particular meanings and interpretations that confirm previously held opinions. To avoid bias, I have taken care to provide corroboration (through documentation or using direct quotes from interviews) to support my observations. The long-term impacts, in particular are based on conclusions drawn from archival material since many of the participants and initiators of the participatory activities are no longer involved with the projects and in one case, one of the key initiators of the participatory work is no longer alive.

South End Community Organization,[21] Boston

Boston's South End neighborhood was initially conceived as a high-income residential enclave, modeled after London, intended to counteract the exodus of wealthy Bostonians to the suburbs. However, as early as 1866, the South End had become a mixed-income neighborhood, accommodating an influx of poor residents, and subsequently became home to successive waves of immigrants.

In the 1950s and 1960s, the South End was beginning to be viewed as a neighborhood in decline and ready to be "renewed" by city planners, even though over 8000 South End residents (mostly Black, Hispanic, and immigrant) who considered it home would be unlikely to ever find suitable housing there again, given the prevailing social and economic conditions. The urban renewal projects proposed by city planners sought to remove "blighted areas" by targeting tenement houses and other housing options available to working-class people. This removed about one-fourth of the neighborhood's housing stock (in terms of dwelling units). Medoff and Sklar note, "Neighborhood tensions rose

as the Boston Redevelopment Authority's demolition work outstripped its promises of relocation and affordable housing. The tension wasn't over whether to renew the South End, but how and for whom?" (1994: 20).

At the time this research began in the early 1995, the South End Community Organization (SECO) operated as one of the service centers for Action for Boston Community Development (ABCD). SECO's Housing and Planning Coalition emerged almost as a direct response to the BRA's new planning strategies in the 1980s. The BRA created Planning and Zoning Advisory Committees to help formulate plans for individual districts (Kennedy, 1992: 225). The agency also established a community planning process in which city planners received the input from various neighborhood groups and then came up with a "rational" plan for the district. The BRA also instituted a public review process in which developers presented their design schemes and alternatives to meet public scrutiny and approval. SECO became active in monitoring community planning processes in the South End. Specifically, SECO monitored compliance of developers who had previously established commitments to create low and moderate income housing within their development projects.

In the late 1980s, the BRA and the Flynn[22] administration had began exploring additional opportunities to spur economic development in Boston. The administration argued that developments in the area of biotechnology/biomedical research would create jobs for Boston's unskilled and semi-skilled populations clustered in the neighborhoods of South End/Roxbury. Building on this concept of planned economic development in the area of biotech/biomedical research, the BRA approved the development of South End Technology Square (SETSA). This was a multi-year, multi-phase project initiated by a consortium of private developers, including Boston University.

When SECO became involved with the community planning process for SETSA, the agency found that they lacked information and an understanding of the effects of biotechnology/biomedical research, particularly its potential to generate jobs for South End residents. Subsequently they engaged the services of an independent consultant (a planner) to investigate the issue.

One of the consultant's key findings unequivocally stated,

> 'the expansion of the biomedical industry in Boston will improve the city's economy but its corresponding job growth will not benefit the majority of Boston residents who are in need of jobs because the educational level of [these] residents will not match the educational requirements of the biomedical industry'. (SECO, 1991: executive summary)

The report's thoroughly researched and well-articulated findings (based on comprehensive geo-spatial analyses) provided SECO with a negotiating chip which they used to garner additional community benefits to improve the quality of life of South End residents. At that time, SECO's executive director said:

> We did something, since we knew we would not get jobs, one of the things we asked for was that they use their influence to help locate and finance a new state-of-the-art community health center. The ground will be broken on that this year. (Interview, March 1996)

Maps and powerful graphics are sometimes used to inform, educate, and attract the attention of residents and outsiders towards the work of the organization.

A South End resident observed:

> [Maps] put into graphic form some of the stuff we know, or don't always know, about what's going on around us. The older maps are nice because sometimes they show the configuration of the housing before they took it all away. It's a kind of history ... Then there are those maps that go way back and show changes from various different times .... (Neighborhood resident's interview, 1996)

SECO's executive director and planning consultant were both ardent proponents of map use to communicate ideas and planning issues.

Most people in other neighborhoods and community organizations devalue, not that they devalue; they don't realize the value of graphics. [Our consultant] did a chart ... I remember, in the 1980s ... it showed an affordability gap in this neighborhood between income and cost of housing. And it showed it over several decades. Well, see; I retain [the map] in my mind's eye because of the graphics. I think graphics are undervalued. (Interview, 1996)

> Maps are representations of reality. I customize maps; I include [qualitative] information, pictures, and integrate data and statistics with issues ... like crime, like housing. (Planning consultant's interview, 1996)

SECO fell back on data and information to clarify perceptions, prove or disprove claims and allegations, and measure trends. These observations from one community organization are consistent with national trends from that mid-1990s time period; community-based organizations in several US cities were using data from various sources in order to challenge established planning orthodoxy.

Planning together, Oak Park Illinois

The Village of Oak Park is a small but vibrant community of about 50,000 people. The village, a municipality adjoining the City of Chicago is probably best known for having the largest assemblage of Frank Lloyd Wright homes and buildings including the Unity Temple and Wright's own residence and studio (Village of Oak Park, 2007). The village is known to be politically and socially progressive; for instance, Oak Park is one of the earliest communities in Illinois that passed a fair housing ordinance in 1968 and has worked carefully and proactively to sustain residential integration despite numerous difficulties (Squires et al., 1989; Williams, 2007). The Oak Park diversity statement, adopted by the village president and the board of trustees in May 2005 is a further affirmation of that original commitment to social integration and active citizen engagement in planning and decision-making.

.... Oak Park has committed itself to equality not only because it is legal, but because it is right; not only because equality is ethical, but because it is desirable for us and our children....

Oak Park's proud traditions of citizen involvement and accessible local government challenge us to show others how such a community can embrace change while still respecting and preserving the best of the past. Creating a mutually respectful, multicultural environment does not happen on its own; it must be intentional. Our goal is for people of widely differing backgrounds to do more than live next to one another. Through interaction, we believe we can reconcile the apparent paradox of appreciating and even celebrating our differences while at the same time developing consensus on a shared vision for the future. Oak Park recognizes that a free, open and inclusive community is achieved through full and broad participation of all its citizenry. We believe the best decisions are made when everyone is represented in decision-making and power is shared collectively ... (Excerpt from the Village of Oak Park Diversity Statement, 2005)

The goal of the Planning Together project (the subject of this case study) was to develop character plans for two business districts in two distinct neighborhoods within the village. While the process was initiated by a range of citizens who argued for the need for such proactive planning to spur economic development in these two neighborhoods, the village initiated the action by inviting the local university (University of Illinois–Chicago) to design and implement the planning process. While interest and commitment to integrating new technologies came from early adopters at both community and university, the technology agenda was not driven explicitly by the community or the village's planning staff. Rather, the integration of technology in the project evolved, waxed and waned organically over the lifecycle of the project. The complete project report is available online.[23]

In this brief summary, I describe and discuss aspects of the planning process as well as the interactive digital applications that were developed because they collectively have helped to transform how planning is done. The need for process within participatory planning projects cannot be overemphasized. In this case, the project planning team developed a set of guiding principles that shaped every aspect of the process. These guidelines were not abstract ideals but were adhered to by all members of the planning team. These were:

1 fairness (ensuring that all participants had equal opportunity to express opinions, ideas, and advice);
2 respect (acknowledging and recognizing participation of individuals and groups, regardless of their particular points of view they espoused);
3 inclusion (including the interests and voices of those directly affected by proposed plans, but also making the efforts to include interests and voices of those who did not participate, or whose participation did not receive meaningful attention);
4 relevance (focusing of citizens' testimony, advice, and deliberation on issues related to the purpose and context of the project); and,
5 competence (soliciting, supporting, and using the skills and knowledge of participants to improve the quality of the process and the creation of the plans).

The project planning team helped create and sustain two stakeholder groups, one of each targeted neighborhood development effort. The stakeholder groups were designed to include a broad swath of the community and were seeded with individuals who were part of the community but also had specialized expert knowledge that they could offer to the group. The project planning team developed a series of interactive digital applications. Examples of applications developed for this project include customized web-based visual preference surveys; online sketch planning tools; planning portals; and a project website. Many of these tools have been presented at the PPGIS conferences[24] in Portland (2003) and Madison (2004). Collectively the digital applications assisted in envisioning the immediate and long-term future for these two neighborhoods, discussing the advantages and disadvantages of particular planning changes. For example, a high-impact scenario visually and quantitatively showed how new development could be scaled up to generate new tax revenues that could benefit the village as a whole while highlighting the quality of life issues (traffic, displacement, and so on) that would be compromised in the immediate vicinity of the development in pursuit of these goals (Ramasubramanian and Quinn, 2006).

The project concluded in August 2003. The village board trustees voted to receive the character plans and directed the Plan Commission to review the plan's recommendations. At a hearing about the plans, the chair of the Plan Commission reported that, "among those who participated, there was 'absolute consensus' that it (the year-long effort) was a wonderful process and that it worked well. Many people came together to try to attain consensus about some difficult issues; it was a positive process" (Village of Oak Park, 2004).

Common ground: creating a regional plan for 2040, Chicago, Illinois

The Chicago Metropolitan Agency for Planning (CMAP) has a jurisdiction over seven counties, extending over 3750 square miles and serving a population of eight million people spread over 272 local governments. The agency was created in 2007 bringing together the Chicago Area Transportation Study (CATS) which previously served as the Metropolitan Planning Organization (MPO) for the Chicagoland region and the Northeastern Illinois Planning Commission (NIPC) which was the regional planning agency that focused on regional land-use planning in addition to providing the demographic and population forecasts necessary for the CATS transportation modeling process.

In 2002 NIPC embarked on a bold initiative called Common Ground, which was

essentially a large-scale public participation process designed to engage the citizenry of this disparate region in envisioning the future. The Common Ground process culminated in the development of a document called Realizing the Vision: 2040 Regional Framework Plan. The Common Ground process engaged over 4000 participants (residents, community leaders, elected officials) in a workshop process in order to establish a shared vision for the future and a process to achieve those goals. Citizens collaboratively generated 52 goal statements that were organized into five themes: livable communities, diversity of people, healthy natural environments, global competitiveness, and collaborative governance. The sheer scale of this participatory planning endeavor necessitated the extensive use of geo-spatial technologies and e-participation methods. The Common Ground process was designed and developed at NIPC and included innovative new ideas of process by (1) integrating local land-use planning and regional transportation planning; (2) creating many opportunities for small group meetings in many communities across the region, including targeted involvement of youth, minorities, non-English speakers; (3) and returning to the these groups to show them planning analyses at different stages, and conducting focus groups to solicit feedback.

Regional planning work of the sort undertaken through the Common Ground process is often highly technical and voluminous. The obligations of regional planning agencies to integrate land use and transportation planning with the goal of reducing congestion and providing increased mobility requires participants to become proficient in reading and interpreting the language of land use planners, civil engineers, traffic modelers, and economists. More importantly, participants must become comfortable with the idea of making complex decisions with imperfect information (Stephenson, 1998). Inevitably a credible process becomes an educational process in which experts are involved in providing testimony and advice to non-technical citizens in order that they may make reasonably informed decisions. As a result, the time commitment involved in participating in a regional planning process is far greater than a local project planning effort.

In the Common Ground process, initial work began with developing a shared vision for the future. These participatory visioning exercises consisted of a series of community meetings where groups of participants (ranging from 20 to 100 people) generated goal statements, determined priorities, and developed action steps, using electronic keypad polling. The Common Ground process used Paint the Region, a customized version of a commercially available tool called Index™. The tool was designed to allow individuals with little or no technical knowledge to "paint" land-use preferences and choices in designated areas. Given the technical difficulties (discussed previously), the process was managed by trained technical operators who manipulated the systems taking guidance from citizens. Citizens also generated maps of natural areas and landmarks that were 'sacred' in that they needed to be preserved – in the Chicagoland region, the lakefront, the existing natural preserves, the historical icons, and so on fell into this category. Electronic keypad polling allowed planners to understand tradeoffs that citizens were making to achieve a balance between different plan themes. The combined results were then used to determine population projections and land use changes for 2040.

The Realizing the Vision document is available on the web.[25] It received the American Planning Association's National Plan of the Year award for 2006. The Common Ground process including the innovative use of geo-spatial technologies embedded within it have previously been showcased at the 3rd Public Participation and GIS conference (Craig and Ramasubramanian, 2004) and in other conference venues.

These vignettes provide context to elucidate the evaluation framework which argued that PPGIS implementation can be analyzed in terms of process design, short- and long-term impacts.

PPGIS IMPLEMENTATION AND THE IMPACTS ON PLANNING PRACTICE

Summarizing from the three case studies discussed in the previous section, using the meta-evaluation framework that focuses on process design, short- and long-term outcomes, we can conclude that the introduction of participatory GIS activities gradually foster a more transparent and proactive planning process/practice, the closer they move towards the goals of an ideal participatory planning endeavor. In each of the cases, we can observe that the project leaders paid particular attention to the design of the participatory planning process. In addition, they attempted to build the capacity of the participants to organize, analyze, and discuss planning concepts to the level required by the particular endeavor they were involved; tried to engage participants in every aspect of the planning process, that is, in the framing the project goals, the methods that are selected to examine and investigate these goals, in project implementation, and assessment; and found ways to incorporate participants' views and participant-generated data into formal planning processes; and provided clear and transparent strategies for data generated from the project to be available to the participants.

The design of participatory planning processes is critical because a well-designed process engenders trust (Ramasubramanian, 1999; Witten et al., 2000). Many individuals who participate in community activities get involved because "non-participation" is no longer an option. Consequently, invitations to get involved in planning initiatives often attract well-established community stakeholders most likely to hold entrenched policy positions. The "vocal minority," as these stakeholders are sometimes derisively called, engage in community decision-making processes in order to further a specific policy agenda, thereby avoiding a consensual approach to plan-making at all costs (Innes and Booher, 2004). The literature on participation emphasizes that an inclusive style which gives the membership a vision of a transformed society, combined with a concrete set of proposals to achieve that vision, makes members more willing to risk alternative modes of behavior (Korten, 1986). In addition, institutional and community-based support systems (e.g., translations or interpretations available for non-native English speakers, provision of day care to facilitate participation of parents, permission to attend planning meetings as part of an individual's paid work time) may be essential to securing the participation of traditionally disenfranchised citizens. However, the timing and poor management of present-day *public comment* processes can sometimes cause even the most well-intentioned citizen to take on an adversarial position vis-à-vis the plan being proposed. The format of public meetings usually restricts citizen involvement to brief comments or prepared statements; inadvertently or deliberately curtailing detailed analyses and discussions. Meetings are held on evenings or weeknights, when the average citizen, particularly one juggling multiple family and work responsibilities is often unable to participate.

In the case of Boston's South End Community Association, many of the problems described above were overcome by establishing a neighborhood planning coalition that was staffed and supported by an individual (SECO's executive director). A core group of participants (staff of neighborhood planning agencies and elected officials) met regularly in the evenings and weekends. These participants viewed coalition meetings as part of their job description, even though meetings occurred during evenings and weekends. They set aside some of their work time to take on SECO coalition activities, because they trusted the credibility of the process, SECO provided the meeting space and staff time. SECO is a situation where professional planners (agency staff who also happened to be community residents) were active and successful on behalf of the more vulnerable residents of their neighborhood who could not have made the time to participate in community meetings. There were many short- and long-term benefits to working with a small coalition of 20–25 members over an extended period of time. The group was able to create a neighborhood "kitchen cabinet" that was able to proactively monitor the development and changes in the neighborhood, rather than reacting to events as and when they unfolded. Their continued presence engendered trust both among other neighborhood residents who did not regularly attend planning meetings and among official planners who were responsible for community outreach. If they lost in terms of broad public involvement (a virtue extolled by PPGIS researchers), they gained in establishing a positive and sustainable neighborhood planning group that remains in place, albeit in a different form even 10 years later.

In the Oak Park Planning Together project, the process was engineered to balance face-to-face meetings with opportunities for communication and feedback. In addition, different types of meeting opportunities were intentionally included to include citizens with different levels of interest and expertise (one-on-one conversations by telephone, email and face-to-face, small group meetings (for 6–10 people) on different evenings and weekends, large group (town hall) meetings (for 50–75 people) to showcase major project milestones, telecasts and web-casts of town-hall meetings for those individuals who did not have time to come to meetings, intensive working group meetings with stakeholders (stakeholder groups consisted of 30 appointed members who made a commitment to come to three intensive working meetings), and planning charettes (over 100 people) where design decisions could be finalized. Separate meetings were held with young people to ensure that youth voices were included in the planning process. In the end, over 600 people had participated in the process over the one-year time frame of the project.

So, what happened to the process when the cameras left, when the students and faculty moved on to other projects and lives returned to conventional routines? It is heartening to note that in February 2006, about two years after the Planning Together project concluded, the Village of Oak Park developed Guidelines and Procedures for Participatory Planning that govern the development or redevelopment of any Village-owned land (Village of Oak Park, Board of Trustees Policy, 2006). The guidelines state:

> the purpose of creating the public participatory planning guidelines is to ensure that each village-owned property being considered for development/ redevelopment is reviewed in a consistent and open manner....

The guidelines emphasize open communication and the need to raise awareness about planning issues in the Village across a wide swath of the public and the need to provide multiple opportunities for review and comment. The Planning Together process showed elected officials and planning staff that most citizens understood the need to make trade-offs and were able to balance their interests and commitments to maintaining community character with the needs of growth and economic development.

Even more rewarding is the realization that the Village's current plans for the redevelopment of one of the districts (the Harrison Street Arts District) in Oak Park developed the Lakota Group, a planning consulting firm which incorporates many of the key design and planning recommendations made by the UIC planners. That the UIC team was able to help visualize the design for the district that eventually incorporated into an implementation plan is additional confirmation that the Planning Together process was credible.

NIPC (the land planning agency) merged with CATS (the transportation planning group) soon after the Common Ground process concluded. The success of the Common Ground work is that the commitment to participatory planning survived the agency merger and resulting organizational and staffing changes. CMAP has published their 'Public Participation Plan' as required by federal regulations governing Metropolitan Planning Organizations. CMAP guidelines, developed for northeastern Illinois state:

- the public should have input in decisions about actions that affect their lives;
- public participation includes the promise that the public's contribution will be considered in the decision-making process;
- the public participation process communicates the interests and considers the needs of all participants;
- the public participation process seeks out and facilitates involvement of those potentially affected by local and regional plans;
- the public participation process provides participants with the information they need to participate in a meaningful way;
- the public participation process communicates to participants how their input influenced the decision. (CMAP, Public Participation Plan, 2007)

By emphasizing transparency, open communication, and accountability, these guidelines, as binding policy go a long way in establishing participation within regional planning processes. To a great extent, the success of the Common Ground process has allowed CMAP to be more innovative in preparing their participation plans for the upcoming forecasting challenges.

CONCLUSION

In this chapter I examined three US-based case studies of PPGIS implementation by using a meta-evaluation framework that emphasized (1) process design; (2) short-term outcomes, and (3) long-term impacts. Despite the paucity of comparative evaluations of PPGIS projects in the USA, I have demonstrated that it is feasible and indeed worthwhile to reflectively evaluate PPGIS implementation using a standardized set of criteria. This is a challenging task – PPGIS activities take time, and while we wait for the PPGIS efforts to yield results, people move, memories fade, local political agendas, organizational goals, and community aspirations are likely to shift and sometimes change beyond recognition. Despite these limitations, for the PPGIS field to remain relevant, researchers and practitioners must build in resources for systematic evaluation.

In each of the three case studies discussed, the GIS applications embedded within participatory planning processes allowed for individual and group capacity building (i.e., the tools made it possible for stakeholders to describe their problems and concerns effectively and to learn new ways of viewing their neighborhoods and communities). For instance, the South End community learned that because of the level of education and skills prevalent in their community, the promised hi-tech jobs would be "theoretically" accessible, but practically out of their reach. In Oak Park, stakeholders learned that it was possible to create economic development without destroying community character, and in the CMAP Chicago case, official planners were able to overlay perceptual maps of the region generated by different stakeholder groups to identify activity centers, development corridors, and areas that citizens wanted to protect against over development. Some of this learning was bottom-up (citizens educating official planners), while other aspects of this learning were peer–peer (citizens educating other citizens).

From the project planner's perspective, the impetus for using GIS was different in each of the three case studies – in the case of SECO (Boston), GIS analysis provided rigor and engendered trust to hold the coalition together, generating "what if?" analyses to allow members to create alternative scenarios in a timely manner. In the case of Oak Park, officials sought to energize their public consultation processes to create innovative opportunities for busy citizens to stay involved and engaged in planning without having to physically attend meetings at the Village Hall. In the case of CMAP in Chicago,

it was a realization that public consultations of the depth and intensity that were conducted would have been impossible without the use of digital tools such as Paint the Region, developed specifically for the Common Ground project. In each case, the adoption and use of GIS was seen as a way to create a collective community memory, a way to create spatial stories (Ramasubramanian, 2004). In other words, each project, explicitly or implicitly aspired to create a new community of identity (Israel et al., 2005) that would proactively solve problems.

What does this mean for planning practice? In general professional planners are leery of opening up their work to involve the public because they find it difficult to manage public involvement within the orchestrated timeline of complex planning processes. For example, citizens focus on projects, when plans are associated with formulating policies. One of the major contributions of PPGIS work has been to allow participants to shift away from reactive/oppositional approaches to planning to taking on a more proactive stance where different options, simulations, and alternatives can be considered. By doing so, both groups (citizens on the one hand, and official planners on the other) are beginning to appreciate the advantages of consultation. While we have a long way to go, these three case studies suggest that we are gradually moving away from the 1960s style of participation by protest to a more pragmatic style of participation and problem solving.

NOTES

1 For instance, the National Environmental Policy Act (NEPA) enacted in 1969 requires a thorough analysis of the impacts of any project or activity receiving federal funds. By specifically requiring consideration of social, economic, and environmental concerns, the NEPA process allows for external scrutiny. As the NEPA process has evolved, it includes environmental impact assessments, community impact assessments, health impact assessments, and environmental justice analyses. Collectively, these analyses are intended to prevent unwise and

uninformed agency actions. Many of these analyses make heavy use of GIS analysis to confirm or disconfirm equity claims and to highlight socioeconomic disparities.

2 FHWA, 2007.

3 Joseph P. Day (1930) 'New York City zoning law makes the skyscraper a thing of beauty', *National Civic Review*, 19(12): 812–14.

4 US Supreme Court (1926) Village of Euclid, *Ohio* v. *Ambler Realty Co.*, 272 U.S. 365 (1926). Online resource, available from http://caselaw.lp. findlaw.com/scripts/getcase.pl?court=US&vol= 272&invol=365 (last accessed 1 July 2008).

5 US Supreme Court 2005. *Kelo et al.* v *City of New London et al.*, No. 04–108. Online resource, available from http://caselaw.lp.findlaw.com/scripts/ getcase.pl?court=US&vol=000&invol=04–108 (last accessed 1 July 2008).

6 Interview with practicing planner by author, November 2007.

7 Civic Alliance (2002) *Listening to the City, Report of Proceedings*. New York: Regional Plan Association.

8 Angotti, A. (2007) Plan NYC 2030. *The Gotham Gazette*, February 2007.

9 Obermeyer credits Xavier Lopez, then a student in Orono, Maine with suggesting this term; a fact confirmed by Dr Lopez (2008, pers. comm. with Ramasubramanian).

10 Community development has been defined as a process "designed to create conditions of economic and social progress with the active participation of the whole community and with the fullest possible reliance on the community's initiative" (Rothman, 1974, cf. Levine and Perkins, 1997: 336).

11 The Telecommunications and Information Infrastructure Assistance Program (TIIAP), one of the programs of the National Telecommunications and Information Administration, is authorized by 47 USC.–390–393A (1991) to provide resources to be used for the planning and construction of telecommunications networks for the provision of educational, cultural, health care, public information, public safety, or other social services. It morphed into the Technology Opportunities Program (http://www.ntia.doc.gov/top/, accessed 1 July 2008).

12 East St. Louis Action Research Project (http://www.eslarp.uiuc.edu).

13 Neighborhood Knowledge Los Angeles (http://nkla.ucla.edu) was created in 1998 with a total project cost of over US$1 million with support from multiple sources with over half the support coming from the Technology Opportunities Program of the US Department of Commerce.

14 The London Air Quality Network (http://www.londonair.org.uk/london/asp/default.asp) site allows users to understand the complex phenomena of air pollution monitoring, analysis, and modeling over an extended time frame (1993 to 2007), with data now provided from 33 London boroughs. Users can display, graph, and download data about individual pollution parameters, for particular sites, and compare across sites. Additional information about London's Air Quality Strategy and target pollution reduction goals are also available for easy comparisons.

15 Living Independently in Los Angles (LILA) (http://lila.ucla.edu/) is a regional (county level) approach to addressing the needs of individuals living with disabilities in LA county. LILA includes a map room to assist local resources to create their own database based on their local 'expert' knowledge to identify and map resources that support independent living.

16 Mashups are web-based applications that use data from multiple sources to create a new application to serve a particular purpose (see examples that follow).

17 Chicago Crime Map is a free browsable database of crimes in Chicago, with data gathered from the Chicago Police department and mapped using Google Maps Application Programming Interface (http://www.chicagocrime.org/).

18 The Hiking Trail Database at http://www.trailheadfinder.com/.

HotSpotr, a community driven site that finds wifi hotspots at http://hotspotr.com/wifi.

19 Eg., 2007 Workshop on Volunteered Geographic Information (http://www.ncgia.ucsb.edu/projects/vgi/).

20 Organization and all participants in the SECO project, with the exception of public and elected officials are referred to by pseudonyms as per agreements established when the research was conducted.

21 Raymond Flynn, Mayor, City of Boston.

22 See http://www.oak-park.us/Community_Services/Planning.html for a listing of all plans and studies conducted in Oak Park including the final report of the UIC project "Planning Together: Character Plans for Oak Park Commercial Districts."

23 US PPGIS Conferences http://www.urisa.org/conferences/publicparticipation.

24 http://www.nipc.org/2040/ (accessed 1 July 2008).

REFERENCES

Alexander, E.R. (1992) *Approaches to Planning: Introducing Current Planning Theories, Concepts And Issues*. Philadelphia, PA: Gordon and Breach Science Publishers.

Arnstein, S. (1969) 'A ladder of citizen participation', *Journal of the American Institute of Planners*, 35(4): 216–24.

Barber, B. (2004) *Strong Democracy: Participatory Politics for a New Age*. Berkeley, CA: University of California Press.

Berke, P., Beatley, T. and Stitfel, B. (2000) 'Environmental policy', in C. Hoch, L. Dalton and F. So (eds), *The Practice of Local Government Planning*, 3rd edn. Washington D.C.: International City/County Management Association. pp. 171–200.

Campbell, H. and Masser, I. (1995) *Gis and Organizations: How Effective are Gis in Practice?.* London: Taylor & Francis.

Carp, J. (2004) 'Wit, style, and substance: how planners shape participation', *Journal of Planning Education and Research*, 23: 242–54.

Carver, S. (2003) 'The future of participatory approaches using geographic information: developing a research agenda for the 21st Century', *URISA Journal*, 15(APA I): 61–72.

Chicago Metropolitan Agency for Planning (CMAP) (2007) *Public Participation Plan, 2007*, Downloadable pdf document available at: http://www.cmap.illinois. gov/ (accessed 1 July 2008).

Craig, W. and Ramasubramanian, L. (2004) 'An Overview of the 3rd Public Participation GIS Conference', in *Proceedings of the 24th Urban Data Management Symposium*, Venice, 27–29 October, 2004.

Craig, W., Harris, T. and Weiner, D. (2002) *Community Participation and Geographic Information Systems*. London: Taylor & Francis.

Craglia, M. and Masser, I. (2003) 'Access to geographic information: a European perspective', *URISA Journal*, 15(1): 51–9.

Dalton, L., Hoch, C. and So, F. (2000) 'Introduction: planning for people and places', in C, Hoch, L. Dalton and F. So (eds), *The Practice of Local Government Planning*, 3rd edn. Washington, DC: International City/County Management Association. pp. 3–18.

Davidoff, P. (1965) 'Advocacy and pluralism in planning', *Journal of the American Institute of Planners*, 31 (4): 331–7.

Federal Highway Administration (FHWA) (2006) *Celebrating 50 Years: The Eisenhower Interstate System, 1956–2006*. Available at: http://www.fhwa. dot.gov/interstate/homepage.cfm (accessed 1 July 2008).

Federal Highway Administration (FHWA) (2007) 'The transportation planning process key issues: a briefing book for transportation decision-makers', *Officials, and Staff. Published by the Transportation Planning Capacity Building Program*, (FHWA-HEP-07–039), Available at: http://www.planning.dot.

gov/documents/BriefingBook/BBook.htm (accessed 1 July 2008).

Freire, P. (1970) *Pedagogy of the Oppressed*. New York: Continuum Press.

Friedmann, J. (1987) *Planning in the Public Domain: From Knowledge to Action*. Princeton, NJ: Princeton University Press.

Forester, J. (1989) *Planning in the Face of Power*. Berkeley, CA: University of California Press.

Gans, H. (1969) 'Planning for people, not buildings', *Environment and Planning*, 1(1): 33–46.

Gaventa, J. (1993) 'The powerful, the powerless, and the experts: knowledge struggles in an information age', in P. Park, M. Brydon-Miller, B. Hall and T. Jackson (eds), *Voices of Change: Participatory Research in the United States and Canada*. Westport, CT: Bergin & Garvey. pp. 21–40.

Graham, S. and Marvin, S. (1996) *Telecommunications and the City: Electronic Spaces, Urban Places*. London: Routledge.

Grosshardt, T., Bailey, K. and Brumm, J. (2003) 'Structured public involvement: problems and prospects for improvement', *Transportation Research Record*, 1858: 59–102.

Hall, P. (1996) 'Cities of tomorrow: an intellectual history of urban planning and design in the 20th century', Updated edn. London: Blackwell.

Harris, T. and Weiner, D. (1998) 'Empowerment, marginalization, and "community-integrated" GIS', *Cartography and Geographic Information Systems*, 25(2): 67–76.

Healy, P. (1996) 'The communicative turn in planning theory and its implications for spatial strategy formation', *Environment and Planning B: Planning and Design*, 23: 217–34.

Hoch, C. (1994) *What Planners Do?*. Chicago: APA Planners Press.

Hoch, C. (2000) 'Making Plans', in C. Hoch, L. Dalton and F. So (eds), *The Practice of Local Government Planning*, 3rd edn. Washington DC: International City/County Management Association. pp. 19–39.

Huxhold, W. (1991) *An Introduction to Urban Geographic Information Systems*. London: Oxford University Press.

Huxhold, W. and Levinsohn, A. (1995) M*anaging Geographic Information Systems Projects*. Oxford: Oxford University Press.

Innes, J. (1996) 'Planning through consensus building: a new view of the comprehensive ideal', *Journal of the American Planning Association*, 62(4): 460–72.

Innes, J. and Booher, D. (2004) 'Reframing public participation: strategies for the 21st century', *Planning Theory and Practice*, 5(4): 419–36.

Israel, B., Eng, E., Schultz, A.J. and Parker, E.A. (eds) (2005) *Methods in Community-Based Participatory Research for Health*. San Francisco, CA: Wiley.

Jackson, K. (1985) *The Crabgrass Frontier: The Suburbanization of the United States*. New York: Oxford University Press.

Kennedy, L.W. (1992) *Planning the City Upon a Hill: Boston Since 1630*. Amherst, MA: University of Massachusetts Press.

King, M.H. (1981) *Chain of Change: Struggles in Black Community Development*. Boston, MA: South End Press.

Korten, D. (ed.) (1986) *Community Management: Asian Experience and Perspectives*. West Hartford, Connecticut, MA: Kumarian Press.

Krieg, R. (1995) 'Information technology and low-income inner-city communities', *Journal of Urban Technology*, 3(1): 1–17.

Levine, M. and Perkins, D. (1997) *Principles of Community Psychology: Perspectives and Applications*, 2nd edn. New York: Oxford University Press.

Lowry, M., Nyerges, T. and Rutherford, G.S. (2009) 'Internet portal for participation of large groups in transportation programming decisions', *Transportation Research Record*, 2077: 156–65.

Medoff, P. and Sklar, H. (1994) *Streets of Hope: The Fall and Rise of an Urban Neighborhood*. Boston, MA: South End Press.

Mitchell, W. (1995) 'City of bits', *Space, Place, and the Infobahn*. Cambridge, MA: MIT Press.

Mossberger, K., Tolbert, C. and Stansbury, M. (2003) *Virtual Inequality: Beyond the Digital Divide*. Washington, DC: Georgetown University Press.

Mossberger, K., Tolbert, C. and McNeal, R. (2008) *Digital Citizenship: The Internet, Society and Participation*. Cambridge, MA: MIT Press.

Myers, J., Martin, M. and Ghose, R. (1995) 'GIS and neighborhood planning: a model for revitalizing communities', *URISA Journal*, 7(2): 63–7.

Negroponte, N. (1995) *Being Digital*. New York: Alfred A. Knopf.

Norris, P. (2001) *Digital Divide: Civic Engagement, Information Poverty, and the Internet Worldwide*. Cambridge: Cambridge University Press.

Neuse, S.M. (1983) 'TVA at age fifty: reflections and retrospect', *Public Administration Review*, 43: 491–9.

Obermeyer, N. (1998) 'The evolution of public participation GIS', *Cartography and GIS*, 25(2): 65–6.

Obermeyer, N. and Pinto, J. (1994) *Managing Geographic Information Systems*. London: Guilford Press.

Onsrud, H. and Pinto, J. (1993) 'Correlates of GIS adoption success and the decision process of GIS acquisition', *URISA Journal*, 5(1): 18–39.

Pickles, J. (ed.) (1995) *Ground Truth: The Social Implications of Geographic Information Systems*. New York: Guilford Press.

Ramasubramanian, L. (1995) 'Building communities: GIS and participatory decision-making', *Journal of Urban Technology*, 3(1): 67–79.

Ramasubramanian, L. (1999) 'Nurturing community empowerment: participatory decision-making and community-based problem solving using GIS', in H. Onsrud and M. Craglia (eds), *Geographic Information Research: Transatlantic Perspectives*. London, England: Taylor & Francis.

Ramasubramanian, L. (2001) 'Children's learning through Geo-Information technologies', in R. Gerber, and M. Robertson (eds), *Children's Ways of Knowing: Learning through Experience*. Canberra: Australian Council for Educational Research.

Ramasubramanian, L. (2004) 'Knowledge production and use in community-based organizations: the impacts and influence of information technologies', *CityScape*, 7(1): 165–91.

Ramasubramanian, L. and Quinn, A. (2006) 'Visualizing alternative urban futures using spatial multimedia to enhance community participation and policymaking', in M. Campagna (ed.), *GIS and Sustainable Development*. Florida, FL: CRC Press. pp. 467–86.

Ramasubramanian, L. (2007) 'Access to geographic information', in K. Kemp (ed.), *Encyclopedia of Geographic Information Science*. London: SAGE.

Rheingold, H. (1993) *The Virtual Community: Homesteading on the Electronic Frontier*. Cambridge, MA: MIT Press.

Rivera, F. and Erlich, J. (1992) *Community Organizing in a Diverse Society*. Boston, MA: Allyn and Bacon.

Rogers, E. (1983) *Diffusion of Innovations*. New York: The Free Press.

Sawicki, D. and Peterman, D. (2002) 'Surveying the extent of PPGIS practice in the United States', in W. Craig, T. Harris, and D. Weiner (eds), *Community Participation and Geographic Information Systems*. New York: Taylor & Francis. pp. 17–36.

Schön, D. (1983) *The Reflective Practitioner*. New York: Basic Books.

Schön, D. and Rein, M. (1994) *Frame Reflection: Toward the Resolution of Intractable Policy Controversies*. New York: Basic Books.

Sieber, R. (2006) 'Public participation GIS: a literature review and framework', *Annals of the Association of American Geographers*, 96(3): 491–507.

South End Community Organization (SECO) (1991) *Boston, A Biomedical Frontier: Hype or Hope*. Boston, MA: SECO. (Available from the author.)

Shenk, D. (1997) *Data Smog: Surviving the Information Glut*. New York: HarperCollins Publishers.

Snow, C., Pettit, K. and Turner, M. (2004) 'Neighborhood early warning systems: four Cities, Experience and Implications for the District of Columbia', *Final Report prepared by the Urban Institute's Metropolitan Housing and Communities Policy Center for the Fannie Mae Foundation, March 2004*. Available from the Fannie Mae Foundation.

Squires, G., Bennett, L., McCourt, K. and Nyden, P. (1989) *Chicago: Race, Class, and the Response to Urban Decline*. Philadelphia, PA: Temple University Press.

Stephenson, R. (1998) 'In What Way, and to What Effect is Technical Information Used in Policy Making?', *Findings from a Study of Two Development Plans, Planning, Practice & Research*, 13(3): 237–245.

Talen, E. (2000) 'Bottom-up GIS: a new tool for individual and group expression in participatory planning', *Journal of the American Planning Association*, 66(3): 279–94.

Toffler, A. and Toffler, H. (1995) *Creating a New Civilization: The Politics of the Third Wave*. Atlanta, GA: Turner Publishing, Inc.

Voogd, H. and Woltjer, J. (1999) 'The communicative ideology in spatial planning: some critical reflections based on the Dutch experience', *Environment and Planning B: Planning and Design*, 26(6): 835–54.

Village of Oak Park (2004) *Minutes of the Regular Meeting of the President and Board of Trustees of the Village of Oak Park, Held on Monday, March 15, 2004 at 7:30 P.M. in the Council Chambers of the Village Hall*. http://www.oak. park.us/About_Our_ Village/board_minutes_2004.htm (accessed 1 July 2008).

Village of Oak Park (2005) *Diversity Statement adopted by the Village President and Board of Trustees on 2 May 2005*. http://www.oak-park.us/Living_In_ Oak_Park/Living_In_Oak_Park.html (accessed 1 July 2008).

Village of Oak Park (2006) *Village Board of Trustees Policy, February 2006: Public Participatory Planning Guidelines for Village Owned Properties*. http:// www.oak-park.us/Community_Services/Planning. html (accessed 1 July 2008).

Village of Oak Park (2007) *Village Background*. http:// www.oak-park.us/Village_Background/Village_ Background.html (accessed 1 July 2008).

Werner, A. (2004) *A Guide to Implementation Research*. Washington, DC: The Urban Institute Press.

Williams, S. (2007) 'Evanston and Oak Park: communities still wrestle with integration', *The Chicago Reporter*, 12 September 2007.

Witten, K., Parkes, M. and Ramasubramanian, L. (2000) 'Participatory environmental health research in Aotearoa/New Zealand: constraints and opportunities', *Health Education and Behavior*, 27(3): 371–84.

22

Politics and Power in Participation and GIS Use for Community Decision Making

Rina Ghose

INTRODUCTION

The use of spatial data and GIS is essential to urban planning and policy formation activities, as spatial knowledge production is effective in facilitating the administration of urban government. Today GIS is commonly used in a wide range of planning tasks in federal, state, and local planning agencies. Such use of spatial data and GIS has been difficult for inner-city neighborhood-based community organizations, who are important participants in urban governance. These community organizations tend to be more decentralized and more fragile in financial and staffing support when compared to larger non-profit organizations and public/private sector agencies (Sieber, 2000). Their resource-poor conditions make it difficult for them to afford the cost of implementing GIS in their organizations. Purchase of data, software, and hardware or provision of ongoing GIS training to their staff members continue to be a challenge for these organizations. Moreover, these organizations are also hampered by frequent staff turnovers that result in higher staff training costs (Barndt and Craig, 1994; Barndt, 1998, 2002). Finally, grassroots organizations have faced the additional challenge of not gaining easy access to public database that are often the repository of valuable community-based spatial data at multiple scales. These difficulties have created a technological divide between the planning agencies that are frequent users of GIS and grassroots community organizations that face challenges in using GIS. Class inequalities are then further heightened by inequalities concerning the knowledge of and access to such information technologies, for it is clear that such access and understanding create greater opportunities for conferring political, economic, and social power upon the citizens of distressed neighborhoods (Castells, 1996). Such a digital divide has raised concerns among practitioners, scholars, public policy makers, and formal planning agencies (Hutchinson and Toledano, 1993;

Obermeyer, 1995; Barndt, 1998; Harris and Weiner, 1998; Obermeyer, 1998; Leitner et al., 2002). In response, a range of public participation GIS (PPGIS) implementations have been undertaken in the last decade by governmental and non-governmental organizations and universities, to provide more equitable access to GIS and spatial data for marginalized groups, leading to unprecedented numbers of community organizations adopting and using this technology for planning, problem solving, and service delivery tasks (Craig and Elwood, 1998; Kellogg, 1999; Ghose, 2001; Ghose and Huxhold, 2001, 2002; Sawicki and Peterman, 2002; Ghose, 2003).

PPGIS process in the urban American landscape has emerged primarily to assist citizen groups and planners in their efforts to revitalize inner-city neighborhoods that have undergone heavy deindustrialization and disinvestment, creating problems of deep poverty, unemployment, crime, blighted housing conditions, and a generally degraded quality of life. Because the process of spatial knowledge production helps community organizations to systematically analyze neighborhood conditions and plan for revitalization, PPGIS activities can lead to more effective participation for community organizations in inner-city planning. The shift to undertaking inner-city revitalization through collaborative governance also provides inner-city community organizations with new opportunities of participation as it formalizes participation of community organizations and provides some material resources to assist with participation. Using a model of public–private partnership, collaborative governance emphasizes the involvement of powerful actors such as private sector business community, educational institutes, philanthropic foundations, and intermediary actors that are considered to be stakeholders in the planning process. Through collaborative governance, community organizations thus have an opportunity to form networks of relationship with critical actors.

However, the participation and spatial knowledge production process of marginalized citizens is complex, deeply influenced by local political cultures and agendas as well as the entrenched power relations, particularly because such citizens and their representative grassroots community organizations occupy a subordinate position in the local political hierarchy and power structure. The extent of their participation is deeply dependent on the willingness of local government agencies and other actors to include community organizations as egalitarian actors. Collaborative governance is also strongly influenced by the process of neoliberalization, endure its negative characteristics such as greatly reduced public funding, the devolution of state's responsibilities, and the foisting of state-led priorities upon citizen groups (Brenner, 1998; Brenner and Theodore, 2002; Newman and Lake, 2006; Leitner et al., 2007). While community organizations are given some funding to undertake collaborative planning, they are also expected to be entrepreneurial and actively seek funding from the private sector. In such a political climate, community organizations are required to skillfully navigate the agendas of various actors and emerge as a powerful voice. Contesting neoliberalization is difficult for citizen groups, due to the power and resource imbalance, but research shows that citizen groups can adopt creative methods to do so (Leitner et al., 2007; Mayer, 2007). For community organizations, PPGIS can be a 'best practice' to navigate and challenge neoliberalization. Prior research shows that spatial knowledge is used by community organizations for attaining four functional categories: administrative, organization, tactical, and strategic (Craig and Elwood, 1998). Community organizations can use GIS and spatial data to demonstrate both neighborhood needs and assets to planners and investors. Community organizations can also use GIS analysis through multiple indicators over time to examine the neighborhood's conditions and assess its potentials for its planning and organizing tasks as well as to communicate the information to powerful actors. Philanthropic foundations such as Annie E. Casey foundation or intermediary actors such as Local Initiative Support Corporation (LISC) bringing funds and for profit investment into inner-city are strongly interested in GIS indicator based studies over time which can demonstrate benchmarks of success or failure of a neighborhood to revitalization projects (LISC, 2007). Project accountability is increasingly expected from community organizations and other actors involved in neighborhood revitalization, and regular evaluations using benchmark data on a neighborhood's well-being is expected by private investors. A customized GIS-based community information system (Ghose, 2001) containing rich data gathered both experientially and from public datasets, and provided at multiple scales, can empower a community organization and enable it to insert its voice in inner-city revitalization. However, local political context shapes the issues of data/GIS access, and the presence of a rich network of GIS providers enables community organizations to undertake spatial knowledge production. Even within a political context of GIS support and participation opportunities, community organizations show variable abilities to succeed. This is due to internal organizational characteristics, which affect the ability of community organizations to utilize PPGIS opportunities (Elwood and Ghose, 2004). Consequently, urban PPGIS outcomes are complex, context dependent, and uneven in nature.

In this chapter, I explore the complex process of urban PPGIS practice by discussing the nature of participation and spatial knowledge production among community organizations within the context of neoliberalization. I then explore the internal characteristics of community organizations that significantly affect their abilities to undertake PPGIS activities. Finally, I discuss how spatial knowledge produced through GIS enables community organizations to negotiate and contest neoliberalization. I draw upon the literature on urban geography, planning, and PPGIS and my decade-long investigation of PPGIS activities in inner-city Milwaukee to frame my arguments.

POLITICS OF CITIZEN PARTICIPATION

Urban planning in USA is increasingly undertaken through the collaborative governance model, which is based on the notions of public–private partnership, involving a range of local and national scale actors and stakeholders. A key component of collaborative governance is citizen participation. Within the context of inner-city revitalization, civic engagement and community building are critical components, and inner-city grassroots community organizations are increasingly being included by the government through formalized participation mechanisms. Input from neighborhood residents are also an important aspect of these planning efforts. The participation component of PPGIS thus depends greatly upon the openness of local government to including community organizations as authoritative participants in formal urban planning practices.

While the collaborative governance model has aided the inclusion of traditionally marginalized citizen groups, the process of participation for neighborhood-based community organizations has also been assisted by a scalar shift in urban planning activities, which has shifted in scale from urban level comprehensive planning to neighborhood level planning (McCann, 2001, 2003). Because of such a scalar shift, neighborhood-level planning has received greater attention, in which neighborhood-based citizen groups (block clubs, neighborhood associations, community organizations) have attained greater legitimacy and importance in the eyes of various actors. Such a scalar shift therefore has opened the door to traditionally marginalized citizens and their neighborhood groups to connect with various actors (Kearns, 1995; Kofman, 1995; Painter and Philo, 1995; Pile, 1995; Atkinson, 1999; Isin and Wood, 1999). However, this process also fosters a politics of locality – such as power relations, interest groups, and concerns (Kearns, 1995).

Cities have emerged as critical "spaces of neoliberalization" (Brenner and Theodore, 2002: 20), experiencing uneven economic growth, heightened social polarization, and escalating tensions in an environment of sharply reduced federal government support for municipal and welfare activities and restructured local government agencies with major budgetary cutbacks affecting their service provision. Today, cities are sites of market-led economic growth and of social control of the underclass in which a range of neoliberalized policies and experiments have been implemented to further advance the process of neoliberalization (Harvey, 1989; Healy, 1997; Kearns and Paddison, 2000; Brenner and Theodore, 2002; Gough, 2002; Jessop, 2002). Inter-urban competitions have emerged, creating an emphasis upon urban entrepreneurship. Consequently, urban governmental agencies are encouraged to create strategic partnerships with business actors. In terms of governance, local governments emphasize collaborative governance with shared responsibilities for economic development and social issues (Stoker, 1995; Swyngedouw, 1997; Brenner and Theodore, 2002; Newman and Lake, 2006). The concept of citizenship has changed in this political context, where citizens or citizen groups are expected to gain rights through performative acts and be flexible citizens (Ong, 1999; Staeheli, 1999; Yuval-Davis, 1999; Lepofsky and Fraser, 2003; Purcell, 2003). Non-governmental organizations are vehicles of such citizen participation (Desforges, 2004).

Inner-city neighborhood-based community organizations have largely been the citizen groups that have been involved in these collaborative urban governance efforts, and their participation process has been complex and political. Participation in collaborative governance model emphasizes community organizations to be cooperative with the government agencies, and as such, discourages opposition such as protests, marches, and so on. Participation into formal collaborative planning programs is not automatic for all community organizations. Rather, community organizations are selected by planning agencies and powerful actors, based on a range of tangible and intangible factors such as their mission goals, size, capacity, and leadership.

The effectiveness of their participation in urban governance is dependent upon their ability to be entrepreneurial, to take advantage of new neighborhood planning programs such as the Neighborhood Revitalization Program in Minneapolis or Neighborhood Strategic Planning program and Area Plan program in Milwaukee (which are accompanied by some material resources) and engage with private sector 'stakeholder' actors, while flexibly negotiating the challenges of governmental funding cutbacks (Elwood, 2002; Ghose, 2005, 2007). However, as seen in the case of Milwaukee, community organizations are also competing with each other to seek limited government funding, as well as seeking funding from private sector entities (Ghose, 2005). They operate within a climate of constant fiscal insecurity, budget cutbacks, staff reductions, and overall state of insufficient resources and are unable to act as egalitarian partners. Simultaneously, budget cuts and restructuring of state and local government agencies have led to a reduction of state-supported services to the inner-city community, causing inner-city residents to appeal to community organizations for critical social services. Thus, community organizations are expected to undertake neighborhood service provision tasks while lacking the resources or experience to do so (Hasson and Ley, 1994; Peck and Tickell, 1994, 2002; Taylor, 1998, 1999; Newman and Lake, 2006).

The role of stakeholders is quite important in collaborative planning, and in PPGIS. Schlossberg and Shuford (2005) define PPGIS participants as "stakeholders who are affected by, bring knowledge or information to, and possess the power to influence a decision or program." Networking with critical stakeholders is crucial both in collaborative planning and PPGIS. Community organizations are not only expected to form relations with actors embedded in territorial networks, but also with the actors in thematic networks (Ghose, 2007). Such relationships provide community organizations with opportunities for obtaining resources from actors located at multiple scales, or those who are not in the immediate geography. But it also provides powerful stakeholders opportunities to influence community organizations into following pre-set agendas.

As such, the planning priorities set out in collaborative governance ultimately reflect the agendas of the powerful stakeholders and the state, thus channeling the energy of citizens and their representative groups into pre-ordained paths. Housing and economic development, for instance, are two major goals, and special funds are allocated to community organizations in order to pursue those goals. Improvement of housing conditions is a major goal due to the involvement of the federal agency Housing and Urban Development (HUD), as well as various state and local actors who prioritize housing development in inner-city revitalization. Blighted housing conditions are a serious problem and are connected to issues of low owner occupancy, resulting in most houses being rental units which are owned and operated by absentee landlords. Targeting such problems is a worthy endeavor, but housing improvement goals have tended to get far more attention than goals of social service provision, at a time of high poverty and unemployment within inner-city areas. This is primarily because built landscape is a site of capital accumulation, and thus is a good strategy for bringing capital into these neighborhoods. Similarly, economic development is a major goal, highlighted by both public and private sector actors. Many community organizations are urged to not only entice private sector investment into inner-city areas, they are also asked to undertake income-generating activities, such as owning business incubators, rehabilitating old houses, and selling or renting them and so on. Yet goals such as after-school programs, youth development, job training are equally important given the high unemployment and crime rates in inner-city areas, which remain under-funded and under pursued.

Participation in collaborative planning is also shaped by the nature of the community organization. While a range of grassroots groups are engaged in community revitalization, they can be classified into two major types: community development corporations (CDCs) or community-based organizations (CBOs). CBOs tend to have a stronger orientation toward community-organizing activities, greater reliance on public funding, and lesser focus on large capital investment projects. CDCs tend to have a strong economic and housing development focus, stronger links to the private philanthropic sector and the corporate community for funding and technical support, and more involvement as direct sponsors of large capital investment projects (Stoecker, 1997; Gitell and Wilder, 1999; Stoecker and Vakil, 2000). But within a neoliberal framework, community organizations that follow the CDC model have an advantage over the CBO model, and also possess the experience to undertake certain economic development projects (Elwood and Ghose, 2004). Consequently, many CBOs are trying to undertake economic activities typically pursued by CDCs, while maintaining their social service component. Due to the immense demand for social support from inner-city residents, many CDCs are also involved in social service provision.

Collaborative planning can also create a fragmented system of governance, which creates difficulties in the state's administration of programs and coordination of services. Within USA, inner-city revitalization is undertaken by two separate planning agencies: the City Hall, and the Community Block Grant Administration (the local arm of the HUD), whose planning activities remain separate. Community organizations have to participate in separate planning processes for inner-city revitalization, leading to duplication of their efforts and duplication in citizen input (Ghose, 2005). A politics of turf thereby emerges, dividing citizen groups in their allegiance to different political entities. Such a situation compromises citizen participation and affects the morale of both inner-city residents and community organizations, leading to a feeling of powerlessness within the process of collaborative planning.

Finally, the ability to navigate neoliberalization and find opportunities of participation, spatial knowledge production, is deeply shaped by organizational factors. Community organizations have differing abilities to utilize opportunities, or navigate the complexities of collaborative governance. Elwood and Ghose (2004) have examined the variable outcomes of PPGIS initiatives among community organizations in Milwaukee, undertaken within the same political context of participation and GIS access. They have identified four major internal organizational factors: organizational knowledge and experience of political strategies and resource acquisition, organizational ability to form networks of collaborative relationship with powerful actors, organizational stability, and organizational priorities, strategies, and status. Table 22.1, taken from Elwood and Ghose (2004) provides a summary of internal organizational characteristics that affect the success or failure of a community organization to participate in PPGIS.

Within the current climate of financial crisis, community organizations that are stable, form networks of relationship with

critical actors, have the knowledge and experience to pursue politically successful strategies, and have organizational missions that fit with those of powerful actors, are likely to survive.

POLITICS OF GIS ACCESS AND SPATIAL KNOWLEDGE PRODUCTION

Use of spatial data and GIS are integral to urban planning activities as urban governance is inherently spatial in nature. With the shift to collaborative governance, inner-city community organizations are now participating formally in planning activities, for which they require access to a range of spatial data at multiple scales. This access has been historically difficult for marginalized citizen groups in inner-city areas, owing to the digital divide that exists along class and race lines. Because of their 'resource poor' nature, community organizations have strong financial constraints that affect their abilities to purchase expensive spatial data, GIS software, and hardware (Sawicki and Craig, 1996; Barndt, 1998). However, greater inclusion of citizens through collaborative governance has provided the political context that

Table 22.1   Internal organizational characteristics for participating in PPGIS

Organizational Knowledge and Experience
- Staff and resident knowledge of local support resources for PPGIS (funds, data, hardware, software)
- Knowledge/experience of locally successful resource acquisition strategies
- Knowledge/experience of locally successful political strategies

Network of Collaborative Relationships
- Relationships with public and private support institutions for community organizations and PPGIS
- Formal collaboration with resource institutions
- Informal personal relationships with local political actors, public agency staff, community organizers

Organizational Stability
- Duration of leadership/low rates of staff turnover
- Consistency of organizational mission and goals
- Consistency of funding support

Organizational Priorities, Strategies, Status
- "Fit" between organizational priorities/strategies and those of local government priorities
- "Fit" between GIS/data needs for these strategies and publicly available GIS resources

Source: Elwood, S. and R. Ghose, 2004, Cartographica, vol. 38, 3&4, Fall/Winter. Reprinted by permission of University of Toronto Press Incorporated. www.utpjournals.com.

encourages urban PPGIS initiatives to take place, with federal agencies (such as HUD), local planning agencies, and universities providing access to GIS and spatial data created by government agencies to citizen groups.

For inner-city community organizations, PPGIS is most strongly affected by the local political conditions (Sieber, 1997; Elwood, 2000; Ghose and Elwood, 2003). Easy and inexpensive access to spatial data produced by government agencies is dependent upon its willingness to consider community organizations as important actors in inner-city revitalization. As well, a cordial relationship must exist for community organizations to gain such access, for confrontational attitudes or past activities can alienate data providers and hinder access (Sieber, 2000). Facing fiscal crisis, many local government agencies are increasingly charging fees for providing spatial data, as a cost recovery measure, which may be unaffordable for community organizations.

The attitude of local government agencies in providing access to spatial data among grassroots citizen groups appears to be quite variable and inconsistent. Collaborative planning programs in Milwaukee, for instance, have greatly facilitated access to GIS and spatial data for inner-city community organizations (Ghose, 2005, 2007). Local planning agencies in Milwaukee advocate participation of community organizations in inner-city planning activities, and have emphasized to community organizations the benefits of GIS use to identify issues, recognize patterns, and create planning strategies. Consequently, the planning agencies have facilitated data access to inner-city community organizations. Milwaukee also enjoys a robust network of GIS actors who champion PPGIS, and work with inner-city community organizations to facilitate it (Ghose and Huxhold, 2001). However, both the city and the GIS providers control the data/GIS provision process, deciding on what type of data to share and at what resolution. Thus, the subordinate position of community organizations is still evident in Milwaukee. Nonetheless, access to

GIS and spatial data for inner-city community organizations has become relatively easier in Milwaukee. In contrast, Elwood (2008) has noted that in Chicago, local government agencies have an informal manner of data sharing with the city's community organizations. In part, this is due to the attitude of the City of Chicago, which does not perceive the neighborhood-based community organizations as stakeholders in planning, data development, and data sharing activities. The subordinate position that community organizations occupy in the local political structure makes them vulnerable both in their access to data and access to participation opportunities. As Elwood (2008) notes, even requests for public data by community organizations have been denied regularly by data stewards in Chicago. When data stewards in Chicago agree to share data, they require community organizations to negotiate with each new request, thereby taking up valuable time and staff resource among community organizations that are seriously understaffed due to funding cutbacks.

Appropriateness of spatial data is another issue concerning data access in urban PPGIS. There are many examples where a range of spatial data may be accessible to community organizations, but the format or resolution are inappropriate. Barndt (2002) presents a model for assessing the value of primary and secondary data used in a PPGIS project. The model asks the following questions: Are the data and material produced appropriate to the organization issues? Can the organization use the information in action-oriented way to support decisions, enhance communication, and inform actions? Is information available to the organization in a timely manner? Is the information pertinent to organization issues? Do the results have temporal and cross-comparison component – that is, a time perspective? Owing to their subordinate power position, community organizations have little control over these issues. Yet, these are vital for the effectiveness of their spatial knowledge production process.

Another pertinent factor concerning access to spatial data is the issue of data accuracy.

Barndt (2002) emphasizes the need for assessing the available data to test its accuracy, as community organizations are expected to demonstrate the accuracy of their data when they interact with powerful actors to obtain grants or to reshape policy. There are inevitable data quality problems in highly detailed local government data, such as property data. A parcel of land often contains a number of data inaccuracies involving parcel boundaries, land use, land ownership, structural conditions, tax status, and so on. In such cases, local knowledge by community organizations is often found to be superior to the data collected by the local government agency. Data updating by the local government agencies is often an issue as well, since updating of public records is time consuming in a major metropolitan area, where built environment goes through rapid changes. Moreover, budget cutbacks in planning agencies have reduced the staff responsible for updating records, thus further slowing down the process. Community organizations thus frequently find data updating of public records to be too slow, hampering their efforts to recruit investment in their neighborhoods.

Inner-city community organizations also face difficulty in buying appropriate hardware, software, and providing GIS training to its staff members, owing to the funding cutbacks promoted by neoliberal policies. Consequently, community organizers rely on a network of GIS actors, who not only provide access to data and technology, but also assist in using GIS. Through multiple GIS provider actors, GIS use among community organizations in inner-city neighborhoods across the USA has become more common (Sawicki and Peterman, 2002).

Leitner et al. (2002) are among the few scholars who have explicitly discussed the various models of GIS provision found among urban grassroots organizations. These include: community-based (in-house) GIS, university–community partnerships, publicly accessible GIS facilities at universities and public libraries, Map room, Internet map servers, and neighborhood GIS center (Leitner et al., 2002).

Lin and Ghose (2008) have followed up their study with an exploration of the effectiveness of these models, particularly in terms of their costs of maintaining GIS (hardware, software, and GIS training), their ease of provision of data and responsiveness to community organizations' needs, their stability and longevity, and their ability to support collaborations among stakeholders as well as among community organizations.

Community-based in-house GIS is the most ideal type of GIS provision to community organizations. Both the technology and the data can be customized to the specific needs of the community organizations, which can create and manipulate the database and maps, and can integrate public data with their local experiential knowledge. Here, GIS resides within the office of a community organization, and is readily accessible to both community organizers and neighborhood residents for their planning and organizing tasks. Neighborhood changes can be immediately noted and incorporated into the database. It is thus highly responsive to the needs of community organization and residents. This model thus provides the opportunity to community organizers and residents to be "proactive" users of GIS, in which users have control over the technology as well as the data. However, this model contains some challenges as well. Owing to their resource-poor nature, community organizations can find it difficult to maintain an in-house GIS, due to the cost of hardware and software, as well as the cost of staff training. Retention of technologically skilled staff is also difficult for community organizations, and staff turnovers can challenge the maintenance and use of the in-house GIS. Finally, access to public datasets can be difficult for community organizations if they are required to purchase it at a high price from the local government agencies. Even if they are able to buy the datasets, community organizations can have difficulties dealing with issues of copyrights and licensing. Also, due to issues of confidentiality, certain government agencies are unwilling to share their data with the community organizations. As a result of these difficulties, community in-house GIS model has been relatively sparse. Rather, other models of GIS provision have been more successful in PPGIS initiatives.

GIS provision through university–community partnership is a particularly effective model, as many universities with GIS focus in its curriculum and research agenda are interested in pursuing GIS-based research with community organizations. Through research and class projects, universities provide free customized GIS analysis to inner-city community organizations. Such partnerships emphasize integration of local experiential knowledge with public datasets, and are very responsive to community needs. Several studies show that through university–community partnerships, it is possible to create community in-house GIS that is in effect a customized community information system, where interface and data are customized to an organization's needs (Ghose, 2001; Thayer and Ghose, 2007). Sophisticated multi-scalar GIS indicators projects have also been results of university partnerships, which have reshaped public policy (Ghose and Huxhold, 2002). Partnering with universities is highly advantageous to community organizations, as universities deal with issues of data access, hardware, software, GIS training, and so on. However, universities have limited capacity and serve only a few community organizations. The partnerships are also dependent upon faculty interests, teaching schedules, academic calendar, research agenda, and hence are not long term in nature.

GIS facilities at universities and public libraries are also a model of GIS provision to community organizations. Such facilities provide access to spatial data, base maps, and GIS software as well as expert advice on how to use it at low or no cost. However, available spatial data is limited to public datasets, unless community organizations are able to incorporate their own data. Also, community organizations have to be self-directed and need to know what type of GIS service to ask for.

Government agencies also provide GIS and spatial data to community organizations through map rooms. Map rooms of city planning agencies in particular are a huge resource to community organizations, as these provide detailed government data on land parcels. Customized maps can also be available at a certain cost. However, institutional priorities are reflected in the availability of services to community organizations, and there may be limited advice from map room staff to community organizations. Also, map rooms will not provide maps of spatial data that are bound by confidential issues.

More recently, distributed Internet mapping technologies and online geographic information data provision has been acknowledged to play an increasing role in PPGIS (Weiner et al., 2002). Google Maps™ and Google Earth™ for instance have emerged as a significant mode of GIS provision (Miller, 2006). Implementations of web-based neighborhood information systems through specific university–community partnerships have taken place (Carver et al., 2001; Wong and Chua, 2001; Kingston, 2002; Thayer and Ghose, 2007). In an effort to enhance citizen participation in planning, city governments have also established web-based GIS sites, through which local government data are available to citizens. A vast array of property data (such as ownership, land-use, service requests, violations, zoning, taxation, building structure information, and so on) are usually available, which can be searched through either tax-key, single address, address range, or recorded last name. Data on crime, health, and demographic, economic conditions are also provided at an aggregated level. Through the Internet GIS sites, the local government aims to enable community organizations to be daily users of spatial data in their planning, service delivery, and organizational tasks. It effectively erases the barriers of distance, time, cost, and technical expertise for the average citizen. However, the datasets are typically not downloadable, and the selection of the data as well as its resolution is controlled by the provider. Incorporation of neighborhood data with public datasets is only allowed in limited cases, such as in the Housing Coalition in Milwaukee where neighborhood organizations formed a partnership with the City Hall to include their neighborhood survey data with public datasets through password protected Internet site (Ghose, 2007). Additionally, old computer hardware and a lack of high-speed Internet connections adversely affect the ability of community organizations to use Internet GIS.

In their study, Leitner et al. (2002) identify the Data Center program in Milwaukee as the only example of a neighborhood GIS center, a distinct model of GIS provision that is experienced in understanding the needs of the community organizations and very responsive to their requests for assistance. Its services range from routinized spatial data provision and mapping to sophisticated analysis to customized applications (Lin and Ghose, 2008). It also strongly believes in a bottom-up approach, and works actively with grassroots organizations to create spatial knowledge. Because of its partnership with Community Block Grant Administration which funds it to provide free GIS-based analysis to resource-poor grassroots organizations in inner-city Milwaukee, Data Center has been able to provide their services for free. But as a nonprofit organization, the Data Center program has also been strongly affected by government funding cutbacks, and without adequate number of staff members, it finds itself stretched thin to accommodate the needs of all community organizations in the inner-city areas.

In their assessment of the various models of GIS provision, Leitner et al. (2002) praise this model for its stability, high responsiveness to community organizations' needs, and its ability to foster collaborations among community organizations. As their research demonstrates, a combination of such attributes is difficult to obtain among the rest of the models (Leitner et al., 2002). For instance, a key issue with the other GIS providers is that their responsiveness to community organizations has been variable. A number of

these (such as the public library, map room, or Internet map servers) are stable organizations that provide ready access to free spatial data. However, they do not provide customized analysis to grassroots groups that lack the GIS-trained staff to make use of such data. Furthermore, they usually provide only public data at a certain resolution which may not be preferred by community organizations (e.g., data are provided at a city-wide scale rather than at a particular neighborhood scale). A notable exception is the university–community partnerships which provide customized analysis at the desired resolution. Also, the university is able to devote greater attention and greater resources in their community partnerships. Even though university partnerships are based on faculty interests and academic calendars, some campuses have ongoing community partnerships precisely because of faculty commitment to PPGIS research and community service oriented GIS courses.

Overall, GIS provider actors vary widely in terms of their support, and networks of support can be tenuous (Leitner et al., 2002; Laituri, 2003; Tulloch and Shapiro, 2003). There are different levels of responsiveness to the needs of community organizations among different GIS providers, shaped strongly by their agendas, budgetary constraints, and time schedules. An unequal power relation is prevalent in the networks connecting GIS provider actors with community organizations, in which community organizations have little control over the access to appropriate data and technology in a timetable set by the needs of a community organization. In the context of PPGIS practice, if one defines a sustainable model of GIS provision as a process in which an institute will provide low cost or free customized spatial data and GIS analysis to grassroots community organizations at the time of their need, then it is clear that most GIS provisions are not sustainable. In a climate of funding cutbacks and reduced federal money for social welfare tasks, community organizations are even more dependent on GIS providers for their spatial knowledge production.

VALUE OF SPATIAL KNOWLEDGE IN COLLABORATIVE GOVERNANCE

Neoliberal ideology has deeply shaped collaborative urban governance and inner-city revitalization activities. Emphasis on the creation of a lean and efficient state structure has meant cutbacks in local planning agencies, shifting many responsibilities upon citizen groups who increasingly act as shadow-state institutions. Simultaneously, deep federal funding cutbacks have required community organizations to compete with each other for dwindling funds. Community organizations are urged to be entrepreneurial and secure funding from non-governmental sources for their survival, as well as attract economic investment from the private sector in the inner city. The incorporation of a range of actors from public and private sectors in collaborative governance means that community organizations must negotiate with a range of agendas. Community organizations must also deal with changing expectations. Both public and private sector actors expect a level of professionalization from community organizations, with an emphasis on rational planning, technical expertise, and demonstration of outcomes through measurable indices. Spatial knowledge produced through GIS can enable community organizations to meet such expectations, as it is widely recognized as expert knowledge by powerful actors. This spatial knowledge is particularly powerful and effective when community organizations integrate their experiential knowledge with public datasets. The resulting knowledge is deeply empowering and superior to knowledge gleaned only from public datasets, enabling them to insert their voice in decision making activities. Visualization of their spatial knowledge through maps and charts are powerful tools for community organizers, and enable them to legitimize their claims.

Prior research shows that community organizations use spatial data and GIS to (1) confirm and legitimize existing experiential knowledge to obtain action and formulate strategies, (2) monitor neighborhood conditions and predict changes, (3) prepare for organizational tasks and funding recruitment efforts, (4) generate new information based on their own experiential knowledge to enhance service delivery tasks, and (e) explore spatial relations to challenge or reshape urban policy (Elwood and Leitner, 2003; Ghose, 2003; Elwood, 2006). These studies show that integration of neighborhood knowledge with public datasets represented through thematic maps enabled community organizations to obtain their objectives. The findings from Ghose (2003) discussed below demonstrate the value of spatial knowledge usage for inner-city community organizations.

First, community organizations use spatial knowledge to confirm and legitimize existing experiential knowledge to obtain action and formulate strategies. Garbage accumulation is a typical problem in inner-city neighborhoods, creating sanitation problems. But in order to obtain actions from the city hall, community organizations are required to prove a problem exists. Conducting local surveys to identify property sites where garbage, abandoned cars, yard waste, old tires had collected, and representing this knowledge through thematic maps enabled Metcalfe Park Residents Association and other neighborhood organizations in Milwaukee to demonstrate the validity of their complaints and obtain action from the city hall.

Second, community organizations also use spatial knowledge to monitor neighborhood conditions over time, to create strategies and predict changes. Boarded up properties is a common problem in inner-city neighborhoods, creating blighted landscape and contributing to the devaluation of the area. Many community organizations study the trend of boarded up houses over time in order to monitor this issue and target strategies to stop spreading it to neighboring blocks. Such an action enables a community group to form strategies and resist further spread of blighted landscape. Monitoring vacant lots is also quite common, and certain Milwaukee community organizations (such as Walnut Way) have used this knowledge to strategically create community gardens – both as a resource for healthy living and as a strategy for preventing neighborhood blight. Overall, research shows that community organizers possess rich knowledge regarding the location of vacant lots and boarded up homes, which have proved to be superior to that of the city hall's land-use knowledge as the latter is frequently incomplete and outdated (Elwood, 2008).

Third, community organizations use spatial knowledge to prepare for organizational tasks and funding recruitment efforts. Due to severe funding cutbacks from federal agencies, community organizations need to be proactive in seeking funding from foundations and private investors, for which they are required to create detailed plans. Neighborhood profiles constructed through the use of spatial data and maps assist community organizations to show neighborhood resources (through asset maps) and neighborhood needs. In Milwaukee, multiple organizations utilized spatial knowledge to apply for funding from philanthropic agencies, or to bring investment into the neighborhood. Moreover, spatial knowledge is also useful in demonstrating project outcomes. In Milwaukee, intermediary agencies such as Local Initiative Support Corporation (who bring for profit investment to the inner city) encourage the community organizations to use spatial indicators over time to show outcomes of grant initiatives. Usage of GIS can therefore be greatly beneficial to community organizations in obtaining funding, showing outcomes of grants, as well as recruiting businesses to the area.

Fourth, community organizations can enhance their service delivery tasks to the neighborhood by generating new information. North-West Side CDC in Milwaukee, for instance, urged their neighborhood residents to be aware of neighborhood problems, and report incidences of such problems.

Residents reported on a range of problems by locations such as abandoned vehicles, blighted properties, city service requests, landlord–tenant issues, nuisance problems, and so on to the community organization. Much of this reporting occurred through the cyberspace as residents sent emails to North-West Side CDC organizers from computers that had been donated to them by the community organization. Community organizers responded quickly to such emails and either tried to resolve these problems themselves or forwarded them to the appropriate department in the city hall. Through this type of cyber-organizing, community organizers were able to significantly improve the service delivery to their neighborhood residents.

Finally, community organizations can explore spatial relations to challenge or reshape urban policy (Ghose and Huxhold, 2002). Use of scale jumping has been proven to be effective in contesting urban policies (Smith, 1992) and is now practiced in PPGIS. Through a university–community partnership, WAICO community organization acquired a sophisticated GIS analysis using ten housing indicators at multiple scales (neighborhood scale, inner-city scale, and city-wide scale) to assess the quality of built environment in the Lindsey Heights neighborhood and compare and contrast it with that of the other scales. By using the strategy of scale jumping, WAICO proved to the City Hall that their neighborhood was not only worse off than the city of Milwaukee, it was also one of the most troubled ones in the inner-city Milwaukee. This study led to the creation of the first residential Tax Increment Financing district in Milwaukee, creating affordable new housing in the Lindsey Heights neighborhood.

Inner-city community organizations need to be skilled navigators within the currents of neoliberalization to survive. Using spatial knowledge proactively through a customized community information systems can help them to achieve their goals. Such a system should be built with data and interface shaped by the needs of community organizers, and should integrate neighborhood knowledge with public datasets. While past efforts to establish an in-house community GIS have failed, recent initiatives show some success. Elwood (2006: 324) has shown how a sustainable and effective community in-house GIS can be built through university–community partnership among two neighborhoods in Chicago, who have used them to create "flexible spatial narratives ... to strategically navigate the institutional, spatial and knowledge politics." She demonstrates how these community organizations use maps, photos, and charts to create multiple narratives about their neighborhoods, their conditions, and capacities. These are then used for diverse projects and decisions. In particular, she shows how the same data (such as vacant lots) was used in multiple ways by community organizers to construct needs narrative, assets narrative, injustice narrative, accomplishment narrative, and reinterpretation narrative. In needs narrative, vacant lots were shown as sites of problematic activities (such as drug dealing, loitering, violence), which needed resolution from the city. However, in assets narrative, vacant lots were depicted as sites for new houses or businesses, and used to attract investment. In injustice narrative, vacant lots in multiple neighborhoods and at multiple scales were drawn to show inequalities between neighborhoods, or places at multiple scales. Vacant lots that were acquired by community organizations to create affordable housing became part of their accomplishments narrative to potential funding agencies. Finally, in reinterpretation narrative, community organizers demonstrated how certain lots designated as vacant in the city database could actually be reinterpreted as community gardens. Thus, a single map of the vacant lots was framed to develop diverse narratives. Such interpretive framings were done through use of different titles and texts on the map, or through discussions and presentations to diverse actors, or through its inclusion and discussion in a grant proposal. These examples show that a GIS that integrates local knowledge and public database, is bottom-up in approach, and sensitive to neighborhood needs, is empowering. In the Chicago case, it has enabled the community organizers to navigate Chicago's infamous machine politics and secure rights for the disenfranchised residents.

CONCLUSION

Citizen participation and spatial knowledge production through a grounded, bottom-up process is a laudable goal in the efforts towards achieving social and environmental justice. However, participation of traditionally marginalized citizens and their groups is complex and deeply affected by political ideology and power relations, where the agendas of the powerful actors greatly shape the participation of powerless marginalized citizen groups. Spatial knowledge production as a result is also a messy and uneven process. While collaborative governance provides new opportunities to inner-city community organizations for participation in urban revitalization, it also contains a number of constraints such as funding cutbacks, devolution of state's responsibilities, and foisting of agendas set by powerful actors. Despite facing such bleak conditions that are beyond their control, these community organizations remain deeply committed to their goals of improving the lives of inner-city residents. Spatial knowledge produced through bottom-up PPGIS can greatly assist community organizations to navigate the complexities of collaborative governance. However, internal organizational factors shape the abilities of community organization to do so, leading to some being more successful than others in obtaining rights and resources, in order to transform spaces of despair into spaces of hope.

REFERENCES

Atkinson, R. (1999) 'Discourses of partnership and empowerment in contemporary British urban generation', *Urban Studies*, 36: 59–72.

Barndt, M. (1998) 'Public participation GIS: Barriers to implementation', *Cartography and Geographic Information Systems*, 25(2): 105–12.

Barndt, M. (2002) 'A model for evaluating public participation GIS,' in W. Craig, T. Harris and D. Weiner (eds), *Community Participation and Geographic Information Systems*. London: Taylor & Francis. pp. 346–56.

Barndt, M. and Craig, W. (1994) 'Data providers empower community GIS efforts', *GIS World*, 7(7): 49–51.

Brenner, N. (1998) 'Between fixity and motion: Accumulation, territorial organization and the historical geography of spatial scale', *Environment and Planning D: Society and Space*, 16: 459–81.

Brenner, N. and Theodore, N. (eds) (2002a) *Spaces of Neoliberalism: Urban Restructuring in North America and Western Europe*. Oxford: Blackwell.

Brenner, N. and Theodore, N. (2002b) 'Cities and the geographies of "actually existing neoliberalism"', in N. Brenner and N. Theodore (eds), *Spaces of Neoliberalism: Urban Restructuring in North America and Western Europe*. Oxford: Blackwell. pp. 2–32.

Carver, S., Evans, A., Kingston, R. and Turton, I. (2001) 'Public participation, GIS, and cyberdemocracy: Evaluating on-line spatial decision support systems', *Environment and Planning B: Planning and Design*, 28(6): 907–21.

Castells, M. (1996) *The Rise of the Network Society*. Oxford: Blackwell.

Craig, W. and Elwood, S. (1998) 'How and why community groups use maps and geographic information', *Cartography and Geographic Information Systems*, 25(2): 95.

Desforges, L. (2004) 'The formation of global citizenship: International non-governmental organizations in Britain', *Political Geography*, 23: 549–69.

Elwood, S. (2000) 'Information for Change: The Social and Political Impacts of Geographic Information Technologies', PhD dissertation, University of Minnesota, Minneapolis.

Elwood, S. (2002) 'Neighborhood revitalization through "collaboration": Assessing the implications of neoliberal urban policy at the grassroots', *GeoJournal*, 58: 121–30.

Elwood, S. (2006) 'Beyond cooptation or resistance: Urban spatial politics, community organizations, and GIS-based spatial narratives', *Annals of the Association of American Geographers*, 96(2): 323–41.

Elwood, S. (2008) 'Grassroots groups as stakeholders in spatial data infrastructures: Challenges and opportunities for local data development and sharing', *International Journal of Geographic Information Science*, 22(1): 71–90.

Elwood, S. and Ghose, R. (2004) 'PPGIS in community development planning: Framing the organizational context', *Cartographica* 38(3/4): 19–33. Published in March 2004, but publication date given as 2001 due to backlog.

Elwood, S. and Leitner, H. (2003) 'GIS and spatial knowledge production for neighborhood revitalization: Negotiating state priorities and neighborhood values', *Journal of Urban Affairs*, 25(2): 139.

Ghose, R. (2001) 'Use of information technology for community empowerment: Transforming geographic information system into community information systems', *Transactions in GIS*, 5(2): 141–63.

Ghose, R. (2003) 'Investigating community participation, spatial knowledge production and GIS use in inner city revitalization', *Journal of Urban Technology*, 10(1): 39–60.

Ghose, R. (2005) 'The Cof citizen participation through collaborative governance', *Space and Polity*, 9(1): 61–75.

Ghose, R. (2007) 'Politics of scale and networks of association in public participation GIS', *Environment and Planning A*, 39: 1961–80.

Ghose, R. and Elwood, S. (2003) 'Public participation GIS and local political context: Propositions and research directions', *Journal of the Urban and Regional Information Systems Association*, 15(APA II): 17–24.

Ghose, R. and Huxhold, W.E. (2001) 'The role of local contextual factors in building public participation GIS: The Milwaukee experience', *Cartography and Geographic Information Systems*, 28(3):195–208.

Ghose, R. and Huxhold, W.E. (2002) 'Role of multiscalar GIS-based indicators studies in formulating neighborhood planning policies', *Journal of Urban and Regional Information Systems Association*, 14(2): 5–17.

Gough, J. (2002) 'Neoliberalism and socialisation in the contemporary city: Opposites, complements and instabilities', in N. Brenner and N. Theodore (eds), *Spaces of Neoliberalism: Urban Restructuring in North America and Western Europe*. Oxford: Blackwell. pp. 58–79.

Harris, T. and Weiner, D. (1998) 'Empowerment, marginalization, and community-oriented GIS', *Cartography and Geographic Information Systems*, 25(2): 67–76.

Harvey, D. (1989) 'From managerialism to entrepreneurialism: The transformation of urban governance in late capitalism', *Geografiska Annaler*, 71(B): 3–17.

Hasson, S. and Ley, D. (1994) *Neighbourhood Organisations and the Welfare State*. Toronto: University of Toronto Press.

Healy, P. (1997) *Collaborative Planning: Shaping Places in Fragmented Societies*. Vancouver: University of British Columbia.

Hutchinson, C.F. and Toledano, J. (1993) 'Guidelines for demonstrating geographical information systems based on participatory development', *International Journal of Geographical Information Systems*, 7(5): 453–61.

Isin, E. and Wood, P. (1999) *Citizenship and Identity*. Thousand Oaks, CA: Sage.

Jessop, B. (2002) 'Liberalism, neoliberalism and urban governance: A state-theoretical perspective', in N. Brenner and N. Theodore (eds), *Spaces of Neoliberalism: Urban Restructuring in North America and Western Europe*. Oxford: Blackwell. pp. 105–25.

Kearns, A. and Paddison, R. (2000) 'New challenges for urban governance: Introduction to the review issue', *Urban Studies*, 37: 845–50.

Kearns, A. (1995) 'Active citizenship and local governance: political and geographic dimensions', *Political Geography*, 14(2): 155–75.

Kingston, R. (2002) 'Web-based PPGIS in the United Kingdom', in W.J. Craig, T.M. Harris and D. Weiner (eds), *Community Participation and Geographic Information Systems*. New York: Taylor & Francis.

Kellogg, W. (1999) 'From the field: Observations on using GIS to develop a neighborhood environmental information systems for community-based organizations', *URISA Journal*, 11(1): 15–32.

Kofman, E. (1995) 'Citizenship for some but not for others: Spaces of citizenship in contemporary Europe', *Political Geography*, 14(2): 121–37.

Laituri, M. (2003) 'The issue of access: An assessment guide for evaluating public participation geographic information science case studies', *URISA Journal*, 15(APA2): 25–32.

Leitner, H., Elwood, S., Sheppard, E., McMaster, S. and McMaster, R. (2002) 'Models for making GIS available to community organizations: Dimensions of difference and appropriateness', in W. Craig, T. Harris and D. Weiner (eds), *Community Participation and Geographic Information Systems*. London: Taylor & Francis. pp. 37–52.

Leitner, H., Peck, J. and Sheppard, E. (eds) (2007) *Contesting Neoliberalism: Urban Frontiers*. New York: Guilford Press.

Lepofsky, J. and Fraser, J.C. (2003) 'Building community citizens: Claiming the right to place-making in the City', *Urban Studies*, 40(1): 127–42.

Lin, W. and Ghose, R. (2008) 'Complexities in sustainable provision of GIS for urban grassroots organizations', *Cartographica*, 43(1): 31–44.

LISC (2007). Personal interview.

McCann, E. (2003) 'Framing space and time in the city: Urban policy and the politics of spatial and temporal scale', *Journal of Urban Affairs*, 25(2): 159–78.

McCann, E. (2001) 'Collaborative visioning or urban planning as therapy? The politics of public–private policy making', *Professional Geographer*, 53(2): 207–18.

Mayer, M. (2007) 'Contesting the neoliberalization of urban governance', in H. Leitner, J. Peck and E. Sheppard (eds), *Contesting Neoliberalism: Urban Frontiers*. New York: Guilford Press.

Miller, C. (2006) 'A beast in the field: The Google maps mashup as GIS/2', *Cartographica*, 41(3): 187–99.

Newman, K. and Lake, R. (2006) 'Democracy, bureaucracy and difference in U.S. community development politics since 1968', *Progress in Human Geography*, 30(1): 44–61.

Obermeyer, N. (1995) *The Hidden GIS Technocracy. Cartography and Geographic Information Systems*, 22(1): 78–83.

Obermeyer, N. (1998) 'The evolution of public participation GIS', *Cartography and Geographic Information Systems*, 25: 65–6.

Ong, A. (1999) *Flexible Citizenship: The Cultural Logics of Transnationality*. Durham, NC: Duke University Press.

Painter, J. and Philo, C. (1995) 'Spaces of citizenship: An introduction', *Political Geography*, 14(2): 107–20.

Peck, J. and Tickell, A. (2002) 'Neoliberalizing space', in N. Brenner and N. Theodore (eds), *Spaces of Neoliberalism: Urban Restructuring in North America and Western Europe*. Oxford: Blackwell. pp. 33–57.

Peck, J. and Tickell, A. (1994) 'Too many partners … the future for regeneration partnerships', *Local Economy*, 9: 251–65.

Pile, S. (1995) 'What we are asking for is decent human life: Splash, neighbourhood demands and citizenship in London's docklands', *Political Geography*, 14(2): 199–208.

Purcell, M. (2003) 'Citizenship and the right to the global city: Reimaging the capitalist world order', *International Journal of Urban and Regional Research*, 27(3): 564–90.

Sawicki, D. and Craig, W. (1996) 'The democratization of data: Bridging the gap for community groups', *Journal of the American Planning Association*, 62(4): 512–23.

Sawicki, D. and Peterman, D. (2002) 'Surveying the extent of PPGIS practice in the United States', in W. Craig, T. Harris and D. Weiner (eds), *Community Participation and Geographic Information Systems.* London: Taylor & Francis. pp. 17–36.

Schlossberg, M. and Shuford, E. (2005) 'Delineating "public" and "participation" in PPGIS', *URISA Journal*, 16(2): 15–26.

Sieber, R. (1997) 'Computers in the grassroots: Environmentalists' use of information technology and GIS', Working Paper #121. New Brunswick, NJ: Center for Urban Policy Research.

Sieber, R. (2000) 'GIS implementation in the grassroots', *Journal of the Urban and Regional Systems Association*, 12(1): 15–29.

Smith, N. (1992) 'Geography, difference, and the politics of scale', in J. Doherty, E. Graham and M. Malek (eds), *Postmodernism and the Social Sciences.* London: McMillan. pp. 55–79.

Staeheli, L. (1999) 'Globalization and the scales of citizenship', *Geography Research Forum*, 19: 60–77.

Stoecker, R. (1997) 'The community development corporation model of urban redevelopment: A critique and an alternative', *Journal of Urban Affairs*, 19: 1–23.

Stoecker, R. and Vakil, A. (2000) 'States, culture and community organizing: Two tales of two neighborhoods', *Journal of Urban Affairs*, 22: 439–58.

Stoker, G. (1995) 'Regime theory and urban politics', in D. Judge (ed.), *Theories of Urban Politics.* London: SAGE. pp. 54–71.

Swyngedouw, E. (1997) 'Neither global nor local: "glocalization" and the politics of scale', in K. Cox (ed.), *Spaces of Globalization.* New York: Guilford Press. pp. 137–66.

Taylor, M. (1998) 'Combating the social exclusion of housing estates', *Housing Studies.* 13: 819–32.

Taylor, M. (1999) 'Influencing policy: A UK voluntary sector policy perspective', in D. Lewis (ed.), *International Perspectives on Voluntary Action: Reshaping the 3rd Sector.* London: Earthscan. pp. 182–201.

Thayer, B. and Ghose, R. (2007) 'Developing a Community Information System (CIS) to Assist Neighborhood Revitalization Efforts', paper presentation at the annual meeting of AAG, 4/17/ 2007 to 4/21/2007.

Tulloch, D. and Shapiro, T. (2003) 'The intersection of data access and public participation: Impacting GIS users success?', *URISA Journal*, 15(APA2): 55–60.

Yuval-Davis, N. (1999) '"The multi-layered citizen": Citizenship at the age of " glocalization"', *International Feminist Journal of Politics*, 1: 119–36.

Weiner, D., Harris, T. and Craig, W. (2002) 'Community participation and geographic information systems', in W. Craig, T. Harris and D. Weiner (eds), *Community Participation and Geographic Information Systems.* London: Taylor & Francis. pp. 3–16.

Wong, S. and Chua, Y.L. (2001) 'Data intermediation and beyond: Issues for web-based PPGIS', *Cartographica*, 38(3/4): 63–80.

Value, Fairness and Privacy in a GIS Context

23

Geographic Information Value Assessment

Roger Longhorn

INTRODUCTION

Linking information to a location on the earth adds extra value to that information, yet assigning that geographical component is a costly process (Van Loenen, 2006). Some of these costs have been reduced in the digital age thanks to advances in a range of technologies, from the ever decreasing cost–performance ratio of computing power and mobile devices, to increased GPS accuracy, high-resolution remote sensing imagery, advances in sensor technology, web technology and so on. Yet assigning value to something called *geographic information* (GI) is fraught with difficulties due to the myriad ways in which such information can be used. The view presented here is that information provided for different uses, presented in different ways via differing mechanisms, covering different time frames, of differing quality, producing results of widely differing values, will have different perceived values for different users from the outset.

Information is a non-rival economic good, that is, consumption by one person does not diminish the amount of information available to others. GI, which is expensive to collect and maintain leads to natural monopolies, that is, having produced the first copy of the data, producing further copies has low marginal cost of dissemination (Shapiro and Varian, 1999). As technical information, GI is also an 'experience good' (Krek and Frank, 2000), that is, often the user must try it out to see if it is fit for purpose and thus has value for the intended use. This also requires special expertise in assessing the information, which adds to the transaction cost for finding and acquiring such information, a negative impact on its potential value commercially and to society, if this deters use (Krek, 2003; Krek, 2009).

Information value can be assigned, assessed or evaluated in different ways. These include commercial or market value (monetary or exchange value) of an information product or service; socio-economic value, when underpinning economic development; cultural value, helping citizens to understand their society; political value, in aiding governance or supporting democracy.

Information assumes value because it is needed to inform decision makers, be those decisions trivial or vital. Information is also required in the public sector, for satisfying legal mandates of government bodies, for example, in health care, education, land ownership and security. It is in relation to decision making that assigning value to information becomes fraught with difficulties, because of the myriad types of decisions to be made, from trivial to life saving, by millions of decision makers. Yet models have been produced that make it possible to quantify the value of geographic information in specific decision making situations, as demonstrated for example by Krek (2002) in relation to navigation information.

Because information has different types of value, determining value is dependent upon many factors, not least of which is cost of information, including all those processes needed to make information useful to different users. Perceived value (of the owner/seller and buyer) affects pricing which in turn affects not only the commercial (monetary) value of information, but also economic and social value, if for example pricing deters use.

This chapter does not contain a formal economic analysis of the value of GI or of public sector information (PSI). Many excellent texts exist that examine information economics in more detail, spanning more than 30 years of research (Hirshleifer and Riley, 1979; McCall, 1982; Shapiro and Varian, 1999; Birchler and Bütler, 2007). Nor does the chapter contain an analysis of the on-going debate over charging for PSI, the price to be paid where such charging exists (cost recovery), or the added value that freeing up PSI access and re-use may bring to a society. Rather, the chapter focuses on identifying the complexities that surround assigning different types of value to geographic information in an information-based society. First, the role of the location attribute that underpins all geographic information is defined, as it is important to know to what one is trying to assign a value. Different ways to value information are explored. A value chain for geographic information is proposed, focusing on the decision-making value of geographic information. The contribution to the value of geographic information of its different attributes or management is also explored.

WHAT IS GEOGRAPHIC INFORMATION – AND DOES THE DEFINITION MATTER?

To what are we trying to assign a value, that is, what is GI? For purposes of this chapter, I refer not only to topographic or cartographic data describing features on the earth – the traditional definition (AGI, 1991, 1999) – although such data, products and services comprise an important sector of the GI market. Rather, this chapter includes in the definition the *location attribute* associated to myriad types of data, since 'location' has taken on new importance in more recent definitions of GI (ANZLIC, 2006; EU, 2007).

These definitions acknowledge a focus on location, or place, in regard to spatial data and services, encouraged in part by technological advances and technology convergence bringing the ability to assign location to ever more types of information, for example, GPS-enabled cameras, mobile devices (smartphones and PDAs) and sensor networks. Just one indicator of the shift in focus is evidenced by the UK government revising its former geographic information infrastructure strategy in November 2008, to become a national location strategy titled 'Place Matters' (Communities and Local Government, 2008b), complete with a Location Information Infrastructure Blueprint (DEFRA, 2009) and official government appointed Location Council. Similarly, in the USA, NASCIO (2008) – the National Association of State Chief Information Officers – noted that 'location awareness' was at an all time high and would only increase in the future.

Datasets defining real world features, such as urban or rural landscapes, or road, rail and river networks, are often treated as the underpinning for information products or services such as maps (digital or paper) or navigation systems. Records in datasets in which location is only one attribute, for example, a person's address, while other attributes describe that person's medical record, financial or employment status or educational achievements, are not usually thought of by their creators as being 'geographic'. Yet the location attribute does offer the ability to use such information in spatial analysis. Longhorn and Blakemore (2007: 5) define 'geographic information' as:

> Geographic Information is … a composite of spatial data and attribute data describing the location and attributes of things (objects, features, events, physical or legal boundaries, volumes, and so on), including the shapes and representations of such things in suitable two-dimensional, three-dimensional or four-dimensional (x, y, z, time) reference systems (for example, a grid reference, coordinate system reference, address, postcode, and so on) in such a way as to permit spatial (place based) analysis of the relationships between and among the things so described, including their different attributes.
>
> *Corollary* to the definition: The format of portrayal or use does not exclude one type of information from being considered 'geographic'. Geographic Information may exist in any number of forms and formats, for example, an aerial image of a house or street, showing its relationship to other houses and streets, qualifies as 'geographic information' just as would the vectors describing the boundaries of the house or centreline of the road in an x-y coordinate system.

Why is the definition important? In order to assign value to something, it is necessary to agree on what that 'something' is or is not. If any information with an associated location attribute is considered to be 'geographic', then many more types of information are brought into the realm of geographic information, increasing the difficulty in assigning different types of value to that information, since value assessment is closely related to use.

THE VALUE OF GEOGRAPHIC INFORMATION

Value is defined by Larousse (1997) as "worth; intrinsic worth or goodness; recognition of such worth; that which renders something useful or estimable; relative worth; high worth; price; the exact amount of a variable quantity in a particular case."

The term 'value' has many formal definitions, yet all share a common factor in the concept of 'worth'. The challenge in valuing information arises in determining what type of worth is important to different actors in society at different times – monetary, economic, social, civil or governance related.

Valuing information through use

The difficulty in valuing information is that the same information can have different values when used in different ways. Information by itself is of little intrinsic value; rather value is related to use, and the nature of that use, by the value it adds to decision-making processes or their results. Longley et al. (2001: 376) note that "the value of the same information differs hugely to different people and for different applications." Barr and Masser (1996: 27) claim that information "has no inherent value, it is only of value once used and that value is related to the nature of the use rather than the nature of the information. Thus, information has very different values for different users." According to the US Federal Highway Administration (1998) information has value "determined by its importance to the decision maker or to the outcome of the decision being made … professionals require information that is not only accurate, timely, and relevant, but also presented and interpreted in a meaningful way."

If one accepts that information only assumes value through use, then different value propositions need to be examined depending upon different types of use. Macauley (2005) presents a value of information framework relating to earth science data collected from space, a prime example of an important type of geographic information. The purpose of the framework was to provide a common basis to conduct and evaluate studies of the value of earth science information for three communities: consumers and producers of information, public officials and the public at large.

Drawing on the premise that value arises from a desire to remove uncertainty from decision making, Macauley (2005) proposes that value depends on such factors as:

- the degree of uncertainty involved in the decision;
- what is at stake as an outcome of the decision;
- the cost to use the information to make the decision; and
- the price of the next-best substitute for the information on offer.

The value of the information needed to reduce the degree of uncertainty in reaching a decision has also been shown to depend partly on the type or range of actions that can be taken in regard to the decision in question. If, for example, the information simply informs a decision maker that something will happen over which they have no control, then the value of such information is much reduced, even if the information is of very high quality. On the other hand, if a range of actions can be taken based on the same information, especially if these have different costs and outcomes, then the information assumes a higher level of value in the eyes of the decision maker.

Outcomes from a decision can have a wide range of values, to persons, businesses, economies or societies as a whole, for example, in the case of health and safety or monitoring and managing environmental impacts. Macauley's value of information model indicates that the greater the value of the outcome based on the information used by the decision maker, the higher is the value of the information to that decision maker. Macauley (2005: 30) sees this level of willingness to pay as "... derived demand – demand emanating from value of the services, products, or

other results that in part determine this worth."

Information can be of high value in reducing uncertainty and in delivering high-value outputs, yet still be too costly to find or use, financially or in terms of human resources, skills, or time of the decision maker. For example, Krek (2009) found that tangible and intangible transaction costs (the cost to find, assess and use specific information) for buildings-related geographic information in three European cities often exceeded the (monetary) cost of the information itself or prevented it from being used by decision makers, thus further reducing the value of that information from the outset.

If alternative sources or types of information exist that would aid the decision maker, and these are considered adequate in the perception of that decision maker, then the cost of such substitutes will affect the perceived value of the information available. If the cost of the next-best substitute is lower than the original information against which it is being compared, then that lowers the decision maker's perceived value (as measured by willingness to pay) of the initial information resource.

Value varies with intended use

A single piece of data may be used in many different ways, each use creating new information, especially if combined with other data, which are then collectively referenced or analysed in different ways depending upon the application and the user's information requirements. This virtuous circle wherein data begets information and information begets new information strains our ability to assign any one value to the original data.

For example, 1 kilometre of road centreline location data collected by the original data holder may be sold to a user for a specific amount, representing the producer's cost recovery and return on investment targets and the buyer's willingness to pay, which are the main determinants of market price for goods or services. Yet the real value of that road centreline to society may vary considerably, depending upon the final uses to which it is put, for example in creating new products and services. The centreline data is of high value to the vendor of a GPS-enabled navigation system, yet the ultimate value differs significantly among users of that system, from trivial to life saving.

MEASURING DIFFERENT TYPES OF VALUE

Value should be measurable, yet if information has multiple types of value depending upon perceived worth, then the same measure or metric will not apply equally to all information in all circumstances. Commercial value of an information product, determined by the information market, is quite different from the value arising from the use of GI in myriad applications, to economies and to society as a whole.

Commercial value of GI

In the commercial information market, the principle measure of worth is monetary value, that is, sales revenue related to production cost recovery, profit margins and return on investment, which relates also to what Lash (2002) refers to as exchange value. Financial value can also apply to public sector GI if the information delivers cost savings from operations, although in this case the numeric value does not necessarily relate to exchange value, that is, the cost savings could far exceed the acquisition cost.

Monetary value recognizes that information costs are real, for example, for data collection, processing, dissemination and management, and must be recovered by someone, somehow. That someone may be a commercial vendor or a government body. The somehow may be via selling GI at a price or using tax payers' money to cover the costs.

Monetary value applies to both raw data, as a commodity to be traded, and to value-added products and services. Costs for acquiring and providing data can usually be computed with some degree of accuracy. Thus monetary value can also be determined reasonably well, related to the price at which the data is traded (exchange value) and the consumer's willingness to pay that price. The sales price in the information marketplace becomes a financial surrogate for monetary (exchange) value. Joffe and Bacastow (2005) propose that the cost or price that a user is willing to pay is a valid surrogate for perceived value for that user, in a specific format, of specified quality, for a stated purpose, typically under legally binding contractual terms. Their scenario suggests that the user's cost depends upon the data owner's policy and other costs that arise from different delivery methods or optional services. Note that because willingness to pay is linked directly to the purchaser's intended use, the same information can have widely varying values when presented to multiple users.

The value of information for a vendor is typically solely monetary, that is, based on a sales price that covers all costs plus an acceptable return on investment. To different types of users, the value might be financial, social, economic, cultural, political or personal (Bryson, 2001). The value could equate to simply added convenience, for example, finding a point of interest more easily, to enabling a new information service offered for financial gain. There is also value to the vicarious user, that is, location-based data for an emergency vehicle routing system that may help save the life of an accident victim (the vicarious user).

So value depends very much upon different actors' viewpoints. A vendor making a profit from sales of GI is probably satisfied with the monetary value of the GI on offer, from their viewpoint. A user of the same information product, who is disappointed with the results of that use, for a specific purpose in certain circumstances, will consider that information to be of lesser value.

Socio-economic value of GI

Numerous studies over 15 years indicate that GI plays an important role in society (Price Waterhouse, 1995; Hardwick and Fox, 1999; OXERA, 1999; PIRA, 2000; CIE, 2000; Baltimore County, 2001; Environment Agency, 2003; Halsing et al., 2004; Booz Allen Hamilton, 2005; OFT, 2006; GeoConnections, 2008; OPSI, 2008; ACIL Tasman, 2008; Communities and Local Government, 2008a; ACIL Tasman, 2009). Location-based information is alleged to help deliver more efficient government, especially in e-government regimes. Accurate spatial (location) attributes found in many types of information help plan, operate and maintain many forms of infrastructure, for example, transport, food production, health, education and many areas of governance generally, at all levels. The studies above suggest that use of location information supports myriad sectors of the economy, helps improve quality of life for citizens, improves business efficiency and helps generate new business and employment opportunities. Each of these outcomes or benefits indicates a certain value for the underpinning information used, which can far exceed sales-generated monetary value.

Socio-economic value, the value of a good or service in achieving societal goals, is much more difficult to quantify than monetary value because of the multiple ways the same information can be used in regard to a wide range of societal goals. There have been attempts to assign socio-economic value to geographic information, yet these face difficulty when translating into something quantifiable the acceptable measures of success in providing often intangible benefits to society as a whole. The study conducted for Land Information New Zealand on the value of spatial information (ACIL Tasman, 2009: ix) states that "Other (non-productivity) benefits linked to the increasing use of spatial information are probably worth a multiple of this (the 1.2 billion NZ$ that GI already is estimated to save). Uncertainties around the likelihoods of future events and valuation

methodologies limit the ability to express such benefits in dollar terms."

The economic value of information derives from its use in making decisions affecting the economy. Various attempts have been made to define a value for GI, in relation to economies or as a component of the total market for all types of information, or especially for public sector information (OXERA, 1999; PIRA, 2000; Weiss, 2002). These studies focus on added value for GI due to the ease of access to the information and ability of others to easily acquire and exploit public sector GI at minimal cost. A study by Pluijmers and Weiss (2001: 21) focused on 'maximizing economic and social benefit from the dissemination of information and data already acknowledged by governments as not confidential, and ... fair terms for commercialisation of government data and competition with the private sector.'

A UK Office of Fair Trading (OFT, 2006) study investigated how PSI becomes value added information, how the pricing of PSI and access to it affects competition between public-sector bodies and the private sector, and the effectiveness of existing guidance and laws in managing the public–private data provider interface – specifically UK implementation of the 2003 EU Directive on re-use of PSI via the Re-use of Public Sector Information Regulations 2005 (APPSI, 2006). The study concluded that improving access to and exploitation of PSI in the UK could "double in terms of the value it (i.e., PSI) contributes to the UK economy to a figure of £1 billion annually" (OFT 2006: 4).

Economists look at economic impacts in financial terms, while socio-economists focus on the social impact of economic change, such as advances in information and communications technology (ICT), changes in intellectual property (IP) law or changes in information access or privacy laws. To analyse socio-economic impacts, socio-economists use metrics such as improvements in literacy, employment and shifts in employment between sectors, which are related to greater access to, and use of, information, while acknowledging negativities due to the "digital divide."

Cultural value of GI

Information also has cultural value, separate from social or economic value, yet difficult to measure except in social terms, and perhaps the most difficult of all types of worth to assign to GI or other types of information. Yet considering the significant sums that nations assign to cultural budgets, for example, for museums, libraries and archives, orchestras or national monuments, one could conclude that cultural information is considered to be a valuable national asset.

Cultural identity is maintained via information, and "place" is a key attribute for much cultural information. Preservation of place-based information, for example, old maps, helps us to understand history and our place in history, in our own society and in the global society, today and in the past. Maps with journey lines explain historical change such as exploration and settlement. A sequence of maps can show how the same place changed over time, helping to develop our understanding of how cities evolve, how continents move or how a local neighbourhood has grown.

Cultural value does not lend itself at all well to monetarization, given the subjective nature of the perceptions of the body of citizens comprising a culture. Adding to the complexity of assessing cultural value of GI is the fact that some types of GI that are very important in one culture may have little importance in another, for example, the role that maps play in visual literacy.

Political value of GI

Bryson (2001) proposes that the political value of information derives from its usefulness in communicating ideas, principles and commitments. Information can be used and misused by individuals, politicians or organisations to promote specific viewpoints, usually to sway opinions or votes over contentious issues. The location attribute of much information used in planning (urban and rural) is valuable to conservation organisations for achieving their goals for land or heritage preservation. When planning decisions have a spatial context, such as running a road bypass through a site of special scientific interest, then geographic information assumes political value – and its use can be a powerful persuader in lobbying.

Geographic information also has political value when it is used to manipulate a specific outcome or promote a particular viewpoint or provide place-based information, with both positive and negative impacts. For example, the high-resolution digital terrain model produced by one UK insurance company to help assess flood risk was of high positive value to the company and its shareholders, but of negative value to policy holders now refused flood protection insurance based on their location. Yet availability of the new dataset provided an important new GI resource for all involved in flood planning, remediation and disaster management – certainly of positive value for society.

Other types of value

In Krek's (2002) agent-based model of geographic information economic value, she distinguishes between the cognitive and functional value, where only functional value, equal to the value of use, can be objectively measured.

Functional value is based on the functional characteristics of a product, that is, does it satisfy the functional needs of the user. The functional value of geographic information is in its use in the decision making process. Krek and Frank (2000: 10) claim that "the required information is highly specialized by the current goal and the spatial situation, and usually only a small set of data is relevant for a decision." Thus, GI functional value can be measured by the degree to which it improves the decision-making process. However, that requires formalizing ways to measure values for improved decision making, that is, the difference in expected value between best actions before and after the information is obtained.

Cognitive value accrues to subjective characteristics of a product and the provider. Krek (2002) demonstrates that GI users first satisfy their functional needs and then may activate cognitive valuation. In economic theory, cognitive value is considered to be a subjective, emotional valuation of a product or service, including such things as brand names, advertising, delivery terms or warranty conditions which raise the perception of the value of a good or the providing firm.

THE ECONOMIC CONTRIBUTION OF PUBLIC SECTOR GI

Public sector GI is necessary for governance of society and efficient operation of the state, which is the rationale behind data collection, processing and management using tax-payers' money. Public sector GI is produced as part of a public agency's legally mandated responsibilities, or in order to carry out those responsibilities more efficiently. Monetary value based on the cost to acquire that data or service may be irrelevant, since the data must be collected and/or used in order to fulfil legally mandated tasks. The actual value of the information lies in the efficient completion of thee tasks. Bryson (2001) notes that it is important to "identify and manage different value propositions from a financial, political, corporate, social, cultural, personal and community values perspective ... to exploit the total worth of the information and knowledge age."

According to a PIRA International Ltd (2000) study into the exploitation of European public-sector information, investment value in European PSI was estimated at €9.5 billion per annum in 2000, and €19 billion per annum in the USA. Investment value was defined as the investment in the acquisition of PSI and economic value was defined as 'that part of national income attributable to industries and activities built on the exploitation of PSI ... the value added by PSI to the economy as a whole'. PIRA estimated that PSI economic value was €750 billion in the USA, compared to €68 billion in 2000 in Europe, at that time of comparable size and population to the USA, and that GI in Europe accounted for €36 billion of this total. The discrepancy for two regions of approximately the same population and level of development was ascribed to the open exploitation policy for most PSI in the USA due to freedom of information legislation at federal level. However, since the US Freedom of Information Act applies only to federal data, and not that created at state, county or municipality level, this contention should still be questioned.

PIRA's methodology differentiated between investment value, that is, what governments invest in acquiring PSI, and economic value, the portion of national income "attributable to industries and activities built on the exploitation of PSI" (PIRA, 2000: 15). Economic value of €68 billion far surpassed investment value at €9.5 billion. Because the normal source for economic value figures, that is, national accounts information for traditional industries, was not available for the information marketplace, PIRA made the assumption that "estimates of the value added by users to PSI ... provide figures for the economic value of PSI." However, investment value, relating directly to costs spent in acquiring PSI, was quite accurately estimated at €9.5 billion– of which GI was the largest single sector at 37 percent – while the economic value reported was actually a central estimate based on a very wide range of values – from €28 billion to €134 billion. This range of variation causes one to consider the reported figures with some uncertainty.

Geoscience Australia highlighted the benefit-cost ratio of public provision of national to regional scale fundamental geoscientific datasets in a 2002 submission to the Australian House of Representatives. The report contends that such datasets are an important foundation on which private-sector mineral and petroleum extraction industries depend in conducting more focused geological surveys in an industry that accounted for AUS$ 55.3 billion to Australia's economy in 2001–2002. The publicly available information provides this regional-scale, pre-competitive knowledge base, online for free or at cost of distribution, to reduce risks in selecting areas for new exploration work by industry, thus "providing a competitive advantage for Australia" (Geoscience Australia, 2002: 2). In trying to quantify the value of the public release of this geographic information, the report quotes exploration expenditure by private industry of AUS$5 or every AUS$1 invested by government in pre-competitive geoscientific data collection. This investment results in AUS$ 100 to AUS$ 150 of in-ground resources being discovered, resulting in a benefit-ratio of 5:1 for industry investment based on the public sector GI and ratios of 100:1 to 150:1 for additions to the proven mineral wealth of Australia for every dollar of government investment in geoscience information provision.

The relationship between cost and value is only one aspect of value of geographic information. Changing information policies can alter the value of GI, reducing potential monetary value for some data owners, while increasing value to users or perhaps to society as a whole. A policy offering cheaper, wider access and liberal exploitation rights to public sector GI may reduce the market value of some pre-existing value-added services offered by commercial data providers, yet create new value-adding actors in the industry or permit easier access by citizens' groups to GI of value in achieving their goals. Consider these basic points.

- Geographic information manifests itself in many different forms and formats, for myriad uses, often in combination with other non-geographic information.
- All information has a range of costs associated with it, which must be covered by someone, although cost recovery alone is not the only measure of value.
- The location attribute that defines information as being geographic is only one of many attributes for that information, each of which has its own unique impact on information value.
- The value of information varies with time and according to use – and user.

EXAMINING THE INFORMATION VALUE CHAIN

The value chain is the set of value-adding activities an organization performs in creating and distributing goods and services, including both direct and indirect activities. In Porter's (1985) classic production value chain for manufacturing enterprises, goods progress from raw materials to finished products via a number of stages, during each of which new value is added to the original input by various activities. If the price of outputs at any stage is higher than the cost of inputs to that stage, then value has been added and a profit margin earned within that stage. The sum of all these margins, at the end of the chain, equals the total 'value added'. For a product or service to be successful, not every stage needs to have a positive value-added, as long as the net result at the end of the chain is positive.

The information value chain

An information value chain has been proposed in which value is added to information by various activities as it progresses from raw data to a new form of information or information service. The US Office of Management and Budget (OMB, 2005: 17) defines an "Information Value Chain Model" as the "set of artifacts within the describing how the enterprise converts its data into useful information." Information and communications technologies (ICT) have a direct impact on virtually all the activities in the information value chain.

Does GI adhere to value chain concepts for determining the value of information, especially in relation to similar information, for example, scientific, technical, medical information? Since an estimated 80 percent of all government information has a geographic component, what are the similarities and dissimilarities between private-sector and public-sector GI regarding perceived value, based on the many criteria that determine value? When value is added to an initial piece of geographic information, then this new information has its own unique value, distinct from that of the original information. Wehn de Montalvo et al. (2004: 2) point out that "location-based mobile services will come to be fully integrated and seamlessly available to end-users seeking localised and customised content, which has value-adding implications for the location-aware component of the content."

What happens in the value chain when private firms exploit public-sector GI or when GI produced by the private-sector becomes public, that is, when governments outsource data collection to the private sector? Do access, exploitation and intellectual property (IP) rights impact on the value of public sector GI any more so than they do on the private sector? What does the term 'value added GI' mean – does GI itself have 'value added' or only the services that use

GI? These are some of the questions that need exploring in regard to GI and the information value chain.

A proposed GI value chain for decision makers

Many authors have proposed different information value chains for different types of information and from different viewpoints. Spataro and Crow (2002) propose a five-stage value chain that progresses from creation (of a product), through management, integration, transaction and finally distribution. Oelschlager (2004) defines a six-stage information value chain in terms of enterprise-wide information integration that converts unstructured data arising from business processes to 'actionable information'. The stages proceed from unstructured data to structured data, then contextual information to business information, leading to knowledge and finally active insight.

Phillips (2001) proposes a management information value chain (MIVC) based on six types of value-enhancing activity, as shown in Figure 23.1. The goal of the MIVC is conversion of raw data into useful information that is then acted upon by management, contributing to corporate value or enhanced organisational efficiency. New value is created at each stage of the MIVC value chain by activities that require expenditure of resources, that is, money, human capital, ICT infrastructure and so on. Such expenditure

Stage 1	Stage 2	Stage 3	Stage 4	Stage 5	Stage 6
Data Acquisition	Initial Transformation	Dissemination	Modelling Tools & Presentation	Decisions	Actions
IT Actions				Management Activities	

Least Value ➔ ➔ ➔ ➔ ➔ ➔ ➔ ➔ ➔ ➔ ➔ ➔ Highest Value

Figure 23.1 MIVC Value Chain according to Phillips (2001)

will not be undertaken unless the result is information of value greater than the combined cost of the value-adding activities in each stage and the cost of the information as it entered that stage.

MIVC assumes that management information systems provide information to enable better decision making resulting in value equal to increased profitability or greater efficiency. The value added to raw data by intermediate activities is measured by the extent to which each activity contributes to the main goal. Transformation includes aggregating and filtering raw data, and integrating multiple data sources. Dissemination involves getting appropriate information to the right people in a usable format when needed. Modelling and presentation activities transform the integrated information into the necessary format for immediate use to different levels of decision maker. In the final two stages of the MIVC, IT-oriented activity is replaced by humans making and acting on decisions based on the information presented to them.

MIVC is a useful model for the GI value chain because a great deal of the GI collected by government and private industry employs a location attribute as an important part of the decision-making process. In that sense, this value chain would apply to any data with a location attribute. There are quite specific, often expensive and complex, activities taking place in the data acquisition, transformation, modelling and dissemination stages that are unique to GI compared to other forms of information to which the MIVC also applies. Also, the decisions and actions corresponding to stages 5 and 6 of the MIVC can have very different values commercially, socially or economically.

For GI, Van Loenen and Zevenbergen (2010 state that the value added can include improving the quality of a data set, integrating several topographic data sets into one layer, linking a framework geographic dataset with several thematic layers or providing user-friendly access to the dataset or other information intermediary services that help

users. They note that the value adding may also be performed equally by government bodies, operating on public sector information datasets, as well as by commercial actors. Their research also indicated that value adding was influenced by the different roles that government and the commercial market play in the GI enhancement chain, which "impact on the appropriation of value flows to the players in the chain." (Van Loenen and Zevenbergen (2010: 259).

Value chain networks

Crompvoets et al. (2010: 96) propose that "the value of spatial data is added through a complex value network rather than a sequential chain." They argue that the spatial context of data matters differently at different spatial levels and that different decision-making contexts and styles require different types of spatial information. This implies that different value-adding activities may be needed to enhance the value of a chain, performed by different actors at different times, where the final information used by the decision maker is the output of a network of value chains, not a single sequential chain.

VALUE COMPONENTS FOR GI

Based on the above considerations for value of GI, it is possible to enumerate several components to contribute to value. The value of GI is a complex relationship between location data and other information, attributes and context, plus timeliness, quality and other factors that add value. For example, a single point relating to a feature, specified in some meaningful spatial reference system, is a piece of location data. More attribute information is needed to add meaningful context to that point, for example, its definition as being part of a boundary line, rather than simply some random point on the surface of the earth. Yet more attributes add context to the original data point, for example, its accuracy, precision, provenance, history or method by which it was measured. These additional information elements add value to the raw location data, resulting in a more robust information package that can be used in a range of contexts, many of which may be in areas other than that for which the location data was first collected.

Value of the location attribute

In the information model of Spataro and Crow (2002), data is defined as 'transaction-based information' while content is 'context-sensitive information'. Raw data acquires more value, as context-sensitive information, by wrapping an information package in a metadata wrapper, resulting in a 'content component'. For geographic information, the location attribute provides spatial context to the other attributes in the information package, thus increasing the value of the data for applications where spatial awareness is key.

Is it possible to set a value on just the location-based component of geographic information? Some economic analyses (OXERA, 1999; ACIL Tasman, 2008; Communities and Local Government, 2008a; ACIL Tasman, 2009) claim that geographic information has special value as an underpinning framework for other information and services, for example, location information as an important attribute in a larger information package. Yet records recording the spread of disease, path of a storm or locations of road accidents have many important attributes other than just location. These non-geographic attributes are valuable in their own right, for example, the severity of storms and resulting damage they may inflict on society and the resultant cost to insurers or property owners. The mixture of attributes, locational and non-locational, that typifies much that is called geographic information further complicates the process of setting a value on such information.

An economic paper of the UK government (Communities and Local Government, 2008a) lists four reasons why 'place matters' from the economic perspective.

- Drivers of productivity come together in places, for example, combinations of assets that can boost the productivity of firms and attract the skilled workers occur in certain physical locations and not others.
- Where something is or occurs, that is, place, has impact on economic, environmental and social outcomes of government policies, for example, policies can have unintended spatial impacts or failures of the market can have different impacts in different places depending upon the conditions existing in those places.
- There are mobility limits on the ability of people to move or commute in response to changing socioeconomic conditions, that is, financial and social costs of mobility can act as a barrier to mobility itself.
- Groups of citizens that need special attention are often concentrated in particular places, thus managing place information offers a way of targeting services to such groups and of co-ordinating multiple policies impacting on particular places.

Granularity value of GI

The location attribute for crop growth rate data in a single farmer's field is of great value to that farmer, who can act on it by applying fertiliser at different rates across fields, thus increasing yields. Yet the location attribute data only has value if used in relation to other attributes of crop data, for example, type and variety of crop, local plant height or density or grain kernel size. Also, information on crop growth rates for a single farm, aggregated for an entire region, can be valuable in setting crop subsidy levels. The same information is important in regard to the regional in situ capacity for crop processing and distribution services that may be needed, with ramifications for local employment levels and purchase of local supporting services.

This example demonstrates the difference in value of geographic information based on its granularity. Point data, that is, the location where a single reading was taken, has one value, but field-wide or farm-wide data (aggregated point data) has another value, and regional data (data aggregated across many farms) has yet another value. Each type or range of values is dependent upon the intended use and the perceived value to the user of the information package as a whole. Moving from point data to higher aggregations also involves value-adding work, with an impact on the MIVC value chain final stages 5 and 6 leading to different types of decisions and actions.

Changing value over time

Information value changes over time. The value of certain types of geographic information may depend on whether it is real-time, near real-time, relatively static or historical data. The decision as to when to make that information available, to whom and at what price, assumes different values for the same data depending upon user needs and perceptions of the value of the intended uses. For example a satellite image can have high value today, for example, in monitoring forest fires so that resources can be best allocated to save human life, property and the environment. Those same images are of less value once the fire has been extinguished, at least for fire fighting purposes. Yet the images may have different value a year from now, or a decade or many decades in the future, for analysing environmental problems and trends, such as potential remediation (replanting) costs for deforested areas, or the impact of deforestation on wild life conservation and biodiversity, or the potential impact on global climate change due to lost carbon sequestration capacity represented by the amount of forest destroyed.

Similar time-related effects apply to traffic congestion information and meteorological data, and transport planning and climate-change decisions arising from use of such data at different times in its lifespan. Information from a decadal population census

"declines in value as it ages in the 10 years between censuses" but the value rises again following the next census, when it forms the benchmark against which change is determined over the preceding decade (Longley et al., 2001: 376).

Value created by mandatory use requirements

Some information has a legal status for certain types of transactions, for example, the location-based boundary data in cadastral or land registration systems. Even if the historical, legal boundary line drawn on a cadastral map is not reconcilable with the actual boundary on the ground between properties today, the cadastral map typically takes precedent legally. Data from officially recognised sources, such as national mapping agencies, land registries or official address or gazetteer owners, must often be used in other civil applications as well. This practice can confer a monopolistic, or near monopolistic, position for such data, with a direct impact on its value to different types of user for different purposes, including for those wishing to add value for commercial exploitation of the original data.

Value due to quality of an information resource

For geographic information, data quality issues are also part of value determination. What is sufficient quality for one user or type of use may be wholly insufficient for another user or type of use. Data quality is often the reason for not using volunteered geographic information (VGI), that is, location-based data collected by other than officially recognized data collection practitioners, such as surveyors. The local success of citizen-centric projects such as the Openstreetmap project (http://www.openstreetmap.org) are exemplars of what can be accomplished using non-official GI data sources as opposed to official ones in producing location-based information that is useful to large groups of users, even if it may not be of the same quality as that obtained from official sources.

What determines "quality," especially in regard to different consumers and uses for geographic information? Completeness of the dataset, timeliness of the information and provenance or reputation of the information provider may all be important, as they can add or detract from the value, or the willingness to pay, as perceived by different consumers for different applications. The Australia New Zealand Land Information Council states (ANZLIC, 2005) "Australia's and New Zealand's economic growth, and social and environmental interests are underpinned by quality spatially referenced information. Note: 'quality spatially referenced data' means spatially referenced information that is current, complete, accurate, affordable, accessible, and integratable."

AREAS FOR FURTHER RESEARCH

Much of the past research into the value of GI has been driven by development of spatial data infrastructures (SDI) at national and regional level across the globe. Creating an SDI is a very costly business, involving most departments across government and third parties in industry. The funding agencies want to know if they are getting value for money from such efforts. Commercial actors want to know where best to invest their resources in adding value to existing GI, that is, where are the markets.

A high proportion of the authors of the papers referenced in this chapter acknowledged that there is great difficulty in assessing value for geographic information partly because of its ubiquity (if one assumes that any information with a location attribute is included in the term) and because geographic information underpins so many other products and services that add value to our economies and personal lives in innumerable ways.

The research presented in this chapter appears to indicate that it is not possible to assign a single, definitive value to any one piece of GI or to a dataset or service or even for specific types of GI, because ultimately value depends upon use, and there are myriad uses for different types of GI. However, many areas of value research have seen progress in the past five years and need to be extended with more empirical work, model building and testing via case studies and applications. Some of these areas are:

- Re-examining the value chain approaches to assigning value to GI used in decision making, to including more work on value chain networks and value chains that operate in parallel as opposed to the classical sequential value chain analysis, plus sectoral specific value chains (Krek, 2002; Crompvoets et al., 2009; Van Loenen and Zevenbergen, 2009; Macauley et al., 2010);
- Developing and agreeing on an evaluation framework for GI value that better accommodates sectoral needs, that is, the private/commercial versus public sector actors (Macauley, 2005, Genovese et al., 2009);
- Conducting more case studies of documented GI value impact on sub-national or national SDI development across the globe, since SDI creation affects whole economies as opposed to select sectors or industries (Castelein et al., 2009; Craglia and Campagna, 2010; Genovese et al., 2009; Halsing et al., 2004);
- Conducting further work linking the perceived value of GI (use) by users with wider socio-economic benefits, such as those attained in regard to earth observation, including development of appropriate models that could be applied across multiple sectors or disciplines (Rydzak et al., 2010); and
- Developing a clearer understanding of the value of public sector GI to economies as a whole, including empirical studies demonstrating the value of proposed valuation models (ACIL Tasman, 2009; Craglia et al., 2010; Navarra, 2009).

REFERENCES

ACIL Tasman (2008) *The Value of Spatial Information.* Melbourne: ACIL Tasman.

ACIL Tasman (2009) *Spatial Information in the New Zealand Economy*. Melbourne: ACIL Tasman.

AGI (1991) *GIS Dictionary: A Standards Committee Publication – Version No: 1.1*. London: Association for Geographic Information.

AGI (1999) *GIS Dictionary* (online). London: Association for Geographic Information.

ANZLIC (2005) *ANZLIC's Vision: Strategic Plan 2005–2010*. Australia New Zealand Land Information Council. http://www.anzlic.org.au/about_ANZLIC_strategic2005–2010.html

ANZLIC (2006) *Glossary of Spatial Information Related Terms*. ANZLIC Spatial Information Council website. http://www.anzlic.org.au/glossary_terms.html.

APPSI (2006) *Realising the Value of Public Sector Information: Annual Report 2006*. Norwich: Advisory Panel on Public Sector Information.

Baltimore County (2001) 'Cost benefit geographic information systems', *Baltimore County Office for Information Technology Business Application Unit Geographic Information Systems,* November.

Barr, R. and Masser, I. (1996) 'The economic nature of geographic information: a theoretical perspective', *Proceedings of the GIS Research UK 1996 Conference.*

Birchler, U. and Bütler, M. (2007) *Information Economics*. London: Routledge.

Booz Allen Hamilton (2005) *Geospatial Interoperability Return on Investment Study*. Washington, DC: National Aeronautics and Space Administration, Geospatial Interoperability Office.

Bryson, J. (2001) 'Value and performance in the IT society', *Proceedings of ALIA 2000 Conference, Capitalising on knowledge: The information profession in the 21st century*, 24–26 October 2000, Australian Library and Information Association. http://conferences.alia.org.au/alia2000/proceedings/jo.bryson1.html

Castelein, W.T., Bregt, A.K. and Pluijmers, Y. (2009) 'The economic value of the Dutch geo-information sector', *International Journal of Spatial Data Infrastructure Research*, (5): 58–76.

CIE (2000) *Scoping the Business Case for SDI Development*. Canberra: Centre for International Economics.

Communities and Local Government (2008a) 'Why place matters and implications for the role of central', *Regional and Local Government, Economic Paper 2*. London: Communities and Local Government Publications.

Communities and Local Government (2008b) *Place Matters: The Location Strategy for the United Kingdom*. London: Communities and Local Government Publications. http://www.communities.gov.uk/publications/communities/locationstrategy.

Craglia, M. and Campagna, M. (2010) 'Advanced regional SDIs in Europe: Comparative cost–benefit evaluation and impact assessment perspectives', *International Journal of Spatial Data Infrastructure Research*. 5: 145–167.

Crompvoets, J., de Man, E. and Geudens, T. (2010) 'Value of spatial data: Networked performance beyond economic rhetoric', *International Journal of Spatial Data Infrastructure Research*. 5: 96–119.

DEFRA (2009) *UK Location Information Infrastructure Blueprint*. London: Department for Environment, Food and Rural Affairs Publications.

Environment Agency (2003) *Contribution to the Extended Impact Assessment of INSPIRE*, Craglia, Max and INSPIRE FDS Working Group (eds), Environment Agency England and Wales, 24 September 2003.

EU (2007) *Directive 2007/2/EC of the European Parliament and of the Council of 14 March 2007 establishing an Infrastructure for Spatial Information in the European Community (INSPIRE), 25 April 2007*. Luxembourg: Official Journal of the European Union.

Genovese, E., Roche, S., Caron, C. and Feick, R. (2009) 'The ecogeo cookbook for the assessment of geographic information value', *International Journal of Spatial Data Infrastructure Research*. 5: 120–144.

GeoConnections (2008) *The Dissemination of Government Geographic Data in Canada: Guide to Best Practices, version 2*. Ottawa: GeoConnections Canada.

Geoscience Australia (2002) *House of Representatives Standing Committee Inquiry into Resources Exploration Impediments – Submission by Geoscience Australia, July 2002*. Canberra: Geoscience Australia.

Halsing, D., Theisen, K. and Bernknopf, R. (2004) *A Cost-Benefit Analysis of the National Map, Circular 1271*. Reston, VA: US Dept. of the Interior, US Geological Survey.

Hardwick, P. and Fox, B. (1999) *Study of Potential Benefits of GIS for Large Fire Incident Management*, 10 February 1999. USDA Forest Service by Pacific Meridian Resources.

Hirshleifer, J. and Riley, J.G. (1979). 'The analytics of uncertainty and information – an expository survey', *Journal of Economic Literature*, 17(4/12): 1375–421.

Joffe, B. and Bacastow, T. (2005) 'Geodata access while managing digital rights: The open data consortium's reference model', *URISA Journal*, under review.

Krek, A. (2002) 'An agent-based model for quantifying the economic value of geographic information', PhD Dissertation, Institute for Geoinformation, Technical University Vienna. http://ftp.geoinfo.tuwien.ac.at/krek/krekPhD2002.zip.

Krek, A. (2003) 'What are transaction costs and why do they matter', *Proceedings of 6th AGILE Conference*, 24–26 April 2003, Lyon.

Krek, A. and Frank, A.U. (2000) 'The economic value of geo-information', *Geo-Informations-Systeme– Journal for Spatial Information and Decision Making*, 13(3): 10–12.

Krek, P. A. (2009) 'Methodology for measuring the demand geoinformation transaction costs: Based on experiments in Berlin, Vienna and Zurich', *International Journal of Spatial Data Infrastructure Research*. 5: 168–193.

Larousse (1997) *Larousse English Dictionary*. Larousse CD.

Lash, S. (2002) *Critique of Information*. London: Sage.

Longhorn, R. (2007) *Report on Cost-Benefit Analysis Methodologies, MOTIIVE Project Deliverable D11*. European Commission. http://www.iode.org/marinexml/files/Motiive_D11a_CBAReport_R2r0.pdf.

Longhorn, R. and Blakemore, M. (2007) *Geographic Information: Value, Pricing, Production and Consumption*. Boca Raton, FL: CRC Press.

Longley, P., Goodchild, M., Maguire, D. and Rhind, D. (2001) *Geographic Information Systems and Science*. Chichester: Wiley & Sons.

Macauley, M.K. (2005) *The Value of Information: A Background Paper on Measuring The Contribution of Space-Derived Earth Science Data to National Resource Management, Rff Dp 5–26*. Washington, DC: Resources for the Future (RFF).

Macauley, M.K., Maher, J. and Shih, J.S (2010) 'From science to applications: Determinants of diffusion in the use of earth observations', *RFF DP 10–03*, Washington, DC: Resources for the Future (RFF).

McCall, J.J. (ed.) (1982) *The Economics of Information and Uncertainty*. Chicago, IL: University of Chicago Press.

NASCIO (2008) *Governance of Geospatial Resources: Where's the Data? Show Me – Maximizing the Investment in State Geospatial Resources*. Lexington, KY: National Association of State Chief Information Officers. http://www.nascio.org/publications/documents/NASCIO-GovernanceGeospatialResources.pdf. (accessed October 14, 2010).

Navarra, D. (2009) 'Understanding geo-ICT and their value for public sector governance: Implications for e-government policy', *International Journal of Spatial Data Infrastructure Research*, under review.

Oelschlager, F. (2004) 'Enterprise information integration: Enabling the information value chain to achieve business optimization', paper presented at Primavera 21st Annual Conference, 3–6 October 2004, New Orleans, Louisiana.

OFT (2006) *The Commercial Use of Public Information (CUPI)*. London: Office of Fair Trading.

OMB (2005) *Enterprise Architecture Assessment Framework Version 1.5, May 2005*, Office of Management and Budget, FEA Program Management Office, Washington, DC.

OPSI (2008) *The United Kingdom Report on the Re-use of Public Sector Information 2008*. London (Kew): Office of Public Sector Information.

OXERA (1999) *The Economic Contribution of Ordnance Survey GB*. Oxford: Oxford Economic Research Associates.

Phillips, R.L. (2001) 'The management information value chain', *Perspectives*, issue 3.

PIRA (2000) *Commercial Exploitation of Europe's Public Sector Information – Executive Summary and Final Report*. PIRA International Ltd and Univ. of East Anglia for the European Commission, D.G.: Information Society, September 20 2000. Luxembourg: Office of Official Publications CEC.

Pluijmers, Y. and Weiss, P. (2001) *Borders in Cyberspace: Conflicting Government Information Policies and their Economic Impacts*. Washington, DC: PricewaterhouseCoopers for National Weather Service.

Porter, M. (1985) *Competitive Advantage*. New York: The Free Press.

Price Waterhouse (1995) *Australian Land and Geographic Data Infrastructure Benefits Study*. Australia New Zealand Land Information Council (ANZLIC).

Rydzak, F., Obersteiner, M. and Kraxner, F. (2010) 'Impact of Global Earth Observation – Systemic View across GEOSS Societal Benefit Areas', *International Journal of Spatial Data Infrastructure Research*. http://ijsdir.jrc.ec.europa.eu/index.php/ijsdir/article/download/170/208 (accessed October 14, 2010).

Shapiro, C. and Varian, H. (1999) *Information Rules*. Boston, MA: Harvard Business School Press.

Spataro, J. and Crow, B. (2002) 'A framework for understanding the information management market', *The Gilbane Report*. Cambridge, MA: Bluebill Advisors.

US Federal Highway Administration (1998) 'Value of information and information services, publication no. FHWA-SA-99–038, volpe national transportation systems center'. Washington, DC: US Department of Transportation, Research and Special Programs Administration. http://www.fhwa.dot.gov/reports/viiscov.htm#toc (accessed October 14, 2010).

Van Loenen, B. (2006) *Developing Geographic Information Infrastructures*. Delft: Delt University Press.

Van Loenen, B. and Zevenbergen, J. (2010) 'Assessing geographic information enhancement', *International Journal of Spatial Data Infrastructure Research*. 5: 244–266.

Wehn de Montalvo, U., van de Kar, E. and F. Maitland, C. (2004) 'Resource-based interdependencies in value networks for mobile internet services', *ACM International Conference Proceeding Series; vol. 60*, Proceedings of the 6th International Conference on Electronic Commerce.

Weiss, P. (2002) *Borders in Cyberspace: Conflicting Public Sector Information Policies and their Economic Impacts: Summary Report*. Washington, DC: National Weather Service.

24

Geovisualization of Spatial Equity

Emily Talen

INTRODUCTION

Geovisualization of spatial equity is of key importance because it communicates a fundamental concept in relatively straightforward, easily recognized terms: who has access to things and who does not. To the degree that people can relate access to goods, services, and environmental hazards in a spatial (mapped) way, geovisualization quickly reveals the implications of the varying patterns of distribution found to exist across the urban landscape. One can visualize quite readily whether poor people are living near environmental hazards, or whether people of a particular class or race seem to have a higher number of public goods in their neighborhoods. The power of visualization, as revealed in the work and writings of Edward Tufte (1983, 1997), can be an effective tool for addressing issues of social justice. Equity in geographic terms is fundamentally about access – not only who gets to live closer to desirable things, but also who has to live closer to undesirable things. While the

concept of access may be defined in terms of affordability, acceptability, availability, and spatial accessibility (Penchansky and Thomas, 1981, cited in Apparicio et al., 2008), this chapter focuses on spatial accessibility. Access in spatial equity terms is defined as the ability to reach a given destination based on geographic distance: locations that have desirable facilities or services close by are said to have better access than locations that have facilities and services far away. The geovisualization of these varying patterns of access gets to the heart of spatial equity. Importantly, it contributes to the public discussion of resource distribution issues, how access changes when inputted variables change, and what those variations mean for economic, social, and environmental health.

Whether or not the patterns observed are "equitable" requires an understanding of who has access to a particular good or service and who does not, and whether there is any systematic bias to these varying levels of access. Thus, in a distance-based analysis, the purpose of visualizing – that is, mapping – spatial equity might address the question of whether access to a particular good is discriminatory. Such inquiries might entail an examination of the extent to which there is a spatial pattern to varying levels of access, and whether that spatial pattern varies according to spatially defined socioeconomic patterns. This is especially important because, for locally oriented populations, that is, residents who rely on modes of transport other than the automobile (e.g., the elderly and the poor), accessibility to urban services may be more important because distance is not elastic (Wekerle, 1985).

Practically, the geovisualization of spatial equity relies on the visualization techniques embedded in geographic information systems (GIS). GIS is used to map distributions of (1) access to facilities and (2) socioeconomic characteristics or other factors that indicate level of need. Both are mapped in an interactive process using the techniques of exploratory spatial data analysis. The process often utilizes procedures in which dynamically linked windows allow the analyst to fully exploit the display capabilities of GIS (Anselin et al., 1993; Batty and Xie, 1994). The implementation is straightforward. All that is required is the necessary software: a standard GIS package capable of importing data and performing overlay functions, and a statistical package; locational information on any appropriate public facility or resource; and socioeconomic data such as population and housing characteristics, readily available in digital format from the census bureau or a local library. It is now fairly straightforward to have the data necessary to map varying patterns of access to resources – that is, social equity. At a minimum, needed data consists of three types: locations and characteristics of origins (places of residence), destinations (e.g., facilities, shopping, or employment), and the routes between them. Specific data requirements under each of these categories are determined based on what measurement factors are deemed important (or obtainable) for the analysis.

PRINCIPLES OF SPATIAL EQUITY

The achievement of equity in the distribution of public resources

The achievement of equity in the distribution of public resources is a goal of paramount importance. Deciding the distribution of benefits ("who gets what") and costs ("who pays") is something policymakers have a great deal of control over as they attempt to guide the allocation of scarce public resources. Equitable distribution entails locating resources or facilities so that as many different spatially defined social groups as possible benefit – that is, have access. It is inherently a geographic question (Hay, 1995).

The allocation of public resources was once termed the "hidden function of government" (Jones et al., 1980), but in the last several decades it has received increasing attention. Crompton and Lue (1992) attribute the change to judicial involvement (the oft-cited case of *Hawkins* v. *Town of Shaw*), the perception of scarcity, the increase in citizen action groups, improved techniques to evaluate benefits and costs, and a rising insistence that patrons bear some portion of delivery costs. Recent literature has investigated the increased government role in the analysis of access to public resources. For example, Higgs (2004) reviews the use of GIS-based measures of access to health care among government entities intent on increasing a "social justice policy agenda" (p. 119). Health organizations are also involved, participating in "mapping audits" of health service provision.

The complexities involved in the equitable allocation of public resources include not only methodology (how can equity be measured?), but also a multitude of value judgments about who should benefit, the nature of social justice, and the definition of political consensus. Measures have become more and more complex and nuanced, for example in the application of indices of "relative wellbeing" that are thought to more carefully account for inequalities (Albrecht and Ramasubramanian, 2004: 371). The stakes are high: since public resources are, in some sense, part of each individual's income, their spatial distribution directly affects the distribution of public welfare (Pahl, 1971; Harvey, 1973).

Considering these complexities, it is not surprising that distributional equity has, until recently, often been approached in a rather ad hoc fashion. Examples of distributive policy explicitly based on equity criteria, such as that in Savannah, Georgia (Toulmin, 1988) are not common. While there is an increase in the use of GIS tools to evaluate spatial equity, usually resources are distributed according to predefined standards such as per capita allocation (e.g., 1 acre of park land per 1000 residents) without conscious attention to distributional fairness. While such an approach minimizes the costs of decision making, it ignores the social geography of urban areas. Alternatively, resources may be allocated in response to political activism or the ability of neighborhood groups to mobilize support for a particular facility. While this method may appear superior to a unidimensional distributional standard, it rewards political savvy at the expense of legitimate need.

The question then arises: how can the spatial equity of public resource distribution be analyzed? There is a need, first, to recognize the distributional principles underlying any geographic arrangement of public resources. The use of maps can elucidate equity variation and perhaps demystify it. By analyzing the spatial incongruity between resource need and resource distribution, we can explicitly reveal the distributional choices being made about "who gets what." Revelations about who benefits, presented in visual, spatially oriented terms, enable communities to evaluate their distributional preferences and see whether or not they are in line with broader community goals and with notions of fairness.

The role of equity in resource distribution has engaged the efforts of a wide array of disciplines. It is possible to discuss both the definition and the measurement of equity, as well as empirical demonstrations of geographic variations in the accessibility of desired facilities.

An overview by Marsh and Schilling (1994) on the measurement of equity in facility location analysis lists the contributions of political scientists, sociologists, economists, geographers, and management scientists. Many divergent modes of analysis are discernible. Health care professionals are often interested in the degree to which access to healthcare is properly distributed not only to prevent health crises, but to ensure that overall population health is maintained (Guagliardo, 2004). Policy analysts discuss the morality of political choices in resource allocation, the preferred structure of government for fulfilling service needs, the fiscal requirements, and the administration of service production (Merget, 1979).

Much research has focused also on the political ramifications of planning for locally unwanted public facilities (sometimes criticized as "environmental racism"), which presents an entirely different set of impact assessment methodologies and locational strategies (Seley, 1983; White and Ratick, 1989; Chakraborty, 2001). Many researchers have investigated the relationship between minorities and low-income groups and unwanted environmental hazards. For example, Grineski et al. (2007) looked at the class and ethnic environmental injustices of air pollution, attributing the higher exposure to hazards suffered by marginalized populations. The relationship between air pollution levels and socioeconomic status is especially conducive to geovisualization, whereby the "critical equity interpretation of environmental policy" leads to an investigation of who is most benefiting from reductions in air pollutants (Buzzelli et al., 2003: 557). Other studies of the locations of environmental hazards and population sub-groups in a geovisualization framework include studies of chemical accidents (Derezinski et al., 2003), air toxic releases (Mennis and Jordan, 2005), and hazardous materials transport (Verter and Kara, 2001).

In the purest sense, equity can be achieved only after society has arrived at a consensus about what is fair. This state is virtually unattainable, however, since what one group

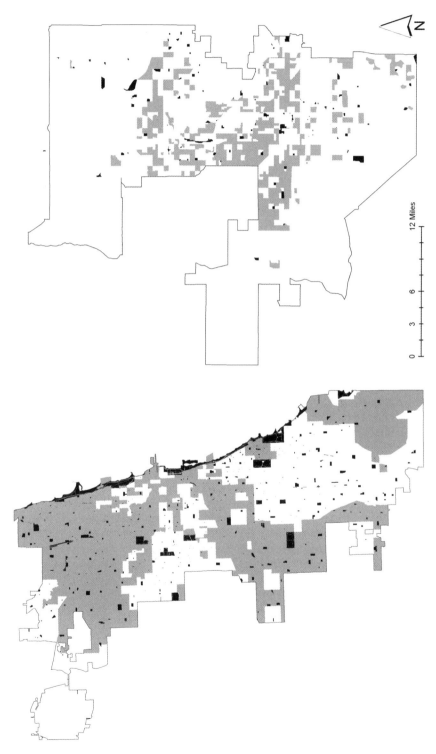

Figure 24.1 One distributional principle of spatial equity is to give areas with higher population density greater access to public resources, like parks. These maps of Phoenix and Chicago show little such relationship between parks (in black) and higher density areas (shaded).

deems equitable may be seen as inequitable by another (Harvey, 1996). In other words, many different definitions of equity could be operationalized in defining distributional equity. This is analogous to Arrow's impossibility theorem (1951), which showed that a community welfare function cannot be logically derived. It is also important to note the conflicts inherent in equity definitions: for example, how social equity conflicts with territorial justice (Pinch, 1985), and how equity in risk distribution conflicts with equity in access to services (Humphreys, 1988). There is also the complicating factor of political intent. Staeheli (1989) has analyzed the reasons for providing services in certain locations in terms of their ability to maintain the legitimacy of capitalism. Indeed, the multidimensionality of equity in providing services or facilities takes on many different political, social, cultural, and economic implications.

Four conceptions of spatial equity

The provision of resources according to locational equity has been variously interpreted. Lucy (1981) identified five categories of equity that are relevant to planning for local services. Subsequent taxonomies relevant to planning have been offered by Crompton and Wicks (1988), Truelove (1993), and Marsh and Schilling (1994). At least four separate categories are distinguishable. In the first category, equitable distribution is defined as equality, in which everyone receives the same public benefit, regardless of socioeconomic status, willingness or ability to pay, or other criteria; residents receive either equal input or equal benefits, regardless of need. In the second category, equity in the distribution of public benefits can be according to need, termed "compensatory" equity by Crompton and Wicks (1988). This is often the starting point of equity distribution. Lucy (1981) refers to this as "unequal treatment of unequals," which is based on indicators such as poverty and race, and ideally would factor in the nature of the benefit.

Definitions of need will vary depending on the resource being analyzed. In the study of public transport equity, for example, need may be based on choice constraints in combination with the level of existing transportation and the dispersion of services (Murray and Davis, 2001). Often equity distribution based on need is a matter of matching resources and facilities to target populations. Toronto, for example, has used geovisualization methods to evaluate HIV service providers relative to target populations (Fulcher and Kaukinen, 2005). Montreal has been evaluated for its ability to spatially connect food supermarkets to socially deprived areas, or to those who could benefit most from having access to food retailers (Apparicio et al., 2007). Savannah, Georgia, is one of the few places that has acted on the geovisualization of spatial resources to direct city resources into the neighborhoods judged to be "the worst off" (Toulmin, 1988). These efforts can be seen as forebears of the notion of equity planning – a procedure for mitigating the inequity of class distinctions – which has been promulgated through the writings of Norman Krumholz (1975, 1982), and more recently by Krumholz and Forester (1990).

The third category is the equitable distribution of services or facilities according to demand. Demand may be conceptualized as economic (demonstrated use) or political ("vociferous advocacy"; see Crompton and Lue, 1992). Distribution based on demand could be interpreted as a matter of surveying the spatial distributions of specific kinds of facilities and matching those distributions to the specific populations who need access to them, but it is not always clear that such a spatial match is actually occurring, or actually satisfying demand. For example, a study of access to the services needed by public housing residents, based on mapping levels of demand and need, concluded that almost half of public housing residents were not having their demands met (Apparicio and Seguin, 2006). Perhaps more often, active participation in distributive decisions is "rewarded" by increased user benefit, and low-income populations may be less likely to participate in any kind of decision-making capacity. This is not particularly good for spatial equity, since the determination of access may be based on nothing more than "squeaky wheels". The distributional outcome based on demand differs sharply from need-based distributions. For example, Mladenka and Hill (1977) concluded that according to the demand criterion, library location patterns should favor wealthier neighborhoods, since consumption is higher there. A need-based criterion would produce an entirely different equitable arrangement.

Finally, equitable distribution can be defined by market criteria that use the cost of the service as a key factor in distribution. In particular, willingness to pay may be operationalized, in which case the equitable distribution of services is defined according to the degree to which people use (and therefore pay for) a particular service. Alternatively, allocation may be based on the amount of taxes paid or on least cost (on the basis of lower land costs, for example). Applying this approach summons up the conflict between efficiency and equity, which pits aggregate quantities of services (output) against considerations of who the beneficiaries are. It is unlikely that distributions based on efficiency can be made to coincide with need-based distributions.

The need-based distributional standard is probably most germane to the geovisualization of spatial equity. First, although the concept of need can be entirely relative, involving individual assessments of deprivation (Harvey, 1973), it is nevertheless valid to characterize need on the basis of the socioeconomic characteristics of the population, and in fact this has become fairly established practice in the geographic literature. The data to obtain this kind of assessment is becoming widely available, especially given that the characterization of equity can be accomplished easily from census data, and easily evaluated in a GIS framework. In contrast, the determination of equity based on demand or market considerations relies on data that may not be readily available or easily interpreted. For example, without rigorous analysis of constituency preferences and demonstrated use surveys (which are beyond the means of many government agencies), or knowing where people with special health needs like HIV are spatially located, achieving equitable distribution as defined by demand is not likely.

On a more conceptual level, defining equity without regard to socioeconomic status may offer equality of opportunity, but leaves in place the inequalities of the existing social structure. Equity, by contrast, is now readily perceived to be related to offsetting the burdens imposed by unchecked "free" market economies, and one approach to this is to administer territorial equity in a compensatory way. Geovisualization of spatial equity, as now emerging in the literature, is virtually synonymous with a need-based approach.

THE IMPORTANCE OF ACCESS

As already mentioned, consideration of spatial equity issues revolves largely around the evaluation of access (Talen, 1998). The issue is one of who has access to a particular good or service and who does not, and whether there is any pattern to these varying levels of access. As discussed above, in a distance-based analysis, the purpose of research on access might address the question of whether access to a particular good is discriminatory. Such inquiries might entail an examination of the extent to which there is a spatial pattern to varying levels of access, and whether that spatial pattern varies according to spatially defined socioeconomic patterns. This is also important because, for locally oriented populations – residents who rely on modes of transport other than the automobile (e.g., the elderly and the poor) – accessibility to urban services may be more important because distance is not elastic (Wekerle, 1985).

Elevating the role of spatial accessibility is closely tied to the view that settlement patterns should increase access between humans, their places of work, and the services they require. In this regard, accessibility is not conceptualized as an issue of private mobility, but is refashioned as a community-wide public problem. This is why spatial equity in accessibility to resources has a close working relationship to the principles of smart growth, sustainable urbanism, new urbanism, livable cities, and related notions in which pedestrian access to daily life needs is viewed as essential.

All of these social and environmental movements are tied to the idea that quality of access and its ability to promote the integration of activities is a basic component of good urban form (see in particular Jacobs, 1961; Lynch, 1981; Jacobs and Appleyard, 1987; Duany and Plater-Zyberk, 1991). Most notably, Kevin Lynch (1981) held "access" as a key component of his theory of ideal urban form. In the broadest sense, Lynch argued that access could be used as a measure of "settlement performance" (i.e., a measure of what makes a "good" city) by factoring in (1) the feature to which access is being given and (2) the person receiving access. From these basic categories, Lynch delineated a large number of additional complexities, for example, the flow of information, access variation by time and season, the fact that access is not always a quantity to be maximized, the need to be able to shut off the flow of access, perception of access, and the benefits of moving to as well as arriving at a given destination. More recently, New Urbanists have developed a specific town planning manifesto (Congress of the New Urbanism, 2000) based on enhancing access at the level of region (by promoting a variety of transportation alternatives), metropolis (by promoting compact urban form), and neighborhood (by promoting mixed uses and housing density).

Of course, there are also factors working against the idea that accessibility is a crucial goal. Notably, there is recognition of the fact that physical distance is lessening in importance, that technology is lessening the need for centered settlements, and that low-density dispersed development is merely the inevitable outcome of the post-Fordist urbanization process (Feldman and Jaffe, 1992; Dueker, 1996; Bruegmann, 2005). With the emphasis on information technology and digital methods of social connection, the idea of access may be downplayed as tangential, despite the importance of pedestrian-oriented access for those who lack mobility (the elderly and disabled, the poor, working parents). The downplaying of physical access may mean that access is not deemed relevant, or that market forces are deemed too difficult to overcome. In practice, the role of accessibility in transportation planning has sometimes taken a back seat to concepts such as congestion reduction, although there is recognition that accessibility ought to be about maximizing land use and transportation choices (Levine, 1998), and that changes to transportation systems have profound consequences for environmental justice (Chakraborty et al., 1999).

Accessibility as the key to understanding spatial equity

We can visualize spatial equity by looking at just two aspects of access: the ability to reach urban places, and the quantity and quality of places that can be reached. Together, these two aspects provide a powerful indicator of urban access – and constitute the geovisualization of spatial equity. The approach relies on the power of maps and the visualization of quantitative data to allow conclusions to be made about how access varies across the urban landscape. Exploration of this data in a visual way is an important tool for making comparisons about the urban pattern, and for assessing the degree to which places are geographically equitable.

Some have advocated an interactive, participatory approach to the exploration of these issues, and this fits well with the notion that geovisualization of equity is, increasingly, an essential tool used by local government for planning the distribution of resources. Urban planners often find it useful to evaluate proposed (i.e., planned) as well as achieved distributional patterns (Talen, 1996). Analyzing the "equity map" of proposed plans reveals the distributional preferences of a community. Understanding changing levels of access has become an important part of decision support tools used in local government planning. Examples include "Community Viz," developed by the Orton Family Foundation, and "Index," a software tool developed by Criterion Planners of Portland, Oregon. Both use indicators to measure the conditions and performance of communities, including the geographic distribution of services and facilities relative to various populations. Such approaches may not be as ideal as survey-based approaches, since plans quickly become outdated, and distributions shown in plans do not necessarily reflect constituent preferences adequately. However, to the extent that plans are developed to reflect community intent, they are a useful proxy for community preference. Comparing planned accessibility patterns (based on the planned distribution of facilities) with actual (achieved) accessibility patterns offers insights into the achievement of equity goals.

Outside of the planning field, GIS-based mapping tools have been developed for health professionals who seek to evaluate varying levels of exposure to environmental factors. Environmental risk factors and their associated health outcomes are interactively displayed for health professionals to allow them to "integrate environmental health assessment skills into their professional practices" (Choi et al., 2006: 381). Related to this, Ghose and Huxhold (2002) investigated the use of GIS-based neighborhood indicators to assist with the examination of neighborhood conditions in inner-city areas. Interactive use of a "multi-scalar" approach to monitoring neighborhood conditions is a way to keep tabs on deteriorating conditions and better understand the geographic range of services and facilities distribution.

MEASURING ACCESS

The basic methodological approach to the geovisualization of spatial equity is to map both the distribution of accessibility measures and the distribution of socioeconomic data in such a way that spatial variation in access can be scrutinized. This method is essentially spatial univariate, bivariate, or multivariate analysis, which analyzes the mapped distribution of spatial patterns in order to characterize spatial association. Most commonly, indicators of socioeconomic status are mapped relative to access (high or low access) as a way of discovering any indication of distributional bias.

Essentially, deriving a measurement standard for the spatial equity of resource distribution depends on the definition of equity being used, and how it is measured. If equity is predicated on expansion of choice for disadvantaged groups, measurement methods will focus on access to facilities by spatially distinct socioeconomic groups. Assuming that the location of these groups can be agreed upon – for example, from census data – the task for communities is to agree upon how to measure access.

Accessibility can be measured in a variety of ways. At one end of the spectrum, accessibility measures can be based on random utility theory, where access is based on the desirability or utility of a set of destination choices for an individual (Handy and Niemeier, 1997). Another similar approach uses travel diaries of individuals to estimate "personal accessibility," based on daily movement patterns (Kwan, 1999). At the other end of the spectrum, accessibility is characteristic of place. Ultimately, how access is measured should be based on how the measure is to be used. For the visualization of spatial equity, it may make sense to focus on the measurement of "place-based" accessibility – a measure that serves as a characteristic of a place. This conceptualization of access carries with it a number of variations. These variations have been discussed more extensively in Lucy (1981),

Pacione (1989), Handy and Niemeier (1997), Talen (1998), and Hewko et al. (2002).

A study by Knox (1978) was perhaps one of the earliest examples of how mapped accessibility patterns can be used to assess the equity of resource distribution. Using several gravity-based measures of proximity to urban services, Knox demonstrated how they could be used as indicators of social well-being in cities. Territorial variations in opportunity were assessed in terms of proximity to urban resources, in order to obtain an overall measure of "relative personal accessibility" to be used for comparisons. An isometric map was produced that indicated the relative levels of access to a specific urban service (in this case, medical care).

One of the most widely used measurement methods is known as the "container" approach, which is simply a count of the number of facilities within a given area such as a census tract, political district, or municipal boundary. Related to this, the "covering" approach, sometimes referred to as the "cumulative opportunities" of a given location, counts the number of facilities within a given spatial unit or range. It has been used in many different applications, since the straightforward approach of counting up the number of facilities or services in a given area is conceptually simple (and therefore easily understood). The basic approach to mapping spatial equity was demonstrated by Truelove (1993). To demonstrate how spatial equity is evaluated, Truelove presented several maps showing regions of Toronto that are not "covered" by day-care facilities. He then compared the socioeconomic characteristics of the areas with divergent spatial proximities, to characterize distributional bias. Counting the number of opportunities within a defined range of a particular facility can identify regions that are locationally advantaged (or disadvantaged) (see also Toulmin, 1988).

More complex formulations can be included depending on how the indices are constructed and weighted (Albrecht and Ramasubramanian, 2004). Alternatively,

a "minimum distance" approach measures access as the distance to the nearest facility (often used in research on access to health care services), whereas the "travel cost" approach calculates the distance (cost) between an origin and all included destinations (often the preferred method for calculating access to amenities such as parks within a city). Using the basic idea of "proximity as a measure of access," Lindsey et al. (2001) looked at the equality of access between urban greenways and population groups, finding that "minorities and the poor have disproportionate access to trails."

Another option is to use the gravity "potential" measure, where facilities are weighted by their size (or other characteristic) and adjusted for the frictional effect of distance. Pacione (1989) examined differences in access to secondary schools by compiling mapped indices of access using a gravity-based model, whereby the author revealed different "undulating" surfaces that could be used as a basis for comparing the effects of school closings on access. In addition to visual comparison of spatial variation, Pacione derived an overall coefficient of variation, by which the aggregate effect of different spatial patterns of facilities can be compared. The socioeconomic characteristics of the neighborhoods that fared better and those that fared worse, in terms of facility provision, were presented to reveal any underlying patterns of distributional bias. Geertman and Ritsema Van Eck (1995) also showed how to produce maps of "potential surfaces," using the gravity potential method of measuring accessibility. Although socioeconomic variables were not included, the authors showed how the maps can be used to visually identify, for example, potential building sites with adequate public transport.

Some researchers have compared the results of using multiple access measures. Brabyn and Gower (2004), for example, compared the ratio, least-cost path and allocation methods to compare how the interpretation of access to medical providers changes. Luo and Wang (2003) synthesized two accessibility measures, a gravity-based method and a floating catchment area method, to analyze accessibility to health care in a GIS-based visual assessment.

A primary issue to be decided is: what characterization of access is most suitable? Largely, this boils down to a decision about how distance between the user and the facility should be characterized. If evaluating access to amenities, the value of the facility to the user declines with distance. If the analysis concerns emphasizing the effect of distance as a deterrent, then the gravity model may be appropriate. Alternatively, it may be appropriate to compare access to facilities as an average of all distances to all facilities (travel cost measure), which treats the resources of a city as a complete package of public goods. If the goal is to assess how to minimize the inequality of nearest distance between origin and destination, then a minimum distance measure may be applied. Finally, if the goal is to maximize the number of people "covered," and if it is decided that beyond a given radius, users acquire no benefit, then a covering approach may be warranted.

If the purpose of access measurement is for determining neighborhood service provision, "covering" and "minimum distance" are probably the most appropriate. This is because the access at that scale essentially revolves around two concepts of access: how far does one have to walk to reach a destination, and second, how many urban opportunities are within walking distance? For the first question, minimum distance is measured between some point of origin (such as a block centroid) and the point location of the given facility. For the second question, a covering radius is drawn around the point of origin, and the number of facilities within walking distance, is determined.

For each measurement approach, there are a number of different measurement factors that have to be considered. As a first step in the analysis of urban access, points of origin have to be selected. This could range from point locations of individual housing units on a parcel, to centroids of larger geographic units (e.g., blocks, block groups, or tracts). An obvious issue in this selection is the potential introduction of aggregation error that results when a single point is chosen to represent an entire area. At a minimum, researchers will need to address the problem of ecological fallacy and the modifiable areal unit problem (MAUP). Hewko et al. looked at spatial accessibility for neighborhoods and found that the measures used were "susceptible to numerous methodological problems" (2002: 1185), particularly when the amenity being investigated had many locations.

Another fundamental issue has to do with obtaining resident attributes for the analysis. If the goal of the analysis is social equity analysis – involving a determination of need – analysts will want to consider the socioeconomic characteristics of a population in looking at access, since such information allows some assumptions to be made about both level of need as well as transport mode choice. Mode choice factors into the accessibility equation. For example, it is likely that residents in poorer areas are more dependent on public transit, have lower access to private automobiles, and therefore require greater access. Even though distance is the most critical factor in determinations of access when the goal of evaluation is assessment of urban spatial pattern (regardless of mode of transport), it is prudent to factor in that for poorer areas, there is a higher distance decay factor, access is not elastic, and lower levels of accessibility are particularly detrimental.

Generally speaking, the greater the level of disaggregation of data, the higher the level of precision in measuring access. Thus individual parcels may be most appropriate for analyzing urban spatial patterns and, visualizing pattern of spatial equity. However, the disadvantage with using parcel level data is that socioeconomic attributes are not easily obtained for a given parcel. If a census geographic entity is used, such as a block, block group, or tract, socioeconomic characteristics for that block can be used in the assessment of spatial equity (this aspect of analyzing accessibility is discussed in more detail below). While it is possible to interpolate characteristics of a given census region to a lower level of aggregation such as land parcel, this approach engenders the ecological inference problem, and can be invalid (King, 1997). The problem has to do with reconstructing individual behavior from aggregate data. Specifically, it is not always valid to attribute a characteristic measured for an entire geographic area to an individual residing in that area.

Thus the trade-off to be made is this: if smaller geographic units are used, the locations are known, but the characteristics of the individuals within those locations can only be assumed. If larger census geography such as the tract is used, individual locations are compromised by using centroid locations, but socioeconomic characteristics can be determined.

Another measurement factor to consider is the determination of destinations. This involves determining what qualities in an urban environment are important to have access to. Obvious categories would be employment, public amenities, such as parks, healthcare facilities, and shopping opportunities. Often the best data for characterizing facilities is parcel-level data, or data at the level of an individual building or street address. Fortunately, parcel-level data that includes the primary use of the parcel is available in many cities from the tax assessor's office.

The amount, type, and quality of a given destination could also be factored in, and some of this data (such as size or square footage) may be available from the tax assessor. It should be noted that some consideration of the relevance of these characteristics is warranted, since different socioeconomic groups have different sets of destination opportunities, either because of their perception of access or because of monetary or cultural constraints (Hanson and Schwab, 1986).

Mode of travel and travel route characteristics are also elements that could be factored

in. If bicycle access is being considered, factors that affect the route include topography, design speed, bike lane width, and number of lanes of traffic. For pedestrian access, perceived safety, sidewalk quality and width, parking, and traffic volume are important factors. Such factors, and their affect on walking and accessibility, have been researched extensively in the past few years as part of an effort to evaluate the built environment for health effects (Greenwald and Boarnet, 2001; Moudon and Lee, 2003). Tools such as the Bradshaw Walkability Index (Urban Quality Communications, 1999) use criteria such as density, off-street parking places, "sitting spots," and sidewalk "dips" at each driveway to measure the walkability of an area. In the past decade a number of tools for measuring walkability have been developed and these can be useful in measuring access for the purpose of visualizing spatial equity (Livi and Klifton, 2004).

Travel route characteristics are readily incorporated in a GIS-based analysis, most likely as weights that quantify the walkability of a given street segment. A significant drawback to their use is that detailed data about walkability factors, such as sidewalk quality, requires significant human resources to obtain, since reliable data require extensive field work that needs to be continually updated. One possible remedy to this problem is the use of high-resolution remotely sensed images or aerial photography. The finer geographic resolutions required to assess things like sidewalk width and quality are becoming more widely available.

Measuring the distance between two spatial locations can be based on several different metrics. First, a route can be based on the shortest straight-line distance between destination and origin ("Euclidean distance"). This is straightforward, but may not approximate actual travel routes very accurately. A second approach is to calculate distance along an existing street network, factoring in such attributes as street direction. A major disadvantage of this approach is that it can be very computationally intensive. A third option is to compute distances within a spatial framework – not along a street network but using an approximation of one. This can be justified if the area being analyzed is covered by a fairly dense street network, and thus distance can be approximated fairly readily. This approach also has the advantage of being much less computationally intensive. One way to calculate distance using a spatial framework rather than a network is to calculate distance based on either latitude/longitude locations ("arc distance"), or Manhattan block distance. The latter computes distances between two locations such that the distance between origin and destination is measured along a grid that approximates a street network.

Once the distances are computed, either along a street network or using arc, Euclidean or Manhattan distance, the access measure can be computed. There are several options available for computing the distances between origins and destinations. First, if a street network is available, GIS software such as ArcGIS can be used. In the case of the former, there is an extension that can be run to compute distances between multiple origins and destinations. The procedure is very straightforward. The user is prompted to enter two layers representing origins and destinations, in addition to a network coverage consisting ideally of streets. Of course, the computational requirements can be very large if parcel-level data is used. Even for a small city, the number of origins and destinations can run into the thousands, and for larger cities, hundreds of thousands. However, the procedure itself is straightforward.

A third option is to use GeoDa software (Anselin et al., 2006), which computes distances between locations based on their latitude/longitude coordinates. With locational data inputted as an ASCII file for two sets of points, GeoDa computes the distance between each origin and each destination by either calculating the Euclidean distance, the arc distance (in which the curvature of the Earth is accounted for), or the Manhattan distance (measured along a grid).

METHODOLOGICAL ISSUES

If spatial equity is more widely defined as the quality of having interaction with, or passage to, a particular good, service, or facility, the visualization of spatial equity opens up a wider range of conceptual and methodological issues. There is the emerging view that spatial equity must be redefined for the information age, whereby many transactions take place in virtual as opposed to physical space or some hybrid form. There is also the view that spatial equity need not be based on distances between two or more locations in space, but may instead be based on social factors, cultural barriers, or ineffective design. For example, there may be barriers to access based on whether or not an individual possesses a certain subjectively defined level of "citizenship" (Staeheli and Thompson, 1997). Access to public spaces like parks may be severely limited by social and cultural boundaries as opposed to physical ones (Mitchell, 2003).

Methodologically, this makes the visualization of spatial equity quite complex, depending on how it is to be used. For example, it may be necessary to factor in the interaction effects of age, ability, or perception of environmental safety in order to accurately account for individual behavior and how it in turn effects notions of spatial equity. Another complication is that not everyone agrees that physical (i.e., distance based) accessibility is essential for maintaining spatial equity, viewing it instead as an inevitable outcome of urbanization processes.

Finally, while the measurement of access does not have to be methodologically complex, there are conceptual issues raised by the notion of quantifying access as a measure of urban quality. Quantified measures can seem arbitrary, entailing a false sense of precision that can be misused. Quantification in measuring access necessarily sets up the problem of defining spatial areas and boundaries, thus arbitrarily dissecting the urban pattern into zones that are "in" or "out."

These are difficulties that must be acknowledged. Yet the value of evaluating access quantitatively remains, for several reasons. First, the political reality of spatial equity is that people respond to numbers because they are an efficient and direct way to make evaluations. This is particularly true in the evaluation of urban quality (and thus urban quality indicators are largely quantitative). Second, the approach used in the evaluation of access depends fundamentally on relative measurement; that is, the numbers derived provide a way to critically assess whether one area has better access than another. The ability to make relative judgments is an important aspect of visualizing spatial equity. Third, the quantified measure of access entails different parameters that can be varied, thereby facilitating different approaches for how access is conceptualized. It is thus possible to legitimize the use of quantified measures in the evaluation of spatial equity by emphasizing flexibility in approach, exploration and visualization of data, and continually bearing in mind the limitations involved in quantified approaches.

Despite these complexities and doubts, spatial equity and its visualization remain tied to the physical urban pattern, as reflected in a wide range of ongoing urban scholarship. Studies of public service provision hold increasing relevance as society becomes more spatially segregated and more unequal. And if the level of spatial equity is mostly a result of increasing or decreasing physical accessibility, or maximizing land-use and transportation choices for certain groups, the visualization of these patterns and how they vary across space will produce highly relevant insights with explicit policy implications.

INTERPRETING SPATIAL EQUITY

Once variations in spatial access have been measured and mapped, it is necessary to establish a framework for interpreting the results. A framework for geovisualization could be organized as a series of questions to be answered. For example, looking at the accessibility patterns of an urban area, one could structure the analysis in terms of three main evaluative questions. How accessible is the city, overall? Who in the city has good access and who does not? And, do areas with higher access need to have higher access?

The initial question to be answered is whether, in general, an urban environment is performing well in terms of access – for example, just how accessible are its blocks and neighborhoods to urban amenities and services? How well does the city measure up in terms of a minimum standard of access? While many factors affect travel behavior, how supportive is the spatial structure to begin with? The answer to these questions provides an interesting basis with which to evaluate the urban pattern.

Obviously, in order for such information to be meaningful, it is necessary to establish some standards against which the citywide access data can be evaluated. Lynch (1981) stressed the need to set minimum standards for accessibility and to use a variety of measures that take into account population need and other factors. One standard of relevance is the willingness and ability of residents to reasonably walk to their destinations. There is some variation, but the walking distance parameter is usually defined as ¼ to ½ mile (Congress for the New Urbanism, 2000), depending on what the specific destination is and the resulting frictional effect of distance (less for certain destinations since people are willing to walk further for some types of uses).

The application of standards is just one way to evaluate citywide access. There are at least three other approaches to assessing how well a city is performing in terms of access: by time – have the figures changed over time, and in what direction? By place – how do the computed measures compare to other cities? By population – how do the figures compare to the population needs of the city as a whole? The third measure requires making some assessment of the accessibility needs of the population. This can be done by, for example, calculating the percentage of children, elderly, or poor in the area under study, and making the assumption that, at a minimum, the percentage of accessible blocks should be similar to the percentage of the population that could be characterized as having a high need for access. This is a fairly basic representation, but it can be an effective way of beginning the task of evaluating access in a city-wide sense.

The second main question has to do with intra-urban variation – determining what kind of variation exists in access levels for different parts of the metropolitan area. The purpose of such an investigation is to identify areas with more versus less access, such that relative comparisons of access can be made. This kind of inquiry is more conducive to geovisualization methods.

The question is fairly simple: how much overall variation in access is there? Even without considering population parameters, what kind of dissimilarity exists? Is it highly skewed in different directions, or is there an even distribution? What parts of the city fare better? This is not always intuitively obvious. For example, denser downtown areas would seem to offer the greatest access to retail facilities, but some densely populated inner city areas lack essential retail services.

One appropriate metric for visualizing intra-urban variation is to assess variation by neighborhood. This can be accomplished by constructing a neighborhood index, the results of which can be mapped to look at spatial variation. One example is an index used by Murray and Davis (2001), who used the following notation:

τ_i = the neighborhood index, equal to the percentage of the block groups (area i) in the neighborhood having a minimum standard of access;

N_i = set of neighborhoods l in area i;

λ_{il} = proportion of population in the block group (area i) found in neighborhood l;

d = distance between block group centroid and nearest park;

S = a minimum standard for access, in this case 1 mile.

Using this notation, the index of neighborhood access can be defined as follows:
  where

$$\tau_i = \sum_{l \in N_i} \lambda_{il} \, f(\bar{d}_1, S)$$

$$f(\bar{d}_1, S) = \begin{cases} 1, \text{ if } (\bar{d}_1 \leq S) \\ 0, \text{ otherwise} \end{cases}$$

The variable τ_i gives the proportion of the population in the neighborhood that has a minimum distance of 1 mile to the nearest amenity (e.g., a park). In other words, first it is determined what percent a particular area in a particular neighborhood contributes to the total population of the neighborhood. This percentage is included only if that block reaches the minimum standard, S, for access (e.g., within 1 mile). The summation produces an index measure and a way to evaluate intra-urban access variation among different neighborhoods. Maps are produced that identify the neighborhoods that have relatively low versus high access levels.

A final question to consider could be called "targeted access" and essentially considers population need more explicitly in the evaluation of intra-urban variation. It asks do areas with a higher population needing access have, correspondingly, greater access to facilities? Presumably, areas with greater access would have populations with greater access need, as the result of a self-selection process, but as the empirical results discussed above show, this is not always the case.

As the review of empirical studies discussed above showed, the measurement of access need factors in the attributes of the individuals who seek access. Characteristics of individuals are usually derived using the characteristics of a given spatial unit, such as a census block (the degree of disaggregation of the spatial unit varies widely). Factors that might affect access include socioeconomic status, age, gender, and employment status. Certain assumptions can be made about the attractiveness or relevance of travel to certain facilities (and the likely mode of travel) based on these characteristics. The frictional effect of the available travel mode is also likely to be predicated on the characteristics of residents. For example, lack of bus service may adversely impact access for low-income individuals but have only a marginal effect on higher income groups. At a minimum, constraints based on age and income are taken into account, such that the needs of children, the elderly, and low-income populations are accounted for. Another relevant variable is percent occupied housing units with no vehicles available. Note that indicator variables can be weighted. For example, some kind of decision-making process could be used to determine whether the lack of a vehicle is a more important indicator of access need than household income.

Construction of a need index involves determining what variables are to be used, whether the variables or indicators are equal in importance in determining a measure of need, and how the variables can be combined (either in a linear or non-linear fashion). A multivariate index can be simply a linear function of a derived value for each indicator (Murray and Davis, 2001), formally expressed as:

$$\Phi_i = \sum_j w_j R_{ij}$$

In order for the index to be meaningful, weights need to be used (represented here as w_j), or the indicator variables need to be transformed and standardized so that their linear combination makes sense. If weights are not used, as in this example, R_{ij}, a derived value, can be constructed based on where a particular value falls within a distribution. For example, each of the need variables could be arranged from high to low, corresponding with high to low need (or, in the case of income, low income corresponds to high need). Each census area, for example, could then be assigned a score of 1, 2, 3, or 4, depending on where its value was located in the distribution. Interval values could be assigned in any number of classes, and could be based on standard deviations,

quantiles, natural breaks, and so on (Murray and Davis, 2001).

Thus the index of need for each census area like a block group is simply obtained by summing its derived value (an assignment of 1–4, depending on where it falls in the distribution) for each of four indicator variables. Mapping the index shows the specific areas in the city were access is low and access need is high. If different cut-off points were used, more or fewer areas would be highlighted. One strategy may be to determine ahead of time how many census areas should be reasonably selected, and then determine the threshold levels that produce the desired number of selections.

A final approach in the analysis of targeted access is to combine the access need scores for census areas, for example, block groups, into a neighborhood measure. The process is the same as above, with different parameters. For the determination of need, in which the block group score is multiplied by "1" or "0," the cut-off used can be a combined need score of 14, based on the median. The percent population that each block group contributes to a particular neighborhood is therefore added to the total score (i.e., multiplied by 1) if it is in the top half of the distribution of need variables. If its total need score is in the bottom half of the distribution, it is multiplied by 0 and not counted. This is simply one approach, and, again, the cut-off criteria could change to result in a different number of neighborhoods in each category of need.

Each neighborhood therefore receives a need index score, and the mapped distribution categorizes these scores into different classes. The need index by neighborhood can then be combined with the neighborhood access scores to determine a final outcome: the determination of specific neighborhoods that have high need and low access. Maps will readily identify where the population is likely to have greater need for access to services relative to other parts of the city, and, at the same time, where the existing distribution of urban services is relatively low. Again, more neighborhoods could be selected by changing the cut-off criteria and other parameters.

Figures 24.2, 24.3 and 24.4 show one example of this process. Figure 24.2 is a map showing selected locations – public schools, parks and libraries – in Portage Park, a neighborhood in Chicago, Illinois, and a 1/4 mile radius around each. Areas within the shaded buffer have good access; areas in white do not. This map can be compared to a map of high-priority areas – areas that would most benefit by being proximal to these desirable facilities and places. The series of maps shown in Figure 24.3 are maps showing the distribution for selected "need" variables by census block group. For each variable or map, darkly shaded areas are high priority – that is, darker shades have higher density, higher social diversity, lower-income, higher numbers of children, and higher numbers of

seniors. The objective is to find those areas with the most need on the most number of variables.

There are many different ways to interpret these maps. Each census area could receive a score, for example, 1 through 5 depending on shade of gray, and then the scores for each variable could be added together to get a composite score for each block group. A slightly more sophisticated approach would be to give each layer a weighted score, for example, if the community determined that low income was a more important variable to consider than density.

Another approach, used here, is to find those block groups that are in the highest category of need for at least two criteria. All block groups in red on Figure 24.4 are areas that had high need (shaded darkest) on two or more variables. The map combines this information with the proximity layer, showing those areas

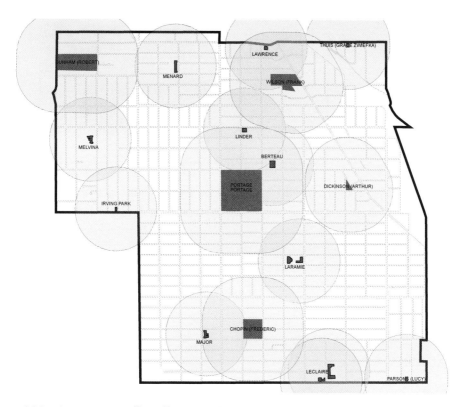

Figure 24.2 One-quarter mile radius around schools, parks, and libraries in the Portage Park neighborhood of Chicago, IL

| Social diversity | % under 18 | % over 65 | Density | Median income |

Figure 24.3   Variation of density, diversity, income, children, and seniors, by block group

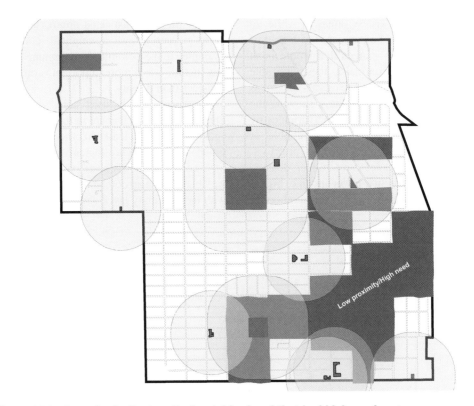

Low proximity/High need

Figure 24.4   Areas in the Portage Park neighborhood that had high need on two or more variables

that simultaneously have high need but low proximity – red areas that are not covered by shading. These are the areas to focus on in order to increase spatial equity.

FUTURE DIRECTIONS

The geovisualization of spatial equity will have an increasingly significant role to play on a number of policy fronts in the coming decades. In the past, we may have seen a lack of practical application of accessibility measures due to conceptual complexities, extensive data requirements, and demanding computations. But this situation is changing rapidly. The geovisualization of spatial equity can be readily made with a GIS of origins, destinations, distances, and corresponding attribute information. In part as a result of these advances, we have seen a significant increase in the role of government in mandating and monitoring spatial equity issues in a visualized environment. Federal and state agencies now often require assessment of environmental justice as a component of project implementation, and these kinds of analyses are likely to take place in a geovisualization environment. As more emphasis is placed on resource need, deprivation, and uneven access, the ability to monitor changes in access and the policy implications involved will warrant continued refinement of geovisualization techniques.

While government involvement has stimulated an increase in research on spatial equity, researchers have also recognized the need to take stock of this activity and assess whether it is actually producing useful, and accurate, results. While there is growing use of mapping to assess inequities in spatial distributions of resources, some have questioned the degree to which we can reliably use these results as a basis for policy change. Toward that end, there have been efforts to investigate the claims made regarding spatial inequity and environmental racism. This is a special concern in public health policy research, where methodological issues can have a significant impact on results and public policy. What is needed, researchers say, are rigorous methods to test the functionality and reliability of spatial equity output. Maantay (2002) notes problems with database accuracy, indices that measure exposure levels, the ability to gauge the extent of impact, and the inability to find reliable health assessment data. Ultimately, the real need is to better connect research on environmental hazards with actual effects, rather than just distribution. As Maantay notes, the critical need is to show "the disproportionate *effects* of pollution rather than just the disproportionate *distribution* of pollution sources" (2002: 161; emphasis added).

Researchers in other fields have also recognized that methodological improvement is essential given the potential policy impact of spatial equity research. Data that is of high enough resolution and accuracy will become increasingly important as policymakers stake their claims on equity analyses.

Recent methodological improvements include the ability to combine statistical techniques in a GIS environment. For example, Ji and Sunil combine statistical clustering, spatial overlay analysis, and non-parametric testing in order to counter what they see as the "simplification" (2001: 36) of environmental equity research.

Ultimately, the heightened relevance of geovisualized spatial equity will serve the populations it is most often concerned with – minorities, low-income groups, and other disadvantaged populations. The physical design of cities and neighborhoods affects quality of life in significant ways: in particular, access to facilities profoundly affects the poor, the immobile, and children. Injustice in allocation, if visually meaningful, can help empower these groups and give them ammunition to fight injustice. This is especially relevant in an economic environment in which wealth inequality has increased, and access to resources has become increasingly a matter of access to wealth.

Another topic of great relevance to the geovisualization of spatial equity is in the area of sustainability. The issues of urban sprawl, global warming, oil scarcity, and the resulting increased pressure on cities to increase population density are all trends likely to increase the importance of visualizing the spatial relationships between goods, services, and populations. Equitable access to resources and opportunities in the urban environment is seen as an essential aspect of sustainability, and visualizing inequality in maps has been seen as a significant analytical tool (Kawabata and Shen, 2007). Sustainability is also an area of research that requires the intermixing of varying notions of equity – for example, the linkages between health, environment, facility location, and notions of justice. Visualization in a GIS context is vital for helping to make these complex connections. Work by Pastor et al. (2006), for instance, is a good example of how GIS can be used to explore the environmental justice implications of such interrelated factors as children's health and school locations.

The evaluation of neighborhood-level, walking access to the goods and services people require in their everyday lives is, for many people, an essential feature of sustainability. Spatial equity analysis of the kind described here can readily show the degree to which neighborhood residents are able to walk to neighborhood level services, far beyond a simple accounting of the total number of services that exist in sub-sections of the city. The result of this kind of analysis is a series of maps that can be very effective planning tools. Geovisualization allows a comparative appraisal about which neighborhoods in fact have longer distances to travel to reach needed services, and which neighborhoods do not. Most importantly, it allows us to make intelligent recommendations about which neighborhoods are in need of better access to facilities relative to population needs. This constitutes a basis for action, allowing residents to actively seek development where it is most needed. By providing a non-arbitrary evaluation of relative deficiency and need, it may be possible to target the development of needed facilities in a more pro-active way.

Finally, there will be increased emphasis on the geovisualization of spatial equity in an interactive and investigatory capacity. This means greater public involvement in the creation and utilization of spatial equity mapping tools. This will include developing the capacity to map data on the internet for ready use by practitioners such as health care providers (Maclachlan et al., 2007). Similar efforts are being made to put "advanced technologies in service to vulnerable communities," essentially the web-accessible GIS visualization of equity (Pezzoli et al., 2007).

Publicly accessed visualization tools will require an interactive approach. This makes sense since often the results of one type of spatial equity analysis – for example, mapping park accessibility and housing value – leads to exploration of other types of relationships. The process is dynamic: maps do not yield definitive answers; they expose relationships and guide the investigator to probe further

correlations. Input variables to be changed include: locational information (e.g., distance between residents and amenities or disamenities); population/housing characteristics (socioeconomic data); and facility characteristics. In the interactive process of constructing GIS-based maps, these data are modified to reflect alternative measurements of access and definitions of need. For example, the accessibility measures can vary in terms of the spatial unit used or how the measure is computed. Population/housing characteristics may be variables indicative of potential discrimination (race and housing value, for example), or may simply reflect certain types of needs (based on age of population, for example). Facilities can be characterized by size, range of services, or quality. If park facilities are being analyzed, the data may characterize the more intensive space needs of higher-density areas. Areas with smaller lot sizes, or areas with fewer opportunities for recreation, can be identified, leading the analyst to interactively investigate how modifying the data changes the observed equity patterns. Variation in how equity is characterized drives the analysis. Any of these definitions can be employed in the interactive process of constructing equity maps.

Spatial data analysis techniques will continue to be developed, refined, and made to be simultaneously sophisticated and user friendly. For example, software tools like GeoDa (Anselin et al., 2006) have been developed for the explicit purpose of fostering interactive data exploration. GeoDa is an intuitive software program – exploring the geovisualization of spatial data based on an architecture that supports brushing and linking to visualize data in different views (windows). Specifically, it includes an intuitive interface to the analysis of local spatial autocorrelation (Anselin, 1995) which can be used to detect clusters and outliers in the provision of services. With multimedia support such as high-definition screens, it can readily be used as an analytical support for public participation GIS. Using these kinds of tools, the geovisualization of spatial equity is likely to become an indispensable part of the politically charged process of resource allocation.

REFERENCES

Albrecht, J. and Ramasubramanian, L. (2004) 'The moving target: A geographic index of relative well-being', *Journal of Medical Systems*, 28(4): 371–84.

Anselin, L. (1995) 'Local indicators of spatial association', *Geographical Analysis*, 27(2): 93–115.

Anselin, L., Syabri, I. and Kho, Y. (2006) 'GeoDa: An introduction to spatial data analysis', *Geographical Analysis*, 38(1): 5–22.

Anselin, L., Dodson, R.F. and Hudak, S. (1993) 'Linking GIS and spatial data analysis in practice', *Geographical Systems*, 1: 3–23.

Apparicio, P. and Seguin, A.M. (2006) 'Measuring the accessibility of services and facilities for residents of public housing in montreal', *Urban Studies*, 43(1): 187–211.

Apparicio, P., Cloutier, M.S. and Shearmur, R. (2007) 'The case of Montreal's missing food deserts: Evaluation of accessibility to food supermarkets', *International Journal of Health Geographics*, 6, 4. http://www.ij-healthgeographics.com/content/6/1/4 (accessed 10/10/10).

Apparicio, P., Abdelmajid, M., Riva, M. and Shearmur, R. (2008) 'Comparing alternative approaches to measuring the geographical accessibility of urban health services: distance types and aggregation-error issues', *International of Health Geographics*, 7(7): 14. http://www.ij-healthgeographics.com/content/7/1/7 (accessed 10/10/10).

Arrow, K.J. (1951) *Social Choice and Individual Values*. New York: John Wiley and Sons.

Batty, M. and Xie, Y. (1994) 'Modeling inside GIS: Part 1. Model structures, exploratory spatial data analysis and aggregation', *International Journal of Geographical Information Systems*, 8(3): 291–307.

Brabyn, L. and Gower, P. (2004) 'Comparing three GIS techniques for modeling geographical access to general practitioners', *Cartographica*, 39(2): 41–9.

Bruegmann, R. (2005) *Sprawl: A Compact History*. Chicago, IL: University of Chicago Press.

Buzzelli, M., Jerrett, M., Burnett, R. and Finkelstein, N. (2003) 'Spatiotemporal perspectives on air pollution and environmental justice in Hamilton, Canada, 1985–1996', *Annals of the Association of American Geographers*, 93(3): 557–73.

Chakraborty, J., Forkenbrock, D.J. and Schweitzer, L.A. (1999) 'Using GIS to assess the environmental justice consequences of transportation system changes', *Transactions in GIS*, 3(3): 239–58.

Chakraborty, J. (2001) 'Acute exposure to extremely hazardous substances: An analysis of environmental equity', *Risk Analysis*, 21(5): 883–95.

Choi, M., Afzal B. and Sattler, B. (2006) 'Geographic information systems: A new tool for environmental health assessments', *Public Health Nursing*, 23(5): 381–91.

Congress for the New Urbanism (2000) *Charter of the New Urbanism*. New York: McGraw-Hill.

Crompton, J.L. and Wicks, B.E. (1988) 'Implementing a preferred equity model for the delivery of leisure services in the U.S. context', *Leisure Studies*, 7: 287–403.

Crompton, J.L. and Lue, C.C. (1992) 'Patterns of equity preferences among Californians for allocating park and recreation resources', *Leisure Sciences*, 14: 227–46.

Derezinski, D., Michael, D., Lacy, G. and Stretesky, P.B. (2003) *Social Science Quarterly*, 84(1): 122–43.

Duany, A. and Plater-Zyberk, E. (1991) *Towns and Town-Making Principles*. New York: Rizzoli.

Dueker, K.J. (1996) 'Neotraditional design: Resisting the decentralizing forces of new spatial technologies', in H. Couclelis (ed.), *Spatial Technologies, Geographic Information and the City*. Santa Barbara, CA: National Center for Geographic Information and Analysis. pp. 56–8.

Feldman, R. and Jaffe, M. (1992) 'Reformation and counter re-formation', *Inland Architect*, 36(5): 62–70.

Fulcher, C. and Kaukinen, C. (2005) 'Mapping and visualizing the location HIV service providers: An exploratory spatial analysis of toronto neighborhoods', *AIDS Care*, 17(3): 386–96.

Geertman, S.C.M. and Ritsema Van Eck, J.R. (1995) 'GIS and models of accessibility potential: An application in planning', *International Journal of Geographical Information Systems*, 9(1): 67–80.

Ghose, R. and Huxhold, W.E. (2002) 'The role of multi-scalar GIS-based indicators studies in formulating neighborhood planning policy', *URISA Journal*, 14(2): 5–17.

Greenwald, M.J. and Boarnet, M.G. (2001) 'Built environment as a determinant of walking behaviour', *Transportation Research Record*, 1780.

Grineski, S., Bolin, B. and Boone, C. (2007) 'Criteria air pollution and marginalized populations: Environmental inequity in metropolitan Phoenix, Arizona', *Social Science Quarterly*, 88(2): 535–54.

Guagliardo, M.F. (2004) 'Spatial accessibility of primary care: Concepts, methods and challenges', *International Journal of Health Geographics* 3. http://www.ij-healthgeographics.com/content/3/1/3 (accessed 10/10/10).

Handy, S.L. and Niemeier, D.A. (1997) 'Measuring accessibility: An exploration of issues and alternatives', *Environment and Planning A*, 29 (7): 1175–94.

Hanson, S. and Schwab, M. (1987) 'Accessibility and intraurban travel', *Environment and Planning A*, 19: 735–48.

Harvey, D. (1973) *Social Justice and the City*. London: Edward Arnold.

Harvey, D. (1996) *Justice, Nature and the Geography of Difference*. Cambridge: Blackwell.

Hay, A. (1995) 'Concepts of equity, fairness and justice in geographical sciences', *Transactions of the Institute of British Geographers*, 20: 500–8.

Hewko, J., Smoyer-Tomic, K.E. and Hodgson, J.M. (2002) 'Measuring neighbourhood spatial accessibility to urban amenities: Does aggregation error matter?', *Environment and Planning A*, 34: 1185–206.

Higgs, G. (2004) 'A literature review of the use of GIS-based measures of access to health care services', *Health Services and Outcomes Research Methodology*, 5: 119–39.

Humphreys, J.S. (1988) 'Social provisions and service delivery: Problems of equity, health, and health care in rural Australia', *Geoforum*, 19(3): 323–38.

Jacobs, A. and Appleyard, D. (1987) 'Toward an urban design manifesto', *Journal of the American Planning Association*, Winter: 112–20.

Jacobs, J. (1961) *The Death and Life of Great American Cities*. New York: Vintage Books.

Ji, M. and Sunil, T.S. (2005) 'Regional assessment of environmental equity through GIS-based clustering and non-parametric statistical testing: A case study of Dallas County, Texas, USA', *International Journal of Risk Assessment and Management*, 5(1): 36–49.

Jones, B.D., Greenberg, S. and Drew J. (1980) *Service Delivery in the City*. New York: Longman.

Kawabata, M. and Shen, Q. (2007) 'Community inequality between cars and public transit: The case of the San Francisco Bay Area, 1990–2000', *Urban Studies*, 44(9): 1759–80.

King, G. (1997) *A Solution to the Ecological Inference Problem*. Princeton, NJ: Princeton University Press.

Knox P.L. (1978) 'The intraurban ecology of primary medical care: Patterns of accessibility and their policy implications', *Environment and Planning A*, 10: 415–35.

Krumholz, N. and Forester, J. (1990) *Making Equity Planning Work: Leadership in the Public Sector*. Philadelphia, PA: Temple University Press.

Krumholz, N. (1975) 'The Cleveland policy planning report', *Journal of the American Planning Association*, 41(3): 298–304.

Krumholz, N. (1982) 'A retrospective view of equity planning', *Journal of the American Planning Association*, 48(2): 163–74.

Kwan, M.P. (1999) 'Gender and individual access to urban opportunities: A study using space-time measures', *Professional Geographer*, 51(2): 210–27.

Levine, J. (1998) 'Rethinking accessibility and jobs-housing balance', *Journal of the American Planning Association*, 64(2): 133–49.

Lindsey, G., Maraj, M. and Kuan, S. (2001) 'Access, equity, and urban greenways: An exploratory investigation', *The Professional Geographer*, 53(3): 332–46.

Livi, A.D. and Clifton, K.J. (2004) 'Issues and methods in capturing pedestrian behaviours', *Attitudes and Perceptions: Experiences with a Community-Based Walkability Survey*. http://www.enhancements.org/trb/trb2004/TRB2004–001417.pdf (accessed 10 June 2004).

Lucy, W. (1981) 'Equity and planning for local services', *Journal of the American Planning Association*, 47(4): 447–57.

Luo, W. and Wang, F. (2003) 'Measures of spatial accessibility to health care in a GIS environment: Synthesis and a case study in the Chicago region', *Environment and Planning B: Planning and Design*, 30: 865–84.

Lynch, K. (1981) *Good City Form*. Cambridge, MA: MIT Press.

Maantay, J. (2002) 'Mapping environmental injustices: pitfalls and potential of geographic information systems in assessing environmental health and equity', *Environmental Health Perspectives*, 110(2): 161–71.

Maclachlan, J.C., Jerrett, M., Abernathy, T., Sears, M. and Bunch, M.J. (2007) 'Mapping health on the Internet: A new tool for environmental justice and public health research', *Health and Place*, 13: 72–86.

Marsh, M.T. and Schilling, D.A. (1994) 'Equity measurement in facility location analysis: A review and framework', *European Journal of Operational Research*, 74(1): 1–17.

Mennis, J. and Jordan, L. (2005) 'The distribution of environmental equity: Exploring spatial nonstationarity in multivariate models of air toxic releases', *Annals of the Association of American Geographers*, 95(2): 249–68.

Merget, A.E. (1979) 'Equity in the distribution of municipal services', in H.J. Bryce (ed.), *Revitalizing Cities*. Lexington, MA: Heath and Co.

Mitchell, D. (2003) *The Right to the City: Social Justice and the Fight for Public Space*. New York: Guilford Press.

Mladenka, K.A. and Hill, K.Q. (1977) 'The distribution of benefits in an urban environment', *Urban Affairs Quarterly*, 13(1): 73–94.

Moudon, A.V. and Lee, C. (2003) 'Walking and bicycling: An evaluation of environmental audit instruments', *American Journal of Health Promotion*, 18(1): 21–37.

Murray, A. and Davis, R.T. (2001) 'Equity in regional service provision', *Journal of Regional Science*, 41(4): 577–600.

Pacione, M. (1989) 'Access to urban services – the case of secondary schools in Glasgow', *Scottish Geographical Magazine*, 105(1): 12–8.

Pahl, R. (1971) 'Poverty and the urban system', in M. Chisholm and G. Manners (eds), *Spatial Policy Problems of the British Economy*. Cambridge: Cambridge University Press.

Pastor, M. Jr, Morello-Frosch, R. and Sadd, J.L. (2006) 'Breathless: Schools, air toxics, and environmental justice in California', *The Policy Studies Journal*, 34(3): 337–62.

Penchansky, R. and Thomas, J.W. (1981) 'The concept of access: Definition and relationship to consumer satisfaction', *Medical Care*, 19(2): 127–40.

Pezzoli, K., Tukey, R., Sarabia, H., Zaslavsky, I., Lynn, M., William, M.A., Suk, A.L. and Ellisman, M. (2007) 'The NIEHS environmental health sciences data resource portal: Placing advanced technologies in service to vulnerable communities', *Environmental Health Perspectives*, 115(4): 564–71.

Pinch, S. (1985) *Cities and Services*. London: Routledge & Kegan Paul.

Seley, J.E. (1983) *The Politics of Public-Facility Planning*. Lexington, MA: Lexington Books.

Staeheli, L.A. (1989) 'Accumulation, legitimation, and the provision of public services in the American metropolis', *Urban Geography*, 10(3): 229–50.

Staeheli, L.A. and Thompson, A. (1997) 'Citizenship, community and struggles for public space', *The Professional Geographer*, 49(1): 28–8.

Talen, E. (1996) 'Do plans get implemented? A review of evaluation in planning', *Journal of Planning Literature*, 10(3): 248–59.

Talen, E. (1998) 'Visualizing fairness: Equity maps for planners', *Journal of the American Planning Association*, 64(1): 22–8.

Toulmin, L.M. (1988) 'Equity as a decision rule in determining the distribution of urban public services', *Urban Affairs Quarterly*, 23(3): 389–413.

Truelove, M. (1993) 'Measurement of spatial equity', *Environment and Planning C*, 11: 19–34.

Urban Quality Communications (1999) *Urban Quality Indicators, Issue 14*. Ann Arbor, MI: Urban Quality Communications.

Verter, V. and Bahar, Kara Y. (2001) 'A GIS-based framework for hazardous materials transport risk assessment', *Risk Analysis*, 21(6): 1109–20.

Wekerle, G.R. (1985) 'From refuge to service center: Neighborhoods that support women', *Sociological Focus*, 18(2): 79–95.

White, A.L. and Ratick, S.J. (1989) 'Risk, compensation, and regional equity in locating hazardous facilities', *Papers of the Regional Science Association*, 67: 29–42.

25

Natural Resource Conflicts, Their Management, and GIS Applications

Peter A. Kwaku Kyem

THE NEED FOR GIS IN MEDIATION

The need to develop strategies for resolving conflicts over natural resource use and management has arguably never been greater than today. Land-use conflicts and attendant disputes threaten resource institutions in communities throughout the world. Competition among individuals and groups for the use of local resources has made the resource management process very contentious and complex. As a result, resource managers are expected to widen the range of interests they consider before resource policy decisions are made. Global demands for the protection of the local environment also compel the managers to integrate more of the factors that bear on the uses and abuses of ecological systems into resource policy decisions. Public participation has consequently become critical for sound resource management but the support for public involvement has opened up the decision-making process to more conflicts. The disagreements strain relations in communities and prevent collaboration and the peaceful implementation of projects. Effective management of resources has therefore come to depend on the ability to identify conflicts and adopt strategies that prevent the disagreements from becoming intractable disputes.

At the same time as traditional resource management strategies have proven ineffective and the search for new approaches has intensified, implementation of community-based GIS projects has spread into communities throughout the world. Propelled by advocacy, favorable developments in the computer industry, availability of digital data, and support from grant-awarding organizations, GIS applications has spread into several remote locations on the globe under a movement often described as participatory GIS (PGIS).[1] Within the communities, PGIS applications offer interactive participatory planning tools for ordinary citizens to meet and collaborate on projects, search for consensus and reach agreements over issues that divide them. The spatial analytical capabilities of the GIS technology makes it a particularly suitable tool for handling many of the land use problems (e.g., land-use conflicts, resources allocation, and environmental problems) that confront local resource institutions throughout the world. PGIS projects offer tools for local resource organizations to structure resource decisions to open up the processes and make them iterative and less controversial than before. In a GIS, natural features, processes, and activities can be georeferenced through sets of geographic coordinates that represent their locations. Once in the computer, the data can be combined with other information such as land ownership and analyzed to help clarify conditions that underlie specific land-use problems to facilitate their management and resolution. Thus, as GIS adoption in local communities has grown in significance, the capabilities of the system have increasingly been deployed or sought to address land-use conflicts and disagreements that result from competition for, and access to local resources. Implementation of PGIS projects therefore remains vital to attempts being made to harness community assets for peaceful and effective resources management. This chapter contributes to this task by reviewing the role that GIS plays, or can play in the management of resource conflicts.

DEFINITION OF CONFLICT

A conflict is a disagreement in which the parties involved perceive a threat to their needs and interests (UW-Madison, 2008). Disagreements ensue from incompatible interests, values, or actions[2] (Moore, 1996; Susskind and Field, 1996) and may originate with individuals, or they can arise among groups in a society and thereby create public conflicts (Deutsch, 1977). Public conflicts refer to situations where sections of the community are in disagreement over public choices. Many such disagreements develop over equity issues regarding the unequal distribution and allocation of local resources. This happens because the multiple and varied interests in society occasionally clash and sometimes the disagreements develop into major disputes. The clash of human interests over natural resource use is also due to the fact that a piece of land is generally suitable for multiple uses. It can be used for a housing project, developed as a farm, or be preserved as a national park. Land-based resources therefore attract multiple interests and the competition for such resources often lead to conflicts. Whether such conflicts of interest are over species preservation or the allocation of land for farming, the disputes restrain relations in society and must therefore be addressed to restore normal relations between the parties.

Causes of resource conflicts

The potential for conflict exists whenever two or more people come together in some form of organization to pursue a common course. Conflict is a characteristic of human existence and is therefore common within human society and in all human endeavors. Some conflict is therefore inevitable in a human relationship. According to Coser (1967), it would be extremely unlikely that two or more people who live and work together in close proximity over a long period of time would not disagree on anything. Absence of conflict, he argues, would probably suggest that some people are being suppressed or that they are subordinating their views to others. Conflicts occur within competitive or cooperative contexts (Coser, 1967; Deutsch, 1977). Competition may imply opposition in the goals of stakeholders such that the chance of one party attaining its goal decreases the probability of success for the other party. It could also happen that the goals sought by the parties may not contradict one another but the simultaneous achievement of these goals may not be feasible, thereby igniting competition and hence conflict between the parties. Competition generates conflicts but not all conflicts reflect competition. For example, a disagreement between members of an organization over how much each should pay as a membership fee reflects a difference in opinion which is often devoid of competition.

A major cause of natural resource conflicts is land, not just as a commodity, but also, as a cultural and spiritual factor in human existence. Conflicts arise over natural resource use for a number of reasons. At the local level, a resource conflict might be driven by a sense of grievance which may result from inequality, the unfair allocation of resources, cultural or moral differences, or competition for scarce resources (Kriesberg, 2002). Besides being the source of livelihood and therefore demanded by all people in society, natural resources are embedded in an environment where the action of one group of people adversely affects the interests of other groups, or create unforeseen adverse impacts on resources used by other members of the community (Warner, 2000). For example, when farmers clear a forest to cultivate new crops, their actions undermine the activities and needs of loggers, cane basket weavers, and others who rely on timber and non-timber resources in the forest for livelihood. Disagreements may then develop between the farmers and other forest user groups within the community. In other situations, individuals and groups with the greatest access to economic and political power (e.g., public officials) may influence resource decisions in favor of their friends and relatives thereby attracting protests and opposition from aggrieved elements in society.

Conflicts over natural resources have class dimensions as well, such as when owners of a resource turn against those who apply their labor to produce the resource or make it more productive. Additionally, resource scarcity brought about by rapid environmental changes, increased demand, or unequal allocation and/or distribution can generate conflicts among members of a community. Furthermore, perceptions, access, and use of

natural resources vary in every community according to gender, ethnicity, age, and other factors, and the clash of these differences can cause conflicts (Moore, 1996; Susskind and Field, 1996).

Impact of conflict

Just as much as a conflict destroys relations it also offers opportunities for positive change and long-term peace and cooperation among groups if it is handled properly and timely. A conflict reveals potential problems in existing human relations and as such engaging the disputing parties in mediation can reveal possible disagreements and thereby pave the way for resolving the dispute to restore normal relations between the parties (Brahm, 2004; Kriesberg, 2002). A timely management of the conflict can also provide a safety valve for clearing a potentially damaging disagreement in a less destructive manner than might otherwise occur without the intervention (Brahm, 2004). Additionally, a conflict can be a catalyst for social cohesion. A conflict or its resolution can give rise to new rules that a community may adopt to not only govern future social behavior of its members, but also, use it to promote peace and cooperation among social groups within the community (Kriesberg, 2002). Besides, conflicts are often the root causes of social change (Coser, 1967). Without conflict, human attitudes might stay the same regardless of changing social conditions and irrespective of whether existing social relations are just and fair (Burgess and Burgess, 1996). A conflict management process therefore assists individuals and groups to adjust to social norms that are consistent with changing relationships in society. A conflict over resources might even be the pre-condition that is needed to motivate stakeholders to engage in a cooperative resolution of their long-held disagreements. The impact of resource conflicts therefore depends on how and when society intervenes to find a resolution. It is during the attempt to resolve the conflict that GIS applications become necessary for the exploration of the conflict, assisting the disputants to get past initial misconceptions and work together to create common gains.

THEORIES OF CONFLICT AND GIS APPLICATIONS

Debates about whether or not GIS is an effective interventionist tool ensue from two main theories – the competitive and cooperative approaches to conflict resolution. While the competitive approach (outlined in conflict theory) assumes irreconcilable antagonistic values and as such dismisses GIS applications in mediation, the cooperative approach (expounded by consensus theory) emphasizes common interests and hence welcomes GIS applications for the management of conflicts.

The competitive approach to conflict

Both the competitive and cooperative approaches to conflict recognize the role culture plays in structuring the way people think and act in a society. Yet, the competitive approach dismisses common bonds between social groups and rather focuses on the extent to which individuals, groups, and social classes are in competition with each other for whatever is considered important and valuable in the society. Perhaps best explained in Max Weber's (1968) discussion of instrumental rational behavior, the competitive approach emphasizes self-interest and competition as the main factors that sustain conflicts. Weber challenged claims about the objective reality upon which stakeholders are expected to reach agreements over conflict in values. He argued that rational arguments succeed in eliminating only superstitions, errors, and prejudices but cannot transform beliefs and values that form the basis of an individual's behavior. Weber maintained that rational exchange is possible only when individuals are expected to benefit from it or, when they are compelled to do so by some 'recognized economic power'. He contended that competition and conflict occur within the sphere of power and not of reason and as such arguments based on values are 'ends rational' because individuals cannot be swayed from their beliefs (Weber 1968: 246).

Proponents of the competitive approach therefore make a distinction between conflicts over facts and conflicts over interests and values. They view cognitive (fact) conflicts as the relatively superficial disagreements about facts behind a dispute and describe value conflicts as disagreements over the social values and beliefs held by stakeholders (Berry, 1995). Supporters of the theory explain that GIS use is best in a context where there is disagreement on the facts surrounding a conflict. In situations where facts agree but values disagree, GIS might be adopted to inspire or persuade parties about the reasoning supporting a position, but not to resolve conflicts (Obermeyer and Pinto, 1994; Berry, 1995). Accordingly, the authors maintain that increased availability of data about a conflict situation, as would be the case with a GIS application, elevate rather than lower the level of a dispute (Obermeyer and Pinto, 1994). This claim raises questions about the validity of GIS applications in mediation. Are stakeholders' behavior grounded in information that is available to them? If they are, can skilful applications of a data-driven technology such as GIS influence the decisions disputants' make during a conflict? Answers to these questions are explored below in a review of the perspectives on conflict and GIS applications.

The cooperative approach to conflict

Conversely, the cooperative approach to conflict stresses common values and sees cooperation as the starting point of social organization. That viewpoint assumes that elements of a conflict are malleable and that meaningful communication between stakeholders can clarify the conflict condition, erase misconceptions, and induce mutual agreements. In his thesis on communicative action, Habermas (1984, 1987) viewed society as a self-regulating system in which human actions are coordinated through functional interconnections geared at maintaining order and harmony. He observed that in many societies rational and goal-directed individuals use communication to reach agreements over disputed claims by way of argument and insight and without recourse to force (Habermas, 1984: 17). He argued that communication allows stakeholders to incorporate the opponents' interpretation of the conflict into their own views until the divergent definitions are brought 'to coincide sufficiently' (Habermas, 1984: 100). Supporters of the cooperative approach therefore argue that because validity claims can be criticized and defended, it is possible to use speech and other tools of communication such as GIS maps to correct the mistakes and misunderstandings between stakeholders and prepare them for mutual agreement. By choosing communication as the medium for coordinating actions that produce consensus, proponents of the cooperative approach to conflict recognize that instruments of communication (including GIS and other multimedia) are important tools in the resolution of resource conflicts. As media that permit direct expression of rival claims, spatial communication technologies such as GIS offer opportunities for disputants to reach agreements and compromise on divisive issues by helping to identify and eliminate sources of friction.

Review of perspectives on conflict and GIS applications

Both the competitive and cooperative approaches to conflict provide frameworks for understanding aspects of stakeholders'

behavior during the conflict. However, they do not fully address factors that motivate parties involved in a conflict to prolong or resolve the disagreement between them. Both theories fail to account for the fact that successful mediation requires strategies for handling both the competitive and cooperative forces that sustain a conflict. They also fail to consider whether a conflict occurs between groups within a common sociopolitical environment (where institutional forces often restrain competition and promote cooperation), or, whether the disagreement occurs between groups affiliated with different sociopolitical environments where the urge to protect one's self-interest ('we against them'), and hence competition is very strong. Moreover, neither of the theories account for changes that occur during the lifetime of a conflict which may either facilitate or restrain both competition and cooperation.

Competition can either be a driving or a restraining force in conflict resolution (Whetten, 1975; Gray, 1989). When a conflict is driven by competition over scarce resources, or when the conflict is over highly valued resources such as diamonds and gold, or over life-supporting resources such as farmlands in a rural community, consensus is often difficult to attain (Whetten and Gray, 1984). This is because such conflicts are sustained by concerns for survival and hence by interests over which there might be little room for trade-offs and compromise. In such cases, self-interest can drive disputants to hold on to their positions as a way of protecting their means of livelihood. Still, stakeholders can reach an agreement to avoid a conflict while also retaining some independent rewards. In a situation where individuals or groups have a strong common interest, competition can create motives for strategic cooperation such as when stakeholders enter into a negotiated agreement for the sole reason of dealing with a threat to their common interests[3] (Gray, 1989).

Moreover, competitive forces that are derived from self-interest foster a zero-sum game that brings rewards to one party while leaving the other party very aggrieved (Rubin and Brown, 1975). Thus, in many communities, as conflict intensifies, so do the effort at cooperation.

The reductionist approach to defining the conflict problem in terms of a difference in the interpretation of facts and values ignores the world views, experiences, knowledge, and expertise of stakeholders. These are equally important factors in determining the complexity of a conflict (Jankowski and Nyerges, 2001b). Almost all conflicts have negotiable interests and values but when people define a dispute in terms of the positions they have taken, conflicts often appear to be intractable because each party wants something that the other completely opposes (Forrester, 1999). By focusing on underlying interests rather than the overt positions that appear to drive the dispute, apparently intractable conflicts often become solvable (Forrester, 1999).

A heightened level of conflict during GIS use might not necessarily signify a failure of the GIS project. Often in conflicts over values, the original cause of the conflict may be related to spatial issues (e.g., land use) but over time as the conflict develops, the original motive may become entangled with derivative issues (interests and values) that are not directly connected to the land use problem that caused the conflict (Northrup, 1989). In such a situation, skillful applications of GIS technology can help avoid the distraction of derivative issues and help focus the mediation effort on the actual spatial problem. As noted earlier, GIS applications are limited to issues that are distributed in space and can be mapped and analyzed (e.g., property boundaries) so the technology is constrained more by the types of conflict (spatial or non-spatial) than by the nature of the disagreement (cognitive or value-driven conflicts). Regarding the validity of GIS applications in mediation, it is important to note that the availability of spatial data about a conflict often raise stakeholders' awareness of the conflict situation to drive home the real import of the choices the parties make to either escalate or resolve the conflict.

This can temporarily raise the level of the conflict but such a development is part of the normal collaborative decision-making process (Jankowski and Nyerges, 2001a). The coincidence of intense conflict level with the analytical phase of a conflict management process often marks the break point in the resolution of a dispute (Jankowski and Nyerges, 2001a) and hence is a necessary part of the progress toward final resolution of a conflict (Kyem, 2004). It is also important to remember that conflict is sometimes the result of faulty perceptions or a distortion of issues (Susskind et al., 1999) so that changes in positions may be induced by the GIS application through the introduction of new information about the conflict situation, or a clarification of the disagreement that sustains the conflict.

In contrast to the competitive forces, the institutional factors that drive conflicts in society are characterized by elaborate rules of behavior to which groups and individual members of the community must necessarily conform. The factors include webs of social networks and relationships, customary practices, and group expectations that are developed with little reference to competition and self-interests. Examples include marriage and membership to ethnic groups and social organizations. Pressure from these institutions can either stimulate or impede the resolution of a conflict. Generally, when people are involved in mutual interactions and long-lasting relationships, they often find it necessary to make adjustments in the values or interests they cherish to maintain those relationships (Uwazie, 2000). The combination of social networks and shared norms of trust and reciprocity create conducive environments for civic engagement. Thus, although the competitive move to advance self-interest is present in resource conflicts, group expectations, sanctions, and shared commitments are equally important factors in conflict resolution and its prevention in society.

However, notwithstanding the binding influence of cultural forces, the cooperative approach fails to anticipate situations where competition resulting from scarcity of resources (e.g., food) in a local community can compel individuals and groups to focus entirely on their self-interests. The cooperative and competitive approaches to a conflict are therefore inextricably intertwined. Raiffa (1982), Lax and Sabenius (1986, 2000) have thus described the mediation process as an effort to manage a tension between the cooperative move to create values jointly and the competitive urge to claim individual rewards. It is therefore necessary for mediators to recognize the dual elements that drive resource conflicts. When a conflict is viewed from this perspective, communication between disputants, and hence GIS applications, become necessary for negotiating joint values to facilitate the resolution of the conflict.

MAPPING AND THE RESOLUTION OF CONFLICTS

There is a long history of the use of maps in direct and informed negotiations and in promoting consensus building among community groups (Gupta, 1989; Mascarenhas and Kumar, 1991; Neela, 1992; Peluso, 1995). Development scientists and other advocates have integrated a variety of simple mapping techniques with participatory methods to facilitate consensus building among heterogeneous groups (Chambers, 1994; Rocheleau, 1997; Fox, 1998). Embedded in the participatory methods are simple mapping strategies that facilitate information interchange, promote consensus building, and enhance collaboration among groups with diverse interests (Craig and Elwood, 1998; Herlihy and Knapp, 2003). The community mapping methods are used by advocates to prepare communities for collaboration, joint management of local resources; and the implementation of community projects (Chambers, 1994). Rocheleau et al. (1995) along with other scholars Poole (1995) and Fox (1998) have explained that feature categories in

maps produced by local groups represent their preferences and negotiated compromises that they reach after thorough deliberations. Thus, community maps are powerful communication tools that assist with the choice selections that individuals and groups make during group discussions (Rocheleau et al., 1995; Eghenter, 2000). The maps equip groups with the power to realize their priorities in cooperation or in competition with other members of society (Turnbull, 1997; Fox et al., 2005).

Counter mapping and conflict management

Community mapping strategies have sometimes been used to generate *counter maps* that provide an alternative to authoritative mapping by state agencies (Peluso, 1995; Poole, 1995; Fox et al., 2005). Historically, official maps of local resources have been drawn with little or no consideration for the interests of under-represented groups in society (e.g., gender perspectives on resource use or native claims to land). *Counter mapping* is therefore widely applied to produce maps representing the experiences, interests and spaces of children, class and caste, gender, age, and religious groups. The mapping strategies recognize the varying spatial and environmental knowledge of such community groups, and transform such experiences into conventional forms to make them visible (Turnbull, 1997). The counter mapping project enables under-represented groups to draw detailed maps of their experiences, lands and resource use as a way of countering information contained in official maps, or they may do so to document and formalize their claims to local resources. Counter maps therefore are a response to official maps that may alienate poor and marginalized groups in society (Peluso, 1995; Rocheleau, 1997). When community maps are used to counter information in official maps that historically represent the political and economic interests of the state, they reveal information about conflicting claims, overlapping interests, and areas where rights and responsibilities are not clearly defined (Fox et al., 2005). The counter maps therefore raise questions and then trigger actions and collaborative efforts that ultimately produce answers to the questions. Counter mapping is thus a powerful medium through which community groups negotiate with state and external agencies over issues such as community forest access and land use rights (Peluso, 1995; Turnbull, 1997; Leila and Hazen, 2006).

GIS and conflict management

GIS is a very advanced tool for depicting and producing relations among spatial entities and hence a far more persuasive device than ordinary community maps (Johnson, 1999). For example, in a conflict management exercise, satellite imagery, three dimensional elevation map, and other GIS data layers can be analyzed together to show land areas that are in dispute, the types of resources involved in the conflict, and groups that are affected by the dispute. The spatial data layers can be utilized to show impacts of positions that stakeholders have adopted in a conflict. Based on such positions, 'what if' scenarios of proposed solutions to the conflict can be generated to help the parties evaluate the impact of each solution on the positions they have taken in the conflict. Once mapped, suggested solutions can be modified by changing critical spatial parameters (e.g., of land use or local resources) and immediately demonstrate visually the changes relating to stakeholders' positions in the conflict. Mediators can pause and gauge the responses of stakeholders before new proposals are introduced. The spatial variables can also be modified in accordance with ongoing changes in the goals of stakeholders and progress in the mediation process. New information can be incorporated when it becomes available and maps can be re-created when situations change. The GIS applications may also involve audio, video, and three-dimensional

viewing of virtual reality simulations of the conflict situation or resource allocation scenarios. These can have major impacts on the stakeholders' involvement in the process and their understanding of the conflict (Al-Kodmany, 2002). It can be possible through the creative use of GIS to get the parties to agree on compromises that previously appeared unreachable.

The mapping capability aside, the opportunity that GIS technology offers for stakeholders to meet and jointly collect and analyze data creates a healthy environment for the parties to exchange views on the conflict and develop trust for each other. The technology also brings with it a sense of impartiality that can be tapped to lend credibility to the conflict management process. Furthermore, GIS is closely linked to centers of power and influence in society so its applications can bring some needed recognition to the conflict management process. The system has therefore been used to explore the strategic choices that stakeholders make during a conflict (Kyem, 2004), to address questions about group decision making (Jankowski et al., 1997), to facilitate the analysis and resolution of conflicts between public officials and forest user groups (Eastman et al., 1993; Jordan, 1999; Kyem, 2000), and to examine pre-defined alternative solutions to land suitability assessment (Pereira and Duckstein, 1993; Eastman et al., 1995). Decision support tools embedded in a GIS have also been utilized in association with multi-objective models to map potential environmental disputes (Brody et al., 2004, 2006), and to suggest alternative possible solutions for facilitating the resolution of land use conflicts (Eastman et al., 1993; Kyem, 2000, 2004).

Information and belief formation

GIS's role in conflict resolution ensues from the critical functions that information and its analysis perform in the formation of beliefs, values, and interests that govern stakeholders' behavior during a conflict. Information is not only important in the formation of our beliefs and interests but it also exerts considerable influence on the choices that disputants make and hence the actions that emanate from their decisions. Familiarity with the role information plays in choice selections is important for understanding stakeholders' behavior during a conflict. A model of the basic structure of an individual's belief formation and the role GIS analyses play in bringing about behavioral changes in individuals is presented in Figure 25.1. The model rests on the assumption that an individual's behavior or actions are dictated by his or her beliefs and interests. In the figure, these behavioral elements are located in the 'Personal World' area. Since an individual's rational behavior depends partly upon the clarity of beliefs from which the actions are derived, we assume that the individual will invest in the optimal information available before he or she will decide on a course of action. This information is found within 'The Model World' area represented by GIS in Figure 25.1. The courses of action that result from an individual's analyses of information which pertains to the problem at hand are shown in the 'Real World' area.

The figure suggests that beliefs provide guides to the formation of interests that are expressed externally as opinions, behavior, and actions. Our values and interests therefore embody behavioral elements because they lead to action when we activate them.

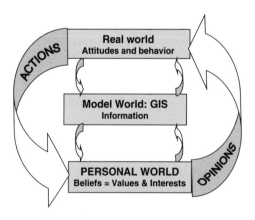

Figure 25.1 GIS, beliefs, and human actions

Source: Kyem, 2004.

An opinion therefore forms a bridge between the 'personal world' of beliefs and interests on one hand, and the 'real world' of behavior and actions on the other. As shown in Figure 25.1, information exerts an influence on both the personal and real worlds. Values and interests, or the opinions and attitudes that emanate from them are based on information that is available to an individual. The individual uses the information to clarify situations and then decides whether or not to act. Expressed opinions are therefore the overt behaviors that reflect our attitudes and hence the values and interests we hold and treasure. Thus, an opinion provides a window to the core of one's beliefs. For example, when stakeholders draw objects on maps, or speak about features on a GIS-derived map that is being used to facilitate mediation, they make decisions that are influenced by values which dictate their goals in the conflict. Questioning stakeholders' opinion about conditions represented on the maps therefore taps into their beliefs and can help reveal values that underlie the choices disputants make during the conflict management process. Rarely do rational human beings make important decisions that affect their lives without considering the information that is available about the issue. Thus, our beliefs and interests, or the opinions and actions that emanate from them are based on information that is available to us. We can therefore use information to clarify a situation surrounding a dispute to either facilitate or impede consensus building (Habermas, 1984).

The production and analysis of data that relates directly to some value or interest can therefore influence the belief itself. For example, when new information about a conflict becomes available, it could help stakeholders change their positions about the conflict and decide to prolong or end the dispute. Consequently, if a GIS analysis focuses on conditions that affect the values and interests in conflict, stakeholders will likely respond to the situation. Again, stakeholders will respond if the GIS application reveals that a position the parties have taken about the conflict can jeopardize their long-term interests or enhance their fundamental values. In such cases, the GIS application will be the source of motivation for the change in stakeholders' positions about the conflict. Engaging disputants in open discussion of issues that sustain a conflict can also lead to the revelation of the real motives that drive a dispute. The information gleaned from such GIS-led discussions can be used to design applications that will help the parties understand the conflict in a new way and therefore prepare them for a mutual agreement that will ultimately resolve the conflict.

Participatory 3D model and conflict management

Participatory three-dimensional model (P3DM) is a relatively new communicative GIS method which supports mediation and collaborative processes related to problems in land use and land tenure (Rambaldi and Callosa-Tarr, 2004; Maling, 2006). The technique has been extensively used in Southeast Asia where it has been successfully adopted to address inter-tribal territorial disputes in the Philippines (Rambaldi et al., 2002) and to resolve conflicts between indigenous people and the government of Thailand (Srimongkontip, 2000; Hoare et al., 2002). The scaled relief model has also been applied in Vietnam to resolve conflicts and facilitate land use planning (Rambaldi et al., 2002; Hardcastle et al., 2004). P3DM integrates the environmental knowledge of local people and contour lines of the local relief to produce three dimensional representation of the land (Rambaldi and Le Van, 2003; Maling, 2006). Several members of the community and hence a great number of potential stakeholders in a dispute join in the construction of the model. On completion, a scaled grid derived from a source map is applied to help incorporate georeferenced data onto the model to facilitate its integration into a GIS. The three-dimensional representation of the

landscape creates opportunities for real (not just imaginary) new 'perspectives' on the conflict scene. The realistic view of the land provided by the model establishes a common ground for effective discussion of the conflict condition and for viewing and interpreting features and conditions that sustain the dispute. Accordingly, the model bridges communication barriers between the literate and illiterate and people from different ethnic backgrounds to prepare them for dialogue (Rambaldi and Callosa-Tarr, 2000). Alongside the stimulation of several senses (sighting, hearing, and feeling), the P3DM model presents an excellent view of the landscape that is very helpful for dealing with conflicts associated with territorial claims and land use (Rambaldi and Callosa-Tarr, 2004).

A REVIEW OF DECISION SUPPORT PROCEDURES IN GIS

Generally, conflict management strategies in a GIS are contained in a collection of inter-linked procedures that the technology offers to facilitate group decision making. For a long time, GIS technology lacked elaborate decision support tools for supporting group decision-making processes that include conflict management (Carver, 1991; Heywood et al., 1995). Currently, commercial GIS software such as Idrisi Taiga (Clark University, Worcester, MA, USA), ArcGIS Community Viz (ESRI), and ILWIS 3.4[4] (ITC, Enschede, the Netherlands) contain procedures for supporting group decision making. MapTalk, the Diamond Touch Table, and a host of GIS-based spatial communication tools also offer interactive participatory planning platforms for supporting small group collaborations. These systems offer a range of decision support strategies ranging from multi-user touch and gesture-activated screens (Diamond Touch), visual and spatial-analytical procedures for group interaction (MapTalk), to specific functionalities for group decision-making based on multicriteria evaluation methods (IDRISI and ILWIS).

Multicriteria evaluation techniques and conflict management

Multicriteria evaluation (MCE) methods involve the qualitative or quantitative weighting, scoring, or ranking of criteria in terms of a single or multiple sets of objectives (Voogd, 1983; Jankowski, 1995; Malczewski, 1999). There are currently different approaches to multicriteria evaluation in GIS but generally, the technique involves all or several of the steps described below (Eastman et al., 1993; Malczewski, 1999; Kyem, 2000).

- The articulation of objectives based on positions stakeholders have taken in a conflict is often the first step in a multicriteria evaluation process. The competing perspectives (that are responsible for the discrepancy in stakeholders' interests) are often the driving force behind stakeholders' positions in the conflict.
- Criteria (factors and constraints) that are relevant for the evaluation of the competing objectives are identified and processed.
- For each evaluation criterion, a map that translates the attributes into a measure of suitability for the given objective is developed in the GIS.
- Weights are assigned by stakeholders and incorporated into the evaluation criteria to reflect the relative importance of each factor and constraint regarding the objective under consideration.
- A decision rule is applied to weigh each criterion and calculate a suitability map for the objectives. The feature category that maximizes conditions in all the evaluation criteria under an objective is then chosen.

Decision rules in multicriteria evaluation

A decision rule can be as simple as a threshold designed to exclude some criterion scores from being considered for the activity (e.g., selecting slope gradients below 30 percent for farming). This is the Boolean overlay technique where all criteria are converted into true/false (or 0/1) logical statements of suitability for the objective under consideration.

The Boolean constraint maps are finally summed up by some combination of intersection (logical AND) or union (logical OR) operators to produce a final map from which a decision may be made. A decision rule can also take the form of a mathematical function such as in linear programming (LP) or a logical procedure such as in MCE. Early attempts to model the decision-making process in GIS resulted in the integration of linear programming techniques from decision theory into the system. The LP technique attempts to choose the most desirable plan of action from a set of possible options based on the assumption that all the alternatives among which a choice can be made and the consequences of choosing any alternative are known (Zeleny, 1982; Lootsma, 1989). The approach works very well with a small number of choice alternatives and in cases where maximization of variables is possible and relevant to the problem under consideration. The massive data sets contained in grid cells of raster GIS images create storage problems and delays in computing (Eastman et al., 1993). Also, the technique cannot accommodate inconsistencies in human values and perceptions that characterize the decision making process. Mathematical programming techniques have consequently found limited applications in GIS compared with choice heuristic algorithms.

The most common procedure for multiple criteria evaluation is the weighted linear combination of factors and constraints (WLC) (Voogd, 1983; Malczewski, 1996). The WLC is a choice heuristic algorithm that provides logical procedures for evaluating decision alternatives[5]. The technique breaks down the decision process into evaluations of sets of criteria and constraint maps that allow for choice alternatives to be assessed (Eastman et al., 1995). The result is often a suitability map for the objective under consideration.

Analyzing conflict of interests in a GIS

The suitability maps that result from single-objective evaluations are later used to resolve areas of conflicting claims. In explaining this

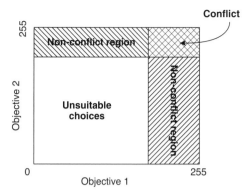

Figure 25.2   Allocating cells between conflicting objectives

procedure, Eastman et al., (1995) have assumed a multidimensional decision space where two suitability maps developed under conflicting objectives are laid over each other. Four possible allocations that result from this are described below (see also Figure 25.2).

- Areas selected by objective 1 and not by objective 2 and hence non-conflicting.
- Areas selected by objective 2 and not by objective 1 and hence non-conflicting.
- A sizeable area not selected by either of the two objectives (unsuitable choices).
- Areas selected by both objectives and hence in dispute (conflict zone).

It is often the case that conflict of interest cases in land use focus on only small portions of the land (as in Figure 25.2) where the opposing interests overlap each other. The marking out of the conflict zone helps to refocus the discussion in the conflict management process.

The final stage of the conflict management process involves the allocation of cells within the conflict zone. First, criterion scores in each suitability maps are rank ordered. Next, each of the ranked suitability maps is considered to have an ideal point defining the case of a cell that is maximally suited for that objective but minimally suited for all others. As illustrated in Figure 25.3, the single line (a hyper plane in the multidimensional space) defines the best allocation for each ranked cell based upon a minimum-distance-to-ideal-point logic. In the process, suitable cells in one objective that happen to be marginally more suited to the other objective are traded off so that the area target for that objective would be met. The single decision line moves further down into the zone of poorer choices until an exact solution is attained.

MCE procedures in GIS are valued for breaking down the complex decision-making process into workable units to facilitate the unraveling of veiled positions and hidden problems (Voogd, 1983; Roy, 1996;

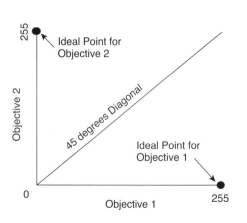

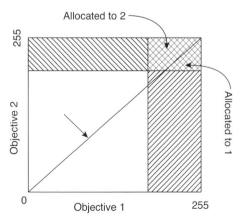

Figure 25.3   Allocating conflicting cells in a multidimensional decision space

Jankowski, 2006). The speedy analyses of evaluation criteria in a GIS enhances interaction between stakeholders and creates opportunities for them to be actively involved in the determination and revision of criterion weights and preferences (Eastman et al., 1993). However, there is uncertainty about the degree to which errors in the evaluation criteria and vagueness about their quality propagates through the MCE process (Malczewski, 2000). Concerns have also been raised about the conflict problem definition, the independence of the criterion maps, and the robustness of the method (Carver, 1991; Heywood et al., 1995; Malczewski, 1999).

CRITICAL FACTORS IN GIS APPLICATIONS IN MEDIATION

The success of a GIS application in conflict management depends upon several factors, some of which are discussed below.

Sociocultural and institutional influences and GIS applications

The inflexibility of stakeholders' positions in a conflict which may dictate the success or failure of the GIS application in mediation is influenced by several factors, including historical events and cultural, political, and legal institutions within the community (Gray, 1989; Jankowski and Nyerges, 2001b). One cannot fully understand the causes of a conflict or deal effectively with it without understanding the sociopolitical and cultural context within which the disagreement occurs. The context provides the knowledge that imbues human action with a meaning. It also provides the background experience upon which stakeholders evaluate the GIS maps, their values, interests, and situations, and decide to either curtail or prolong a conflict. In some cases, the norms and networks of social interaction embody past

experiences with conflicts that serve as cultural templates for the resolution of disagreements within the community. According to Jankowski and Nyerges (2001b), if and when there is a common interest between the parties as is the case in many local communities, it helps to bring the parties together. Such a condition also helps to create a conducive climate for setting the agenda and focus of the group discussion. Other factors that influence the success of the GIS application include recognition and mandate from sociopolitical institutions within the community, a facilitator of the process who is respected and trusted by both parties, and the adequate representation of key stakeholders in the discussions (Jankowski and Nyerges, 2001b).

The type of conflict

The inflexibility of values, interests, and goals that sustain a conflict depends upon several factors, including whether or not the disagreement occurs between groups who live within the same or in different sociopolitical units. The need for cooperation and hence the urge to resolve disputes is stronger among individuals and groups who live in the same sociopolitical environment than it is with groups located within different cultural and political systems (Zartman, 2000). This is because the sociopolitical context plays an important role in the resolution of conflicts and as such a full understanding of GIS's role in the management of conflicts will require familiarity with the social context in which the disagreements occur.

Between-system conflicts
Between-system conflicts are disagreements that occur between individuals, organizations, or subgroups located in different sociopolitical environments (Zartman, 2000). As shown in Figure 25.4, the stakeholders in a between-system conflict may live in different geographic locations, share few or no values in common, and may not be engaged in any intimate and long-term relationships such as

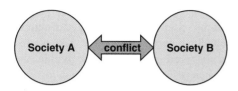

A disagreement between individuals and groups who live in different communities. The stakeholders may ...

- live in different territories
- have different beliefs and values
- live under different political entities and. . .
- have few or no relationships between them

Figure 25.4   A between-system conflict

A disagreement between individuals and groups who live together in a community. The feuding parties may share many things in common.

- language
- territory
- identity
- social values and . . .
- networks of social interaction

Figure 25.5   A within-system conflict

marriage or being members of a local religious group. An example is a conflict between two countries. In the absence of a binding relationship, the parties in a between-system conflict will feel less motivated to work toward the resolution of conflicts between them. Prolonging a conflict could even be a way for the parties to ascertain the relative strengths of their antagonistic values. Thus there is a strong competitive urge for the parties to protect their independent values and as such between-system conflicts are more difficult to resolve than conflicts that occur between parties who are members of the same sociopolitical unit. For example, in between-system conflicts that occur over forests, oceans, species, and the environment, the disagreements arise mainly from the negotiation of rights to the resources and less from the spatial allocations of such resources. In view of the predominantly non-spatial nature of between-system conflicts, and the fact that often no strong binding relations exist between the feuding parties, their resolution requires negotiation rather than mediation which may involve a GIS strategy (Mastenbroek, 1989; Druckman, 1997).

Within-system conflicts

In contrast, conflicts between individuals and groups within a common sociopolitical environment (within-system conflicts) occur amid a constellation of relationships, common values, and group expectations. Individuals or groups within the same sociopolitical unit are often engaged in long-lasting relationships including inter-marriages, common ethnic backgrounds, allegiance to a common authority, and a long history of cooperation between them. Within-system conflicts therefore pit individuals or groups against each other and strain relationships between them. Conflict management strategies (including GIS applications) and mediators can therefore take advantage of referents in values and binding relationships to induce compliance, cooperation, or consensus by essentially calling the parties to order to preserve relationships within the community (Osaghae, 2000; Zartman, 2000). Several community-based GIS projects occur within the context of within-system conflicts. For example, in South Africa, a PGIS project involving the use of interviews, participatory workshops, and global positioning system (GPS) boundary identification was conducted by Harris and Weiner (2002) to highlight competing interests and prepare the groups for land reforms in the former apartheid state. The author also adopted participatory GIS strategies to mediate conflicts between local groups and foresters to facilitate the protection of reserved forest estates in Southern Ghana (Kyem, 2000, 2004). The success of the GIS applications was partly due to the fact that the disputes occurred between groups who live in a community within the same sociopolitical context.

Some within-system conflicts do not pose a direct threat to the ultimate political authority in the community. Such disputes (termed inter-group conflicts) result from competition over scarce resources, power, or recognition among individuals and groups located within the sociopolitical system. There are however some disagreements within society that pitch individuals or groups against the status quo. Such conflicts (termed against-system conflicts) occur between individuals or groups in a community against part of, or the complete sociopolitical system in the state (Zartman, 2000). Of the two cases of disagreement, against-system conflicts are more common but also more difficult to resolve because of the imbalances of power and resources between social groups and the overall political authority. A large number of community-based GIS applications in conflict management have occurred in against-system conflicts between marginalized groups and public officials. Many of the projects in counter mapping also occur in the context of against-system conflicts. For example, GIS has been adopted to assist some Native American tribes of North America in preparing claims to their territories and ancestral lands (Beltgens, 1995; Smith, 1995) and to also facilitate the bottom-up transformation of political structures and public discourse to make room for the views of indigenous groups (Forbes, 1995). GIS mapping is also the tool of choice for activism organized at local and national scales (Sieber, 2002; Tulloch, 2002). Together, these applications suggest that creative applications of GIS can play a beneficial role in reconciling seemingly intractable disagreements over values that occur between groups located within the same sociopolitical system.

Data provision and analysis of the conflict situation

The undertaking to resolve conflicts through GIS applications requires that stakeholders do not become mere consumers of spatial information. Providing information is only the first step in creating a congenial atmosphere for a dialogue that is intended to forge an agreement between disputants. Passing on information to stakeholders makes no distinction between what Moemoka describes as providing raw facts and figures about an issue, (the 'talking-to model'), and exchanging ideas about the problem (the 'talking-with model') (2000: 12). In the former model, emphasis is placed on data capture and its dissemination, while in the 'talking-with model' the focus is on data capture, analyses, and a discussion based on the factual information. Without effective analyses of the data to guide the discussion, it is likely that stakeholders will interpret the information to confirm their pre-existing beliefs about the conflict. In such a situation the GIS application will elevate rather than lower the level of a dispute in the manner described by Obermeyer and Pinto (1994). If a GIS application is to bring about a change in human perceptions that may lead to a change in behavior that is favorable for a mutual agreement, then data provision efforts must be accompanied by rigorous data analyses geared toward exploration of the spatial condition that caused and sustains the disagreement. There are also further requisites for, a GIS application is insufficient when simply added to the mix of conflict management strategies without adequate provision of important complementary factors. These include effective dialogue, commitment of the parties to the mediation, representation of all key stakeholders, and the support of people and institutions within the community.

On-site interaction versus online collaboration

Advances in spatial technology opens up new opportunities but also imposes fresh limitations on GIS applications in conflict management. Current infrastructure for wireless communication networks is capable of carrying not only voice traffic but also video and data traffic. The convergence of voice communication, spatial data processing, and imaging technologies has ushered in the era of multimedia in which voice, images, and data analyses and display can be combined in a GIS to present a realistic image of a conflict situation. Web GIS is one such technology where the Internet is used as a platform for integrating multimedia into GIS applications (Al-Kodmany, 1998; Kingston et al., 1999; Carver et al., 2001). Given the universality of the Internet, the group of participants who have a stake in a resource conflict may no longer be locally defined. Participation can expand to include those who live hundreds of miles away from the project site but respond to issues from within cyberspace (Carver et al., 2001). There is therefore the possibility that a great number of affected people can be brought into the conflict management process. However, the majority of people in disadvantaged and indigenous communities around the world remain either poorly connected, or not connected at all to broadband communication networks, especially the Internet (ITU, 2006). Added to the problems of web-based GIS applications are technical difficulties related to lack of effective procedures in GIS and the Internet for supporting collaborative interactions among stakeholders (Steinmann et al., 2004).

The online project may also not be able to sustain collective action and face-to-face interactions that are essential for consensus building. In a traditional GIS application, acknowledgement is expressed by non-verbal channels of communication such as nodding, facial expressions, eye blinking, and supportive sounds (e.g., 'ya,' 'uh,' 'u-huh'). These gestures (that are indicative of approval and/ or disapproval) are absent from online discussions. Instead, stakeholders must record their responses online in a written or spoken form via multimedia. The possibility that a respondent's recorded statement may be later used against her can limit her participation in the discussions. Furthermore, investigations into the behavior of groups engaged in online discussions confirm the fear of many that online GIS applications limit participation to a few 'professional' participants. The majority of participants in an online discussion forum never contribute to any discussion besides reading others' comments (Nielsen, 2006). Online collaboration may therefore produce results that are not shared by majority of stakeholders. The Internet may also create exclusive sophisticated user communities beyond the reach of the majority of people in the place-based community whose involvement may be critical to the resolution of the conflict. Thus, even though the Internet aims to expand GIS applications in conflict management by addressing some of the access, representational and epistemological limitations of traditional PGIS projects, the technology may simultaneously re-inscribe the limitations on participation and public access to information as well as weaken interaction and effective collaboration among stakeholders (Wong and Chua, 2004).

Timing of the GIS application in mediation

As a product of social interaction, resource conflicts undergo changes over time. Social interactions are not only initiated by motives but also, with the passing of time, the interaction generates new intents and alters existing motives (Moore, 1996). The changes exert significant influence on the outcome of a GIS-mediated conflict management process (Cormick, 1982; Moore, 1996). For example, there are situations when parties engaged in a conflict may need to develop some basis of power prior to the GIS application to be able to assert their influence during the group decision-making process. Such power is developed in a number of ways, including legal challenges, grassroots organizations, and even the use of negative or disruptive tactics such as strikes and protests (Cormick, 1982). Under these circumstances, an early intervention through any strategy could inhibit the development of sufficient power to ensure true mutuality and equal participation (Cormick, 1982). It might even be necessary to hold back the conflict management process until after the development of intense emotions that significantly raise the level of threat to the parties before the right political atmosphere develops for the mediation to be successful. The right timing of a GIS application, and for that matter any mediation strategy, is therefore critical for a successful outcome of the process.

The institutional and competitive forces that create the context for the disagreement also undergo changes during the lifetime of the conflict. In the course of time, the forces driving the conflict either subside with new information and a deeper understanding, or they turn into negative forces that restrain cooperation. The environmental context itself changes over time. For example, changes in the environment brought about by floods, threats from wildfire, and hurricanes or a bumper harvest after a period of dwindling food resources can lead either to the strengthening of stakeholder positions that sustain the conflict, or they can undermine and weaken the positions that stakeholders have taken and thereby make it easy for the parties to agree on the issues that divide them.

ASSESSMENT OF GIS APPLICATIONS IN MEDIATION

GIS applications can help clarify the conflict situation and thereby pave the way for a better understanding of the conflict. On the other hand, GIS is not a perfect conflict management tool because applications of the technology are subject to several restraining conditions that can reduce the effectiveness and outcome of the project. In the sections that follow, I discuss some beneficial and negative impacts of GIS applications in conflict management.

Potential negative influences of GIS applications in mediation

If a GIS application is not handled well, it can restrict fair and open discussions in a conflict management process. The competency requirements that the technology impose on users limit active participation to individuals and groups who have some experience with GIS technology or those who are familiar with computers. This narrowing of the group discussion and evidence about the conflict to the analyses of spatial data may reinforce the hegemonic position of a GIS technology that is usually not equally available and accessible to majority of people within a local community (Harwell, 2000). Consequently, if the conflict management process is based mainly on GIS applications, it is possible that some important voices will be filtered out, the individual experiences of some key stakeholders (i.e., the poor and illiterate members) will be ignored, and alternative representations (i.e., local knowledge and voices of underrepresented groups) may be excluded from the mediation process (Kyem, 2004). This is irrespective of the fact that such views and representations from those deprived from the mediation may be vital to the final resolution of the conflict.

In addition, a GIS application might not in itself ensure a fair, participatory or a deliberative conflict management process (King, 2000; Hogson and Shroeder, 2002). Participation requires a conscious effort to make it happen. Short of a deliberate effort to ensure fair and equal participation in group discussions, the party with prior knowledge of the conflict situation, those stakeholders with some experience of spatial data analysis, or those close to positions of power, will dominate the discussion and alter the outcomes in their favor. GIS applications occur within existing power structures in society and the injection of the technology into the mediation process does not automatically change the dynamics of power relations between groups in the community. Generally, GIS applications are most effective when they are implemented in a political atmosphere of good-faith negotiations (Johnson, 1999).

GIS models are also abstractions of reality that may represent a simplified and inaccurate form of the natural conditions that sustain a conflict. It is therefore possible that the maps produced to facilitate the conflict management process may highlight some issues (i.e., property boundaries) and omit others (such as land claims) entirely. When this occurs, the maps will fail to capture the root causes of the conflict and thereby cause the mediation process to fail. In addition, the powerful appeal of the technology, particularly, the production of brightly colored and professionally looking maps, can distract stakeholders' attention and obscure rather than illuminate the true basis of their decisions. Consequently, GIS applications might not necessarily lead to the resolution of conflicts by virtue of the insights stakeholders garner from spatial data analyses (Harwell, 2000).

Potential positive influences of GIS applications in mediation

The problems with GIS applications described in the preceding section may not limit the potential and proven capabilities of the technology to be appropriated for the management of resource conflicts. The technology can be the battleground as well as the medium in which different viewpoints may compete and disagreements resolved. Innovative visual representations of the conflict condition gleaned from P3DM map displays for example, may allow disputing parties to concentrate on fresh ideas, and the issues that need

immediate attention. Generally, in group decision making, GIS applications promote a search for evidence to substantiate opinions, allegations, and accusations. This evidential requirement can help reduce the number of times stakeholders rely on speculation and as a result, more factual considerations may form the basis for their decisions. With the maps and other data serving as points of reference in the group discussion, the expression of dissenting views will be directed more toward the search for evidence (contained in maps and other GIS products), than at persons with whom there was disagreement. Ultimately, it will be ideas rather than proponents of viewpoints that will become the objects of discussion in a GIS-mediated conflict management process.

Furthermore, the GIS applications provide opportunities for stakeholders to meet and jointly collect and analyze data, share resources, and exchange ideas about the conflict. The joint search for data and the group mapping exercises create a congenial climate that encourages the parties to develop trust, cordial relations, and friendships between them. Such coalitions may later become the building blocks for collaboration and hence, the foundation upon which a compromise solutions is reached. The technology also equips the parties with the capability to draw links between subjective values that triggered and may sustain the conflict, and the external conditions about the conflict. A computer screen projection of maps or remote-sensing images showing resources that are in dispute will create a common focal point for discussions (Ozawa, 1999). With their eyes fixed on the screen, the parties often become physically, as well as mentally engaged in the discussions. Through such map representations, the GIS expert is able to bridge perception gaps between the parties to facilitate a common interpretation of the conflict situation. Thus, if the provision of spatial data is well organized and the data is effectively utilized in the mediation, the GIS applications can lead to a deeper understanding of the conflict to prepare stakeholders for mutual agreement.

An important GIS contribution to conflict management that is not possible with manual approaches is the assurance of consistency in the processing of information about the conflict. Even if a GIS application fails to make an initial impact on the conflict, it leaves behind valuable feedback information that can be used for further analysis of the conflict situation. Once spatial information has been registered to a common geometry, it could be propagated uniformly across all support systems, would not change without intervention, and would not be affected by subsequent viewing and use (Johnson, 1999). An added advantage is the capability that GIS brings to process data more easily and consistently than with manual methods (Ozawa, 1999). GIS applications in conflict management have the additional benefit of providing a record of the process that can be conveniently replicated, stored, printed, and shared with all concerned parties.

CONCLUSION

The intricate and complex task of allocating resources among competing interests and the rapid rate at which community groups are being integrated into the official decision-making process have generated new requirements for appropriate information and analytical tools. However, creating a supportive climate within GIS projects for the management of resource conflicts requires not only digital spatial data and computer hardware enhancements, but most importantly, simple GIS procedures that provide direct support for dialogue and effectively involve all parties in the conflict management process. Meeting the demands for such a GIS-mediated dialogue also requires group decision support techniques that are flexible and allow for questioning, repetition, and re-evaluation of choices such that the changing and evolving thoughts of stakeholders can be captured and incorporated into the conflict-mediation process.

I note also that although GIS technology's reputation as an interventionist tool has been undermined by competing explanations offered by the competitive and cooperative approaches to conflict, the theories do not adequately capture the dynamics of the conflict management process. A reduction of the conflict problem to a mere difference in the interpretation of facts or values is an over-simplification that generates skepticism about the potential for resolving certain conflicts. Rather, conflicts involve crucial and unavoidable interdependencies between the cooperative move to create values jointly and the competitive push to gain an independent advantage. GIS applications are however limited to issues that exhibit a spatial dimension and as such, the technology remains a poor medium for resolving ideological or value-laden conflicts that usually occur between parties located within different sociopolitical systems. It could also happen that issues that caused the conflict and may be sustaining the dispute lack a spatial component, or that the GIS application occurs amid intense suspicion, skepticism, and distrust. Under these conditions, a GIS application may only succeed in fueling the dispute through the provision of data which the parties may use to defend the positions they have already taken in the conflict. Failure to make a positive contribution to the resolution of a value-rational conflict with a GIS application may therefore be due to factors other than the irreconcilability of the values that sustain the disagreement. Almost all conflicts have negotiable interests and values and as such GIS applications may be utilized to explore a conflict situation and prepare disputants for a better understanding of the disagreement, search for common interests, delve into common concerns, and facilitate the creation of joint gains. Ultimately, the management of resource conflicts depends upon a combination of factors within and outside communities where the disagreement occurs.

There is also an interesting convergence that is currently taking place between multimedia, the Internet, and GIS applications. An increasing number of practitioners are using the Internet as a platform for hosting GIS applications. With the integration of the worldwide web into GIS applications, the tools for group decision making has expanded to include online tools for visualization, three dimensional viewing, text, audio, and video. The use of multimedia in Internet GIS applications can motivate participants and generate a high level of responsive feedback and individual involvement in the conflict management process. GIS applications in mediation can also be programmed as part of an interactive system on the web to expand access to citizens affected by the conflict but who may not be physically present at meetings organized to resolve it. Internet GIS therefore has the potential to expand public participation in conflict management but also poses a great challenge to PGIS applications in mediation. Among other things, there are concerns about how a genuine communication and effective interaction can be maintained between stakeholders, the mediator, and community groups in a web-based GIS application. The uneven development of structures for Internet access between people in rich and poor communities means that relatively little participation in the conflict management process will occur among those in poor communities. Advances in spatial information technology therefore raise prospects as well as concerns for the future of GIS applications in mediation. In the end, the choices we face today regarding advances in spatial technology, the uses we design for those technologies, and the institutional arrangements in which spatial technologies may be embedded will determine the future of GIS applications in conflict management.

ACKNOWLEDGMENT

I would like to express my gratitude to the Connecticut State University (CSU) System for its support in funding the research for this paper through its University Research Grant Program.

NOTES

1   A survey of GIS literature reveals the following additional terms have been used to describe community-based GIS Applications: Public Participation GIS (PPGIS), Participatory GIS (PGIS), Community Integrated GIS (CIGIS) and recently, Participatory Three-dimensional Modeling (P3DM).

2   Several terms have been used to describe conflict types based on the sources of the disagreement. The terms include: 'value conflicts' and cognitive (fact-based) conflicts (Obermeyer and Pinto, 1994), conflicts induced by affectual behavior and value-rational conflicts (Weber, 1964) and conflicts in facts and value conflicts (Berry, 1995: 11–7).

3   An example is the development of the nuclear bomb. Even at the height of the cold war, the Soviet Union and the USA could not face each other in a war. This is mainly because a war involving nuclear arms would never benefit any country. The nuclear arms therefore served as a deterrent for war and might have played a major role in getting the two powers to enter into direct negotiations to control the development and deployment of nuclear arms.

4   As of 1 July 2007, ILWIS Open 3.4 is available as 52°North free and open source software, http://52north.org/index.php?option=com_content&task=view&id=47&Itemid=70.

5   Some MCE techniques that have been integrated into GIS include the ordered weighted average (OWA) available in Idrisi GIS (Jiang and Eastman, 2000), the Technique for Order Preference by Similarity to Ideal Solution (TOPSIS) designed by Hwang and Yoon and Multiple Criteria Group Decision Making (MGDM) introduced by Malzewski (1996).

REFERENCES

Al-Kodmany, K. (2002) 'Visualization tools and methods in community planning: From freehand sketches to virtual reality', *Journal of Planning Literature*, 17(2): 189–211.

Beltgens, P. (1995) 'Resource information training program', *Cultural Survival Quarterly*, 18(4): 21–2.

Berry, J.K. (1995) *Spatial Reasoning for Effective GIS*. Fort Collins, CO: GIS World Books.

Brahm, E. (2004) 'Benefits of intractable conflict', in G. Burgess and H. Burgess (eds), *Beyond*

Intractability: Conflict Research Consortium. Boulder: University of Colorado. http://www.beyondintractability.org/essay/benefits/ (accessed 25 July 2007).

Burgess, G.M. and Burgess, H. (1996) 'Constructive confrontation theoretical framework', in G. Burgess and H. Burgess (ed.), *Beyond Intractability: Conflict Research Consortium.* Boulder: University of Colorado. http://www.colorado.edu/conflict/peace/essay/con_conf.htm.

Brody, S.D., Highfield, W.A., Sudha, D.H., Bierling, D.H., Roubabah, M., Ismailova, Lai Lee and Butzler, R. (2004) 'Conflict on the coast: Using geographic information systems to map potential environmental disputes in Matagorda bay, Texas', *Environmental Management*, 34(1): 11–25.

Brody, S.D., Grover, H., Bernhardt, S., Tang, Z., Whitaker, B. and Spence, C. (2006) 'Identifying potential conflict associated with oil and gas exploration in Texas state coastal waters: A multicriteria spatial analysis', *Environmental Management*, 38(4): 597–606.

Carver S.J. (1991) 'Integrating multi-criteria evaluation with geographic information systems', *International Journal for Geographic Information Systems*, 5(3): 221–39.

Carver, S., Evans, A., Kingston, R. and Turton, I. (2001) 'Public participation, GIS and cyberdemocracy: Evaluating on-line spatial decision support systems', *Environment and Planning B: Planning and Design*, 28(6): 907–21.

Chambers, R. (1994) 'The origins and practice of participatory rural appraisal', *World Development*, 22(7): 953–69.

Coser, L. (1967) *Continuities in the Study of Social Conflict.* New York: Free Press.

Cormick, W.G. (1982) 'Intervention and self-determination in environmental disputes: A mediator's perspective', *Resolve*, 11: 1–7.

Craig, W.J and Elwood, S.A. (1998) 'How and why community groups use maps and geographic information', *Cartography and Geographic Information Systems*, 25(2): 95–104.

Deutsch, M. (1977) *The Resolution of Conflict: Constructive and Destructive Processes.* New Haven, CT: Yale University Press.

Druckman, D. (1997) 'Negotiating in the international context', in I.W. Zartman and L. Rasmussen (eds), *Peacemaking in International Conflict.* Washington, DC: US Institute of Peace.

Eastman, J.R., Kyem, P.A.K. and Toledano, J. (1993) *GIS and Decision Making.* Geneva: UNITAR.

Eastman, R.J., Jin, W., Kyem, P.A.K. and Toledano, J. (1995) 'Raster procedures for multi-criteria/ multi-objective decisions', *Photogrammetric Engineering and Remote Sensing*, 61: 539–47.

Eghenter, C. (2000) *Mapping Peoples Forests: The Role of Mapping in Planning Community-Based Management of Conservation Areas in Indonesia: Peoples, Forests and Reefs Program Discussion Paper Series.* Washington, DC: Biodiversity Support Program.

Forbes, A.A. (1995) 'Heirs to the land: Mapping the future of the Makura-Barun', *Cultural Survival Quarterly*, 18(4): 69–71.

Forrester, J. (1999) 'Dealing with deep value differences', in L. Susskind, S. McKearman and J. Thomas-Learner (eds), *The Consensus Building Handbook: A Comprehensive Guide to Reaching Agreements.* Thousand Oaks, CA: Sage Publications. pp. 463–94.

Fox, J. (1998) 'Mapping the commons: The social context of spatial information technologies', *The Common Property Resource Digest*, 45: 1–9.

Fox, J., Suryanata, K., Hershock P. and Hadi Pramono, A. (2005) 'Mapping power: Ironic effects of spatial information technology', in J. Fox, K. Suryanata and P. Hershock (eds), *Mapping Communities: Ethics, Values, Practice.* Honolulu: East-West Center.

Gray, B. (1989) *Collaborating: Finding Common Ground for Multiparty Problems.* San Francisco, CA: Jossey-Bass.

Gupta, A.K. (1989) 'Maps drawn by farmers and extensionists', in R. Chambers (ed.), *Farmer First: Farmer Innovation and Agricultural Research.* London: Intermediate Technology Publications. pp. 8–92.

Habermas, J. (1984) 'The theory of communicative action. Vol 1: Reason and the rationalization of society', trans. T. McCarthy. Boston, MA: Beacon Press.

Habermas, J. (1987) 'The theory of communicative action. Vol 2: *Life World and System: A Critique of Functionalist Reason*', trans T. McCarthy. Boston, MA: Beacon Press.

Hardcastle, J., Rimbaldi, G., Long, B., Lanh, L.V. and Son, D.Q. (2004) 'The use of participatory three-dimensional modeling in community-based planning in Quang Nam province, Vietnam', *PLA Notes*, 49: 70–6.

Harris, T.M. and Weiner D. (2002) 'Implementing a community-integrated GIS: Perspectives from South African fieldwork', in W.J. Craig, T.M. Harris and D. Weiner (eds), *Community Participation and Geographic Information Systems.* New York: Taylor & Francis. pp. 246–58.

Harwell, E.E. (2000) 'Remote sensibilities, discourses of technology and the making of Indonesia's natural disaster', in M. Doornboss, A. Saith and B. White (eds), *Forests, Nature, People and Power*. Malden, MA.: Blackwell. pp. 299–32.

Herlihy, P.H. and Knapp, G. (2003) 'Maps of, by and for the peoples of Latin America', *Human Organization*, 62 (4): 303–14.

Heywood, I., Oliver J. and Thompson, S. (1995) 'Building and exploratory multi-criteria modeling environment for spatial decision support', in P. Fisher (ed.), *Innovations in GIS 2*. London: Taylor & Francis.

Hoare, P.B., Maneeratana, W., Songwadhana, Suwanmanee, A. and Sricharoen, Y. (2002) 'Relief models, a multipurpose tool for improved natural resource management: The experience of the upper NAN watershed management project in Thailand', *Asean Biodiversity*, 2(1): 11–6.

Hogson, D.L. and Shroeder, R.A. (2002) 'Dilemmas of counter mapping community resources in Tanzania', *Development and Change*, 33: 79–100.

International Telecommunications Union (2006) *World Telecommunication/ICT Development Report*. http://www.itu.int/ITU-D/ict/publications/wtdr_06/index.html (assessed 20 June 2007).

Jankowski, P. (1995) 'Integrating geographical information systems and multiple criteria decision-making methods', *International Journal of Geographical Information Systems*, 9: 251–73.

Jankowski, P. (2006) 'Integrating geographical information systems and multiple criteria decision-making methods: Ten years after', in P. Fisher (ed.), *Classics from IJGIS: Twenty years of the International Journal of Geographical Information Science and Systems*. Boca Raton, FL: Taylor & Francis. pp. 291–6.

Jankowski, P. and Nyerges, T. (2001a) 'Methods, models and GIS-supported collaborative decision making: Results of an experiment', *Annals of the Association of American Geographers*, 91(1): 48–70.

Jankowski, P. and Nyerges, T. (2001b) *GIS for Group Decision Making*. New York: Taylor & Francis Publishers.

Jankowski, P., Nyerges, T.L., Smith, A. and Moore, T.J. (1997) 'Spatial group choice: A SDSS tool for collaborative spatial decision making', *International Journal of Geographic Information Systems*, 11: 577–602.

Jiang, H. and Eastman, R.J. (2000) 'Application of fuzzy measures in multi-criteria evaluation in GIS', *International Journal of Geographic Information Systems*, 14: 173–84.

Johnson, R.G. (1999) 'Negotiating the dayton peace accords through digital maps: United States institute of peace (USIP)', *Virtual Diplomacy Report*, Washington DC, 25 February.

Jordan, G. (1999) 'Maximizing the benefits of participatory GIS in technology poor countries: Case studies from Zambia and Nepal', paper presented at Geographic Information and Society Conference at University of Minnesota, Minneapolis, MN, 20–22 June.

King, B.H. (2000) 'Towards a participatory GIS: Evaluating case studies of participatory rural appraisal and GIS in the developing world', *Cartography and Geographic Information Sciences*, 29(1): 43–52.

Kingston, R.S., Evans, Carver A. and Turton, I. (1999) 'Virtual decision making in spatial planning: Web-based geographical information systems for public participation in environmental decision making'. http://www.geog.leeds.ac.uk/papers/99–9/index.html (assessed 22 July 2008).

Koassi, E.K. (2000) 'West coast diplomacy among the Akan and their neighbors', in I.W. Zartmann (ed.), *Traditional Cures for Modern Conflicts: African Conflict Medicine*. Boulder, CO: Lynne Reinner. pp. 6–78.

Kyem, P.A.K. (2000) 'A choice heuristic algorithm for managing land resource allocation problems involving multiple parties and conflicting interests', *Transactions in GIS*, 5(2): 113–32.

Kyem, P.A.K. (2004) 'Of intractable conflicts and participatory GIS applications: The search for consensus amidst competing claims and institutional demands', *Annals of the Association of American Geographers*, 94(1): 37–7.

Kriesberg, L. (2002) *Constructive Conflicts: From Escalation to Resolution*. 2nd edn. New York: Rowman and Littlefield.

Lax, D.A. and Sabenius, J.K. (1986) *The Manager as Negotiator: Bargaining for Cooperative and Competitive Gain*. New York: Free Press. pp. 29–45.

Lax, D.A. and Sabenius, J.K. (2000) 'The negotiators dilemma: Creating and claiming value', in F. Paul Levy and J. Thomas-Learner (eds), *Negotiating Environmental Agreements: How to Avoid Escalating Confrontation, Needless Costs and Unnecessary Litigation*. Washington DC: Island Press. pp. 227–39.

Leila, M.H. and Hazen, H.D. (2006) 'Power of maps: Counter mapping for conservation', *ACME: An International E-Journal for Critical Geographies*, 4(1): 99–130.

Lootsma, F.A. (1989) 'Optimization with multiple objectives', in M. Iri and K. Tanabe (eds), *Mathematical Programming, Recent Developments and Applications*. Tokyo: KTK Scientific, Publishers.

Maling, A. (2006) 'Mapping the forest in three dimensions', *The WWF Cambodia Newsletter*, 1(2): 3.

Mascarenhaus, J. and Prem Kumar P.D. (1991) 'Participatory mapping and modeling user's notes', *RRA Notes*, 12: 9–20.

Mastenbroek, W. (1989) *Negotiate*. London: Basil Blackwell.

Malczewski, J. (1980) *The Analytical Hierarchy Process*. New York: McGraw Hill International.

Malczewski, J. (1996) 'A GIS-based approach to multiple criteria group decision making', *International Journal of Geographical Information Systems*, 10: 955–71.

Malczewski, J. (1999) *GIS and Multicriteria Decision Analysis*. New York: John Wiley.

Malczewski, J. (2000) 'On the use of weighted liner combination method in GIS: Common and best practice approaches', *Transactions in GIS*, 4(1): 5–22.

Malczewski, J., Chapman, T., Flegel, C., Walters, D., Shrubsole, D. and Healy, M.A. (2003) 'GIS-multicriteria evaluation with ordered weighted averaging (OWA): Developing management strategies for rehabilitation and enhancement projects in the cedar creek watershed, Ontario, Canada', *Environment and Planning A*, 35(10): 1769–84.

Moore, C. (1996) *The Mediation Process: Practical Strategies for Resolving Conflicts*. San Francisco, CA: Jossey-Bass.

Moemeka, A.A. (2000) 'Development, social change and development communication: Background and conceptual discussion', in A. Anderw Moemeka (ed.), *Development Communication in Action: Building Understanding and Creating Participation*. Lanham, MD: University Press of America. pp. 1–16.

Neela, M. (1992) 'Villagers, perceptions of rural people through the mapping methods of PRA', *PRA Notes*, 15: 21–6.

Nielsen, J. (2006) 'Participation inequality: Encouraging more users to contribute', *Alterbox: Current Issues in Web Usability: Bi-weekly Column*. http://www.useit.com/alertbox/participation_inequality.html (accessed 9 October 2006).

Northrup, T.A. (1989) 'The dynamic of identity in personal and social conflict', in A. Terrell, J. Northrup, S. Thompson and L. Kingsbergy (eds), *Intractable Conflicts and their Transformation*. Syracuse, NY: Syracuse University Press.

Obermeyer, N.J. and Pinto, J. (1994) *Managing Geographic Information Systems*. New York: Guillford Press.

Osaghae, E.E. (2000) 'Applying traditional methods to modern conflict: Possibilities and limits', in I.W. Zartmann (ed.), *Traditional Cures for Modern Conflicts: African Conflict Medicine*. Boulder, CO: Lynne Reinner. pp. 201–18.

Ozawa, C.P. (1999) 'Making the best use of technology', in L. Susskind, S. McKearman and J. Thomas-Learner (ed.), *The Consensus Building Handbook: A Comprehensive Guide to Reaching Agreements*. Thousand Oaks, CA: Sage Publications. pp. 401–34.

Peluso, N.L. (1995) 'Whose woods are these? Counter-mapping forest territories in Kalimantan, Indonesia', *Antipode*, 27(4): 383–406.

Pereira, J.M.C. and Duckstein, L. (1993) 'A multiple criteria decision-making approach to GIS-based land suitability evaluation', *International Journal of Geographical Information Science*, 7(5): 407–24.

Poole, P. (1995) *Indigenous Peoples, Mapping and Biodiversity Conservation: An Analysis of Current Activities and Opportunities for Applying Geomatics Technologies*. Washington, DC: Biodiversity Support Program.

Raiffa, H. (1982) *The Art and Science of Negotiation*. Cambridge, MA: Harvard University Press.

Rambaldi, G. and Callosa-Tarr, J. (2000) 'Exploring the synergies of GIS and participatory 3-D modeling to increase local communication capacity', paper presented at the 5th Seminar on GIS and Developing Countries, GISDECO 2000, Malaysia.

Rambaldi, G. and Callosa-Tarr, J. (2002) 'Participatory 3-dimensional modeling: Guiding principles and applications', *ASEAN Regional Center for Biodiversity Conservation*. Los Baños: Philippines.

Rambaldi, G. and Callosa-Tarr, J. (2004) 'Participatory 3-D modelling: Bridging the gap between communities and GIS technology', in A. Neef (ed.), *Participatory Approaches for Sustainable Land Use in Southeast Asia*. Bangkok: White Lotus.

Rambaldi, G. and Van, L.Le. (2003) 'The seventh helper: The vertical dimension: Feedback from a training in Vietnam', *PLA Notes*, 46: 77–83.

Rambaldi, G.S., Tiangco, Bugna A. and de Vera, D. (2002) 'Bringing the vertical dimension to the negotiating table, preliminary assessment of a conflict resolution case in the Phillipines', *Asean Biodiversity*, 2(1): 17–26.

Rocheleau, D. (1995) 'Maps, numbers, text and context: Mixing methods in feminist political ecology', *The Professional Geographer*, 47(4): 458–66.

Rocheleau, D. (1997) *Musings on Mapping Against Power: Comments, Questions and Selected Examples*, Paper Presented at the Ford Foundation-Sponsored Conference on Representing Communities: Histories and Politics of Community-based Resource Management. Helen, Georgia.

Rocheleau, D., Thomas-Slayter, B. and Edmunds, D. (1995) 'Gendered resource mapping: Focusing on women's spaces in the landscape', *Cultural Survival Quarterly*, 18(4): 62–8.

Roy, B. (1996) *Multicriteria Methodology for Decision Aiding*. Dordrecht: Kluwer Academic.

Rubin, J.Z. and Brown, B.R. (1975) *The Social Psychology of Bargaining and Negotiation*. New York: Academic Press.

Sieber (2002) 'Geographic information systems in the environmental movement', in W. Craig, T. Harris and D. Weiner (eds), *Community Participation and Geographic Information Systems*. New York: Taylor & Francis. pp. 153–72.

Smith, R.C. (1995) 'GIS and long range planning for indigenous territories', *Cultural Survival Quarterly*, 18(4): 43–8.

Srimongkontip, S. (2000) 'Building the capacity of watershed networks to restore natural resource conflicts: Field experiences from CARE, Thailand project', *Asia-Pacific Community Forestry Newsletter*, 13: 2.

Steinmann, R., Krek, A. and Blaschke, T. (2004) 'Analysis of on-line public participatory GIS applications with respect to differences between the US and Europe', *Proceedings of Urban Data Management Symposium 04*, Chioggia, Italy.

Susskind, L.S. (1999) 'An alternate to Robert's rules of order for groups, organizations and ad hoc assemblies that want to operate by consensus', in S. Susskind, L. S. McKearman and J. Thomas-Learner (eds), *The Consensus Building Handbook: A Comprehensive Guide to Reaching Agreements*. Thousand Oaks, CA: Sage Publications. pp. 3–60.

Susskind, L. and Field, P. (1996) *Dealing with an Angry Public*. New York: Free Press.

Susskind, S., McKearman, L.S. and Thomas-Learner, J. (1999) *The Consensus Building Handbook: A Comprehensive Guide to Reaching Agreements*. Thousand Oaks, CA: Sage Publications.

Tulloch, D.L. (2002) 'Environmental NGO's and community access to technology', in W. Craig, T. Harris and D. Weiner (eds), *Community Participation and*

Geographic Information Systems. New York: Taylor & Francis. pp. 192–204.

Turnbull, D. (1997) 'Reframing science and other local knowledge traditions', *Futures*, 29(6): 551–62.

Turnbull, D. (1998) 'Mapping encounters and (en) countering maps: A critical examination of cartographic resistance', *Knowledge and Society*, 11: 15–44.

Uwazie, E.E. (2000) 'Social relations and peace keeping among the Ibo', in I.W. Zartmann (ed.), *Traditional Cures for Modern Conflicts: African Conflict Medicine*. Boulder, CO: Lynne Reinner. pp. 15–30.

UW-Madison (2008) *Conflict Resolution*, Academic leadership support; joint efforts of the Office of Human Resource Development and Office of Quality Improvement at University of Wisconsin at Madison. http://www.ohrd.wisc.edu/onlinetraining/resolution/index.asp (assessed 5 July 2008).

Voogd, H. (1983) *Multicriteria Evaluation for Urban and Regional Planning*. London: Pion.

Warner, M. (2000) *Conflict Management in Community-Based Natural Resource Projects: Experiences from Fiji and Papua New Guinea*. Working Paper 135 April 2000 Overseas Development Institute, London.

Weber, M. (1968) *Economy and Society: An Outline of Interpretive Sociology*, (ed.) G. Roth and C. Wittich. New York: Bedminister Press.

Whetten, D. (1975) 'Inter-organizational relations: A review of the field', *Journal of Higher Education*, 52: 1–28.

Whetten, D. and Gray, B. (1984) 'Policy coordination and inter-organizational relations: Some guidelines for sharing power', paper presented at the Conference on Shared Power, Humphrey Institute and School of Management, University of Minnesota, Minneapolis.

Wong, S. and Liang Chua, Y. (2004) 'Data intermediation and beyond: Issues for web-based PPGIS', *Cartographica*, 38(3/4): 63–80.

Zartman, W.I. (2000) 'Introduction: African traditional conflict medicine', in I.W. Zartmann (ed.), *Traditional Cures for Modern Conflicts: African Conflict Medicine*. Boulder, CO: Lynne Reinner. pp. 1–14.

Zeleny, M. (1982) *Multiple Criteria Decision Making*. New York: McGraw-Hill.

26

Legal and Ethical Issues of Using Geospatial Technologies in Society

Daniel Z. Sui

INTRODUCTION

Geospatial technology, along with bio- and nano-technologies, has been recognized by the scientific community as one of the three leading technologies that will shape the development of science, technology, and society in the years to come (Gewin, 2004). Generally speaking, geospatial technology is an amalgamation of several technologies, including (but not limited to) remote sensing (RS), geographic information systems (GIS), global positioning systems (GPS), location-based services (LBS), and related fields such as computer mapping, spatial modeling, and data visualization. Not very long ago, an editorial in the *Wall Street Journal* alerted its readers that "… tools of geographers are changing society today as much as the tools of physicists did at the time of the atomic bomb" (Gomes, 2003: B1). Indeed, the atomic bomb could serve as an illuminating metaphor for the mixed, far-reaching, broad social impacts we are just beginning to appreciate for geospatial technologies. On the one hand, it has been demonstrated that geospatial technologies can be used to document cases of gross human rights abuses, find land mines, and identify concentrations of the poor and the hungry in dire need (AAAS, 2007). On the other hand, recent years have witnessed a growing outcry by the general public on the increasing use of geospatial technologies for tracking people (CNN, 2003; Edmundson, 2005; USA Today, 2008).

Indeed, the growing applications of geospatial technologies have contributed to a new geography of hope and fear (Klinkenberg, 2007), which concomitantly raised a series of legal and ethical issues. During the past five years, we have witnessed an increasing coverage by both popular media and scholarly articles on the issues brought by the breathtaking development of geospatial technologies and their expanding capabilities for surveillance purposes (NRC, 2007a, 2007b). Since its very early days, geospatial technology has been characterized as a major tool for surveillance (Holz, 1973), and today it has become an integral component of the surveillance infrastructure (Levin et al., 2002). Not surprisingly, concerns about unintended consequences have also grown with the increasing sophistication of these surveillance capabilities. The social implications of GIS have always been one of the major research areas in geographic information science. Scholars in many fields have contributed to our understanding of GIS from legal and ethical perspectives, but the scholarly work on this topic has been scattered throughout a large interdisciplinary literature (O'Harrow, 2005; Rushkoff, 2005; Dobson and Fisher, 2007). The primary goal of this chapter is to present a synthesis of the literature on the legal and ethical issues of using geospatial technologies in society. In doing so, I aim to bring the legal and ethical dimensions of geospatial technologies to a broader audience and help open more dialogues and discussions among the stakeholders in this area. To achieve this goal, I shall first review the key elements of the new geospatial technologies that have enhanced our surveillance capabilities, followed by a synopsis of the legal and ethical problems these technologies have brought to society in the third section. The fourth section discusses some possible remedies for these problems, and the last section contains a summary and conclusions.

THE CHANGING TECHNOLOGICAL LANDSCAPE FOR POSITIONING, TRACKING, AND MAPPING: FROM SURVEILLANCE TO SOUSVEILLANCE

Although concerns over legal and ethical issues of geospatial technologies were voiced throughout the 1990s (Onsrud et al., 1994; Goss, 1995; Cho, 1998), these discussions were confined to the scholarly community and did not gain much public attention. This was primarily due to two reasons. First, earlier applications of geospatial technologies focused disproportionately on environment and resource applications at a crude spatial resolution (10 m by 10 m or coarser). Those dealing with socioeconomic applications were conducted mostly at the aggregate

level, not focusing on individuals explicitly. Second, high-resolution satellite remote sensing or aerial imageries (sub-meter resolution) were tightly controlled by government (mostly classified), and GPS, although in use from 1972, was not declassified for civilian applications or commercialization until 1983.

The developments of geospatial technologies during the past 15 years have dramatically changed the technological landscape. Recent advances in surveillance capabilities of geospatial technologies have rendered science fiction movies, such as *Enemy of the State* (produced in 1998), more like a documentary in the early days of the twenty-first century. The new technological breakthroughs have not only equipped Big Brother with the ability to conduct extensive surveillance on citizens, but have also empowered individual citizens to conduct surveillance among themselves or inverse surveillance on the watcher (Dobson and Fisher, 2007). Furthermore, under the new paradigm of citizens as sensors (Goodchild, 2007), individuals, and informal groups of individuals popularly known as smart mobs (Rheingold, 2002), can record, describe, and disseminate information on activities at either the individual or collective level from the perspective of the participants – a new form surveillance called sousveillance (Mann et al., 2003). Several key components of the geospatial technologies have contributed to the transition from surveillance to sousveillance.

Throughout human history, a variety of different location technologies, ranging from mechanical, acoustic, optical, radio, and electromagnetic, have been developed (Beresford, 2005). Generally speaking, geotracking – obtaining the locational coordinates of the target being tracked – has mostly relied on three primary techniques for determining location: (1) triangulation, which can be done via either lateration (using multiple distance measurements between known points) or angulation (using measured angles or bearings relative to points with known separation); (2) proximity, which measures nearness to a known set of points; and (3) scene analysis, which examines a view from a particular vantage point. Different geotracking technologies use different combinations of these three techniques (Hightower and Borriello, 2001). These different technologies have different coverage, spatial-temporal resolution, and accuracy, and have increasingly been embedded into a variety of consumer products such as car navigation systems, smart cellular phones, printers, underwear cosmetics, and so on (Table 26.1). Custom-designed tracking devices have also been available in the market, such as Digital Angel, Wherify child locator and various other types of WhereWare (Pfeiffer, 2003). Among the many technological breakthroughs during the past 15 years, the following are particularly relevant when we discuss the legal and ethical implications of geospatial technologies:

Global navigation satellite systems and high-resolution remote sensing

Among these different positioning technologies, perhaps the most significant one is the global navigation satellite system (GNSS), which was instrumental in promoting the development of location-based industry. As of 2009, the US NAVSTAR GPS is the only fully operational GNSS. However, the global dominance of positioning systems by the USA is eroding with rapid development of GNSS by the EU, Russia, China, Japan,

France, and India. The European Union's Galileo positioning system is a GNSS in the initial deployment phase, scheduled to be operational in 2013. The Russian GLONASS is a GNSS in the process of being restored to full operation. China has indicated it may expand its regional Beidou navigation system into a global system. The current Beidou-1 system (made up of four satellites) is experimental and has limited coverage and application. However, China has planned to develop a truly global satellite navigation system consisting of 35 satellites (known as Compass or Beidou-2). The Quasi-Zenith Satellite System (QZSS) is a proposed three-satellite regional time transfer system and enhancement for GPS covering Japan. The first satellite is scheduled to be launched in 2010. Doppler Orbitography and Radio-positioning Integrated by Satellite (DORIS) is a French precision navigation system. Indian Regional Navigational Satellite System (IRNSS) is intended to be completed and operational by 2012. Obviously, more and more countries have recognized the growing importance of GNSS to their military operations as well as various civilian applications, which explains their growing investment in the global navigation infrastructure to develop their own independent systems.

Advances in remote-sensing technologies have made high resolution (sub-meter) commercially available satellite from GeoEye and DigitalGlobe (see http://www.vterrain.org/Imagery/commercial.html for a more complete list of vendors). The corporate sector is increasingly interested in collecting

Table 26.1 Location/positioning technologies

Technology	Coverage	Accuracy	Updates	Location Data
GPS	Earth	0.01m – 100m	< 1s	x, y, and z coordinates
Mobile phone (tower triangulation)	Populated areas	120m – 30km	4.6ms – 2hrs	x, y coordinates
CCTV	City centers	1m	1/30s	Camera location
RFID	Near readers	1m	Sporadic	Distance to reader
Credit card	Payment kiosk	1m	Sporadic	Kiosk location

information at the local and individual level. Google™ and Microsoft® are investing in Street View (http://www.everyscape.com/). Satellite navigation systems and high-resolution remote sensing are instrumental in contributing to what Regan (2004) called the creeping legibility of both people and places.

Radio-frequency identification and biometric systems

Radio-frequency identification (RFID) technology relies on storing and remotely retrieving data using radio waves. An RFID tag can be attached to or embedded in a product, animal, or person for identification or tracking. An RFID chip typically is composed of a tiny antenna attached to a tiny ID chip, and it can be passive (without an internal power source) or active (with a built-in power source). As GPS signals are usually too weak to be used for tracking purposes inside a building, the development of RFID technology, especially once it is fully integrated with GIS, may potentially track and map everything on surface of the earth. EPCglobal, a system of tags to create globally unique serial numbers for all products using RFID technology, may be a concrete step forward toward stitching together a new electronic skin for the Earth.

Since each individual is identifiable spatially and temporally via GPS and RFID, we are subject to the linkage of our positioning information to other types of biometrics such as finger prints, iris/retina scans, face recognition scans, or thermal maps of the body, as well as to detailed genetic information at the individual level (http://www.23andme.com). GPS and RFID especially in the form of sub-dermal implantation, along with biometric and genetic information, have brought surveillance to a new level of unprecedented detail ranging from genetic all the way to global levels. One particular interesting recent trend is the integration of GPS with RFID. The two complementary systems could potentially close the location positioning gaps for the entities we aim to track and map.

People-based GIS, participatory sensing, and the development of sensor webs

One of the most significant advances is the development of people-based GIS (Miller, 2007). Until the mid 1990s the development of GIS had been driven by a place-based paradigm, in which environmental and socioeconomic data are aggregated to spatial units of various sizes (e.g., census tracts, traffic analysis zones, or grids of varying sizes). We often rely on place-based, aggregated information to infer information about individuals. Advances in information and telecommunication technologies and related changes in peoples' activity patterns have increasingly made such inferences problematic. Inspired by Hägerstrand's time geography and activity theories, Miller (2007) proposed the concept of people-based GIS, which is capable of monitoring, tracking, analyzing, and visualizing people's activities in space and time. Many real-world applications such as transportation planning, emergency evacuation, and disease surveillance all demand people-based, rather than place-based GIS. The development of people-based GIS represents a major conceptual departure from place-based GIS. The increasing applications of people-based GIS are made possible because of a growing array of location-aware technologies (Weaver, 2006).

People-based GIS is made possible partially by the location-aware technologies such as the smart cellular phones people carry with them. Detailed spatial and temporal information is recorded, thus making the spatial and temporal analysis of trajectories possible (Raper and Livingston, 2001). Humans are becoming sensors for collecting data about other people and the environment. The so-called participatory sensing – individuals using cellular phones to collect data – has emerged in recent years with growing areas of applications (Burke et al., 2006). Participatory sensing is an integral part of the emerging sousveillance.

Ubiquitous computing, Web 2.0, and volunteered geographic information

The explosive growth of Web 2.0 technologies and the concomitant growth of user-generated content marked a new era for the development of geospatial technologies and their surveillance applications. Perhaps the most significant development for this new era is the dazzling growth of volunteered geographic information contributed by citizens using Web 2.0 technologies through the new paradigm of cloud computing (Sui, 2005, 2008). In addition to its contributions to a bottom-up process for the growth of spatial data infrastructure, VGI is also contributing rather significantly to the social transition from surveillance to sousveillance, as a large amount of VGI reflects extreme details about personal experiences voluntarily provided. Besides the explicitly geocoded data that citizens contributed to VGI sites such as openstreetmap.com or wikimapia.com, the past five years have also witnessed the rapid growth of geotagged, user-generated content on the web, ranging from twits, blogs, and photos, to YouTube™ videos and online social networking activities on Facebook™ or MySpace™. Nowadays even Twitting is increasingly geotagged and readers can tell where you are twitting from. The emerging new infrastructure for ubiquitous computing (ubicomp) has increasingly become context- or location-aware, which contributes to both surveillance and sousveillance capabilities unprecedented in human history.

Indisputably, ubicomp will embed more conventional GIS functions into various kinds of enhanced LBS. Location-aware computing, or more broadly "context-aware" computing, will equip information infrastructure of all kinds with special capabilities to recognize and react to real-world contexts in which it operates. "Context" encompasses a plethora of factors, including user identity, time, physical location, and environmental conditions (such as local weather, and so on). The two most critical aspects of context are location and identity. Context-aware computing systems respond to a user's location, either spontaneously (e.g., a friendly reminder of approaching a favorite restaurant, or warning of a nearby hazard) or when activated by the user's request (e.g., is this area prone to traffic jam or accidents?). With the continual growth of a variety of LBS, many GIS functions that were previously confined to desktop PCs may become embedded as part of ubicomp or ambient intelligence.

The development of ubicomp will also entail another round of explosive growth of data of many kinds with greater spatial and temporal resolution. Real-time data acquisition (RTDA) will become a reality in the age of ubicomp, which will make just-in-time mapping (JITM) a routine operation in the near future. For example, the development of smart "dust sensors" – devices that combine microelectromechanical sensors with wireless communication, processing, and batteries into a package about 1 mm^3 in size – could potentially revolutionize RTDA and JITM. Although currently still in their infancy, prototype smart sensors have demonstrated their capabilities to monitor environmental conditions that are hazardous to humans, determine the velocity and direction of passing vehicles in remote areas, or to be attached to humans, animals, or even insects to record where they travel (Pister, 2002). The data transmitted wirelessly in real time from these sensors increases not only the volume but also the complexity of available geospatial data. To store and analyze these colossal data sets obviously demands more storage space and computers more powerful than ever for data mining and research. So paradoxically, the age of ubicomp will also simultaneously create new demands for more powerful mainframe and personal computing as well. The theoretical foundations and functional capabilities of GIS in data acquisition, storage, analysis/ modeling, and visualization need to be expanded to accommodate the new demands created by ubicomp.

Data mining, knowledge discovery, and geographic profiling

The growing availability of massive amounts of geocoded information has contributed to rapid development of a variety of new data mining and knowledge-discovering techniques. These techniques are capable of conducting integrated analysis of heterogeneous data sets to detect meaningful structure and patterns (Dykes and Mountain, 2003). In addition to techniques for handling quantitative data, recent developments have also led toward breakthroughs in text mining (Feldman and Sanger, 2006) and photo synthesis (http://photosynth.net).

The increasing availability of geocoded data, coupled with our improved capabilities in data mining and knowledge discovery, has resulted in new spatial practices called geographic profiling (Rossmo, 2000). Geographic profiling originally developed as a criminal investigative methodology that analyzes the locations of a connected series of crimes to determine the most probable area of offender residence (Canter, 2003). Geographic profiling helps police prioritize information in major crime investigations that often involve hundreds or thousands of suspects and tips. Most recently, techniques of geographic profiling were used to zero in the possible location for Osama Bin Laden (Farmer, 2009). Although typically used in criminal investigation, such as in cases of serial murder, rape, arson, bombing, robbery, and other crimes, geographic profiling techniques can also be used in several other areas such as marketing, location-allocation analysis, political campaign/fund raising,

real estate development, environmental health, archaeology, and so on.

One very important fact that must be kept in mind is the existence of a massive infrastructure (such as Echelon) that is classified and controlled by the government for surveillance purposes. Although the project for total information awareness (TIA) was stopped due to strong public opposition, the government's capability to conduct surveillance has vastly improved with the passing of the Patriot Act following the events of September 11, 2001 (Taipale, 2007).

The vastly improved technical capabilities in real-time tracking have led to diverse applications, such as tracking children, the elderly, Alzheimer's patients, animals, employees, students, and those on parole. It is these diverse applications that have created many new legal and ethical issues for us to ponder.

GEOSPATIAL TECHNOLOGIES AND SOCIETY: LEGAL AND ETHICAL ISSUES

As demonstrated by several high-profile lawsuits and news reports involving the wide-range applications of geospatial technologies in society, legal, and ethical issues have increasingly been on the public radar screen (Blumenfeld, 2003; Sui, 2006a; Aday and Livingston, 2007; Sui, 2007a; Dobson, 2009; Perez, 2009). There have been calls for a broader public debate and dialogue on these issues in order to develop new legal and ethical guidelines for geospatial technology practices in this new, pervasive computing environment with massive surveillance capabilities (Dobson and Fisher, 2007; Sui, 2007b). To begin with, a distinction between legal and ethical issues should be helpful.

Legal versus ethical issues

Human conduct in society can be classified as legal or illegal (the circle in Figure 26.1).

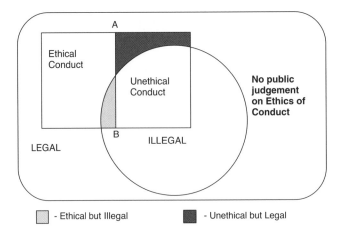

Figure 26.1   Legal and ethical dimensions of societal conduct [after Onsrud (2001)]

We also judge people's conduct as ethical or unethical (the rectangle in Figure 26.1). Under normal circumstances, a clear distinction can be made between legal and illegal and usually also between ethical and unethical conduct in society (Onsrud, 1995). Each society has set up its own rule of laws that bans certain behaviors. Violations of laws are subject to sanctions imposed by the judicial system.[1] Ethics refers to values that deal with human conduct or practices with respect to the rightness of certain actions and to the goodness or badness of the motives and ends of such actions. Each society has its rule of ethics and morality, which are widely accepted by that society but not clearly coded into law.

Two grey areas complicate the legal versus ethical behavior issue in society. Certain human behaviors are illegal but ethical, whereas some others are legal but unethical. For example, to prevent a murder from happening, one may break the speed limit or break into somebody's house. To some pacifists, the use of geospatial technologies on the battleground is regarded as unethical, but its use is legal in most cases except when geospatial technologies are used in war crimes such as committing genocide or purposefully targeting civilians.[2] Similarly, to some environmentalists, using geospatial technologies to facilitate oil drilling in environmentally sensitive areas (such as Alaska's wildlife refuge) may be legal but unethical. These distinctions are helpful when we discuss the legal and ethical issues of geospatial technologies. But in reality, as Olson (2006) so vividly documented, there exists a vast murky terrain of moral limits in spying for the purpose of national security. The same moral dilemmas, although perhaps at a different intensity level, also exist for the general use of geospatial technologies in society.

Major legal issues

Recent media coverage on legal issues relating to geospatial technologies has focused predominantly on tracking people and invasion of privacy, but the legal issues of geospatial technologies are broad and complex. In general, all legal issues related to applications of geospatial technologies are concerned with collection, ownership, access, retention, use, and dissemination of georeferenced data at either individual or collective levels. Major legal issues relating to geospatial technologies can be roughly grouped into three categories: (1) privacy and data accessibility issues; (2) intellectual property, copyright, and data licensing issues; and (3) international law issues.

Privacy and data accessibility issues

At the individual level, the possible invasion of privacy has been a growing concern owing to the growing use of geospatial technologies to track people and commodities in real time (Aaron, 2002; Armstrong and Ruggles, 2005). Traditionally, privacy has been defined as an individual's right to be left alone (Warren and Brandeis, 1890). Over the past century, extraordinary technological development has dramatically redefined the boundary and the domain of what is normally considered as a private realm (Curry, 1997a, 1997b). The meaning of privacy has also changed from the right to be left alone, to the right to enjoy anonymity, to the right to control information about oneself, and so on. The recent development of geospatial technologies has moved locational (spatial or geographical) privacy to the forefront of privacy concerns. Purely locational information in terms of latitude/longitude or other types of coordinates (site information) may not be that meaningful, but people can make a reasonable inference about the surroundings of a particular location (situation information), which could be embarrassing or harmful. This is in large part why most people would prefer their whereabouts to remain private. For example, each year, one million American women and half million American men are being stalked (http://www.ojp.usdoj.gov/bjs/abstract/svus.htm), and geospatial technologies can play a very important role in stalking.

In terms of legal protections, the Fourth Amendment of the US Constitution provides that: "The right of the people to be secure in their persons, houses, papers, and effects, against unreasonable searches and seizures, shall not be violated, and no Warrants shall issue, but upon probable cause, supported by Oath or affirmation, and particularly describing the place to be searched." Constitutional protections for privacy, derived primarily from the Fourth Amendment,

restrict government intrusion into our personal life through searches of persons, personal space, and information. For law enforcement officials, a search warrant is usually required before a private property can be search or seized.[3] Although, in general, the Fourth Amendment places restrictions on government intrusions into the private realm of ordinary citizens, it has not been interpreted to provide an effective means of protecting physical and locational privacy outside of the home or other quarters. In the seminal case *Katz* v. *United States* (1967), the United States Supreme Court held that government eavesdropping of a man in a public phone booth violated a reasonable expectation of privacy because the Fourth Amendment protects people, not places (Herbert, 2006). The Supreme Court has interpreted the Fourth Amendment as protecting individuals from government intrusions without a warrant only where the individual has an objectively reasonable expectation of privacy. The reasonable expectation standard has been adopted by the state courts when interpreting state constitutional and common law protections of privacy. However, in a recent case involving Google™, a Pennsylvania judge recently dismissed a law suit against Google™ for posting some very private photos on Google Earth™ Street View (Perez, 2009).

As a worst-case scenario, some scholars have also contemplated the possibility of geoslavery in this age of ubiquitous computing (Dobson and Fisher, 2003). The growing applications of geospatial technologies, especially through the development of human tracking devices and various kinds of LBS, has introduced a new potential for real-time locational control and monitoring that extend far beyond privacy and surveillance per se. Scholars have warned that society must address a new form of slavery characterized by location control – geoslavery, now looming as a real, immediate, and global threat (CNN, 2003; Nichols, 2007). According to Dobson and Fisher, geoslavery refers to "a practice in which one entity (the master) coercively or surreptitiously monitors and exerts control over the physical location of another individual (the slave)" (2003: 47). With the current geospatial technologies readily available and affordable (US300–500), an individual can routinely control the time, location, speed, and direction of another individual for each and every movement, even without the permission of the individual being monitored. The fact that child slavery, sex slavery, and other abusive behaviors (such as stalking) are still rampant worldwide (e.g., http://www.iabolish.com/slavery_today.htm) begs one to ponder where the increasing use of geospatial technologies and location-aware computing will lead us in the near future. The potential of geoslavery has raised the issue of whether locational privacy should be universally protected as a fundamental human right (Monmonier, 2002; Fisher and Dobson, 2003). Although legally speaking, the Thirteenth Amendment of the US Constitution, which states: "Neither slavery nor involuntary servitude, except as a punishment for crime whereof the party shall have been duly convicted, shall exist within the United States, or any place subject to their jurisdiction," has clearly outlawed slavery since 1865, recent incidents involving individuals serve as painful reminders of the potential for geoslavery (Dobson, 2009).

Although the Fourth (and possibly the Thirteenth) US Constitutional Amendments have been invoked in legal cases regarding the use of geospatial technologies, legal scholars have argued that it is unlikely that workable limitations on the use of human tracking devices will grow out of criminal appeals under these Amendments (Herbert, 2006). Many legal issues, such as who can track whom, under what circumstances, and whether a warrant is needed (in the case of police tracking citizens) also have to rely on other federal and state laws.

Several federal legislations have been cited in recent legal cases. While the Electronic Communication Privacy Act 1986 protects against unauthorized interception and disclosure of electronic communications,

it excludes tracking devices. However, the Wireless Communication and Public Safety Act 1999, explicitly protects location information in wireless devices, requiring customer approval for disclosure. This protection does not extend to deriving location information from communication devices. Transaction information such as telephone numbers is not protected (*Smith* v. *Maryland*, 1979), but providers are prevented from releasing information that discloses the physical location of an individual (CALEA, 1994/2000; *US Telecom* v. *FCC*, 2000). However, using mobile communication devices as tracking devices to derive location information is not constitutionally prohibited (*US* v. *Meriwether*, 1990; *US* v. *Knotts*, 1983; *US* v. *Forest*, 2004), as courts have ruled that individuals using cell phones, beepers, and pagers do not have a reasonable expectation of privacy when moving from place to place (although this interpretation continues to be challenged). Several related federal regulations, however, have been enacted: Telecommunication Act 1996; Children's On-line Privacy Protection Act; Children's Bullying law; Privacy for Consumer and Workers Act 1993; and the Video Voyeurism Prevention Act, as well as other legislations aimed at eavesdropping and Internet websites.

Recently, however, the Patriot Act 2001 has nullified some of these protections, granting broad authorities for government surveillance, including the ability to use roving wiretaps, which has caused grave concerns to both the public and legal scholars (Taipale, 2007). The Patriot Act has vastly increased government power for surveillance (in some cases even warrantless). Taipale (2007) describes the nature of modern communication networks and certain related technology developments, and examines how three situations – transit intercepts, collateral intercepts, and automated monitoring – cannot be accommodated by the Foreign Intelligence Surveillance Act (FISA) as currently constituted. It remains a legal challenge to fix foreign intelligence surveillance so that it preserves existing Fourth Amendment principles and protections while still addressing these failures. To get beyond backward looking recriminations, we need to craft new progressive consensual solutions.

Invasion of privacy due to the use of geospatial technologies can also be dealt with through common law and state constitutions. Tort laws are often invoked. A tort is a wrongful act or damage (not involving a breach of contract) for which a civil action can be brought. Following the doctrine established by Warren and Brandeis (1890), there are four kinds of privacy torts:

- Misappropriation of one's likeness – use of a person's name, likeness, or identity for trade or advertising purposes without consent.
- Intrusion upon a person's seclusion – a physical, electronic, or mechanical intrusion into someone's private space. This is an information-gathering, not a publication, tort. The legal wrong occurs at the time of the intrusion; no publication is necessary.
- Public disclosure of embarrassing private facts – publication of non-newsworthy, private facts about an individual so intimate that they outrage the public's sense of decency, or that would be highly offensive to a reasonable person (true defamation).
- Publicity in false light – publication of false, highly offensive (but not necessarily defamatory) information about an individual.

However, the public disclosure tort is limited by the clause that if an event takes place in a public place, the tort is unavailable. The courts have generally ruled that a person traveling in public places voluntarily conveys location information. But courts have also recognized that a person does not automatically make public everything he or she does merely by being in a public place. Most states give common law or statutory recognition to some or all four of the privacy torts.

According to Herbert and Tuminaro (2008), case law has interpreted these locational privacy rights more specifically, examining intrusions of technology into the private sphere, government searches that are technologically enhanced, and the use of mobile devices and telecommunication information to derive locational information. While Fourth Amendment protection does not extend to that which is knowingly disclosed to the public, the courts have ruled that the use of technologies not available to the general public can violate the privacy one reasonably expects (*Kyllo* v. *US*, 2001). However, the courts have also shown a willingness to allow law enforcement to use technologically enhanced means for searches, including flying over properties such as a fenced backyard (*California* v. *Ciraolo*, 1986), a greenhouse (*Florida* v. *Riley*, 1986), or an industrial plant (*Dow Chemical* v. *US*, 1986), suggesting that the open fields doctrine [3] brings no reasonable expectation of privacy.

In summary, legal protection for location privacy in the USA is inconsistent and sectoral, providing coverage only under certain situations and for specific technologies. Recently, legal public privacy issues raised by Nissenbaum (1998) and the further development of geospatial technologies have certainly added quite a bit of urgency to this issue. Conflicting rules exist, such as the need to obtain a warrant for police to start tracking somebody, despite the lack of legal protection for privacy in public.

Intellectual property, copyright, and data licensing issues

In addition to privacy issues, recent advances in geospatial technologies have also raised many challenging issues related to copyright, liability, and intellectual property rights on diverse geographic information. Under the current culture of mashing-up practices, which is part of the larger emerging remixing culture (Lessig, 2008), "who legally owns the geospatial data" emerges as a burning issue for further discussion and clarification. The recent development of VGI poses new interesting questions about data ownership, intellectual property rights, and copyright, as recently demonstrated by the Facebook™

data ownership dispute (see http://www.japantoday.com/category/technology/view/facebook-does-about-face-in-content-ownership-dispute).

Licensing of geographic data and works has increasingly become a common practice because of the limited protection afforded by copyright and other intellectual property doctrines in the digital environment (NRC, 2004). *License* or *licensing* of geographic data or a geographic work means a transaction or arrangement (usually a contract, in which there is an exchange of value) in which the acquiring party (e.g., the licensee) obtains information with restrictions on the licensee's rights to use or transfer the information. More and more data providers also have turned to technological means to control access and copying, measures that are reinforced by the Digital Millennium Copyright Act, for works that have at least some copyright protection. Moreover, courts have upheld contracts or licenses that limit the uses that a licensee can make of data, or that prohibit further distribution. Data providers' rights are likely to be further strengthened if Congress adopts database protection.

Federal agencies almost always distribute geographic data at or below marginal cost of distribution. Cost recovery has been the norm in dealing with spatial data in Europe and it has held GIS development back. In the USA, Landsat pricing has also attempted to follow the cost recovery path, which has held back the development of remote sensing. Since the 1990s however many state and local governments have experimented with the distribution of data using licenses to generate revenue from them. As we move further into the ubiquitous computing age of the twenty-first century, many of these entities have concluded that fee programs (1) cannot recover a significant fraction of government data budgets, (2) seldom cover operating expenses, and (3) act as a drag on private-sector investments that would otherwise add to the tax base and help grow the economy (NRC, 2004). The use of licenses to

provide data to users may, however, be useful to enforce proper attribution, minimize liability, enhance data security, and formalize collaboration.

Licensing has become commonplace because of the realization that many geographic data, as opposed to geographic creative works, are difficult to protect through copyright alone. There have been growing concerns over potential liability and a desire to limit liability through explicit license language. Sharing costs through various data maintenance partnerships has also become common practice.

This has facilitated a shift away from supplying distinct datasets to providing access to databases, and the rise of business models that stress multiple subscribers despite the reality of digital networks and media that allow others to distribute perfect and inexpensive copies.

Confusion and uncertainty have arisen in recent years as a result of a proliferation of nonstandard licensing arrangements. The geospatial community has recognized the difficulty of designing licenses that can (1) track the legal, economic, and public interest concerns of different levels of government, and (2) accommodate all sectors of the geographic data community. There also exist no effective license tracking and enforcement mechanisms. Different sectors of the geospatial community also have different practices and standards in the licensing process.

The wikification of GIS has also raised another important legal issue on who is qualified to create geospatial data (Sui, 2008). In January 2007, the Management Association for Private Photogrammetric Surveyors (MAPPS) filed a lawsuit seeking to limit competition for federal mapping contracts of nearly every type, including GIS services, to firms of licensed architects, engineers, and surveyors alone. In June 2007, Judge T.S. Ellis III of the US District Court in Alexandria, Virginia, ruled against MAPPS, finding that MAPPS failed to "establish that an injury in fact was suffered by the individual [licensed] surveyors or their firms" (http://www.ucgis.org).

This is a significant legal victory for the continuing democratization of GIS, which will hopefully ensure all qualified professionals – not just licensed engineers and surveyors – can compete for government contracts related to mapping and GIS activities. Recent innovations in technologies have drastically flattened the learning curve for geospatial and mapping technologies. The development of Google Maps™/Google Earth™ and Microsoft®'s Virtual Earth®, along with their precursors Mapquest, Yahoo Maps, Multimap, StreetMap, and so on, have democratized the application of massive online geospatial information. Additionally, the new wave of technological innovations has even democratized the production of maps and online geospatial information. The accelerated democratizing process for mapping and GIS has put powerful mapping technologies into the hands of the masses, which now can perform rather complex mapping tasks (once requiring years of training) with little or no training at all. Although Judge Ellis' ruling in the case of *MAPPS* v. *US Government* has been widely applauded by the geospatial community, the fast growing collaborative mapping by amateurs (or citizen cartographers) does raise new questions and concerns about the authority and trustworthiness of geographic information production.

Drawing on an analogy of the tragedy of the commons in the environmental domain, Onsrud (1998) warned of a possible tragedy of the information commons unless innovative mechanisms for sharing information and licensing geographic data are developed. The recent democratization of geographic data collection and dissemination in the age of Web 2.0 further complicates the liability issue of geographic data information. Obviously, the wide-ranging applications may be disadvantageous to some people, such as users of the software or data or those affected by decisions taken on the basis of GIS applications. Liability is a creation of

the law to support a range of important social goals such as avoidance of injury, encouraging the fulfillment of obligations established by contracts, and the distribution of losses to those responsible for them. Generally speaking, liability of GIS is related either to contract liabilities (warranties/implied vs. defined) versus tort liabilities (negligence, fraud, and product liability).

Liability in data, products, and services related to GIS is likely to be determined in most instances by resort to contract law and warranty issues (Onsrud, 1999). If decisions are made based on geographical data or products produced by someone other than the user, there will always be liability exposure. Minimizing losses for users of geographical data products and reducing liability exposure for creators and distributors of such products is achieved primarily through performing competent work and keeping all parties informed of their obligations. But new data-licensing practices, value-added operations, plus volunteered geographic information via mashing up and wiki sites have made it increasingly difficult, if not entirely impossible, to track the creators and distributors of geographic data. Establishing liability in case something goes wrong is thus becoming even murkier. Recent road accidents also raised the issue of whether GPS or navigation systems should be blamed for fatal crashes (Hawrey, 1999; Masnick, 2008; Musgrove, 2008).

International dimension

When Google Earth™ was first launched in 2005, several countries, including India, China, Pakistan, and Israel, immediately expressed security concerns posed by the high-resolution satellite imagery taken over their sovereign territory, which renewed discussions on the legal issues of geospatial technology at the international level. In fact, such have been a concern of the international community since the early days of remote sensing technology in the 1960s (Deibert, 2003), as geospatial technologies have always played an important role in international affairs (Livingston and Robinson, 2003).

The basic legal framework for all space activities is provided by the 1967 Outer Space Treaty, signed by major countries in the world with space technology capabilities (Okolie, 1989). This treaty ensures the freedom of exploration and use of outer space by all states, including for satellite remote sensing. The treaty further articulates the principle of non-appropriation of outer space by any single state. This treaty also makes it clear that any limit to the freedom of exploration and use can be established only at the international level, that is, by the community of states via treaty provisions or, as the case may be, by customary international legal rules. Finally, the treaty provides for the application of general international law to outer space, in particular by establishing general principles such as the freedom of information gathering from outer space.

The United Nations Declaration on Principles Relating to Remote Sensing of the Earth from Outer Space, Resolution 41/65, adopted on 3 December 1986, sets out the main legal principles (15 in total) specifically pertinent to remote sensing. Resolutions passed by the UN General Assembly do not per se constitute binding legal documents; however, they may over time evolve into reflections of customary international law. Resolution 41/65 was adopted by consensus, and in any case UN General Assembly Resolutions carry considerable weight in the political/moral sphere, so that this resolution may indeed be considered customary law.

The key principles contained in the resolution deal with the issue of access to data gathered by remote sensing activities for land-use purposes, in particular, by states other than the one(s) generating the data in the first place. Here, Principle IV provides for the conduct of activities on the basis of respect for the sovereignty of so-called "sensed states." Principle V calls for offering opportunities of cooperation to sensed states, and Principle VII requires so-called "sensing states" to make technical assistance available to other interested states on mutually agreed terms. Most importantly,

however, Principle XII provides for a right of access by the sensed state to data concerning its territory "on a non-discriminatory basis and on reasonable cost terms." While these two qualifications already allow for considerable flexibility for sensing states ultimately to disallow sensed states access to certain data, it is also clear that the sensed state has no right of precluding its territory from being sensed, nor any right of exclusive, or even priority access to such data. In the last resort, freedom of information-gathering has thus prevailed over a principle of sovereign control over data regarding one's own territory.

In terms of obligations binding on states concerned, Principle X lays down the need for states to convey relevant information regarding threats to the "Earth's natural environment" to other states concerned; and Principle XI calls upon states in the possession of relevant information regarding natural disasters to duly inform other states concerned. Principle VIII furthermore envisages a key role for the United Nations: it "shall promote international cooperation, including technical assistance and co-ordination in the area of remote sensing." Once again, freedom of information-gathering reigns supreme over data control.

The above framework, being very general, already raises a number of legal issues at the highest level when it comes to applying it to the "real world" of satellite earth observation (von der Dunk, 2005). Two of these will be briefly touched upon as generic issues requiring treatment before moving on to legal details. Such details would namely also involve particular intellectual property rights issues pertaining to satellite data, compensation for damage caused by erroneously interpreted data, the potential value as evidence in court cases, and a number of other matters, all involving specific legal regimes and questions which are clearly beyond the scope of this article.

The two "real world" issues concern international responsibility and liability, respectively in specific cases of involvement of intergovernmental organizations and private entities as categories of players in addition to that of the states. First, under Article VI of the Outer Space Treaty, states are responsible for national activities in space, even if conducted by non-governmental entities, and for ensuring that these activities conform to the law (Litfin, 2001). Second and along similar lines, under Article VII of the Outer Space Treaty and the 1972 Liability Convention, states are specifically liable for damage caused by space objects. Both are, therefore, clearly focused on states as "undertakers" of space activities, a focus which made sense historically but is increasingly subject to discussion.

The role of intergovernmental organizations results in some particular ramifications of responsibility and liability. As to state responsibility, it also applies when activities are carried on in outer space by an international organization, although in such cases jointly with the responsibility of the international organization itself (von der Dunk, 2005). As a result, member states of intergovernmental organizations are effectively prevented from hiding behind these organizations in the case of their earth-observation activities violating applicable rules of international law; it is their duty and responsibility to ensure that the organizations themselves do not undertake any such violating activities.

As to liability, under the 1972 Liability Convention, intergovernmental organizations equally enjoy a secondary status effectively allowing them to qualify to some extent as liable entities, and a similar construction under the 1975 Registration Convention allows them to themselves register satellites and exercise concomitant competencies over them. The European Space Agency (ESA) actually enjoys the relevant status, as it has deposited relevant Declarations in respect of both conventions, but for most organizations, any liability would revert directly to individual member states.

As far as the liability stemming from geospatial data is concerned, this is still a murky terrain in international law (Onsrud, 1999). Some legal scholars have argued that international liabilities regarding geospatial data are most likely handled by international agreements and frameworks such as the General Agreement on Tariffs and Trade (GATT) developed by the World Trade Organization (WTO). Dispute resolution over international liabilities of geospatial data may also be addressed by various existing and proposed EU laws regarding electronic databases, or other bi-lateral/multi-lateral agreements such as the North America Free Trade Agreement (NAFTA) or the Mercado Común del Sur (MERCOSUR).

Critics argue that the existing rules of international law regarding geospatial technologies are outdated and no longer can deal with the complexities of their international dimensions. Both the Outer Space Treaty and the UN Resolution of 41/65 reflect the legacy of the Cold War with heavy emphasis on states as players. Their dominant concern is military/national security instead of commercial goals (Cloud and Clarke, 1999). They have also been criticized as overtly favoring those developed countries with space capabilities, whereas the rights of developing countries are not properly respected according to the international rule of law.

Ethical issues

As indicated earlier, not all of the social issues brought about by the advances in geospatial information science and technology can be resolved according to the rule of law. Some of these issues fall into the realm of ethics and moral judgment. Ethics deal with society's moral code on human behavior and practices in terms of right and wrong, which varies greatly according the culture, history, and customs of the country concerned. Generally speaking, discussions on ethics can be conducted at three levels: normative, meta-, and descriptive/applied. Normative ethics deals with issues related to what should be considered as right or wrong behavior/practices in society, whereas meta-ethics is concerned with the ontological foundation and justification for the normative practices. Descriptive/applied ethics concentrates primarily on what specific actions we should take under specific circumstances. Some scholars have raised and discussed ethical issues pertaining to GIS from normative and meta-ethical perspectives, but for the general public, the applied/descriptive perspective on ethics is perhaps more relevant. We have yet to define what actions are acceptable and under what circumstances our use of geospatial technologies is ethical and moral.

One particular ethical dilemma we face is the so-called exterior surveillance vs. interior sousveillance. Recent technological advances seem to point to a paradoxical trend involving the general public and the rapid diffusion of geospatial technologies. On the one hand, millions of Internet users worldwide voluntarily contribute very large amounts of information by the hour (if not by the minute) using Web 2.0 technologies in different formats of user-generated content. The blogs, photos, videos, and twitss contributed by users on the Web often expose people's lives in excruciating detail. There is a vast literature in psychology about this aspect of human nature, which is closely related to exhibitionism and voyeurism (Calvert, 2004). In fact, most people not only want and enjoy surveillance, but also play with it and use it for comfort (McGrath, 2004). On the other hand, we have repeatedly seen headlines in various news media on the growing public concerns and outcry about the danger of surveillance, invasion of privacy, and a looming geoslavery on the horizon. Although fragmented studies and reflections have been reported (Levin et al., 2002; Koskela, 2003; Dobson and Fisher, 2007; Obermeyer, 2007), there exists no comprehensive study so far linking these two separate lines of inquiry to address this love–hate reaction by the public to surveillance in general, and geosurveillance in particular.

We need more research and attention to this area, which may facilitate the development of applied ethics for geospatial technologies (Sui, 2007c).

The dilemma seems to derive from the fact that human existence is often characterized by the paradoxical desires of trying to be both private and public. The question is when, where, how, and whether the parties involved have the choice of disclosing or not disclosing. On the one hand, we are all afraid of the darker scenarios of repressive obsession and the invasion of privacy through the relentless logistics of data gathering and database linkages. Dystopian depictions of a future totalitarian state run by a super-panopticon is also too Orwellian to be real. On the other hand, the seemingly new fascination with certain forms of surveillance as a source of pleasure and entertainment is manifested in the increasing popularity of webcams, the proliferation of claims to real-time/live broadcasting, and the global success of the reality TV genre, which has resulted in the dramatic proliferation of surveillance both as subject matter and as narrative structure in contemporary cinematic production. The risks of aestheticizing surveillance can potentially trivialize its irreducible and all-too stark political dimensions.

Another ethical issue is related to the so-called first law of geographic information: information is often the most scarce when it is needed the most (Taylor and Overton, 1991). Have the applications of geospatial technologies helped to narrow or widen the digital divide? The new surveillance infrastructure, of which geospatial technologies are an integral part, mediates the production of social knowledge and action toward individuals. The potential uses of locational infrastructure redistribute the power to negotiate the meanings and uses of public places (Phillips and Curry, 2002). Non-reciprocal visibility is one of the greatest inequities in contemporary surveillance (Brin, 1998). Who is being constantly surveilled? The news reports seem to point to the young, the sick, the elderly, and the vulnerable.

The on-going war on terrorism raises another ethical dilemma. High-resolution satellite images available on Google Earth™ have reportedly been used by terrorists in Yemen in 2006 and insurgents in Iraq in 2007 to plan attacks on allied troops. True, committed terrorists could find all this information in most public libraries, but the increasing availability of online geospatial databases has made some of the sensitive information a lot easier to access. In other words, by making more geospatial information available online, we have inadvertently created an infrastructure that can be used counterproductively by terrorists to plan and launch attacks against us (Baker et al., 2004).

In his classic essay "The Tragedy for the Commons," Hardin (1968, p.1243) somberly warned "ruin is the destination toward which all men rush, each pursuing his own best interest in a society that believes in the freedom of the commons. Freedom in a commons brings ruin to all." This raises the question, should society impose certain limits and guidelines in terms of who can collect, access, use, retain, and disseminate geospatial data?

SEEKING REMEDIES: DISCUSSIONS AND PROSPECTS

Evidently, the recent developments in geospatial technologies and their wide-ranging applications have raised a series of challenging legal and ethical issues. Although existing laws and regulations can be applied to some limited extent, we need a combination of legal, ethical, and technical approaches in order to address these issues effectively.

New legislation

Most legal issues regarding the use of geospatial technologies in society revolve around the issues related to geospatial data/information at the individual or collective levels, and include: (1) data collection; (2) data retention; (3) data access; (4) data

use and integration with other information; (5) data dissemination; and (6) data ownership and licensing. Comprehensive legislation is needed to clearly address these issues at local, national, and international levels. The European Union framework, as implemented in the Netherlands, strikes a balance between protecting consumer privacy versus offering adequate services, while at the same time the new legal frameworks are also widely accepted by the general public (Van Loenen and Zevenbergen, 2007). In the USA, former North Carolina Senator John Edwards initiated new federal legislation on locational technologies in 2003, but the new law was not brought to the Senate floor for a vote due to his subsequent vice-presidential nomination in the 2004 presidential campaign. Generally speaking, the USA has taken a more *laissez-faire* approach to markets, which tends to restrain government, whereas EU tends to regulate third parties.

A core concept that much of the new legislation hinges upon is locational privacy, which suggests individuals have rights to their signature in space and time and can determine when, how, and to what extent location information is communicated to others (Armstrong and Ruggles, 2005). For further legal protection Sui (2006b) proposed that location be treated as an integral part of a person's identity, as where we are often reflects and defines who we are. By treating location as part of identity, Sui (2006b) argued that many existing laws regarding identify theft can be invoked when a person's location information is collected, used, and disseminated without the person's permission.

In recent years, more than 13 US states have passed laws restricting RFID adoption and application. Texas, for example, passed laws prohibiting school districts from requiring students to use an RFID device for identification. Wisconsin made it illegal to implant RFID chips into human bodies. Also, New Mexico and Tennessee require the disclosure of RFID chips to consumers and the removal or deactivation of tags at the point of sale of RFID-chipped merchandise (http://rfidprivacy.mit.edu/access/happening_legislation.html).

There also have been efforts in recent years to develop measures of self-regulation by industry. Although industry self-regulation is a welcome step toward protecting personal privacy, these rules and regulations by service or data providers often focus on relieving themselves of legal liabilities, thus avoiding potential law suits in case something goes wrong. It is also hard to enforce those industry self-regulations.

Many businesses offering LBS or geospatial information have increasingly realized the importance of the legal and ethical issues that a suite of powerful geospatial technologies has brought to individuals and society. Industry leaders have recognized that safeguarding sensitive personal information is not only important to consumers, but also of paramount importance for the sustainable growth of their business. Most LBS or geospatial data providers have developed their own privacy policies and protocols posted on their web sites, most of which warn users of the potential risks of using their data or services.

One particular area that has attracted much public attention in recent years is the legal limit of an employer's right to conduct surveillance on employees (Herbert and Tuminaro, 2008). As the boundary between work and non-work is increasingly blurred in the digital economy, how to track employees for their productivity, although understandable and legitimate, has caused considerable privacy concerns in recent years. Furthermore, inspired by Garrett Hardin's tragedy of the commons thesis, Onsrud (1998) argued for the existence of what he called the information commons. Drawing from experiences in developing laws to protect the environmental commons, he proposed to develop new legal frameworks for the information commons.

New ethics

Legal remedies are expensive and notoriously slow, and not every potential problem caused by geospatial technologies can be litigated. Therefore, in addition to legal solutions through new legislation, scholars have also been calling for the development of new ethics rules and social norms at both the individual and societal levels suitable for the age of pervasive computing. In addressing many of the social issues brought by new technologies, new ethics and moral practices are perhaps more effective, because as humans we are more likely to be seduced by new ethics rather than coerced into compliance with new laws.

To resolve many social problems, Dodge and Kitchin (2005) advocated a new ethics of forgetting, which clearly articulates a new set of rules on "how" and "when" to "forget," and even "delete," the massive electronic information in the age of pervasive computing. The rapid development of pervasive computing in general and geospatial tracking in particular has led to the widespread sousveillance, which complements surveillance, through the development of life-logs. We now have a new cyber-infrastructure for socio-spatial archives that can document every action, every event, every conversation, and every material expression of an individual's life. A new ethics of forgetting needs to be developed and built into the development of life-logging technologies. Rather than seeing forgetting as a weakness or fallibility, Dodge and Kitchin (2005) argued that the new ethics of forgetting could be an emancipatory process that will free pervasive computing (of which geospatial technologies are part of) from burdensome and pernicious effects.

Recently, Google™ has already started a new business of blurring or deleting sensitive targets on Google Maps™ or Google Earth™ (ITSecurity, 2008). Although the benefits of a new ethics of forgetting cannot be denied under certain circumstances, it is not always possible, or even desirable, to adhere to forgetting as a new social norm. Inspired by Asimov's "Three Laws of Robotics" (Table 26.2), Durocher (2002) formulated a set of three laws of LBS (Table 26.3), which

Table 26.2 Asimov's Laws of Robotics

First Law of Robotics:
A robot may not injure a human being, or, through inaction, allow a human being to come to harm.

Second Law of Robotics:
A robot must obey orders given to it by human beings, except where such orders would conflict with the First Law.

Third Law of Robotics:
A robot must protect its own existence as long as such protection does not conflict with the First or Second Law.

Table 26.3 Durocher's Laws of LBS

First Law of LBS:
Location, through its availability or non-availability, must not allow a human being to come to harm.

Second Law of LBS:
The availability of one's location must be in one's complete control, except where such control would conflict with the First Law.

Third Law of LBS:
The providers of location-based services must be allowed to create a profitable business from these services as long as such business does not conflict with the First or Second Law.

he contends that the LBS industry should adopt. Overall, LBS should have ethical laws regarding (1) its use during emergency situations; (2) its voluntary status; and (3) the appropriate/beneficial use of the locational data.

Since its original publication in a short story called "Runaround" in 1942, Asimov's three laws of robotics have been continuously debated and fine-tuned. Although still controversial, several extensions have been made (Clarke, 1993, 1994), Asimov's laws have been widely accepted as a reasonable guide to discuss the moral issue of robotics (Warrick, 1980). Even Asimov himself admitted that "there was just enough ambiguity in the three laws to provide the conflicts and uncertainties required for new stories, and to my great relief, it seemed always to be possible to think up a new angle out of the sixty-one words of the three laws" (cited in Warrick, 2002: 175).

Although significant fine-tuning is needed, Durocher's three laws of LBS offer a reasonable guideline for the use of LBS in the near future – provided that an enforcement mechanism can eventually be established.

The first LBS law addresses the requirements of LBS in emergency situations. It is consistent with enhanced 911 (E911) services as mandated by the new FCC regulation. It is reasonable to expect improved emergency services if all 911 calls are locationally explicit. The first law of LBS also requires that no services should put mobile users in danger.

The second law would ensure that LBS services are voluntary, and therefore that privacy should be preserved for individuals subscribing to these services. Under normal circumstances, a subscriber should be able to prevent others from locating him or her. But totally complying with this could also put the user at risk, since in emergency situations it might be impossible for the user to provide all the necessary life-saving authorization-Alaso, in some cases, the police will want to (and already do) track cellular phone usage to locate dangerous criminals.

Finally, the third law stresses the fact that providing location information alone is not sufficient to sustain business growth. Service providers must find a way to develop the right business models and charge the appropriate fees for the right services. Applications must bring real value that consumers and business users will be willing to pay for. However, the third law also ensures that no business should be able to benefit from the availability of location data to the detriment of a LBS user's right to complete privacy and safety.

As Fisher and Dobson (2003) illustrated in their seven different scenarios regarding the use of LBS (Table 26.4), the legal and ethical implications of LBS are complex and contingent upon many uncertain parameters in the real world. Nonetheless, I believe that the three LBS laws provide reasonable guidelines for most civilian applications, as tested by the Fisher and Dobson's seven scenarios (Table 26.4). The ethics of forgetting is only one of the seven possible real world scenarios defining practices that may be viewed as desirable.

Technical solutions: steps toward trustworthy geospatial technologies?

Legal and ethical strategies for remedying the problems brought about by geospatial technologies are trust-based mechanisms for delimiting unacceptable uses of location information (Myles et al., 2003). However, trust can be breached, making sensitive information still vulnerable to unintentional and intentional disclosure. Therefore, the research community also suggests development of technical solutions. A range of previous research on location privacy has addressed the issue of adapting the level of spatial detail in location information as needed to protect an individual's location privacy. This concept is termed spatial generalization by Mascetti and Bettini (2007), but has also been variously termed in the literature as "spatial cloaking" (Gruteser and Grunwald, 2003), "obfuscation" (Duckham and Kulik, 2006), the "need-to-know principle" (Hutter et al., 2004), and the "principle of minimal asymmetry" (Jiang et al., 2002).

Generally, two major strategies have been well-developed and adopted: anonymity and obfuscation (Duckham and Kulik, 2006). Anonymity is often regarded as one of the privacy-sympathetic technologies (PST). Anonymity detaches or removes an individual's locational information from electronic transactions. Anonymity is normally quite effective in protecting individual privacy. However, with recent advances in data mining techniques, GIS can integrate locational

Table 26.4 Surveillance scenarios and laws of LBS

Scenarios	Examples	Legal/Ethical issues	Laws of LBS
They didn't know where you were	Normal life for ordinary citizens	Personal privacy/ethics of forgetting	Obeyed (violated if the person is suicidal?)
They know and you want them to	On call, emergency, alibi	Consent	Obeyed
They don't know but you thought they did	Faulty signal, signal blocked, physical density	Ignorance	Violated
They know and we wanted them to	Criminal activity, unethical conduct	Public interest	Ambiguous
They know and you didn't want them to	Nuisance calls, stalking, monitoring	Geo-identity theft	Violated
They know and we thought we wanted them to	Abusers, hostage takers	Coercion	Violated
They know and can physically keep you there	Forced labor or domestic abuse	Geo-slavery	Violated

Note: The first three columns were modified from Fisher and Dobson (2003).

information with other data such as remotely sensed imagery, georeferenced social, economic, and cadastral data, point of-sale data, credit-card transactions, traffic monitoring and video surveillance imagery, and other geosensor network data, allowing identity to be inferred (Monmonier, 2002; Miller, 2007). Obfuscation techniques deliberately degrade locational information, using error and uncertainty to protect privacy, which is part of the privacy enhancing technologies (PET). They also include geographic masking for static data (Armstrong et al., 1999). Duckham and Kulik (2006) extend the obfuscation approach to mobile objects. They also consider ways to counter potential threats from third parties who can refine their knowledge of a mobile object and compromise the obfuscation.

Reactions by the international community

Facing the threat of freely available high-resolution satellite images in various digital globes such as Google Earth™, Microsoft®'s Virtual Earth®, NASA's WorldWind, and so on, many countries have taken a variety of steps to protect their national interests. According to a confidential report recently issued by the CIA's Open Source Center and made public by the Federation of American Scientists (http://www.usatoday.com/tech/news/surveillance/2008–11–06-googleearth_N.htm), the following reactions have been reported by the international community in response to the recent advances of geospatial technologies.

- Negotiation – some nations have asked Google™ and other companies to keep certain images off the market. For example, Google Earth™ uses older imagery for several areas of Iraq based on British concerns about exposing its military sites. Some commercial imagery providers – typically those providing pictures from planes, not satellites – blur sensitive images before they are provided to Google™, usually in accordance with local law or at the request of local authorities.
- Bans – China issued a new government regulation barring websites selling "unapproved" commercial imagery in 2008. Similar rules were also implemented in Bahrain, but the move has been mainly to prevent exposure of elaborate residences and land holdings of the country's rich and powerful.
- Buying in – several countries, such as China and Thailand, are getting into the satellite imagery business themselves, and India sells its spy photos commercially. Many countries without their own satellites have become enthusiastic purchasers of commercial imagery to meet intelligence and security needs, and international demand for high-resolution satellite imagery has been growing steadily in recent years.
- Evasion – many countries have stepped up efforts to conceal sensitive facilities, either by putting them underground or camouflaging them. Others, such as India, have improved their ability to discern when satellites pass overhead, which allows them to conduct sensitive military activities when cameras are not watching. (For more details, see http://www.fas.org/irp/dni/osc/google.pdf).

However, these actions are ad hoc. There is an urgent need for the international community, perhaps under the umbrella of the United Nations, to update the rules and resolutions regarding the use of geospatial technologies at the international level in order to narrow the global digital divide between the information rich versus the information poor countries.

SUMMARY AND CONCLUSION

It is abundantly clear that recent technological advances in geospatial technologies have created a complex set of legal and ethical issues that deserve a broader dialogue in society about their short- and long-term implications. Mark Poster (2004) argued that networked digital information "humachines" should be understood as the central part of the evolving, unavoidable aspect of globalization. The new technological cornucopia tends to erode privacy, create new forms of inequality, and diminish the mechanisms of accountability. Indeed, a broader dialogue is needed to awaken humanity from its technological somnambulism. Whereas these humanchines bring with them countless risks and afford considerable resources for highly dangerous agglomerations of power, they also offer serious points of resistance to those powers and may serve as a base for developing auspicious, decentralized, multicultural global networks.

Technological advances provide us with hope for trustworthy computing that is capable of giving users more secure control of their own personal information, but technical remedies are not sufficient for the legal and ethical challenges discussed in this chapter. We also need broader legal and ethical frameworks that can effectively deal with issues at individual, institutional, and international levels. Similar to the dilemmas brought by bio-tech innovations, how to capitalize on the benefits of geospatial technologies and deter (even diminish) the emergence of a dystopia of Orwellian, or a monster of Frankenstein, proportions remains one of the grand challenges for our technological society. Obviously, we all want to savor the fruits of the latest advances in geospatial technologies without succumbing to their most dangerous temptations. Whether this delicate balance can be achieved is far from clear at this point.

Geographers have long been interested in studying complex issues at the intersection of geography and law (Delaney et al., 2001; Blomley et al., 2001, Blomley, 2003), geography and ethics (Proctor and Smith, 1999), geography and morality (Tuan, 1989; Sack, 1997), and the education of the next generation of geographers (Griffith, 2008). The widespread applications of geospatial technologies in society and our individual lives have opened new avenues for intellectual inquiries that will have far-reaching impacts. Geographic information scientists need to work closely with other geographers and with scholars in other disciplines facing similar legal and moral concerns in order to

address many of challenging issues reviewed in this chapter.

ACKNOWLEDGMENTS

Critical comments from Mike Goodchild, Don Janelle, John Kelmelis, Bill Herbert, and two anonymous reviewers have vastly improved this chapter. The author is responsible for any remaining errors. Thanks are also due to Chen Xu for his research assistance.

NOTES

1   There are criminal laws that make conduct illegal and then there is civil law (statutes, constitutions, and common law) that make conduct subject to lawsuits for damages and injunctions. Criminalizing conduct (such as prohibiting implanted chips and passing privacy statutes) is a legislative function which defines the contours of acceptable behavior and sets the situations where someone can be jailed or fined as a criminal sanction. Civil law (interpretation of constitutions and common law by courts) evolves on a case by case basis. For example the US Supreme Court's decisions interpreting the Fourth Amendment limitations has changed over time.

2   See AAAS's on-going project on "Geospatial Technologies and Human Rights" for more details: http://shr.aaas.org/geotech/.

3   Two contradictory findings were handed down regarding GPS tracking recently. In Wisconsin, an appellate court found that no warrant would be required, while a New York Court of Appeals found that a warrant would be required.

REFERENCES

AAAS (2007) 'Geospatial technologies and human rights: What can geospatial technologies do for the human rights community?', http://shr.aaas.org/geotech/whatcanGISdo.shtml.

Aaron, R. (2002) 'Satellite tracking and the right to privacy', *Hastings Law Journal*, 53(2): 549–65.

Aday, S. and Livingston, S. (2007) 'NGOs as intelligence agencies: The empowerment of transnational advocacy networks and the media by commercial remote sensing', paper presented during 2007 AAG meeting, San Francisco.

Armstrong, M.P., Rushton, G. and Zimmerman, D.L. (1999) 'Geographically masking health data to preserve confidentiality'. *Statistics in Medicine*, 18(5): 497–525.

Armstrong, M.P. and Ruggles, A. (2005) 'Geographic information technologies and personal privacy', *Cartographica*, 40(4): 63–3.

Baker, J.C., Lachman, B.E., Frelinger, D.R., O'Conneil, K.M., Hou, A.C., Tseng, M.S., Orletsky, D. and Yost, C. (2004) *Mapping the Risks: Assessing the Homeland Security Implications of Publicly Available Geospatial Information*. Santa Monica, CA: RAND and National Defense Institute.

Beresford, A.R. (2005) *Location Privacy in Ubiquitous Computing (Technical Report UCAM-CL-TR-612)*. Cambridge: University of Cambridge.

Blomley, N.K. (2003) 'From "what?" to "so what?" Law and Geography in retrospect'. in J. Holder (ed.), *Law and Geography*. Oxford: Oxford University Press.

Blomley, N.K., Delaney, D. and Ford, R.T. (eds), (2001) *The Legal Geographies Reader: Law, Power and Space*. New York: Wiley & Blackwell.

Blumenfeld, L. (2003) 'Dissertation could be security threat', *Washington Post*, 8 July. http://www.washingtonpost.com/ac2/wp-dyn/A23689–2003Jul7?language=printer (accessed on July 7, 2007)

Brin, D. (1998) *The Transparent Society: Will Technology Force us to Choose between Privacy and Freedom?* Reading, MA: Addison-Wesley.

Burke, J., Estrin, D., Hansen, M., Parker, A., Ramanathan, N., Reddy, S. and Srivastava, M.B. (2006) 'Participatory sensing', *Proceedings of WSW'06 at SenSys '06, Boulder, Colorado*. http://peir.cens.ucla.edu/wp-content/participatory-sensing.pdf (accessed 15 January 2009).

Calvert, C. (2004) *Voyeur Nation: Media, Privacy and Peering into Modern Culture*. Boulder, CO: Westview.

Canter, D. (2003) *Mapping Murder: The Secrets of Geographic Profiling*. London: Virgin Publishing.

Cho, G. (1998) *Geographic Information Systems and the Law: Mapping the Legal Frontier*. New York: John Wiley & Sons.

Clarke, R. (1993) 'Asimov's laws of robotics implications for information technology (I)', *IEEE Computer*, 26(12): 53–61.

Clarke, R. (1994) 'Asimov's laws of robotics implications for information technology (II)', *IEEE Computer*, 27(1): 57–66.

Cloud, J. and Clarke, K.C. (1999) 'Through a shutter darkly: The tangled relationships between Civilian, Military and Intelligence remote sensing in the early U.S. space program'. in J. Reppy (ed.), *Secrecy and Knowledge Production*. Occasional Paper no.23. Ithaca, NY: Cornell University Peace Studies Program.

CNN (2003) 'Will GPS tech lead to "geoslavery"?', CNN.com Technology Section 11 March 2003. http://www.cnn.com/2003/TECH/ptech/03/11/geo.slavery.ap/ (accessed 27 November 2006).

Curry, M.R. (1997a) 'Digital people, digital places: Rethinking privacy in a world of geographic information', *Ethics and Behavior*, 7(3): 253–63.

Curry, M.R. (1997b) 'The digital individual and the private realm', *Annals of the Association of American Geographers*, 87(4): 681–99.

Deibert, R.J. (2003) 'Unfettered observation: The politics of earth monitoring from space'. in J.C. Baker, K.M. O'Connell and R.A. Williamson (eds), *Space Policy in the Twenty-first Century*. Baltimore, MD: The Johns Hopkins University Press. pp. 89–114.

Delaney, D., Blomley, N. and Ford, R. (2001) 'Where is law?', in N.K. Blomley, D. Delaney and R. Ford (eds), *The Legal Geographies Reader: Law, Power, and Space*. New York: Wiley & Blackwell. pp. xiii–xxii.

Dobson, J.E. (2009) 'Big brother has evolved', *Nature*, 458: 968.

Dobson, J.E. and Fisher, P.F. (2003) 'Geoslavery', *IEEE Technology and Society Magazine*, 22(1): 47–52.

Dobson, J.E. and Fisher, P.F. (2007) 'Panopticon's changing geography', *Geographical Review*, 97(3): 307–23.

Dodge, M. and Kitchin, R. (2005) 'The ethics of forgetting in an age of pervasive computing', *Working paper, CASA Working Papers, (92)*. Centre for Advanced Spatial Analysis (UCL), London, UK.

Duckham, M. and Kulik, L. (2006) 'Location privacy and location-aware computing'. in J. Drummond, R. Billen, E. Joao and D. Forrest (eds), *Dynamic and Mobile GIS: Investigating Change in Space and Time*. Boca Raton, FL: CRC Press. pp. 35–51.

Durocher, J.M. (2002) 'Webraska CEO proposes 'Laws of LBS'. http://www.m-travel.com/20614.shtml (accessed on May 8, 2008).

Dykes, J.A. and Mountain, D.M. (2003) 'Seeking structure in records of spatio-temporal behavior: Visualization issues, efforts and applications', *Computational Statistics and Data Analysis*, 43(4): 581–603.

Edmundson, K.E. (2005) 'Global positioning system implants: Must consumer privacy be lost in order for people to be found?', *Indiana Law Review*, 38: 207–37.

Farmer, B. (2009) 'Geography professor claims to have found Osama bin Laden'. http://www.telegraph.co.uk/news/worldnews/asia/pakistan/4681736/Geography-professor-claims-to-have-found-Osama-bin-Laden.html (accessed 15 May 2009).

Feldman, R. and Sanger, J. (2006) *The Text Mining Handbook: Advanced Approaches in Analyzing Unstructured Data*. New York: Cambridge University Press.

Fisher, P.F. and Dobson, J.E. (2003) 'Who knows where you are, and who should, in the Era of mobile geography?', *Geography*, 88(4): 331–37.

Gewin, V. (2004) 'Mapping opportunities', *Nature*, 427: 376–77.

Gomes, L. (2003) 'The newest road to fame and fortune is mapping the road', *The Wall Street Journal, B1,* 14 July.

Goodchild, M.F. (2007) 'Citizens as sensors: The world of volunteered geography', *GeoJournal*, 69(4): 211–21.

Goss, J. (1995) 'We know who you are and we know where you live: The instrumental rationality of geodemographic systems', *Economic Geography*, 71(2): 171–98.

Griffith, D.A. (2008) 'Ethical considerations in geographic research: What especially graduate students need to know', *Ethics, Place and Environment*, 11(3): 237–52.

Gruteser, M. and Grunwald, D. (2003) 'Anonymous usage of location-based services through spatial and temporal cloaking', *Proc. MobiSys '03I.* pp. 31–42.

Hardin, G. (1968) 'The tragedy of the commons', *Science*, 162(3859): 1243–48.

Hawrey, L.L. (1999) 'GPS: charting new terrain – legal issues related to GPS-based navigation and location systems'. http://www.constructionweblinks.com/Resources/Industry_Reports__Newsletters/April_1999/april_1999.html (accessed on June 8, 2008).

Herbert, W.A. (2006) 'No direction home: Will the law keep pace with human tracking technology to protect individual privacy and stop geoslavery?', *I/S: A Journal of Law and Policy*, 2(2): 409–73.

Herbert, W.A. and Tuminaro, A.K. (2008) 'The impact of emerging technologies in the workplace: Who's watching the man (who's watching me)?', *Hofstra Labor and Employment Law Journal*, 25(2): 355–93.

Hightower, J. and Boriello, G. (2001) 'Location sensing techniques', *IEEE Computer*, 34(8): 57–66.

Holz, R.K. (1973) *The Surveillant Science: Remote Sensing of the Environment*. Boston, MA: Houghton Mifflin. http://www.technologyreview.com/articles/print_version/pfeiffer0903.asp (accessed on May 27, 2008).

Hutter, D., Stephan, W. and Ullmann, M. (2004) 'Security and privacy in pervasive computing: State of the art and future directions'. in D. Hutter, G. Miiller and W. Stephan (eds), *Security in Pervasive Computing, volume 2802 of Lecture Notes in Computer Science*. Berlin: Springer. pp. 284–89.

ITSecurity (2008) 'Blurred out: 51 things you aren't allowed to see on Google maps', http://www.itsecurity.com/features/51-things-not-on-google-maps-071508/ (accessed on June 9, 2008).

Jiang, X., Hong, J.I. and Landay, J.A. (2002) 'Approximate information flows: Socially-based modeling of privacy in ubiquitous computing'. in G. Borriello and L. E. Holmquist (eds), *Proc. 4th International Conference on Ubiquitous Computing*, volume 2498 of Lecture Notes in Computer Science. Berlin: Springer. pp. 176–93.

King, G. (1997) *A Solution to the Ecological Inference Problem: Reconstructing Individual Behavior from Aggregate Data*. Princeton, NJ: Princeton University Press.

Klinkenberg, B. (2007) 'Geospatial technologies and the geographies of hope and fear', *Annals of the Association of American Geographers*, 97(2): 350–60.

Koskela, H. (2003) '"Camera"– the contemporary urban panopticon', *Surveillance and Society*, 1(3): 292–313.

Lessig, L. (2008) *Remix: Making Art and Commerce Thrive in the Hybrid Economy*. London: Penguin.

Levin, T.Y., Frohne, U. and Weibel, P. (2002) *Rhetorics of Surveillance from Bentham to Big Brother*. Cambridge, MA: MIT Press.

Litfin, K.T. (2001) 'The globalization of transparency: The use of commercial satellite imagery by non-governmental organizations'. in J. Baker, K. O'Connell and R. Williamson (eds), *Commercial Observation Satellites: At the Leading Edge of Global Transparency*. Santa Monica, CA: RAND. pp. 463–84.

Livingston, S. and Robinson, L. (2003) 'Mapping fears: The use of commercial high-resolution satellite imagery in international affairs', *AstroPolitics*, 1(2): 3–25.

Mann, S., Nolan, J. and Wellman, B. (2003) 'Sousveillance: Inventing and using wearable computing devices for data collection in surveillance environments', *Surveillance and Society*, 1(3): 331–55.

Mascetti, S. and Bettini, C. (2007) 'A comparison of spatial generalization algorithms for LBS privacy preservation', *International Conference on Mobile Data Management*, 1(1): 258–62.

Masnick, M. (2008) 'Driver blames GPS for driving on railroad tracks, getting hit by train'. http://techdirt.com/articles/20080104/141128.shtml (accessed on June 25, 2008)

McGrath, J. (2004) *Loving Big Brother: Performance, Privacy, and Surveillance Space*. New York: Routledge.

Miller, H. (2007) 'Place-based versus people-based geographic information science', *Geography Compass*, 1(3): 503–35.

Monmonier, M. (2002) *Spying with Maps*. Chicago: University of Chicago Press.

Musgrove, M. (2008) 'Bus accident blamed on driver's GPS distraction'. http://blog.washingtonpost.com/posttech/2008/04/bus_accident_blamed_on_drivers.html.

Myles, G., Friday, A. and Davies, N. (2003) 'Preserving privacy in environments with location-based applications', *IEEE Pervasive Computing*, 2(1): 56–64.

National Research Council (NRC) (2004) *Licensing Geographic Data and Services*. Washington, DC: The National Academy Press.

National Research Council (NRC) (2007a) *Putting People on the Map: Protecting Confidentiality with Linked Social-spatial Data*. Washington, DC: The National Academy Press.

National Research Council (NRC) (2007b) *Engaging Privacy and Information Technology in a Digital Age*. Washington, DC: The National Academy Press.

Nichols, M. (2007) 'NY Scanners spark union cries of "geoslavery"'. http://www.msnbc.msn.com/id/16832030/.

Nissenbaum, H. (1998) 'Protecting privacy in an information age: The problem of privacy in public', *Law and Philosophy*, 17: 559–96.

O'Harrow, R., Jr (2005) *No Place to Hide: Behind the Scenes of our Emerging Surveillance Society*. New York: Free Press.

Obermeyer, N. (2007) 'Thoughts on volunteered (geo)slavery'. http://ncgia.ucsb.edu/projects/vgi/docs/position/Obermeyer_Paper.pdf (accessed 10 September 2008).

Okolie, C.C. (1989) *International Law of Satellite Remote Sensing and Outer Space*. Dubuque: Kendall/Hunt Publishing.

Olson, J. (2006) *Fair Play: Moral Dilemmas's of Spying*. Washington, DC: Potomac.

Onsrud, H.J. (1995) 'Identifying unethical conduct in the use of GIS', *Cartography and Geographic Information Systems*, 22(1): 90–7.

Onsrud, H.J. (1998) 'The tragedy of the information commons', in F. Taylor (ed.), *Policy Issues in Modern Cartography*. Oxford: Elsevier Science. pp. 141–58.

Onsrud, H.J. (1999) 'Liability in the use of geographic information systems and geographic data sets'. in P. Longley, M. Goodchild, D. Maguire and D. Rhind (eds), *Geographic Information Systems: Principles, Techniques, Management, and Applications*. New York: Wiley. pp. 643–52.

Onsrud, H.J., Johnson, J. and Lopez, X. (1994) 'Protecting personal privacy in using geographic information systems', *Photogrammetric Engineering and Remote Sensing*, 60 (9): 1083–95.

Perez, J.C. (2009) 'Judge dismisses Google street view case', *PC World*, 19 February. http://www.pcworld.com/article/159740/judge_dismisses_google_street_view_case.html (accessed on Sept. 7, 2008)

Pfeiffer, E.W. (2003) 'Whereware', *MIT Technology Review*. http://jrichardstevens.com/articles/pfeiffer-whereware.pdf (accessed 13 November 2009).

Phillips, D.J. and Curry, M. (2002) 'Privacy and the phenetic urge: Geodemographics and the changing spatiality of local practice'. in D. Lyon (ed.), *Surveillance as Social Sorting: Privacy, Risk, and Automated Discrimination*. London: Routledge. pp. 137–52.

Pister, K. (2002) 'Smart dust: Autonomous sensing and communication in a cubic millimeter'. http://robotics.eecs.berkeley.edu/~pister/SmartDust (accessed 30 January 2005).

Poster, M. (2004) 'The information empire', *Comparative Literature Studies*, 41(3): 317–34.

Proctor, J. and Smith, D.M. (1999) *Geography and Ethics: Journeys in a Moral Terrain*. New York: Routledge.

Raper, J.F. and Livingstone, D.E. (2001) 'Let's get real: Spatio-temporal identity and geographic entities', *Transactions of the Institute of British Geographers*, 26: 237–42.

Regan, P. (2004) 'Emergency response systems and the creeping legibility of people and places', *The Information Society*, 20(5): 1–13.

Rheingold, H. (2002) *Smart Mobs: The Next Social Revolution*. Cambridge, MA: Perseus.

Rossmo, D.K. (2000) *Geographic Profiling*. Boca Raton, FL: CRC Press.

Rushkoff, D. (2005) 'Honey, I geotagged the kids', *The Feature*. http://www.thefeaturearchives.com/101490.html (accessed 2 May 2008).

Sack, R.D. (1997) *Homo Geographicus: A Framework for Action, Awareness, and Moral Concern*. Baltimore, MD: Johns Hopkins University Press.

Sui, D.Z. (2005) 'Will UBICOMP make GIS disappear?', *Computers, Environment, and Urban Systems*, 29(1): 361–67.

Sui, D.Z. (2006a) 'The streisand law suit and your stolen geography', *GeoWorld*, 12: 26–9. http://www.geoplace.com.

Sui, D.Z. (2007c) 'GIS, Hollywood and the surveillance space', *GeoWorld*, 6: 18–20. http://www.geoplace.com.

Sui, D.Z. (2008) 'The wikification of GIS and its consequences: or Angelina Jolie's new tattoo and the future of GIS', *Computers, Environment, and Urban Systems*, 32(1): 1–5.

Sui, D.Z. (2006b) 'The location of identity: Reclaim your stolen geography', paper presented during the 2006 AAAS Symposium on 'Orwell's Wolf is Back: Tracking kids, dogs, old people, and everybody in between,' St Louis, 18–20 February.

Sui, D.Z. (2007a) 'Mapping by the creative commons? Or how wiki can GIS become', *GeoWorld*, 12: 21–3.

Sui, D.Z. (2007b) 'Geospatial technologies for surveillance: Tracking people and commodities in real-time', *Geographical Review*, 93(3): 3–9.

Taipale, K.A. (2007) 'The ear of dionysus: Rethinking foreign intelligence surveillance', *Yale Law and Technology*, 9: 128–61.

Taylor, P. and Overton, M. (1991) 'Further thoughts on geography and GIS', *Environment and Planning A*, 23: 1087–94.

Tuan, Y.F. (1989) *Morality and Imagination: Paradoxes of Progress.* Madison, WI: University of Wisconsin Press.

USA Today (2008) 'Truant students to be tracked by GPS anklets in Texas'. http://www.usatoday.com/news/education/2008–08–27-gps-truancy_N.htm (accessed 4 September 2008).

Van Loenen, B. and Zevenbergen, J.A. (2007) 'The impact of the European privacy regime on location technology development', *Journal of Location Based Services*, 1(3): 165–78.

von der Dunk, F.G. (2005) 'Legal aspects of geospatial data-gathering in space: Eyes in the sky or big brother'. http://www.gim-international.com/issues/articles/id528-Legal_Aspects_of_Geospatial_Datagathering_in_Space.html (accessed 15 October 2008).

Warren, S. and Brandeis, L. (1890) 'The right to privacy', *Harvard Law Review*, 4: 193–220.

Warrick, P.S. (1980) *The Cybernetic Imagination in Science Fiction.* Cambridge, MA: MIT Press.

Warrick, P.S. (2002) 'Asimov and the morality of artificial intelligence'. in J. G. Cunningham (ed.), *Science Fiction: Literary Movements and Genres.* San Diego, CA: Greenhaven Press. pp. 169–77.

Weaver, S.D. (2006) 'The visualization of my digital footprint: A system to evaluate the societal consequences of ubiquitous computing with emphasis on homeland security and privacy erosion', MS thesis, Pennsylvania State University, State College, PA.

PART III

Conclusion

27

GIS and Society Research: Reflections and Emerging Themes

Helen Couclelis, Timothy Nyerges
and Robert McMaster

INTRODUCTION

When the first geographic information system (GIS) appeared in the 1960s as a program for plugging map coordinates into a computer, few would have thought that at some point in the not too distant future a *Handbook of GIS and Society Research* would become necessary. The chapters in this handbook reflect the inroads that GIS has made into most aspects of society in industrialized nations, and also increasingly in the developing world. GIS applications deriving from years of research are now part of everyday life. They are fully integrated in the workings of a wide range of organizations and institutions, and they facilitate public participation in community affairs even in situations where more conventional attempts to involve stakeholders in local decision-making have failed. An increasing range of applied sciences now use GIS routinely, and disciplines such as urban, landscape, and environmental

planning are now unthinkable without it. At the same time, the ubiquity of GIS in society has raised legal and ethical issues that cover the spectrum from the very practical to the philosophical, as questions ranging from liability and pricing to privacy, fairness and value have come to the fore. On the conceptual and theoretical side, GIS as geographic information *science* has led to a rethinking of the nature of geographic space, and also to the realization that different representations of that space are needed not just to display different themes but also to convey meaning to different kinds of users. Cognitive science, computer science, linguistics, philosophy, and logic are among the fields that have contributed fundamental insights to geographic information science, insights that led to more versatile GIS software and more appropriate applications just as they have helped develop a highly exciting new intellectual domain. While the section titles in this handbook as well as the chapters under these could have been other, what would unquestionably be a constant among all possible organizations of such a work is the breadth and depth of the issues covered by the 'GIS and society' theme. In the following we offer some more specific thoughts on each of the six sections in this handbook, and close with a handful of thematic threads that cut across the diversity of perspectives and topics that this volume reflects.

SECTION 1: FOUNDATIONS OF GIS AND SOCIETY RESEACH

Section 1 set the tone for the rest of the book by presenting four different perspectives on how scholars working within the theme of geographic information and society view the conceptual foundations of that domain. The views represented there are among the current ones at the time of the handbook's publication. It is worth stressing that such views are to a large extent a function of time, as the meaning and content of each of the components of the phrase 'geographic information systems and society' keep evolving. First, what was originally fully captured by the acronym 'GIS', to be read as geographic information *systems*, eventually saw the meaning of the 'S' expand to also include services, science, and society. Second, and even more obviously, our understanding of society in all its aspects (community, daily life, science, education, business, government, institutions, politics, the military, and so on) has also greatly evolved since the time when the first GIS were used to make the updating of cadastre maps for forest resources more efficient. Third is the 'and' that connects 'geographic information' and 'society' in the title of this handbook, which stands for all the applications and services that form a two-way bridge between these notions, but also for their on-going transformative dialectic. Here too, technical and conceptual advances over the years have led to a much broader range of socially

relevant applications that are ever more accessible to non-expert users, just as concerns about the pervasive power of related technologies continue to rise.

The four perspectives on the 'fundamentals of GIS and society' that were represented in that first section reflect the diversity of approaches to the subject. How is that phrase to be understood? For the authors of the first contribution the answer lies in the tradition of the classic conception of geography as the science of space *par excellence*. From this perspective geographic information is the basic ingredient out of which we construct geographic representations, which can then be used in different applications to serve society. These representations rest on a handful of key spatial concepts, such as distance, area, and location, along with other concepts specific to GIS. But the main message of that chapter was that, since everything happens in space as well as time, these same concepts underlie most if not all of social science – whether its practitioners are aware of this or not. This means that geographic information in fact permeates society through the spatial concepts that enrich our understanding of social phenomena. The notion of 'spatially integrated social science' promoted by the authors conveys this idea that spatial concepts, and thus geographic information, should be part and parcel of practically all social science research.

A more abstract perspective on the fundamentals of geographic information and society was presented in the second chapter, a perspective that is closer to both philosophy and computer science. But the authors' discussion of geographic information ontologies stressed the need to move that domain of inquiry beyond the rarified realm of concepts and relations meaningful only to experts, towards the representation of commonsense knowledge and less formal, more intuitive specifications of things. In a sense this call for the 'democratization' of geographic ontologies is closer to the original meaning of ontology as the study of what exists in the world, because clearly the world that geographic ontologies strive to describe also includes the purposeful social actors that interact with it.

While the first two chapters in that section approached the question of the fundamentals of geographic information 'from the inside out', so to speak, the next two presented a view 'from the outside in', focusing on the changing roles of GIS in society and moving from there to the changing character of the technology itself. These two perspectives reminded us of the contributions of critical theory, feminism, and participatory/emancipatory projects to the shaping of the more socially inclusive forms of GIS that we have today. They both characterize GIS primarily as a communicative medium facilitating spatially informed societal dialectics capable of supporting sometimes contrasting forms of discourse – discourse that simultaneously operates through, and strengthens a complex web of social relationships among people and institutions. These last two perspectives on the foundations of geographic information and society highlighted the need to be critically mindful of how the technology both enables and constrains these societal relationships.

Despite some major differences in approach, all four chapters in this section implicitly or explicitly made the point that GIS is much more than 'just a tool', and geographic information is much more than spatially referenced data that one collects, manages, and analyzes. The chapters in the five sections that followed have illustrated these critical points by presenting more targeted discussions of the myriad of ways (usually benign, on occasion questionable) in which geographic information and GIS have penetrated society, just as they have been shaped by it.

SECTION 2: GIS AND MODERN LIFE

In industrialized societies, geographic information has become part of everyday life in a myriad ways both visible and invisible. The chapters in Section 2 examined but a small sample of the contributions that geographic information has made to modern life, some of them in the hands of experts who then deliver specific services to people, others directly in the hands of individual non-expert users, as is literally the case with some location-based services. These are of course part of the broader information revolution and yet distinct from it, set apart by the explicit geographical perspective they embody. As spatial data and associated analysis and visualization techniques become more available and accessible, the original small group of societally relevant applications of geographic information has exploded in size and significance. From national security and the military to local government, from science to business, from transportation to agriculture, there is hardly a domain today that has not been touched by geographic information in its various manifestations. The increasing spatial awareness in society places additional demands of efficiency, pliability, scientific quality, and technical sophistication on the services and products delivered by the geographic information community. These qualities were reflected in the four chapters of Section 2. Two of these highlight the kinds of technical advances that facilitated the integration of geographic information and GIS with everyday life, while the other two focus on its contribution to scientific applications of great benefit to society.

Since the early twenty-first century sizeable investments in information-related infrastructure ('cyberinfrastructure') have been made in Europe, the USA, several technologically advanced countries in East Asia, and more locally elsewhere in the world. These investments have primarily involved upgrades of Internet hardware so as to allow the transfer of massive amounts of data across space, along with the provision of specialized web software tools necessary for handling all that information. On the research front, 'big science' was first to make use of these computational resources to address questions of unimaginable complexity, but applications directly relevant to society's own complex problems are already in the works, many of them involving geographic information. Novel kinds of geographic information systems, services and science are being developed around the new cyberinfrastructure, aiming to address societal needs and problems at all relevant spatial scales. Research on 'information utilities' is beginning to blossom, involving questions about how best to provide these newly enabled web services while also protecting privacy and confidentiality when sensitive data are transmitted over the invisible, inscrutable network that now circles the globe.

At the other end of the macro–micro spectrum, location-based services (LBS) provide real-time access to information supporting on-the-go decision making. LBS have been called 'the services that know where they are' – but also 'at what time'. Made possible by mobile computing technologies, they range from those that present local maps of services centered on the current location of individual consumers, to those that allow emergency personnel to locate victims of accidents or other targets of interest. But LBS can serve more than individuals. At places and times when disasters hit, or in developing nations, LBS can also be used to monitor food or medication shortages and the progress over space and time of re-supply efforts. On the theoretical side, LBS research is part of the broader agenda involving space–time modeling, a research tradition well established in geography. The idea is that as people move in space, they also move in time, so that 'where', and 'when' should be considered together. This notion is more and more relevant in today's dynamic, accelerating world, which is largely defined by change and movement. Research that situates and times relevant changes and movements is becoming increasingly important across all spatial and temporal scales, from those of daily activities to the global flows of capital, of the next

flu pandemic, or of human trans-continental migrations.

The other two chapters in Section 2 addressed two major scientific areas with direct societal relevance and considerable needs for geographic information: these areas are environmental sustainability and population health. Since the publication of the Brundtland Report (World Commission on Environment and Development, 1987) on environment and development, researchers have been deploying GIS tools that can be put to use in the cause of sustainable development. Global problems are intrinsically geographic. With the widespread recognition that global climate change will likely influence peoples' lives around the world in different ways, researchers heavily depend on geographic information to explore how communities and societies can address their climate-related vulnerabilities while also continuing on the path to development. Clearly, environmental issues of great relevance to society go well beyond climate-related concerns. Whether it is research on the health of ecosystems, on species preservation, deforestation, water pollution, the depletion of marine resources, or soil erosion, it is increasingly difficult to avoid using GIS and associated tools. Next (and not unrelated) to the health of the environment, the health of human populations is another area where the value of geographic information is beginning to be appreciated. Health GIS research has not yet attracted the amount of attention it deserves, though this is changing. For example, exposure to environmental contaminants is a geographic issue strongly involving the notions of collocation and proximity, and generally, even small hot-spots of ill health may be identified with spatial statistics. Similarly, the spread of a contagious disease is a spatial process that has been modeled for at least half a century. Spatial epidemiology, of which health GIS is part, is a research area ripe for expansion. In order for health GIS to deliver the societal benefits expected of it, a more favorable funding climate may be all that is still missing.

SECTION 3: ALTERNATIVE REPRESENTATIONS IN GIS AND SOCIETY RESEARCH

Computer visualization in science has been an extraordinarily successful endeavor, harnessing the mind's innate ability to apprehend and interpret patterns, colors, and movement literally at a glance, and helping stimulate higher cognitive functions such as problem solving and scientific discovery. As a research area computer visualization is exploding, helping make the invisible visible, the hidden manifest, and the inert come alive. Scientists can now rotate, magnify, distort, dissect, and probe objects represented on the computer screen, fly past nebulae towards the primordial depths of the universe, or explore the inside of atoms. Inevitably, these feats of software development and creative imagination have also touched the world of geographic information, which appears especially well suited to graphical computer displays since these share with geographic reality the property of being essentially spatial.

GIS gave geography its very own computer visualization revolution. At first there was computer mapping or computer cartographics. However, the theme of geographic information and society goes well beyond what may be represented on a computerized map and other such obvious artifacts. Researchers have needed to show phenomena that are invisible as well as visible, and images that are inside the human mind as well as out in the world. In the past decade the terms geographic visualization, geovisualization, and geovis were coined to indicate more advanced forms of visualization emphasizing a more user-centered, more exploratory, and cognitively adequate view of maps and other, more abstract kinds of representations. The chapters in the third section of the handbook took us on a brief tour of alternative approaches in that general area, with the understanding that the possibilities for thoughtful, creative representations are practically endless.

A striking example of the need for alternative representations was given by the chapter about uses of GIS by indigenous peoples, which focused on the existence of diverse cultural perspectives, each of which may foster a different way of viewing the world. This cultural focus makes the consideration of alternative representations unavoidable. Different cultures may categorize the things and events in the world in different ways, and these differences are often expressed in language. Thus the categories and concepts needed to meaningfully represent an indigenous reality may not have appropriate equivalents in the mainstream culture's GIS databases, requiring alternative representations that are subtly or even radically different from what may be taken for granted elsewhere. But different cultures are not only found in far-away places. Different sciences also have their own 'cultures' – their own ways of categorizing, prioritizing, defining, interpreting, analyzing, and doing things – and so do organizations. The latter sometimes write down their 'cultural mores' in documents, creating organizational guidelines. Geographic information visualization from an organizational perspective, and more specifically map-making that is adopting certain conventions and symbolizations over others, has been researched for some time. The result of these cultural choices often amounts to organizations speaking different 'languages', making communication among them an issue. It will be interesting to see how this line of research develops as more and more people appreciate the importance of shared understanding among organizations.

The research on alternative cultural representations of geographic information strives to externalize the understanding of space and geography that lies inside the collective minds of indigenous groups or organizations. By contrast, the computational representation of social networks explores a spatial phenomenon that is out there in the world but invisible. Given the extraordinary growth of social networking fostered by the Internet, research on computational networks is now recognized by the US National Science Foundation as being among the most promising areas for funding. The investigation of networking relationships among and within organizations is even emerging as a new subfield, called *virtual organization* research. But whether the focus is on virtual organizations or on social, professional, or interest-based networks, computing and representing their structure leads to new understanding of how individuals, groups, communities, and societies organize themselves for diverse activities and purposes.

The phrase 'alternative representations of geographic information' is usually understood to mean visual representations, and this is indeed the best known kind. However, viewed as a system, GIS involves two additional kinds of representations: database, and computational. Database representations are developed based upon database technologies that are used to store, manage, and retrieve GIS data. Computational representations in the form of spatial data structures support geospatial analysis. The development of geospatial analysis software is one of the major contributions that geographic information researchers have made to the GIS industry. All three kinds of representation – database, computational, and visual – are involved in research about GIS and society, and the chapter on representing human activities in a space-time context explicitly addressed all three. New types of data management techniques and data models are being developed to support space–time data used in dynamic representations of social phenomena. Spatiotemporal process modeling using large-scale computational resources such as the Open Science Grid architecture or the TeraGrid architecture (Wang and Liu, 2009), now being called CyberGIS, is on the verge of expanding into mainstream social science. Computing and visualizing the relationships among virtual and physical activities in society will greatly enhance our understanding of ourselves in a complex, fast-moving world.

SECTION 4: GIS IN ORGANIZATIONS AND INSTITUTIONS

Organizations and institutions of every kind are an essential part of modern society. In geographic scope these may be focused on a neighborhood or span the globe. In social significance they may range from the esoteric to the fundamentally important. They may be public or private, large or small, governmental or not, technology-intensive or not, but one thing they definitely have in common is that they all handle data. We saw how networking within and among organizations has become a prime topic of research in the GIS and society area. The far-flung implications of newly possible forms of virtual networking and data collecting, sharing, and use have pushed the question of data within, for, and by institutions to the forefront of researchable topics. Clearly not all data are spatial data, but given the growing awareness that all data are collected *somewhere*, and the growing ease to geocode data, they increasingly are geospatially enabled.

Geospatial data have been a raw material of the knowledge society for many years. Organizations and institutions have been primarily users (the majority) or primarily producers of such data, though many are both users and producers, or distributors. The geospatial data production and distribution system is closely linked to (geo)spatial data infrastructures (SDI) which have been developing for the past two decades in the more technologically advanced regions of the world. Generally speaking, national-scale infrastructures are more developed than state and local ones, mainly because national-level organizations are able to put forth more human and financial resources in a systematic manner. On the other hand, local-level data tend to be more useful to communities because of their much finer resolution, which may go down to individual parcel details. At the same time such fine-grain data are more likely to raise privacy concerns. There are thus many challenges beyond resource availability in enhancing SDI at the local level, as more and more people expect increased efficiency in local services through on-line access to geospatial data, while at the same time being fearful of privacy infringements. Balancing openness of access to data with the protection of privacy is a delicate act with no obvious technological solutions.

From the viewpoint of organizations and institutions (as well as individuals) that are primarily data users, the issue of access to geospatial data has at least four major dimensions. One is simply the issue of locating the desired data, even if they do exist somewhere. Metadata (data describing the contents of databases) are being continuously created but it is often still hard to find what one needs as available datasets continue to grow in number. Another is the problem of technical access, considering the size of many spatial databases and the sophistication of today's computational infrastructure. Yet another is the issue of ensuring their release if they are protected for privacy reasons; and a fourth is the question of cost, since private suppliers as a rule, and public suppliers often, will charge for the data they provide. On the whole geospatial data in the public (government) domain tend to be easier to find and obtain since many governments make it their business to make data available on SDI, though there too cost can be a problem. The reverse situation tends to arise in the scientific domain, where the data are usually free but access technology can be quite primitive.

Workflow technology, an emerging technology that is currently more readily available for business applications than for scientific and public activity workflows, would greatly benefit from more open access to data and provide a basis for better regional and urban planning. It would allow planners to more easily assemble and analyze materials for plans, and could help enhance participation in the planning process of diverse stakeholder groups. Increasingly, attacking large-scale, complex problems would be possible, involving scientific and not-for-profit organizations as well as different levels of government. For example, large-scale problem-solving for emergency management requires the active, coordinated participation of national, state, and local governments and other organizations to address issues arising at different geographic scales. Once workflow technology in the geospatial domain is enabled by better access to data, research about its social implications will be needed to better understand its strengths and weaknesses, and to support large-scale interdisciplinary science studies.

SECTION 5: GIS IN PUBLIC PARTICIPATION AND COMMUNITY DEVELOPMENT

Research about individuals, groups, and organizations participating in community decision situations has been one of the most visible research areas for GIS and society over the past decade. Now well in their second decade, participatory GIS (PGIS) and public participation GIS (PPGIS) are mature enough for retrospective assessment and critique. The difference between these two terms is subtle and has to do with whether the participation refers to some specific group of stakeholders or collaborators, or to the public at large. For other researchers, the distinction has to do with whether the decision-making process incorporates values identified primarily by the community (bottom-up approach), or by professional planners acting on behalf of a government agency (top-down approach). There is some disagreement in the literature as to whether, and to what extent, these approaches have fulfilled their promise and realized their potential, considering the great hopes that researchers and community leaders had pinned on them for fostering more democratic processes in local decision making and empowering the marginalized. As is usually the case with complex matters, it turns out that both critics and defenders have a point.

In assessing the successes and shortcomings of research in that area, a number of conceptual frameworks that have been proposed in the past decade can be of help. There is considerable consensus among researchers that three components: people, group processes, and GIS technology can capture the general similarities and differences between and among three realms of research: grassroots GIS, collaborative GIS, and web GIS. These three realms always include all three components, but with different emphases. Thus *grassroots GIS* emphasizes people, especially marginalized populations who can be empowered through participatory processes using mostly off-the-shelf GIS technology. *Collaborative GIS* emphasizes group process, with a focus on face-to-face meetings and social-behavioral science research designs for studying participatory processes and outcomes. Finally, *web GIS* emphasizes the technology, especially new tool development and methods, with a focus on broader access, interactivity, and the use of multimedia in what some have referred to as 'GIS2'

Reflecting on the research outcomes involving the three realms, one could conclude that small-group participation has been enabled with GIS and thus a potential fulfilled for an approach (PGIS) that brings together in specific structured ways people, processes, and technology. On the other hand, proper public participation using GIS (PPGIS) has not yet been achieved. This is indeed a bigger challenge and further research is needed. As for web GIS, a very different kind of participation has recently taken form, known as *volunteered geographic information* (VGI). VGI involves spontaneous online geospatial information contributions from individuals who might or might not be organized in any particular manner (Goodchild 2007). Exciting research is already underway exploring how people, process, and technology come together in VGI, and striving to better understand how new forms of activity relating to geographic information emerge within societies. What motivates people

to contribute? How valuable is the contributed information for society? How reliable is it? What places and thematic areas attract the most contributions, and which are left blank? What would a mature geospatial Wikipedia look like? How could that volunteered effort by growing numbers of contributors be channeled to the benefit of society? The VGI phenomenon is so new that the key research questions are only now beginning to be formulated.

SECTION 6: VALUE, FAIRNESS AND PRIVACY IN A GIS CONTEXT

In the sixth section of the book, four chapters tackled some of the most challenging issues that connect GIS and society: issues of fairness, privacy, conflict, ethics, as well as the value of the geographic information itself. These issues are inter-related. Although they are the last ones to be treated in the handbook, they are among the most compelling in GIS and society research.

Valuing geographic information has been a research interest for decades, at least since map use became an important research topic, becoming even more critical after the emergence of GIS. There are two aspects to this issue. The first has to do with the marginal utility of the new knowledge acquired through the use of the information, but also with the disutility associated with breaches of privacy made possible by its careless or malicious use. What do people gain from using geographic information? How do they value that information within various contexts? What justified fears do people have concerning the growing public availability of geographic information? No absolute answers can be given to these questions because information use is context-dependent and so is therefore the value of information for different users at different times. Nonetheless, some degree of generalization across contexts is possible and has been an ongoing research interest. At the very least, the value of information is tied to the ability to access needed data, or to protect data that should not be in the public domain. We saw earlier how the issue of data access has several dimensions: the data must exist and the user must be able to locate them; data access must be technically possible for the user; access must be restricted if and only if this is justified by the sensitivity of the data; and there is also the question of cost. At least two of these dimensions of access raise issues of equity and fairness. Obviously cost is one of them. Technical access is the other, since this requires not only a suitable computational infrastructure but also the technical expertise to put the data to good use. Thus, while people talk about an information glut, this does not mean that the appropriate data are available equally to everyone where and when needed. As in so many areas in society, there are 'haves' and 'have-nots' also in the geographic information domain.

A second aspect of value and fairness associated with GIS concerns the many possible direct applications of geographic information towards the investigation and on occasion, remediation of inequities in society, and its use in promoting collaborative solutions to problems that often lead to serious conflicts among groups. Spatial equity, that is, the fair distribution of resources, services, and burdens across space has been a major area of concern in GIS and society research. This concern is best encapsulated in the notion of environmental justice, with its focus on the lack of access to the goods, and especially proximity to the 'bads' of society. This is a fundamentally geographic topic that is very well suited to geovisualization and spatial analysis with GIS, and which has become an important research area in democratic societies. Related to this is GIS-based research about natural resource conflicts and their management, a strand that will grow in importance as growing populations put more pressure on scarce natural resources. More generally, there are many kinds of spatially based conflicts in society, and many GIS-aided approaches that

can be used to study and mediate these. This is largely the realm of collaborative and participatory GIS discussed earlier.

Value differences, perceptions of (un)fairness, and conflicts at various geographic scales also give rise to many legal issues. Actually, the legal and ethical problems relating to geographic information go well beyond the issues discussed in this section. Like other powerful technologies, geographic information technologies develop faster than society's ability to handle the issues that arise in their wake. These technologies enable new modes of behavior (and misbehavior) and create new societal problems just as they help resolve others. As much as we would like to see it otherwise, society's ability to address new problems of fairness, equity, privacy, fraud, and conflict – whether spatial or not – will inevitably continue to lag behind the emergence of the problems themselves. There is good reason to hope however that in the case of geographic information and associated technologies, the balance between beneficial and problematic developments will continue to be strongly on the positive side.

CLOSING THOUGHTS

When reaching the end of a handbook such as this one, characterized by topical breadth and considerable diversity of research perspectives, it is prudent to refrain from drawing general conclusions or venturing predictions about research paths yet to be followed and discoveries yet to be made. These closing thoughts have a more humble goal, to bring out a handful of major themes that weave together the 27 chapters gathered here.

Not surprisingly for a volume on GIS and society, these themes span the technology–society spectrum. In a sequence from the mostly technological to the thoroughly social, they may be identified as follows: (1) part-whole relations of GIS with other information technologies; (2) geographic information technology in the service of society and science; (3) concern for the user's viewpoint; (4) enhancing the social dialectic through improved communication; and (5) the social construction of science. No doubt other readers might discern different threads, but these five spell out an instructive story.

Let us take these observations in that order. To begin, it is quite obvious that GIS is not – could not have been – a free-standing technology conceived independently of the broader computational and information revolution. As goes information technology so goes *geographic* information technology. Few of the achievements detailed in the pages of this book would have been possible without remote sensing, GPS, wired and wireless Internet, mobile computers, smart phones, Microsoft®, Google™, and a host of other companies and technologies. Only now are we beginning to see developments in the reverse direction, where instead of capitalizing on other existing technologies, GIS helps foster new ones of its own. An example is LBS, which strongly depend on GIS maps. In light of other revolutionary technologies already within reach (microsensors, wearable computing, augmented reality, ubiquitous computing, and so on), it would be tempting to speculate on how geographic information technology might use these to tighten its relationships with society even further. But we shall leave that to the reader, and move on.

Since 'services' is one interpretation of the 'S' in GIS, the notion of services to society is already built into geographic information technologies. This handbook included numerous examples of such services provided directly to individuals, groups, organizations, and communities, as well as of those provided to applied fields such as planning, emergency preparedness, and the environmental and health sciences. What is not immediately obvious, or clear, is the extent to which this is a two-way relationship of influence, where GIS not only provides services that society needs or wants, but is itself shaped by evolving currents of social and political thought. One significant contribution of this handbook was to highlight that point, both in the chapters on the foundations of geographic information and society and elsewhere, as in the discussion of alternative representations, of participatory GIS, or of that of ethics and values. The extent of this two-way relationship is yet to be fully explored.

A related theme cutting across most chapters is a concern for the user's viewpoint. That strand grows out of the very first handbook section as a desired expansion of geographic information ontologies, and weaves its way through discussions of alternative social group perspectives, alternative representational needs for different cultures and organizations, the views and information needs of different stakeholders, the value of geographic information to the user, to examples of the provision of individually tailored LBS. The challenge no longer seems to be how to present 'the facts' most accurately but rather, how best to select and re-present what is most relevant to the user in the context of the task at hand. The shift here is not one from scientific objectivity to subjectivity but rather, to intersubjectivity and the recognition that the user's purpose is the filter that helps decide what information is needed under what circumstances, and in what form. Emerging from this conceptual and practical re-orientation is a geographic reality that is more malleable, more fluid, more dynamic, but also much more interesting as it evolves, just like society itself is evolving in its concerns, needs, and wants.

A societal value that had been somewhat lost in the mechanistic single-mindedness of the modern era, and that is being revived in the post-modern age, is that of communication among the individuals, groups, organizations, and institutions that make up society. Every section of this handbook reflected deep concern for helping enhance the social dialectic by facilitating networking, participation, collaboration, or empowerment of the marginalized, and provided concrete examples of how GIS is being used to that end. This emphasis on viewing GIS as a tool for community building and democratization is remarkable, considering how many successful business, transportation, military, and other such applications of GIS are out there that the authors could have written about. Few would deny that these domains are also part of society, and yet the handbook is silent about them. It is for the reader to decide whether this gap can be explained by the academic (rather than professional) credentials of the authors, or whether there is some tacit understanding in the field at large that the most enduring contributions of GIS to society are those that promote social harmony and fairness in a sometimes ruthless world.

The last thread of the five is not about technology even though it is to a large extent technology that helped bring it about. That thread may be called the social construction of science. The phrase is borrowed from science and technology studies but it is used here in a more restricted sense, to mean literally the view of science as a communal project where individuals and groups actively contribute to knowledge generation and sharing. In the geographic information domain, while the more flashy manifestations of this phenomenon get the most attention (think of VGI, Wikimapia, neogeography, and other neologisms along these lines), it is the deeper undercurrents of this opening up of traditionally exclusive expert domains that has the greater significance for society. The supporting trends are an increasing public spatial awareness, the recognition of spatial intelligence as a separate form on a par with mathematical and verbal intelligence, the greater appreciation of local and indigenous knowledge, and a concern for including the experiences of space and place of groups outside the scientific or social mainstream. These trends are accelerated by the increasing democratization of the languages that geographic information technologies 'speak': ways of expressing meaning through programming, modeling, map-making, annotating, animating, displaying, presenting, and other such computational skills that are now often simple enough to be mastered by children. One wonders what the relationship between geographic information and society might become when these children grow up and start contributing to the communal project in earnest. But again, it is prudent not to speculate, as we leave that for the reader, and hope that future editions of this handbook can take up this discussion.

REFERENCES

Goodchild, M.F. (2007) 'Citizens as sensors: The world of volunteered geography', *GeoJournal*, 69(4): 211–221.

Wang, S. and Liu, Y. (2009) 'TeraGrid GIScience gateway: Bridging cyberinfrastructure and GIScience', *International Journal of Geographical Information Science*, 23(5): 631–56.

World Commission on Environment and Development (1987) *Our Common Future*. http://www.un-documents.net/wced-ocf.htm (accessed 9 March 2010).

Index

Note: When the locators are in bold following an author's name, this indicates the page range of the chapter they have authored within this volume.